T3-BWY-564

BORDERLANDS

BORDERLANDS

Mike Dash

THE OVERLOOK PRESS
WOODSTOCK & NEW YORK

First published in the United States in 2000 by
The Overlook Press, Peter Mayer Publishers, Inc.
Lewis Hollow Road
Woodstock, New York 12498
www.overlookpress.com

Library of Congress Cataloging-in-Publication Data

Dash, Mike.
Borderlands / Mike Dash.
p. cm.
Includes index.
1. Curiosities and wonders. I. Title.
AG243.D36 1999 081.02—dc21 99-37203

Manufactured in the United States of America

ISBN: 0-87951-724-7

1 3 5 7 9 8 6 4 2

Contents

List of Illustrations vii
Preface ix
Introduction 1
1 Strange Planet 21
2 Lands of Gods and Angels 41
3 World of Spirits 73
4 Alien Universe 126
5 Where the Wild Things Are 176
6 The Good Earth 217
7 Reign of Frogs 244
8 Hoax 276
9 Hard Evidence? 314
10 Answers from Inner Space 355
11 Strange Fashions 388
12 A Sense of Wonder 438
Notes 444
Index 502

Illustrations

1 An image of Christ in clouds over Korea, photographed from an American bomber during the Korean War.
2 Vision of the Virgin Mary in the skies over the French village of Pontmain in January 1871. Note the scroll at Mary's feet on which the words of her message were seen to appear.
3 Vision of the Virgin Mary which appeared on the rooftops of a Coptic church at Zeitoun in Egypt in 1968 – one of the Virgin's very few appearances in a non-Catholic country.
4 The stigmatic Therese Neumann, who manifested the wounds suffered by Christ on the cross every Friday from 1926 until her death in 1962. Therese claimed to have lived for three decades on nothing but wine and Communion wafers.
5 The Norwegian psychic Einar Neilson at a seance in September 1921 – one of many mediums who were pictured producing ectoplasm during the heyday of physical mediumship.
6 The Irish medium Kathleen Goligher photographed materialising a 'psychic rod' from her vagina.
7 Eleonore Zugun displays wounds her investigators concluded were inflicted on her by an invisible assailant.
8 One of the many faces which appeared on a concrete floor in the Andalusian village of Belmez – one supposedly built directly over an old graveyard.
9 Samples of the 'Martian' script produced by late nineteenth century mediums convinced they were in touch with inhabitants of the Red Planet.
10 A photograph taken at Raynham Hall in Norfolk during the 1930s, which is often said to portray the 'Brown Lady' who is supposed to haunt the house.
11 An artist's impressions of some of the dozens of radically different alien races encountered by UFO witnesses in the last 50 years:
- 11a a Grey – by far the most commonly reported alien of the last two decades.
- 11b one of the hairy dwarfs encountered by Jose Antonio de Silva in Bebedouro, Brazil, in May 1969.
- 11c one of the minuscule aliens reported by six Malaysian schoolboys in August 1970. The entity closely resembled a character in a local comic book.
- 11d one of the grey, mummy-like aliens which reportedly abducted two fishermen at Pascagoula, Mississippi, in October 1973.
- 11e the huge, fleshy alien which attacked Fortunato Zanfretta in a house near Genoa in December 1978.

11f one of the small, silver-coloured 'goblins' which besieged a farmhouse in Kelly, near Hopkinsville in Kentucky, in August 1955.

11g a 'Mince-Pie Martian' – one of three tiny beings who visited Jean Hingley in her home in Rowley Regis in January 1979 and accepted a seasonal plate of pies.

11h one of the strange fleshy aliens with skin like aluminium which abducted bus driver Antonio La Rubia in Rio de Janeiro during September 1977.

12 A sketch by Captain James Hooton of the airship he saw at Homan, Arkansas in April 1897. It was on the ground, and Hooton spoke to the occupants before they flew away.

13 The McMinville photograph, obtained by Mr and Mrs Paul Trent at McMinville, Oregon, in May 1950, is generally regarded by ufologists as the most convincing picture ever taken of a UFO.

14 The giant head which washed ashore at Tecolutla, Mexico, early in 1969. It weighed one tonne and was thought to be part of the body of a sea serpent.

15 This photo, thought to show a wake produced by the Loch Ness Monster, was taken by RH Lowrie in the summer of 1960. Thanks to the recent exposure of several better-known images of the monster as forgeries, it is now probably the best monster photograph not seriously suspected of being a hoax.

16 One more than 1,000 footprints left by the 'Bossburg Cripple' – a Bigfoot with a club right foot – in Washington State in October 1969. Bigfoot hunters suggest no hoaxer would go to the trouble of producing such an unlikely fake.

17 A giant snake reported from Siracusa, Italy, in August 1954.

18 This controversial satellite photograph procured by pulp magazine editor Ray Palmer supposedly shows the gigantic north polar opening to a hollow earth. In fact the 'hole' is simply the area of the Arctic in perpetual winter darkness.

19 Two of the Devil's Arrows, a group of megaliths in northern England which form part of the longest generally accepted ley line in Britain.

20 A patch of damp in Christ Church, Oxford, which bore a striking resemblance to the late Dean Liddell and appeared a quarter-century after his death in 1898.

21 Some of the fish which fell from the sky over East Ham in 1984 and were recovered by Bob Rickard, editor of the *Fortean Times*.

22 One of the 'Holy Aubergines' which appeared across the Midlands in 1990, bearing in their seed patterns verses from the Koran.

23 The charred remains of Helen Conway, whose body was destroyed in as little as six minutes – by spontaneous combustion?

24 Official police photofits showing phantom social workers who appeared at homes in (left to right, top to bottom) Hampton, Bristol, Portishead and Leicester.

25 A performance said to show the fabled Indian Rope Trick in the 1920s.

26 An artist's impression of the bizarre Goatsucker, which plagued Puerto Rico in 1995 and 1996. Other witnesses described the creature as bipedal and apparently alien.

Preface

You are about to enter the borderlands, an enigmatic world where almost anything seems possible.

It is important to realise, however, that very little of what appears in this book is verified 'fact'. There is no doubt that some of the cases that will be discussed are hoaxes, others honest misperceptions. It could be – and indeed has been – argued that most of the rest have no basis in physical reality, and are the products of hallucinations and other altered states of consciousness. But by the same token, the sceptical arguments that have been advanced to explain away the more contentious reports are themselves generally based either on the fragile foundations of witness testimony, or on unsupported assertion. They may be no more 'true' than the wildest assertions of the believers.

For this reason, almost every case cited in the book could be, and perhaps should have been, peppered with qualifications such as 'alleged', 'is said to', 'supposed', 'claimed', 'apparent' and 'assuming'. As the constant use of such phrases tends to become tedious, they have frequently been omitted, but cautious readers may wish to insert them mentally as they go.

This is a long book, but it could have been very much longer. Perhaps the most difficult task was to distil whole libraries of theories and information into single chapters, and to select just a handful of representative cases from the many thousands of compelling narratives that exist. In addition, I have chosen not to overburden the work with an extensive scholarly apparatus. This has entailed stripping the text of numbered footnotes, but anyone who wishes to follow up any of my cases, or who doubts any of my assertions, will nevertheless find a section of notes at the back of the book. Most are simply source references; occasionally, however, the reader will encounter a passing mention in the main text which glosses over an entire subject and, where possible, I have tried to expand a little on such matters in the notes.

I have adopted one other practice which may irritate scholars in choosing not to indicate every piece of excised text in quoted passages with ellipses (. . .). Where ellipses are present in the text, the reader should assume that further short passages may have been excised elsewhere in the quotation.

Like any author, I owe great debts of gratitude. Many friends and fellow researchers have contributed, directly or indirectly, to the writing of this volume. Among those who went out of their way to help were Brian Chapman, Hilary Evans, Luigi Garlaschelli, Ted Harrison, Patrick Huyghe, Alice Keens-Soper, Karen Krizanovich, Kevin McClure, Joe McNally, Steve Moore, Bob Rickard, Paul Sieveking and Dennis Stacy. I would, however, like to dedicate this book to John Brown and to my wife Penny, who between them made it possible for me to write it; and to Ffion, who I hope may one day read it.

Mike Dash

London, February 1997

Introduction: At a Border Crossing

It may be a peculiar coincidence or a freeze-framed moment of deja-vu; it may be something much less common – an odd light in the sky, or a statue drinking milk. But we have all experienced something that we cannot quite explain.

This simple observation is the key to understanding our consuming interest in the unknown. Whatever we are told by the authorities, by science, by sceptical friends or our own common sense, we know that strange things happen because we have witnessed them ourselves.

Everyone visits the borderlands at least once in their lives.

Tom D'Ercole was leaving home one morning when he happened to glance skywards. There, hovering not far above the roof of his house, he saw a small, round, basketball-sized cloud quite unlike the occasional cirrocumulus wisps far above it. As he watched, the cloud began to float back and forth over his home, slowly growing and darkening, until, to his amazement, it appeared to gather itself up, pursed its 'lips', and squirted a substantial jet of liquid over him and his car. After a few moments, the unusual shower came to an end and the strange cloud immediately vanished. Changing out of his sodden clothes, D'Ercole drove to the school in Garden City,

New York, where he worked as a science teacher and ran a pH test on the liquid that had soaked him. It was water.

Borderlands are territories where this sort of thing is not unusual, where the known shades into unknown, occurrences can be both terrifying and hilarious, and fiction mutates slowly into fact. They are the grey areas, though the things that go on there are frequently intensely colourful. We have always known that they exist, and have been exploring them for centuries, but they remain a largely trackless territory to which existing guidebooks are often inadequate and sometimes dangerously misleading. Yet we cannot ignore them. The borderlands surround us, and the expansion of knowledge in almost any direction requires us to probe and understand them.

Indeed, this *terra incognita* is vast and fast-expanding, despite the treasury of proof and data that has already been collected, since most answers suggest questions, every science has its anomalies, each history its revisionists, and all religions their schismatics and heretics. Passing into it can be easy: for all the mumbo-jumbo favoured by occultists, the majority of crossing points are guarded not by massive gates opened only with a coded word and careful ritual, but by ordinary doorways which stand permanently ajar. At such a border crossing, reality and the unreal stand so close together we are not always aware we have moved from one world to another.

No one could have been more prosaically rooted to reality than Tony Clark, a civil engineer hired to build a cement factory in Iran, and he had no idea he had crossed into the borderlands when he left Manjil, near the Caspian Sea, to drive the 150 miles back to Teheran. At that time – it was the mid-1950s – Manjil was an isolated place, and Clark and his Iranian companion had eaten only some unleavened bread and *dugh*, a type of liquid yoghurt, before they left. They were hungry, but as their vehicle crawled upwards to a plateau some fifty miles from the nearest town, the men had to concede that their chances of finding a substantial meal were slight. At best they might find a *tchae khana* – a roadside cafe where the principal dish was a glass of weak tea strained through a sugar lump held between the teeth. All at once, they came upon a distinctive pile of rocks, topped by one stone balanced precariously on the others, beyond which lay a village that boasted just such an establishment. This *tchae khana* was a long, cool building, full of Iranian lorry drivers drawing on hubble-bubble pipes, and run by an Armenian who hurried forward to offer them a meal and introduce himself, in flawless English, as Mr Hovanessian.

Delighted at the opportunity to fill their empty stomachs, Clark and his companion gratefully accepted, and before long Mr Hovanessian served them two bowls of the most delicious iced soup, based on cucumber, raisins and yoghurt. This was followed by delicately flavoured stuffed vine leaves and an equally superb *chelo kebab*, the national dish of Iran. The men rounded off the meal with Turkish coffee drunk in a glow of contentment. The atmosphere, Clark recalled nearly forty years later, was hazy, almost unreal, and when the time came to leave, the bill for what was surely the best meal the engineers had ever eaten turned out to be ridiculously small. Mr Hovanessian invited the men to call again and, as they left the village, they noted down the mileage they had driven from Manjil.

Naturally, Clark told a number of his friends about his remarkable find; many were sceptical that it was possible to obtain such superb cuisine in so unlikely a location. So it was with no small measure of satisfaction that he found himself making the same journey three months later with one of the principal doubters, another Englishman, as his passenger. The circumstances were nearly identical; again the men in the car were hungry and tired as they ascended to the plateau. Checking the mileage, Clark announced they were only five miles from his village, and sure enough the little hamlet soon came into view, marked as before by the distinctive pile of stones. But the fabulous *tchae khana* of Mr Hovanessian had disappeared; nor was there any sign it had ever existed. Questioning the villagers was useless. '*Tchae khana?*' one told Clark. 'There's never been one in all the time I've been here, and that's forty years.'

Tony Clark never could explain what had become of his phantom diner or how he had come to enjoy that remarkable meal in what he thenceforth called the world's best restaurant. He advanced no theory of a ghostly encounter, hallucination or vivid dream and, four decades later, it would be difficult, if not impossible, to reinvestigate his experience satisfactorily. It will always seem as unreal to us as it was real to him.

However, no one should doubt that things that happen in the borderlands do have real effects. The consequences may be rather personal, as they were in the case of a Swedish woman who used a coil for contraception. Shortly after watching Uri Geller perform on television, she discovered she was pregnant; investigation showed that her IUD had straightened inexplicably; she blamed the metal-bender for her predicament. Occasionally they are melodramatic: half a world away, a road worker, Edward Baldock, lost his life because a Brisbane woman named Tracey Wigginton convinced three friends she was a vampire who could read minds and make people disappear, except for their eyes. Anxious to please her, they helped Wigginton entrap and murder the drunken Baldock, then watched as she frenziedly sucked blood from his neck.

Sometimes, though, strange events change history, as they did when Joan of Arc's celestial visions inspired her to lead the counter-attack that eventually expelled the English from France, or when a young Xhosa girl named Nonquawuse, standing in her family's fields one day in 1856, saw two figures apparently standing in a bush next to her garden.

Calling her over, these ghosts gave Nonquawuse a disturbing message to impart to her people: that they had sinned, and that as a consequence all their cattle and their crops would be blighted. The only solution, the girl was told, was for her people to slaughter their animals and destroy their crops; if they did so the dead would arise from their graves, the sick and the crippled would be healed, healthy cattle, horses and fowl would rise from the earth, and the entire Xhosa nation would grow rich and fat on the proceeds of their faith.

Slowly, gradually, the prophetess Nonquawuse gathered converts to her cause. Several chiefs declared for her, then Sarhili, the king of the Xhosa, became a convert. With his influence behind her, the girl was able to persuade almost the whole nation to carry out the instructions of the spirits. Some 400,000 head of cattle were slaughtered, the crops were all burned – but, even so, Nonquawuse's prophecies were not fulfilled. As a result, an estimated 40,000 of the 105,000 Xhosa people slowly starved to death, as many again were forced to abandon their lands in order to survive, and nearly the entire territory was absorbed into the British colony of South Africa. The vision one young girl saw in her garden was directly responsible for one of the most cataclysmic events in the history of Africa.

What should we expect, then, as we stand at one of these unguarded crossings? Within the borderlands we may glimpse silver discs that glide across the sky, statues that weep, move, drink and menstruate. Big cats live there, real as any in the jungle, and share the land with ghostly jet-black dogs with eyes the size of dinner plates; fish, frogs and hay rain from the sky; the flames of a combusting man belch without warning from his belly; the living receive phone calls from the dead; and phantom ships patrol the seas with masts and spars aglow with phosphorescent light.

Some of what we'll see or hear is real: one might cite the minor mystery of homing pets as an example of this category of phenomena. These determined animals have made journeys of hundreds, and sometimes thousands, of miles to rejoin their human owners – returning not only to their homes, which might be accounted for by exceptional senses of memory and direction, but sometimes to masters who left them behind in moving to another district or country, which is altogether harder to explain. The best-known such case was that of Prince, a collie/Irish terrier cross who lived with James Brown and his wife in Buttevant, Ireland, in 1914. When war broke out, Brown left for France and his wife moved to London, taking Prince with her. Some time later, the dog disappeared, only to turn up two weeks later at Brown's quarters at Armentieres, near the front line in France, where he was, unsurprisingly, adopted as a lucky mascot. Another collie, Bobbie, was taken by his owner on a 3000-mile trip from Silverton, Oregon, to Wolcott, Indiana, in August 1923. There he was chased away by a pack of local animals and could not be found when the time came to return home. Six months later, Bobbie returned to Silverton, having crossed three major rivers, the Rocky Mountains and the Great Plains to get there. He was found asleep on the grave of a fox terrier who had been his companion in puppyhood, and recognised by a scar and an old hip injury. As a reward, Bobbie received a gold collar, medals, and a new kennel in the shape of a bungalow. The dog's journey became so celebrated that witnesses who had encountered him on his travels began to come forward; from their accounts it seemed that he had cast about in a thousand-mile arc, making many false starts before somehow hitting on the correct road home.

At the other extreme lie phenomena made up of wishful thinking, poor research and misidentification, such as the fabled Bermuda Triangle. This supposed graveyard of ships and planes was promoted by writers in the early 1970s, who fixed the Triangle's amorphous boundaries to include the maximum possible number of cases and copied from one to another with little regard for accuracy. Then Lawrence Kusche, a reference librarian at Arizona State University, took it upon himself to check each report against the original sources. He discovered that many of the best-known cases had rational explanations – one derelict had been in harbour when she was struck by a hurricane and broke free from her moorings, and a number of the vessels that vanished without trace were known to be at risk from structural failure. Worse, several of the Triangle's supposed victims had disappeared thousands of miles away, in locations varying from the Pacific shores of Mexico to the coast of Brazil. The Triangle was exposed as a myth – which is not to say that mysterious disappearances do not take place at sea, simply that there is no evidence that they regularly occur in definable locations.

As for the bulk of what occurs within the borderlands, and is reported as real, much of it is fascinating but not proof of anything in the scientific sense of the word. Accounts of strange and unusual phenomena tend to be subjective, not objective; indeed the very subjectivity of some events is a key to their understanding.

A good example of a subjective phenomenon – but one that is all too real, and terrifying, to those who have experienced it – is the 'bedroom invader', an entity that materialises inside a home without opening any windows or doors, often when the witness is dozing or asleep. These invaders tend to be female; many are vividly described as hideous and withered old hags who crouch upon their chosen victims' chests, half-suffocating them. Still more bizarre creatures are also seen, however, sometimes when the witness seems wide awake.

One such case occurred when thirteen-year-old 'Randy P.', who lived with his family in a trailer home in Simi Valley, California, returned from school to find a creature sitting in one of the chairs in the living room. 'It was a small, pot-bellied figure,' he recalled, 'with a large head, and roughly two feet tall. It was jet black, had glowing red circles for eyes, two small white fangs that protruded from its wide mouth, and pointed ears.' Strangely, perhaps, Randy did not feel particularly frightened and he did not think the creature was malign. He walked towards it, noticing that it turned its head to watch him, and had approached to within five feet when he blinked, and the being instantly vanished. A few months later it reappeared, again in broad daylight, sitting cross-legged on a shelf in the boy's bedroom and grinning broadly at him before pulling the same vanishing trick. That was the end of the little pot-bellied demon, but some years later, at college, Randy returned to his dormitory room, tired, at about ten p.m., only to be kept awake by the noise of a party going on outside. At midnight the revellers departed, but Randy found himself still unable to sleep. He sat on his bed reading, with the main lights on, until, at about one a.m. he sensed something entering the room by coming through the wall above his head. It was invisible, but Randy heard, or sensed, the distinctive snap and whoosh of leathery, batlike wings as his visitor flew across the room and exited through the opposite wall. This 'invasion', which certainly did scare him, lasted no more than three or four seconds.

This is not to say that all such bizarre experiences occur when the witness is asleep, or nearly so. Some occur in broad daylight and in the most familiar of surroundings. For example, the *Guardian* of 30 November 1976 contained the following rather remarkable letter, signed by 'A Wiltshire Teacher':

> In East Anglia a few years ago . . . I was teaching in a small village school and the caretaker's husband declared that he had seen strange orange lights in the school field as he walked the dog home at about 10.30 p.m. Cynics suggested that he had seen more light ale than anything else. I thought little of it.
>
> Next day a little lad brought me a small plastic toy pistol which he had found near the school. I popped it into my drawer until such time as someone claimed it. Near the end of the afternoon of hectic pre-Christmas activities I felt I could not tolerate the compulsive and ceaseless chatter of one Sandra, and on impulse I pointed the pistol at her, saying mentally, 'Got ya!'
>
> To my astonishment she immediately vanished. The other children, conditioned to ignore her perpetual trivialities, didn't even notice.
>
> At the end of the session I dismissed the class and sat down in the ill-lit room to ponder over the unprecedented situation. I was suddenly aware of the figure of a man standing by me dressed in some kind of boiler-suit protective clothing. I assumed he was a parent on his way home from work. He extended his hand, lying in the palm of which was another toy pistol. Wordlessly, I passed the first one over to him. He examined it briefly, clicked a small ratchet at the side, pointed it towards the corner of the room and pulled the trigger.
>
> To my utter amazement Sandra reappeared immediately in full spate, breaking off only to observe that it was time to go

home. And as I sat there, Sandra and the stranger independently disappeared into the evening gloom.

Nothing could be more personal, no experience harder for a sceptic to concede a basis in reality, for it seems inconceivable that the other children would not have noticed their classmate's disappearance and that the teacher would wait until the end of the lesson before contemplating a search. Yet the experience seemed real enough at the time, and even the best-witnessed phenomena can remain just as indefinite and frustratingly difficult to interpret.

This was certainly the case on 30 October 1917, when an estimated 70,000 people packed themselves into a 500-yard-wide depression at Cova da Iria, near Fatima in Portugal, in the hope of seeing what was widely expected to be the sixth and final apparition of the Virgin Mary to a trio of peasant children. At noon, on cue, the children saw a flash of light, and Mary appeared and conversed with them. None of the people in the crowd saw or heard anything of what passed between them. At the end of the brief conversation, however, ten-year-old Lucia Santos (and perhaps the other two children as well) saw Christ and other holy figures appear with the Virgin in the sky. Following a prompt from the children, the crowd stared up towards the sun and at that point the general miracle that had been promised did seem to occur. To a portion of the vast gathering – though less than half of them, it seems – the sun appeared to whirl about and dance in a sky that changed from grey to vivid blue.

This might have been a fantasy induced by expectation, or a collective hallucination, except that it was also seen by several independent witnesses standing up to two miles away. On the other hand, it is indisputable that the sun did not leave its place in the sky that day, and few of those present seem to have agreed on what, precisely, occurred. Some saw the sun sway from side to side in the sky like a falling leaf, others watched it spin violently in circles, like a catherine wheel. And although there are pictures that show members of the crowd witnessing the miracle, no one seems to have photographed this dance of the sun; the only snapshot sometimes said to depict it has been identified as a picture of a pre-1917 solar eclipse. Nothing should be less personal than a vision seen by 30,000 people in the presence of scientists and members of the press, yet – setting its religious significance aside – the solar miracle of Fatima, which was the best-witnessed phenomenal event of this and probably any other century, might just as well have occurred to Randy P., alone in his trailer home, for all the sense that can be made of it.

The differences in emphasis and interpretation that divided the throng at Fatima are certainly not confined to those who have personally witnessed peculiar events. The re-examination of historical sources often proves equally problematic. Thus, several decades of close study persuaded Iman Wilkens, a Dutch scholar, that the events reported in Homer's *Iliad* and *Odyssey* occurred not in Asia Minor, where they are ostensibly set, but in the fenlands of East Anglia. Troy, for Wilkens, is not the dusty archaeological site in Turkey identified and excavated by Heinrich Schliemann, but Wandlebury Ring in the Gog Magog hills, close to the junction of the A11 and A604 roads – an identification that at least allowed one newspaper to run the attention-grabbing headline 'Troy Relocated to Happy Eater off the A11'. Similarly, Kamal Salibi, a Lebanese-Christian scholar, resolved some of the inconsistencies of the Bible to his own satisfaction by relocating events to the southern Hejaz, in Saudi Arabia – a suggestion that would have been disputed by Comyns Beaumont, a prominent *Daily Mail* journalist, who wrote a book to show that Galilee was in Somerset and that Edinburgh had once been called Jerusalem.

The problems with such theorising – Salibi and Beaumont cannot both be right, after all – must be borne in mind whenever we seek to enter the borderlands through ancient chronicles and histories. Such sources can certainly be rich in suggestive parallels to the cases and concerns of the present-day investigator, but they are also potentially misleading, if taken out of context. The latter point is well made by recent reassessments of one of the most peculiar of such stories, which appears in two early thirteenth-century chronicles: 'The Tale of the Green Children'.

These infants, a boy and a girl, were found in wolf traps dug around the village of Woolpit in Suffolk, probably some time during the reign of King Stephen (1135–1154). Not only their clothing but their skin was of greenish hue, and at first their only diet was green beans. Communication was difficult, since they spoke only an unintelligible language of their own; before much could be learned about them the boy died. The girl, however, grew up, adopted a mixed diet (after which her skin assumed a normal colour), learned English and eventually married a man from King's Lynn. From her, questioners learned that the children had come from a Christian land they called St Martin's which existed in perpetual twilight, and had walked from there to the place where they were found through an underground passage, following the sound of church bells. This story could be a symbolic invention, or mean that the children came from an underground kingdom or a parallel universe of some sort, but it has also been interpreted more mundanely as the tale of two malnourished waifs from the Suffolk village of Fornham St Martins, caught up in the civil war of Stephen's time and arriving in the vicinity of Woolpit after walking through passageways in the Neolithic flint mines in Thetford Forest. According to this explanation, the skin that alarmed the chroniclers was caused by a form of anaemia called green chlorosis, which is known to give flesh a greenish tinge, and the unintelligible language was merely a thick local accent.

Similarly, zoologists in search of the Great Sea Serpent have welcomed the discovery of early sighting reports, sworn before magistrates, among the legal records of Norway; who, after all, would risk perjuring themselves in court in order to testify to such an experience? Yet the same records also contain sworn accounts of what would today be regarded much less plausible encounters with trolls: in Jamtland, in 1671, one Peter Rahm made a notarised complaint that his wife had been abducted by such creatures to serve as a midwife. It seems arbitrary to accept one report as evidence and reject the other, simply because the former accords better to current notions of reality.

The study of strange phenomena, in short, must sometimes be allied to study of the witnesses and an understanding of what they themselves believe. There are, for example, differences in the way that UFOs are perceived between the US and Europe and some African societies which suggest that, whether or not the objects are alien spacecraft as is popularly supposed, the details that are picked up on and reported owe something to cultural conditions; in the same way, the frequency of the reports seem related to the degree to which western influences have penetrated the local culture. There are also percipients who are capable of interpreting the mundane as unexplained in quite spectacular ways – looking at the moon, but seeing a flying saucer, in one extreme case. In another, which occurred during a British panic about sinister impostors who posed as health visitors to inspect and abduct new-born children, a mother reported a visit from bogus 'social workers' who, on investigation, turned out to be a television crew, complete with cameras, making a documentary.

One part of the problem is the conditions created by a climate of expectation. Where one phantom social worker has been reported, others may be lurking; and one is more likely to assume the worst in matters of identification when something as precious as a child's safety is at stake. The same principle, perhaps, applies to UFO abductions; in one recent, Scottish, case, the two primary witnesses described how they had been motoring across a lonely moor at night when they observed a strange light in the sky. Presently the light got closer; the next thing the men were aware of was that it was considerably later and they were rather further down their road – a typical 'missing time' experience, one which frequently can, and in this case did, turn into a full-blown abduction under hypnosis. Yet the key to this particular case may lie in a tiny, incidental detail that one of the witnesses mentioned to the man investigating their experience: that on first seeing the strange light, he and his companion had leaned over and locked their doors, the suggestion being that strange lights equal UFOs, and UFOs equal abductions and the forcible removal of victims from their vehicles. With expectations so high, it is not, perhaps, surprising that the men did indeed report being taken on board an alien spacecraft.

Still, there are many apparently credible witnesses to the unknown. On 11 July 1881, Edward, Duke of Clarence, and his brother, Prince George, the future king, were on board HMS *Inconstant* as she sailed through the Bass Straits on passage from Melbourne to Sydney. 'At four a.m.,' the princes noted in their journal, 'the *Flying Dutchman* crossed our bows. A strange red light as of a phantom ship all aglow, in the midst of which the masts, spars and sails of a brig 200 yards distant stood out in strong relief as she came up on the port bow.' Another royal, His Highness Jigme Dorgi Wangchuk, King of Bhutan, reported seeing the 'great, white, fast-swimming shape' of a monster in one of his country's northern lakes. Then there are other respectable witnesses: presidents, priests, and policemen. Jimmy Carter reported his own UFO sighting a few years before his election, and an Anglican priest, Father William Gill, was the chief witness in what remains one of the most baffling of UFO reports, a multi-witness encounter with a craft that hovered over a mission in Papua New Guinea on two successive evenings in October 1953. A few years later Jeff Greenhaw, the police chief of Falkville, Alabama, discovered and photographed a silver-suited robot, which outran his car as he chased it down a dirt road.

Any of these men might be regarded a reliable witness, too sober to be easily confused, too responsible to make wild guesses, and with far too much to lose to tell a lie. Yet every one of their accounts is open either to doubt or serious criticism. There is no firm proof that either of the royal princes on the *Inconstant* were among the fourteen sailors who saw the phantom ship, while some evidence suggests that the account was probably elaborated and the identification of the phantom as the *Flying Dutchman* was made on no very good authority. The King of Bhutan may well have seen the white shape he described, but his account does little to support the reality of the sort of monsters said to dwell in Loch Ness, which are always described as black, brown or grey in colour. Jimmy Carter's UFO has been explained as either a misidentification of Venus or a mirage of the star Altair; Father Gill, too, may have seen a mirage, though this is far less likely – and as for Jeff Greenhaw, an investigation showed he had participated in a hoax involving a man dressed in a silver firefighters' outfit.

There are, in short, no unimpeachable witnesses to the unexplained, and few things that even apparently respectable people will not do for publicity, for fun, or to make a point. Still more remarkably, some of those who deliberately mislead seem undeterred by the serious consequences of their actions. Greenhaw's hoax, in October 1973, cost him his job, and his marriage broke up shortly thereafter. Perhaps he failed to anticipate these consequences, but one can only wonder at the actions of Paul Ingram, another police chief – from Washington State this time – who voluntarily admitted to raping and abusing his own daughters, and coercing them into an incestuous relationship with their brother, as part of the activities of a satanic coven that he supposedly ran with the help of his wife and several other policemen. His vivid confessions led the judge to impose twenty-year jail sentence, even though he subsequently retracted his testimony, and demonstrated that many of the outlandish events he described were invented. Nor are such actions confined to the United States. In the little Yorkshire town of Halifax, in 1938, a dozen men and women reported they had been attacked, and cut, by a mysterious razor-wielding slasher. An investigation by two detectives seconded from Scotland Yard soon proved that, while the wounds were real enough, the maniacal attacker did not exist. His supposed victims had slashed themselves, for reasons they could never adequately explain. If apparently sensible and normal people are capable of such extreme actions, the only conclusion to be drawn is that hoaxing is likely to be considerably more common than most investigators care to admit.

If neither memory nor reputation are proper safeguards, what certainty is there that anything occurring in the borderlands is real? The occasional piece of physical evidence has been preserved, and sometimes the proof is of somewhat spectacular nature. At Uniontown, Alabama, in the spring of 1956, hundreds of living fish fell from the sky onto a patch of farmland around 200 feet square. They came from a small, dark cloud that formed in the sky on an otherwise clear day, and their descent was witnessed by Mrs Para Lee Phillips and her husband. When the remarkable shower subsided, about fifteen minutes after it had begun, the couple were able to gather enough fish – catfish, bass and bream – to fill a washtub three feet in diameter and about a foot deep.

In the rare cases where a phenomenon persists for weeks, months or years, much more may be achieved: at Hessdalen, in Norway, and Gulf Breeze, in Florida, the repeated appearance of strange lights in the sky has drawn investigators from miles around and produced a substantial body of film and sighting records for study. Very occasionally, it is even possible to predict when something strange will occur: stigmatics – people who bear the wounds that Christ suffered on the cross – tend to bleed most profusely on high days and holy days, especially Good Friday. And, finally, there are some cases where evidence for the peculiar is embarrassingly abundant, there were once, for example, three rival Veronicas – pieces of cloth said to have been miraculously imprinted with the face of Jesus when he wiped his face on the road to Calvary – and two survive today, one of them in the Pope's study in Rome. There are likewise three heads of John the Baptist preserved in various churches, and several dried scraps of skin which purport to be the Holy Prepuce, Christ's foreskin, severed in the Temple. (One of these, kept in the parish church of Calcata, north of Rome, was stolen in 1983 from the wardrobe of Don Dario Magnoni, the parish priest, drawing unwelcome attention to a category of relic the Church prefers not to discuss.)

It is more usual, though, for evidence to be less physical and more ambiguous than this. Photographs and films of a wide variety of strange phenomena exist, as do a handful of tape recordings, radar traces, plaster-casts of footprints and statements made under hypnosis. All of them can be challenged. Of the myriad UFO photographs, most are clumsy hoaxes – pieces of paper pasted onto windows or hubcaps tossed into the air. It has been suggested that the most famous of all these snapshots, a domed flying saucer with portholes and three spherical 'landing pods' photographed from below by an amateur astronomer and hot-dog salesman named George Adamski, is actually either a cut-down pith helmet, or a chicken brooder. Then again, there had never been a photograph of a living sea serpent – not one that had been published, at any rate – until an eccentric named Doc Shiels produced several dramatic examples in the late 1970s and early 1980s, most of them shot in Falmouth Bay during a wave of sightings of the local 'sea giant', Morgawr; a lengthy investigation later suggested that Shiels's long-necked, double-humped monsters were Plasticine shapes placed on a plate of glass and held between the camera and the horizon. And, during the heyday of photography in the mid nineteenth century, dozens of photographers specialised in the production of so-called 'spirit photographs', which portrayed a sitter surrounded by the ghosts of the dear departed, using either double exposure or the crudest of *papier mache* models to achieve their effects. Today, even a credulous person would be hard-pressed to believe that such pictures showed what they purported to, but in their day the claims were widely believed.

In a world in which the Flat Earth Society (and some other, less obviously biased, commentators) continue to argue that America's moon landings were faked in a film studio, not even the most apparently conclusive proofs can expect to go unchallenged. In 1988, the Vatican agreed to submit the fabled Shroud of Turin – the reputed burial cloth of Christ – to scientific examination. A series of carbon-dating tests were planned, with the aim of establishing whether the shroud really was a first-century winding sheet, or dated from the middle ages, when the earliest historic records of its existence appear and when, sceptics argued, the image of a crucified man that appears on it was painted by a cunning forger. In order to conduct the tests, small fragments of the cloth were cut away and, to ensure both fairness and accuracy, sent to three different, carefully-selected laboratories in the United States and Europe. The dates produced by the experiments were then collated and averaged, allowing the investigators to announce 'with a 95 per cent probability', that the shroud was woven between 1260 and 1390, and must, therefore, be a fake.

Almost instantly, the test results were challenged. It was suggested that carbon dating can give anomalous results if samples become contaminated (on one occasion, one of the laboratories chosen for the experiments dated a Viking cow horn to A.D. 2006), which might have occurred when the shroud was caught in a fire in Turin cathedral in 1532; also that a burst of energy accompanying the Resurrection might have artificially dated the cloth. One might add that, had the results suggested that the shroud genuinely was of first-century origin, the sceptics would merely have regrouped and fallen back on the argument that the shroud was that of some other crucified man, or an ancient piece of cloth obtained by a medieval forger.

Perhaps, though, this lack of consensus, this absence of agreement on what constitutes an objective reality, is one of the keys to what goes on within the borderlands. In this world, precision and clarity can be suspicious: the clearest UFO photographs, for instance, are generally the least convincing. In addition, there is always the temptation for believers and sceptics alike to bolster their cases by stating as fact what is only supposition, or make definite figures that can only be tentative. For many years, an earnest enquirer would be told that there have been 3000 (or sometimes 10,000) sightings of the Loch Ness Monster, when, in point of fact, careful enquiry has revealed only 600 in the whole period to 1985. And, told by occultists that 133,306,688 demons fell with Lucifer, and that at Vienna, in 1583, no fewer than 12,652 of these were expelled from a single possessed girl, we are entitled to ask who counted, and how carefully?

In truth, it seems that the real and the unreal are closely intertwined throughout our territory – so closely that they sometimes change from one into the other. The folklorists who study urban legends have coined the term 'ostention' to describe a fiction that becomes a reality, and indeed there are now documented cases of poodles exploding while being dried in microwaves, a story that had been doing the rounds as a piece of folklore for many years. But the same sometimes applies in reverse. It was always assumed that tales of alligators living in the sewers of New York, surviving off debris and vermin, and slowly mutating into half-blind albinos, were nothing more than myth – until a researcher named Loren Coleman discovered a report in the *New York Times* of 10 February 1935, which described how a group of young boys investigating strange sounds from a sewer on East 123rd Street found a young gator thrashing feebly in the slushy water beneath a manhole cover. This particular piece of solid evidence was dragged from the sewers and beaten to death with sticks.

We have travelled far, but perhaps only in a circle. In the end, we regain our border crossing convinced of one thing above all others: this is a pliable realm. Though hundreds, or millions, of people may be visiting the borderlands at any given time, most of the things that happen here happen in private, and become known only through the possibly unreliable testimony of a single witness. Almost all the evidence for the rest is, by definition, contentious, and for every expert there seems to be an equal and opposite expert. In such a situation, everyone is free to make up their own mind about the evidence and testimony, though it helps to realise from the start that no two people will draw precisely the same conclusions from the same evidence.

What, then, is the point of studying something so ephemeral? Because if only half of one per cent of what is said to happen in the borderlands actually occurred, the chances are that some sciences will be revolutionised and some histories rewritten. Because if the other ninety-nine-and-a-half per cent did not, the witnesses still thought their experiences were real; not all of them are fools or liars, which makes the cases worthy of study in their own right for what they may tell us about perception, memory, and belief. And, of course, because all of us are curious. Everyone visits the borderlands at least once in his or her life.

I

Strange Planet

Red snow. It stains the virgin purity of sterile Antarctica: a pinprick of the peculiar in the howling fastness. Red spots, like blood drip-dripping from a blank-faced statue of the Virgin to speckle the freshly laundered crispness of an altar cloth. An alien redness in the whitest world – something that doesn't belong.

For a while, when the first explorers reached the fringes of the southern polar regions, the patches of red snow they found along the edges of the continent remained a minor mystery. Then the mystery was solved. The Antarctic whiteness had been stained by penguin droppings, coloured red by the shellfish that the birds had eaten. Nothing strange about the redness now.

Except that it appeared elsewhere. In the province of Macerata, Italy, at the end of the last century, a myriad small, blood-coloured clouds blew over, covering the sky. When the storm broke, those clouds dumped a hundred-thousand seeds upon the ground – seeds that came from a tree found only in central Africa and the Caribbean. In dusty Baghdad, on the night of 20 May 1857, a heavy darkness fell, succeeded after midnight by a red and lurid gloom. As panic seized the inhabitants, a dense shower of sand began to rain upon the city. More redness fell upon the little town of Stroud in Gloucestershire on 24 October 1987, this time in the shape of hundreds of thumbnail-sized, rose-coloured frogs, which tumbled from the sky, bouncing off umbrellas and pavements amid townspeople going about their business.

Three red things, all coming from the sky. Such patterns may be found wherever unexplained phenomena occur, combining, piece by piece, to form the fragmentary portrait of a truly colourful world, haunted by aliens and fairies, miracles and wonders, monsters and ghosts, all the way from Alaska to Argentina and from Britain to Japan.

We can explore this strange planet in many ways: by continent, listing the phenomena of each country, dating and placing them, and feeding the information into a computer that might confirm that ghosts appear near running water, and that odd things tend to happen on Wednesdays; by category, concentrating first on monsters, then on ghosts and, finally, on possible connections between the two; or by colour, in the hope that this unorthodox approach may yield unexpected insights.

Choose another colour. Yellow: a yellow rain fell in Afghanistan during the Soviet occupation in the 1980s. Some feared it was a Russian chemical warfare agent, but it was later positively identified as a blizzard of dung from a million bees. Green: a disc-shaped UFO glowed green as it hovered over a weapons depot near Astrakhan on the night of 28 July 1989, watched by servicemen from two army units in the area. Blue: thirteen-year-old Jean Bernard saw the Virgin Mary in the village of Vallensanges, near St Etienne in France, on 19 July 1888. She wore a white dress and a blue cloak spangled with stars, and encouraged him to kill a lizard. Silver: the colour of the Big Muddy Monster, an eight-foot-tall ape-creature that haunted Murphysboro, Illinois, between 1972 and 1988. Two men saw it at about one-thirty a.m. one night, moving through the rustling treeline at the edge of a salvage yard full of decaying cars and angled shadows. It had glowing red eyes and yellow teeth, and smelled of sewers and skunk.

Choose another continent – it makes no difference. From a vision of the Virgin in a Patagonian bedroom to an encounter with the devil in an Irish pub; from the great sea serpent of the North Atlantic to giant wheels of phosphorescent light spinning slowly beneath the tranquil waters of the Persian Gulf; from the ghost riders of the Mesopotamian desert to Christ's grave – in Japan; from the planetary barcode stretching hundreds of miles across the Australian wilderness to the poltergeist-haunted toilet of a German dentist, Dr Bachseitz . . . this earth is uniformly rich in wonders.

A world away from Antarctica, far in the frozen north, a phantom township appears in the sky over the Muir Glacier, Alaska. This is the bewitching 'Silent City', one of the strangest and most spell-binding sights to be seen at the top of the world: a chaos of weird architectural forms, from clusters of glittering spires to gables, obelisks, monoliths and castles, all shimmering over the 700-foot-deep crystal waters of Glacier Bay, all beautiful beyond description. Some say it is a vision of a real and ancient city, now covered by the icy waters of the inlet; others that it is a mirage, either of Bristol or perhaps of the capital of an undiscovered civilisation situated near the pole. It is certainly not the only ghostly settlement to be seen in the far north. During the Cold War, when the Americans built bases in Greenland to study ways of fighting in Arctic conditions, soldiers from the baking dustbowls of the Great Plains sometimes saw 'medium-sized mid-western cities' on the white horizon, in such detail on at they could identify individual buildings and churches.

It was in the skies over Alaska, on 17 November 1986, that a Japanese Airlines Boeing 747 cargo plane on a flight from Paris to Tokyo had an alarming close encounter with a gigantic UFO. It was dark and the aircraft's experienced pilot, Captain Kenju Terauchi, first noticed some unusual lights as he passed over the north-eastern part of the state, flying at about 35,000 feet. The lights were to his left and about 2000 feet below him; he assumed they might be military aircraft. However, the visitors seemed to keep pace with him, and as the aircraft turned left they appeared directly in front of it. They seemed closer now, and Terauchi and his crew could see they formed two pairs, each made up of about 120 rectangular lights arranged in rows. The glowing shapes appeared to be as little as 400 yards from the plane, each pair somewhat smaller than his 747.

Worried now, the Japanese crew contacted air traffic control at Anchorage to ask if the objects were appearing on radar. They were not, but did seem to be interfering with radio transmissions between the plane and the ground, which became increasingly garbled. Shortly afterwards, the light arrays moved off to the left and Terauchi was able to discern what seemed to be a third UFO some seven or eight miles away. This object appeared on the 747's instruments and was also detected on two ground radars. Slowly it fell astern; then, as the crew craned to see if it was still behind them, they realised to their alarm that it had placed itself right on their tail, where it flew, dimly illuminated by the reflections of lights on the ground. To Terauchi, this UFO seemed huge – perhaps the size of two aircraft carriers is how he put it – and was shaped like the planet Saturn. Suddenly frightened, the aircrew sought their controller's permission to take evasive action. It was granted, but the giant object kept its station behind them despite all their attempts to shake it off. Finally, as air traffic control directed another jet into the area to see if it could confirm the sighting, this monster among UFOs disappeared, leaving, in Terauchi's words, 'nothing left but the light of the moon'.

South now, to Canada, where strange aerial detonations, or 'skyquakes', were afflicting the residents of Burlington, Ontario, in the mid-1970s, despite the absence of supersonic aircraft in the area and of blasting operations on the ground; where a sea monster nicknamed 'Caddy' haunts the waters around Victoria, British Columbia, and, on the other side of the country, where three burning, ghostly ships sail the Northumberland Strait between Prince Edward Island and Nova Scotia, travelling at impossible speeds, sometimes attracting crowds that watch them hurtling towards inevitable disaster on the rocks. In the Saskatchewan town of Gravelbourg, in 1910, a line of human footprints was found in granite that was formed millions of years before man appeared on earth, while in Clarendon, Quebec, in December 1889, an investigator named Percy Woodcock held a conversation lasting several hours with an invisible entity which the daughter of a family named Dagg had discovered in their wood shed. Speaking in gruff tones, from a spot that appeared to be in the middle of an empty floor, this being first claimed to be the Devil and to have set various mysterious fires which had plagued the family. After a while its tone changed, and, as the phenomenon continued into a second week, the voice became kinder, although still prone to embarrass its questioners by recounting details of their private lives or spitting out volleys of blasphemy. Finally, on the day it had promised to leave, it claimed to be an angel, and sang along with hymns in such a 'beautiful, flute-like voice' that it was begged to stay – which it did not.

South again, to the United States, where apelike monsters prowl, where the modern age of flying saucers began in 1947 and where, during the Second World War, the little Illinois town of Mattoon fell victim to the 'Mad Gasser', a phantom anaesthetist who sprayed a mysterious paralysing gas into people's homes at night, leaving them nauseous and unable to move for up to forty minutes. The Gasser, whom one witness described as a man, 'tall, dressed in dark clothing and wearing a tight-fitting cap', and another as 'a woman dressed in man's clothing' who left the imprints of high-heeled shoes on the ground outside a bedroom window, evaded capture and neither robbed nor molested anyone. The paralysing gas, the witnesses reported, smelled of flowers.

To Houston, Texas, where in 1983 a curious panic spread among children in the city. A vicious gang of Smurfs were said to be marauding through the city's schools, massacring pupils and slaughtering headmasters. The murderous cartoon characters, armed with knives and machine guns, were thought by some to be killing anybody wearing sky blue; others insisted only those who put on blue clothes were safe. In the Aldine school district, mental torment was supplemented by acute physical discomfort when a rumour spread that the Smurfs were lying in wait in the school toilets. Investigation suggested that the panic began after a television news report on the arrest of several youths from a street-gang named 'The Smurfs', became embroidered with fantasy; the police insisted they had no reports of massacres in any schools, though they did arrest nearly fifty people for 'Smurf-related goings-on', mostly petty theft and burglary.

Further south, to Central America. Here there remains a tradition that races of pointy-heeled dwarves, called Dwendis (a corruption of the Spanish *duende*, or goblin), live in the rainforests. Standing up to four-and-a-half feet tall, and with yellow, flattened faces, they dwell close to human settlements and steal the children. Here, in Mexico City in the autumn of 1593, a soldier who had been standing guard in Manila a moment or two earlier, materialised in the Plaza Mayor, having presumably teleported (or, as some of his contemporaries preferred, been carried by Satan) over the intervening expanse of the Pacific Ocean. Naturally, he was thrown into prison and interrogated as a possible devil-worshipper. Here too, on the island of Puerto Rico in the Caribbean, a devilish man-beast named *chupacabras*, Goatsucker, which 'sucked dead' five goats and twenty parakeets on Hallowe'en 1995, climbed into a house in the town of Caguas, where it destroyed a stuffed teddy bear and left a puddle of slime on the windowsill. Artists' impressions showed it as a biped, with red eyes, claws, and a line of spikes or spines running down its back. Some said Goatsucker also had a forked tail and cloven hoofs; within a few months *chupacabras* attacks were being reported along the shores of the Caribbean and the Gulf of Mexico, from Venezuela in the south, through Vera Cruz in Mexico and as far north as Florida.

Giant snakes are said to dwell in the great wildernesses of South America; in April 1949, an apparently dead specimen reckoned to be 150 feet long was photographed floating down the Abuna River. This animal is known as the *sucuriju gigante*, or giant boa, and there are also reports of a 98-foot specimen being killed around 1933 on the Rio Negro, and one 115 feet long being despatched in the ruins of Fort Tabatinga on the River Oiapoc, both by machine-gun fire. Also in Brazil, shortly after midnight on 16 October 1957, a 23-year-old farmer's son named Antonio Villas Boas watched as a large red 'star' fell from the sky onto the field he was ploughing by lamp light. An egg-shaped object landed no more than fifty feet away from him; his tractor engine died, he was seized by three small entities and dragged on board their craft. After a medical examination of sorts, and a failed attempt to communicate with barks and yelps, his captors left him in a room equipped with a couch. A short while later, a door opened to reveal a naked female about four feet five inches tall. She was apparently human and exceptionally beautiful, although the hair on her head was almost white while her pubic hair was the colour of blood. She would not kiss Antonio but nibbled his chin; they made love, twice, after which the woman patted her belly and pointed at the sky, as if to indicate that their child would be born on another planet. Villas Boas was returned to his field and the UFO took off, listing to one side as it did so. It was nearly dawn.

South, south to Patagonia and the uttermost part of the earth. Here, in 1897, a Chilean farmer who lived on the shores of White Lake told Dr Clementi Onelli, of the zoo at Buenos Aires, that strange noises could be heard at night – a sound like a heavy cart being dragged along the shingle shores. When the moon was full, the farmer added, a huge, long-necked monster could be glimpsed in the half-light, swimming across the still and ink-black waters of the lake. This was not the only sighting Onelli recorded of the so-called Patagonian plesiosaur; in 1922, an American prospector friend named Martin Sheffield was searching for gold in the Chubut territory when he came across a lake so isolated it had no name. Here he found strange tracks in the scrub along the shore, and deep marks, which he thought had been made by a heavy animal, leading down to the water. Then, said Sheffield, 'I saw in the middle of the lake an animal with a huge neck like a swan, and the movements made me suppose the beast to have a body like that of a crocodile.' Onelli, who by now had been made director of his zoo, led an expedition to the lake. His party watched from the shore for weeks, until the onset of the southern winter; then they exploded eleven dynamite charges in its depths in the hope of forcing the monster to the surface. The waters boiled, but no prehistoric monsters emerged and the party returned empty-handed to Buenos Aires.

There is no further to go. South of Patagonia there is only Tierra del Fuego, the icy Land of Fire, and then the freezing waters of the Southern Ocean. And there is little in the Southern Ocean but a dozen 'doubtful islands', lumps of wind-swept rock in the numbing sea, sometimes reported and surveyed by the most competent of mariners, which nevertheless elude rediscovery by later explorers. Many, no doubt, never existed, and were the result of misidentification and poor navigation; but even today, some may still await rediscovery and perhaps harbour their own strange and unknown forms of life. At Kerguelen, an undoubtedly real island just north of the Antarctic Circle, the hoofmarks of some large and unidentifiable animal, that apparently came from the sea, were discovered by a naval surveying party in May 1840.

Another continent? Africa. In the time of Idi Amin, Uganda was home to a talking tortoise which roamed the country, prophesying trouble for the dictator. On one occasion, it was reported, it entered a local police station and demanded to be taken to the town of Jinja, near Kampala, where it held a meeting with the provincial governor and the police commissioner. These worthies were quick to deny that any such thing had happened; Amin issued a statement denouncing his people for being 'drunk with rumours' and threatened to put anyone trafficking in tortoise tales before a firing squad. Fourteen years later, when the country was in the grip of an AIDS epidemic, a talking goat arrived in the village of Kyabagala to announce, 'in a loud, terrifying voice', that the disease was a divine punishment for failure to observe the Ten Commandments. In Burundi, the people believe that Lake Tanganyika and the Lukuga River are infested by vampiric mermaids known as *mambu mutu*, which kill people to eat their brains and suck their blood; there are also tales of land-locked, though less deadly, merfolk from Nigeria and Zambia. In Zanzibar, the men live in occasional terror of the attacks of a bat-winged flying dwarf – a bedroom invader of sorts – which in 1972 and again in 1995 appeared inside homes at night. *Popobawa* – the name is derived from the Swahili for 'bat' and 'wing' – pins its victims down, sodomises them, then warns that it will be back if they fail to tell their friends what has happened, a tactic that led to bizarre scenes on the island's streets as violated men accosted total strangers to tell of how they had been buggered by the bat-man. The scare even influenced the local elections: Zanzibar's chief minister blamed the opposition for the *popobawa's* depredations, while his opponents responded by suggesting that he was really the dwarfish sodomite himself.

To the east, in Kenya, on 23 December 1982, showers of stones, which seemed to materialise from thin air, began to strike the home of Peter Kavoi and his family in the town of Machakos. The bombardment persisted for weeks, despite the continual presence of investigators at the home. 'My life has become an unbelievable nightmare,' Kavoi told one of the investigators trying to help him. 'I have been struck by them and my face cut. My son and his children were so frightened they fled, and our neighbours are saying we are bewitched. I can tell you honestly that we are being driven mad by what is happening.' One odd feature of the case was that the stones came from many different directions – some were flung horizontally, others fell, some landed gently, and some with such force that they shattered. Several samples were gathered: they were no different to the other pebbles and rocks that littered the area.

But we are back to falling things again. Another country? Indonesia, where on the island of Seram in the Moluccas *orang bati*, or 'flying men' – devilish creatures human in form, with red skin, black wings and long, thin tails – swoop from their lairs in the mountains to carry off the unwary children of the coast. Russia, where in 1987 an expedition set out for the Kamchatka peninsula, in the furthest reaches of Siberia, to search for the monstrous *irkuiem*, an unidentified mammal which looks like a polar bear but moves like a caterpillar. Spain, where two years earlier, farmers working on the land around Pulpi, on the south-east coast, experienced a protracted drought, which they blamed on the activities of mysterious light planes; every time black thunderheads rolled over the horizon, bringing with them the promise of a break in the dry spell, the planes would take off from their secret airfields, and appeared overhead spewing chemicals to disperse the rain-clouds. Their sponsors were rumoured to be local tomato barons, or possibly astronomers fanatically clearing the atmosphere to ensure optimum observational conditions. In Iceland, belief in nature spirits is so strong that a succession of bulldozer accidents prompted the national road authority to negotiate with the malevolent elves whom they believed were causing the problems; with the help of psychic mediators, the problem was solved. In Mauritius, in the 1770s, a wizard beacon-keeper named Bottineau accurately predicted the arrival of sailing ships at the island up to four days before they were visible to watchers on shore; his discovery, *nauscopie* – the art of discerning the movements of vessels by interpreting changes in cloud patterns and other subtle atmospheric effects – was demonstrated successfully for years, but lost shortly after his death, never to be rediscovered. In Germany, a man named Orffyreus once built a machine that persuaded many learned observers that he had discovered the secret of perpetual motion, and the above-mentioned and unfortunate dentist Karl Bachseitz had his experience with the talking toilet . . .

Let's halt for a moment to consider the Bachseitz case in more detail; it is rather more complex than it first appears, and typical in its reluctance to offer easy solutions. Dr Bachseitz, an eminently respectable sixty-year-old, operated a dental surgery in the small German town of Neutraubling with the help of his seventeen-year-old secretary, Claudia Judenmann. One day in the spring of 1982 a female patient leant over to make use of the dental spittoon. 'Shut your mouth,' said the spittoon. A few days later, a male patient, prostrate in the dentist's chair, heard the wash basin command: 'Open your mouth wider, stupid.' The next victim was a woman using the surgery toilet; no sooner had she sat down than voice from beneath her commanded: 'Move your behind, I can't see a thing.'

For the next eleven months Dr Bachseitz was a tormented man. The voice broke in on his work up to ninety times a day, taking over phone calls, abusing him and his patients in a guttural Bavarian accent, and hinting that it was planning terrible fates for his wife. It gave itself a name, Chopper, and hurled a rich stream of obscenities around the surgery, but at the same time talked sweetly to Claudia, enquiring if she had enjoyed her weekend and seeming to know a lot about how she had spent it.

By February 1982, the desperate Dr Bachseitz had had enough. He filed a suit against persons unknown for harassment and injury, and called in Germany's most distinguished poltergeist hunter, Hans Bender, as well as the police, the Post Office, and a television crew. Bender held a conversation with the voice, which begged him: 'Help me. Release me.' The Post Office men disconnected the telephone – not that that stopped its ghostly ringing – and the television people filmed the voice as it spoke to Claudia from a plughole and over the phone. But it was the police who made the greatest progress. Early in March, the public prosecutor at nearby Regensburg, Elmar Fischer, announced that his men had solved the case: it was a hoax, perpetrated by Bachseitz and Claudia, using 'voice projection'.

Eventually Claudia appeared on a television show to agree

that this had indeed been pretty much the case; she and Dr Bachseitz had been playing along with an unknown man who used to phone the surgery several times a day, adopting Chopper's distinctive voice. Naturally this explanation satisfied most people, and the police case against the dentist and his assistant was dropped, though both were nominally liable to up to three years in prison for 'feigning a crime'. It is of course entirely possible that the whole episode was an elaborate practical joke. Yet the official explanation left many questions unanswered. It did not explain why the respectable Dr Bachseitz should endure a year's worth of obscene phone calls and draw attention to himself in so bizarre a fashion, simply to humour a dangerously eccentric third party whom he did not even know. It did not explain how the peculiar voice appeared to emanate from sinks and toilets, light fittings and spittoons, nor how it knew so much about Claudia's activities at the weekends. And there was no good reason for the dentist to risk exposure by calling in the police, unless he was so vain that it amused him to test his wits against those of the authorities. So there may be more to the Bachseitz case than German television audiences were told.

At the very least, Dr Bachseitz's story offers an intriguing contrast between the mundane and the remarkable – the clinical familiarity of the dental surgery and the outlandish reality of the events that occurred within it – and a reminder that there is nowhere so mundane it cannot also be bizarre, nowhere so comprehensively explored that it cannot produce the unexpected. Still more importantly, it recalls a dozen other cases – such as the peculiar phenomena that occurred in a woodshed at Clarendon, Quebec. Links and patterns begin to emerge from such eddies in the unknown.

For example: flying pigs, surely the most ridiculous and improbable of strange phenomena. One was seen over Llangollen one night during the great Welsh religious revival of 1904–5; it had short wings, four legs and seemed to be moving at about twenty miles per hour. A misinterpretation, perhaps, despite the use of 'powerful field glasses' by observers, since the object was estimated to be two miles up in the atmosphere; but if there are no flying porkers, what left the gigantic pig's droppings that appeared on the first floor balcony of 325b Sparkler Drive, Huntingdon Beach, California, on three occasions in January and February 1982? And if giant domestic animals do not exist, what made the impression of a chicken's foot, eight feet long and sixteen feet across, in Gianpiero Baizi's maize field outside Milan in the summer of 1985?

Such bizarre stories strain the outer limits of credibility, even by the dubious standards of the borderlands. Yet we cannot entirely laugh them off or ignore them, for there are also tales, perhaps a little better evidenced, of phenomena that are nearly as outlandish. One Maryland monster, Goatman, who has roamed the back lanes of Prince George's County since 1957, certainly seemed to be a creature of folklore. Local people could not agree on whether he was an ancient hermit with a long white beard, a mad scientist from the Beltsville Agricultural Farm, or a were-creature of some sort, though his principal purpose seemed to be to scare courting couples from Prince George's Community College in the local lovers' lane. Persistent research into the origins of the story, however, eventually revealed that they appeared to have their source in an August 1957 sighting of a hairy ape, seen in the Upper Marlboro area by Mr and Mrs Reverty Garner of Brown Station Road. A similar man-beast was seen twice in the autumn of 1976, and again in March 1977, by three different witnesses. It was described as gorilla-like, six feet tall, round-shouldered, and covered with grey-brown hair. The Goatman legend, then, may be based on real sightings of an ape-creature: Bigfoot in Maryland.

Repetition makes any phenomenon more interesting. In the summer of 1970, a silver thread, or wire, appeared in the sky over the home of Mr and Mrs A.P. Smith of 85 Forest Avenue, Caldwell, New Jersey. It hung there, as though suspended from some invisible supports, throughout the month of August, to the bafflement of the Smiths, their neighbours, and the local police. A few days after the thread's first appearance, the local newspaper reported:

> It looks rigid, as if it were a wire, not a string. It appears silver when the sunlight strikes it. On Monday it hung about 150 feet above the houses on Forest Avenue and Hillside Avenue. By Tuesday, it seemed limper to Mrs Smith and other observers, as if one of its ends – wherever that is – had loosened. It also seemed lower in the sky.
>
> The Caldwell police tried to trace it on Monday, found signs of it up Hillside and down towards West Caldwell, but lost it in the clouds before tracking down the origins. They looked again on Tuesday with the same nebulous results.

The silver thread's provenance remained a mystery; the best explanation the locals could proffer was that it was a line that had fallen from the Goodyear blimp as it passed over the town. But the thread just hung there, day after day, long enough for the noted investigator Berthold Schwarz to visit the Smiths and confirm its presence. On the afternoon of 31 August, the family heard a loud explosion, or sonic boom, and shortly afterwards noticed that the line had fallen to earth and was now lying on the ground outside their home. Mrs Smith phoned the police, who arrived and took the thread away. It proved to be a stiff, translucent nylon fishing line.

Whatever its significance, however, this eccentric story is not unique. In September 1978 a car worker named John Wright saw something snagging a bush behind his home in Greensburg, Ohio. It was fishing line, trailing off into the sky, and he hauled in a single length of about 1000 feet of it, enough to fill eight reels. At that point the line snapped and the remainder floated off into the sky until it was lost to view.

Parallels and echoes of many other phenomena can be found in the annals of the unexplained. Some come from countries and peoples that share a culture or a history. The Black Dog, a gigantic, shaggy, ghostly dog with blazing red eyes, is primarily reported from the north of England, East Anglia and the west country, but such creatures are also encountered in northern

Europe, Nova Scotia and parts of the United States. Descriptions of these beasts are remarkably similar wherever they are encountered, though there is some dispute as to whether they are benevolent ghosts or are indifferent or hostile to man. In County Londonderry, in 1928, a student from Trinity College, Dublin, who had never even heard of the Black Dog (or *pooka*, as it is generally known in Ireland) was fishing on a riverbank, when a huge dog came padding along the shallow stream. Feeling an intense sense of menace, the student dropped his rod and bolted up the nearest tree, from where he observed the animal as it went past. It looked up at him, a friend later recorded, with eyes like blazing coals and 'almost human intelligence, and bared its teeth with a mixture of snarl and jeering grin.' Similarly, the people of rural Mississippi, in the 1930s, told of encounters with gigantic black dogs 'with big red eyes glowing like chunks of fire', and in France the author Pierre van Paassen tried to set his own fierce dogs on a large black specimen that appeared in his home. This, he wrote,

> led to a horrible scene . . . they retreated growling back into my room, baring their fangs and snarling. Presently they howled as if they were in excruciating pain, and were snapping and biting in all directions, as if they were fighting some fierce enemy. I have never seen them in such mortal panic. I could not come to their aid, for I saw nothing to strike . . . The battle with the invisible foe lasted less than two minutes. Then one of my dogs yelled as if he were in his death throes, fell on the floor and died.

Such accounts, as well as exhibiting striking similarities, also parallel (and may have been influenced by) the Black Dogs that appear in folk tales and literature, from the tales of Hans Christian Andersen to the adventures of Sherlock Holmes. Alternatively, of course, the ghost dogs of folklore may record real encounters with phantom canines in the past.

Apparently related cases become still more interesting when the reports come from different countries and different periods. Reports of giant ape-creatures have come from cultures as distinct as aboriginal Australia and twentieth-century California. Most lake creatures resemble the Loch Ness Monster. But there are many lesser-known examples of intriguing similarities, too. In the Swiss, Bavarian and Austrian Alps, mountaineers and travellers sometimes encounter an aggressive, hole-dwelling lizard known as the *tatzelwurm*, or 'worm-with-feet'. In some areas it is known as the 'spring-worm' because of its alarming leaping ability – it can jump, witnesses say, up to nine feet, and attacks and wounds cattle. Descriptions of this miniature monster vary, but witnesses generally agree that it is between eighteen inches and three feet long and cylindrical in shape, with two or four short, stubby legs and a blunt and heavy head. Although it is well enough known in its homeland, few outsiders have heard of the *tatzelwurm*, despite a considerable tradition of sightings and a discussion of the evidence for its existence in the cryptozoologists' bible, Bernard Heuvelmans' *On the Track of Unknown Animals*. Yet descriptions of it resemble those of an equally mysterious Japanese snake, known as the *tzuchinoko*, which has been reported from the mountainous areas of all the main Japanese islands, and also from Korea, since the thirteenth century. Like the *tatzelwurm*, the *tzuchinoko* is credited with large eyes, large scales and a prodigious leaping ability; there are also some differences in the description, particularly an absence of legs in the case of the Japanese monster. These parallel traditions could indicate the existence of a single type of unknown animal on opposite sides of the world, the evolution of two similar creatures – one a skink, perhaps, and the other a species of snake – or an intriguing independent development of an equivalent folklore among two very different peoples.

Cryptozoology is not the only borderland discipline in which such thought-provoking parallels may be discovered. Welsh historians of the Tudor period record the extremely peculiar tale of the *cochion*, or 'red ones', a people who lived in *Coed y Dugoed Mawr*, the Great Dark Wood. They built no houses, but used their considerable skills with the bow and arrow to terrorise the local people, some of whom set scythes into the brickwork of their chimneys to prevent the *cochion* from climbing down them to murder the inhabitants in their beds. In some Welsh stories the *cochion* are given the attributes of fairies, though in others they are real enough; they are, for instance, supposed to have set an ambush for the local landowner, Baron Owen, in the 1530s, and slain him. In consequence, it has recently been suggested that they may have been a tribe of Red Indians who had somehow contrived to cross the Atlantic. It seems appropriate, therefore, that the Piute Indians of Nevada have a mirror tradition concerning a tribe of red-haired cannibals, the Siwash, who had lighter skin than any of the native people and preyed on the Piute until they were defeated in a three-year war. The few remaining cannibals hid themselves in a cave; when they were found, the Piute piled wood across the entrance and burned or asphyxiated the survivors. Little or no evidence now remains to prove the existence of the Siwash, whom some present-day Piutes suspect of being a band of misplaced Europeans or Egyptians.

Another Native American tribe, the Navajo, have a traditional belief in a society of evil-doers called 'skin-walkers'. Skin-walkers have something in common with the European werewolf; they are humans who have the ability to change into animals, though they possess other strange powers in addition, such as the ability to move much faster than a car. But the notion that they band together in a group, and wear the skins of animals, is reminiscent of European traditions of witches' sabbats, as well as of the most terrible of secret societies, the Brujeria, a brotherhood of warlocks who dwell in a labyrinth of caves beneath the impenetrable forests of Chiloe, a large island off the coast of Chile.

Members of the Brujeria wear waistcoats of human flesh flayed from the torsos of Christian corpses, which give off a gentle phosphorescence that guides them as they pick their way along their secret forest paths by night. The society owns a ghost ship, the *Caleuche*, which is officered by witches and crewed by shipwrecked mariners. This frigate, which is often portrayed as a burning ghost-ship, of the sort that haunts the Northumberland Strait, can sail into the wind and even submerge, useful attributes for a vessel chiefly used to smuggle cargoes up river for the Brujeria's merchant allies. When the strange vessel suffers engine trouble, she puts into a cove for repairs; should her crew be disturbed at their work, she is transformed instantly from a ship into a gigantic log.

The Brujeria's principal occupation, however, is plotting the downfall of mankind. The brotherhood is guarded during its deliberations by two monsters, the *chivato* and the *invunche*, both gradually moulded from human children. The *chivato* is part goat, part man, the *invunche* an even stranger creation: over many months a young boy's head is twisted with a tourniquet until it has been turned through 180 degrees and looks directly back; his right arm is then sewn into an incision under the shoulder blade. The new *invunche* sprouts bristles and is fed on human flesh. He is kept naked in the Brujeria's headquarters cave, where he acts as both a guardsman and a talisman in certain of the society's rituals.

The Brujeria are not simply part of the rich folklore of Spanish Chile. On at least two occasions – in 1743 and again in 1880 – alleged members of the society were captured and tried as witches. In the great trial of 1880, one of the main witnesses was an old man named Mateo Conuecar. He named one Jose Merriman as king of the witches and explained that he had entered the sacred caves of the Brujeria through a passageway that led from a camouflaged door in Merriman's cellar. There are also interesting similarities between the monster-manufacturing practices of the Brujeria and those of the Dacianos, a particular caste of European gypsies who specialised in the manufacture of freaks. These Dacianos had their headquarters in the Gorge de Pancorbo, near Victoria in Spain, though they also met near Diekirsch, Germany, Bourbonne-les-Bains in France, and at an old square tower near Cleveland in Yorkshire. They were nicknamed 'the child-buyers' and specialised in kidnapping children, three or four years old, whom they lamed and disfigured before selling to vagabonds and blind men to be used as beggars. Chile, of course, was, for centuries, the colonial possession of Spain. Perhaps a few Dacianos emigrated there from their gorge near Victoria, and founded the society; perhaps it was only traditional stories of the gypsies' methods that reached South America, to be elaborated over the years in Chilean memories.

Naturally there are significant differences between the phenomena reported in foreign lands, as well as significant parallels. The vampire of the Philippines, for example, is a different creature from the blood-sipper of western Europe. The Filipino *manananggal* is a woman who can cut her own body in two, sending the top half flying through the night in search of babies to devour. The *manananggal* does not seem to be bothered by garlic, but it can be repulsed by the touch of a dried stingray's tail and, like a western vampire, it is vulnerable to daylight; the two halves must rejoin before dawn if the vampire is to survive. There was a *manananggal* scare in Manila during the local election campaign of May 1992; a woman named Martina Santa Rosa came forward to say that she had been savaged by just such a creature. 'She attacked me – I was lucky I was able to get free,' Santa Rosa said. 'I saw half of her body. It was naked. She had long, scraggly hair, long arms, nails and sharp fangs.' A neighbour, Alfonso Bernardo, backed up the account, coming forward to assert that he had seen the *manananggal*'s top half flying away from Santa Rosa's house. Similarly, the feminine mermaid of Scottish tradition is very different to Burundi's vampiric *mambu mutu*, and accounts of 'little people', which abound all over the world, vary subtly from country to country. The western elf is related to, but distinct from, Far Eastern equivalents such as the Javanese *tuyul*, an entity that looks like a bald and naked child with big eyes and red skin. Like most oriental spirits, the *tuyul* moves without touching the ground, but it resembles its European counterparts in defying all attempts to relegate it to the realm of folklore, and continues to be seen occasionally in the modern world. In 1985 a Japanese *tuyul*-hunting expedition visited the Indonesian island and interviewed a clothing designer in Jakarta. 'I saw a *tuyul* about three years ago,' the man told his interviewer. 'It was real; it looked like a little naked boy and tried to steal my money.'

Finally, there are phenomena that remain specific to a particular people, though they may travel with them throughout the world. Sudden Unexplained Nocturnal Death Syndrome, a mysterious but real and very deadly illness that has defied attempts to isolate and identify it, is a good example of this kind. The disease, if that is what it is, is almost wholly confined to men from south-east Asia – Thailand, Cambodia, Vietnam and Laos – but it strikes both at home and among migrant communities, such as those in the Middle East. The symptoms of the illness are rather remarkable; the victims, who are generally young and apparently fit, die abruptly and inexplicably in their sleep, sometimes frothing at the mouth in a manner that suggests they have been killed by sheer terror.

Although SUNDS has claimed hundreds of victims, doctors do not understand it, nor can they explain why it strikes within this particular community; the syndrome's very name is little more than an elaborate confession of ignorance on the part of the medical community. In Thailand, though, complex explanations have evolved to explain the peculiarities of the illness. There, the deaths are sometimes interpreted as the work of evil female spirits, out hunting for suitable husbands; once dead, the victims are forcibly married in the spirit world to their murderers. In order to avoid this unpleasant fate, some Thai males have taken to going to bed wearing women's clothing and make-up in the hope of fooling any prowling female spirits.

Another example of an alarmingly specific phenomenon was the American killer kangaroo scare of 1934, which involved the appearance of a creature like a giant kangaroo in the farming community of South Pittsburgh, Tennessee. The monster killed and partially devoured several police dogs, some geese and a few ducks; it was tracked up a mountainside to a large cave, where it appeared to vanish, and it was never identified or caught. But when it hopped into oblivion, it left this strange planet just a little stranger.

2

Lands of Gods and Angels

This is a book about strange phenomena. It is a book about evidence and belief. It is also a book about explanations.

Nevertheless, it is not really a book about what is true and what is false. These concepts, so essential to other disciplines, can become clumsy weapons when brought to bear within the borderlands, capable of crushing and destroying a witness whose testimony might have yielded valuable insights or a piece of evidence that might have pointed us towards an explanation, were it handled with greater sensitivity.

Let me make myself clear. I am not suggesting that we uncritically accept every story we are told, adopt theories that are not supported by any evidence, ignore science or dismiss the arguments of sceptics out of hand. I have had neither the time nor the inclination to make a proper study of occultism or mysticism, and I do not want to involve us here in issues that are solely a matter of faith.

What I want to do is argue that 'fact' and 'fiction' are inadequate categories when it comes to sifting strange phenomena. I am not denying that thousands of fakes and hoaxes litter our way, nor even that some unusual events may be physically real, and just as thoroughly peculiar as they first appear to be. I am suggesting that many strange events occur somewhere on a continuum that runs from 'real' to 'unreal'; that they may be real to their witnesses without necessarily being physically real; that each truth begs as many questions as it answers, and that every falsity can tell us something about the psychology of a witness, the problems of perception, the propensity to fantasy or self-deception, and the influence of the witness's background and culture.

Experiencing Strange Phenomena

Time and again in the following pages we will find ourselves wondering not only what to believe and who to trust, but, more fundamentally, whether we are dealing with something that is physically real or something that is – in a sometimes indeterminate way – the product of a witness's imagination.

It is important to realise that this problem applies not only when there is obviously scope for the human imagination to play tricks, such as in sightings of ghosts or encounters with fairies, but in cases that are generally presumed to involve physical phenomena. If, for example, you are asked the question, 'Do you believe in UFOs?', the chances are that what is meant is, 'Do you believe that UFOs are alien spacecraft?' This is a valid suggestion, and many able researchers do believe that extraterrestrial visitors are responsible for the hard core of flying saucer reports. But there are other possible explanations for UFO sightings. Some unidentified flying objects may be secret weapons, covertly flown by our own or someone else's government. Many, certainly, are the products of simple misidentification, and others are produced by more complex illusions, such as mirages. A fair number appear to result from observations of unknown or poorly understood natural phenomena, and more than a few seem to be experienced by witnesses who have entered an altered state of consciousness of some sort – anything from a dream to an hypnotic trance.

Nor are any of these explanations complete in themselves. Suppose, for example, a sincere and intelligent witness sees the planet Venus – a bright but stationary light just above the horizon – yet reports that he watched a brilliantly-lit UFO, which may well have seemed to move about the night sky before finally darting off at high speed: a surprisingly common experience. Having recognised the mistake, we could close the case file and forget all about it. On the other hand, we could put the experience to better use by observing that many witnesses have a tendency to see something strange in the essentially mundane. If another percipient recalls, under hypnosis, that she was lifted from her bed in a city apartment by an invisible force field in the middle of the night, teleported through a closed window and into a waiting UFO, subjected to a medical examination and then returned to her room, all without disturbing her husband, who was sleeping next to her, we might ask whether there is any physical evidence to support such claims – marks left by the examination, or witnesses outside the apartment who saw the abduction take place – and also whether there is any reason why the experience itself might not have been a dream of some sort, or even a false memory produced under hypnosis.

Moreover, it is not enough to ask, in such complex cases, only the obvious questions: 'What was it that this witness saw?' and 'Was the experience real?' If the abduction experience *was* real, why was the husband not disturbed? How was it possible for the experient's body to pass through a solid object such as a window? If it was illusory, then how did the witness come to concoct – and apparently believe – such an eleborate story? Had she entered an altered state of consciousness, and, if so, what sort of altered state was it, and why did this particular witness experience it at this particular time? How did it affect her perceptions, and why did the aliens who examined her appear to be the same as those encountered by dozens of other people who also remember being abducted? Did the witness know enough about abduction cases to fabricate her story, consciously or unconsciously? Was her account influenced by a desire to please the UFO investigator handling the case or by leading questions put to her by her regression therapist?

Did her conscious memories in any way match those recalled under hypnosis?

Let me stress now that some of the mysteries we will be encountering will have purely physical explanations. For example, a number of reported falls of frogs, fish and other unusual objects from the sky may be attributed to the actions of whirlwinds and waterspouts, which suck up the contents of a stream or pond from one location and dump them later on another. UFO researchers can point to a significant handful of cases which resulted in the appearance of physical traces such as apparent 'landing marks' and burns on the faces and bodies of witnesses who came too close to an unidentified flying object. Similarly, the recent discoveries of several new and unusual species of deer in the forests of Vietnam suggest that at least some of the 350 or so unknown animals currently being hunted around the world, ranging from Bigfoot to unidentified species of water monsters, really might exist.

Indeed, it may well seem both easier and more realistic to accept that most strange phenomena are physically real. After all, most of the witnesses on whose memories we are relying make that assumption. The Loch Ness Monster looks and behaves much as a real animal would. Alien abductors may be alien, but they also appear to be flesh-and-blood creatures flying metallic spacecraft, and preoccupied with physical procedures such as medical examinations. Moreover, it is always possible to explain the more bizarre and improbable aspects of such encounters by suggesting that we are simply failing to understand an alien technology superior to our own.

Nevertheless, the fact that several hundred witnesses believe they have seen large, moving objects in Loch Ness and that the loch appears to contain enough fish to support a small population of aquatic monsters does not prove that there are monsters in it. There may be, but if there are, how are we to explain the very similar sightings of apparently identical beasts in other lochs and Irish lakes too small to support even a single large animal, much less a breeding herd? Are these 'monsters' ghosts of some sort, or are witnesses misidentifying strange wave formations or diving birds? If so, if the unreal can seem so real, can we be sure there even is a 'real'? In short, to what extent are we, ourselves, the phenomenon?

Wondrous Events

One researcher who has supplied noteworthy insights into the reality of strange phenomena is David Hufford, a folklorist whose field work in Newfoundland and elsewhere has led him to propose a particularly interesting model for assessing supernatural events.

Hufford's speciality, which he discusses at length in his book *The Terror That Comes in the Night*, is the 'bedroom invader,' an entity that gains access to a room, generally at night, and badly frightens the occupant. We have already met one: the invisible, bat-winged creature which so scared 'Randy P.', alone in his college room. But Randy's entity was not representative of the breed. Most bedroom invaders are far more terrifying.

In the course of his research, Hufford discovered that bedroom invader reports occur in many different cultures, from America to Japan. A typical case involves the witness waking from sleep to become aware that something is approaching his room. He may hear footsteps moving towards the door, or perhaps even see a strange entity closing in on him from a great distance – far greater than the furthest limits of the room. The entity comes nearer and nearer, looming over the witness's bed, until eventually it is crouching on his chest. Its weight pushes him down into the mattress but, when he tries to struggle free, he will find himself paralysed and unable to do anything to fight off the attacker. His assailant may even speak, often mocking its victim with the words 'You knew that I would come.'

Most bedroom invaders are visible and adopt a human form, though witnesses often feel there is something strongly animal or alien about them. They are seldom recognisable. Some are no more than a vague blur; others may be better defined, but have a blank where their face should be. Almost without exception, however, they seem menacing, evil and powerful, even though they never actually harm anybody. Lying there, unable to move, utterly vulnerable and at the mercy of a malevolent and apparently supernatural being, is often the most hideous experience of the witness's life.

Hufford discovered many variants in the bedroom invader experience. In Newfoundland the entity is known by the generic name of the 'Old Hag', and is thought to be an ancient, evil woman. In Japan it may more closely resemble a demon from local mythology. A number of witnesses have reported small alien figures in their rooms, much like the 'Greys' which some UFO researchers believe are abducting humans in order to carry out medical experiments on them. Others undergo a less-well-defined but equally unsettling experience. During a recent correspondence on the subject on an internet e-mail group, Paul Vincent, a computer analyst on the staff of the University of Central England, recalled

> a period of about a year in my early twenties during which, several times a week, I'd come awake with the awareness that the bedclothes were being lifted off me: not rolled back, or a corner being lifted, but the whole bedclothes lifting a few inches . . . Next, I'd become aware of deep, heavy breathing from near the bed. Then I'd start to feel fear – an icy cold hand would grab my scrotum and squeeze. No pain was caused by this, but it certainly wasn't pleasant.
>
> Around this time, I'd try to move and discover that I was completely paralysed – I could feel my fingertips but I couldn't even twitch them. Next, the squeezing would stop, and I'd feel the bedclothes drop back on me – I even felt a draft of warm air gust over my face as this happened. Then the final section would come as the feeling of being pressed down on, all over, by a great force from above . . . At this point I'd suddenly succeed in twitching a finger. Once I could do this, I'd be able to move my whole body, and would come 'properly' awake, usually panting for breath.

Sometimes there are clues which seem to explain the origin of the phenomenon. Steve Howells of South Wales remembered reading his way through his uncle's collection of books by Dennis Wheatley – a novelist who specialised in tales of witchcraft and demonology – after which he 'awoke in the night with my head side ways on the pillow so that one eye could see around the room, the other being buried in the pillow. Though my free eye could see the room around me, my buried eye could see down into a pit at the bottom of which was the big red guy himself, horns and all, reaching up to me.' Another correspondent, Bill Jacobs, of San Diego State University, recalled watching a film about Frankenstein and then waking 'to find a translucent Frankenstein's monster (the classic movie version) standing in my bed. I say "in" because he was standing on the floor under the middle of my bed, his legs extending through it.'

Hufford came across many similar cases during his own research. (In Newfoundland he discovered that almost one in four of the population had experienced a visit from the 'Old Hag'.) Yet he did not believe that the bedroom invader could be a purely cultural phenomenon, since few of his informants had discussed their experiences with anyone and almost a third had never previously heard of the phenomenon and were surprised to discover that the experience was shared by others and that their encounters followed a recognisable pattern. Instead, Hufford looked deeper, suggesting that his witnesses were undergoing an experience common to every society around the world, but interpreting it in a manner appropriate to their own culture, their own beliefs and their own experiences. In other words, he identified the Old Hag experience as a source, rather than a product, of belief.

We will return to the question of what the Old Hag actually is in a later chapter. For the moment it is enough to note that later researchers, following Hufford's lead, have identified other phenomena, common to many cultures, which also appear to be in some sense 'real' and which can be analysed using the same experience-centred approach.

Of these, probably the most important are what James McClenon terms 'wondrous events'. McClenon, a research fellow at the Pennsylvania State University College of Medicine, has collected more than a thousand first-hand accounts of extrasensory perception, apparitions, out-of-the-body experiences (OBEs), psychic surgery and spiritual healing, and shown that they recur, with certain identifiable characteristics, in cultures from Europe to Japan and from Africa to China. (For example, a survey published in 1978 demonstrated that OBEs have been reported in nineteen out of twenty societies.) Furthermore, such anomalous experiences have been recorded throughout history and have played an important role in the development of concepts of an afterlife, paranormal powers, ghosts, spirits and the human soul. In his book *Wondrous Events: Foundations of Religious Belief*, McClenon suggests that similarities between Buddhist and Christian views of the afterlife may be, at least in part, the product of common experience of such phenomena.

There can be no doubt that strange phenomena have always been associated with religious practices, as they still are today. Indeed, inexplicable events have been incorporated into religion at the most basic levels. Every faith owes its foundation to one or more 'wondrous event' and the key figures in the major religions – men such as Moses, Christ and Muhammad – all experienced such events themselves. In short, it is possible to argue not that strange phenomena are the product of faith and religion, but that religion and faith have their roots in the stimulus of – to all appearances real – strange phenomena.

Encounters with the Divine

Of all religious phenomena, the most significant and, surely significantly, the most common, are visions of gods and angels, devils and saints. Throughout recorded history, the deities of almost every religion have manifested themselves on earth to bestow favour on their chosen instruments, instruct their peoples and (perhaps most frequently of all) to warn of the consequences of deviation from the letter of their laws. These 'visions' may take the form of voices that seem to come from nowhere; alternately, the gods may appear in dreams or as visions, or perhaps disguise themselves as humans and let slip their divinity only by the manner of their sudden disappearances or through the miracles they work.

Such accounts are of great antiquity. The Greeks and Romans thought the inhabitants of Hades and Mount Olympus could and did move freely about on earth in animal and human form. This belief helped shape their rich mythologies, but also found its way into some sober contemporary histories of the period. There are, for example, at least a dozen surviving records of what one writer has termed 'classical encounters of the third kind' with the twins Castor and Pollux, who were the patron deities of Sparta and also oversaw travel, hospitality and the conduct of war. For this reason they seem to have frequently appeared to reward kind hosts, take part in battles or announce the outcome of a campaign. According to Cicero, when the Romans fought Perseus of Macedonia in 167 BC, one P. Vatienus, who was travelling by night along the Salarian Way, met two young men on white horses (later presumed to be the twins) who confided that Perseus had been taken prisoner that day. When Vatienus told the Roman senate the news he was thrown into prison 'for speaking inconsiderately on a state affair', and not released until news of the victory reached Rome by conventional means some time later. As well as freeing the visionary, the senate agreed to recognise the truth of his tale by awarding him land and immunity from taxes in a decree which still existed in Cicero's day, one hundred years later.

Looked at objectively, there does not appear to be any great difference between the peculiar encounter of Vatienus, who was sufficiently certain that something remarkable had happened to him to risk ridicule by approaching the Roman senate, and the experiences of religious leaders who receive visions and visits from their own deities. The only real distinction between them is that the Roman appears to have made no claim to have been especially favoured by his gods, whereas the founders and prophets of monotheistic religions are regarded as very special people whose experiences offer them privileged insights into the will of God, and thus some secular power over their co-religionists.

Because this power tends to be ceded willingly – albeit after the prophet encounters some initial resistance – the religious visions of a handful of men have greatly influenced the entire course of history. Around 1250 BC, the prophet Moses was tending sheep in Midian when the voice of God, issuing from a blazing bush, commanded him to lead the Israelites out of Egypt and restore the Jews to their promised land. He obeyed, with consequences that are still being felt today. Muhammad received his call around the year 610 while meditating on Mount Hira, above the plain of Mecca (again, it came in the form of a voice speaking from nowhere, rather than a vision). Further revelations came to the prophet in similar fashion for the rest of his life (initially in a variety of different voices, and occasionally as a sound like 'the reverberating of bells'), and, put together, now constitute the text of the Koran. With his word and this book to guide them, the Muhammadans burst forth from the desert in 633 and within a few decades had not only shattered the ancient Persian empire and nearly destroyed that of Byzantium, but introduced their new religion to half of Asia and half of Africa.

Today it is usual for liberal religious leaders to suggest that the ancient and extraordinary traditions of such encounters with the gods are symbolic and need not be taken too literally. But there is in fact every reason to think that, for those concerned, these experiences were not only the most important of their lives, but very real indeed.

We know this because, within the last two hundred years, two modern prophets have reported comparable visions and left contemporary records of what occurred which are still available for inspection by historians, unlike those written in the very earliest days of Judaism, Christianity and Islam. The first of these visitations is said to have occurred in 1819 when God and Christ appeared together to a farmer's son from Palmyra, New York and warned him not to join any of the established churches. Four years later a second vision, this one of an angel called Moroni, guided the young man, Joseph Smith, to a cache of gold tablets buried on a hillside above his log cabin. According to Smith, the tablets were covered in a mysterious and indecipherable text, but in September 1827 Moroni appeared once more and gave him two magic stones to help him translate the ancient language on the tablets. By placing the two stones in his hat, burying his face in the crown and pulling a blanket over his head, Smith was able to read the golden hieroglyphics and dictate the words that became the foundation of a new religion: Mormonism.

Smith's claims to divine favour, believed absolutely by his followers, were greeted with derision by many of his contemporaries. The enemies of the new religion savagely attacked Smith as a charlatan, pointing out that his discovery of the strange gold tablets came at the height of a mania for treasure-hunting that had swept across the state, demonstrating that he was only one of many engaged in setting up new religions at the time, and poking fun at his claim that he could not produce the mysterious tablets as evidence, because Moroni had returned and taken them from him as soon as the translation was complete. They even collected statements from neighbours who claimed Smith had told them the Book of Mormon had been intended as a novel and that he was startled to realise that people were taking it seriously. The Book itself, essentially a history of America from 500 BC to AD 400, which includes the claim that Christ himself descended from heaven following his crucifixion to preach to the inhabitants, runs counter to other written records and the evidence of archaeology, yet Mormons accept it as readily as other Christians accept the Bible, and converts to this fast-growing religion testify both to its inspirational qualities and to the fact that, with its tales of treachery and visions, and many a bloody battle, it makes exciting reading.

Even more remarkable is the story of Hong Xiuquan, a failed civil servant from Guangdong province in China, who was handed a translation of passages from the Christian Bible during a visit to Canton in 1836. The verses of the New Testament helped Hong to make sense of a strange dream he had had in which he fought demons alongside an elder brother on behalf of a man with a golden beard. He now understood that his 'dream' was actually a vision of God and Christ, and that he, himself, was Christ's younger brother and thus God's Chinese son. Preaching this alien doctrine in the hills north of Canton, Hong gradually made converts to a movement that somehow swelled until it became a general rebellion of the southern provinces of China against the rule of the Manchu emperors in the north.

The rebellion – ironically called the Taiping, or 'Heavenly Peace', after one of Hong's slogans – took the Chinese government fifteen years to suppress. Throughout this period, Hong continued to have visions in which his father and elder brother spoke to him. In addition to this – and unusually for a man in his position – he accepted, for a while, the claims of a few of his followers that they were also conduits for celestial edicts. One, a charcoal burner named Yang Xiuqing, would enter a trance state and allow God to speak through him; another, a peasant, Xiao Chaogui, had visions of Jesus and sang songs newly-composed in heaven for the Taiping congregations. Fuelled by such visions, the rebellion became the greatest in the long history of China and led to the deaths of an estimated 60 million people in battle or from starvation and disease.

In the west, visions such as Hong's have, thankfully, had less serious consequences, though they have nevertheless been influential in their own way. True, Joan of Arc, who was guided by the voices of St Catherine and the Archangel Michael, helped the French to throw off English rule during the Hundred Years' War. But Joan was a unique figure, not least because, rather surprisingly, few Christian visionaries have claimed that they have seen Christ or any of the saints. The vast majority are visited by the Blessed Virgin Mary, who acts as an intermediary between heaven and earth, conveying messages and interceding with her son on behalf of humanity. This may be because the greater percentage of this majority are Roman Catholics, for whom the choice of Mary as messenger is a logical one since she (alone, with Christ, of the inhabitants of heaven) is believed to have a physical body in which to appear on earth. Yet to non-Catholics there is something highly questionable about the manner in which the Virgin goes about her work on earth.

To begin with, Mary appears to have spent virtually all of the first 1800 years after her death in heaven, yet for some reason she seems to have made the return journey to earth with ever-increasing regularity since 1830. Setting aside the figure 'clothed with the sun' who appears in the Book of Revelation, the earliest vision for which a record exists dates to AD 432, and the first for which we have significant detail only to 1061, when the lady of the manor of Walsingham in Norfolk was shown a vision of the house where Christ had lived in Nazareth and ordered to build an exact copy. (Intriguingly, the supposed facsimile was completed in an eleventh-century Saxon architectural style and not in the manner of first-century Palestine.)

A further five centuries then elapsed before the next vision of any importance, which occurred, in 1531, not in Europe but in only partly-Christianised Mexico. There an elderly Indian convert named Juan Diego was waylaid on his way to church by the vision of a beautiful young girl who ordered him to build a chapel on the spot where she had appeared. The vision was forced to work a miracle in order to convince the local bishop of Diego's sincerity, and she did so by imprinting her image on the Indian's cactus-fibre cloak, which still exists and now hangs above the altar in a spectacular new basilica in the nearby town of Guadeloupe. Largely on the strength of this miracle, the indian's vision has been accepted as genuine by the church, the first of a total of only ten such experiences to be accorded official recognition, and the only one to date to before 1830. Yet even some contemporary Catholic sources claimed that the full length figure on the cloak was really a painting, and sceptics have pointed out that the Church used the miracle to help convert some eight million Mexicans to

Christianity in the next six years, and that the image bears little resemblance to Diego's own description of his vision. Indeed, perhaps the strangest thing about the whole incident was the account the indian gave of Mary: she looked, he said, like a young Mexican girl of about fourteen. This detail has been variously interpreted: believers suggest that the Virgin had chosen to appear in a form that would not frighten Diego, while sceptics argue that the vision was a fantasy and that Juan's Mary was the product of a specific time and a specific place.

It was not until the mid nineteenth century that visions of the Virgin began to assume the form they generally follow today. Before then, the few visionaries there were had tended to be adult, exceptionally religious and reasonably well educated. This made sense both to the religious, who assumed that Mary's visits were a suitable reward for piety, and the irreligious, for whom such visions were signs of nothing so much as an over-active imagination. In the 1840s, though, a new pattern emerged in which visions of the Virgin were increasingly vouchsafed to young, frequently illiterate, peasant children, some of whom appear to have received little religious education. Both believers and disbelievers have struggled to explain this peculiar *volte face*.

The vision that changed everything occurred near Grenoble, in the French Alps, on 19 September 1846. The two witnesses – fourteen-year-old Melanie Mathieu and Maximin Giraud, aged eleven – were peasants who were looking after cattle in the hills above the settlement of La Salette. They had just awoken from a nap when, at about three o'clock in the afternoon, Melanie saw a light 'far more brilliant than the sun' appear near a spring. The light came from a woman who was sitting with her head in her hands. She was crying. As the curious children approached, the figure stood, commanded them to come closer, and warned:

> If my people will not submit, I shall be forced to let go the

> hand of my son. It is so strong, so heavy, that I can no longer withhold it.
>
> Six days I have given you to labour, and the seventh I have kept for myself, and they will not give it to me. It is this which makes the hand of my son so heavy. Those who drive the carts cannot swear without introducing the name of my son. . . If the harvest is spoilt, it is all on your account.

The vision continued in similar vein for some time, speaking both in French and in the local *patois*, and warning of a disease that would strike the children of the area, and of the imminent failure of the grape and walnut harvests. At length, she concluded: 'Well, my children, you will make this known to all my people,' after which the figure swept up the hillside – hovering, Melanie recalled, just above the level of the grass – and vanished.

If the warnings the vision had issued seemed conventionally calculated to terrify an agricultural community living at subsistence level, the manner of her disappearance was quite extraordinary. Rather like the Cheshire Cat in Lewis Carroll's *Alice in Wonderland*, the vision disappeared in stages, though in this instance it was from the head down, so that after a few seconds only the feet remained visible and a moment or two later these too had vanished, leaving merely the vestiges of the brilliant light that had surrounded the figure. (For sheer strangeness this description is rivalled only by that of a later vision, which occurred, during the Franco-Prussian war, in the French village of Pontmain. On that occasion the Virgin appeared in the sky surrounded by an oval frame, and her words, far from being spoken, inscribed themselves slowly on a twelve-foot-long strip of 'parchment' that had materialised beneath her feet. She then disappeared from the feet up into 'a kind of bag'.)

It is difficult, now, to determine quite what Melanie and Maximin thought about the things they saw at La Salette. Though it seems clear enough, from the vision's references to the power of her son, that she was hinting she was the Virgin

Mary, the children spoke of her only as 'The Lady' and made no specific claims as to her identity. Neither did they enjoy any particular good fortune in later life; Melanie joined a number of religious orders, one after another, without feeling at home with any of them, while Maximin drifted from one poor job to another. On the other hand, it has been claimed that all the vision's predictions of disease and blight were quickly fulfilled, though the earliest source we have to support this dates only to 1854, eight years after the vision.

It was only a few years later that perhaps the most influential of all the several hundred known visions of the Virgin Mary – and another of the handful formally accepted as genuine by the Roman Catholic Church – occurred, this time in the backwater French town of Lourdes. The visionary was a young and sickly girl, Bernadette Soubirous, whose background certainly recalled those of the visionaries of La Salette. She lived in extreme poverty with her drunken father (a former miller who worked as a casual labourer), an equally inebriated mother and three brothers and sisters. The family had so little money at the time the visions began, early in 1858, that they were living, rent free, in an old gaol which had been condemned as unfit for habitation by the dregs of the French prison system, and had so little food that Bernadette's infant brother was caught eating candle wax from the floor of the local church.

At midday on 11 February 1858, the fourteen year-old girl was scavenging for animal bones along the banks of a stream just outside the town. Her two young companions decided to cross to the opposite side and Bernadette paused in front of a small grotto in the cliff face to remove her shoes and stockings. As she did so, she told her confessor a day or two later, she noticed a white object in the shape of a woman or girl inside the cave. This vision seems to have sent the girl into a state of ecstasy, since she proceeded to paddle across the stream without being bothered by the freezing waters. For further details of what occurred on that winter's day, however, we have to rely on the more detailed account Bernadette recorded more than three years later. According to this later statement,

> I heard a noise. I turned towards the meadow and I saw the trees were not moving at all. I went on taking off my shoes and stockings. I heard the same noise. I raised my head and looked at the grotto. I saw a lady dressed in white, she was wearing a white dress and a blue sash and a yellow rose on each foot the colour of the chain of her rosary. When I saw that I rubbed my eyes – I thought I was seeing things. I put my hand in my pocket and found my rosary in it. I wanted to make the sign of the cross but I could not get my hand up to my forehead, it fell back. The vision made the sign of the cross, then my hand shook. I tried to make it and I could, I said my rosary. The vision ran the beads of hers through her fingers but she did not move her lips. When I had finished my rosary, the vision disappeared all of a sudden.

Three days later, Bernadette returned to the grotto, this time accompanied by about a dozen witnesses. It seems that the girl had been doing some thinking about the vision she had seen, since she came equipped with a vial of holy water to throw at the apparition, should it reappear. Her aim seems to have been to establish whether her lady in white might have been created by the devil in order to tempt her. It had also been suggested that the apparition might be the ghost of a devout Catholic woman named Elisa Latapie, who had died a few months earlier.

Bernadette saw her vision again that day, and on a further sixteen occasions between February and July, though the increasingly-large crowds who followed her down to the grotto never saw the white-clad figure and had to rely on Bernadette's description of her. On the second visit, the apparition spoke for the first time, declining to give her name but telling the girl: 'I do not promise to make you happy in this world, but in the next.' This was enough for some of Bernadette's neighbours to decide that the lady in white was probably the

Virgin Mary, an identification that seems to have been fairly readily accepted by Soubirous and by the people of Lourdes.

Both the police and the local curate took a more sceptical view of events, subjecting Bernadette to a stern three-hour interview without shaking her conviction that the visions were genuine. Despite the disapproval of her parents, the girl continued to visit the grotto, as she had promised the Virgin she would, and by 25 February she was being followed to the cliffs by about 300 people. On that day the throng who gathered around her watched as Bernadette broke off from saying her rosary and began stuffing handfuls of earth from the grotto floor into her mouth. As she later explained, the apparition had pointed to the muddy soil and ordered her 'to drink at that spring'. Any doubters who harboured suspicions that the girl was either an hysteric or a liar were doubtless disconcerted when, at the point where Bernadette had scrabbled on the ground, an undiscovered spring did, indeed, burst forth and was soon yielding eighteen gallons a day. The spring still flows, and is now the focal point of the major shrine of Lourdes, supplying healing waters that have been credited with working many miracles.

As the procession of visions continued, the Virgin began to issue a stream of warnings to sinners and ever more ambitious orders through Bernadette. At the beginning of March the girl went to see the sceptical parish priest, Father Peyramale (who had steadfastly refused to visit the grotto) and informed him that he was to build a chapel at the site. He dismissed the request and told the girl to find out more definitely who her mysterious lady in white actually was. In consequence, after an unexplained three-week gap during which no visions occurred, Bernadette returned to the grotto under the cliff and three times requested the figure, 'Madame, will you kindly tell me who you are?' At the third time of asking, the figure in white extended her hands to Soubirous, replied: 'I am the Immaculate Conception', and vanished.

Although they were pretty much the last significant occurrence in the series of visions vouchsafed to Bernadette, those five words were enough to raise the sense of excitement permeating Lourdes to a new pitch. The Catholic doctrine of the Immaculate Conception, asserting that Mary was preserved from the effects of original sin from the moment of her conception, had been proclaimed by the Pope only four years earlier. With that short statement, the woman in white not only implicitly identified herself as the Virgin, but signalled divine approval for what was, in 1858, still a novel item of faith.

To the devout, who were already willing to accept Rome's claim to dictate the articles of faith, the Virgin's words were confirmation, if any were needed, that the visions at Lourdes were genuine. Within a matter of a few weeks, a shrine began to grow up around the grotto and the first of many hundreds of miraculous cures were being attributed to the powers of its waters. Bernadette herself, who had been a nonentity before her experiences began, became both a celebrity and an object of some devotion. In due course she entered a convent and took her vows as a nun; after her death in 1879, she was canonised, one of only two of the several hundred visionaries known to church history to be elevated to the sainthood.

To the more sceptical, though, the same evidence that convinced the faithful that the Virgin really was appearing at Lourdes suggested that Soubirous's visions (though doubtless real enough to her) may have had a psychological origin. To begin with, the figure that appeared in the grotto did not look like a Palestinian woman of the first century AD. Indeed she was hardly a woman at all, being described by the fourteen-year-old Bernadette as a girl of about her own age and height. Her dress – white with a blue sash, and with yellow roses on each foot – was reminiscent of Melanie and Maximin's description of the lady of La Salette, who wore a white robe and cape and white shoes decorated with brightly coloured roses. Even more intriguingly, contemporary sources record that shortly before the visions at Lourdes began, a priest had remarked to Bernadette's teacher in reference to Bernadette herself, that 'If my mental picture of the children of La Salette is exact, this little shepherdess must resemble them', a comment which, if it reached Soubirous's ears, might certainly have suggested to her that she, too, might not be beneath the Virgin Mary's notice.

It also seems at least possible that the Virgin's remarkable confirmation of the new doctrine of the Immaculate Conception (in a phrase which was, incidentally, grammatically incorrect – as Peyramale observed, the correct form should have been 'I am the Virgin of the Immaculate Conception'), may have had something to do with the fact that Bernadette had been sent, directly before the initial vision, to stay with another family who had agreed to teach her her catechism, and that these preparations for her first communion may have awakened both religious feelings and, perhaps, a sense of expectation in the young girl, which had not been present earlier.

Those who argue that religious visions are not really divinely inspired make a number of other valid comments about the Virgin Mary's appearances on earth, pointing out, for example, that once Bernadette had experienced a whole series of visions, the pattern of such encounters changed to reflect this. There were six major visitations at Fatima, in 1917, and the principal visionary, Lucia de Jesus dos Santos, later claimed to have had another six in 1915 and 1916, involving the apparitions of an angel and a 'statue made of snow'. At Beauraing, in Belgium, in 1932, five child witnesses were involved in a series of more than two dozen further visits from the virgin. Subsequently, Mary is supposed to have appeared more or less regularly for five years (1961–65) at Garabandal in Spain and for well over a decade at Medjugorje in Croatia, beginning in June 1981. Other, less well-publicised encounters continued elsewhere at the same time; indeed at one point in 1987 it was being claimed that Mary was appearing regularly at six-thirty p.m. each evening at the village of El Repilade in Andalusia, and at six-forty p.m. to the visionaries of Medjugorje, more than a thousand miles to the east. Those who had argued that the Virgin appears rarely on earth, and for a specific reason, have been at something of a loss to explain the sheer fecundity of contemporary visions.

Indeed, Mary's reasons for appearing at the times she does, and to the witnesses she chooses, can hardly fail to strike an agnostic as inexplicable. On several occasions – notably at Fatima – the Virgin has made it clear that she had messages of great importance to impart, intended for the local bishop or perhaps the Pope. Yet, on this and other occasions, she has chosen to give her instructions to young children, who often have great difficulty in convincing anyone to take them seriously. Their task is seldom helped by the great selectivity with which the Virgin reveals herself. Even when there are adults present, Mary is generally visible and audible solely to the small group of chosen children, who have to communicate her words to the rest of those gathered. Believers have argued that Mary's visits are intended to bring faith and comfort to poor rural communities where they are most needed, but, even so, a variant of the old argument of the 'space-ship on the lawn' – which suggests that real aliens would be more likely to land their flying saucer in front of the White House than confine their attentions to the small rural communities where they often seem to appear – can be applied to Marian visions: the Virgin would surely make an enormously greater impression if she chose to appear at St Peter's, Rome.

On other occasions, Mary's requests seem oddly low-key – an order to build a chapel here, a plea for prayers to be said there – for such a powerful figure, and her willingness to submit to questioning and even allow herself to be ordered about by young children is remarkable. The witness Jean Bernard, whom we met in the last chapter, not only asked for, and claimed he was granted, private favours by his vision, but was gratified by her decision to change the times of her appearances from seven o'clock in the morning to the more civilised eleven a.m. Although Jean passed on a number of requests that the Virgin grant a miracle, the vision was reluctant to comply, and when the throngs who gathered around him got too large, she also ceased her gracious practice of individually blessing rosaries offered up by members of the crowd. As one commentator wryly observes: 'Have we the right to speculate that Jean himself was growing bored with the practice?'

Acceptance of any of these plausible suggestions leads us inexorably to the conclusion that it is as important to study the witnesses to such remarkable events as it is to record what is supposed to have happened to them. This is, in fact, one of the cardinal rules of research into strange phenomena, as important when it comes to the study of UFO abductions or lake monster sightings as it is when contemplating religious visions, and its application can yield rewarding insights and help make sense of the most perplexing of cases.

For example, a witness-centred approach can explain why the Virgin appears with comparative regularity in conventionally Catholic countries (most cases occur in either France or Italy), but apparently hardly at all in Protestant or Orthodox territories and practically never in the much more alien cultures or China or India, where one would think that a few apparitions might help to convert the local people from their existing beliefs. Pursuing this line of reasoning, it at once becomes significant that the one known series of Marian visions recorded by the Church of England – which occurred at Llanthony Abbey in Wales during the early autumn of 1880 – happened in a fringe establishment run by an eccentric aristocrat whose devotion to the Virgin was the principal driving force in his life.

Perhaps the most important question raised by such religious visions, though, is how 'real' they are. It seems they cannot be wholly real – that is, the result of a physical manifestation of the Virgin Mary in a human body – since that would suggest that the 'vision' would be visible to anyone looking in the right direction, rather than to the very select group of witnesses at the centre of most such events. It is possible, though needlessly complicated, to argue that Mary does take on a physical form on her visits to earth, but then uses divine powers to hide herself from most of her audience. An intermediate position –

one which the Catholic Church would support – is that a small minority of the visions are divinely inspired, and the remainder the product either of self-delusion or active intervention by the forces of evil. While this is a difficult proposition to prove, evidence of successful prophecies by the Virgin, or of demonstrably miraculous healings at a Marian shrine, would certainly help. Finally, there is a case for considering all such visions to be either experience-centred events, or simply internally-generated fantasies.

Exploring the latter possibility first, a focus on the witnesses certainly has the effect of calling into question many of the more remarkable claims that they make, or that have been made on their behalf. There are, for example, substantial discrepancies between the accounts that Lucia de Jesus dos Santos, the Fatima visionary, gave immediately after her experiences in 1917, and the version of events she set down in her memoirs in 1942, two decades after taking her vows as a nun. As well as doubling the total number of visions she had previously claimed, Lucia set down, for the first time, two of the three famous 'secrets of Fatima' said to have been entrusted to her and her two companions. These included a horrifying vision of hell, and prophecies concerning the future of Russia. All of this material must be of questionable reliability. As the author Kevin McClure, one of the most sympathetic and sensitive of authorities on such matters, observes, 'Spending over 20 years in the quiet and seclusion of a religious house, cut off from the normal run of daily life, undoubtedly reliving the events of 1917 time and again, is not the best background for recalling precise details of what must have been deeply traumatic events in the life of a young and innocent child. It would have taken a staggering degree of objectivity for those memoirs to have been an accurate record of what actually happened.'

The more sceptical Joe Nickell harbours graver doubts about Lucia's reliability as a witness, labelling her 'petted' and 'spoiled', not to mention the possessor of 'a gift for telling stories', and pointing out that her own mother is said to have called her 'nothing but a fake who is leading half the world astray'.

There are, nevertheless, problems with the presumption that visions of gods and angels have a purely psychological origin. The internal fantasy hypothesis undoubtedly works best in cases involving a solitary witness. However, the majority of the religious visions described above occurred in the presence of two or more witnesses. This may suggest that one witness is dominant and somehow leads the others to experience something they are not really seeing – a phenomenon familiar to psychologists and known as the *folie a deux*, though this is really little more than a label, and certainly not an explanation for how such a lead is either offered or accepted.

The *folie a deux* theory might certainly explain the early Fatima visions, since it is at best highly doubtful whether the two subsidiary witnesses, Francisco Marto (who was ten in 1917) and his sister Jacinta (who was only six), actually saw and heard all the things that the older Lucia described. On the other hand, all such visions may be seen as evidence for the experience-centred hypothesis, which suggests that the witnesses are reacting to some, at best hazily-understood, phenomena in a manner dictated by their religion and culture. 'Proving' this suggestion would require a lengthy comparative study of religious apparitions in several different cultures.

The experience-centred approach would explain not just the very similar descriptions of Mary offered by different witnesses (which, it is only fair to add, might also be the product of exposure to religious iconography), but why essentially similar events seem to occur in very dissimilar environments. Compare, for example, the vision vouchsafed to Bernadette Soubirous, aged fourteen, at Lourdes in 1858 with the 'ghosts' encountered two years earlier by the fifteen-year-old Xhosa prophetess Nonquawuse – she of the terrible cattle-killing movement. Like Bernadette's 'lady in white', Nonquawuse's 'ghosts' issued warnings of the dire consequences that were about to befall her people and explained the gestures of devotion that were required to avert such a fate. They appeared on successive days at the same spot, and, when Nonquawuse appeared there accompanied by her guardian, they remained visible only to her. The girl's friend Nombanda has left us an account of the circumstances surrounding these events that might equally describe a Marian vision: 'I frequently accompanied Nonquawuse to a certain bush where she spoke with people – and although she frequently informed me when I was with her at this bush that she saw people and heard them speak to her, I neither saw them nor did I hear them speak till after I had constantly visited the bush with her.'

Other equally intriguing parallels may be noted. Where Christian Europe has its legend of the Wandering Jew, for example – an unfortunate man cursed, because he had dared to mock Jesus on his way to Calvary, to wander the earth testifying for Christ until the Day of Judgement – the Mormon church has a tradition that three disciples of the Nephite tribe, who followed Jesus when he visited America after the Resurrection, were granted permission to remain on earth preaching the gospel. In the last two hundred years, a number of apparently sincere Mormons have reported encounters with bearded men dressed in white whom they took to be one or other of these wandering Nephites.

Instructive comparisons may also be drawn between religious experiences and other strange phenomena. There were, for example, many more visions of the Virgin than usual in 1947, the year that flying saucers were first reported in the skies over America. Might this suggest either that Catholics were responding to some external stimulus in their own particular fashion – somehow perceived by others as mechanical UFOs – or even simply that the anxieties that accompanied the onset of the Cold War were manifesting themselves in culturally diffuse ways? What, too, should one read into the testimony of a Spanish visionary, Amparo Cuevas, who, in 1982, told her confessor she had been warned that 'the celestial ships are already prepared which will carry the chosen ones to the promised land. They will come surrounded by blue light' – a prophecy that sits uneasily in a Christian context, but makes a great deal of sense to anyone familiar with the history of flying saucer contactees?

The fact is that there are many cases involving visionaries whose experiences seem to have a psychological basis of some sort – who see angels as a child, for example, but go on to experience erotic hallucinations at a later date – and few, if any, that seem wholly resistant to such interpretations. Is there any evidence, then, that there is more to visions of the Virgin than the fantasies of a witness? The answer to this question must be, 'Perhaps'.

It is, for instance, true that the one prophecy made by the Virgin of Fatima that Lucia revealed while the sequence of visions was still going on turned out to be false: on 13 October 1917 she announced that Mary had told her that the Great War was over: 'The war ends even today; wait here for the very brave soldiers.' In the event, the conflict dragged on for a further 13 months. As we have seen, it also seems to be true that fewer than half the 70,000 or so people present that day witnessed the 'solar miracle' that their companions somehow failed to see. On the other hand, two of the clerical witnesses to the fifth Fatima apparition, on 13 September that same year, 'clearly and distinctly' saw a luminous globe of light move from east to west across the site, and observed that, even when it had disappeared from their view, one little girl 'dressed like Lucia and of about the same age, continued to cry happily: "I see it! I see it! Now it's coming down towards the bottom of the hill."' It also seems possible (though the evidence is confusing) that some of the witnesses to the apparition at Pontmain described what was happening independently of each other. Therefore the case that some apparitions of the Virgin are genuinely supernatural in character, while weak, might still be made.

Photos of the Gods

Of all the problems associated with such visions, surely one of the hardest for the uncommitted to accept is the enormous difficulty of actually witnessing such an event. Merely being in the right place, at the right time, and in the presence of the visionaries themselves, is seldom enough; and for this reason there is very little photographic evidence to back up claims that such experiences occur.

Nevertheless, a handful of images that claim to be photos of the gods do exist. Of these, the earliest appears to have been taken around the year 1920 and shows a bearded, Christ-like figure standing against what looks like a hedge, his right hand raised in a gesture of benediction. Sir Arthur Conan Doyle seems to have received a copy of the photo in 1926 with the explanation that it had been obtained by a Seattle housewife named Mildred Swanson when she put her camera down facing a flowerbank only to hear the shutter click of its own accord. When she wound on to the next exposure, the same thing happened again, and when the film was developed she discovered that the strange image of Christ had appeared on both the rogue frames.

This is only one version of the origin of this picture, however. Over the years more than a dozen further, mutually exclusive, accounts have appeared in print. The claims have varied from the assertion that the image was secured in a First World War trench in 1917 to the suggestion that it had been shot by a Bristol hairdresser. Over time, repeated reprintings led to a gradual loss of detail in the photo, which eventually became a stark black and white image that the *Sunday People* newspaper was able to represent as 'quite simply, a snow scene in the Alps, taken from an aircraft [showing] the face of Christ etched in the melting snow'. As such, this particular photo of Jesus may be regarded as evidence for the astonishing ability of strange phenomena to generate accompanying legends, but of little else.

Nevertheless, several other supposed photos of Jesus appear to show remarkable natural formations. The best-known is a snapshot of clouds, which precisely resemble an outline of a bearded Christ giving a blessing. It first appeared in a Kentucky newspaper in the 1960s and is supposed to have been taken from an American bomber during the Korean War. At least two further pictures of supposed cloud formations that circulate in south-east Asia are said to show visions of a Buddhist goddess, Kwanyin, and in 1982 there was great excitement in Thailand at the appearance of what was said to be a genuine photograph of the Buddha meditating. Investigation showed that there were at least eleven different accounts of the origin of this picture. Several of these stories included the detail that the black and white image had appeared unaccountably on a colour roll of film.

All of these photographs are unacceptable as evidence, in that nothing is really known about the people who took them, or the circumstances in which they were taken. However, two quite remarkable accounts of further photos of Christ that have come to light within the last few years seem at first glance to be better evidenced. One was reportedly taken inside the Vatican by a 32-year-old African nun, Sister Anna Ali. Sister Anna is housekeeper for the Zambian archbishop Emanuel Milingo, who has been accused of sorcery by several fellow bishops and has attracted considerable disapproval for his practice of holding mass open-air exorcisms for his flock. She announced in 1991 that Jesus had been visiting her in her cell each Thursday and that she had been granted permission to photograph him. The resultant shot featured a conventional portrait of a young, bearded Christ with handsome, but decidedly European, features. It is certainly quite unlike the Christ who appears in the second modern portrait – an apparently Semitic figure, swathed in a turban, who appeared in Nairobi among a crowd that had gathered to hear the faith healer Mary Ataska. Witnesses to this extraordinary event reported that Jesus blessed onlookers in Swahili before uttering a Hebrew curse and ducking into a car driven by a Mr Gurnam Singh. Questioned later, Singh said he had driven his passenger to the bus terminus for route 56, where the Son of God asked to be dropped off so he could 'head for heaven'.

It must be admitted, then, that all supposed photos of the gods are dubious at best. Mystery almost always surrounds their origin, and most of the images are so conventional in appearance that it seems reasonable to ask whether they were not originally photos of existing portraits or icons. As matters stand, they certainly cannot be regarded as proof of any religious phenomena.

Miraculous Relics

Even before the invention of photography, a good number of churches possessed their own physical proof of the power of God in the shape of a miracle-working relic of Christ or one of the saints. Such relics typically became the centre of their own cults of veneration, and miraculous cures were frequently attributed to them. In times of crisis they would often be taken from their churches and paraded before the people in order to inspire them – each relic in its own elaborate reliquary.

Today, many hundreds of religious relics are still preserved in temples and churches around the world. They range from pieces of the True Cross and fragments of the Buddha's finger bones to what is said to be the miraculously seamless tunic worn by Christ on his way to Calvary, now preserved in the cathedral church of Trier in Germany, in a thin rubber solution which unfortunately also renders it impervious to carbon dating. Saints' bones are also popular – so much so that the head of Saint Teilo, which resides in Llandaff Cathedral in South Wales, is one of three rival skulls, each famed for its ability to drive out whooping cough.

Unfortunately, however, religious relics are rarely solid evidence for anything. Though they may generate remarkable tales of miraculous cures, hardly any of these much-venerated artefacts can be satisfactorily traced to its original owner. Trier's holy tunic, for example, first appears in the historical record as late as 1196, leaving more than a thousand years of history quite unaccounted-for.

One particular variety of relic, however, does seem worthy of further investigation. The bodies of a surprisingly large number of especially religious people appear to have resisted the usual processes of decomposition and decay, remaining incorrupt for anything up to several hundred years after death. Such corpses are sometimes put on display when they are discovered, and as a result incorruption is one of the better-documented religious mysteries.

The phenomenon is often thought of as an essentially Christian one, and the earliest case on record relates to the corpse of St Cecilia, who is said to have been martyred by the unusual method of being partially beheaded and then locked in a steam bath around AD 177. In 822 Pope Pascal I completed a cathedral church in her memory and – guided, it is said, by a vision of the saint – relocated her supposed tomb and disinterred the corpse, reburying it under the altar of the new church. There it was rediscovered during repair work in 1599, and when the casket was opened Cecilia's body was observed to be both incorrupt and perfumed by a 'mysterious flower-like odour'.

Among several dozen similar cases might be mentioned that of St Theresa of the Sacred Heart, an Italian nun who died of a gangrenous infection in 1770. Given the nature of her illness it might be supposed that her body would decay rapidly and unpleasantly, but it was exhumed twice, in 1783 and 1805, and on both occasions was found to be in a good state of preservation. The doctors who conducted the 1805 exhumation reported that the body was then of a 'healthy flesh colour, somewhat dry, but, nevertheless, surprisingly elastic and pliable, even in the soft parts between the rib and groin; the colour of the hair on the head livid and fresh, that of the eyebrows golden-blond, with the appearance of life in it; the wound in the right foot by the surgeon that bled her still visible, but healed and of good colour.' This body, now mummified, but still intact, is preserved in a chapel dedicated to the saint in Florence.

The phenomenon of incorruption is, indeed, closely associated with the sainthood. Many of the cases on record came to light with the disinterrment of a corpse during the processes of beatification and canonisation in the apparent hope of discovering just such evidence of sanctity. Several noteworthy cases involved the discovery of incorrupt bodies – such as that of St Catherine of Genoa – in decaying and mildewed coffins that really ought to have accelerated the normal process of putrefaction. Others involve partial incorruption. When St Anthony of Padua was dug up, for example, his body was found to have crumbled to dust, while his tongue alone remained incorrupt and was found lying on the bottom of the coffin 'red, soft and entire'. Though the records of his life that still exist give no hint that he enjoyed any special prowess as a preacher, the Congregation of Sacred Rites, assembled to consider the case, accepted it as a 'miracle of the second class'. It is also well worth noting that the bodies of the only two Marian visionaries to be canonised, St Catherine Laboure (who saw a vision of the Virgin in Paris in 1830) and that of St Bernadette Soubirous herself, are supposedly incorrupt.

The principal difficulty in accepting the phenomenon of incorruption at face value is a general lack of evidence for cases in which the supposedly holy corpse has remained in a perfect condition for many years after its rediscovery. Again and again, as the sceptic Joe Nickell points out, a body is observed to deteriorate over the years. Saints who have been found incorrupt on one disinterrment have become mere piles of dust when they are dug up again a few hundred years later; others, kept above ground, slowly mummify or decay. The history of St Bernadette is a case in point. During her first disinterment in 1909, thirty years after her death, her body was found to be somewhat damp. It was thoroughly washed and reclothed, an action that seems to have precipitated a degree of decay, since, ten years later, a second examination found that the saint's face had become discoloured and action had to be taken to preserve it. Because of this, although the corpse remains on display in a glass coffin in the French town of Nevers, Bernadette's apparently flawless face is actually a wax mask. St Catherine Laboure's body, meanwhile, was more thoroughly dealt with on its disinterrment: her hands were amputated and placed in a reliquary, and her heart and also her kneecaps removed by surgeons before the remainder of the body was preserved by the injection of an embalming fluid and put on display in a special chapel.

Such actions caution against accepting the many available photographs of incorrupt corpses at face value. Nor is it readily apparent *why* the bodies of some saints seem to be preserved from decay, while those of others, no less holy, rot away like any sinner's – a problem which bothered the great Jesuit writer on religious phenomena, Father Herbert Thurston. Indeed, the whole notion of incorruption as a proof of sanctity is thrown into doubt by the preservation of the corpses of a number of pagans and reprobates. In 1485 the body of a Roman woman, Julia, the daughter of Claudius, was exhumed and found to be well-preserved, with 'the bloom of youth still on her cheeks'. The corpse, like that of St Cecilia, was surrounded by the smell of perfume, a phenomenon known as 'the odour of sanctity', though it seems at least as likely that it is really the odour of antique embalming fluids. The discovery of Julia's incorrupt remains caused such a sensation that the Pope, Innocent VIII, quickly ordered the corpse to be secretly reinterred by night. A similar case occurred in 1895 at Stade in Hanover, when the 'perfectly preserved' body of an eighth-century warrior was reportedly discovered. Even the notorious magician Aleister Crowley happened across an apparently incorrupt corpse in Mexico, in the shape of the mummified body of a man who had been dead for about three weeks and lay in the open air untouched by vultures and coyotes. Crowley attributed the condition of this corpse to the man's consumption of 'chillies and other pungent condiments'.

It has, in short, never been possible to regard the incidence of strange occurrences as a reliable barometer of holiness or sanctity. That is the principal mystery of religious phenomena. It is also, perhaps, a compelling argument for regarding strange events not as mere ammunition for the religious, but as subjects worthy of study in their own right.

3

World of Spirits

One morning in the middle of the nineteenth century, four men walked into the courtyard of a Brussels prison where an execution was scheduled to take place and concealed themselves beneath the guillotine, close to where the condemned man's severed head would roll into its basket. One of the men was Antoine Joseph Wiertz, a well-known Belgian painter and also a fine hypnotic subject. With him were his friend, Doctor D— , a physician who practised hypnotism, and two witnesses.

Their purpose that day was to conduct a unique and extraordinary experiment. Wiertz, who had long been haunted by the desire to know whether a head remained conscious after a guillotining, had agreed to be hypnotised and instructed to identify himself with the man who was about to be executed for murder:

> He was to follow [the murderer's] thoughts and feel any sensations, which he was to express aloud. He was also 'suggested' to take special note of mental conditions during decapitation, so that when the head fell in the basket he could penetrate the brain and give an account of its last thoughts.

Wiertz became entranced almost immediately and...

manifested extreme distress and begged to be demagnetised, as his sense of oppression was insupportable. It was too late, however – the knife fell.

'What do you feel? What do you see?' asked the doctor. Wiertz writhed convulsively and replied, 'Lightning! A thunderbolt falls! It thinks; it sees!' 'Who thinks and sees?' 'The head. It suffers horribly. It thinks and feels but does not understand what has happened.'

As Wiertz spoke, the witnesses saw the head which had fallen into the basket and lay looking at them horribly; its arteries still palpitating. It was only after some moments of suffering that apparently the guillotined head at last became aware that it was separated from its body.

Wiertz became calmer and seemed exhausted, while the doctor resumed his questions. The painter answered: 'I fly through space like a top spinning through fire. But am I dead? Is it all over? If only they would let me join my body again! I remember all. There are the judges in red robes. I hear the sentence. Oh! my wretched wife and children. If only you would put my body to me, I would be with you once more. You refuse? All the same, I love you, my poor babies. Miserable wretch that I am I have covered you in blood. When will this finish! – or is not a murderer condemned to eternal punishment?'

As Wiertz spoke these words, the witnesses thought they detected the eyes of the decapitated head open wide with a look of unmistakable suffering.

The painter continued his lamentations. 'No, such suffering cannot endure for ever; God is merciful. All that belongs to earth is fading away. I see in the distance a little light glittering like a diamond. I feel a calm stealing over me. What a good sleep I shall have! What joy!' These were the last words the painter spoke. He was still entranced, but no longer replied to the questions put to him by the doctor. They then approached the head and Dr D— touched the forehead, the temples and teeth and found they were cold. The head was dead.

In the Wiertz Gallery in Brussels are to be found three pictures of a guillotined head, presumably the outcome of this gruesome experiment.

Whether or not Antoine Wiertz really was able to penetrate the mind of a dying man that day (and the somewhat melodramatic tone of his utterances suggests that a vivid imagination may have played at least a part in the experience), his bizarre and perhaps dangerous experiment was of at least symbolic importance. As they crouched together beneath the guillotine, the artist and the man of science had sought to enter the world of spirits, which, for many centuries, had been the province of shamans and mystics. They had done this, moreover, not by relying on prayer or ecstasy, but by using what they thought were the tools of science and reason. Henceforth, the borderlands would be open not merely to a chosen few, but to anyone who wished to make the journey.

Dr Mesmer and the Spirit Rappers

The hypnotism practised by Wiertz and Dr D— had its roots in the eighteenth-century and the work of Franz Mesmer, a physician from the Swiss–German border. Mesmer was one of several practitioners who believed that magnetism could be used to cure all manner of illnesses, and he developed a 'magnetic tub', the *baquet*, which he filled with magnetised substances. Iron rods leading to patients were supposed to carry the healing energy, while Mesmer and his assistants walked around, pointing other iron rods at various parts of the sufferers' bodies.

The results were remarkable. Not only did Mesmer report many cures; his patients often fainted, began laughing or weeping uncontrollably, or were seized by convulsions. Whilst in these 'twilight states', a number developed what appeared to be clairvoyant abilities, 'seeing' not only their own diseased organs but those of other people, including some who were many miles away. Mesmer himself considered such symptoms dangerous, but it was not long before one of his pupils, the Marquis de Puysegur, encountered one patient who fell asleep under the influence of his 'magnetic fluids' and began to talk. Upon waking, the man remembered nothing of his experience. Thus was discovered the new phenomenon of 'somnambulism' or 'Mesmeric sleep', which later became more widely known as hypnotism.

Although the value and even the very existence of hypnotism are still hotly debated today, Puysegur's discovery was of great significance. Somnambulism was the first altered state of consciousness – excepting sleep – to be accessible to the ordinary person, and the first to offer a real opportunity for experimentation. Though religious initiates had long entered trances to secure their revelations, it was only now, in the first half of the nineteenth century, that the idea of the trance state gradually established itself. It seems probable that, without this gradual preparation of the ground, spiritualism and psychical research (the scientific investigation of psychic phenomena) could not have flourished as they did later in the century.

The spiritualist movement was the first to be born – on 31 March 1848, at the home of John Fox and his family in Hydesville, New York State. This house already had a weird reputation, and for several weeks raps and sounds like furniture scraping over the floor had been heard in the bedroom occupied by Maggie Fox, aged ten, and her sister Kate, seven, which the girls announced were made by the ghost of a murdered peddler. On the day in question, though, the whole family were shaken by clatterings of unprecedented fury. Suggesting that the windows might be rattling in the wind, John Fox got up and shook the sashes to see if they were loose. Immediately, the clattering noise recurred, and Kate observed that it seemed to be answering her father's rattles. Calling out, 'Mr Splitfoot, do as I do,' she clapped her hands several times – and at once the same number of raps came back. Before long, using a simple 'yes and no' code of knocks, the family succeeded in establishing contact with the entity responsible for the sounds. Very much as Kate and Maggie had predicted, it claimed to be the ghost of a 31-year-old peddler named Charles Rosma, who had had his throat cut in one of the bedrooms five years earlier and been buried in the basement.

Before long, half the neighbourhood had visited the haunted house and heard the spirit raps, and the Fox sisters were well on their way to celebrity. Further bangings and knockings, apparently made by other spirits, accompanied them when the family moved on to other homes. With the introduction of an alphabet code, it became possible to receive more complex messages from the other side, beginning, in 1849, with the promise: 'Dear friends, you must proclaim this truth to the world. This is the dawning of a new era; you must not try to conceal it any longer. When you do your duty God will protect you and the spirits will watch over you.'

Gradually the phenomenon became more orderly. Other 'mediums' between this world and the next sprang up, each apparently able to summon up her own spirits, and soon regular seances were being held, at which tables rocked, objects moved, and musical instruments were played. Though the Fox sisters had not gone through any particular preparation in order to communicate with their spirits, many of their successors explained that they entered a trance state in order to become a channel through which the dead could speak.

Spiritualism, as the new movement became known, spread with great rapidity through the United States and then Europe, so that by 1851 there were a hundred mediums in New York. By the turn of the century the movement numbered its members in the tens-of-thousands. Its appeal was the same as that which had been held by mesmerism for an earlier generation: the possibility of general and regular contact with other realms, something hitherto vouchsafed only to the elect and the saved. As one of the movement's critics, John Mulholland, observed, 'And so the next big step in spiritism was reached. Those of the spirit world did not need to be unhappy to come back to earth, they did not need to have been murdered nor to have left unrighted wrongs . . . It was just as easy to call back Grandmother or Aunt Hattie. Naturally when a person's own dead could be brought back to him, spiritualism became of interest to every one.'

The movement reached its height during and after the Great War, when many of the hundreds of thousands who had lost a member of their family in the fighting sought comfort in the idea that they might be contacted in the afterlife. Hundreds of helpful mediums ensured that they succeeded. Possibly the best known of all these sitters was Sir Oliver Lodge, a noted physicist and past president of the British Association, whose son Raymond had died in 1915. A leading medium produced so much private information that Lodge was satisfied that his son had indeed survived death.

Nevertheless, the idea of contact with the dead was already an old one at the time of the Fox sisters. The ancient Greeks practised a form of magic known as 'theurgy', which they believed made it possible for an entranced medium to contact the dead. Theurgist seances appear to have featured many of the phenomena that became familiar to the spiritualists, including the production of a substance resembling ectoplasm, and the occasional levitation of the medium. Nor were the spiritualists the only ones propagating supernatural and mystical doctrines in the late nineteenth-century: in France, a man named Allan Kardec added a belief in reincarnation to the spiritualist credo to produce a movement known as spiritism, which is still one of the major religions of Brazil. At about the same time, a Russian called Helene Petrovna Blavatsky introduced her own brand of eastern mysticism to Europe and the United States in the form of Theosophy, a religion in miniature, which provided the template for a great many of the occult orders of the twentieth century. Purporting to be based on esoteric Buddhism, it drew its inspiration from telepathic messages received from a group of 'Hidden Masters' in Tibet. Both Kardec, who was himself a medium, and Blavatsky, who used to hypnotise pigeons and appeared to display psychokinetic powers, owed a substantial debt to the spiritualists and their ideas.

The historian James Webb, who wrote a penetrating study of this strange interlude in religious and intellectual history, labelled the years 1820 to 1910 'the Age of the Irrational', and suggested that it represented an abandonment of reason and a betrayal of the rationalist ideals of the eighteenth century. There is much truth in this interpretation. But not every claim made by the spiritualists was devoid of all foundation, and not every man and woman of intellect either rejected the evidence for strange new powers, or found themselves seduced by the new religions. In 1882 a group of scholars established an organisation dedicated to the investigation of strange events. This was the Society for Psychical Research (SPR), which, for more than a century, has conducted research into all manner of psychic phenomena, from apparitions to predictions, and from hallucinations to hypnotism. It is thanks largely to the SPR and similar organisations that we have much of the evidence we do for the causes and effects of such enigmas.

The Medium and the Message

Much of the SPR's early work concentrated on a detailed exploration of mediumship. By the 1880s two distinct varieties of seance-room phenomena – physical and mental – had emerged, though at this time the majority of mediums produced both sorts of effect.

Feats of physical mediumship included inducing the spirits present to lift and play musical instruments, the materialisation of objects ('apports'), the levitation of tables and chairs or the movement of items in the seance room by psychical means, and, perhaps most excitingly of all, the production of the strange substance known as ectoplasm, which streamed from the orifices of a medium's body. In some cases ectoplasm was reported to have formed itself into the faces or even the full bodies of the deceased; in others – with praiseworthy economy – it restricted itself to simulating the human vocal apparatus, so that disembodied voice boxes floated about the seance room, a technique known as 'direct voice'. Ectoplasm was also thought to shape itself into prods that moved objects scattered on the seance table.

Mental mediumship, on the other hand, consisted simply of receiving messages from the beyond. Mental mediums might be possessed by the spirits of the dead, who made use of their physical bodies to speak or write out messages, receive visions and pass on the messages they were given, or even see nothing but hear spirit voices in their ears.

Much of a psychical researcher's work in this early period involved determining whether or not a medium's effects were the product of deception and fraud. Rooms were searched for accomplices and secret compartments, and some psychics were trussed hand and foot to their chairs in the expectation that this would stop them from manipulating concealed apparatus. Many – perhaps most – of the mediums who were investigated in this way were caught in trickery at least once in their careers. Harry Bastien, a well-known American, was exposed on no fewer than three occasions: during a seance in Vienna before Archduke John of Austria-Hungary, when a 'spirit' that had entered the room was found to be the medium without his shoes; again when a female sitter discovered the medium's hand where a 'spirit hand' had been; and finally during a direct voice experiment when, despite having successfully produced spirit messages while his mouth was filled with water, the voices ceased as soon as corks were rammed up his nostrils.

There can be no doubt that many of the phenomena produced by physical mediums, particularly rappings and the movement of objects in the seance room, were simple conjuring tricks, employed to deceive sitters who were often positively anxious to believe that they were contacting the spirits of their loved ones. An especially dramatic exposure of just this sort of fraud occurred in 1888, when, after four decades as professional mediums, Kate and Maggie Fox jointly confessed that the Hydesville rappings – the very foundation-stone of spiritualism – had been produced by cracking the joints in their toes. They demonstrated this ability on stage before large audiences, and also admitted to rigging simple devices around the house to produce other bumps and knocks: their intention had simply been to frighten their mother. 'Spiritualism,' Kate Fox announced, 'is a humbug from beginning to end.'

The new religion might have been expected to wither away in the face of such a devastating expose, but in fact it was far too well-established by then to be badly affected. Not only were many thousands of sitters already convinced that they had been placed in contact with the dead; some very prominent psychical researchers had satisfied themselves that some of the phenomena of mediumship could not be explained as mere trickery.

The claims of several leading mediums to produce ectoplasm proved particularly controversial. Professor Charles Richet and Baron Schrenck-Notzing, two psychical researchers who conducted several thousand seances between them, became convinced that it was a real substance, albeit a very peculiar one; it could be black, grey or white, moist and sticky or hard and dry, slow-moving or quick as lightning. A few physical mediums proved able to produce the stuff in reasonable light; in the case of the German medium Maria Vollhardt, it was observed to bear the marks of her teeth, suggesting that it was formed of some plastic substance. Another researcher, W.I. Crawford, an engineer by profession, produced some remarkable results by weighing his mediums before and after a materialisation. He reported that one, Kathleen Goligher, appeared to lose up to half her body weight (some fifty-four-and-a-half lbs) during a seance, a phenomenon he vigorously asserted was genuine. The determined Schrenck-Notzing, meanwhile, was eventually able to film a materialisation performed by the Polish medium 'Stanislawa P.', and in 1916 he even trapped a fragment in a test-tube. A chemical analysis showed that this ectoplasm was an unsavoury concoction of human fatty matter, leukocytes (white blood cells) and cells from the mucous membranes.

Oddly enough, such materialisations are unknown today and, in retrospect, ectoplasm seems to be one of those curious enigmas that recur throughout the short history of psychical research: a phenomenon that flourished for a time, only to practically disappear thereafter. It can hardly be denied that most photographs of materialisations now look frankly unconvincing: in most cases the so-called ectoplasm resembles either rough cloth, *papier mache* or paper cut-outs. The case for its reality thus rests largely on the eyewitness testimony of the researchers who investigated it. Their jobs were made the more ticklish by the problems of detecting fraud in such cases: a number of physical mediums produced the effect with the help of a supply of butter muslin concealed in a bodily orifice – sometimes the mouth, but also, in the case of female mediums, the vagina. Very much the same problem applies to the assessment of mediums who specialised in the materialisation of fully-formed figures. Of these, perhaps the most remarkable was a Pole who went by the name of Franek Kluski. As well as being a proficient mental medium, Kluski was photographed materialising a bird-like creature resembling a pterodactyl, and even a hairy ape-creature, smelling strongly of 'wet dog', which went about the seance room attempting to lick the faces of his sitters. Sadly, surviving pictures of the latter being show an object that resembles nothing so much as a couple of sacks.

Spectacular though their effects were, the physical mediums were, in truth, far less significant than their purely mental colleagues when it came to producing real evidence of the survival of death. By acting as channels and allowing the dead to speak, mental mediums offered not only comfort to the bereaved, but the very real possibility that a message might be communicated which contained information known only to the sitter and the spirit. This, it was generally agreed, would constitute the best possible *prima facie* evidence for the survival of bodily death.

The problem with all such communications, as psychical researchers have been quick to recognise, lies in the difficulty of excluding any possibility that the information could not have been obtained from a living source by some form of extra sensory perception. Even if outright fraud can be dismissed, all the information in such messages is generally known to the sitter, at least, and often to friends and relatives as well. It is, thus, at least possible to argue that the medium is obtaining his or her information not from the spirit worlds, but telepathically, by reading the sitter's mind. This is known as the

'Super-ESP' theory, and it constitutes the principal barrier to the recognition of seance-room evidence as proof of survival.

Although it is quite impossible to devise an experiment that excludes Super-ESP altogether, several attempts have been made to show that the theory must be stretched to such extreme lengths that survival seems an altogether simpler solution. Among the most convincing experiments of this kind were the 'cross correspondences', an extremely lengthy series of trance writings produced by mediums who were mostly unknown to each other, and in some cases resident on different continents, which contained fragments of messages that made sense only when assembled by the SPR. In addition, a large number of so-called 'book tests' were conducted in the early years of the twentieth-century.

The problem with the cross-correspondences is that they were in general both vague and extremely cryptic, and thus open to a wide variety of interpretations. In contrast, book tests involved the medium passing on a spirit message comprising only a reference to a particular book owned by one of the sitters. Thus a communication might consist of an instruction to find 'the ninth book on the third shelf counting from left to right in the bookcase on the right of the door in the drawing-room as you enter; take the title, and look at page 37'. In the best of these cases, the book might not even have been read by the sitter, but, when consulted, would be found to contain a passage of obvious significance, perhaps relating to some family joke or an intimate personal detail that could not have been known to the medium. (The reference given above, which purported to come from a son killed in the Great War, led the dead man's father to a book titled *Trees*, and a passage about a tunnelling beetle. The father's obsession with 'the beetle' was a long-running family joke.)

Even in these cases, there would seem to be some room for the powers of suggestion to come into play. In the example above, the father appears to have selected one sentence from a whole page and ascribed it special significance, though he had received no precise instructions as to where on the page to look. Nevertheless, when one of the SPR's leading lights, the formidable Eleanor Sidgwick, published an analysis of 532 book tests in 1921, she concluded that at least seventeen per cent could be classified as wholly successful. When 1800 'control' book tests were subjected to a similar analysis, the number of 'hits' fell to under two per cent.

Despite such impressive results, however, there are still difficulties in accepting mental mediumship as a genuine phenomenon. One is that when psychical researchers are asked to identify the most important mental mediums they will almost always cite two women, Mrs Leonard (who came to prominence when she acted for Sir Oliver Lodge in the Raymond sittings, and who later conducted some notably successful book tests) and her American counterpart, Mrs Piper. Both participated in the cross-correspondences, and both were the subject of numerous controlled sittings and concerted investigations by the SPR and its American sister organisation, which included the employment of private detectives to discover whether they made any attempt to ferret out information about their subjects before a seance (they did not). Yet these great mediums were born in 1882 and 1859 respectively, and had done all their best work by the end of the 1920s. It seems fair to say that not one of their hundreds of successors has come close to satisfying so many eminent researchers, for so long a period, with so little apparent recourse to fraud. If mediumship really is the genuine, and generally accessible, phenomenon portrayed by spiritualists and, to a lesser extent by psychical researchers, there seems no reason why this should be so.

Another difficulty encountered in any attempt to assess mediumship is that of knowing where to draw the line between cases that may involve contact with an external intelligence, and those that may be the product of the medium's own mind. There are obvious parallels between mediums who claim to contact the dead through intermediary 'spirit guides' (who appear, with suspicious frequency, to be wise old American Indians), and New Age psychics, who channel the disencarnate spirits of ancient Atlantaens or, in one extreme case, the plastic essence of Barbie (her first message was 'I need respect') – yet few serious psychical researchers accord channellers the respect they reserve for mediums. Moreover, not every communication received by mental mediums has proved to be accurate or even purported to come from the spirit world.

During the 1890s, four women separately claimed mediumistic contacts with the inhabitants of the planet Mars. Some were in contact with 'actual' Martians, while others reported that the planet was merely the home of some formerly earthbound spirits; but each was able to elaborate a more or less sophisticated vision of life on a planet that we now know to be barren and apparently lifeless. Two of the mediums, a Swiss woman named Catherine Muller and an American, Mrs Willis Cleveland, even spoke and wrote a 'Martian' language (though not the same one) which, when analysed, proved to be their own unconscious invention.

It is, of course, highly unlikely that any of the supposed Martian communications were in any way 'real', but, even so, they displayed an astonishing internal cohesion and complexity, which suggests that the brain is fully capable of producing many of the phenomena commonly ascribed to mental mediumship. Muller, in particular, manifested a full range of spiritualistic powers, including raps, apports and incidences of psychokinesis. She painted 'inspired' pieces of art and worked in harness with a typically overweening spirit guide called Leopold, who claimed – demonstrably falsely – to be the notorious eighteenth-century mystic Cagliostro.

The investigators of three of the Martian mediums – the psychologists Carl Jung and Theodore Flournoy, and the psychical researcher James Hyslop – concluded that the phenomena were the product of secondary personalities, in one case an adult persona that was in the process of taking over from the child. But they also concurred that the mediumship was not pathological, nor merely a form of hysteria, and indeed was possible only because the women enjoyed good health and possessed normal and balanced personalities.

What else distinguishes a medium? Psychical researchers concede that there is little proof that mediumship is hereditary, or that mediums possess any physical distinguishing marks, while sceptics argue, with some justification, that two other supposedly common characteristics – the ideas that they are in some way 'delicate', and thus unable to produce their phenomena consistently or under controlled conditions, and that their powers wax and wane unpredictably, permitting great displays of genuine powers on some occasions and forcing them to cheat, so as not to disappoint sitters, on others – are little more than excuses for fraud and deception. It may, however, be significant that there are more female mediums than there are males, and there is, as we shall see in a later chapter, some interesting evidence that sincere (rather than patently fraudulent) mediums do share certain traits of personality that help to explain why they experience unusual phenomena.

Extrasensory Perception

The second broad group of phenomena studied by psychical researchers has been given the collective name 'psi', though it is nearly synonymous with the better known term ESP – extrasensory perception. The term psi covers the phenomena of telepathy ('mind-reading'), clairvoyance (visions of objects and events occurring at a distance from the clairvoyant), precognition (foretelling the future) and psychokinesis (the movement of objects by mental means alone), among others.

Many thousands of anecdotal accounts of such strange phenomena exist, and they may be divided into four broad categories: waking intuitive impressions, devoid of imagery ('hunches', in other words – the feeling that 'something is wrong'); hallucinations (waking experiences accompanied by visual impressions of objects that are not physically real); and realistic and unrealistic dreams. The great majority concern instances of telepathy and clairvoyance. A simple, but fairly typical, example was recorded by the psychical researcher Rosalind Heywood, who found herself unexpectedly stranded one day, many miles from the place where she had arranged to meet her husband. As she walked, exhausted, along a road, he drove up in his car and explained that he had 'felt quite suddenly that you needed me here, at once'. Many of the most intriguing instances of telepathy seem to have been prompted by similar or greater crises: the mother who suddenly 'knows' that her child has been hurt, for example. Another extremely common category concerns telepathic or clairvoyant dreams. F.W.H. Myers, one of the founders of the SPR, gave the example of an acquaintance who was visiting a friend when the man lost a treasured watch while working in a pasture. The friend, who had never ventured far into the field, 'could not keep his mind off the watch, and after two or three days' thinking of it, went to bed one night still thinking of it. During the night he had a dream . . . . and saw the watch lying on the ground with the chain coiled in a peculiar position; rocks, trees and all the surroundings were perfectly plain to him. Telling his story at the breakfast table he was, of course, well laughed at, but being so convinced that he could go straight to the watch, he saddled a horse and found it exactly as he expected to.'

This example of clairvoyance is particularly interesting, in that it appears to exclude the possibility of telepathy: it is unlikely that the watch's owner or anyone else had seen it lying in the position in which it was found. But the subject is an extremely broad and complex one. Psychical researchers have shown that people from all walks of life experience supposed telepathic incidents, and have noted instances of telepathy with unborn children, with the dead, and among close relatives, particularly twins. The latter phenomenon will be familiar to many families, and may be more common than is generally supposed. The psychologist Berthold Schwarz, who made a practice of keeping a daily record of apparent instances of telepathy between himself, his wife and their two offspring, reported that, by the time his children had reached the ages of fourteen and twelve, his notebooks listed a total of 1520 incidents. There have also been instances of telepathic healing, of telepathy manifesting itself under hypnosis, and of precognitive telepathy. It is nevertheless apparent that such spontaneous cases occur unpredictably and that most do not particularly benefit the person who experiences them: our 'sixth sense', if it does exist, is plainly much less useful to us than the other five.

The same seems to be true of precognition, another extremely common phenomenon, and one that really ought to be of the utmost value. Here again, a principal problem is that many of those who do experience flashes of foreknowledge fail to act on them or – most unfortunately for the researcher – record them before the event that was foreseen actually occurs. This is surely because experience has shown us that most instances of precognition do not come true, or are so vague as to be nearly useless.

Nevertheless, there are a handful of spectacular incidences in which people have benefited from glimpsing the future. One concerns the British horse racing enthusiast Lord Kilbracken who, while a student just after the Second World War, 'dreamed' the names of a succession of winners. The dreams were not completely accurate, but contained enough information for Kilbracken to make some very advantageous bets: one night, for example, he dreamt of a winning horse called Tubermore, and two days later noticed that an animal named Tuberose was running at Aintree. It was a rank outsider, but won at odds of 100 to 6; even more remarkably, Kilbracken wrote, 'I have watched its fortunes since, and it has never won another race.'

This case is regarded as an especially good one, because the dreamer shared his knowledge with a group of friends, all of whom benefited financially as a result. Even Kilbracken, though, never dreamed of winners to order, and many years passed between successful 'hits' during which nothing untoward occurred at all. Furthermore his final prediction, filed in advance with the SPR, that the 1972 Grand National would be won by a horse called Neat Turn, failed to come true, and indeed no horse of that name ran in the race.

Of course, Kilbracken was a keen racing enthusiast and it is at least possible that he was knowledgeable enough to select likely winners himself, and that his dreams were simply alerting him to these selections. This objection is, however, more difficult to apply to another common sort of precognition, the premonition of disaster. In the particularly well-documented case of the Aberfan catastrophe of October 1966, in which an entire infant school was submerged by a collapsing Welsh coal tip, killing 128 children and 16 adults, the parapsychologist J.C. Barker made a newspaper appeal for premonitions of the event and received almost eighty replies, thirty-five of which he concluded were genuine instances of precognition.

Similarly, it is rare for a plane to crash or a ship to sink without at least one prospective passenger coming forward to say that they had been warned not to travel, by a dream or a 'feeling' of some sort. In the early 1960s the American parapsychologist William Cox collected detailed statistics, which compared the number of passengers travelling on trains that had been involved in a collision or an accident with the number travelling on the same train on each of the preceding seven days, and on three sample days in the previous month. His results showed that, in each case, there were fewer passengers on the damaged or derailed trains than normal; analysing his figures, he concluded that the odds against this effect happening by chance were more than 100 to 1. This suggests, of course, that some prospective passengers had experienced premonitions and chosen not to travel on the fateful day.

Despite Cox's statistics (which have not been confirmed by other experimenters), the real problem with precognition is, again, its unpredictability. If all disasters were prefaced by premonitions as a matter of course, it might be possible to act in time to prevent at least some of them. This was, in fact, Barker's conclusion, and he followed up his study of Aberfan by establishing premonition bureaux in London and New

York, in the hope of creating a sort of psychic early warning system. Unfortunately, while a handful of the 1200 reports received by his London bureau between 1967 and 1973 did appear to anticipate subsequent events, the majority of predictions followed no obvious pattern, and no flood of precognitive experiences was ever recorded before a disaster took place.

In fact, the evidence for precognition of impending disaster is essentially negative: in other words, there are no accurate predictions of events that one might reasonably expect to have been predicted. Of all the catastrophes of the twentieth-century, the greatest were the two world wars. Yet not only do there appear to have been no good predictions of the coming disasters, each destined to affect many millions of families around the world, but throughout the tense months leading to the outbreak of the Second World War, when even lay people were becoming increasingly certain that a conflict was inevitable, the massed ranks of the spirit guides consulted by mediums continued to insist that there would be no war. The same failure occurred in 1982, when Argentina invaded the Falkland Islands. On the other hand, the leaders of a variety of cults and religious movements have given several dozen, very specific dates for the end of the world, ranging from 1843 to 2012 – predictions that seemed real enough to persuade thousands of their followers to devote themselves to preparing for the doomsday. To date, it goes without saying, not one of those predictions has been fulfilled.

The last major category of psi is psychokinesis, the power of mind over matter. This also has a considerable history, having been associated with poltergeist-type phenomena since ancient times. Physical mediumship is a form of psychokinesis, as is 'spoon-bending', and a number of mediums have claimed to be able to move or levitate objects more or less at will. One, a Polish woman named Stanislawa Tomczyk who flourished shortly before the Great War, appeared to be able to stop clocks, affect the fall of a roulette wheel and levitate small objects such as a matchbox or scissors, even under controlled conditions. She attributed this power to rigid, invisible 'rays' which shot from her fingers.

Remarkable though the phenomenon of psychokinesis may appear, however, it must again be remarked that the effects that are produced are hardly in proportion with the efforts expended to obtain them – it would be much easier simply to pick up the matchbox or scissors. Psychics who have attempted to demonstrate psychokinesis on a larger scale have sometimes come to grief. In September 1989, the driver of a freight train nearing Astrakhan, at the mouth of the Volga river, noticed a man in a white shirt walking beside the line. As the train approached, the man stopped, dropped his briefcase, and walked into the path of the train, where he stood with his arms raised, head bowed and body tensed until the locomotive struck and killed him. A police investigation determined that he was Alexei Frenkel, a man with a local reputation as a faith healer, and his apparently suicidal behaviour was explained by a note found in the briefcase: 'First I stopped a bicycle, cars, and a streetcar. Now I am going to stop a train. Only in extraordinary conditions of a direct threat to my organism will all my reserves be called into action.'

Finally, it should be added that small-scale psychokinetic effects are so similar to those produced by stage magicians, that it is quite likely that most, if not all, are the product of nothing more than simple conjury. The Russian psychic Ninel Kulagina, who, in the 1960s, produced effects very similar to those of Tomczyk – moving a salt cellar and levitating a table tennis ball – was eventually caught by Soviet parapsychologists using concealed magnets and invisible thread to effect her tricks. Sceptics have repeatedly observed that parapsychologists are generally ill-equipped to spot such fraud, and psychics who have performed before stage magicians have fared poorly. In one embarrassing case, two American conjurors who posed as men with psychokinetic gifts were able to convince researchers at the McDonnell Laboratory for Psychical Research at Washington University that their 'powers' were genuine, despite deliberately leaving clear evidence of their tampering and trickery.

In conclusion, parapsychologists have been forced to concede that it is so difficult to rule out the possibility of fraud, coincidence and poor reporting when considering ESP that anecdotal cases and uncontrolled experiments do not constitute sufficient evidence for phenomena that all, in some way, violate important scientific laws. The recent history of psychical research is thus, largely, the history of protracted attempts to produce scientifically acceptable evidence that psi even exists. The idea of finding some special subject who can spontaneously and unerringly produce psi phenomena under laboratory conditions having been long ago abandoned, the aims of such studies are now simply to meet the basic scientific requirement of producing a repeatable experiment, while obtaining 'statistically significant' results (in other words, a controlled study in which the subject, while failing to produce results that are consistently predictable, does at least obtain a better proportion of 'hits' than would be expected by chance alone). In its first hundred-or-so years, parapsychology has signally failed to attain these relatively modest goals, though it has certainly succeeded in producing a large number of papers that make dull and difficult reading for anyone without a background in statistics.

Much of the experimentation has concerned attempts to detect telepathy and clairvoyance under laboratory conditions. One of the pioneers of this approach was an American parapsychologist, J.B. Rhine, who developed what are known as Zener cards – a 25-card pack featuring five symbols: a cross, a star, a circle, a square and a series of wavy lines – in an attempt to produce statistically acceptable evidence. He asked subjects seated in his laboratory to guess which of the five cards had just been dealt. The chance result – what a subject might be expected to achieve by guessing – was one correct answer in five, but after thousands of experiments Rhine believed he had discovered a handful of subjects whose results were beyond chance. Further experiments suggested that similar results could be obtained when the experimenter and his subject were anything up to 100 miles apart, and that stimulants could enhance test scores.

Persuasive though Rhine's results were, however, they did not prove to be repeatable. In one intriguing case, the British parapsychologist Samuel Soal, frustrated by his inability to duplicate Rhine's work, re-analysed his subjects' results, looking for other possible correlations. He discovered that one sitter, Basil Shakleton, appeared to be demonstrating precognition by sometimes guessing one card ahead of the one the experimenter had actually dealt. Soal's research was hailed as the best available proof of psi for three decades, until a painstaking check on his results by an SPR member named Betty Markwick finally proved that he had faked some of his results by adding spurious 'hits' to the tests. When these hits were removed, Shakleton's performance fell to chance levels.

No one has suggested that Rhine faked his results, but he did employ Soal's technique of searching apparently negative tests for forward or backward displacement of psi. The sceptic Martin Gardner has observed that

> such displacement of ESP may even be two or three cards ahead or behind! Clearly if [a parapsychologist] can choose between all these possible relations, there is a strong likelihood one of them will show scores above average. If no displacement is found, however, a chance score may be attributed to some disturbance of the subject's mental state. . . Even the experimenter, if he is in any of these regrettable states, may inhibit the subject by unconscious telepathy. . . Of course, when the scores are high, no one is likely to look for 'subtle influences'. But if the scores drop low, the search begins. Naturally they will not be hard to find. Usually if low scores continue, the tests are discontinued. If the scores are extremely low, they are regarded as a *negative* form of ESP.

In this way, it is possible for sincere psychical researchers to account for apparent 'misses' and increase their number of 'hits'.

Another of Rhine's experiments attempted to test for psychokinesis. He asked subjects to try to influence the fall of dice, and again produced a string of positive results. Further analysis suggested that there was also a noticeable decline in psychokinetic ability as an experiment continued, suggesting that psi might be affected by the subject's tiredness. However, though a few other experimenters produced results similar to those of Rhine, others obtained nothing that could not be explained by chance.

More recently, parapsychologists have turned to attempts to influence random number generators in the hope of producing less fallible experiments. Indeed, many different techniques have been tried in an effort to eliminate all the possible explanations for apparently paranormal effects. For some time, it seemed that the elusive repeatable results could be produced by searching for telepathy in the 'Ganzfeld' ('total field'), a state in which the subject is subjected to mild sensory deprivation by having half table tennis balls placed over their eyes and white noise pumped into their ears through headphones. Then a row erupted over whether the Ganzfeld researchers had been randomising their targets correctly, and, as a result, the viability of this approach is now open to question.

Another obvious problem is the possibility of suggestion influencing results, or even unconscious collusion between the experimenter and his subject, so some parapsychologists have experimented on animals instead. In one rather gruesome test, Robert Morris of the Psychical Research Foundation put nineteen numbered rats into a large arena, having determined in advance that he would kill all the odd-numbered rats in ten minutes' time, then studied the movements of all nineteen over a two-minute period. He found that the rats selected for death appeared to 'freeze' and were much less active than their fellows – apparent evidence for animal precognition. When two other laboratories attempted to duplicate the experiment, however, one obtained nothing of significance (other than a lot of dead rats) and the other produced results that ran directly counter to Morris's: the doomed rodents were *more* active than their favoured brethren.

One further suggestion, which has the virtue of allowing for the general uselessness of ESP, is that psi might be a vestigial ability, which adults learn to suppress, and which is more pronounced in children. In the 1980s Ernesto Spinelli, an Italian researcher, conducted some 1200 Zener-style sessions with subjects aged from three upwards, and concluded not only that they could guess cards at a rate up to 27 per cent greater than chance, but that this ability was enhanced when children of the same age were paired, and that it declined as the children grew older, so that by the time they were eight it had disappeared. Even here, there appears to be some question over whether Spinelli's tests adequately allowed for the likelihood that children of a similar age group might obtain apparently good results because of similarities in experience and taste. In a much smaller experiment conducted in 1993, Susan Blackmore and Frances Chamberlein tested twelve sets of twins and twelve non-twin siblings in an attempt to discover whether they could transmit numbers, photographs and pictures by telepathy. They discovered that the twins scored well above chance on the tests – but only when they were allowed to choose which numbers, pictures and photos to transmit. When the targets were selected with the help of random number tables, the results fell to just above chance. This suggests that the results were due to 'thought concordance' – the likelihood that children raised in the same environment will have similar preferences and think in similar ways – rather than ESP.

In short, despite many years of hard work and much research, parapsychology has still to produce a viable and repeatable experiment, demonstrating the existence of any variety of psi. As Blackmore, one of the best modern psychical researchers, puts it, 'the non-repeatability of psi is parapsychology's only repeatable finding'. This is a state of affairs that offers far more comfort to sceptics than believers.

Into the Astral

In recent-years, both parapsychologists and physiologists have also devoted considerable effort to the study of two phenomena that appear to be related to ESP: the out of the body experience (OBE) and near death experience (NDE). Both appear to involve the projection of some form of consciousness from the physical body, allowing the person experiencing them to witness events at a distance and from a different perspective. Surveys have shown that the out of the body experience, at least, is relatively common: somewhere between eight and fifteen per cent of the general population have had at least one OBE. Moreover, instances have been collected from most countries and all periods of history. It has been suggested that medieval witches who insisted, even under torture, that they had left their bodies and flown through the air in spirit form, may have had out of the body experiences, and there are obvious parallels with some feats of mediumship, including those of Catherine Muller. The notion of the 'astral body' has also become a staple of many occult movements, particularly Theosophy. In short, the out of the body experience is among the most commonly reported of all strange phenomena, and believers and sceptics agree that this means it is likely to be a 'real' experience of some sort.

But what sort of experience is it? OBEs tend to have several identifiable stages. Typically, the witness suddenly and unexpectedly finds himself 'outside' his physical body, perhaps looking down on it from a vantage point near the ceiling. (Some people are able to deliberately induce OBEs, and they often report unusual sensations such as clicks or vibrations at the beginning and end of their 'journey'. Those who have only a single OBE rarely report such experiences.) At this point about half the witnesses become aware that they are now inhabiting a second body, which resembles their own. The two may be joined by an infinitely elastic silver cord, but this is rare, and appears to occur mainly in cases where the witness was previously aware that there is an occult tradition that the physical and astral bodies are joined by such a cord.

Now, and with little effort, many witnesses report that they are able to move about at will. They generally perceive the world as solid and realistic – if anything, it seems clearer, brighter and altogether more vivid than usual – and they may be able to visit distant places practically instantaneously. While all this is happening, those who are with the witness report that the physical body remains still and that the subject appears to be in some sort of trance state.

Susan Blackmore's early interest in parapsychology was confirmed by her own OBE, which happened while she was at college. The experience began late one night in 1970 when she was very tired. She had also smoked a small quantity of hashish.

> . . . After seeing my own body down below I began to travel around the room. It all seemed quite real and quite natural. I could see my body sitting on the floor, and 'I' seemed to be another self up on the ceiling.
>
> 'Can you fly around?' asked Kevin's calming voice from down below.
>
> 'Yes, I can go anywhere I want,' answered a second voice. The odd thing was that I could actually see my own mouth opening and closing down there on the floor. It seemed to be giving sensible replies but equally seemed to have nothing to do with me at all.
>
> 'But I'm joined to the body by a cord,' I added . . . a wonderful glowing greyish-white cord snaking down from my tummy 'up here' into the head 'down there' . . .
>
> In this state anything was possible by thought alone. I reached out a hand, and then, with a leap of pleasure, two hands, and three, and half a dozen! I could have 20 hands. I could fly and float and change shape and move just as I liked.

With this realisation, Blackmore set out to explore the world beyond the college room. She flew across the Channel to France, and on to the Mediterranean, where she visited a star-shaped island with a hundred trees. She knew there was no such island in that sea. 'Something inside me reckoned this must be someone's idea of an island,' she recalled. When she finally returned to her body, some three hours later, she found she had difficulty re-entering it. At first her new form seemed too small, then much too large for her physical body. At length she 'climbed' through a gap in some clouds and came to a plain filled with thousands of people. 'With that, it was obviously time to come back, but I had no idea of what a struggle it would be and how long it would take. Some time later, I was still repeating to myself, "I must go behind the eyes and look out through them". It wasn't easy.'

There are several possible explanations for the out of the body experience. One is that the occurrence represents the separation of the soul from the body and that it is objectively real. Another is that the OBE is an externalisation of a psi experience – a construct created by the subconscious to persuade the conscious mind that it is capable of gathering information remotely by telepathy. The third is that the experience is psychophysiological in nature – a product, in other words, of the way in which the human brain functions.

In recent years, the psychophysiological theory has gained ground and become the generally accepted explanation for OBEs. Broadly, the theory suggests that the out of the body experience is the brain's response to a disruption of the normal sensory inputs, which serve to anchor the perception of consciousness within the body. This may occur in the early stages of sleep, and also in conditions of deep relaxation or, conversely, extreme physical excitement. In this altered state of consciousness, purely mental imagery, created within the mind, comes to the fore; Blackmore suggests that the vivid world through which the witness travels is actually the brain's own mental map, which it usually refers to for the purpose of orientation. This explains why the world of the out of the body experience so closely resembles the real world, while sometimes – particularly in far-off, unvisited lands – containing elements of pure fantasy. Because the mind is used to receiving a sensory input that identifies its physical location, the shock of perceiving itself to be in some other position is often enough to allow normal bodily sensations to reassert their control of the body image, ending the OBE early on. Even if the experience persists, a change in the conditions that allowed the witness to enter his altered state of consciousness is enough to bring the OBE to a sudden halt: the 'astral' and physical bodies are abruptly reunited.

If either the occult or parapsychological view of the out of the body experience is correct, it should be relatively easy to disprove the psychophysiological hypothesis. All a witness would need to do would be to travel from his physical body and find and remember some piece of information that he could not otherwise have known – a number written on a piece of paper and displayed in someone else's home, for instance – or to return with a precise description of an incident that occurred in a distant city during the OBE. Psychical researchers have attempted to conduct such experiments, without obtaining irrefutable evidence.

Celia Green records a case in which a correspondent who was in hospital had an OBE in which she saw a 'big' woman sitting up in bed with her head wrapped in bandages, 'knitting something in blue wool'. It was claimed that the 'big' woman in question did in fact exist, but there was no evidence that the witness had not seen her previously, while walking through that ward. Charles Tart reported a case in which one of his subjects apparently succeeded in noting a five-digit number hidden from her view, but he later agreed she might have glimpsed it earlier in the day. On the other hand Blackmore notes an incident in which a Canadian architect, 'Mr C', travelled not only across the Atlantic but apparently back in time to the mid-Victorian era during an OBE. He was able to supply a precise description of a street in the Fulham area of London that he had visited. Unfortunately, at that period in history, Fulham was not part of London. It was still a rural area and consisted of green fields, not streets. The architect's OBE appeared to be a fantasy.

Nevertheless, the potential implications of the out of the

body experience are obviously profound. Should it ever be proven that the OBE is in some way 'real', it should be possible to train suitable subjects to use the 'remote viewing' component of the experience to assist search and rescue operations, or to create a new breed of uncatchable super-spy.

The latter possibility has not escaped the US government. In the early 1970s – already concerned by rumours that the Soviet Union was investing resources in an exciting programme of defence-related ESP studies – it initially backed two scientists at the Stanford Research Institute, Harold Puthoff and Russell Targ, and later its own panel of psychics and testers, in an official attempt to develop its own capacity for psychic warfare.

Puthoff and Targ's experiments involved feeding map co-ordinates to a number of psychics, of whom the most prominent was a New York artist named Ingo Swann, and asking them to record their impressions of the unknown locale. Some initially interesting results were obtained. On one occasion Puthoff gave Swann co-ordinates for the middle of Lake Victoria. The psychic responded that he was receiving a mental picture of land to the right of a large lake. A check on a large scale map confirmed that there was an island in the lake at the relevant spot, a fact Puthoff did not know. Later the experiment was improved so that neither the experimenter nor the remote viewer were told what lay at the co-ordinates selected. Again Swann seemed to supply some impressive responses, of which the most interesting involved a site on the east coast of America. Given the co-ordinates, he sketched a plan showing several buildings, a flagpole and a tower – details not shown even on large scale maps of the area in question. Yet Puthoff and Targ concluded: 'Not only was Swann's description correct in every detail, even the relative distances on his map were to scale!'

The problem with such experiments, of course, is that they can only be assessed subjectively. There is no way of determining empirically whether results are 'hits' or 'misses'. Nevertheless, emboldened by the initial trials, the remote viewing programme, now known as Operation Stargate, was taken over by America's Defense Intelligence Agency and the National Security Agency, who ran it from the NSA's headquarters at Fort Meade, Maryland, for a further two decades. During that time, between three and six psychics were maintained on US government payrolls, and a total of about $20 million was spent on remote viewing projects. (This is actually an extremely modest budget for a US military project.)

One component of the programme was a systematic attempt to produce viable and repeatable results from remote viewing experiments conducted under controlled conditions. When the results of these trials were finally released for analysis by outsiders in 1995, there was a clash between the two scientists on the assessment panel. One was convinced that the results did demonstrate the validity of remote viewing; the other strongly disagreed. Perhaps the most significant finding, though, was the admission that even if the experiments had been conducted correctly, the number of 'hits' obtained over a twenty-year-period was little more than one in three. While this would, in theory, be sufficient to demonstrate the existence of psi – it is above chance expectation – it is not enough to suggest that remote viewing is a particularly useful technique.

A second component of the same programme was an attempt to train psychic spies. Stargate's best years came in the late 1970s and early 1980s, when its staff included six remote viewers known as 'The Naturals'. A varied list of claims have been made for successful 'hits' produced by the mystics of Fort Meade, including detection of a major Soviet submarine project in 1979, the position of secret PLO training bases, Russian radar establishments and nuclear testing areas, and also the locations of Saddam Hussain during the Gulf War, General James Dozier, an American general kidnapped in Italy in 1981, and a Soviet TU-95 'Backfire' bomber which had crashed in Africa. On the other hand, the same sources also spoke of the programme deteriorating in the mid-1980s under the influence of New Agers and 'kooks'. There was speculation that new psychics were being brought in to communicate not only with the crews of submerged submarines and astronauts in space, but with aliens in UFOs. One member of the team was retired after he became convinced there was a Martian colony beneath the New Mexico desert.

In retrospect, Operation Stargate can be seen to have suffered from two insuperable problems. Because they were running an intelligence operation and not a scientific study, the DIA had no compunction in making as much background information available to its psychics as possible, and then attempting to fit the information generated by remote viewing to the known facts. This practice made it impossible for outsiders to assess the true usefulness of the OBEs. Furthermore, the nature of the targets meant that any successes the 'Naturals' and their colleagues did enjoy could be appreciated only if their predictions were confirmed by conventional intelligence. This problem rendered the entire programme essentially worthless, and when it was finally shut down in 1995 it was conceded that remote viewing had never provided an adequate basis for 'actionable' intelligence operations.

While Operation Stargate was running, another variant of OBE, the near death experience, was attracting even more controversy. Like the out of the body experience, the NDE has been reported throughout history and in many different cultures. It has, however, become far more common in recent years, thanks, perhaps, to the advent of advanced techniques of resuscitation. It is difficult to know how many of those who come close to death have the experience – estimates vary between seven and seventy-two per cent – but what is clear is that NDEs seem to occur no matter how death is approached, whether it be through illness, accident or suicide, and that the experience almost always has a profound effect on the witness's subsequent life.

The reason for this is simple: the near death experience appears to offer proof that humans have a 'soul' and that it does survive bodily death and journey towards heaven. Like the out of the body experience, the NDE has identifiable stages, though not every witness goes through every stage. It generally begins like an OBE, with the witness suddenly aware that he is looking down on his body from above. In a stereotypical incident the next stage is a rapid journey through a long, dark tunnel, at the end of which appears a bright light (this stage is in fact reported only by about one in four of those who have experienced an NDE). About half the witnesses next report encountering a supportive 'presence', which may take the form of a recognisable religious figure, such as Christ, or might appear simply as an amorphous 'being of light'. If the experience continues, it is normal for the witness to proceed to some heavenly realm at this point; typically one featuring imposing architecture and beautiful gardens. It is not uncommon to encounter dead relatives, and about one NDE in four involves a rapid 'life review' akin to the old notion that a drowning man's life flashes before his eyes.

Once again, there are competing explanations for the NDE. Most people who undergo the experience are convinced that they have proof of survival, but physiologists point out that many of those who approach death but are revived do not recall an NDE at all. Near death experiences may be better understood as a biological response to some forms of approaching death. It has been suggested that some components of the NDE are the product of oxygen starvation affecting the brain and producing hallucinations, while the feeling of serenity reported by most witnesses may be accounted for by the release of endorphins – natural painkillers secreted by a body that is injured or under stress. The 'tunnel' effect might be explained as an opthalmological phenomenon known as 'form constants': images produced by the actions of the human visual nervous system itself, independently of signals received via the retina, often in response to stress. One of the most recognisable form constants is 'a luminous, tunnel-like image appearing in the middle of the visual field'.

Some apparently peripheral surveys do lend support to the physiological hypothesis. One was conducted by a mountaineer named Albert Heim as early as the 1880s. Heim had fallen seventy feet from a mountain face, surviving only because he landed on a snow-covered ledge. During the fall he experienced a strange sensation of time slowing up, accompanied by a sensation of peacefulness and calm; surveying thirty other climbers who had suffered similar accidents, he found that such experiences were fairly common, perhaps because the plummeting mountaineers were being calmed by endorphins. But as would be expected if the physiological theory of NDEs was correct, there was no mention of the sort of phenomena apparently caused by oxygen starvation, such as 'the being of light'.

Experiences closely resembling NDEs have also been reported by witnesses who were not in fact close to death, including women in childbirth and people undergoing night terrors. Robert Baker, a psychologist at the University of Kentucky, has concluded: 'The human brain, it seems, whenever it is subjected to unusual mental or physical stresses and strains, responds appropriately and typically, that is, neurochemically, with hallucinatory defensive reactions. These we colour with our religious beliefs, our folklore, and our hopes and fears.'

Some psychical researchers counter that the physiological hypothesis cannot explain some of the more extraordinary aspects of the near death experience. Some NDEs have occurred in patients registering no brain activity whatsoever, and it has been suggested that this proves the journey to the afterlife must have been experienced by the astral body. Nearly a century ago, Sir William Barrett collected a number of cases in which the dying witness was greeted in heaven by relatives whom they thought were still alive, but who were in fact dead. He thought this might constitute proof that the experience was real, though it may also be explained by ESP or, indeed, flawed memory on the part of a witness who had been told of his relative's death.

Perhaps the most damning argument in favour of the physiological hypothesis, however, is the discovery that classic near death experiences can be induced under controlled conditions by the administration of small doses of the anaesthetic ketamine. The German physiologist Karl Jansen has concluded from studies of dying patients that specific conditions, including low oxygen, low blood flow and low blood sugar, result in the release of a flood of the substance called glutamate within the brain. The glutamate blocks a category of drug binding sites in the brain's nerve endings, which can result in the death of cells; to counteract this, the body's defence mechanisms respond to the possibility of lockage by releasing natural chemicals, resembling ketamine, which protect the threatened sites by binding to them. It is this final process which has the side effect of inducing an altered state of consciousness in which the NDE takes place.

Complicated though the process may sound, the key finding of Jansen's research is that near death experiences can be induced at will in a perfectly healthy subject by the intravenous admission of between 50 and 100 mg of the anaesthetic. If he is correct, NDEs cannot be taken as evidence for life after death, and the ketamine theory must also be considered as a possible explanation for out of the body experiences.

Life After Life

Suppose, for a moment, that some part of our personalities does indeed survive death. What happens next? One possibility is that the soul is reincarnated, either immediately or after an interval, and enters another body to begin a new life. This extremely ancient belief is central to two of the world's great religions, Hinduism and Buddhism, and was accepted by the early Celtic Christian church. It is also found in many other cultures, from the Aborigine to the Zulu.

Even in the twentieth century, many people have claimed a conscious recall of past lives. One standard criticism is that far too many of them speak of incarnations as well-known historical figures: during the 1930s a British woman called Joan Grant won fame for her fictionalised recollections of a succession of glamorous lives in ancient Egypt (a popular destination for many past life stories), and in other well-known cases one woman has recalled living as James IV, king of

Scotland, and another as Charles II's famous mistress, Nell Gwynn. However, one recent survey of no fewer than 1088 American cases showed that most subjects recalled past lives of considerable inconsequence and squalor. This suggests that there may be more to the problem of reincarnation than pure braggadocio.

Though the conscious recall of past lives has contributed significantly to the total number of cases available for study, the rebirth of western interest in reincarnation stemmed from the discovery, in the early 1950s, that hypnotic subjects could be regressed past the moment of their birth, and into previous lives, where they produced unparalleled quantities of information about everyday life in earlier times. The first significant case of what became known as past-life regression occurred in Colorado in 1952, when an amateur hypnotist, Morey Bernstein, took a young woman called Virginia Tighe back to a previous existence as a middle-class Irish woman – Bridey Murphy – who had lived from 1798 to 1864. To Bernstein's delight, Tighe immediately dropped her mid-western accent for a consistent Irish brogue and proceeded to spill forth a wealth of convincing detail about the mundanities of life in Cork and Belfast in the first half of the nineteenth-century.

Checking her story proved difficult – few Irish records survive from the period in question – but when Bernstein published an account of the case in 1956, it caused a sensation and made hypnotic regression suddenly fashionable. Others were irresistibly drawn to the idea of conducting their own experiments with the new technique, among them a Welsh hypnotherapist named Arnall Bloxham. During the 1960s and 1970s, he regressed more than 400 people and tape recorded their recollections of past lives.

Among Bloxham's most impressive cases were those of Graham Huxtable – a Swansea swimming instructor whose recall of an eighteenth-century sea battle ended most realistically with him screaming in agony as he re-lived having a leg blown off by cannon fire – and a female subject given the pseudonym 'Jane Evans', who produced detailed recollections of seven past lives ranging from that of a Romano-British woman of the third century AD to a nineteenth-century American nun. The most dramatic of these, however, was Evans's recall of her incarnation as a Jewish woman named Rebecca who lived in twelfth century York.

This story came to a climax in 1190, when the York mob rose and massacred the Jewish community of the city. Under Bloxham's guidance, Evans relived Rebecca's last moments as she and her daughter sought sanctuary in a small church outside the gate:

> . . . We can hear the screaming and the shouting and the crying – 'Burn the Jews, burn the Jews.' . . . Oh God – they're coming – they – they are coming – Rachel's crying – don't cry – don't cry – don't cry. [*Pause.*] Aah, they've entered the church – the priest is loose – the priest has got free – he had told them we are here – they're coming – they're down. [*Pause and voice almost incoherent with terror.*] Oh not – not not not Rachel! No don't take her – don't – stop – they're going to kill her – they – don't – not Rachel, no, no, no, no – not Rachel, oh, don't take Rachel.'
>
> Bloxham [*shocked*]: 'They're not going to take her are they?'
>
> Rebecca [*grief-stricken voice*]: 'They've taken Rachel, they've taken Rachel.'
>
> Bloxham: 'They're not going to harm you are they?' [*Silence*]
>
> Bloxham: 'Are you all right? They have left you alone have they?'
>
> Rebecca: 'Dark . . . dark . . .'

What impressed Bloxham about this case was the fact that the story contained many details that could be checked by historians. To begin with, a massacre of Jews really had occurred in much the way that Rebecca described, though Evans (a Welsh housewife who had not studied history beyond 'O' level) was adamant that she had never heard of it before. Furthermore, though no record survived of Rebecca herself, an historian who had studied the incident confirmed that Evans's account was essentially credible. Working from her descriptions, he even identified the church – St Mary's Castlegate – that he felt must have been the one Rebecca and her daughter had hidden in.

There was one problem: Evans had specifically described concealing herself in a crypt. Yet none of York's medieval churches, including St Mary's, was known to possess one. Then, six months after the historian had delivered his opinion, workmen renovating St Mary's discovered what appeared to be a crypt under the chancel.

It was just the sort of evidence that regression researchers had been hoping for – a detail that seemed to fit the memory of a past life exactly, but could not possibly have been known to the subject. Even now, nearly a quarter of a century later, it remains one of the most compelling arguments in favour of the reality of reincarnation. Yet there is still room to doubt that Evans really was recalling a previous existence. To begin with, the discovery of the crypt was never confirmed – it was sealed up immediately, and only a single workman peered down to see what had been uncovered. It is possible that the workmen had found nothing more than the remains of an earlier church on the same site. Furthermore, one or two of the details that Evans gave of twelfth-century York were not accurate; she described Coppergate as a real gate, when in 1190 it was actually a street.

The real problem with the case however, and all such past life regressions, is ruling out any possibility that the witness (placed in a highly suggestible state by hypnosis) is not taking cues from the hypnotherapist or simply elaborating a fantasy around a known event. The massacre of 1190 is not quite the utterly obscure event suggested by proponents of claims for reincarnation; turning, for example, to the relevant volume of the *Oxford History of England*, a standard work available in many schools and local libraries, we find several lines devoted to the incident in a longer passage concerning King John's persecution of the Jews. Even if Evans had never seen the description in that book, or another, it does not seem inconceivable that some novelist or playwright had made use of such a dramatic incident and that, in this way, Evans had become aware of the event years before she was regressed – so long ago, in fact, that her conscious mind had forgotten all about it.

One way of tackling this question is to search accounts of reincarnation for possible anachronisms. One subject, Harry Hurst, recalled an existence in the Egyptian city of Thebes during the reign of Rameses III (c.1150 BC); among other details, he spoke of holding a sestertius, a common Roman coin. But an Egyptologist, asked to verify the details of the experience, pointed out that Thebes was a name given to the city by Greek writers of a later period – an Egyptian of Rameses' time would have called it 'On'. Furthermore, the Egyptians did not number their pharaohs but distinguished between rulers of the same name with a complex scheme of birth, throne and reign names, and the first sestertius did not come into circulation until a thousand years after Rameses' rule.

Such evidence may be intriguing, but it is not entirely convincing. If reincarnation is a reality, we cannot know to what degree memories of past lives are filtered through modern experience. It is difficult, for example, to know for sure whether the recollections of an 'Italian' are given in English for the benefit of the therapist, or because the subject is engaging in a fantasy and cannot actually speak Italian. A surer way of assessing the reality of the past life memory is to look at the few cases where the subject actually did speak in another language. There have been instances of poor and ungrammatical attempts at ancient Egyptian and modern German; but on the other hand, the psychologist Ian Stevenson encountered an apparently good case in which a subject spoke in fluent period Swedish with the correct admixture of Norwegian.

Other researchers have combed mouldy old records in the hope of confirming or disproving some of the precise details recalled under hypnosis. Perhaps the most fascinating evidence that regressions are based on unconscious fantasies was discovered by Ian Wilson. He was researching the account of a subject called Jan, a young woman from Merseyside who recalled a dramatic former life as Joan Waterhouse, a girl standing trial for witchcraft at Chelmsford assizes in 1556. This was the first significant English witch trial and, sure enough, Wilson confirmed that Joan Waterhouse had been tried as a witch at the assize. What intrigued him, though, was the discovery of a significant discrepancy in the date given for the trial. Contemporary sources clearly stated that it had actually occurred in July 1566, ten years after the date given by Jan. Wilson soon discovered the probable source of this confusion: during the nineteenth-century, a learned society had reprinted the sixteenth-century chap-book record of the assizes, but the compositor had made one vital error. In re-setting the title page he had wrongly transcribed the date as July 1556, an error that was repeated by later authorities who consulted the reprinted pamphlet rather than the single surviving copy of the original. Wilson concluded:

> We may not able to pinpoint exactly the source from which Jan obtained her Joan Waterhouse memories – it may have been a comparatively minor radio play or a story from a girl's comic that would be a needle-in-a-haystack task to identify – but since Joan's historical information is so accurate in all other respects, we can be virtually certain that her single mistake derives from someone writing of the trial *after* the error by the nineteenth-century typographer. Jan's Joan Waterhouse may confidently be attributed to nothing more out of the ordinary than something she has read or heard.

Summing up his findings, Wilson suggested that the memories of past lives obtained under hypnosis were actually examples of the psychological phenomenon of cryptomnesia, or 'hidden memory', which occurs when the brain retrieves material that it does not recognise as a memory. He further suggested that the different lives recalled under hypnosis could be likened to the multiple personalities manifested by some mentally ill people, generally as a result of childhood trauma. Multiple Personality Disorder, as it is commonly known, can result in anything up to forty different personalities appearing to inhabit the same body. Typically, one is the sufferer's true personality and another a 'control', which may be identified as the patient's conscience, while other, perhaps less well-developed, characters symbolise childishness, artistic characteristics and so on. If questioned, each personality will insist that it is an independent, fully conscious entity, though it may well be aware of at least some of the other personalities and even interact with them.

Wilson's appeal to MPD as a possible explanation for the past life phenomenon is controversial, because multiple personality disorder is still not properly understood and there is still considerable debate about its causes and the increasing willingness of psychotherapists to diagnose it. Like regression therapy itself, MPD is a modern phenomenon. Very few cases date to before the 1950s, but today there are thousands on record. Nevertheless, it must be admitted that the evidence for past lives obtained through hypnosis remains inconclusive, at best, and that there are object lessons to be learned both about the power of the human mind to weave utterly compelling fantasies in the depth of the subconscious, and the dangers of using regression therapy to explore the unknown.

One further group of cases suggestive of reincarnation does exist, however. It comprises accounts collected – and in many cases personally investigated – by Ian Stevenson, a parapsychologist from the University of Virginia. It is generally accepted that Stevenson's case files – he has assembled several thousand accounts from as far afield as Alaska, India, Burma and Turkey – constitute the best available evidence for the past life phenomenon. This is not just because his cases avoid the pitfalls of relying on hypnosis, but because they are frequently accompanied by convincing supporting testimony.

One of the peculiarities of Stevenson's sample is that his cases are drawn from the testimony of young children. Again and again, he found that infants as young as two years old experienced vivid memories of past lives. These recollections faded as they grew older, so that by the time the witness was eight or nine, the past life was pretty much forgotten.

Some of the most interesting of these accounts come from Sri Lanka, where reincarnation is, of course, widely accepted. One involved a boy called Sujith, who was born in August 1969. Before he was two years old, the child informed his mother that his real home was not at Mount Lavinia, where they lived, but eight miles to the south in Gorakana. He added that his name was Sammy Fernando and that he had worked on the railway, become an alcoholic, and died after being struck by a lorry.

Stevenson's investigation revealed that Sammy had been a real person, who lived and died in the manner Sujith described. In total, fifty-nine apparent correlations emerged between the child's statements and the recollections of witnesses in Gorakana. This sort of evidence, Stevenson concluded, was too elaborate to be the product of cryptomnesia:

> Cases attributed or actually traced to cryptomnesia have lacked the behavioural features of the richer cases [in which] the child sustains an identification with the previous personality over an average period of seven years, but without other obvious alterations of consciousness or personality. Moreover, in the richer cases cryptomnesia cannot account for the transmission of much intimate information about one family to a child of another family without supposing that much more contact had taken place between the families than either can remember.

Not surprisingly, sceptics have challenged Stevenson's work. Wilson has pointed out the problems of gathering accurate information through interpreters (Stevenson speaks French and German, but no Asian language) and found it suspicious that two in three of the Indian and Sri Lankan cases involved children from poor backgrounds who recalled previous lives as members of higher castes. Not only is this suggestive of wishful thinking on the part of the child; there is also the obvious possibility that the reincarnated personality might be able to claim some of the wealth of his former family. In one interesting case, a child called Veer Singh openly asked his 'past life father', Laxmi Chand, for a third of his wealth, then lost interest in his former family when Chand suffered such misfortune that he became much poorer than Singh's new father. In the Sujith case, further investigation showed that the child might have obtained his information from three of Sammy Fernando's relatives who lived in Mount Lavinia – one of them in a property that backed onto the Sujith household.

In many ways, Stevenson's best case concerns Imad Elawar, a Lebanese Druze child born in December 1958. (The Druzes, originally an heretical Moslem sect, accept the doctrine of reincarnation.) On this occasion, unusually, the investigators reached the scene before the boy had made any contact with his presumed past life family, which made the possibility of collusion much less likely. When the meeting took place, moreover, Stevenson found an impressive total of some fifty-seven correspondences between the boy's recollections and those of his previous family.

Nevertheless, the sceptic Leonard Angel alleges a remarkable discrepancy in the case:

> Stevenson presents the original information he received concerning the boy's memories, according to his parents, as follows: 'They believed he was claiming to have been one Mahmoud Bouhamzy of Khriby, who had a wife called Jamilah and who had been fatally injured by a truck after a quarrel with its driver.' . . . Amazingly enough, the boy's memories are in the end held to be good enough evidence for reincarnation in spite of the fact that the best past-life candidate Stevenson found was not named Mahmoud Bouhamzy, did not have a wife named Jamilah, and did not die as a result of an accident at all, let alone one that followed a quarrel with a driver.

Reviewing Stevenson's evidence, Angel adds that Stevenson asks leading questions and that the key supporting witness is found to have given misleading information on at least one occasion.

This sort of criticism brings us up against some general

problems of assessing eyewitness descriptions, particularly at second hand. Stevenson's rejoinder to the first claim depends on a subjective interpretation of the subject's statements: 'It turned out that Imad had never actually said the fatal truck accident had happened to him; he had merely described it vividly. Nor had he specifically said that Jamilah was his wife; he had simply often referred to her . . . Although I tried to learn exactly what Imad had himself said, his parents passed on to me as having been said by Imad some of those inferences that they themselves had made.'

It does not appear likely that we will ever get to the bottom of this sort of problem, and it is fortunate, therefore, that Stevenson has some intriguing physical evidence to back up his claims. A number of his best cases feature children who bear on their bodies birthmarks that correspond to scars inflicted in a previous life. One concerns Ravi Shankar, an Indian boy who claimed to have been a child called Ashok Kumar in a previous existence. Kumar had been brutally murdered and beheaded. Stevenson found that Shankar bore a long, thin mark, resembling a knife scar, under his chin.

Not all of these special cases are so impressive, however. An Alsakan Indian named Derek Pitnov had a prominent diamond-shaped birthmark on his abdomen, which he told Stevenson might correspond to a fatal spear-wound delivered to an ancestor, Chah-nik-kooh, though he had no recollection of such a past life and there was no evidence that Chah-nik-kooh had been stabbed in that particular place. Stevenson included this case among his twenty strongest, apparently on no better evidence than the aversion Pitnov displayed towards knives. Birthmarks, in short, are hardly conclusive evidence of the reality of reincarnation, and it is possible that some past life recollections are invented specifically to explain such marks. They do, however, at least indicate that reincarnation studies is a field still rich with possibilities.

Life after Death

Ghosts, I think, are probably the single most commonly encountered strange phenomenon of all. Every culture has its own spectres, and accounts of hauntings have been preserved from every period of history. In consequence, a uniquely large and diverse body of evidence exists to make a detailed and complex analysis of the enigma possible. One of the Society for Psychical Research's earliest and most ambitious projects, the *Census of Hallucinations*, published in 1894, analysed a total of 17,000 cases broadly classifiable as 'hauntings', which had been submitted in response to published appeals. Subsidiary censuses conducted during the twentieth century added several thousand further reports. Nor does this effort even begin to allow for the many hundreds of purely anecdotal cases published every year.

If nothing else, an examination of this vast quantity of evidence quickly demolishes the popular preconception that ghosts are simply spirits of the dead. In fact there appear to be many different sorts of ghosts. One of the most intriguing categories identified by psychical researchers is the 'phantasm of the living' – in other words, an apparition that is identified as someone still very much alive. Such ghosts often feature in 'crisis' cases, in which witnesses encounter the ghost of someone who is, at that moment, dying or undergoing great stress. Another discovery is that reports of classically haunted houses are comparatively rare and most modern ghosts appear not as sheet-clad phantoms but as apparently real figures, clad in everyday clothes, which behave entirely normally.

Neale Mounsey, a former prison officer who served at Lancaster Prison – a former castle with a history going back to the Roman period – recently recorded some anecdotal evidence for the wide variety of ghostly phenomena witnessed in the prison:

> During my many years on the staff of the prison, a number of unexplained phenomena occurred. One morning I unlocked a

cell to allow the prisoner to get ready for his discharge that day. Instead of the usual whoops of joy, the man quietly beckoned me inside and explained that, more than once, he had woken during the night to see a hazy light near the door. The light formed clear images of a woman and a young girl wearing coarse, old-fashioned clothes. The figures became fainter as they moved towards him, and faded completely in the centre of the cell. The appearance and the timing did not vary. He had experienced no fear, feeling more of an observer than a participant.

I was on duty in the same wing three years later. On unlocking the same cell, the current inmate came hurtling out and stood, white and trembling, at the far end of the landing. After I calmed him down, he told me the same story. The only difference was that he had seen an old witch, warts and all, together with a demure young maiden. The first man had found the faces barely discernible.

On another occasion, a cell bell rang furiously. The cell was occupied by an ex-SAS hard man. I unlocked his door with caution. The man dashed past me, wide-eyed and ashen-faced. It took me 10 minutes of talking and two mugs of tea to get any sense out of him.

He had been lying on his bed, reading, when he decided to roll himself a cigarette. As he was about to put some tobacco on the paper, it floated to the floor. He tried again, with the same result. To stop the supposed draught, he pushed his mat across the bottom of the door and his towel across the window ledge, then sat down to resume rolling his cigarette. As he did so, a wire coat-hanger, holding his jacket and trousers, began to swing slightly from side to side on the wall opposite. The arc increased, suddenly stopping when the clothes were horizontal. They remained, as though frozen stiff, at 90 degrees to the floor. At this point he leapt up and rang his bell in terror.

As night orderly officer, I visited the dungeon in the witches' tower, now a workshop. There were some iron rings on the walls and one very large one fixed, loosely but securely, to the floor. I lifted the ring and dropped it back to its original position, lying towards the door. It must have weighed at least 2 lbs.

I made my way back to the stairs and, on reaching the doorway, heard a metallic 'clunk' behind me. In my torch beam

I noticed the central ring was now lying away from the door. I was also aware of the foul stench of human filth. I didn't investigate further.

One night I awoke with the feeling I was not alone. I checked everywhere, but finding nothing returned to my bed where I lay wide awake. It was then that I heard snoring close beside me. It sounded like my father, but I decided it was probably the pipes beneath the floor.

I shuffled around the room trying to trace the exact location of the noise. I realised it was coming from below me. Putting my left ear to the floor, I was startled to find that the noise came from a few inches above my right ear – just about bed level. As the noise was quite soothing, I lay down and slept soundly. Next morning the noise had gone. I mentioned it to the head of the Works Department who checked his plans and assured me that no pipes or cables ran beneath that room.

Mounsey's recollections cover a wide variety of what might be called typical hauntings, with visual, auditory, olfactory and physical effects, but there are also many more eccentric cases on record. In October 1817 another tower warder, Edmund Swifte, the keeper of the Crown Jewels at the Tower of London, saw 'a cylindrical figure like a glass tube, seeming about the thickness of my arm, hovering between the ceiling and the table; its contents appeared to be a dense fluid, white and pale azure' appear in his dining room. Many witnesses have reported apparitions of animals – a problem for those who believe that spectres are spirits of the dead and that animals do not have souls – and several people have reported having sex with ghosts. And at Belmez, a small village in southern Spain, a large number of faces have appeared on the concrete hearth of Maria Gomez Pereira. The first was reported in August 1971; unable to scrub it off, Pereira had the hearth covered with an inch of cement. More faces appeared on top of this new layer. The house is supposed to be built over an old graveyard, and tape recorders left running in the room overnight are said to pick up whispered snatches of ghostly conversation. Although the faces are hardly life-like, it does not appear that they are painted or drawn; sceptics have suggested they may be etched with acid or silver nitrate and argue that the motive is profit (visitors to the house are charged for entry). This matter has yet to be resolved.

The Faces of Belmez are most unusual in that they are purported to be permanent records of ghosts, available for examination by scientists. There is otherwise very little physical evidence for the reality of the phenomenon; only one or two photographs (we will discuss them in a later chapter), and a number of broadly unsuccessful attempts to measure changes in temperature, electromagnetic activity and so on, in a possibly haunted house. Furthermore, the great majority of reports involve only one witness and no communication between the ghost and the witness.

These sorts of cases generally feature what might be termed 'automatic' behaviour on the part of the ghost. Not only does it not seem to notice or react to the witness in any way; it fails to exhibit any sign of independent intelligence either. Typically, it appears, perhaps moves a short distance (maybe even passing through the proverbial wall), and then disappears having apparently accomplished nothing.

C.D. Broad, a philosopher and sometime president of the SPR, commented of such accounts: 'When one studies the details of the best cases of "hauntings", they do not, I think, on the whole suggest the presence of any persistent desire or intention. They suggest, rather, an aimless mechanical repetition of the dreams or waking fantasies of a person brooding over certain incidents and scenes in his past life.'

Several explanations have been advanced to explain these cases: that they are examples of hallucination, or 'thought forms' projected, perhaps unconsciously, from the mind of some living person. At present, however, the most generally accepted is probably the suggestion that this particular variety of ghost is neither a spirit nor a vision, but a 'memory' of someone who used to frequent the place in question, which has somehow become imprinted on the environment rather as if it were a tape recording. Because most such cases centre on dwellings of one sort or another, this has sometimes been termed the 'stone tape' theory. Some psychical researchers extend it by suggesting that the recording may be accessed purely telepathically, but only by a suitably sensitive person. This might explain why ghosts that appear in a room with more than one occupant are often visible only to one.

Very little can be done to prove or disprove the stone tape theory. Though the identity of the ghost may well be guessed at, it is extremely rare for such apparitions to be positively identified with any particular person, which makes it difficult to place great faith in the 'prior occupant' hypothesis. Hallucination is an obvious alternative, particularly in cases where only one person in a group is able to see the spectre. On the other hand, there are examples of what appears to be the same phantasm being witnessed independently, and these must be accounted for if the hallucination theory is to be preferred, even if the explanation is simply suggestion prompted by the knowledge that the house in question is supposed to be haunted.

There is general agreement that the best 'haunted house' case is that of the Cheltenham hauntings, which occurred between 1882 and 1889. It concerns the repeated apparitions of a tall, weeping 'woman in black', holding a handkerchief to her face. The ghost appeared at St Anne's House, a modern property on the corner of All Saints and Pittville Circus Roads, and was seen by a total of seventeen people, as well as being heard by perhaps a further twenty. The principal witnesses were the tenants, Captain and Mrs Despard, and their six children. Most significantly, there were several witnesses to some of the apparitions, the ghost was seen in daylight at very close quarters (passing through a pair of outstretched hands at one point) and gave the impression of being a physically real person. Intelligent attempts were made to determine whether or not the case was a hoax – on two occasions the ghost glided through a thread stretched across the stairs. The chief weakness of the case appears to be the lack of definite corroboration from outside the circle of the Despards and their servants: the only other first-hand witness known to the SPR was a former occupant of the house who wrote up his encounter more than fifty years later, when the details of the case had been published, and who must have been no more than four years old at the time of the experience.

Still more interesting are reports in which the ghost is readily identifiable and there is some form of intelligent communication between it and the witness. A good example is the case of David McConnel, a pilot killed in a crash on 7 December 1918. The impact of the crash stopped his watch at 3.25 p.m. – an important detail, because at some time between 3.15 and 3.30 p.m. McConnel's room-mate, Lieutenant J. J. Larkin, was sitting in their room sixty miles from the crash site when 'the door opened with the usual noise and clatter which McConnel always made and Larkin heard his greeting ("Hello, boy!"). He half turned round in his chair and saw McConnel standing in the doorway, half in and half out of the door, holding the doorknob in his hand. He was dressed in his full flying clothes but wearing his naval cap – an unusual item of apparel. The two young men exchanged a few words, [and] McConnel said, "Well, cheerio!", closed the door noisily and went out.'

The incident is an important one, because no more than half-an-hour later another officer called to enquire whether McConnel had returned and was told by Larkin that he had. Larkin thus had some proof that a strange event had occurred when news of McConnel's fatal crash reached him later that evening.

What, though, is the explanation for the incident? Hoax and simple misidentification may probably be ruled out. On the other hand, the meeting was so inconsequential that it seems hard to believe it was a conscious attempt by a dead or dying man to confirm the reality of an afterlife: if McConnel's ghost could say, 'Well, cheerio', why not communicate a more interesting message?

The other possibility is that the ghost was a construct either of McConnel's mind, or of Larkin's. If the latter, the case might be written off as no more than an interesting hallucination, perhaps occasioned by the fact that Larkin was actively anticipating his colleague's return. But if it was the former, we would have some evidence for the reality of 'crisis apparitions', which might be accounted for either by a need on the part of the dying man, or as a form of telepathic contact between two friends, to which Larkin's mind responded by creating the ghost itself. Perhaps only a better idea of the coincidence between the times of McConnel's death and Larkin's vision would help to resolve the problem.

So far, all the ghosts we have encountered are what might be termed 'western' ghosts, traditional spectres of a sort recognisible to any American or European. But it is vital to understand that people brought up in other cultures may see different sorts of spectre. For example, Native Americans and Africans make many more reports of animal ghosts, presumably because they believe that the spirits of the dead possess the bodies of animals.

Historical Chinese cases commonly feature ghosts that appear with the specific purpose of righting wrongs and that communicate intelligently with the living in a way that modern western ghosts do not. In Japan, the term for spirit is *tama*, a word that denotes something round, such as a pearl. A living person's *tama* is thought to detach itself from the body in crises and roam independently about the countryside; after death, it takes on the form of a round, floating ball of light, which must be nourished by physical offerings made by its descendants. Many Japanese cases thus involve reports of 'ghost lights'. On the other hand, the ghosts of people who die violently or in disgrace become *onyro*, angry spirits of an especially powerful kind. They are able to possess the bodies of the living – an ability rarely attributed to ghosts in the west, where possession is generally the province of demons. In the West Indies, ghosts are known as *duppies* and are uniformly evil. They are blamed for many of the accidents that take place. *Duppies* live in large chambers beneath cotton trees and are heard congregating in the branches, where they hold raucous parties. When travelling further abroad, *duppies* may take on the form of animals, particularly reptiles.

It is clear, then, that not all ghosts behave in the same way. On the other hand, not all 'hauntings' need be the work of ghosts. One particularly large sub-category of cases involves rappings, bangings, clatterings and the movement of objects around rooms – much the same phenomena, in other words, as those that the Fox family reported in Hydesville in 1848. In 1929 the Regulski family of Charlottenburg, a suburb of Berlin, were subjected to repeated and powerful rappings by day and night. Objects were seen to lift themselves from their resting places and fly across rooms; dolls danced; bedsheets levitated and formed themselves into the shape of heads, rearing up again each time they were pressed down. The Regulskis attributed these incidents to Albert Regulski's recently deceased brother, particularly after the daughter of the family encountered a glowing phantom waiting for her in the toilet, carrying a scythe, and with nothing but two blazing eyes where its head should be. (For some reason she was sure this was her uncle.) Similar, but much less spectacular, events occurred in the dead man's own home.

Such incidents are generally ascribed to poltergeists, a German word that means 'noisy ghost'. Those with only a casual interest in the unknown may perhaps consider 'ghost' and 'poltergeist' to be merely different terms for what is essentially the same phenomenon, and it is true that it can be hard to distinguish one from the other; a significant minority of ghost stories involve the sort of physical effects supposedly created by poltergeists, such as the moving iron ring described by Neale Mounsey. In general, though, there are significant and predictable differences between hauntings by ghosts and poltergeists, of which the most obvious is that ghosts appear to haunt a place and poltergeists appear to haunt a person. If a family move out of a haunted house, for example, it is generally supposed that the ghost will either disappear, or stay put and haunt the next people to move in. If, on the other hand, the 'epicentre' of a poltergeist case moves, the phenomena may follow to another location, though they will often diminish in intensity. Another difference that is often commented on is that hauntings may be of much greater duration than poltergeist 'infestations', which generally last only a few days or weeks. It might be added that, in the majority of cases, poltergeist phenomena seem to centre on children or adolescents, and that while – in general – poltergeists probably display greater apparent intelligence than ghosts, there are a small number of cases in which ghosts display considerably greater purpose than any poltergeist.

Although some authorities point to aspects of poltergeist infestations that suggest they really are caused by mischievous spirits, the majority theorise that they are somehow manifested by their epicentres. It is certainly interesting to note that, though poltergeists often appear to be extremely violent, it is practically unheard of for anyone to be injured by the objects that fly around the room and smash into walls. This fact seems to support the 'epicentre' theory. There is a sub-category of what might be termed 'phantom attacker' incidents, in which the subject is indeed injured, but these wounds generally take the form of scratches, bites or pinches, which might be self-inflicted, either deliberately or – it has been suggested – psychosomatically, as a result of either masochism or self-loathing. In the best-known such case, which occurred in 1925–26, a Romanian girl called Eleonore Zugun had her hair pulled out, her face, neck, arms and chest scratched with marks, in some way comparable to stigmata, and her hands pricked as if by needles.

One problem that poltergeist cases pose psychical researchers is the source of the copious amounts of energy that seem to be expended. The explanation preferred by most is that the phenomena are in fact examples of 'recurrent spontaneous psychokinesis' (RSPK) manifested by the children at the centre of a case, which are in some way externalisations of the stresses of puberty. This theory has the virtue of appearing to account both for the epicentre phenomenon and for the fact that a significant number of cases centre on adolescent girls, in whom the changes occasioned by sexual maturity are most pronounced. On the other hand it must be admitted that in many cases – about one in five – no adolescent of either sex appears to have been involved; that rather more than ten per cent of apparent poltergeist cases centre on houses, not people; and, of course, that no scientifically acceptable mechanism that would allow the manifestation of RSPK has ever been proposed.

Whether or not RSPK actually exists, however, poltergeist cases are of special interest because they involve physically real events – the movement of objects and so on – which have, in many cases, been witnessed by large groups of people and recorded as they occurred. The only really plausible alternative explanation for such accounts is that they are either bizarre errors or frauds.

The idea that witnesses to a protracted infestation could simply be mistaken may sound unlikely, but Susan Blackmore investigated one apparently impressive poltergeist case which proved to be caused by nothing more than a conflation of unusual circumstances. A family in Bristol had heard odd noises. Then their television began to change channels of its own accord and they saw a clock jump along the mantelpiece. It was discovered that the television's remote control receiver was reacting to metal in the family dog's collar, and that the movement of the clock was caused by a faulty mainspring. The strange noises seemed to be perfectly ordinary sounds that can be heard in any home, but which had been co-opted into the 'poltergeist' case by the much stranger behaviour of the television and the clock.

Many other poltergeist cases are outright frauds, or perhaps a genuine phenomenon 'helped along' by a witness, as is argued surprisingly frequently. Eleonore Zugun, for example, was detected injuring herself on occasion, but her investigators continued to insist that some of her other injuries must have been inflicted paranormally. Alan Gauld and A.D. Cornell, the authors of the best work on the subject, estimated that eight per cent of their reports were hoaxes; moreover, the sort of phenomena said to occur in such incidents, do not seem to differ from those in 'real' cases.

The difficulty in explaining all poltergeist accounts in this way is that a handful of the best were investigated as they occurred by intelligent and able people, who left accounts of such precision, about incidents involving physical effects, that the possibilities of hallucination or fraud appear slim indeed. Some people will still prefer to seize on that possibility, while others see evidence for the paranormal.

'True' ghost sightings, on the other hand, may be explained in many different ways. Joe Nickell, one of the principal investigators employed by the sceptical Committee for Scientific Investigation of Claims of the Paranormal, believes many are the products of the human imagination, and he is clearly right to do so. (We will consider exactly what the term 'human imagination' means in a later chapter.) He is also critical of multiple witness cases, having investigated a number in which it transpired that a second witness (often a spouse) had seen and heard nothing, but agreed that their home was haunted simply to keep the peace. Heightened expectation, too, must play a role, particularly where the witness is well aware that he or she is staying in a supposedly haunted house. In such cases, it is particularly easy to misinterpret shadows as ghosts, and the ordinary noises of a sleeping home or the local wildlife as spectral sounds. Finally, the opportunities for fraud, mischief and tall-tale-telling must always be considered when investigating ghosts and – perhaps more so than ever – when researching another category of mystery: unidentified flying objects.

4

Alien Universe

At three in the morning on the night of 27 October 1975, the sky exploded over the little settlement of Norway, Maine. A sharp detonation drowned out the sound of music blaring from inside a trailer home on the edge of town and, alarmed, the two men inside raced to the door, flung it open and clattered out into the cold night, searching anxiously for the source of the blast.

Thus begins perhaps the strangest UFO report of all – a story so bizarre that today it is seldom cited in the myriad books and articles that explore the mystery of unidentified flying objects. This is a pity. Barely remembered though it is, the Maine encounter is among the most complex and complete of cases, at once unique, yet also somehow typical of all the many thousands of reports that have been logged in the fifty years since flying saucers first entered the public consciousness.

David Stephens, twenty-one, and Glen Gray, eighteen, were both shift-workers, so it was hardly unusual for them to be awake at three in the morning. Nor, as they stood uncertainly outside their home, thoroughly awake but unable to see anything that might have caused the explosion, did they feel at all like retiring to bed. Instead, Stephens suggested going for a short drive, and the men arbitrarily decided to head for the shores of Lake Thompson, about twelve miles away. Gray took the wheel and they motored off down Route 26.

The two men had travelled no more than a mile when, they later recalled, their car turned off the main road onto a deserted lane, apparently of its own volition. Gray, who had a firm grip on the steering wheel, found himself powerless to do anything as the vehicle accelerated over the increasingly rough terrain.

Several strange things were now happening at once. Not only was the vehicle out of control, it seemed to be moving much more quickly than the men realised, covering the five miles to the town of Oxford in little more than two minutes rather than the usual ten. And despite their break-neck speed, the men slowly realised that the ride, over what was little more than a rugged track, seemed unnaturally smooth.

The car sped on, travelling through Oxford and on towards the lake. It passed one field in which some cows – the first living creatures Stephens and Gray had seen since leaving Route 26 – were shaking their heads in unison from one side to the other, before drawing to a halt alongside a cornfield. Two bright lights were shining from the field across the road.

At first, Stephens and Gray thought that someone was sitting out in the field in a truck; but then the lights began to rise into the air. Reasoning that the object must be a helicopter, they switched off the engine and wound down their windows to listen for the clatter of an engine or the chop of spinning rotor blades. But the strange night air was still, and, as the lights moved slowly towards the road, they realised that they were mounted on an elongated cylinder, which was hovering in the air twenty or thirty feet away from their car.

It was only now that Stephens and Gray seem to have thought of UFOs, and their natural reaction was to escape. Gray gunned the engine. For whatever reason, the car appeared to be under their control again and they raced off, winding up the windows and locking the doors as they went, Gray struggling with the wheel and Stephens craning to see what the lights in the sky were doing. To his great alarm, they were following the car. There was no escape. The two men were no more than a mile further down the road when what Stephens remembered as 'the brightest lights I've ever seen' surrounded them. Blinding whiteness enveloped them, and both men lost consciousness.

When the friends came to, they were a mile further down the road, their windows had been wound down, and the car doors they had locked were open once again.

From Flying Ships to Flying Saucers

It seems that people have always seen strange things in the sky. Records of unidentified flying objects appear in the earliest written histories, as do accounts of many other signs and portents. Most of these reports appear to involve comets, meteors and fireballs, or perhaps the visions of an early mystic, but a handful seem to describe quite a different category of phenomenon: manned vehicles in the sky.

In 215 BC, for example – at least according to a much later Roman history – things 'like ships' were seen in the air over Rome. Several dark age and medieval chroniclers used the ship simile to describe the aerial phenomena of their own day, and by the ninth century AD, the churchmen of France were busy trying to stamp out some quite elaborate pagan beliefs on the subject. In one text, the *Book Against False Opinions Concerning Thunder and Lightning*, Agobard, the bishop of Lyons, recorded that many of his flock lived in fear of an alliance between the people of the clouds and earthly sorcerers, who raised high winds and hailstorms and then sold the wrecked crops to their confederates:

> We have seen and heard a lot of people so mad and blind as to believe and to assert that there exists a certain region called Magonia, from which ships, navigating on clouds, set sail to transport back to this same region the fruits of the earth ruined by hail and destroyed by the storm . . . We have even seen several of these senseless fools who, believing in the reality of

> such absurd things, brought in front of an assembly of men four persons in chains, three men and one woman, who said they had fallen from these ships. They retained them in irons for some days, before they brought them before me, followed by the crowd, to have them stoned to death.

An even more elaborate sky-ship story, which exists in several chronicles in alternate versions, describes one of the occupants of these strange craft in greater detail. The tale first appears in an early Irish history, where it is said to have occurred in Clonmacnois (a small town on the Shannon, south of Athlone), but it also features in the chronicle of Gervase of Tilbury, which relocates the events to Gravesend, Kent, and gives the year as 1211. The story is quite a detailed one. According to Gervase, one Sunday, during mass, the congregation of a church saw an anchor descend from the sky and catch on a tombstone. The churchgoers ran outside and found a sky-ship floating overhead and members of its crew milling about on deck. As they watched, a crewman from the ship jumped overboard and 'swam' down the anchor cable, apparently to free the vessel. He was seized by the people on the ground, and only spared upon the intervention of the bishop. The man then paddled back up through the air to his vessel and his companions cut the anchor rope, at which point the sky-ship flew away.

Agobard's account of the Magonian sky-ships is perhaps the best-known of early UFO records and is frequently cited as evidence that flying machines roamed the skies of medieval Europe. Yet it is important to note that the bishop did not believe the story he recorded and made it clear that he berated the members of his flock who took it seriously. Nor do the sky-ships sound much like flying machines. In Gervase's more precise description, they really are ships, which float in the air as easily as they would at sea – not, as some ufologists prefer, spaceships described in the only terms comprehensible to medieval minds. Moreover, if the strange sailor who swam to earth in dark age Clonmacnois (or was it medieval Tilbury?) actually existed, his behaviour had nothing in common with that of modern UFO occupants. It makes more sense to assume that the sky-ships were part of an old tradition of things seen in the sky, which also includes the occasional accounts of peculiar clouds and sky creatures that pop up in the records as late as the nineteenth century – accounts that may throw considerable light on unidentified flying objects of the apparently mechanical variety, and which at least show that UFOs are not the only strange things that infest our skies.

At their simplest, these reports seem only a little strange: for example, small, round clouds that moved against the prevailing winds and discharged showers of stones appeared over France in September 1814 and October 1815. But some are more bizarre. In 1872 the barque *Lady of the Lake* was in mid-Atlantic, close to the equator, when 'a curious-shaped cloud' appeared from the south. It was well-defined, circular and light grey in colour. The barque's captain, Frederick Banner, noted in his log that the rear portion was divided into four segments and trailed a hooked tail 'very similar to that of a comet'. Unlike a comet, however, the strange cloud sailed slowly through the sky, remaining in sight for about half an hour. It flew lower than any other clouds, and it too travelled against the wind.

Finally, there are a handful of accounts of truly odd visions in the skies, such as the red 'sky serpent' seen undulating over Oklahoma in 1978, or the 'jellyfish-like white floating object' that appeared in a Japanese cowshed on 4 January 1991 and sailed off into the sky, leaving behind it a cow with a smashed hind leg. Perhaps the best-witnessed of these cases occurred in Crawfordsville, Indiana, where a luminous white 'sky serpent' some twenty feet long and eight feet wide, equipped with flapping fins, appeared over the town on the nights of 4 and 5 September 1891. The writer Vincent Gaddis, who interviewed surviving witnesses many years later, noted: 'All the reports refer to this object as a living thing. At times it "squirmed as if in agony." Once it swooped low over a group of witnesses who said that it radiated "a hot breath".'

Yet, only a few years later, before the turn of the century, reports of sky-ships and sky-creatures gave way to a new wave of sightings that indicated, perhaps for the first time, that unidentified flying objects might be mechanical in origin. The new reports, probably significantly, came at a time when man had at last solved the problem of aerial navigation himself, abandoning unpowered balloons – which were at the mercy of the winds – in favour of powered airships; and they took the form of sightings of similar, but apparently much more advanced, craft of this type.

In the early evening of 17 November 1896, a light that resembled 'an electric arc lamp propelled by some mysterious force' passed over Sacramento, California. People on the ground saw the light manoeuvre to pass buildings, and some claimed to have discerned a large, dark shape looming behind it. A few heard voices coming from overhead, passing comments such as 'Go up higher'; on one occasion they were 'singing in a chorus, a rattling song', and on another announcing, in English, 'Well, we ought to get to San Francisco by tomorrow noon.' Next day the *Sacramento Evening Bee* recounted the various reports and the rest of the Californian press chipped in with speculation, arguing either that a mysterious inventor had perfected some sort of airship, or that the whole affair was a hoax.

The Sacramento sightings were only the first reports in what became the great airship wave of 1896–7, which lasted for six months and included several hundred sightings from witnesses in the Pacific, mid- and south-western United States. The dirigibles that they described were certainly remarkable. Not only were they bigger, faster and more robust than anything then produced by the aviators of the world; they seemed able to fly enormous distances, and some were equipped with giant wings.

Despite the great excitement produced by such reports, the number of sightings did eventually tail off. By the end of 1897, the American airship wave was nearly forgotten, even in the towns that had been at the heart of the mystery. But the strange aerial craft returned several times in the next fifteen years, flying over Denmark in 1908, and appearing in Britain in 1909 and 1913, New England in 1908 and 1909, and New Zealand in 1913. In South Africa, in 1914, there were many sightings of mystery 'aeroplanes', even though there were no serviceable aircraft and no airfields in the country at the time. Reports of strange flying machines continued to appear periodically after the First World War. Many came from Scandinavia, where between 1933 and 1937 there was a substantial wave of 'ghost flier' sightings over Norway.

During the Second World War, pilots on both sides began to notice strange lights, which appeared in the sky and kept station with their aircraft during missions. Both sides assumed that the lights, which the Americans named 'foo fighters', were enemy secret weapons; as there were no accounts of the objects actually attacking anyone, it was supposed they were part of an experiment in psychological warfare. (The mystery was not resolved.) In the early post-war years, the number of unidentified flying objects reported was even greater. This time they were again frequently seen over Scandinavia, where they were christened 'ghost rockets' and thought to be Soviet secret weapons developed with the help of captured German scientists. Unlike the foo fighters, ghost rockets sometimes left tantalising physical traces of their presence. In Sweden, on 10 July 1946, a glowing object trailing smoke crashed on a beach at Bjorkon, leaving a small crater, fragments of metal and a mass of slag as evidence of the impact. The material was gathered up by military personnel, who later announced that it was junk that had been lying on the seashore for some time – an explanation that was greeted with incredulity by the witnesses to the crash. Nevertheless, the Swedish defence staff conducted an official investigation of more than 100 other reports. It decided that about twenty per cent remained mysterious and probably represented secret weapons tests by a foreign power – presumably the USSR, since two-thirds of the objects flew in from the east. But in the days before the invention of sophisticated guidance systems, there seemed to be no simple explanation for the minority that came in from the south and west.

The Twenty-Fourth of June, 1947

The mystery of the ghost rockets did receive some publicity in a United States worried about the Soviet Union's growing military capability – but nothing to compare with the furore that greeted an incident that occurred over Washington State on 24 June 1947. Kenneth Arnold, an Idaho man who owned his own fire control equipment business, was flying his light plane over Mount Rainier when his attention was drawn to a series of flashes in the sky. Looking more closely, he noticed a diagonal formation of nine bright objects jinking between the peaks ahead of him at an incredible speed. One was crescent-shaped, but the other eight were discs that moved, in Arnold's telling phrase, 'like a saucer would if you skipped it across the water'.

Arnold's sighting is generally regarded as the first 'modern' UFO report, but something remarkable was happening over the United States that month. Thousands of similar reports were recorded in the next few weeks as speculation about the mystery of the saucers exploded, first across the American and then throughout the world's press. Some were simply strange lights in the night sky, but most of the sightings were of 'daylight discs' that gave every impression of being structured craft of some kind, though they often moved at 'impossible' speeds or executed manoeuvres that no human pilot could match – a sharp ninety-degree turn in mid-air was a particular favourite.

Whatever the explanation, it gradually became apparent that this time unidentified flying objects had come to stay. The 1947 'flap' would never be forgotten, as the mystery airships, the ghost fliers and the ghost rockets had been. After 1947 there would be years when little seemed to happen, and investigators puzzled over a sharp decline in reports, but flying saucers entered the public consciousness in the wake of Arnold's report and have remained there ever since.

Understanding why the encounter over Mount Rainier excited such interest, and why the UFO phenomenon permanently seized the imagination of the public in 1947, rather than in 1896, 1934, or 1946, may thus be one of the keys to the whole mystery. To begin with, Arnold had the makings of a reliable witness. He was a respected businessman and an experienced pilot – not to mention a qualified Eagle Scout and a one-time Olympic hopeful in 'fancy diving', as the sighting report he filed with the US Air Force proudly announced – and seemed to be neither exaggerating what he had seen, nor adding sensational details to his report. He also gave the impression of being a careful observer. As he watched the formation of bright lights pass his aircraft, he tried to gauge their speed by measuring the time it took them to travel from one mountain peak to another, calculating from this that the objects were moving at the then astonishing speed of 1700 miles per hour. He then estimated their size by comparing them to a DC4 airliner visible in the distance, concluding that they were rather smaller than the jet. These details impressed the newspapermen who interviewed him and lent credibility to his report.

Even so, Arnold himself was hardly solely responsible for the sudden explosion of reports, nor for the hold they quickly took on the public imagination. It is true that the invention of the evocative term 'flying saucer' provided a convenient and appealing label for the phenomenon, but that, in itself, is not enough to explain the wave of sightings that occurred. The year 1947 must have some additional significance, and three main theories have been proposed to explain what that was.

To those who believed UFOs were physical craft, the dropping of the first atomic bomb in 1945 and the appalling threat of a devastating war suggested that the 'saucers' were craft sent by an alien civilisation to investigate man's new potential for destruction and perhaps warn of the dangers; indeed, over the next few years many so-called 'contactees', who claimed to have met and talked to the beings from outer space and to have returned with messages for mankind, claimed that they had been lectured on just this point by concerned 'space brothers'.

Other investigators, equally worried about the future but searching for an explanation closer to home, hinted that UFOs were Soviet super-weapons developed with the help of captured rocket scientists from Hitler's secret weapons programme. Finally, those who concluded that UFOs had no physical reality acknowledged the potency of both arguments, but suggested that it was the very prevalence of such fears that lent the Arnold sighting a special glamour and encouraged others to report ambiguous sightings as encounters with flying saucers. To these researchers, UFOs came not from outer space but from the pages of the popular pulp science fiction magazines of the 1930s and 1940s – with their tales of encounters with aliens – and from the sci-fi movies of the 1940s and 1950s, whose invaders from space were a handy metaphor for the equally alien forces of the Soviet Union. According to this theory, the airships of 1896 failed to hold the interest of the public precisely because they were so novel that it was easier to dismiss them as the work of mysterious inventors or as hoaxes – neither explanation having the same power to captivate the mind as the idea of extraterrestrial spacecraft.

Unidentified Flying Objects

Though both Kenneth Arnold – acting as a reporter for one of the pulp magazines of the day – and the United States Air Force did attempt to investigate some of the earliest sightings, it was only after 1947 that UFO reports were studied in any depth. The USAF, which had an obvious interest in any aerial craft that might pose a threat to national security, began by setting up an investigative team under the code-name Project Sign to research the subject. It commenced its work by looking into the 122 flying saucer reports received by the Air Force during 1947. Of these, 110 were identified as aircraft, stars and so on, and 12 remained unidentified.

A year or two later, the growing band of civilian enthusiasts began to form themselves into 'flying saucer clubs' and to conduct their own investigations. During the 1950s and 1960s, in an attempt to distance themselves from their naive origins, the surviving clubs began to give themselves serious-sounding names – the two largest were NICAP, the National Investigations Committee on Aerial Phenomena, which pressed for congressional hearings into the mystery, and APRO, the Aerial Phenomena Research Organisation – and the saucer buffs took to calling themselves 'ufologists'. The new subject nevertheless remained an amateur pursuit, and the standard of investigation varied from the competent to the extremely credulous. Many UFO researchers were unable even to correctly identify reports of lights in the sky that were actually sightings of shooting stars or the planet Venus, although astronomical objects were by far the most common source of misidentifications.

It is hardly surprising, then, that some of the most enduring and important UFO cases have been reported by 'trained observers' such as pilots, who might be presumed to be both sober and reliable. As early as January 1948, the death of a National Guard fighter pilot named Thomas Mantell created a sensation when the press discovered that he had died while pursuing 'a metallic object of tremendous size' over Kentucky. Although the authorities were convinced that Mantell had blacked out while pursuing a rogue weather balloon to 25,000 feet, causing his plane to go into a steep dive, many newspapers and members of the public found it hard to believe that the pilot could have made such a mistake. Soon, rumours abounded that the fighter had been shot down when it got too close to a flying saucer, that Mantell's body was missing or riddled with bullets, and that the wreckage was radioactive.

UFO sightings by pilots have persisted to the present day. In one of the best-known cases of the 1970s, a four-man US army helicopter crew on a night flight near Mansfield, Ohio, noted a bright, fast-moving light manoeuvring nearby. The helicopter pilot, Lawrence Coyne, estimated its length at sixty feet and noted that it appeared metallic and had a red light at one end. As the object approached, he was forced to put his helicopter into a steep dive to avoid it. Descending rapidly from 1700 feet, he levelled out 650 feet above the ground and, looking up, was horrified to find the object directly over him, sweeping his aircraft with a green beam of light.

One of Coyne's crewmen, Robert Yanacsek, remembered: 'The object may have hovered over us for 10 to 12 seconds. It seemed like a long time. It seemed like it was there for so damn long. It was just stopped, for maybe 10 to 12 seconds, and I mean stopped. It wasn't cruising, it was stopped. It didn't waver, it didn't just put on the brakes, it didn't gyrate – it was just like in a cartoon. It was coming at us, and then, in the next frame, it was there, just like that.' At the end of the encounter, the object accelerated again and headed off, leaving the helicopter alone in the sky. When Coyne looked down at his controls, he was startled to discover that although his joystick was still pushed right forward, he was now at 3500 feet. He could only assume that the strange object had somehow pulled him up from his previous height.

A not dissimilar incident occurred as recently as 6 January 1995, when the pilot of a British Airways Boeing 737 passenger jet reported being overtaken at high speed by a wedge-shaped craft as he began his descent to Manchester airport. Although nothing appeared on radar to confirm the sighting, the pilot, Captain Roger Wills, was convinced that the object was covered in small white lights, and his first officer noted a black stripe on its side.

Both these cases have been carefully investigated. Coyne's airborne encounter was the subject of a detailed report by Jennie Zeidman of the Center for UFO Studies, who not only questioned the crew but located independent (though frustratingly anonymous) witnesses on the ground who claimed to have watched the incident. She concluded that the encounter was genuinely mysterious, although the sceptical UFO writer Philip Klass has proposed that the UFO was actually a meteor, a suggestion both Coyne and Zeidman reject. The British Airways jet's experience, meanwhile, was investigated by an official body called the Independent Joint Airmiss Working Group, which could find no likely explanation.

Even better evidence for the reality of flying saucers – at least in the eyes of the ufologists – became available from the late 1940s in the shape of photographs and even the odd scrap of film. Many of these pictures were highly dubious – convincing UFO photographs are remarkably easy to fake with the help of commonplace items such as hub-caps and saucepan lids – but a small number have continued to perplex. Among the best known are a pair of photographs snapped at McMinville, Oregon, on 11 May 1950. The photographer, Paul Trent, captured a large silvery UFO with what appeared to be a small protrusion on its roof as it flew silently past his farmhouse. It resembled, he said later, 'a good-sized parachute canopy without the strings, only silvery-bright mixed with bronze,' and he assumed it was some sort of army secret weapon.

Although sceptics have always been suspicious of the McMinville photos, which show the UFO hovering under some telephone wires from which the Trents might have hung a model, an investigation by a group called Ground Saucer Watch concluded that the object was at least sixty-five feet in diameter and some distance from the camera.

An equally famous sequence of four pictures of a fuzzy, disc-shaped UFO with what appears to be a thick ridge separating its two hemispheres, taken by a photographer on board the Brazilian naval survey ship *Almirante Saldanha* off a tiny pinnacle of rock in the South Atlantic called Trindade Island, have aroused even greater controversy since they were taken in January 1958. According to the photographer, Almira Barauna, they show a solid object that flew in a parabola over the island and (an odd detail, this) moved 'like a bat'. Members of the ship's crew who were on deck at the time confirmed that they had seen a bright light in the sky, which a Brazilian navy investigation concluded made a hoax unlikely.

The only likely natural explanation is a mirage, and it has

been suggested that the object in the pictures is a 'double merged and magnified mirage' of the planet Jupiter. Yet critics of the sceptical perspective have pointed out that the photographs were taken shortly after noon, when Jupiter is simply not bright enough to be visible to the naked eye.

If the controversy that has raged for decades over practically all the most interesting UFO photographs settles anything, it is that such images prove little or nothing. It is almost always possible to produce either a natural explanation for the photos, or to suggest that they are frauds. And, in fairness, it should be noted that there are often worrying discrepancies in the published accounts of how such images were obtained. In the McMinville case, Trent and his wife stated that the photos were taken at about 7.45 p.m., but two separate analyses of the lighting and shadows in the pictures have suggested that they must have been snapped in the morning, perhaps up to an hour apart. That alone would be enough to cast enormous doubt on the shots, but others have answered the attack by arguing that cloud conditions could have caused the lighting anomalies. In the Trindade Island case, it has never been established how many other people on board the *Almirante Saldanha* saw the UFO – believers say forty-eight, sceptics only two – and there are discrepancies between the eyewitness descriptions of a 'bright light in the sky' that have been published, and the strange object in Barauna's pictures.

Today, as computer retouching techniques reach ever greater heights of sophistication, UFO photographs are of progressively less value as evidence. Proving fraud may become more difficult, but the very existence of the new technology is enough to make still photos, in particular, almost worthless. Sceptics will always be able to argue that such pictures are fakes, no matter how apparently sincere the witnesses may be.

In consequence, evidence that some unidentified flying objects are physically real must be sought elsewhere. Ufologists have, in fact, identified several different categories of cases, which seem to offer such proof. There are, for example, a number of what are known as 'radar/visual' reports on record, in which UFOs seen by witnesses are also picked up and tracked on radar. Further evidence is provided by what are known as 'Close Encounters of the Second Kind' – cases defined by the astronomer and ufologist J. Allen Hynek as those in which a UFO 'has a measurable physical effect on either animate or inanimate matter'. A CE2 might involve traces of a landing left in the soil; electromagnetic effects, such as saucers' apparent ability to stop car engines; and even burns inflicted either on the environment or an unfortunate witness.

Probably the best known of radar/visual cases occurred in August 1956, when no fewer than six military radars at the Lakenheath and Bentwaters air bases in Suffolk picked up several unidentified flying objects that appeared to be travelling at speeds of up to 4000 mph. The incident lasted for almost ninety minutes, and visual confirmation came from the pilot of a USAF transport plane who saw a fuzzy light flashing towards the ground. An RAF night fighter directed towards the contact reportedly found itself in what appeared to be a simulated dogfight; the UFO circled rapidly to place itself on the British plane's tail and could not be shaken off for more than five minutes.

Although it has been suggested that the Lakenheath-Bentwaters incident can be explained as a meteor sighting that happened to coincide with some anomalous radar reflections, a report commissioned by the US Air Force famously concluded that 'a mechanical device of unknown origin' was the most likely explanation for the case. The best argument against the reality of radar/visual reports, in fact, seems to be a spectacular decline in the number of cases that have been recorded over the last quarter-century. It is not entirely clear whether this pattern is caused by the increasing sophistication of modern radars, which are less likely to be deceived by spurious returns, or greater secrecy on the part of the military, who operate most of the equipment.

There is certainly no such shortage of car-stop reports. There appears to be abundant proof that UFOs can interact with a vehicle's electrical systems, causing engines and radios to cut out and then come back to life. According to a catalogue compiled in 1981, more than 440 have been reported in total, dating all the way back to 1909, when a British motorcyclist's headlamp cut out as a glove-shaped light passed overhead. A comparative analysis of this data shows that many cases involved a chase between a vehicle and a UFO, the presence of a light-beam, and the loss of control of a car or truck by its driver. The same analysis suggests that most such cases took place (like the Maine UFO encounter) in deserted, rural areas in the small hours of the morning – perhaps because such locations are ideal for concealing surreptitious activity by real aliens in real spacecraft, or perhaps because the witnesses are simply more tired and more suggestible in lonely places at that time of the night.

Possibly the most spectacular vehicle interference report is the multiple-witness case that occurred at Levelland, Texas, during the great UFO wave of 1957. Shortly before midnight on 2 November, Pedro Saucedo, who combined work as a farm-hand with a career as a part-time barber, was driving with a friend along Route 116, about four miles to the west of the town, when he saw a flash of light in a nearby field. The light rose and headed towards his truck at increasing speed. As it did so, the truck's engine and headlights cut out. Saucedo got out to investigate but, as the UFO passed directly overhead, he felt such an intense heat that he threw himself to the ground. From the glimpse he had got of the object, he thought it was torpedo-shaped, about 200 feet long and 6 feet wide, and had yellow flames spewing from its rear. When it had gone, Saucedo had no trouble restarting his engine.

The significant thing about the Levelland case is that Saucedo was not the only one to have problems with his vehicle there that evening. Jim Wheeler, who was about eight miles away, but driving along the same road as Saucedo, came across a brightly-lit, 200-foot-long, egg-shaped object on the highway. As he approached, his engine and lights died and the object shot into the air. Its light blinked off, and Wheeler's engine immediately restarted. The local police received similar reports from Jose Alvarez, eleven miles to the north of the town, Newell Wright, ten miles to the east, James Long, some way to the north, and Ronald Martin, back on Route 116. At about the same time that Saucedo reported his sighting, four adults driving down a farm road several miles away saw a brilliant bolt of lightning in the sky; their car headlights and radio died for between one and three seconds. At fifteen minutes past midnight, a driver called Frank Williams came across a pulsating UFO on the ground north of Levelland. Each time the object glowed, Williams's motor died. Finally, between 1.15 and 1.30 a.m., two policeman, despatched to search for the object Saucedo had seen, separately reported strange lights in the sky. One of them also experienced engine problems.

Controversy still rages about the extent and the cause of the Levelland incidents. A US Air Force investigation suggested that only three witnesses – Saucedo and his friend, and Newell Wright – had seen a UFO. It concluded that the glowing object was probably ball lightning or St Elmo's fire, and that the engine difficulties were coincidental and caused by wet circuits. Ufologists have countered by pointing to inaccuracies in the Air Force report and adding that neither natural phenomenon is known to behave in the strange way the witnesses describe.

By now it should be obvious that even effects such as vehicle interference and the appearance of a UFO on radar are too insubstantial to provide ideal subjects for study. Physical trace cases, on the other hand, have the enormous advantage of offering evidence that can be inspected after the fact, and which can often be taken away and subjected to tests in a laboratory.

Even laboratory testing, though, can give rise to controversy. Consider one of the most heavily investigated physical trace cases, the Delphos (Kansas) CE2 of 2 November 1971. Sixteen-year-old Ronald Johnson was tending sheep behind his family home when he heard a rumbling sound and saw blue, red and orange lights flash in a nearby grove of trees. The lights illuminated an object shaped like a button mushroom, about nine feet in diameter, which appeared to be hovering two feet off the ground. Before long the glow grew so intense that it hurt Johnson's eyes and the object then took off with a whine like a jet engine, temporarily blinding the boy as it passed over him.

Johnson's parents arrived on the scene in time to be shown a small blue light fading away on the horizon. Walking into the grove, the family found a grey-white circle glowing in the dark. 'Mr and Mrs Johnson placed their hands inside the circle and found that the soil was not warm, as they had expected it to be. It felt, however, as if it had been crystallised. Even more weirdly, the couple's fingers became numb. When Mrs Johnson tried to rub off the soil residue on her leg, the part of the leg she touched also went numb.'

Unfortunately, neither parent sought medical advice, so there is no second opinion to back up these claims. Soil samples taken from the glowing circle did, however, come into the possession of a ufologist called Ted Phillips, who specialised in physical trace cases, and he arranged for them to be tested by seven independent laboratories. The findings were intriguing: soil taken from the glowing ring did not absorb water and contained more acids, more calcium and more soluble salts than normal. It also contained fibres of white organic material. Attempts to grow seeds in the sample soil suggested that it actively retarded plant growth.

Doubts about the Delphos case emerged when the author Ronald Story pointed out that the soil samples bore all the signs of infestation with common fairy ring fungus, the filaments of which can be so dense that they prevent the soil absorbing water and also inhibit the normal growth of grass. This suggestion is still the subject of debate. Meanwhile, other investigators had looked more closely at the primary witness, Ronald Johnson. They found that he claimed to have acquired psychic powers as a result of his encounter. Shortly afterwards, he reported meeting a strange 'wolf-girl' with wild blond hair, wearing a coat of torn cloth, who escaped him by running away on all fours when he approached. Johnson and his parents subsequently claimed to have had a second encounter with the UFO, which hovered over the grove of trees and then circled their home and flew off, this time in full daylight. These subsequent claims have tended to embarrass ufologists who believe the Delphos case offers real evidence for the existence of UFOs, and the Johnsons did not add to their credibility by declining to take a polygraph test.

What, then, of close encounters that result in UFOs actually wounding or marking the witnesses? On 29 December 1980, Vickie Landrum and her grandson Colby were driving through an oak and pine forest near Houston, Texas, with a friend named Betty Cash when they noticed a bright light hovering over the trees ahead. The three watched as the light gradually resolved itself into a 'diamond of fire'. It seemed to be some sort of unusual aircraft, they decided, of a dull aluminium colour and with a line of blue lights running across its belly. Moreover, it seemed to be in trouble. The object kept dipping towards the treeline, then belching blue flames from its underside and rising briefly. Occasionally, it made a beeping sound.

Betty Cash, who was driving, stopped the car and all three witnesses got out to take a closer look. They estimated that they were no more than forty yards away from the craft, and they could feel a tremendous heat radiating from it, which eventually left the metal skin of their vehicle so hot that they could not touch it. Interestingly, Vickie Landrum interpreted the experience as the second coming of Christ, and reassured her grandson: 'That's Jesus. He will not hurt us.' Perhaps uncertain that Vickie was right, Colby Landrum pleaded with the adults to get back into the car and they drove on. As they did so, Cash and Landrum saw a swarm of helicopters surround the flying 'diamond'. They counted twenty-three aircraft in total.

Within hours of the incident, all three witnesses began to exhibit painful symptoms of their close encounter, including severe headaches, swellings and blisters on their skin, and diarrhoea. Colby Landrum developed a sunburn-like rash, and his grandmother's hair began to fall out. A week later, Betty Cash was unable to walk and her eyelids were so badly swollen that she could not see. She was hospitalised and spent twenty-seven days being treated for a variety of ailments, but the problems did not clear up. Over the next eight years, she returned to hospital a further twenty-five times with eyesight and blood problems, and was subsequently diagnosed with cancer.

The Cash-Landrum case is regarded by many ufologists as among the strongest on record. Doctors who examined the witnesses confirmed that all were suffering from exposure to intense electro-magnetic radiation. Investigators also discovered physical traces on the car, including a mould of Vickie Landrum's fingers in the plastic of the dashboard, which had been partially melted in the heat of the encounter. They were even able to locate other witnesses who reported seeing both the UFO and its accompanying helicopter fleet. An Army investigator reported that these witnesses, and also Cash and Landrum, were credible and sincere.

Even so, the case remains frustratingly unresolved. The US Army and the Marine Corps both denied any involvement. Investigators from the Mutual UFO Network and the Fund for UFO Research were unable to find any military or civil airport that would admit to having put up a fleet of helicopters on the evening in question, and when Cash and Landrum sought compensation for their injuries by bringing a $20 million lawsuit against the American government, it was thrown out on the grounds that 'no such object was owned, operated or in the inventory' of the US armed forces. Peter Brookesmith, a sceptical ufologist, sums up the Cash-Landrum CE2 with the comment: 'To ufologists, the case is perhaps the most baffling and frustrating of modern times, for what started with solid evidence for a notoriously elusive phenomenon petered out in a maze of dead ends, denials, and perhaps even official deviousness. Sceptics have always asked a blunt and fundamental question: what was the trio's state of health before their alleged encounter?'

One special category of physical evidence case remains to be considered. There have always been rumours that a handful of the thousands of UFOs thronging our skies have come to grief, crashing to earth, killing their pilots and leaving hard physical evidence of their reality to be gathered up by astonished governments and their grimly efficient armed forces.

The earliest such report dates to June 1884, when a paper called the *Nebraska Nugget* published an item about a strange occurrence in the remote wasteland of Dundy County in the southern part of the state. According to this story, a group of cowboys engaged in rounding up cattle were alarmed to hear a terrific whirring noise from overhead and looked up to see a blazing object plummeting to earth nearby. When the startled men reached the crash site they found 'fragments of cog wheels and other pieces of machinery lying on the ground . . . glowing with heat so intense as to scorch the grass for a long distance around each fragment.'

One of the largest pieces, the paper reported, resembled a brass propeller sixteen inches wide and three inches thick. When the blazing object finally cooled, it was revealed to be a cylindrical craft more than fifty feet long, made of a remarkably light and strong metal. In the meantime, though, one of the cowboys, Alf Williamson, had been overcome by the heat and collapsed to the ground with blisters covering his face, and his hair 'singed to a crisp'. A day or two later, another paper reported that he had been permanently blinded though 'otherwise he does not appear to have been seriously injured'.

Sadly, the Dundy County 'saucer' turned out to be not just the earliest 'crash-retrieval' story on record, but one of the first UFO hoaxes. Follow-up stories treated the whole tale as a joke and reported that the object had simply melted away in a rainstorm, leaving no trace of its existence. Research undertaken after the story's rediscovery in the 1960s, by members of the local historical society, failed to unearth a single resident who had ever heard of the incident.

Twentieth-century crash-retrieval stories have seldom proved much more reliable than this nineteenth-century hoax. The author Frank Scully, who based parts of his best-selling 1950 book *Behind the Flying Saucers* on an account of a 1948 saucer crash in New Mexico which supposedly resulted in the recovery of the craft and its sixteen 'chocolate-coloured' occupants (each of them incongruously dressed in the fashions of the 1890s) by the American air force, later discovered that he had been hoodwinked by a pair of veteran confidence-tricksters engaged in peddling a complex oil-detection scheme supposedly based on recovered extraterrestrial technology. Leonard Stringfield, who spent years investigating crash reports and set out his findings in no fewer than six 'status reports' covering about fifty individual cases, based most of his work on second-hand or third-hand sources, and chose to disguise the identity of the few witnesses who claimed first-hand knowledge of such dramatic events. This made it nearly impossible for other ufologists to verify his findings.

Only one crash-retrieval case has produced a variety of first-hand witnesses who have been prepared to tell their stories on the record to a number of different investigators: the Roswell Incident of July 1947. Today, after many years of research, no one doubts that *something* fell to earth in the New Mexico desert only a few days after Kenneth Arnold's sighting had ignited the whole flying saucer controversy: the only question is what. The US Air Force initially claimed that the object was a runaway weather balloon. Some researchers think it was really something much more secret – an instrument package mounted on a high-altitude balloon designed to search for evidence of Soviet nuclear weapons tests. But the majority of those who have written about the incident believe that a UFO really did crash near Roswell, and that the government has backed the various rival explanations as part of an extensive cover-up.

One of the few facts about this remarkable case that is not in dispute is that an object fell from the sky eighty miles north of Roswell, perhaps during an electrical storm, and landed on an isolated ranch owned by a man named Mac Brazel, creating a field of debris about a quarter of a mile long and several hundred feet wide. Brazel stumbled across the wreckage on either 14 June or 3 July – accounts differ – but the debris did not look like anything much and he was not sufficiently curious to investigate at first. Later he returned to the field, gathered up some of the fragments and took them home. The debris consisted of struts or beams, wire and brown parchment-like paper, together with a lightweight grey metallic foil; Brazel had never seen anything like it. It was not until he drove in to Corona, New Mexico, on 4 July that he heard for the first time about the wave of flying disc reports and began to wonder whether the material he had collected had something to do with the mysterious saucers. He reported his find to the local sheriff, and before long a team of air force officers had turned up at the ranch and gathered up the wreckage. From Roswell it was flown to the local air force headquarters in Fort Worth, Texas, where journalists were told the weather balloon story; and from there it vanished into history.

Everything else about the Roswell incident is in dispute. Investigating ufologists have gathered witness testimony that appears to support the crashed UFO theory, including evidence suggesting that some alien bodies were recovered from the desert. For example, the Roswell mortician, Glenn Dennis, claims to have received a call from the local air base asking him whether he had any child-size coffins available. When he drove to the base in pursuit of this promising piece of business, he was denied access, but – he insists – a nurse there later told him that three small bodies with concave eyes and four-fingered hands had been recovered from a crashed disc. Recent research, however, has shown that no nurse matching Dennis's description worked on the base at that time.

Still less credible is the testimony of a man named Jim Ragsdale, who claimed to have been out in the desert on the night of the crash romancing a girlfriend with the unlikely-sounding name of Trudy Truelove. They were camping just off Highway 48 when a bright light flared overhead and crashed to earth a mile-or-so away. Next morning the couple drove out to the impact site and found a strange object half-embedded in a ridge. The bodies of the alien crew were scattered about, and lying among them were fifteen helmets made of solid gold. Ragsdale later claimed that he had gathered up some of these helmets and buried them near the crash site.

Incredible as Ragsdale's testimony may be, it does draw attention to one of the principal problems of the Roswell story: the question of just where the UFO that came down near the town was supposed to have landed. At present there are no fewer than six competing crash sites, some of them well over a hundred miles from the Brazel ranch. Some ufologists have suggested that the mysterious saucer was damaged over Brazel's property, shedding debris before crashing elsewhere, and others have been driven to speculate that not one but two UFOs must have fallen to earth in the New Mexico desert. The seven witnesses who claim to have seen alien bodies also disagree on the number of corpses that were recovered: the numbers vary from one body up to five. This conflicting testimony, together with the recent discovery that every record from the local air base has been destroyed, makes it highly unlikely that we will ever know the truth about the Roswell incident.

Indeed the best piece of evidence we do have may well be a classified report written by Colonel Howard McCoy eight months later, which does not even mention the Roswell incident. McCoy, who, as the overall head of US Air Force Intelligence should have been informed about such a sensational development as soon as it occurred, notes, 'I can't even tell you how much we would give to have one of those [UFOs] crash in an area so that we could recover whatever they are.' It is hard to reconcile this plea with the idea that just such an incident had occurred only a matter of weeks earlier.

The discovery that the relevant records were disposed of has proved embarrassing for the US Air Force and the government, which had already been accused of knowing far more than it was admitting about the UFO mystery. There was some reason for supposing that this really was the case. The Air Force's initial 'Estimate of the Situation', a top secret report submitted by Project Sign in August 1946, had reviewed evidence from the most reliable sources available, including scientists and airline pilots, and concluded not just that flying saucers were real, but that they probably came from outer space. Moreover, a few years later the CIA had chosen to involve itself in UFO research by convening a panel of scientists, air force officers and members of the intelligence community to study the saucer phenomenon. Although the panel expressed great scepticism about the extraterrestrial hypothesis, its very existence, when it became known late in the 1950s, convinced many ufologists that some sort of cover-up was underway. This conclusion was only reinforced by the fact that the panel had recommended that the Air Force launch a campaign to convince the public that UFOs did not exist.

British ufologists began to harbour similar suspicions in 1955 when the Air Ministry admitted that the RAF had recently completed a five-year investigation of the mystery, the conclusions of which could never be revealed to the public for security reasons. In the USSR, a committee organised by the Cosmonaut Committee and headed by a retired air force major-general named Porfiri Stoljarov was denied access to the Soviet government's UFO archives. According to one western report, Stoljarov was told that this was because 'this is too big a matter and you are too small'.

Why have governments around the world shown such an interest in the flying saucer mystery? The simple answer is that they have to: any country has an interest in unidentified flying objects that penetrate its airspace – not because they may be alien, but because they may be enemy aircraft. This point of view is not popular among ufologists, however. Many prefer to believe that our governments are fully aware that some UFOs are extraterrestrial spacecraft, piloted by aliens whose intentions may well be hostile.

The Occupants

UFO cases that feature descriptions of occupants are known as 'Close Encounters of the Third Kind'. For many years, such occupant reports were scarce, and those that were made tended to be treated sceptically by the ufologists themselves, principally because it was feared that any apparent endorsement of such 'way out' material would jeopardise their attempts to interest the scientific community in the UFO phenomenon.

Nevertheless, once the idea of flying saucers as extra-terrestrial spacecraft gained currency, it was not long before questions began to be asked about the beings who piloted them. And, once UFO researchers started actively looking, it became clear that there were a significant number of occupant reports around. One modern estimate suggests that up to one in three sighting reports can now be classified as a CE3.

It will be remembered that records of such cases go back to the days of the mediaeval sky-ships, whose crewmen looked and acted like ordinary human beings. Little had changed by the end of the nineteenth century, when some of those who reported mystery airship sightings claimed that they had also seen members of the crew. With no significant exceptions, these people also looked human, and, indeed, sometimes emerged from their cockpits to claim to be Yankee inventors, or patriots on their way to bomb Havana. Basing their reports on this information, quite a few newspapers identified the mystery airship's pilot as a Mr Wilson of New York, though inquiries in that city failed to locate him or any evidence of his existence.

As early as the 1890s, though, not everyone was convinced that the strange aerial craft were built on earth. A small minority speculated that they came from elsewhere in the solar system, and a handful of sightings seemed to support this notion. Even these cases involved near-human pilots, however. One witness, W.H. Hopkins of Springfield, Missouri, told the papers he had been out walking in the hills east of the town on 16 April 1897 when he came upon one of the airships, which had landed in a clearing. A naked woman of exquisite beauty, and with hair down to her waist, was sitting on the ground, plucking flowers and fanning herself, while nearby a nude but heavily bearded man lay in the shadow of their craft. Both exhibited great apprehension as Hopkins approached, gesticulating and talking in an unintelligible language; eventually, though, they calmed themselves and established communication with the help of sign language. Asked by

Hopkins where they came from, the pair 'pointed upwards, pronouncing a word which, to [his] imagination, sounded like Mars'.

Early in the twentieth century, a few close encounters began to feature somewhat more alien creatures. In the forests of Thessalonica, in the late summer of 1938, a Greek man from the village of New Apollonia came upon an egg-shaped object about nine feet tall standing in a clearing. Two occupants, both humanoid but taller than a normal man, were standing alongside; they had big heads, red eyes and sunburned skin, and wore what looked like English military uniforms. When they realised they were being watched, the beings jumped back inside the giant egg. Something resembling a balloon appeared and inflated at the top of the craft, and the object took off vertically and disappeared.

Stranger encounters still were to follow. At the little hamlet of Kelly, near Hopkinsville in Kentucky, a family of nine were besieged, with two friends, in an isolated farmhouse by a group of three- or four-foot-tall 'goblins' with over-sized heads, glowing yellow eyes and huge ears. The creatures, which were a metallic silver in colour, appeared on the night of 21–22 August 1955 and repeatedly approached the house between 7.30 p.m. and 4.45 a.m. The frightened inhabitants tried to beat them off with shotguns, but although the creatures were hit repeatedly, somersaulting backwards from the force of the blasts, they soon returned, uninjured, to the fray.

In May 1969, Jose Antonio da Silva, an off-duty military policeman stationed near Bebedouro, Brazil, reported that he had been attacked by a number of four-foot-tall beings wearing helmets. Dragging him on board a machine shaped like two saucers joined by a vertical cylinder, the beings removed their helmets and revealed themselves to be squat and heavily bearded – much like fairytale dwarves, in fact. As the craft landed again, Da Silva lost consciousness and only came to four-and-a-half days later. On 6 December 1972, at Genoa, a 26-year-old night watchman called Fortunato Zanfretta found himself pushed to the ground by a huge green being some ten feet tall. Its body was a mass of dark grey fleshy folds and its oddly-shaped head, framed with spines, and with two horns on either side of the forehead, was dominated by two triangular yellow eyes, inclined upwards. Zanfretta noticed luminous wrinkles on the forehead, which he thought might have surrounded a third eye. Abruptly, the creature vanished, and a huge triangular craft rose into the sky from behind a nearby building with a loud whistling noise.

These incidents, drawn more-or-less at random from case-books which now contain reports on several thousand close encounters, illustrate the central problem of UFO occupant cases: the ufonauts are at once too human to be truly alien – it is rare indeed for anyone to meet an entity that is not at least humanoid in appearance, with two arms, two legs and a head – and too diverse. If every witness has described the beings he encountered accurately, it would appear that earth is being visited by several hundred different species of aliens. This in itself appears unlikely (though who are we to query alien logic?), the more so when it is observed that CE3s display a noticeable geographical bias. Patrick Huyghe, author of *The Field Guide to Extraterrestrials*, notes:

> From South America came reports of small swarthy dwarves who were fairly aggressive, while from Europe and, in particular, England, many reports were of tall, blond blue-eyed beings with a much friendlier disposition.... This once apparent geographical difference among alien types presents a major stumbling-block to the reality of UFO extraterrestrials. The phenomenon seems to mould itself to conform to the culture and time in which it appears. This implies that the encounters are more likely visions than visitations.

Huyghe's view is shared by many European ufologists, but rejected by the majority of American UFO investigators, where the idea that flying saucers are indeed alien spacecraft – the 'extraterrestrial hypothesis', or ETH – continues to predominate.

Although there are several major difficulties with the ETH

– principal among them the problem that other civilisations would need to make prohibitively lengthy journeys simply to reach earth, assuming (as Einstein presumed) that faster-than-light travel is essentially impossible – most can be circumvented simply by arguing that we cannot possibly know what the technological capabilities of a much more advanced civilisation may be. And if the purely physical objections are set aside, there is no doubt that many flying saucers *appear* to be alien spacecraft, and that the extraterrestrial hypothesis can indeed satisfactorily explain the UFO phenomenon.

The real question, then, is whether the ETH is fatally flawed by the internal contradictions of the evidence. For example, many ufologists find it difficult to understand why there should be so many UFO sightings – at least 100,000, according to one reasonably conservative extrapolation from the collective database of known cases – when a mere handful of aliens ought to be capable of surveying the earth and returning with any biological samples that might be required. There are also problems with the detail contained in many sighting reports: any craft executing the sort of sharp, 90-degree turns often attributed to UFOs, for example, should generate such enormous G-forces that the manoeuvres would be deadly not only to human pilots but to any alien life forms that resemble us.

Again, this argument fails simply because we have no idea what another race may be capable of. Some ufologists have avoided the problem by suggesting that UFOs are pilotless drones, others merely assume that extraterrestrials must be tougher than earthlings. Gerald Heard, whose 1951 work *Is Another World Watching?* was one of the earliest books about flying saucers, argued that the saucers were Martian spaceships piloted by advanced 'super-bees', each about two inches long. Only small insects, Heard believed, could survive the sort of G-forces that would be felt inside manoeuvring saucers.

It seems much more profitable to study what the aliens themselves have told witnesses. One of the most intriguing things about the UFO mystery is the way in which the alien's home planet has moved further and further away from earth as our own knowledge of space has grown. In the 1950s a whole series of witnesses called 'contactees' claimed not only to have seen flying saucers but to have made contact with their occupants, boarded their craft and travelled with them into space. According to George Adamski, the amateur astronomer and sometime hot-dog salesman who was by far the best-known of their number, most of the spacemen he met came from Venus, though they assured him that all but one of the planets in our solar system were inhabited. The space people also looked entirely human; Adamski's initial contact was with a rather beautiful Venusian man, about five feet, six inches in height, with a high forehead, grey-green eyes and pleasing cheekbones.

In later years, once Russian and American probes had shown that Venus is an uninhabitable, gas-filled desert and Mars too barren and desolate to support life, the space people began to claim that they came from further away – from the Pleiades, in the case of the Swiss contactee Billy Meier, or from a planet in the system Zeta Reticuli, if a star-map seen on board one UFO and recalled by an abductee is to be believed. This seems to suggest that the witnesses may be consciously or unconsciously selecting an apparently plausible 'homeworld' for the aliens themselves.

If UFOs are not alien spacecraft, though, what might they be? The sceptical position is that the casebook is made up of a combination of hoaxes, hallucinations and misidentifications. There is no doubt that these explanations account for the great majority of cases; even ufologists estimate that somewhere between 85 and 95 per cent of UFOs become IFOs – identified flying objects – if properly investigated.

From the 1950s on, one man in particular – Donald Menzel, the director of the Harvard College observatory – argued that many 'flying saucer' sightings were astronomical mirages, in which familiar objects such as the planet Venus were distorted by unusual atmospheric conditions, which could turn them into saucer-shaped objects and make them appear to dart about. He had even seen such a mirage himself, while researching the aurora borealis in Alaska. Just before dawn, on 3 March 1955, he was flying towards the town of Fairbanks in an old Air Force bomber when a bright light shot towards him from the horizon and came to a 'sudden skidding stop' about 100 yards away from him. The object had a silvery, metallic sheen, flashing red and green lights and what looked like an illuminated propellor on its roof.

Menzel's initial reaction was to suppose that the object was a meteor, but its strange behaviour ruled that out. He wondered if he was hallucinating, and took off his glasses to see if he was being deceived by an internal reflection, but had to conclude that the object really was outside the plane. Finally, after it had kept pace with the bomber for some time, the light suddenly accelerated away at an unbelievable speed, disappearing over the horizon in about two seconds. It was only when the light reappeared in the same position, but even brighter than before, that Menzel realised he had been watching a mirage of a star – he thought it must be Sirius, the dog star, just below the horizon – which had behaved exactly as many witnesses described UFOs.

There is no doubt that Menzel had identified one of the principal causes of UFO sightings, though ufologists have always argued that such mirages are rarer than astronomers admit and criticised Menzel, in particular, for attempting to apply his theory to many reports which it cannot really explain. It is true that some astronomical explanations stretch credulity, but at the same time a review of typical 'light in the sky' cases does show that even trained observers are capable of the most astonishing misidentifications. Philip Klass, who has assumed Menzel's mantle as the leading UFO sceptic, cites one case in which the crew of a US Navy transport aircraft, flying from Iceland to Newfoundland, reported an 'orange light' moving towards them at high speed which was actually the moon, viewed through a haze of thin cloud.

If experienced airmen are capable of that sort of error, it seems almost pointless to place any reliance on the eyewitness statements of ordinary people. Yet one group of ufologists suggests not only that these statements actually hold the key to the UFO mystery, but that the most ostensibly ludicrous, bizarre and incongrous among them may prove to be the most valuable.

High Strangeness

When David Stephens and Glen Gray came to, that night in October 1975, they were a mile further down the road than they had been before, their windows were wound down, and the car doors they had locked were open once again.

Up to this point, what had happened to the men, frightening and bizarre though it had been, was not untypical of other close encounters reported during the previous decade-and-a-half. Indeed, one of the main features that set the case apart was that the witnesses were used to being awake in the early hours of the morning, unlike those whose late-night encounters took place while they were tired or disorientated. But if their account really was accurately observed, what happened next must have been remarkable indeed.

The first thing the two friends noticed as they came to their senses and looked at each other in the half-light was that their eyes seemed to be glowing orange. (Gray's pupils also seemed to have disappeared.) Then they realised that the UFO was still visible, floating in the sky to the east. Numbed, they drove on, and two miles down the road the light in the sky vanished. At Stephens' suggestion, they turned the car around and returned the way they had come, until Gray, acting on an impulse that he could not explain, spun the wheel and swung down a gravel track that led to Tripp Pond, at the southern end of Lake Thompson.

Immediately he did so, the cylinder-shaped UFO reappeared in front of them, glowing bright white and hovering about 500 feet away from the car. Both the motor and the radio died and could not be restarted. Then the object rose further into the sky and positioned itself about a quarter of a mile away. The men watched it for about three-quarters of an hour – it is another of the many mysteries of the case that neither Stephens nor Gray explained why they sat there for so long – until two other 'craft' appeared in the night sky. The newcomers were disc-shaped and displayed blue, green and red lights as they darted about, putting on what one of the men described as an 'air show', skimming the surface of the pond, turning sharply at right angles and suddenly reversing course.

At the end of the display, the pair noticed that a thick, grey fog was rising from the still waters of Tripp Pond. The car had come to a halt a good half-mile from the water, but to Stephens and Gray it seemed that, suddenly, they were no more than fifty feet away and that the pond – in reality no more than a few hundred yards wide – had grown to the size of an ocean, stretching across the horizon. In the middle of this great expanse of water, an island appeared (the real pond has no island), and one of the disc-shaped UFOs descended to hover over it.

At this point the thick fog rising from the waters reached and engulfed the car. As it did so, the radio blared back into life and an announcer's voice declared, incongruously, that the day ahead would be bright and clear. The cylinder-shaped UFO was still visible overhead, but their engine had returned to life and the men were able to drive away. It was 6.30 a.m. The encounter had lasted for about three-and-a-half-hours.

The bizarre recollections of Stephens and Gray mark their encounter as a 'high strangeness' case – a report characterised by its essential illogicality, the dreamlike quality of its imagery and the unlikelihood that its events actually occurred as described. Such reports often have psychical components, and because their complexity makes them difficult to evaluate and their content means that they are hard to believe literally, they have often been ignored by mainstream ufologists.

Another high strangeness case occurred in Rio de Janeiro, on 15 September 1977. A bus driver named Antonio La Rubia, who was walking to work at 2.20 a.m., saw a bright, hat-shaped object hovering over a football field. Scared, he attempted to run, but found himself paralysed by a blue beam. At that moment, three strange beings materialised close by.

> The entities were about four feet tall and had an antenna more than a foot long jutting out from the middle of their [American] football-shaped heads. The antennae were topped with a teaspoon-shaped tip that rotated rapidly. Across the middle of their heads was a row of what looked like small mirrors in two shades of blue. . .
>
> Their stocky bodies were covered in scale-like clothes or skin that appeared to be made of dull aluminium. They had arms like elephants' trunks that narrowed down to tips as narrow as a finger. Across their 'waist' was a belt with hooks holding syringe-like devices. From the bottom of their rounded bodies emerged a single leg, actually a narrow pedestal that ended in a small circular platform.
>
> As the three identical entities floated around La Rubia, one pointed a 'syringe' at him, whereupon he found himself in a corridor inside the craft.
>
> In a huge hall with only a piano-like device and filled with some two dozen of these entities, La Rubia underwent an examination of some sort. He was also shown a series of 'slides', some of himself both dressed and naked, another of a horse and cart on a dirt road, one of traffic, and one of a dog trying to attack one of the beings. To La Rubia's horror, the dog turned blue and melted. Another slide showed a 'UFO factory' with millions of robots around. During the picture show, one of the entities drew blood from La Rubia's finger with a syringe.
>
> Suddenly, La Rubia thought he had been 'thrown overboard' as he found himself on a street opposite the bus station. One of the robots was standing beside him. When La Rubia looked around, the being vanished.

It seems to be one of the features of high strangeness cases that they do not require an exotic setting. Arguably the strangest close encounter of all occurred in the British midlands town of Rowley Regis, just to the west of Birmingham, in January 1979. The incident began early in the morning of 4 January, when Jean Hingley waved her husband off to work from their home in Bluestone Walk. As she turned to go back indoors, she saw a large orange sphere hovering over the carport and three small figures shot past her into the house, making a high-pitched buzzing noise as they went. Each figure,

Hingley recalled, was about three and a half feet tall and dressed in a silvery tunic with buttons down the front. The heads were covered by a 'goldfish bowl' helmet, through which eyes set in wide, white faces glittered 'like black diamonds'. Still more bizarrely, each had a pair of large, transparent wings covered in small dots. Limbs tapered to points, and the beings hovered and flew with their arms clasped over their chests and their legs hanging stiffly down. Each entity was surrounded by a halo.

The strange creatures made straight for the living room, where two of them began to shake the Hingleys' Christmas tree. At one point during the encounter, two of them flew over to the sofa and bounced on it like children. When Jean asked them to stop, they shone a beam of light at her forehead which seemed to blind and burn her. Nevertheless, the beings did accept the plate of mince pies Jean proffered and, when she spoke to them, they pressed the buttons on their tunics and then replied in gruff, masculine voices. Eventually they flew out of the back door and returned to their 'spacecraft', a sphere with a scorpion-like tail at its rear. The craft took off, leaving a pattern of inch-wide, parallel lines in the snow. Perhaps most strangely of all, two days after the encounter, the Hingley's Christmas tree vanished from their living room. It reappeared on 8 January 1979, in the back garden, minus its decorations and in pieces. The decorations themselves turned up just outside the garden at intervals over the next few days.

Incidents such as the La Rubia and Hingley encounters are quite unique – there is nothing like them in the ufological record. But some high strangeness cases do contain motifs that recur time and again. Perhaps the best example is the problem of the mysterious 'Men in Black' – sinister but ostensibly human agents who turn up periodically to silence witnesses and recover telling evidence of close encounters.

The Men in Black typically travel in groups of two or three, and they are often said to have a somewhat oriental appearance. Although they generally claim to represent the government, one of the strangest things about them is how they come by their detailed knowledge of UFO sightings. Frequently they arrive at a witness's door before he has had a chance to tell anyone else what he has seen; often they know far more about him than they have any right to.

One of the first visits from the Men in Black occurred in 1953, when Albert K. Bender, director of the International Flying Saucer Bureau, the largest early UFO organisation, was visited by three dark-suited men who, he said, first confided the 'solution' to the UFO mystery to him, then threatened him with prison if he told the secret to anyone else. Bender was so badly scared by the visit that he closed down his bureau and ceased all active involvement in the world of ufology.

Over the next few years similar, smartly dressed figures appeared to other UFO witnesses, issuing frightening threats (which never seem to have been carried out) and driving large, black, unmarked cars. And, as time went by, they became increasingly inhuman. In May 1967, a man with an olive complexion and a pointed face calling himself 'Major Richard French' visited a Minnesota UFO witness. When he complained of an upset stomach, the woman offered him a bowl of jelly, which he picked up and attempted to drink. Eventually, she said, 'I had to show him how to eat it with a spoon.'

Perhaps the oddest and most detailed of all MIB incidents actually sprang from the Maine encounter of 1975. About six months after the incident had occurred, a local doctor named Herbert Hopkins was alone in his home when he received a call from a man who claimed to be the vice-president of a UFO organisation. The caller had heard that Hopkins had spoken to Stephens and Gray, and asked if he could call to discuss the case. Hopkins agreed, and within a matter of seconds – far more quickly than seemed possible – a man appeared at his back door. Hopkins let him in, for some reason not even asking his name.

The stranger, he thought, 'looked like an undertaker'. He was dressed in a just-pressed black suit, and when he removed his (black) hat, Hopkins saw that he was not only bald, but lacked eyelashes and eyebrows. His face was white, his lips a vivid red, and he asked his questions about the case in a flat, unaccented voice. At one point, while Hopkins was talking, his visitor brushed his gloved hand against his face and the doctor saw with surprise a red smear appear on the back of the glove. The man was wearing lipstick.

Then came the threats. First Hopkins's visitor executed a bizarre 'conjuring trick', slowly dematerialising a coin the doctor was holding in his own hand, with the comment 'No one on this plane will ever see that coin again.' Next, Hopkins was told to destroy all the tapes and notes he had made of his meetings with Stephens and Gray. If he did not, the man threatened, his own heart would vanish in the same way that the coin had.

'As he spoke his last words', Hopkins remembered, 'I noticed that his speech was slowing down. A bit unsteadily, he got to his feet and said, very slowly, "My energy is running low. Must go now. Goodbye." ' The man walked woodenly out of the house, towards a bright light that was shining in the driveway, and Hopkins did not see him again.

What features do these high strangeness cases have in common? One seems to be a tendency for the witnesses to be alone at the time of their experience. This might mean that physically real entities are awaiting the right moment to initiate an encounter, but, equally, it could suggest that such incidents are in some way the product of the witness's imagination. Bearing this possibility in mind, it is interesting to note that the British ufologist Nigel Watson, who specialises in researching high strangeness cases, believes that many of the witnesses to such events experience a UFO sighting or some other sort of phenomenal encounter at an early age and may tend to have several more dramatic paranormal experiences as an adult.

Such encounters contain a high degree of subjectivity and Watson found that the witnesses are often undergoing some sort of mental upheaval at the time of their experience. Whether or not this pattern applies in the La Rubia and

Hingley cases is difficult to say from the evidence available, but, if Watson is correct, both the personal history and the psychology of the UFO witness begin to assume a critical importance in any attempt to understand the mystery. This observation is especially true when applied to a new phenomenon which was about to turn ufology upside down: abductions by aliens.

The Terror

The strangest aspect of the Maine experience remained the missing time between the first and second phases of the encounter. What had happened to Gray and Stephens while they were unconscious? How did they come to be a mile away from the place where they passed out? And who, or what, had opened the car's windows and doors?

To Shirley Fickett, one of the investigators who made their way to Norway to interview Gray and Stephens, the best way to unlock the mystery of the missing time was hypnosis. The technique had already been employed in a number of earlier UFO cases, going back to 1960, with results so startling that they were revolutionising the subject. Once placed in a trance state, UFO witnesses became capable not only of a much more detailed recall of the experiences they remembered, but of penetrating the frustrating veil of missing time to retrieve memories of terrifying close encounters. In case after case, they remembered being spirited on board the UFO, meeting the occupants of the craft and, when their experience was over, returning to earth with their recollections of the event deliberately masked by the aliens who had abducted them.

Fickett, perhaps, anticipated just such a revelation when she arranged for the Maine witnesses to meet Dr Herbert Hopkins of Old Orchard Beach, the therapist and hypnotist who eventually conducted the eight sessions with David Stephens that laid bare the bones of a typical abduction. At any rate, she gave Hopkins sufficient information for him to tease the details from the witness.

Under hypnosis, Stephens recalled being in the car when it was hit by the light beam of the UFO. Suddenly he found himself sitting on a floor within the strange craft, looking out through a window and watching as his car skidded sideways in the beam, with Glen Gray still at the wheel. Switching his attention to his surroundings, Stephens realised he was in a high-ceilinged room about thirty-five feet in diameter, which contained no furniture of any kind and had only a single door. The door opened and a non-human being entered the room. When Hopkins asked for a description of the alien, Stephens appeared to be under considerable stress. His breathing became laboured and his voice trembled as he described a being four and a half feet high dressed in something resembling a flowing black sheet. Although it had two arms and two legs, it had only three fingers and they were thin and webbed. It had white skin, no facial hair, a mushroom-shaped head and large, slanted, unblinking eyes. Its nose was small and round and it had no noticeable mouth.

The alien communicated telepathically with Stephens. It knew his name, and Stephens was told that the aliens had been watching him and studying him for some time. He was assured that he would not be harmed. Then he was taken into another room, this one equipped like a hospital, where another four beings were waiting. One took two samples of Stephens's blood, using a needle to draw the fluid from his right elbow. But when the aliens attempted to make Stephens lie on what looked like an operating table he rebelled, hitting one of the creatures in the face. The being took a step backwards, but did not react in any other way to the blow, and Stephens subsided, lying down and subjecting himself to a further examination. The aliens produced a machine that slid over his body without touching it, examining every part of him. Small samples of his hair and fingernails were taken, and a button was removed from his sleeve; all these objects were placed in empty containers.

In all, the examination took about forty-five minutes, after which Stephens was escorted back into the empty room. He was given some sort of message or promise, he recalled, and told that he would see the aliens again – but even in a trance state he could not recall exactly what the message was. Finally, Stephens was given some sort of injection near his right shoulder. Almost immediately, he found himself back in the car next to his friend, Gray.

The experience described by Stephens was already all-too-familiar to UFO investigators such as Fickett. Indeed, several accounts of similar abductions were already on record. The earliest came from Antonio Villas Boas, the Brazilian farmer who had been taken on board a flying saucer in 1957 and seduced by a beautiful female occupant. Then a middle-aged American couple, Betty and Barney Hill, encountered a glowing UFO while driving through the White Mountains of New Hampshire one night in September 1961. About two weeks later, Betty experienced a series of nightmares in which she found herself surrounded by a group of small, grey humanoids wearing military-style uniforms. She and Barney eventually sought the help of a hypnotherapist, Dr Benjamin Simon, and, under hypnosis, both recalled being pulled from their car by a group of nearly a dozen aliens – each of them short, with grey skin, black hair, blue lips and long noses 'like Jimmy Durante' – and forcibly taken on board a UFO where they were subjected to medical examinations. Barney had a circular instrument placed over his groin, while Betty was given a 'pregnancy test', though in fact she had undergone a hysterectomy – her dress was removed and a long needle was painfully inserted into her navel. Afterwards, the Hills were returned to their car remembering nothing of their experience.

Unprecedented though such details were in 1961, it gradually became clear that the New Hampshire case was the precursor of hundreds of broadly similar experiences. Starting slowly in the 1960s, the number of abduction reports increased rapidly in the 1970s and by the early 1980s the subject had become the most controversial topic of debate among ufologists. In case after case, abductees reported that they had been taken on board an alien spacecraft, stripped, and subjected to a medical examination of some sort. Some were scanned by floating instruments that hovered over their bodies; others endured the unpleasant insertion of probes. The Gothic novelist Whitley Strieber, who was to become the most prominent of all abductees, recalled having 'an enormous and extremely ugly' triangular object forced into his rectum.

After the examination was over, most abductees were allowed to dress and then, perhaps, shown around the interior of the craft. The UFO was generally described as clinically clean and lit by a bright, diffuse light, which came from some invisible source. Often the witnesses expressed surprise at discovering that the rooms within the craft were bigger on the inside than they seemed to be from outside, or expressed disconcertment at the apparent absence of windows and doors.

Descriptions of the alien abductors varied. Some were small and hairy, with bat-like ears. Others had domed heads and turtle-like lower faces. Gradually, however, reports of beings very similar to those encountered by the Hills came to predominate. They were humanoids with hairless, bulging heads, huge wraparound eyes, narrow jaws which tapered to a point, scrawny bodies, and three-fingered hands. Some were about three feet tall, others six-inches-or-so taller, but because all had characteristically grey-white skin ufologists began to refer to them collectively as 'the Greys'.

Some abductees – about a third – retained a conscious memory of their experience, but in the majority of cases either the whole encounter or the abduction itself could only be recalled under hypnosis. Ufologists soon learned that certain indicators pointed to the possible existence of such repressed memories. The most important clue was often a witness's recall of unaccounted-for periods of 'missing time'. Under hypnosis, the missing time was often identified as the period during which the abduction took place.

In the late 1970s and early 1980s, it gradually became apparent that two broad categories of experience were being reported. One group, which included Streiber amongst its number and centred on abduction researchers such as John

Mack and Leo Sprinkle, were experiencing broadly positive encounters with aliens who showed some concern for humankind. The other, which included the majority of abductees working with the abduction experts Budd Hopkins and David Jacobs, reported increasingly grotesque encounters with disinterested or even hostile aliens. Many now recalled even more overtly sexual aspects of the medical examinations: women had their eggs harvested while male abductees were hooked up to pumping machines that expressed the sperm from their bodies.

Male and female abductees interviewed by David Jacobs recalled these experiences with obvious distress. Under hypnosis, Will Parker described his experience as unpleasantly clinical:

> 'They've got this comb-shaped gimmick over my crotch, and it's a buzzing, vibration type of sensation. It's a very functional kind of thing.'
>
> 'What do you think is happening?' Jacobs asked.
>
> 'Well, they're taking a sperm sample, obviously, because it's not piss they're pulling out of there.'
>
> 'Do you feel something flowing out?'
>
> 'Definitely; there's an erection and there's no sense of release or anything orgasmic; it's just like a literal drawing out.'
>
> 'Can you get a sense of what the apparatus looks like?'
>
> 'It looks like polished stainless steel, aluminium, chromium I guess you'd call it. It fits over the penis and it's got a rounded lower section that fits up over the testicles. And it's like you're enclosed in this thing. It looks like a piece of machinery no good mistress of domination would be without.'

Twenty-year-old Tracey Knapp, meanwhile, remembered that

> 'There's one man here and one man on this side, and there's one man here, and they're pressing. My legs are up, and I'm getting snipped, but internally. Something's snipping . . . Something burned, burned. A fluid burns me.'
>
> 'They're using instruments for this, I guess?'

'Very tiny, tiny, long, very long little itty bitty scissor things, but very, very tiny. It feels like . . . snipping on both sides. Somehow I just feel an uneasiness. I don't like it. They're not taking eggs out of me, they're releasing, they're snipping. It's like they're cutting threads.'

'Do they remove their instruments?'

'Yeah, they removed something out of me. They removed a, like a little baby or something. And they removed the sac or something. But it's tiny, real tiny. It's not a baby.'

'An embryo, you mean?'

'Yeah, it's like . . .'

'What do they do when they remove it?'

'There's a cylinder or something. It seems like it's being placed in this silver cylinder, probably about three inches wide.'

'What do they do with the cylinder then?'

'Well, you know, they got other . . . God! It's like they've got other babies there. They're in like drawers in the walls; it's like little drawers that pull out, and there's babies like little, little somethings in those drawers that pull out like in a lab or something.'

Piecing together the testimony they had gathered, Jacobs and Hopkins began to realise that they were uncovering a sinister motivation that lent purpose to the apparently purposeless abduction phenomenon. The Greys, they discovered, have been visiting earth for many years and repeatedly abducting carefully selected victims. Sometimes abductions 'run in the family', and several generations will undergo similar experiences. All such cases begin in childhood. Victims might be marked with inexplicable scars of have implants of some sort inserted into their nasal cavities. (In one or two cases, such implants have actually appeared to show up on X-rays, though the aliens return to remove their handiwork before any attempt can be made to recover them.) The grand purpose of the abductions is systematically to manipulate the genetic stock of the human race and breed hybrid human-alien babies; a handful of abductees have hinted that these hybrids are to be used to revitalise a dying alien race. Jacobs concludes: 'It is not a programme of reproduction, but one of *production*. They are not here to help us. They have their own agenda, and we are not allowed to know its full parameters.'

The principal argument in favour of the reality of the abduction phenomenon is the great degree of continuity between reports. The abductees seem to undergo similar experiences, and the sex, age or occupation of the witness seems to make no difference to their accounts. Furthermore, although most abduction cases come from the United States, those that are reported from other countries generally follow similar patterns.

Sceptics have countered with the suggestion that the mystery is an essentially sociological phenomenon, drawing its inspiration initially from science fiction films and television shows of the late 1950s and early 1960s such as *The Twilight Zone*, *The Outer Limits* and even *Star Trek*. According to this theory, the rapid growth in the number of reports received from the late 1970s on is probably due to increasing media coverage of abductions and a consequent surge in public awareness of the phenomenon. Although such critics generally stop short of suggesting that most abductees are simply hoaxers, they do suggest that they may be fantasising or hallucinating.

This argument shows little sign of being resolved. Though abduction researchers have argued that early science fiction material is almost devoid of precise parallels to the abduction experience, doubters have countered with the claim that every element of the typical abduction can be found in the early pulp magazines or post-war alien invasion movies. The sceptics have pointed out that hypnosis is not an infallible way of getting at the truth, and that the testimony of witnesses can easily be shaped by leading questions. Ufologists have responded by pointing out that consciously recalled abduction experiences match those recovered under hypnosis in every detail. Scientists have insisted that it would be biologically impossible to breed human-alien hybrids. Abduction experts reply that we cannot state with certainty what an advanced race would be capable of.

Perhaps, then, we should consider the evidence of the abductees in other ways. Is there, for example, a good reason why so many hundreds, or thousands, of abductions are necessary? Why go to the trouble of kidnapping so many human males when it would be simpler to raid a sperm bank? Can the aliens really remove abductees from their beds without waking their sleeping partners, and teleport them through windows and solid walls into their spacecraft, as many reports suggest?

In truth, there are elements of absurdity to some abduction accounts which are hard to reconcile with the idea that all are physically real experiences. One abductee, Leah Haley, has claimed that the UFO on which she was being forcibly detained was shot down by the US Air Force – an incident that the Air Force, unsurprisingly, denies ever happened. In another case, a witness who came across a flying saucer standing in a forest clearing, approached and heard a voice from within the craft cry, 'I am Jimmy Hoffa!' Finally, the farcical failure of various attempts to videotape an abduction-in-progress again argue against the physical reality of the phenomenon. David Jacobs notes that one subject, Melissa Bucknell,

> began to have abduction experiences almost on a daily basis. We decided to use a video camera and VCR on a dresser top pointed at her bed. Melissa had been abducted the night before we set up the equipment. But after we installed it, days went by with no activity . . . Then one day she reported that she thought 'something might have happened'. She had gone to sleep very late and had slept until noon. The tape had run out at 6 a.m. Investigation revealed that the abduction took place sometime between 6 and 12. Weeks later she had another abduction episode. This time she had slept on the living room couch to get away from the noise of the neighbours.

Budd Hopkins tells a similar story:

> One interesting thing happened when a young woman set up a video camera. She woke up in the morning, and felt that something was happening. I think she had physical marks and so forth. But when she went to the video camera, there was no tape in it.

> Let me tell you what happened under hypnosis. She's abducted, she's brought back, put in her room. Then she marches straight over to the video camera, turned it off, takes out the tape, walks downstairs to the basement, takes a hammer and smashes it to smithereens, and puts it in the garbage.

If the Greys really are capable of exerting such control over their abductees, it must be doubted that we will ever be presented with conclusive evidence for the physical reality of the abduction phenomenon.

UFOs and Other Worlds

Suppose, for a moment, that unidentified flying objects are not physically real spacecraft engaged in a systematic programme of abduction and medical experiments. Suppose that the witnesses themselves are the key to the mystery. Suppose the things that they see are actually, in some way, the products of their imaginations.

How could we tell? Perhaps by adopting a witness-centred approach. If UFOs really are extraterrestrial spaceships crewed by a single race, for example, we would expect to find significant similarities in sighting reports from around the world – all should describe similar craft, and descriptions of the occupants should also be consistent. Indeed, members of the 'nuts and bolts' school of ufology have, as we have seen, claimed that this is the case with abduction reports. The witness-centred approach, on the other hand, suggests that reports from Africa or Asia should be significantly coloured by cultures and traditions that differ from those of the west.

There are some signs that the content and quantity of UFO reports are influenced by local culture and the local media. The occupants in one 1970 encounter in Malaysia were only three inches tall and wore brightly-coloured jump-suits. Far from looking like the Greys, which were just beginning to emerge as the dominant UFO entity in the west, they actually resembled characters from a local comic book. On the other hand, the French ufologist Thierry Pinvidic conducted some research in Algeria during the early 1980s which suggested that, despite the country's close links with France, western-style UFOs were practically unknown there. Though there certainly were traditions of strange things seen in the sky, they were interpreted as religious signs and wonders. Pinvidic sought an explanation for this curious problem and concluded:

> My hypothesis is that if a specific interpretation is put on these experiences by a country's own culture (i.e. the Islamic interpretation in Algeria) then the western interpretations of the UFO stereotype will not spread in that country.
>
> This idea forced me to more precise research. I discovered that very few UFO cases can be said to have as witnesses people who can be said to be totally un-westernised. I re-read the major UFO catalogues and about 60 books and magazines in both English and French, and failed to find more than 13, from across the world, from cultures that could be said to be ufologically 'virgin' . . . [This suggests that] the association of a western, 'technological' imagery, coupled with local folklore, can account for UFO experiences worldwide. The decisive factor is mass sensitisation to the UFO motif.

Let's consider the aftermath of the Maine abduction case with this witness-centred approach in mind. Are there signs that the witnesses were familiar with the concept of unidentified flying objects? Is there reason to believe that they may have fantasised, misperceived or exaggerated parts of their experience? Is there evidence that the experience had roots that went deeper than the events of the night of 27 October? The answer to all these questions seems to be 'Yes'.

A few days after David Stephens and Glen Gray experienced their bizarre close encounter, two local ufologists, James Carey and Brent Raynes, heard about the incident and arranged to spend some time with the two witnesses. Carey and Raynes thought both men were frightened and agitated; during the interview, Stephens even announced that three more craft were hovering over the house and pointed out three bright lights in the sky, which Carey readily identified as the planets Jupiter and Mars and a nearby star, Betelgeuse.

Next, Stephens and Gray reported that several peculiar incidents had happened since their encounter: someone (or something) had walked across the roof of their trailer home; both men had suffered sudden bouts of extreme tiredness; both had seen snowflakes and black cubes and spheres flying from the sky and through a wall; 'golden wires' appeared in the air above their TV set; and a disembodied voice, audible only to Gray, had intoned the letters 'U-F-O'. Finally, two days after the encounter had occurred, Stephens answered the door to find a stockily built man with crew-cut hair and sunglasses waiting outside. The stranger asked if he was the person who had seen a 'flying saucer', and warned the young man: 'Better keep your mouth shut if you know what's good for you.'

On the face of it, then, the Maine UFO encounter may well be sinister and extraordinary, but it is also hard to imagine that it occurred just as the witnesses described it. Even Stephens and Gray were inclined to think that some of the things they had seen that night were hallucinations of some sort, but they had never experienced similar things before and did not know why such visions were occurring to them now. Because of these difficulties, the case is not often discussed, even in ufological circles, and is certainly too strange to be included among the handful of 'classic cases' that most researchers would cite as evidence for UFOs. Yet this one incident includes almost all of the key elements that distinguish such classics from run-of-the-mill reports.

The Maine sighting is, for example, simultaneously a close encounter of the first, second and third kinds – that is, a case in which a UFO was observed from a range of less than 500 feet, had a physical effect on its environment (taking control of the car from Gray, and later stopping its engine), and in which its occupants were seen by the witnesses. One leading ufologist has noted that the incident 'is more like than unlike other abduction cases' and that it perfectly follows the 'capture pattern' of a typical abduction.

Certainly, many of the details recalled by the two men had parallels in other cases; as we have seen, incidents of unconsciousness and 'missing time' have become so common that they are regarded as a standard feature of many close encounters. Nor is it uncommon for witnesses to enter a 'zone of strangeness', as one researcher has termed it, and experience the odd sense of unreality that Stephens and Gray felt as they drove down an unexpectedly smooth track at an unnaturally high speed, or watched a small pond turn itself into an ocean.

For all its apparent outlandishness, then, the Maine encounter of 1975 may be considered fairly representative of the more detailed hard core of UFO reports. It does not seem to have been suggested that the entire incident was a hoax, and though it could have been, this would at least have required Stephens and Gray to have built up a fairly detailed knowledge of the main elements of UFO reports. To dismiss the case out of hand is to disregard the similarities between the incident and a much larger body of evidence; to exclude its more remarkable details would seem an act of intellectual dishonesty, while to accept it as it stands creates problems whether one believes UFOs are alien spacecraft or, in the broadest sense, figments of the imagination.

Is there an 'explanation' for the Maine case? One key seems to be the bizarre dream-like quality of much of the encounter. Even setting aside the abduction itself, which was recalled only under hypnosis, the two witnesses appear to have experienced a remarkable shared vision, and to have remained in a heightened or altered state of consciousness for some time afterwards. In such a state it seems possible that Stephens and Gray misidentified some mundane objects. The investigators of the case considered the possibility that the 'mother ship', which apparently hovered in the sky for much of the encounter, was actually the moon, which, in late October 1975, was in its final quarter and quite prominent in a clear night sky. Stephen's later insistent identification of three commonplace celestial bodies as UFOs also suggests that one or other of the men may have become scared, during their drive, by a star or planet, which he became convinced was a brightly lit flying saucer, and that his apprehension somehow triggered a shared hallucination.

If there was a 'leader' among the two it seems, at first sight, that it must have been Gray, since it was his idea to drive to Lake Thompson and later to detour to Tripp Pond, and we have only his word to suggest that the car was out of his control at any time during the encounter. Yet each witness separately experienced elements of the peculiar, parapsychological aftermath of the case; it was Stephens, and not Gray, who underwent hypnosis and relived a solitary abduction and examination; and Gray was both the younger of the two witnesses, and the first to become disillusioned with the attention they were receiving. He told the investigators that he was not interested in being hypnotised after Stephens's first session with Hopkins, and after that gradually withdrew from the investigation, shortly afterwards moving away from the Norway area altogether. Stephens, on the other hand, continued to cooperate fully with Fickett and Hopkins. If Gray was planting ideas in his friend's mind, then Stephens seems to have believed in them wholeheartedly. And the account he gave under hypnosis suggests that he believed them somewhere deep in his subconscious.

5

Where the Wild Things Are

From the endless skies over America to the claustrophobic confines of the Amazonian jungle; from outer space to the ocean's depths; from extraterrestrial spacecraft to living creatures: surely there can be no greater contrast than that between ufology and cryptozoology, the study of unknown animals.

If ufology is the study of the totally fantastic, then cryptozoology is – or should be – the study of the nearly acceptable, indeed the almost mundane. No biologist doubts that thousands of species remain to be identified, classified and named. All that is needed is some physical evidence, and that should be rather easier to secure than elusive fragments from crashed saucers.

In the summer of 1994, for example, a tortoise hunter scouring the Khe Tre watershed – a forest in the mountain borderlands between Vietnam and Laos – stumbled across something unexpected: a small, goat-like creature he did not recognise. Setting his dogs on the little animal, the hunter succeeded in capturing it. It proved to be a female calf, no more than five months old and two feet tall at the shoulder – but it was certainly no goat. It was a living specimen of the *sao la*, or Vu Quang ox, an animal first identified only two years earlier from skulls and antlers found in a nearby nature reserve and quite unknown (to zoologists, that is) in the wild.

The Vu Quang ox is one of only a handful of large mammals discovered and classified this century. Yet it is far from the only surprise to emerge from Khe Tre since the latter became a focus for zoological research. In the last four years, this one small area of near-virgin forest has also produced a new species of muntjac deer (a giant so commonplace that it forms part of the staple diet of the local Vietnamese), two novel species of bird and a new fish, not to mention an unknown tortoise – which must have cheered up the tortoise hunter.

Though zoologists had not been presented with quite such a cornucopia of novelty for well over 100 years, new species are being discovered all the time, at the rate of several hundred a year. The majority are insects, a fair number are fish, and a few are reptiles, amphibians and birds. Only a handful are mammals, and among these, few are as large as the Vu Quang ox, which is not really an ox at all, but a relative of the oryx. Yet each such find is a reminder that our knowledge of the animal kingdom is far from complete and an encouragement to the small band of cryptozoologists that still more spectacular discoveries may yet be made.

The problem, of course, is that the majority of cryptozoologists are not really interested in the minutiae of classifying new variants of beetle, nor even with the rediscovery of fossil fish. They seek bigger game, animals that, in some cases, have been hunted for centuries, yet today seem frustratingly little closer to capture or identification than when they were first reported: lake monsters, ape-men, sea-serpents and giant birds. It is in their belief that such beasts do exist that they part company with their more orthodox colleagues.

In fact, cryptozoologists have three main fields of study. One is the problem of known species that crop up unexpectedly in habitats that are quite alien to them. Such creatures are generally known as 'out-of-place animals' and they are, in fact, surprisingly common. The most celebrated examples are the big cats which have been seen roaming the moorlands of

Britain, Germany, France, Australia and the United States in recent decades. But many even more exotic animals are at large: there are, for example, porcupines in Devon, wild boar in the Home Counties, and perhaps even wolverines on the loose in Wales.

The second field of study concerns animals that are presumed to have died out, but that may still survive in some remote corner of the world. Cryptozoologists have long drawn inspiration from the rediscovery of the coelacanth, a prehistoric fish trawled up off the coast of South Africa in 1938, some 65 million years after its supposed extinction. In more recent years they have gone in search of giant sloths in the South American rain forests and living dinosaurs in the jungles of the Congo. Such expeditions have yet to bring back any irrefutable proof that their quarries exist.

Finally, and most spectacularly of all, cryptozoologists have complied accounts of a range of large creatures which apparently exist, but which remain unrecognised by science. Bernard Heuvelmans, a Belgian zoologist who has devoted himself to the study of such 'hidden animals' since the 1950s, has complied a catalogue of more than 300 species, all of them still awaiting discovery, ranging from unknown tapirs to long-necked seals. Some of these creatures may exist, others will probably remain elusive despite having been seen and sought for many years; and it remains one of the curiosities of cryptozoology that there are far more sightings of its least likely quarries – the lake monsters and the giant ape-men – than there are of many of the more plausible creatures in the menagerie. Appreciating why this is so, may, in fact, be one of the keys to understanding the whole subject.

Cat Flaps and Bear Scares

One cryptozoological mystery for which there is certainly no shortage of evidence is the problem of big cats loose in the British countryside. In the 1990s, sightings have multiplied to the point where there are certainly more than 300 each year.

Most are made at relatively long range: typically a big black cat, perhaps the size of a Labrador, is seen in the middle distance. If the animal becomes aware it is being watched, it makes off immediately. Such reports are generally accompanied by the occasional discovery of an eviscerated sheep's carcass in a farmer's field, or by a hazy photograph, or a short video sequence shot on a camcorder.

Infrequently, though, the encounters are much closer and much more alarming than that. Shortly after midnight on 26 October 1993, a big cat attacked 37-year-old Jane Fuller while she was out walking her dog on Bodmin Moor. She was temporarily stunned, but recovered; next day the remains of two sheep – one of them disembowelled, the other decapitated – were found in the adjoining field. Two months later, a veterinary lecturer named Sally Dyke ventured into the Welsh Marches with her husband, Nick, in search of the Beast of Inkberrow – a big cat that had been seen more than thirty times in the previous four years. The couple laid bait for the creature among the graves at St Peter's, Inkberrow, and returned to the churchyard the next evening. As they made their way back towards the bait, Nick Dyke, who was in the lead, actually trod on a big cat. The startled animal leapt up and tore off down the path. Finding Sally blocking its way, the cat took two swipes at her. One blow caught her below the ribs, penetrating her wax jacket and several other layers of clothing, and knocking her aside. The combination of darkness and extreme surprise meant that neither could positively identify their assailant, beyond saying it was black and very large; but Sally had the claw-marks to show that the animal was no figment of their imagination: three five-inch wounds across the right side of her ribs, which bled profusely and were still visible four months later.

The Beast of Inkberrow is only one of the many mysterious big cats, or colonies of big cats, presently haunting the British Isles. Cambridgeshire has its Fen Tiger, Cornwall, the Beasts of Bodmin and Exmoor, County Durham, the Durham Puma, Nottinghamshire, the Nottingham Lion. Some of these creatures are seen more or less regularly; others – the Nottingham Lion is a case in point – only once or twice, or for a few months, before they vanish back into the undergrowth for good. But all in all, out-of-place big cats of varying descriptions have been reported from some thirty counties in England, Scotland, Wales and Northern Ireland.

The most perplexing thing about the mystery is that it seems to be a relatively modern phenomenon. It really dates only to 1962, when the first and most influential of all the alien big cats, the Surrey Puma, first reared its head.

The borderlands of Surrey, Hampshire and Sussex seem a much less likely home for a population of large, wild cats than do the relatively wild moorlands of Bodmin, Durham and Exmoor. They are part of London's commuter belt, within easy reach of the capital, and heavily populated; there are many fields and woodlands, but they are patrolled by farmers and weekend walkers. Yet these well-trodden acres have generated several hundred big cat sightings, backed up by a few snapshots, droppings, some dead cattle and a number of plaster-casts of tracks, some of which were positively identified as those of a puma. At the height of the flap, the Surrey police logged sightings in the Day Book of Godalming police station; a total of 362 entries were made between September 1962 and August 1964.

Where was the Surrey Puma before the summer of 1962? Was it living quietly and unnoticed in the same fields and woodlands where it would be hunted for the next two years? Was it heading towards the commuter belt from its original home in one of the wilder areas of the south west? Or was it biding its time in a cage in a back garden or a private menagerie somewhere in the Home Counties? Whatever the answer to that question, the puma was far from being alone even in 1962. There was a similar, but older, tradition of out-of-place big cats in Australia, where sightings have been reported sporadically since the 1880s. There were more reports – of tigers and lions – in the 1930s, and the farmers of Emmaville, New

South Wales, reported the killing of more than 340 sheep by a 'panther' between 1956 and 1957.

In the United States, natives such as the cougar appear to share their territories with both lions and black panthers. Here, reports of out-of-place big cats go back at least as far as July 1917, when a butler named Thomas Gullet was attacked at the Robert Allerton estate at Monticello, in central Illinois, by what he described as 'an African lioness'; a male lion was later seen nearby. More recently, big cats have also appeared in Germany, where, in 1988, a 'young puma' was reported in the Saar; a year later, police in Darmstadt issued warnings that a dangerous animal was lurking in the nearby forest, and in the Odenwald, along the border between Hesse and Bavaria, several people from the villages of Furth and Steinback claimed to have seen a black panther. At first the police took these sightings seriously, and insisted that the witnesses they had interviewed were sober and reliable. Later, however, so many reports piled up that substantial discrepancies began to appear. At this point a police spokesman announced that sightings of the Odenwald beast were either hoaxes or delusions.

This pattern – initial sighting, tentative acceptance, inconclusive investigation, further and divergent reports, increasing scepticism and then dismissal – is already becoming a familiar one in the borderlands. And, in truth, there are many problems in assuming that colonies of big cats, or even individuals, lurk in the hedgerows and woodlands of a country such as Great Britain, not least the fact that witnesses, particularly town-dwellers, often over-estimate the size of the animals they have seen. At its most extreme, this tendency can have farcical consequences. In Winchmore Hill, London, on 11 March 1994, eight witnesses independently telephoned the police to warn them that a lioness was stalking the streets of the quiet suburb. Officers with megaphones were dispatched to warn householders to stay indoors while a police helicopter clattered overhead and marksmen from London Zoo, armed with tranquilliser guns, stood by. Eventually, however, the 'lioness' was photographed sunning herself on a garden shed and identified as Bilbo, a large ginger-haired tomcat whose owner, Carmel Jarvis, insisted he was 'not ferocious at all'.

There can, however, be no doubt that some of Britain's mystery felines are real. Over the last decade-and-a-half, two pumas, a pair of jungle cats and five smaller leopard cats have been run over, captured or killed in a swathe of countryside that runs from Cornwall north to Inverness-shire – a total that does not include any of the several known escapees from zoos, menageries and private collections. The real question, then, is not whether big cats are now loose in the British countryside, but where they come from and how many of them there are. In some cases witnesses have reported pairs of cats, or adults escorting infants, and in others, the discovery of a dead body has failed to put an end to big cat sightings in the area, implying that some of these animals are breeding in the wild and are displaying an unexpected ability to adapt to the local climate.

Nevertheless, at least some of these more definite reports have mundane explanations. In October 1980, a Scottish farmer named Ted Noble caught a full-grown puma in a trap set on his land at Cannich in the Highlands, ending almost a year of sightings in the area, and appearing to solve the puzzle of the sheep that had been disappearing from his farm. Yet, on closer examination, this apparently fearsome beast turned out to be an elderly, arthritic female, so tame that she enjoyed being tickled behind her ears and so malnourished that she had evidently had difficulty surviving in the wild since escaping from, or being released by, her human owner.

The absence of an appreciable number of reports dating to before 1960, and the rapid increase in the number of British big cat sightings reported and the number of bodies found since 1980, has suggested to several researchers that the key to this mystery lies in the release of captive animals into the wild, particularly since the introduction of the Dangerous Wild Animals Act of 1976 – a piece of legislation that made it much more difficult for enthusiasts to keep large exotics in captivity and probably encouraged the deliberate introduction of a number of now troublesome big cats to the British countryside.

This hypothesis has much to recommend it, particularly when it is borne in mind just how much meat a large cat consumes. An animal the size of a puma must eat the equivalent of five adult deer each week to survive; and although it sometimes appears that mystery cats are chewing their way through thousands of sheep each year, there is actually little evidence that prey are being killed in the quantities required to sustain a large and stable population of unknown predators. A British government report on the evidence for big cats in central Cornwall – home of the fabled Beast of Bodmin – concluded: 'No verifiable evidence for the presence of a "big cat" was found. There were only four suspected livestock kills reported in nearly six months, none of which gave any indication of the involvement of anything other than native animals and dogs. There is no significant threat to livestock from a "big cat" on Bodmin Moor.'

Though the question of what the Beast of Bodmin might be living on remains unanswered, the provenance of an out-of-place animal is that much more intriguing when the creature in question is less than well adapted for survival in its new home. From this point of view, the most peculiar and most prolific of out-of-place animals is undoubtedly the crocodile. There have been numerous verified discoveries of such creatures at large in the British Isles, including one at Chipping Norton, Oxfordshire, in 1836; more recently, there were sightings in the River Ouse in 1970 and the River Stour in 1975.

The Chipping Norton beast, which was a very young and not particularly deadly animal about twelve inches long, chased a party of ramblers across a common until one of them, braver than his companions, turned and crushed its head with a stone. What made this discovery particularly interesting was that it was only the first of several in this small rural community over the next three decades: a second baby crocodile was found on a farm in the same village around 1856, and killed; and two others were seen, separately, at nearby Over Norton in the

1860s. It might be possible, though it seems unlikely, that some rural farmer had a passion for breeding dangerous reptiles and that he somehow kept his hobby secret for all the years that he lived in the little community. Alternatively, but still more implausibly, it may be that a small colony of crocodiles somehow survived the inhospitable Oxfordshire climate for three decades or more, without alarming any of the local fishermen or leaving a trace of their presence in the shape of the remains of their prey. We will probably never know for sure.

Whatever the explanation, crocodiles, alligators and caimans certainly do turn up in the most unexpected places. On 2 July 1843, one was reported to have fallen from the sky over Charleston during a thunderstorm. Another was found thrashing on top of a gasbag in an airborne Zeppelin, a third at Brooklyn Museum subway station in New York on 6 June 1937, and a fourth turned up in a passenger toilet on board the Munich to Cologne express train in February 1973. In May 1980, police at Preston, Lancashire, received three calls from motorists who had seen a six-foot crocodile crossing the M55 at Lightfoot Lane; one of them believed that he had run over its tail as he passed. Some of these animals were probably pets that had either escaped or were in the process of being smuggled to new homes by their owners, though the continuing proliferation of out-of-place reptile stories (a total of well over 100 cases have been reported since the discovery of the first Chipping Norton beast) suggests that this may not be the only answer.

The 'escaped pet' theory is deservedly popular as an explanation for out-of-place animal reports, but it would be dangerous to attempt to apply it to every case. What are we to make, for example, of the surreal Hackney bear scare of 1981? On the evening of 27 December, four boys, aged between nine and thirteen, out walking their dogs on Hackney marshes, came across a set of three-clawed footprints in the snow, which one of their number identified as bear prints. Soon afterwards, the boys met a middle-aged couple and asked them if they knew there was a bear about. 'They said, "Yes, it's up there," ' thirteen year-old Tommy Murray later told the police, 'and told us to keep away because it was dangerous. And they threw snowballs at us to frighten us.' This, of course, only piqued the boys' curiosity and they pressed on until they came across 'a giant great growling hairy thing' which reared up on its hind legs, sending them running.

Next day, the police searched the 5000-acre wasteland with dogs and a helicopter, finding nothing but several convincing sets of tracks. Oddly enough, though, the tracks started and finished abruptly, and were surrounded by virgin snow. The police evidently suspected a hoax, and sure enough someone did phone the newspapers to claim responsibility and to explain that he had perpetrated a practical joke by hiring a bear suit from a fancy dress shop. It seemed a plausible explanation, until the police admitted they could not find a shop that had hired out any such costume, and one leading costumier pointed out that bear suits are made to fit over ordinary shoes and certainly don't leave three-clawed tracks.

But what was the alternative? Though desolate enough, the marshes are still emphatically part of Greater London and are ringed with industrial estates and council homes. They could hardly provide a safe home for even one bear for long. And what of the curiously knowledgeable, middle-aged couple with the snowballs? The Hackney bear scare is a useful reminder that the annals of cryptozoology contain high strangeness cases, too.

To Catch a Tiger by the Tail

The cryptozoologists' casebook contains many records concerning the possible survival of apparently extinct animals. Living mammoths have been glimpsed far in the distance, moving slowly through the Siberian taiga; live moas have emerged briefly from the bush in New Zealand. It has even been suggested – though, sadly, it is merely speculation – that the dodo may survive on some bleak and unvisited islets north of Mauritius.

Of all the many animals supposed to be extinct, however, the one most likely to have survived is the Tasmanian tiger, or thylacine, a fierce marsupial predator some six feet long, endowed with massive, gaping jaws and a striped rump that gave it its common name. Once common throughout Australia, it is generally reckoned to have been wiped out on the mainland by 1000 BC, thanks to the introduction of dingoes to the continent. The thylacine survived far longer in Tasmania, but it was hunted so ruthlessly by early British settlers, who were convinced it was a menace to their sheep, that it had become rare in the wild by 1910. The last confirmed specimen was trapped in the Florentine Valley in 1933 and died three years later in Hobart zoo; and in 1936 the animal was declared 'probably extinct'.

Yet the thylacine has never entirely disappeared from view. Government-sponsored hunts in 1937–8 and 1945–6 found clearly identifiable tracks, and more than 400 eyewitness sightings have been logged since 1936 – a total that compares more than favourably with the number of reports of most mystery animals. Steven Smith of the National Parks and Wildlife Service, who conducted a further hunt for evidence in 1980, estimated that about a third of these reports were of high quality, and found that in many of the cases the observer was less than thirty feet away from the quarry.

One typical incident occurred in March 1982, when a veteran bushman named Hans Naarding, who was camped near the headwaters of the Salmon River in north-west Tasmania, was woken at about two a.m. Grabbing his flashlight, he shone it around and discovered a large animal about eighteen to twenty feet away. It certainly looked like a thylacine: 'It stood absolutely still, and every part was clearly visible. It was a fully-grown male wearing a fine sandy-coloured coat which was in good condition. I counted 12 black stripes over its back. It had a massive, angular head with small rounded ears. The tail was very slender, but very thick at the butt, quite unlike the tail implant of a dog.' When Naarding moved to fetch his camera, the animal made off; but it had lingered long enough to leave a strong, musky smell, which the bushman compared to the distinctive scent of a hyena.

The idea that a small population of tigers might have survived the sixty-or-so years since their supposed extinction in Tasmania does not seem too outlandish, but zoologists have been troubled by the fact that there are an additional 500 reports describing thylacines on the Australian mainland, where their survival appears far more problematic. Nor are these sightings concentrated in one or two inaccessible areas; they stretch all the way from Queensland south to the environs of Melbourne, where a creature known as the Wonthaggi Monster has been seen more than 100 times in the past four decades, and as far west as the sea, 100 miles south of Perth. There are reports from the north too, including the discovery of a small fragment of leg bone in the Kimberleys, a mountainous region of north-west Australia, which was dated to around 1890 by a radio-carbon analysis of the bones that surrounded it (the fragment itself was not subjected to carbon dating because the process would have destroyed it).

Hard evidence is still scarce, even though one witness, a professional pig hunter named Kevin Cameron, recently came forward with six photographs which appeared to show the tail and hindquarters of a tiger nosing its way through the bush near Yoongarillup. The pictures aroused considerable interest at first, but it was soon pointed out that they had been taken from so many different angles that they could not, as Cameron had claimed, have been photographed in '20 or 30 seconds'. The pig hunter's credibility was further dented by his announcement that, in order to minimise noise as he tracked down his prey, he had stripped off his trousers and hunted the tiger in his underpants. In the absence of a better quality of proof, the case for thylacine survival remains persuasive but unproven.

The Quest for Dinosaur Survivors

The idea that the thylacine could survive a few decades of 'extinction' in Tasmania, or even a few thousand years of competition with the dingo in remote areas of the Australian bush, seems plausible indeed when set alongside the astonishing notion that lost worlds, populated with whole colonies of dinosaurs, which have somehow survived the tens of millions of years that separate us from the age of reptiles, still lie buried deep in the rain forests girdling the equator. Yet reports of dinosaur survival in central Africa go back to the early years of this century – further, if we include curious native rock-drawings of four-legged, long-necked animals, or a 1776 description of three-foot-wide, clawed footmarks, seven feet apart, which a French priest, the Abbe Proyart, observed on the forest floor during a journey through Gabon, the Cameroons and the Congo.

The first real clues to the mystery emerged in 1913, when a German expedition to the Likouala area of the Congo produced reports of a water beast that dwelt in the larger rivers of the area – an animal the pygmies called *mokele mbembe*. According to the local pygmies, it was 'of brownish-grey colour with a smooth skin, approximately the size of an elephant; at least that of a hippopotamus. It is said to have a long and very flexible neck and only one tooth but a very long one; some say it is a horn. A few spoke about a long muscular tail like that of an alligator.' Though the description did not match that of any known dinosaur, the members of the expedition found themselves excited by the prospect that they might be on the trail of prehistoric monsters.

Just after the war, there were further reports of sightings in the Belgian Congo (these proved to be a hoax) and a flurry of interest in a similar body of stories from the area around Lake Bangweulu in Northern Rhodesia (now Zambia), where a hippopotamus-eating, amphibious monster was supposed to dwell. Another tantalising contribution to the meagre store of evidence was made by the explorer Leo von Boxberger. 'The belief in a gigantic water-animal, described as a reptile with a long, thin neck, exists among the natives throughout the Southern Cameroons, wherever they form part of the Congo basin,' von Boxberger wrote. 'The name *mbokalemuembe* [is] given to the animal.'

All in all, though, the case for the Congo dinosaur remained a very long way from being proven when the first cryptozoological expedition to the area was made in 1979. Its leader, a Texan herpetologist named James Powell, had heard tales told by the Fang people of Gabon about a strange animal they called *n'yamala*, which lived in swamps in the interior. To Powell's considerable excitement, the handful of reports that he was able to assemble described an animal closely resembling the gigantic long-necked sauropod diplodocus. The creature was said to dwell only in remote lakes, and to subsist on a local vegetable called 'jungle chocolate'. Powell's principal informant, a local witch doctor, claimed to have seen *n'yamala* himself around 1946 as it emerged from the N'Gounie river. It was over thirty feet long, he said, mostly neck and tail, and weighed at least as much as an elephant. He insisted that, unlike the Germans' *mokele mbembe*, it did not have a horn. Intrigued by these sightings, Powell and Roy Mackal, a Chicago biochemist who was one of the founders of the International Society of Cryptozoology, decided to visit the Congo in the hope of gathering further reports from the local people, investigating the biology of the swamps and, if possible, photographing *n'yamala/mokele mbembe* – they concluded that one creature was probably responsible for both sets of reports.

The first problem was choosing where in the thousands of miles of steaming jungle to look. Hypothesising that *mokele mbembe* was either drifting towards extinction or perhaps withdrawing to ever more impenetrable areas to avoid the encroachment of man, Mackal and Powell identified the weed-clogged Likouala-aux-Herbes river and its surroundings – in particular an isolated body of water called Lake Tele, a full five days' march from the nearest local settlement – as the most likely lair of any dinosaur survivors. The area was so little-known that two separate expeditions failed to reach the lake. Mackal and his colleagues were, however, able to identify other spots in the jungle where *mokele mbembe* reportedly lived: the Ubangi river, Lake Tebeki (a smaller body of water near Tele), and the northern stretches of the Likouala-aux-Herbes. They also collected a number of new eyewitness accounts of sightings of dinosaurs.

One of the most dramatic came from a Congolese hunter named Nicolas Mondongo, who was seventeen when he had his encounter on the banks of the Likouala-aux-Herbes, at around seven a.m. one morning in the 1960s. He was hunting for monkeys when a huge creature reared out of the river only thirteen yards away from him, the river waters cascading down its shoulders as it came. The Likouala-aux-Herbes being only three feet deep at that point, Mondongo got an unusually good look at the monster as it emerged. It had a six-foot-long head and neck, the thickness of a man's thigh and crowned by a frill like that of a rooster, four sturdy legs and a tail longer than its neck. In all, the hunter estimated that the animal was around thirty feet long. He watched it for about three minutes before it disappeared back into the river.

A second, still more important story, was also recorded by Mackal. Interviewing Pascal Moteka, a native of one of the river villages closest to Lake Tele, he was told that his people had once attempted to prevent a group of *mokele mbembe*s from entering the lake and disturbing their fishing by erecting a barrier of stakes across one of the seven streams that link Tele to the local river systems. When one of the animals tried to force its way through the barrier, the pygmies succeeded in spearing it to death. Unfortunately for cryptozoology, the giant corpse was butchered and eaten (perhaps as a kind of celebration of the victory), and there were no surviving witnesses: all those who consumed the monster's flesh soon died.

Collating his data, Mackal reported that the general consensus of the local Congolese was that *mokele mbembe* was a real and very large animal, but one that was only rarely observed. It was generally described as red-brown in colour, with a long neck topped by a small, reptilian head, a thicker body and a long, whip-like tail. The local people believed that it inhabited deep pools in the river bank and emerged, most often, early in the morning or late in the afternoon, particularly during the dry season. On the rare occasions when it came onto land, it left large, three-clawed footprints. Finally, the witnesses asserted that the creature made no noise but could be fearsome if provoked; its preferred method of attack was to come up beneath a canoe, tip the occupants into the water and then kill them with powerful strokes of its tail. When Mackal and Powell showed some of the local people picture-books of dinosaurs, the witnesses identified either sauropods (thick-legged herbivores such as brontosaurus) or long-necked, flippered plesiosaurs, as *mokele mbembe.*

Mackal and Powell were not the only ones to penetrate the Likouala swamps at this time. A former colleague, Herman Regusters, mounted his own expedition while the two crypto-zoologists were in the field, and he and his wife actually succeeded in reaching Lake Tele in the autumn of 1981, becoming, perhaps, the first westerners to do so. As well as returning with sound recordings, plaster-cast footprints and samples of possible dinosaur droppings, the Regusters claimed a sighting on the lake. They were followed by a Congolese expedition led by Marcellin Agnagna, a zoologist from Brazzaville zoo, which arrived at Tele in April 1983. Agnagna, who has been prominently involved with most western dinosaur-hunting expeditions, claimed a spectacular sighting of *mokele mbembe* about 300 yards out on the lake. The creature held its thin, reddish head – tipped with crocodile-like oval eyes and a slender muzzle – about three feet out of the water, and turned it from side to side as though looking for him. Just behind the neck, Agnagna said, there was a long black hump. He thought the animal was definitely a reptile, but not a crocodile, a python or a freshwater turtle. Sadly, he reported, an unfortunate camera problem prevented him from actually securing a film record of the sighting.

The lure of the living dinosaur set at least six further

expeditions trecking through the swamps towards Lake Tele in the next decade. Disappointingly – or perhaps tellingly – little further evidence emerged, though one group was able to confirm the existence of turtles, python and crocodiles at Tele and another returned from the Congo convinced that the sightings were nothing more than misidentifications of forest elephants crossing lakes and rivers with their trunks raised.

The elephant hypothesis is only one of a variety of theories proposed to explain Congolese reports of *mokele mbembe*. The most obvious – that the animals really are dinosaur survivors – requires the climate in the Congo region to have remained unchanged for millions of years, and for the animals themselves to have escaped both the extinction that overtook the rest of the dinosaurs and the notice of predators, including man, as well as to have somehow avoided the problems of disease and, perhaps, inbreeding for all that time. Those who find this impossible to believe, on the other hand, or who wonder why there are not more sightings on record by now, have suggested that some witnesses who do believe they have seen *mokele mbembe* may have actually encountered one of the large freshwater turtles common in the region, or that the native people are describing, not flesh and blood creatures, but jungle deities no more real than visions of the Virgin Mary.

It is certainly noticeable that the people of the Likouala region hold *mokele mbembe* in considerable dread; when the American traveller Rory Nugent did finally sight what he thought might be the elusive monster, far away across the waters of Lake Tele, his guides discouraged him from closing in to obtain a close-up photograph by holding a shotgun to his head.

Though all the evidence suggests that superstition flourishes in the region, it is also worth wondering just how 'primitive' the inhabitants of the interior actually are. Scientists who go on expeditions equipped with dinosaur picture books routinely suppose that the local people know nothing about such creatures, but this seems to be a dangerous assumption. As well as being occupied by western powers for several decades during the colonial period, the Congo is presently home to missionary groups whose activities include many educational projects. The growing wealth of the country has also created opportunities for the people of the interior to visit modern capitals fully equipped with television, libraries and universities.

In short, the image of the 'ignorant savage' is becoming increasingly unrealistic, not just in the Congo but in other undeveloped places, and cryptozoologists may well be forced to make greater allowances for their increasingly sophisticated informants. In the Likouala region, for example, questions have already been raised about the methods employed by some monster-hunting expeditions. As the initially friendly local people became more suspicious of their visitors, and information about the creatures was increasingly hard to obtain, some westerners began to distribute large sums of money. This worrying practice has allowed sceptics to argue that the visitors are being told what their hosts thought they wanted to hear, thus undermining much of all-important eyewitness testimony for *mokele mbembe*. This is a significant problem: though the oral evidence for dinosaur survival is intriguing, physical evidence of almost any sort is noticeably lacking.

Snakes in Green Hell

Several thousand miles to the west, the all but impenetrable rain forests of South America promise to conceal giant unknown animals of almost equal interest. Cryptozoologists have collected isolated accounts of large otter-like creatures, twelve-foot armadillos and even unknown species of apes. One of the most promising leads, however, concerns an animal bigger and perhaps more deadly than any of these.

For the last two decades, Dr. David Oren of the Goeldi Natural History Museum in Belem has hunted a monstrous beast, known to the forest people as *mapinguary*, which is said to roam the Matto Grosso. Though earlier cryptozoologists had tentatively identified the animal as an unknown ape, Oren believes that it is probably a surviving giant ground sloth similar to the prehistoric *mylodon*, which is thought to have become extinct around the time of Christ. Sloths are generally thought of as slow and defenceless herbivores, but the accounts that Oren has collected suggest that the *mapinguary* has an unexpected and devastating defence: a scent-secreting gland in its belly, which emits a stench so foul that the creature is known to the hunters of the rain forests as 'the beast with the breath of hell'. Though the *mapinguary*'s unusual weapon appears to have preserved it from capture so far, Oren has obtained fragments of what he believes are the animal's hair and faeces. It seems possible that DNA tests on the hair might produce enough evidence to allow the animal to be classified.

By far the most dramatic reports with South American mystery animals, however, are those that describe encounters with truly gigantic serpents. The Amazon is already home to the largest known species of snake, the anaconda, a semi-aquatic reptile which hunts largely in the rivers that riddle the rain forests and is known to grow up to thirty feet in length; but this is a mere fraction of the size that the giants of some unexplored areas of Brazil and Venezuela are said to reach. It is, admittedly, notoriously hard to gauge the size of living animals in the wild, and harder still to do so when they are snakes, which lie coiled or move in horizontal undulations; indeed, in such circumstances it is possible for the untrained eye to exaggerate length by up to one hundred per cent. But even if we exclude every report of a living giant, we are left with a number of cases involving dead animals that have been more or less carefully measured and shown to have reached extraordinary lengths.

The celebrated British explorer Percy Fawcett made just such an observation in 1907, during an expedition to explore the borders of the Matto Grosso. His canoe was drifting along the Rio Abuna, deep in the Amazon jungles,

> when almost under the bow there appeared a triangular head and several feet of undulating body. It was a giant anaconda. I sprang for my rifle as the creature began to make its way up

the bank, and hardly waiting to aim smashed a .44 soft-nosed bullet into its spine, ten feet below the wicked head. At once there was a flurry of foam and several thumps against the boat's keel, shaking us as though we had run on a snag.

With great difficulty I persuaded the Indian crew to turn in shorewards . . . We stepped ashore and approached the reptile with caution. It was out of action, but shivers ran up and down the body like puffs wind on a mountain tarn. As far as it was possible to measure, a length of 45 feet lay out of the water and 17 feet in it, making a total length of 62 feet. Its body was not thick for such a colossal length – not more than 12 inches – but it had probably been long without food. I tried to cut a piece out of the skin, but the beast was by no means dead, and the sudden upheavals rather scared us. A penetrating foetid odour emanated from the snake, probably its breath, which is believed to have a stupefying effect, first attracting and then paralysing its prey. Everything about this snake was repulsive.

Fawcett's report was so extraordinary that it exposed him to criticism at the time, and since he disappeared, mysteriously and for good, during another expedition into Amazonia in 1925, it is not possible to verify it now. But in 1947 it was backed up by Serge Bonacase, a Frenchman who joined an expedition to explore the Middle Araguaya river and establish relations with the Chavante Indians. Traversing a swamp between two tributaries, the Rio Manso and the Rio Cristalino, Bonacase's party came across an anaconda asleep in the grass. A volley of rifle fire killed the beast, which was measured with a length of string and proved to be between 72 and 75 feet long. Unfortunately, no one in the party was aware of the significance of their kill at the time, and no attempt was made to preserve a bone or a piece of flesh; nor were any pictures taken.

Four photographs, published in provincial Brazilian newspapers, do purport to show giant boa constrictors in the Amazon jungle. One is a head-on shot of what was said to be a 130-foot-long, five-ton specimen killed near Manaos; another, a snapshot of what is said to be a 100-foot-long corpse drifting downriver at the mouth of the Amazon; a third depicts a giant of 98 feet, killed on the banks of the River Negro; and the last portrays a snake, purportedly 115 feet long, which was despatched in a ruined fort by 500 bullets from a machine gun. All, however, are of limited value as each lacks a convincing indication of scale.

What this scattering of cases from the sweating hell of Amazonia does seem to suggest is that every unexplored wilderness on earth may conceal zoological treasures of extraordinary richness. The Australian outback, for example, has yielded reports not just of thylacines, but of unknown marsupial tiger-cats, twelve-foot giant kangaroos – even monstrous monitor lizards, anything up to thirty feet long. And there can be little doubt that there is plenty of room in the trackless backwoods for such animals to flourish, food for them to catch and eat and, in many cases, an absence of obvious predators to threaten their survival.

Indeed, the real problem, though most cryptozoologists scarcely acknowledge it, is not so much to show that mystery animals could exist, as to explain why there appear to be so very many of them, whether there are good historical records of their presence, and how they can continue to be seen, heard, and photographed from year to year without ever actually providing incontrovertible proof of their reality.

The Apes Among Us

Of all the mystery animals sought by cryptozoologists, giant apes are, in some respects, the most mysterious. This is, in part, because they are astonishingly ubiquitous. Although most people have heard of the Abominable Snowman of the Himalayas and North America's Bigfoot, few realise that similar traditions exist in Australia – where ape-like animals are known as yowies – in Hubei province in central China, and among the Pamir mountains along the Russo-Chinese border. In Japan, the area around Mount Hiba is supposedly inhabited by the 'Hiba-gon monster', a five-foot-tall humanoid with a triangular face. Even little Andros Island, in the Bahamas, is home to the fearsome yay-ho, and populous and thoroughly explored Europe has produced recent sightings in the Pyrenees.

In May 1993, for example, six woodsmen working in the mountains of Aragon were cutting trees when, a worker named Manuel Cazcarra recalled, they came across a strange being some five-and-a-half feet in height: 'Suddenly we heard a scream, some squeals . . . I went up to see what had happened. And when I saw him, he had climbed a pile, was clutching a branch with both arms and legs, and he was screaming. The distance between us was about 90 metres.' Later that week, someone or something broke into Cazcarra's Land Rover, and unknown footprints were found nearby.

In fact, the earliest surviving reports of hairy man-beasts come from Europe. Such cases date back to the Middle Ages, and a time when much of the continent was covered in thick forest and man was still the servant of nature and not its master. Medieval Europe was full of legends of giant, hairy men – the *wodewose*, 'wild man of the woods' or 'lord of the woods' as they were known – who, shunning or shunned by civilisation, preferred to roam the forests. Some were armed with staves, and many seemed to possess a measure of authority over the animals of the forest. They often responded with hostility to any humans who chanced upon them.

There is no doubt that one of the *wodewose*'s functions was to be a symbol of both the literal and the figurative wilderness. The anthropologist Myra Shackley suggests: 'For the mediaeval peasant, the wildman was simultaneously an allegorical figure, the centre of a cult, the real or legendary inhabitant of wild places, and a traditional figure. These ideas cannot be separated. . . . Unable to recognise the existence of God – a catastrophe to the mediaeval mind – wildmen were outside society both physically, because they lived beyond its boundaries, and socially, because they observed none of its conventions.'

It is important to note, at this point, that the one thing the *wodewose* was not was some primitive form of man or relict hominid, though this is the most usual explanation advanced to account for wildman reports today. On the other hand, the lord of the woods was not an entirely legendary being, and there is some reason to suppose that a few men really did live wild in the forests at this time, many of whom were lunatics or mentally handicapped people who were liable to be violent or unpredictable.

The really interesting point is that the tradition of the wild man of the woods survived in Europe as late as the sixteenth century, which makes it quite possible that it was taken to America by early immigrants, perhaps along with the custom of abandoning lunatics and unwanted and handicapped children to the mercies of the wild. This may help to explain some of the earliest reports of wild men of the woods in Canada and the United States.

Records of wildmen seen in the American wilderness go back to the early years of the nineteenth century. Nevertheless, it would be true to say that the modern era of Bigfoot sightings dates only to the summer of 1958. That August, a bulldozer operator called Jerry Crew, who was working on a road-building programme near Bluff Creek, California, reported that he had found a line of huge footprints, which approached and circled his vehicle where he had left it overnight. Each print was of a naked foot some 16 inches long, and the stride varied from 46 to 60 inches – about double that of the average human.

Crew's account was the first Bigfoot report to receive wide press coverage, and it sparked a wave of further reports. Yet although later research was to turn up many earlier accounts, it is important to remember the incredulity with which Crew's report was received by the cryptozoological community of the time. Ivan Sanderson, a British naturalist who was widely regarded as a leading authority on Bigfoot's more famous cousin, the yeti, admitted that at first he found the idea of large ape-men at large in the United States 'quite barmy'. Yet such was the surge of interest in the subject that within no more than a year or two, the idea that Bigfoot did exist was firmly established not only among crpytozoologists, but in the minds of the general public.

One reason for this is that encounters with hairy bipeds can have an immediacy that is hardly matched elsewhere in the cryptozoological canon. In October 1980, for example, Charles Fulton and his family were watching television in their rural home in Mason County, Kentucky, when something turned the back door knob. Fulton and his mother-in-law, Anna Mae Saunders, went to investigate. Opening the door, they found a huge animal standing on their porch holding a rooster. Mrs Saunders took in the bizarre sight. 'It was a big, white fuzzy thing,' she recalled. 'I never saw its face; it was above the [seven-foot-high] door.' As the huge creature backed away, Fulton grabbed his gun and fired two small-calibre bullets into the figure. He was sure he had hit it, but it neither flinched nor made a sound as it made good its escape.

Still, Kentucky is hardly classic Bigfoot territory, and the majority of accounts have come from southern Canada and the north-west United States. The backwoods west of the Rockies are a particularly fertile area for encounters with sasquatch, and one of the more interesting cases on record concerns the experience that William Roe, of Edmonton, had on Mica Mountain in eastern British Columbia. He was climbing through the wilderness towards a deserted mine one October day in the 1950s when he saw what he took to be a grizzly bear about seventy-five yards away. As he recalled,

> I could just see part of the animal's head and the top of one shoulder. A moment later it rose up and stepped out into the open. Then I saw it wasn't a bear.
>
> It came across the clearing directly towards me. It was about six feet tall, almost three feet wide, and probably weighing near 300 pounds, covered from head to foot with dark brown, silver-tipped hair. As it came closer, I saw by its breasts that it was female, yet its torso was not curved like a female's.
>
> It came to the edge of the bush I was hiding in, within 20 feet of me, and squatted on its haunches. Reaching out its hands, it pulled the branches of bushes towards it and stripped the

leaves with its teeth. I was close enough to see that its teeth were white and even. The head was higher at the back than at the front; the nose was broad and flat. Its neck was unhuman, thicker and shorter than any man's I have ever seen.

Finally, the wild thing must have got my scent, for it looked directly at me through an opening in the branches. A look of amazement crossed its face. Still in a crouched position, it backed up three or four short steps, then straightened up and walked back the way it had come, throwing its head back to make a peculiar noise that seemed half laugh, half language.

Few people have come closer to Bigfoot than that, but one who did was Albert Ostman, a Canadian prospector who claimed to have been kidnapped by a sasquatch in 1924. Ostman, who did not tell his story until 1957, explained that he had been camping out at Toba Inlet, opposite Vancouver Island, when his sleeping bag was suddenly scooped up, with him inside it, and he found himself slung over the shoulder of a large ape-like creature, which carried him deep into the woods. Eventually Ostman was thrown down among a family of sasquatch comprising the large male who had abducted him, an adult female and two young. They kept him prisoner for nearly a week until he was able to escape by feeding the male chewing tobacco, disconcerting the creature sufficiently to create a diversion.

Incredible though it is, Ostman's account has been taken seriously by many cryptozoologists. One reason for this is that his descriptions of his captors seem to accord with what is known or suspected about the sasquatch's morphology and behaviour. Although true Bigfoot sightings are scarce, several hundred cases have gone on file since 1958. They generally describe a shaggy, bipedal monster some seven-and-a-half-feet tall, heavily built, and solitary by nature. Most Bigfeet have small or non-existent necks, flat noses and faces crowned by a brow sloping up to a conically-shaped crown. The gigantic footprints they leave in soft ground and snow are seen much more frequently than the animals themselves. They are generally at least fifteen to eighteen inches long, and around seven inches broad.

The creature's habits suggest that it is still extremely primitive. Bigfoot is not generally a tool user and does not seem to be able to communicate other than in growls and yelps. Nevertheless, the sheer range of activities that have been observed is quite remarkable. Janet and Colin Bord summarise some of the more eccentric portions of the casebook as follows: 'Bigfoot has been seen performing a number of likely and unlikely actions, such as tearing open bags of salt, ripping open an electric power box, jumping on a car roof, throwing dirt through a car window, tossing a tyre and rim, smashing 20 feet of sluiceway into pieces against a tree, throwing a goose at a woman, throwing rocks, playing with a camp fire, destroying camping equipment, chasing people but not attempting to catch them, clam-digging on a beach, and spiking fish on sticks.'

Perhaps more tellingly, there are also some peculiar discrepancies in the physical evidence, which cast doubt over the simple conclusion that Bigfoot is simply a large, ape-like animal. For example, not every trail of footprints displays five toes. There have been many reports of four-toed and even three-toed beasts, and plaster casts exist to prove it. Moreover, the American cryptozoologist Mark Hall has collected a number of highly anomalous reports of creatures that he calls 'True Giants', which are up to fifteen feet tall – twice the height of an 'ordinary' seven-and-a-half-foot sasquatch. True Giants, Hall believes, are survivors of the supposedly extinct primate species *Gigantopithecus*. His theory has not been warmly welcomed by the cryptozoological establishment, not least because it strains credulity to imagine man-like apes of such a height escaping notice for long, and most authorities believe that Hall's proposed 'very bigfoot' seems altogether too tall not to be a story. Yet the witnesses that Hall can muster are not obviously less sincere than those who describe Bigfoot as a more acceptable seven and a half feet in height.

Many thousands of miles away, in the soaring mountain

borderlands between China, India and Nepal, dwells the abominable snowman, or yeti, a large, shaggy-haired ape-man, which is seen even more rarely than its American cousin. Like Bigfoot, however, the yeti leaves evidence of its presence, largely in the shape of footprints that appear in the snow covering lonely mountain passes. Unlike the Pacific coast or the Pyrenees, which appear isolated but nevertheless enjoy road and rail links that make it possible for weekend hikers to explore them, the lands of the yeti really are inaccessible, which perhaps explains why they are so rarely seen by outsiders. Another theory is that the creatures are not really mountain dwellers at all, but live in the dense and uninhabited forests that cover the foothills of the Himalayas.

Although only a tiny handful of western mountaineers and explorers have even claimed to have sighted a yeti, belief in the Snowman is widespread amongst the local people. In the old stone monastery of Thyangboche, set, amid firs and birches, on a spur above the Imja Khola valley in the shadow of Everest, Lord Hunt (leader of the expedition that first conquered the world's tallest mountain) was told by an ancient abbot that

> a yeti had appeared from the surrounding thickets, a few years back when the snow lay on the ground. This beast, loping along sometimes on its hind legs and sometimes on all fours, stood about five feet high and was covered by grey hair.
>
> Oblivious of his guests, the abbot was reliving a sight imprinted on his memory as he stared at the scene of this event. The yeti had stopped to scratch – the old monk gave a good imitation, but went on longer than he need have done to make his point – had picked up snow, played with it and made a few grunts – again he gave us a convincing rendering. The inhabitants of the monastery had meanwhile worked themselves into a great state of excitement, and instructions were given to drive off the unwelcome visitor. Conch shells were blown and the long traditional horns sounded. The yeti ambled away into the bush.

Though the yeti's fame has outshone that of other wildmen from the central Asian plateaus, some of the most intriguing cases actually come not from the Himalayas but from the Pamir mountain range to the west. In 1934, for example, the Russian geologist B.M. Zdorick was travelling across a remote plain when he stumbled on what appeared to be a sleeping wildman. The creature was lying face down on the ground, with its shaggy, red-brown legs and feet in view, and its head and torso hidden behind a bush. Some of the ground around its sleeping place had been dug up, and scraps of fur and drops of blood were scattered about. Zdorick and his guide chose to retreat rather than investigate further.

Nearly fifty years later, in 1980, a teenager called Nina Grinyova had a rather better view of the Pamir wildman. She was walking along a river bank when she saw a figure

> standing some 25 metres away, facing me and piercing my very soul with his glance. It was not aggressive, rather well-wishing, but piercing. The eyes were big and glowing. . . . And all his body was sort of glowing. He was dark and at the same time somewhat silvery. I could see his body was covered with hair but it was not shaggy. He was about two metres tall. His figure looked very hefty, square and straight from shoulder to hip, with a short neck, the head put forward, the arms hanging down freely.
>
> I began to slowly advance to him. Having gone about five steps, I held out and pressed two or three times a rubber toy in the shape of a bird to attract [the creature's] attention. But it was this that spoiled our contact. [It] made a sharp turn and quickly went down the slope towards the river. I noted the softness and grace of his walk, though he moved very fast. It was not a human walk.

Many explanations have been advanced to explain reports of Bigfoot, the yeti and their kin. The most popular is that the witnesses are actually seeing bears, which can be a frightening and an imposing sight when rearing on their hind legs. There can be little doubt that some sightings in both the Himalayas and the north-west United States can be explained in this way, as can a number of ambiguous tracks.

Another theory, which deserves some credence, suggests that many early wildman sightings were, quite literally, reports of wild men – hermits who had chosen to live rough in the woods, and whose unkempt hair and tattered if not non-existent clothing lent then an almost supernatural air. The American researcher Michael Shoemaker, who has carefully re-researched every available pre-1900 'Bigfoot' case, found that from a database of sixty-three reports, anything up to thirty-nine could be attributed to wild people, seven to bears and twelve to outright hoaxes. Shoemaker concluded that he had

> uncovered several definite points that weigh heavily against the case for Bigfoot's existence. The most startling is that . . . in almost a third of cases, the descriptions themselves clearly do not correspond to the current conception of a Bigfoot, generally exhibiting an absence of two of Bigfoot's principal characteristics, its great height and terrible smell. Only two cases can be reasonably attributed to a Bigfoot, and even in these the descriptions are exceptional. The search for the historical Bigfoot thus ends with a definite result: no historical Bigfoot has been found, apparently because it does not exist.

Robbed of its historical antecedents, the case for Bigfoot immediately becomes much flimsier. There seems little chance that wildman witnesses are encountering captive animals that have escaped or been released into the wilderness, and less that Bigfoot could have survived in the north-western United States for well over a century without being encountered by trappers, hunters or hikers.

The problem becomes particularly acute when it is realised that the first modern Bigfoot sighting – Jerry Crew's report of the strange footprints that surrounded his bulldozer – has been critically re-evaluated by several leading researchers in the last two years. Suspicions have grown that this key case may in fact have been a hoax perpetrated by Crew's boss, a man called Ray Wallace. Not only has Wallace reported a suspicious number of sightings of his own in the last forty years; he has admitted to hoaxing footprints and even produced dubious photos of a female Bigfoot which he claimed to have purchased from an anonymous photographer.

Mark Chorvinsky, who has researched the Crew and Wallace cases, concludes: 'Wallace's claims have been so over the top that Bigfooters have dismissed him, but his involvement in the Birth of Bigfoot case makes him a key figure – if not the key figure – in the cultural history of Bigfoot. . . . There was no Bigfoot in California before 1958. Bigfoot, a cultural spawn of Mount St Helen's apes and the Abominable Snowman, was brought to California by Ray Wallace.'

Other Bigfoot hunters dispute Chorvinsky's conclusions, pointing to the hundreds of unexplained eyewitness reports, and to the occasional find of suspected ape droppings and the numerous plaster casts of giant footprints that have been collected. It does seem, though, that if proof positive of the existence of giant ape-creatures is to be found, it is most likely to come from China, where a whole series of expeditions searching for the *yeren* of Hubai province resulted in the collection of no fewer than 8000 samples of suspected wildman hair. A preliminary analysis of the hair suggested that it came from a higher primate closely related to *homo sapiens*. Even if they had gone unchallenged – which they have not – the findings are not enough to show exactly what the *yeren* might be, much less prove the existence of wildmen in other parts of the world. They are, however, enough to excite cryptozoologists and suggest that further research might finally demonstrate the reality of one of the most perplexing mysteries of the century.

Paddlers in the Deep

Early on the morning of 1 May 1934, Kathleen MacDonald was standing on the shores of Loch Ness when she saw a 'brownish, drab-coloured' mass rise from the water about forty yards away. As she watched, the object slowly changed shape until it had become one large, central hump with smaller, shallow humps at either end. Splashes could be seen in the water, which MacDonald assumed marked the presence of flippers or legs.

Before long, a fourth hump appeared in front of the other three, and a few moments later this lifted itself clear of the water and showed itself to be an undulating neck, topped by a small head. Then the animal began to move very slowly across the surface, leaving a swirling in the water at its rear, which MacDonald thought might have been produced by a tail. She watched its progress for about ten minutes, until the creature suddenly sank vertically, leaving hardly a ripple on the smooth surface of the lake.

By this time, there was little doubt in Kathleen MacDonald's mind that the animal she was watching was none other than the Loch Ness Monster, a fantastic creature that had attained national prominence a year earlier, almost to the day, after the local paper, the *Inverness Courier*, picked up a story about a Mrs MacKay's sighting of two blue-black humps rolling in the water at practically the same spot that MacDonald's monster had surfaced.

Strong press interest, and a welter of sightings at the lake along the newly cleared north road – more than 30 in 1933 alone – quickly helped to elevate the Monster to an iconic status. It became, first, the subject of cartoons and the butt of jokes, and, later, both the unmistakable symbol of the Scottish highlands and the subject of the most costly and the most protracted search in the annals of cryptozoology. In this way, the Loch Ness Monster achieved an international prominence that no purely local cryptozoological mystery had ever done before.

The Monster's fame – like most mystery animals it is always written of in the singular, though of course it is now generally presumed that there must be a breeding population of animals in the loch – has always tended to obscure the fact that it is not alone. There have been sightings, very similar to those reported from Loch Ness, in nearly a dozen other highland lakes. As recently as September 1996, for example, guests at the Corriegour Lodge Hotel on the shores of Loch Lochy, at the southern end of the Great Glen, watched a creature with three humps swimming in tight circles on the surface. There had been earlier sightings at the lake in 1929 and July 1960. At Loch Canisp, far to the north in Sutherland, Kenneth MacKenzie of Steen was alarmed by a huge animal with a head like a hind's which loomed out of the water over the stern of his boat as he rowed through the gloom one evening in the 1930s. And at Loch Morar, on the west coast, the deepest lake in Europe, there are records of some forty sightings going back to the end of the nineteenth century.

The most dramatic was made by two lorry drivers, William Simpson and Duncan McDonnell, at dusk on 16 August 1969. The men were returning in their small motorboat from a day's fishing. McDonnell was at the wheel when he 'heard a splash or disturbance in the water astern of us. I looked up and about 20 yards behind us this creature was coming directly after us in our wake. It took only a matter of seconds to catch up with us. It grazed the side of the boat.' William Simpson 'came out of the cabin to see my mate try to fend the beast off with an oar. To me he was wasting his time. . . I seen the oar break and I grabbed my rifle and quickly putting a bullet in it fired in the direction of the beast. I then watched it slowly sink away from the boat and that was the last I seen of it.'

Between them, the men estimated the monster's length at twenty-five to thirty feet. It had three shallow humps or undulations, a snake-like head about a foot across, and a rough, dirty-brown skin. McDonnell thought it might have been an overgrown eel.

McDonnell and Simpson saw no blood and no sign that the bullet had struck the animal. But then, there has always been something a little supernatural about Scottish lake monsters. In local folklore, most lochs are haunted by their own water-horse (*each uisge*), a malevolent spirit which often comes ashore in the guise of a beautiful thoroughbred for the principal purpose of luring unwary passers-by onto its back. If they are unwise enough to mount the water-horse, it will instantly gallop back into the loch and drown them. Loch Morar had an especially complex tradition. Its monstrous guardian, *a Mhorag*, was a sort of mermaid with long, fair hair and a snowy bosom, whose infrequent appearances on the surface of the lake foretold doom for the Gillieses on the north shore of the lake.

It is clear from some traditions that the water-horse *could* look much like the modern conception of a lake monster. At Loch Arkaig, in the 1850s, Lord Malmesbury heard his stalker mention that he had recently come across the loch's denizen at close quarters, and that it had a head like a horse and a hollow back. When Malmesbury announced that he would take his hunting rifle with him the next time he walked down to the lake, the stalker 'observed very gravely, "Perhaps your lordship's gun would mis-fire." ' What is less certain is whether, as cryptozoologists tend to assume, the water-horse was a flesh-and-blood animal credited with supernatural powers by the superstitious highlanders, or whether, as some folklorists have argued, modern lake monster sightings are no more than updated versions of an encounter with a water-horse, and about as real.

It is almost certainly true that the great fame of the Loch Ness Monster has influenced the way in which other lake monsters are perceived and reported. There are, today, several hundred lakes scattered around the world which are reputed to be the homes of monsters, and those monsters are almost always described as having small heads, long necks and a series of low humps – the stereotypical description of 'Nessie', which became so familiar in the 1930s. It would, however, be wrong to suggest that the monster of Loch Ness is some sort of archetype on which all other lake monsters are based. There are strong traditions of similar animals in at least two other lakes, which pre-date the first modern reports from Scotland.

One of these lakes is Okanagan, in British Columbia; its denizen, which is known as Ogopogo, has featured in local newspaper reports since the 1920s, and a scattering of earlier sightings have been put on record since then. The other is

Lake Storsjon, the Great Lake, which lies far to the north of Stockholm, amid the forests and the mountains of central Sweden. Storsjon is bigger and deeper than Loch Ness, and was quite isolated until the railway and the logging industry opened up Jamtland province in the mid nineteenth century, bringing with them an influx of new settlers, journalists and newspapers to report on their doings.

Thus it was that, in 1893, the *Ostersund Post*, published in the only large town on the shores of the lake, printed a report on the strange sight seen by Karin and Marta Olssen, two young women who had gone down to the lake to wash clothes. As they did so, they noticed an object out in the lake, which approached them at high speed and stopped only a few yards off-shore. It was the head of a large animal, held just out of the water and round like a dog's. It was grey in colour, with large black spots, and had big, saucer-like eyes and an open mouth, the interior of which was a dark red colour. After a while Karin gathered some stones in the hem of her dress and began to throw them at the creature, which responded by coming even closer in-shore. Terrified, she ran back up the bank while her sister shinned up a nearby tree. From her new vantage point, Marta got a better view of the animal as it churned up the water. It had a neck eight or nine feet long, she thought, a further fourteen feet of body, and two forefeet or flippers. Finally, it turned away from shore and swam off, leaving a large wake.

The Olssons' encounter, and other reports from the lake, encouraged the formation of a company dedicated to trapping the monster. It is said to have hired a Norwegian whaler who waited in a little hut on a specially built jetty for the monster to show itself, without success. A more productive approach was tried by a naturalist, Peter Olsson, who interviewed local people and searched the newspaper archives, unearthing a total of twenty-two sighting reports from Storsjon dating back to the 1820s. He concluded that the monster did exist, and was probably an unknown species of long-necked seal.

Olsson's work highlights the problems that confront cryptozoologists when they attempt to identify water monsters. His theory made sense of the monster's dog-like head and its large eyes, and also of a curious detail noticed by several other witnesses who asserted that the creature had ears, a distinctively mammalian trait. On the other hand, seals have to breathe air every few minutes, which means that any seal-like lake monsters should be seen at the surface far more often than they are. Nor could they survive at a lake such as Storsjon, which freezes over in winter, without leaving clues as to their presence.

Rival theories have their own pros and cons. For more than a century, the most popular has been that water monsters are actually plesiosaurs – long-necked, fish-eating reptiles from the dinosaur era. The fossil records show that plesiosaurs do indeed look more like the popular image of the Loch Ness Monster and its kin than any other animals. Yet the theory requires its supporters to believe, not only that the plesiosaur somehow survived the mass extinction of the dinosaurs and the next 70 million years of history unscathed, but that such reptiles could prosper in the icy waters of the northern lakes in which they are seen. In addition, plesiosaurs, as air-breathers, share many of the drawbacks of long-necked seals when it comes to finding reasonable solutions to the mystery. The same is true of a more recent hypothesis, which suggests that a species of prehistoric whale, the zeugoldon, is responsible for such reports.

The only rival theories that have much merit both take the sensible route of suggesting that some water monsters are fish. There are two plausible candidates – the first an unknown species of giant eel and the second the sturgeon. Both explain why lake monsters are so rarely seen at the surface. An eel might additionally account for reports of long necks thrust above the surface, but on the other hand the animal is generally a bottom-dweller, and to explain the plethora of records that describe lake monsters' backs as 'like an upturned boat', any super-eel would need to exhibit a highly abnormal thickening of its central body. The sturgeon theory, on the other hand, cannot easily explain neck sightings but does have one huge advantage: we know that specimens big enough to explain lake monster sightings do exist. A mature sturgeon can live to be 100 and measure nearly twenty-five feet in length. Fish of this size have certainly been responsible for some lake monster reports: for example, rumours of a giant animal in Lake Washington, near Seattle, were confirmed when an eleven foot sturgeon was found dead there in 1987.

There are, then, a number of animals that might explain the hundreds of reported sightings of lake monsters. But matters become more complicated if we approach the problem from a different angle and wonder whether such animals could enter and survive in the lakes where they are found. In the case of Loch Ness, for example, it is generally said that the lake was formerly an arm of the sea and was cut off from it about 10,000 years ago, at the end of the last ice age. From then on, the only access to the sea was via the River Ness, which is not only extremely shallow for much of its length, but also flows straight through the large town of Inverness, the 'capital of the highlands'. Cryptozoologists, therefore, tend to suggest that, far from entering and leaving the loch from time to time, a small colony of monsters has been cut off there since the retreat of the sea and survived the intervening millennia by interbreeding. It has been estimated that a minimum population of between sixteen and twenty-five animals would be required to sustain the species.

This theory poses some serious problems, which are not, rather remarkably, addressed in the standard works on the subject. The first is the question of whether Loch Ness contains enough fish to support a stable population of such large animals. Estimates of the loch's foodstocks have varied from one tonne to around twenty-six tonnes of fish – the former not nearly enough, and the latter only just sufficient to support large predators. The second question is whether any tiny breeding herd could hope to survive in isolation for 10,000 years without being wiped out by disease, particularly when it is remembered that zoologists estimate that in-breeding would be expected to cause insuperable genetic problems within a mere handful of generations.

Lake monsters, in fact, do seem to flourish in the face of the most astonishing obstacles. At Lake Dakataua, on the Pacific island of New Britain, for example, a creature known as Migo was twice filmed by a Japanese documentary crew in the years 1994 and 1995. The video footage, which lasts for several minutes and is the longest piece of monster film ever shot, appears to show a twenty-foot animal with a low snout, domed head, shallow back and long tail crowned with spines. By any standards, Migo seems to be a large animal, and one which might be expected to have a substantial appetite. Yet Lake Dakataua is a sterile lake, its alkaline content so high that it contains no fish. The only available source of food is the ducks that flock on the surface – yet, if their numbers were being decimated by ravenous lake monsters, one might expect them to seek a safer sanctuary on one of the other lakes on the island. Similar objections can be raised to the suggestion that real animals dwell in 'China's Loch Ness', Lake Tianchi, which lies near the border with North Korea. Although a handful of sightings of a dragonlike creature have been made there in the last decade, it is hard to reconcile them with the fact that the lake fills the crater of a dormant volcano, which last erupted about three centuries ago.

All in all, it seems much more likely that if large water monsters do exist, they survive in the seas and oceans, where food stocks are plentiful and the chances of being photographed or captured are slight. There are indeed several hundred reports of the creature popularly known as the Great Sea Serpent on record. They come from every portion of the globe, date back more than four centuries, and their number includes several highly persuasive accounts made at close range by experienced seamen. In 1848, for example, a huge animal was observed by four officers and three men of the frigate HMS *Daedalus*, south of St Helena, while on passage from the Cape of Good Hope to Plymouth. According to Captain Peter M'Quhae,

> it was discovered to be an enormous serpent, with head and shoulders kept about four feet constantly above the surface of the sea, and as nearly as we could approximate it . . . there was at the very least 60 feet of the animal above the surface. It passed rapidly, but so close under our lee quarter, that had it been a man of my acquaintance I should have easily recognised his features with the naked eye.
>
> The diameter of the serpent was about 15 or 16 inches behind the head, which was, without any doubt, that of a snake, and it was never, during the 20 minutes that it continued in sight of our glasses, once below the surface of the water; its colour was a dark brown, with yellowish white about the throat. It had no fins, but something like the mane of a horse, or rather a bunch of seaweed, washed about its back.

At its closest, the animal came within about 100 yards of the ship.

Similarly, Captain R.J. Cringle of the SS *Umfuli* saw, on 4 December 1893, a large animal surface about 400 yards away. It had three connected humps, the middle one larger than the other two (much like Kathleen MacDonald's monster in Loch Ness), and its long neck soared a full fifteen feet above the surface of the water. It was moving very rapidly, its speed being estimated at about fourteen knots.

On occasion, some evidence has emerged to suggest that sea serpents are indeed flesh and blood animals. Shortly after the Second World War, the liner *Santa Clara*, steaming south off the coast of North Carolina, encountered a large animal that appeared just off its bow. Three of the ship's officers saw it.

> The creature's head appeared to be about two and a half feet across, two feet thick, and five feet long. The cylindrically shaped body was about three feet thick and the neck about one-and-a-half feet in diameter. As the monster came abeam of the bridge it was observed that the water around it, over an area of 30 or 40 feet square, was stained red . . . It was assumed that the colour of the water was due to the creature's blood and that the stem of the ship had cut the monster in two.
>
> From the time the monster was first sighted until it disap-

peared into the distance it was thrashing about as though in agony.

Then there are a number of sea serpent strandings to consider. The most famous incident occurred as early as 1808, when what appeared to be a long-necked, six-legged sea-beast was washed ashore at Stronsay in the Orkney Islands. Its identity remained a mystery for a while, but fortunately a few fragments of its cartilaginous skeleton were preserved, allowing the carcass to be recognised as the decomposing remains of a huge basking shark. This species of shark is responsible for a good number of apparent sea serpent strandings. A rotting basking shark soon loses its lower jaw, its dorsal fin and the upper lobe of its tail, leaving a carcass that bears a remarkable resemblance to a plesiosaur. The outer layer of skin then vanishes too, exposing tough, fibrous white bristles that often cause witnesses to assume that the dead 'monster' possessed feathers.

Dead whales, too, can sometimes be mistaken for sea serpents. Perhaps the most spectacular such case occurred early in 1969, when a twenty-four ton carcass measuring seventy-two feet was washed ashore at Tecolutla in Mexico. Part of the body resembled a monstrous head and neck, some twelve feet tall and more than six feet wide. Eventually, however, the remains were identified as those of a rorqual.

Appropriately enough, one of the very few carcasses that remains mysterious was dragged from the stomach of a sperm whale killed off the west coast of Canada in 1937. It was the remains of a twelve-foot-long serpentine animal with flippers, a serrated tail, and a head somewhat resembling a camel's. On the basis of three surviving photographs taken at Naden Harbour whaling station showing the creature stretched out over a long table and two packing cases, two Canadian scientists have suggested that the carcass was that of an unknown species of reptile. Unfortunately, the animal they describe would be a highly inefficient swimmer, and probably incapable of the sort of high speeds that many sea serpent witnesses report.

Indeed, the whole business of classifying sea serpent sightings has proved highly contentious. Sorting through a total of more than 580 reports, Bernard Heuvelmans, the leading authority on the subject, drew the influential conclusion that it was possible to discern up to nine separate, undiscovered species, ranging from long-necked seals to giant marine crocodiles and from prehistoric whales to enormous eels. In 1996, however, a reanalysis of these findings by the German cryptozoologist Ulrich Magin showed not only that the database from which Heuvelmans worked contained many poor quality reports and outright hoaxes, but that many of the most detailed sightings in the casebook – such as that made by the officers of HMS *Daedalus* – resisted attempts to fit them to Heuvelmans's categories. Furthermore, Magin points out, that the 600 or so sighting reports from tiny, isolated Loch Ness themselves exhibit such a startling variety that it would be possible to argue that all nine species of sea serpent must be present in the lake. In short, Heuvelmans's system of categorisation seems seriously faulty.

Indeed, Magin's persuasively argued paper, while ostensibly of interest only to marine zoologists, is actually of much greater importance than that. Heuvelmans's categorisation of sea serpent reports was one of the foundation stones of cryptozoology's claim to be a reputable science. By demonstrating its considerable inadequacies, Magin leaves open the question of whether the Great Sea Serpent – and by extension its cousins the lake monsters – is an animal at all.

'I think "scientific" cryptozoology is something like "scientific" ufology,' he concludes. 'In both, witness reports are taken literally, at face value, which leads to the most complex, irrational and paranoid belief systems in ufology (for example alien abduction), and to the "discovery" of dozens of uncatchable creatures in cryptozoology.'

Magin may be right or he may be wrong, but he has certainly identified a problem confronting every visitor to the borderlands. Whether or not the things that are seen there should be 'taken literally' is the central problem of the second part of this book. But before we can consider such matters it might be wise to keep our feet on the ground and turn to a consideration of the quite different challenges posed by a group of strange phenomena known collectively as 'earth mysteries'.

6

The Good Earth

In 1985, at the height of a violent series of confrontations between the police and groups of travellers, pagans and greens who wished to celebrate the summer solstice at Stonehenge, the British authorities announced that they were taking steps to prevent alternative festivities being organised elsewhere by stationing guards at other significant sites 'where ley lines intersect'.

The idea that, somewhere among their files on serial killers and terrorists, the police keep notes on the location of major leys may seem ludicrous, but if nothing else the story does demonstrate just how familiar the concept of ley lines has become since the idea was first proposed more than seventy years ago. Today the suggestion that straight lines linking ancient sites stretch not just across Britain but other countries, from Europe to South America, is accepted by thousands of people who have never attempted to plot such an alignment on a map, much less actually gone out to 'walk the ley', as the serious researchers prefer to do. Many are also aware that leys are supposed to act as conduits for a mysterious sort of energy that courses through the earth like blood through the veins of a living animal, and perhaps even that if this energy is somehow blocked or stopped, a so-called 'black ley' is created, resulting in all sorts of psychic mischief and general misfortune for those living nearby.

That is the popular conception of leys, and all most people know of the broader subject of 'earth mysteries' – a discipline that actually deals with far more than mere ley hunting, embracing geomancy (the art of controlling and refining man's interaction with the landscape), dowsing, and the possible existence of ancient civilisations, and touching on archaeology and folklore. Yet the universal notion of leys is far from an accurate reflection either of the way in which such alignments were originally conceived, or of the direction that earth mysteries research is taking today.

Ley lines, as they were initially conceived by Alfred Watkins, the businessman and photographer who first described them, were no more than the remnants of prehistoric pathways: 'the old straight track', which guided travellers from one part of the country to another before the Romans came and built their roads, and helped them to progress in safety from one marker to the next. Watkins's proposition – which he backed up with a considerable amount of fieldwork, mostly carried out in his native Herefordshire – was that ancient man deliberately placed standing stones, cairns, mounds and beacons to link outstanding natural features, such as tumps or notches in hillsides, and create the tracks. The implication, radical enough in the 1920s though much less startling today, was that prehistoric man was no painted savage, who built monuments such as Stonehenge with brute strength and little subtlety, but an able mathematician and a fine surveyor, much more civilised than many contemporary archaeologists believed.

Watkins went further than this, though. He suggested that, while the ancient trackways had, at some point, fallen into disrepair, their upkeep had once been one of the principle responsibilities of the local community, and that the later constructors of paved roads, castles and churches had taken advantage of this well-maintained network of sites when they came to build their own structures. As a direct result, he argued, it is still possible to follow many leys today, despite the havoc wrought on the countryside by the growth of towns, the construction of motorways, and modern intensive farming techniques.

In the seventy years since Watkins first published his theory, several thousand ley lines have been plotted in the English countryside. This is a superficially impressive achievement. Yet it is important to remember that there is no generally recognised definition of what a ley actually is. Many of the lines discovered by casual ley hunters consist of only three or four points, whereas most specialists admit that such leys can easily be produced by chance alignments and agree that, to be valid, a ley should consist of a minimum of five points. There is even less agreement about how wide a line may be. Watkins thought that leys ought to be the width of an ancient trackway – no more than four yards. Modern ley hunters seldom, if ever, work to such tolerances, and some have allowed their 'alignments' to be up to a hundred yards out.

There are real dangers in being so imprecise: the statistician and ley critic Robert Forrest has pointed out that the probability that ley lines are no more than chance alignments increases dramatically if a single marker some fifty yards out of alignment is allowed to form part of a ley. Similarly, the length of a claimed line has a strong bearing on the likelihood that it is genuine: most ley hunters accept that alignments of more than twelve miles are significantly more likely to be the product of chance. This does, of course, have strong implications for Watkins's original theory of straight trackways, since such purely local leys would have been of little use in guiding a traveller. Towards the end of his life, Watkins himself began to suspect that his leys might be more than simple pathways.

Years of statistical analyses have reduced the number of apparently genuine leys to a mere handful. One alignment, which even Forrest agreed seemed beyond mere chance, occurs in Yorkshire, where a group of giant monoliths known as the 'Devil's Arrows' – the tallest standing stones in Britain, bar one, rising to more than twenty-two feet in height and spaced 200 yards apart – is aligned with Nunwick Henge and the three Thornborough Henges, forming a ley eleven miles long. Oddly, even ley hunters concede that the stones at the heart of this most famous of leys are not in a straight line. The northernmost of the three surviving Devil's Arrows is noticeably out of alignment with its sisters and, as Devereux and Thomson concede, 'there is no doubt that they had a definite purpose . . . if the stones are not in a line, then they were constructed that way'.

Hundreds of miles to the south, meanwhile, another well-surveyed ley has been identified running the eighteen and a half miles from Frankenbury Camp to a tumulus north of Stonehenge. As well as Stonehenge itself, this ley passes through Old Sarum, Salisbury Cathedral and an old earthworks known as Clearbury Ring. Again, years of careful work on the alignment of this ley have served to point up slight imperfections in the line: it passes just to the east of Salisbury Cathedral's spire, slightly to one side of the central alignment of Stonehenge, and brushes the edges of Frankenbury Camp and Clearbury Ring. Critics may seize on this discovery, but perhaps it simply confirms that our distant ancestors, who marked out the alignment, were only human, and not guided by the superior technology of aliens or other superbeings, as another popular theory has it.

Local ley lines such as these form the basis of earth mysteries research, but despite the general proscription on more ambitious lines, the existence of much grander alignments (known as 'primary leys') has also been suggested from time to time. One, the 'Great Isosceles Triangle of England', is supposed to have as its apex the Arbor Low stone circle in Derbyshire, a spot from which anything up to 150 separate leys are said to radiate, and which some ley hunters have identified as the centre of Britain's ley network. From there, according to the earth mysteries researcher Philip Heselton, primary leys run south-west 152 miles to St Michael's Church at Orthery in Somerset, and south-east a similar distance to West Mersea in Essex.

Over the years, Watkins and the ley hunters have had to answer two principal objections to his theory. The first and simplest was advanced by O.G.S. Crawford, who edited the journal *Antiquity* in the 1920s. Crawford refused to take an advertisement for Watkins's book on the grounds that the theory could not be correct, since all known surviving prehistoric pathways wended their way through the countryside, as modern roads still do; marching in a dead straight line through and over any obstacles is seldom the easiest way to get from one place to another. Other contemporaries pointed out that some areas were so rich in supposedly significant markers, such as barrows, that it was ludicrous to suggest they were all needed to guide travellers on their way. The second, and still more deadly, objection has been raised by statisticians such as Robert Forrest, who have questioned whether the alignments discovered by earth mysteries researchers even exist. A country as old and as densely scarred by man as England contains so many monuments and mark-stones, clumps of trees, beacons, barrows and churches, they argue, that anyone running a ruler over a map is bound to find an apparently significant alignment sooner rather than later.

Ley hunters have been quick to argue for the reality of their alignments by drawing attention to what they see as similar lines on the landscape elsewhere in the world. While modern earth mysteries research has remained a predominantly British affair (though the subject enjoyed a certain vogue in Weimar and Nazi Germany), it has been argued that ancient cultures had many similarities, perhaps because contact between them was greater than mainstream historians and archaeologists suspected. Watkins cited contemporary references to show that roads in the Chin district of India followed the most direct line between villages, regardless of obstacles, and that, believably enough, the desert peoples of Africa used the few readily identifiable landscape features – a clump of trees here, an oddly shaped hill there – as navigation points. Several American

Indian tribes also seem to have laid out straight tracks, and, in Bolivia, paths marked by cairns of stones have been laid between sites, apparently aligning themselves on mountain tops.

Since relatively little work has been done to research such foreign alignments, it remains a moot point whether some of them really exist and, if so, whether they are straight enough to qualify as leys. Critics of the ley line theory have also expressed concern about ley hunters' willingness to build their lines from what are known as 'mixed markers' – a combination of genuinely prehistoric stones and earth features, and much newer ones such as castles – when there may be no evidence that the newer markers are built over older ones. All too often, the presumption is that modern monuments, particularly churches, have been placed on much older sites with the deliberate intention of usurping pagan places of worship, with the result that the number of acceptable ley markers has multiplied significantly.

If this was all there was to ley line theory, we could safely leave its proponents and opponents to wrangle over whether or not leys actually existed and, if so, what they were for. Yet, from Watkins's day to ours, there have always been mystical, pagan and New Age undercurrents to earth mysteries research. In his published works – notably the 1925 book *The Old Straight Track* – Watkins confined himself to a dry recitation of the facts as he saw them, with plenty of topographical exposition and antiquarian detail thrown in. In private, though, he often confided to his followers that the existence of the whole ley network had become apparent to him in a single moment of mystical revelation on 30 June 1921. As his son Allen recalled it,

> A chance visit to Blackwardine caused him to look at the map for features of interest. He had no particular object in mind, but was just having a look around. He noticed on the map a straight line that passed over hill tops through various points of interest and these points of interest were all ancient. Then

> without any warning it all happened suddenly. His mind was flooded with a rush of images forming one coherent plan. The scales fell from his eyes and he saw that over many long years of prehistory, all trackways were in straight lines marked out by experts in a sighting system. The whole plan of the Old Straight Track stood suddenly revealed.

Watkins and his latter-day followers attributed the vision to five decades of intimate daily contact with the Herefordshire countryside (the discoverer of leys was sixty-six when he experienced his quasi-religious conversion). 'I now know,' he wrote in *The Old Straight Track*, 'that in fully half a century's familiar contact with this region my other self had, quite unknown to me, worked at one subject. . . The "spirit of the British countryside" had surely been hovering near.'

For many modern-day ley hunters, particularly those who participated in the explosion of interest in the subject in the 1960s and 1970s, this intimate, spiritual contact with an unchanging countryside is central to the attraction of earth mysteries research. They champion the purity of rural field-work and decry the corruption that the human spirit suffered in the cities. Like Watkins, they are also drawn to the chance to reclaim the study of archaeology and prehistory from the dry-as-dust specialists. (Indeed, every borderlands discipline, from psychical research to cryptozoology, has always held a powerful attraction for enthusiastic amateurs – intelligent people, perhaps without academic training, who have little respect for the restrictive specialisms of the professionals.) Ley hunting, one social historian has noted, 'transformed the countryside into a place of mystery, in which a mundane and unnoticed landmark might be the key to a great pattern stretching back to prehistory'. It is the patina of mysticism, as much as the exhumation of apparently hidden knowledge, that gives earth mysteries research its place among the disciplines of the borderlands.

Mother with a Hollow Heart

There is, though, nothing new about the reverence with which earth mysteries researchers view the land. A vast body of 'folklore of the landscape' survives to show that many of our ancestors saw the earth as an intelligent, living thing to be treated with respect, left undisturbed where possible, and occasionally beseeched for favours. The Chinese, for example, practised (and still practise) a system called '*feng shui*' ('wind-water') which seeks to maintain a natural balance between negative (*yin*) and positive (*yang*) in the landscape, and urges respect for the energy (*ch'i*) which flows through it. Exponents of the art advise on the correct placement of houses, tombs, and other artificial additions to the landscape, as well as recommending modifications to the countryside – the removal of a mountain-top here, the planting of a clump of trees there – to avoid negative energies and maximise the sought-after harmony of the earth. Nevertheless, the energy lines identified by practitioners of *feng shui*, though as invisible as leys, are curved, not straight.

Other western traditions are linked to beliefs in fairies, who were seen as living guardians of the harmony of the landscape. In Iceland, for example (where belief in elves is still relatively commonplace among the population), there appear to have been several recent instances in which the construction of new roads or tunnels was held up by the supernatural malfunctioning of heavy-duty equipment.

One such case reportedly occurred at Akureyri in the far north of the island in 1984. When inspections showed that nothing was obviously wrong with the machinery, a local psychic named Olafur Baldursson was consulted, and the problem diagnosed as insensitivity to the landscape (notably in attempting to drive a tunnel through a hill inhabited by fairies) and the general failure to placate the local nature spirits. The difficulty was solved by re-routing the road. A related tradition, common in Britain, concerns churches that move overnight from one place to another, usually because the original choice of site offended the little people or upset the landscape geometry of the area. Whether or not such stories are literally true – a recent investigation suggests that the Icelandic case may be no more than a modern version of an ancient legend – they do suggest that old traditions may indeed survive to the present day.

An urbanised, forward-looking, scientific mind may find it hard to believe that such unlikely sounding tales have any real significance. But there is another way of looking at them. Paul Devereux, an influential writer who, for twenty years, edited the principal journal of earth mysteries research, *The Ley Hunter*, has argued that the uncovering and understanding of such traditions is central to our understanding of ourselves: 'Earth mysteries research is an attempt to recover what we have forgotten as a race – a remembering. But it is also very much about developing an understanding of the wholeness of Nature in general, and life on Earth in particular – in this guise it is re-membering, a "putting back together".'

Devereux is, of course, right to point out that man has always had good reasons to accord respect to the landscape. The vital importance of ensuring good hunting or coaxing a fine crop from the soil was one. Another may have been the very human tendency to see patterns in the natural world, finding 'simulacra', as they are known. As man explored the planet, he found rock formations that looked like human heads; trees that grew into the shape of animals; and faces in the ever-changing patterns of the clouds. Simulacra can still be seen everywhere around us today. Some exist in miniature: a quarter-century after the death of the cleric Dean Liddell in 1898, a patch of damp and fungus on a wall at Christ Church, Oxford, was observed to have formed 'a faithful and unmistakable likeness' of his profile, which endured for at least three years. Others are on a much grander scale – so grand, indeed, that ancient man was probably quite unaware of them. A recent aerial survey of Ungava Bay, Quebec, resulted in the discovery that a peninsula on the southern tip of the Iles Radisson bore so remarkable a resemblance to the profile of the playwright George Bernard Shaw that the *Commission du Toponymie du Quebec* gave it the name *Pointe Bernard Shaw.*

The grandest idea of all is, perhaps, the notion that our planet itself is a living creature. A few years ago the idea of a sentient earth was revived by Jim Lovelock, an independent scientist (albeit one of some standing) with no university post to risk, who funded his research from the proceeds of his inventions. Lovelock had come to believe that our planet's ability to maintain its temperature, and the levels of oxygen and carbon dioxide in its atmosphere, within the narrow boundaries necessary for life, for hundreds of millions of years, was so remarkable that the whole globe must form part of a self-regulating organism that he called Gaia, after the Greek earth goddess. While positive evidence for this hypothesis is hard to come by (Lovelock, like the Biblical creationists, essentially could not believe that the diversity of life on earth is the result, merely, of chance evolution), it has struck a deep chord in many pagans and ecologists, and it is certainly worth remembering that similar traditions survived from ancient times into very recent history, as earth mystery scholars suggest the ley system may have done.

One example of this body of belief is the widespread notion that certain stones can move or grow. The Rollright Stones, a large group of monoliths situated near Long Compton in Oxfordshire, which are traditionally said to be the petrified remains of a king and his retinue, are supposed to uproot themselves once a year to drink from a nearby stream, and a local tradition has it that when one lord of the manor tried to remove the king's stone to use it to build a bridge, it took every horse he had to drag the rock downhill. So many ominous signs and wonders occurred at Rollright following its removal that it was decided to return the stone to its original site – at which point it was found that a single horse was easily able to pull it back up into position. Suffolk's Blaxhall Stone, meanwhile, is reported to have grown in the course of a century from a rock the size of a loaf into a five-ton boulder.

There is another theory about our world, equally ancient,

which has greatly influenced the worlds of occultism and ufology: the notion that we live on a hollow earth, or, at the very least, one that is extensively honeycombed with giant caverns and cave systems and inhabited by the dead or, perhaps, by not entirely human beings. Walter Kafton-Minkel, one of the few reliable chroniclers of this strange belief, observes:

> A world within a world is one of the most archaic concepts in world mythology, part of the archetypal image of Gaia, the Earth Mother. Many of our distant ancestors told or heard stories of their distant ancestors germinating in the dark cavern-wombs of the Earth Mother, and being born into the bright, cold world of the surface. They knew they would return again to the Earth Mother's arms again one day in death . . . [and feared] being reabsorbed too soon into those dark places, where all sorts of dim 'things' crept.

In the last two centuries, this old idea of an underworld has been supplemented by an altogether more radical one, based on the ideas of an early nineteenth-century American soldier named John Cleves Symmes, who evolved a system called the 'theory of concentric spheres'. Symmes's central idea was that earth (and indeed every other planet in the universe) was hollow, with a crust no more than a thousand miles thick, 'habitable within', and that access to the interior might be gained through large holes situated at the north and south poles. Inside the earth, he predicted, smaller hollow globes would be found rotating. Symmes sought to prove this theory by leading an expedition to the northern hole (this was nearly a century before the supposed conquest of the pole by Robert Peary) with the explicit intention of claiming the interior for the United States. Unfortunately for him, but probably fortunately for the safety of his would-be companions, he was never able to raise the necessary funding. He died, exhausted from constant lecturing in support of his ideas, in 1829.

Though there were enormous problems with Symmes's hypothesis – not least the remarkable implications it had for gravity, the theory of planetary formation, and geography (he claimed the northern polar opening was 4000 miles in diameter, so big that it would swallow much of Canada, Greenland and Siberia) – the notion of a hollow earth has proved surprisingly tenacious in the years since his death. Various theorists elaborated on it (one, Leonhard Euler, came up with the useful notion that a small 'sun', some hundreds of miles across, floated at the centre of the earth, providing much-needed heat and light to the inhabitants of the interior), but it was not until the end of the nineteenth century that the next significant step was taken, when the idea of a hollow earth was enthusiastically taken up by some of the occult societies that flourished at the time.

Groups such as the theosophists (led by the remarkable Helena Blavatsky, a former circus bareback rider who single-handedly conceived many of the central tenets of modern occultism and the New Age Movement) taught that the interior of the earth was the domain of the Secret Masters – benevolent sages possessed of enormous occult powers who guided the fortunes of mankind. From there it was only a short step to linking the hollow earth theory to the Tibetan legend of an underworld city, called Shambhala, ruled over by the King of the World, from which the destiny of mankind was closely controlled.

During the Second World War another alternative hollow earth doctrine surfaced, in unlikely fashion, in the pages of the American pulp science fiction magazine *Amazing Stories*. This one was the work of a man named Richard Shaver, who promoted it by writing a series of astonishing accounts of his adventures in a vast network of underground caverns which, collectively, had a greater area than all the land masses of the surface. Shaver explained that his contact with earth's secret inhabitants had begun when he heard strange voices calling him from out of thin air while he was working as a welder on an assembly line. Later, he had been guided to one of the many entrances to the underworld by a beautiful inner earth girl who rescued him from a hospital where he had been incarcerated to recover either from injuries or a mental breakdown (Shaver gave both versions at different times). Backed by *Amazing*'s enterprising editor, Ray Palmer, the one-time welder insisted that his stories of the inner world were all true.

It hardly seemed likely. Shaver's tales were amongst the wildest ever spun, even in the pages of the pulp science fiction magazines of the period. According to him, the hollow earth was populated by two races: the benevolent Teros and the malevolent – and unfortunately much more numerous – Deros. Both peoples were supposedly descended from an Atlantaen super-race that had abandoned the surface thousands of years earlier when a sharp increase in solar activity made it uninhabitable. Confined to underground caverns hollowed out by the Atlanteans' advanced technology, the Teros succeeded in maintaining some sense of discipline, while the Deros abandoned themselves completely to vice. Some lived their lives in a perpetual debauch, luxuriating in 'sex rays' produced by so-called 'stim machines'. Others indulged in torture, luring human women from the surface, penning them, raping them and then flaying or roasting and eating them when their usefulness was at an end. (Sado-masochism was one of the prominent themes of Shaver's writings.) The Deros' other great pleasure was causing trouble in the surface world with the help of further items of strange weaponry which caused plane crashes and other accidents, and could even be used to boil an unfortunate victim's brain alive in its own cranial fluids. In short, Shaver charged that the evil dwarfs were responsible for almost every misfortune visited upon humankind.

Hardly surprisingly, critics of the 'Shaver Mystery' were quick to point out that its author was suffering from several of the classic symptoms of paranoid schizophrenia, and that many of the letters that poured into *Amazing* recounting personal experiences that backed up the author's stories patently came from the sort of people who would otherwise spend their time claiming that they were being persecuted by invisible voices or their neighbours' dogs. For example, one woman alleged she had been in a lift in the basement of an office building in Paris when she had pressed the 'down' button by mistake:

> The elevator suddenly plunged down below the basement, falling through space as if the cable had been broken. After a rapid drop, perhaps several hundred feet, it stopped with a sudden lurch . . . Through my terror-stricken mind I heard a loud, guttural noise on the other side. The elevator door was torn open with a sudden slam and I saw the most horrible beast in the world . . . His face was of a pale, whitish colour. His short, twisted body was covered with thick, bristly hair. His eyes? Piggish, insensitive to any emotion, and gleaming with evil lust. The creature was fat, almost bloated. There were terrible scars running over most of his body. He had no neck, so his head was placed squarely atop his muscular shoulders.

The creature was, of course, a Dero. For a month the woman was confined to a cage with a group of other females, most of them in a pitiful physical condition, and periodically raped by one or more of her captors. Her life was saved only by a Tero raiding party, which drove off her captors, treated her wounds and returned her to the surface. When the local representative of the Hollow Earth Society spoke to her, months later, the woman told him she had recently been released from a mental hospital – where she had been confined, she explained, by doctors who found her story unbelievable. The hollow earth enthusiast chose to trust her, though, after checking the lift shaft and concluding that it bore evidence of having been recently concreted over.

Entertaining though such unusual cases are, the legend of a hollow earth would probably be remembered as nothing more than an eccentric myth were it not for two significant contributions that it made to the lore of the unexplained. The first is the dubious suggestion that many of the most prominent Nazi leaders were believers in the hollow earth theory, that Hitler himself had sponsored several expeditions to central Asia in search of an entrance to the interior, and that a number of Tibetan adepts from the inner earth – wearing, some said, green gloves – had been found dead in the smoking ruins of Berlin in 1945.

None of this seems to be true. The second is the no less incredible theory that UFOs come, not from outer, but from inner space, flying from their advanced bases inside the earth through the polar openings and out into our atmosphere, and that some apparently paranormal creatures, such as Bigfoot, are really dwellers in a hollow earth. Ray Palmer was one proponent of an inner earth origin for UFOs, though it is doubtful whether he himself actually believed the theory, and the idea was fashionable for a short while among a small minority of American ufologists, unable to believe that earth could be so formidably attractive to extraterrestrials that they would travel light years to visit us, but unwilling to concede that the flying saucers might not be physically real. From there, the hollow earth theories of Symmes and Palmer (not to mention those of still more eccentric writers such as the puritan, frutarian utopian Dr Raymond Bernard), achieved wider notice. It is a testimony to the power of the notion that they have attracted much greater attention than is warranted by the evidence in their favour ever since.

Evolving Concepts of the Ley

Part of the attraction of the hollow earth theory lies in its mystical elements – the idea that cosmic masters gifted with astonishing powers might be living beneath our feet and controlling our destiny – and it is not too much to suggest that the popularity of ley hunting, when it peaked in the 1970s, owned much to a similar impulse.

The intuitions and investigations of these modern-day ley hunters soon led to the replacement of Alfred Watkins's original conception of leys as a network of ancient trackways with the idea that they channelled subtle energies from one point to another. If they were trackways at all, it was argued, they became so long after they were first identified as lines of energy by an able and mystically inclined prehistoric civilisation. Watkins himself, in the instant that he first saw the ley network laid out beneath him, may have suspected as much: he seems to have described the alignments he saw in his vision as shimmering with some sort of energy.

The notion of leys and megaliths as conduits and beacons for earth energies was originally suggested by dowsers. T.E. Lethbridge, a professional archaeologist and amateur dowser who became interested in earth mysteries when the subject was at its lowest ebb, in the 1950s, was among the first to make the connection. After his retirement in 1957, he spent much of his time dowsing ancient sites. Lethbridge's technique was much more sophisticated than that of the traditional dowser with his forked twig; he dowsed with a pendulum, and believed that all manner of buried or concealed objects, from underground streams to buried metal, could be detected by varying the length of the cord from which the bob swung. After further refinement of the theory (which, it is worth pointing out, was never proven to the satisfaction of any scientist), Lethbridge dowsed the Merry Maidens, a group of nineteen standing stones in Cornwall, and finding that he could sense some sort of electrical current passing through the stones, suggested that the megaliths might be acting as accumulators of some sort.

By the late 1960s there was a general belief that leys and ley markers were associated with energy. Traditional dowsers thought that it might involve underground water courses while others suggested it was electro-magnetic in character, not least the many earth mysteries researchers who had experienced strange sensations at certain sites. Paul Screeton, for example, reported that on touching a mark stone at Hart, County Durham, 'I and several others felt a tingling sensation of varying intensity. My wife received an unpleasant shock when touching it one evening.' There is even a 'tingle stone' in Gloucestershire, which is said to discharge a shock like static electricity at certain times.

The first serious investigation of the energy theory did not come until the mid 1970s, when the author Francis Hitching arranged for a dowser named Bill Lewis to check a standing stone at Crickhowell in Wales. When Lewis reported that he had found a spiral line of energy running up the stone, Hitching arranged for his findings to be checked with a gauss meter, which detects magnetic fields. Eduardo Balanovski, the physicist operating the instrument, found that the stone was surrounded by a magnetic field considerably stronger than the background level, which appeared to ascend the megalith in a spiral path much as Lewis had predicted.

Hitching's findings, limited as they were, inspired Paul Devereux and *The Ley Hunter* to set up a more systematic investigation of energy patterns at ancient sites a year or two later. This was the Dragon Project, which has, for nearly two decades, co-ordinated the monitoring of a number of British megaliths, beginning with the Rollright Stones. In its first dozen years, the project concentrated on monitoring physical effects, noting that some stones seemed to produce measurable effects, such as generating ultrasound emissions at certain times of the year, which are audible only to creatures such as bats. It was also suggested that the energy patterns that Hitching appeared to have detected might have been produced by microwave energy from the sun energising the stones at dawn. Nevertheless, one of the project's most significant findings was that there appeared to be no consistency to the energy patterns detected at various sites. Some had background radiation well above the local average, others gave off less radiation than their surroundings. In addition, the energy patterns that were detected varied greatly over time and even depended on the time of day.

It has become apparent, therefore, that there are no readily detectable and consistently measurable lines of energy flowing along ley lines or spiralling up ancient megaliths. The most that can be said of the Dragon Project's findings – which are the product of many years of protracted field work – is that a great deal of further research will be required to gauge whether there is indeed any significance to such patterns of energy as can be detected at megalithic sites. In consequence, while the project's research has had no impact on the public perception of earth mysteries, the inner core of researchers, led by Devereux, have largely abandoned the 'energy line' theory of leys.

Indeed, the idea of leys as alignments of any sort has come under such withering attack by sceptical statisticians in recent years that honest earth mysteries enthusiasts have been forced to agree, in Devereux's words, 'that more is attributable to chance than any ley hunter – including Alfred Watkins – had ever suspected, and that most of us had not always been as meticulous as should have been the case'. This finding, too, has not penetrated far beyond the core of earth mysteries researchers.

In the last few years, this small group has been concentrating its attentions on 'consciousness research' – the idea that ancient sites were not only used for religious rituals involving altered states of consciousness, whether naturally induced or produced by taking hallucinogenic drugs, but actually built by people whose perception of the world was not, indeed could not have been, the same as ours. The great defect of modern archaeology, researchers such as Devereux argue, is that it views the ancient world with a modern eye, remaining obsessed with the engineering problems of constructing megaliths, for example, rather than attempting to understand how a Neolithic or Bronze Age people may have thought, and chosen to interact with the landscape.

One of the central features of consciousness research, and probably its most promising line of enquiry, is its experience-centred exploration of shamanism – the magical religion practised in different forms by many early races, based on the ability of certain special people to enter an altered state of consciousness and there interact with the gods or other elementals on behalf of their people – and in particular, the ecstatic journeys undertaken by many shamans.

These seem, from various accounts, to have much in common with out of the body experiences, but Paul Devereux has argued that they also involved travel in straight lines: 'What I am suggesting is that the exceptionally ancient and now obscure association between spirit and straight linearity in "ceremonial" landscapes is a common denominator that occurs . . . because of the universality of the human central nervous system. The concept of the straight landscape line originates, I suggest, in a fundamental element of the shamanic experience, indeed, in what is arguably *the* central element of shamanism – *magical flight.*'

Casting around for evidence to back up this contention, Devereux and his followers have suggested that, should such ecstatic experiences occur on anything like a regular basis, it might have been assumed that the spirits of the dead would leave their bodies and proceed to the afterlife in a similar fashion. Such traditions have been found in several European countries. In Britain, coffins were sometimes carried to the graveyard along what were known as corpse ways; in Holland, straight tracks known as 'Death Roads' have been discovered in the area north of Hilversum, and in Sweden the bodies of dead Viking chiefs were carried to the burial ground at Rosaring along a 500-yard-long straight track called a 'cult road', aligned precisely north to south. In Germany, the researcher Ulrich Magin identified straight 'ghost paths' that led to cemeteries, along which the spirits of the dead were believed to thrive.

A great deal of work must still be done before it will be possible to say whether this new theory bears any real relation to the old idea of leys. Already it is becoming clear that there are difficulties in attempting to apply the concept too generally; not all corpse ways are straight, and Magin has pointed out that the physical approaches to German cemeteries are almost invariably curved, possibly a legacy of the old belief that straight lines are unnatural and thus somehow evil. There is no doubt, too, that the whole idea of shamanic ecstasy and spirit paths is far less attractive to the New Age audience than the concept of energy-packed ley lines. Nevertheless, this is the area that earth mysteries researchers will be exploring for the next few years.

The Earth Lights Revolution

It may seem curious, now that earth mysteries is moving closer to an association with psychical research, that the first modern ley hunters were drawn into the subject through the study of UFOs. Thirty or more years on, the original link between the two subjects is now no more than a half-remembered relic of the naive days of ufology in the 1950s. Yet, at the time, it was hoped it was the theory that would light the way towards a scientific and quantifiable way of studying flying saucers.

The principal justification for suggesting that two such apparently distinct subjects were linked lay in the work of a prominent French ufologist, Aime Michel. Taking the great French saucer wave of 1954 as a starting point, Michel plotted the location of each day's sightings and discovered that they appeared along alignments that criss-crossed the country. These alignments, which Michel called orthotentic lines, could be viewed as 'celestial leys', though the Frenchman did not make this connection himself. Indeed Michel took pains to point out that the lines did not appear to mark trajectories, since UFOs popped up in odd places along them in the course of a day. During the late 1950s and early 1960s, however, the theory of orthoteny was very popular in ufological circles, not only because other researchers claimed to have discovered similar patterns in Spain, Brazil, North Africa and California, but also because it seemed to be the testable hypothesis that respectable ufologists craved.

Unfortunately for the proponents of orthoteny, however, its very testability proved to be its downfall. Michel's published data soon came under scrutiny. The whole theory was effectively abandoned less than a decade after it had first been suggested when a re-examination of the 1954 wave showed that his database had been badly corrupted by the inclusion of hoax cases and that the location of even apparently genuine sightings could often not be fixed to within half a mile.

Nevertheless, many earth mysteries scholars continued to take an interest in UFOs, and by the mid-1970s Paul Devereux, one of the most creative and persistent writers in the field, began to evolve a new theory that revived the half-forgotten link between the two subjects. His idea, which has become known as the 'earth lights hypothesis', had something in common with Michel's orthotentic lines, in that it suggested that plotting the exact locations of UFO sightings on a map could yield important results. But it was altogether a far bolder theory, which, at least in Devereux's opinion, may help to explain a range of strange phenomena, including a variety of religious visions and reports of 'ghost lights' from around the world.

In essence, though, the earth lights hypothesis is a relatively simple one. Devereux and his colleagues suggest that strange 'lights in the sky' are actually charged balls of electrical energy generated deep beneath the surface of the planet as the result of 'strain fields' set up in the crust by the crushing and cracking of rocks along fault lines. Such balls of energy produce an electromagnetic discharge that can make them intensely luminous. When they escape up into the atmosphere through the faults, they may be reported as UFOs.

What might such an object look like? In his first major summary of the earth lights hypothesis, Devereux cites a case that occurred in the Welsh town of Bridgend, midway through the 1960s, as 'a superb description of the formation of a UFO from a ground emanation'. A couple were standing in their back garden when they heard a noise like that of a distant jet engine and saw a white patch of sparkling mist appear low on the horizon.

> A reddish light then materialised by the side of the mist, joined up with it and then started to blink. The mist then began to glow and pulsate, dividing into two sections. These sections began to spin round and around. The smaller of the two now moved on top of the larger one, giving the overall impression of an object looking like a squashed bowler hat. Lights of many colours now came on the bottom of the object, which now began to solidify into a metallic-looking disc shape with a dome on top, broken only by a reddish glow underneath.

> After this the object spun around for a few minutes and the noise similar to a jet plane began again. Once again the object became mist-like in appearance and the blinking lights reappeared. Then suddenly the whole thing disappeared.

Scientists have known for some years now that balls of light can be produced under certain conditions. In 1981, for example, Brian Brady of the US Bureau of Mines filmed an experiment in which he applied some 32,000 lbs per square inch of pressure to a granite core, crushing it under laboratory conditions. As the core collapsed under the pressure, small balls of light flitted out from it and shot around the crushing chamber. There is also some evidence that the same phenomenon can occur on a much grander scale. During the great T'angshan earthquake of 1976, a British diplomat in that part of China observed dazzling displays of lights in the sky, and also heard aerial booms reminiscent of the phenomenon of 'skyquakes'. Similar events have been reported from Japan several times this century: a straight line of round balls of light appeared over the Idu peninsula during a major earthquake in 1930, and, on 31 March 1982, strange electro-magnetic emissions were recorded on sensitive monitoring instruments about half an hour before an earthquake occurred, measuring seven on the Richter scale.

Most remarkably of all, there are several special places around the globe where such lights appear with some regularity. One is Marfa, a town in south-west Texas, which has sighting records going back to 1883. Another is Hessdalen, a thinly populated valley near the Norwegian border with Sweden, where strange white or yellow luminous globes, which sometimes hovered overhead and sometimes streaked about at great speeds, were reported between 1981 and 1986, accompanied by unexplained rumbling and banging noises. Scientists and ufologists who came together to investigate the sightings managed to film several of the lights and even tracked three on radar, a result that suggested the lights were either solid objects or very strongly ionised globes of gas. (On a further thirty occasions, the radar picked up signs of an object in the sky, which appeared invisible to observers on the ground.)

Many geologists now accept that earth lights are a reality, that they are produced by strain in the earth's crust and that they are therefore likely to be associated with earthquakes, but many mysteries remain to be solved before we can say we understand exactly when and why the lights are produced, let alone whether or not they are responsible for some of the strange phenomena of the borderlands. Dr John Derr, the head of the Global Seismological Survey, observes: 'There is so little we understand about these lights. We don't know exactly how they are generated. We don't know the precise source of the electricity or how it is conducted to the surface of the earth, or how it is focused into the air to produce these lights. We don't know why some of them last much longer than others. So there is much more work to be done.'

Some of the necessary research has now begun. It has been argued, for example, that rock is generally a good conductor of electricity, and that any balls of lights generated in the crust should be earthed before they can escape. According to Jim Byerlee, a geophysicist with the US Geological Survey, however, it may be possible that the same friction responsible for the lights also generates a 'sheath of steam' which coats the fault line with a non-conductive material: water. 'During an earthquake you then have a vaporised region which is an insulator and a central region, where the charge is generated, which is a conductor,' he argues. Unable to earth themselves along the insulated fault, the luminous charge escapes, instead, into the atmosphere.

By their very nature, such earth lights ought to be a short-lived phenomenon, dissipating their energy and their luminosity into the atmosphere relatively quickly. Indeed the fact that there are a number of reports of such lights persisting for several minutes at least, is one of the biggest stumbling blocks to accepting the theory. In Jim Byerlee's view, 'The main problem is that in order to get discharge to cause the lights, you have to have a charge generated and maintained for however long the lights last – and it is difficult to see how you could maintain that charge for very long.' Logic, therefore, suggests that earth lights produced in this manner should be seen very close to fault lines.

Devereux has devoted much of his energy to plotting a possible relationship between faults and UFO sightings. The first such work, conducted with the help of the geologist Andrew York, was carried out in Devereux's native Leicestershire during the 1970s. Plotting UFO reports logged by the local newspaper since 1953, the two researchers suggested that they occurred mostly in local fault areas, a pattern, distorted but not destroyed by the distribution of the population. Devereux has made similar studies in Dyfed and Cumbria, and delved further back into history to suggest that strange lights in the sky, which appeared over the Egryn peninsula in North Wales during a religious revival in the area in 1904–5, were earth lights generated by the Mochras fault, which runs from Egryn north to Harlech.

Such statistical work is vital to setting the earth lights hypothesis on a firm footing, but it must be added that Devereux's work has been subjected to considerable criticism. The reports cited from Dyfed, for example, were mostly collected during a major UFO flap in the area in the late 1970s, which a later reinvestigation by Hilary Evans showed to be composed principally of hoaxes and simple misidentifications. The researcher Kevin McClure, who lived for several years in Leicestershire and who has researched the Welsh religious revival, has pointed out that Devereux's Leicestershire cases were drawn almost entirely from uninvestigated local newspaper stories, which, according to the conventional ufological estimate, suggests that ninety per cent of them probably have conventional explanations. If so, this would strip Devereux's and York's database down to a mere thirteen cases. McClure also notes that seismic activity in the Egryn area seems to have ceased a year before the religious revival in the area began, and believes that reports of lights in the area are more likely to be explained by the religious fervour sweeping North Wales at the time.

Another critic of the earth lights hypothesis, the sceptical ufologist Steuart Campbell, draws attention to another problem: the sheer number of fault lines present even in a geologically relatively inactive country such as Britain. 'Since Britain is criss-crossed with geological faults', he writes, 'it is not surprising that many reports of UFO sightings come from areas close to them.'

Such criticism focuses attention on one of the fundamental differences that exist between earth lights researchers. Devereux and his colleagues believe that such luminosities should be seen not much more than five or so miles from a fault line. On the other hand the Canadian researcher Michael Persinger, author of a related concept known as the tectonic strain theory, has suggested that strain fields may be transmitted great distances through the earth's crust, allowing earth lights to emerge two hundred miles or more from the fault where they have their origin. While tectonic strain theory thus seems able to explain the appearance of lights in the sky even in seismically quiet areas such as the mid-western United States, it has never been conclusively demonstrated that strain fields can be transmitted in this way, and Persinger has been criticised for attempting to apply his theory in a way that is simply not justified by the available facts.

It is worth pointing out, too, that other theories have been advanced to explain the mystery light phenomenon. The will-o'-the-wisp, which looks and behaves much like one of Devereux's earth lights, is traditionally thought to be a somewhat malevolent spirit. It has also been explained as burning marsh gas. Then again, in the year 1908, there were many sightings of red, white and blue aerial lights throughout East Anglia. It was generally believed that these were caused by luminous owls – birds that had eaten phosphorescent fungus, and thus acquired their own eerie glow. Similar reports came from the same area in 1912 and 1921, after which the luminous owls, if they ever existed, seem to have vanished from the earth.

Assuming, for a moment, that Devereux and Persinger are correct, however, the earth lights hypothesis may do much more than simply hold out the possibility that many 'lights in the sky' UFO cases – by far the largest, if unfortunately also the least interesting, category of 'flying saucer' sightings – could have a natural explanation. Both researchers have suggested that these intensely charged globes of energy might do more than simply whiz about the sky confusing people. Persinger, who combines his studies of geophysics with a university career as a neurophysiologist, has proposed that the intense electromagnetic fields generated by his tectonic strain phenomenon may directly act on the brains of witnesses, producing strikingly realistic hallucinations.

As part of his own studies of epilepsy, Persinger applied electrical and magnetic fields to the temporal lobes of volunteers, who experienced sensations varying from a feeling of dreaminess to something more akin to an anomalous experience. It has been speculated that a more intense electromagnetic field might produce out of the body experiences and possibly even a simulacrum of an alien abduction. Devereux, meanwhile, has suggested that the human mind may be able to interact with the earth lights phenomenon by using its inherent psychic abilities – not only being influenced by a geophysical event, but perhaps, in turn, influencing that event itself. This, he feels, may help to explain not just the many reports of balls of light moving about as though they are under some form of intelligent control, but also reports of ghosts and even poltergeist infestations.

It should go without saying that any such correlations are as yet entirely unproven. The statisticians may, in time, demolish the claim that earth lights and fault lines are in any way connected; indeed earth lights, in the form that Devereux and Persinger conceive them, may not even exist and, if they do, they may have nothing to do with UFOs, ghosts, poltergeists and psi. But there is something strangely familiar about

Devereux's theory of fault lines deep within the earth, coursing with an unexplained energy that can manifest itself at the surface. It is all highly reminiscent of the good old days of ley hunting in the 1970s, when every standing stone might mark an unobserved alignment that channelled earth energies from one point to another. It is a connection that has not escaped Devereux himself. Plotting his own huge database of prehistoric sites against known fault lines, he has observed that every stone circle in England and Wales is sited within a mile of a known fault or a surface intrusion. Perhaps our ancestors really were possessed of a hidden knowledge that still eludes us today.

7

Reign of Frogs

'We shall pick up an existence by its frogs,' the American author Charles Fort announced at the tail end of the 1920s. 'Wise men have tried other ways. They have tried to understand our state of being by grasping at its stars, or its arts, or its economics. But, if there is an underlying oneness in all things, it does not matter where we begin, whether with stars, or laws or supply and demand, or frogs, or Napoleon Bonaparte. One measures a circle, beginning anywhere.'

Fort was interested in the connections between things but, more than that, he was interested in those connections that science had rejected as unreal, unintelligible, or unimportant. So he didn't begin to draw his circle by considering the stars, or the laws of supply and demand, but by writing about frogs – specifically, about frogs that fell from the sky. Between 1916 and 1932, he spent years in the great libraries of London and New York, reading and re-reading his way through the scientific literature of two continents and assembling thousands of notes on all manner of strange phenomena. He used these notes to compile four books about apparently inexplicable events, which chronicled the connections that he found in his material in a difficult style but with humour and a sharp intelligence.

Most cultures have their collectors of strange phenomena. In the past, some were grand, and salaried by the state; today, most are self-appointed, and labour alone in some half-forgotten archive. Imperial China employed an official with the imposing title 'Inspector of Invading Oddities' – an astronomer whose job it was to collect and catalogue omens, portents and reports of strange events from throughout the Empire. It was vital work, for unusual events were considered an important indicator of how well the Emperor was doing his job: a good ruler controlled a land in harmony, and a bad one a country in which strange happenings outraged the natural order on an increasingly regular basis.

In the 1920s the United States had Fort, and it had Robert Ripley, who created the syndicated 'Believe It Or Not' newspaper strip and filled it with the eccentricities of the world, travelling incessantly, while back at home in New York City his researcher Norbert Pearlroth (a man who spoke eighteen languages) read his way through a forest of magazines and journals in search of other oddities. Unlike Fort, Ripley favoured human oddities, such as Weng, the 'human unicorn' – a Manchurian who sprouted a foot-long horn from the back of his head – or the man who could kill, pluck, butcher, cook and eat a chicken in one minute, fifty seconds.

Robert Ripley, thanks to his syndicated newspaper column, was read by millions; Fort by hundreds. But some of Fort's readers were energetic people. Eventually, a group of his admirers banded together to found a Fortean Society, and there are still a few score Forteans around today, performing the same task that Fort had set himself: the collation of all manner of source material dealing with strange phenomena. They are interested in religious phenomena, in parapsychology, ufology, cryptozoology and earth mysteries, but – being Forteans – many have a special affection for the phenomena excluded from consideration by these broad and sometimes insular disciplines and wonder whether, by collecting and studying such data, they may not discover connections that the cryptozoologists, the parapsychologists and the ufologists have missed.

The Opened Heavens

Fort's first work, *The Book of the Damned*, began with a discussion of the strange things that have tumbled from the sky. Falls were perhaps his favourite phenomenon, and he collected, from the scientific press, reports of an astonishing variety of things that had descended from the heavens: everything from alabaster to worms, but particularly frogs, fish and ice. Sometimes they came down in showers or storms, but occasionally they fell from a clear sky, which seemed much more mysterious.

Many people are vaguely aware that strange falls have been reported, but suspect that such accounts are tall tales that cannot possible be true. No one who has actually studied the phenomenon shares this view. It is impossible to dispute that many things do rain from the sky. They did so in Fort's day, and they still do today, in similarly outlandish combinations and in equal abundance. The mystery is not whether, but why and how they come down.

Falls of fish and frogs are still pretty much commonplace: on 22 February 1994, for example, hundreds of spotted perch – each between one inch and two inches long – were found flapping about in the carpark of the Dunmarra Wayside Inn, 370 miles inland in the desert Northern Territory of Australia. A week later there was a second fall of slightly larger fish in the same place during a heavy storm in which about five inches of water fell overnight. But, just as in 1920s, more unusual objects continue to rain from the skies. A piece of grilled halibut plummeted to earth in Barnes, a suburb of London, in February 1981, wedging itself into a garden fence. It was still edible. Amongst a wide variety of other foodstuffs, beans rained down in Joao Pessoa, Brazil, in the summer of 1971. Salvador Targino, on whose farm they fell, thought that they might have come across the Atlantic from west Africa, but it proved difficult to test the theory because he boiled the beans for dinner. Less palatable was the brown shower that descended on spectators at Craiglockhart Tennis Club, near

1. An image of Christ in clouds over Korea

2. Vision of the Virgin Mary in the skies over Pontmain, France, in January 1871.

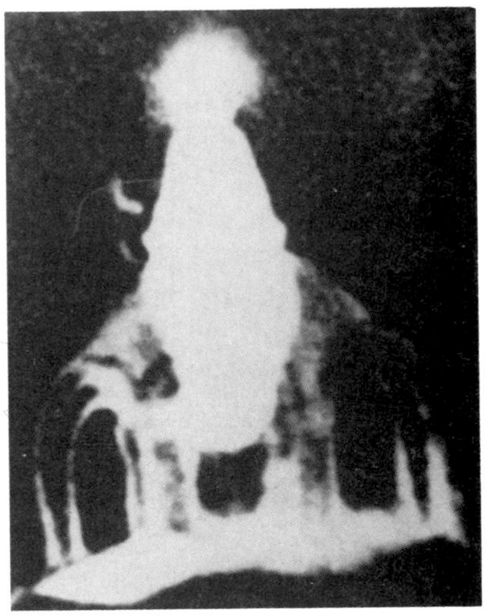

3. Vision of the Virgin Mary above Coptic church at Zeitoun in Egypt in 1968.

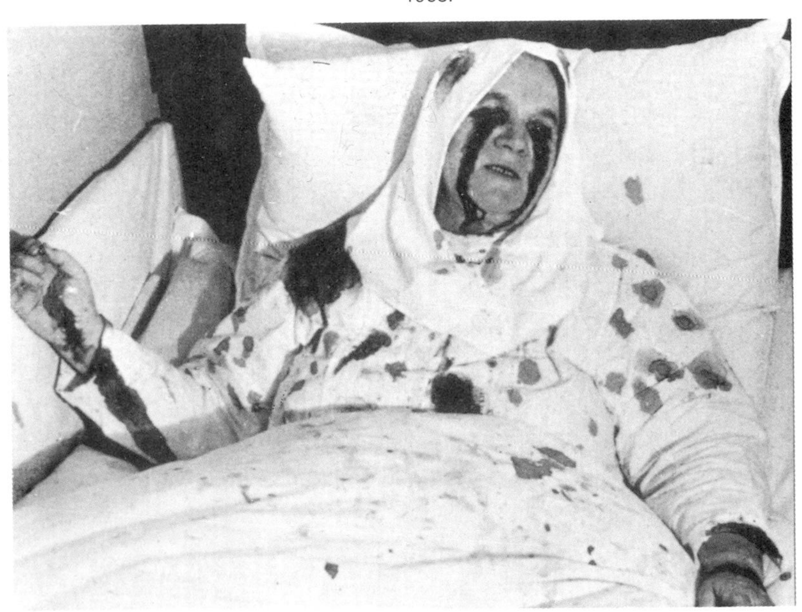

4. The stigmatic Therese Neumann, who bled each Friday for thirty-six years.

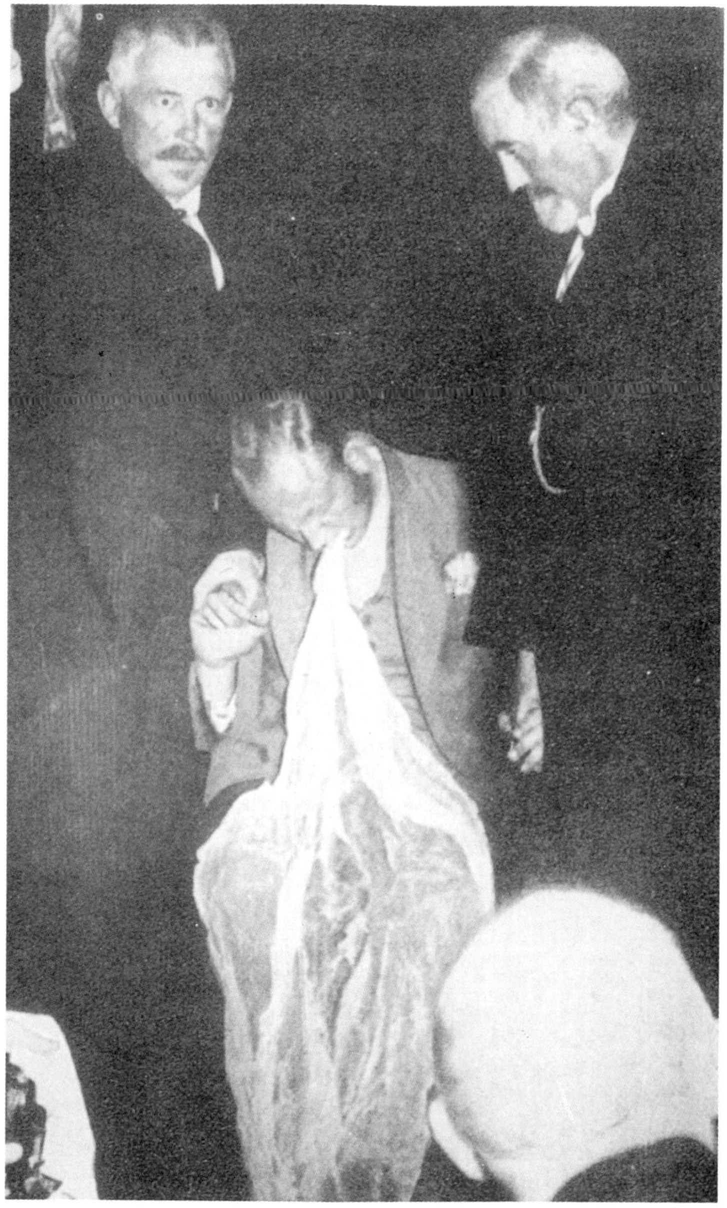

5. The Norwegian psychic Einar Neilson producing ectoplasm in September 1921.

6. The Irish medium Kathleen Goligher materialising a 'psychic rod' from her vagina.

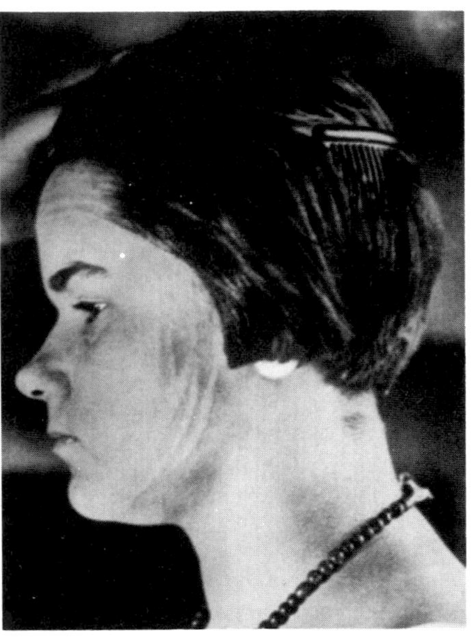

7. Eleonore Zugun displays wounds her investigators concluded were inflicted on her by an invisible assailant.

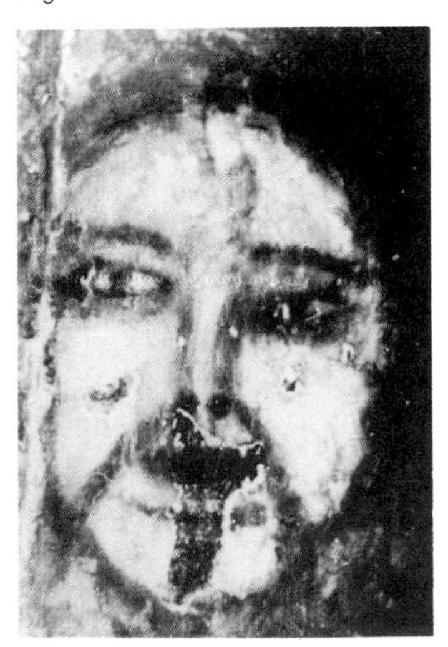

8. One of the many faces which appeared on a concrete floor in the Andalusian village of Belmez – one supposedly built directly over an old graveyard.

9. Samples of the 'Martian' script produced by the late nineteenth century mediums convinced they were in touch with inhabitants of the Red Planet.

10. A photograph taken at Raynham Hall in Norfolk during the 1930s which is often said to portray the 'Brown Lady' who is supposed to haunt the house.

11. An artist's impression of some of the dozens of radically different alien races encountered by UFO witnesses in the last 50 years:

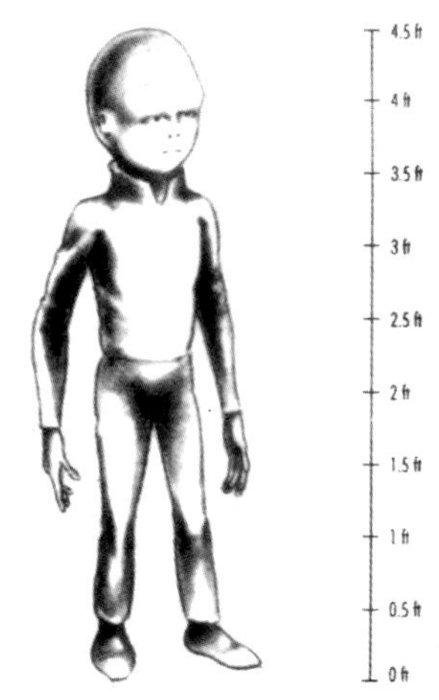

11a. a Grey – by far the most commonly reported alien of the last two decades.

11b. one of the hairy dwarfs encountered by Jose Antonio da Silva in Bebedouro, Brazil, in May 1969.

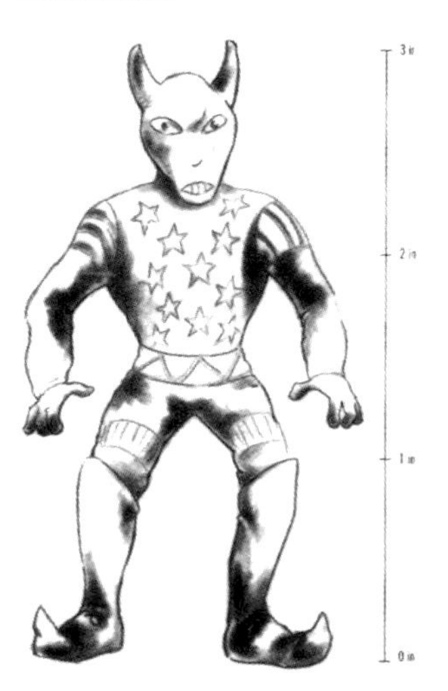

11c. one of the minuscule aliens reported by six Malaysian schoolboys in August 1970. The entity closely resembled a character in a local comic book.

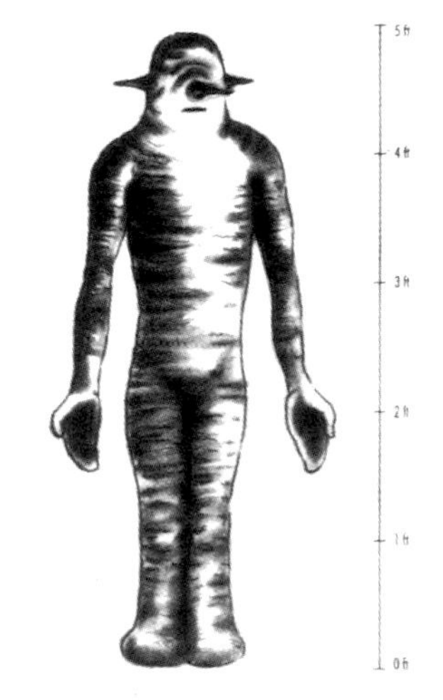

11d. one of the grey, mummy-like aliens which reportedly abducted two fishermen at Pascagoula, Mississippi, in October 1973.

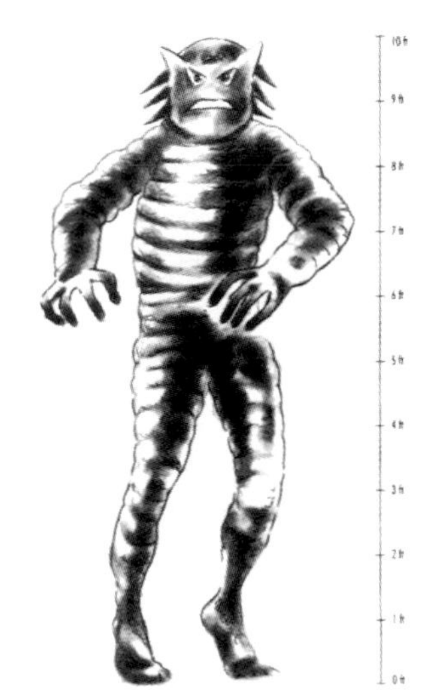

11e. the huge, fleshy alien which attacked Fortunato Zanfretta in a house near Genoa in December 1978.

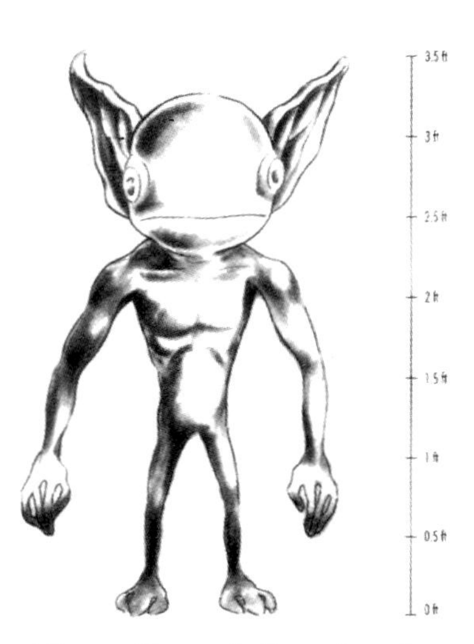

11f. one of the small, silver coloured 'goblins' which besieged a farmhouse in Kelly, near Hopkinsville in Kentucky, in August 1955.

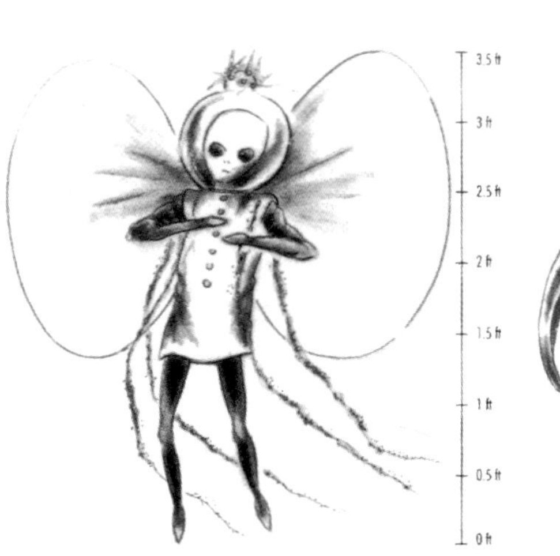

11g. a 'Mince-Pie Martian' – one of three tiny beings who visited Jean Hingley in her home in Rowley Regis in January 1979 and accepted a seasonal plate of pies.

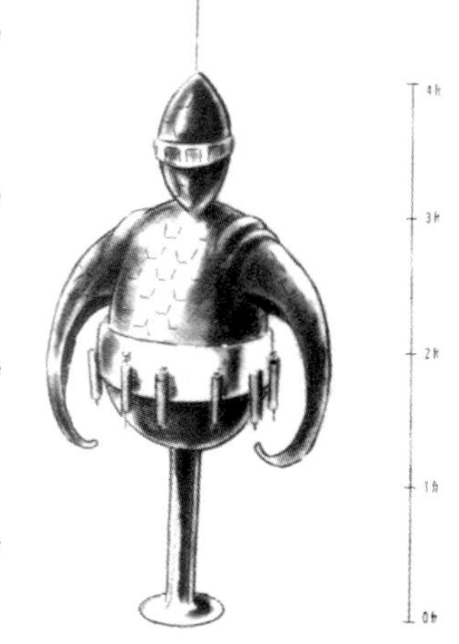

11h. one of the strange fleshy aliens with skin like aluminium which abducted bus driver Antonio La Rubia in Rio de Janeiro during September 1977.

12. Sketch by Captain James Hooton of the airship he saw at Homan, Arkansas in April 1897.

13. The McMinville photograph, obtained by Mr and Mrs Paul Trent at McMinville, Oregon, in May 1950.

Edinburgh, in August 1995. Its stench quickly identified it as human excrement.

Less frequently, something quite unique descends from the sky. There is a Swedish tradition that a strange animal, thought to be a troll, plunged into the streets of Norrkoping in the summer of 1708. Other unusal objects to have descended from the heavens are worms, mussels, straw, nuts and hunks of bloody flesh. Amongst the more peculiar was the silver notecase that fell into Lynn Connolly's back garden in Hull, in December 1973, tapping Mrs Connolly lightly on the head in passing. The notecase, which measured 7.5×1.4 inches and contained a half-used message pad, was marked with the initials T.B. and the word 'Klaipeda'. Klaipeda, it turned out, is the name of an old Lithuanian seaport. In 1973 the port was cut off behind the Iron Curtain, which makes the provenance of the notecase a little more mysterious.

The port of Hull has long sent ships into the Baltic, though, so perhaps the notecase reached England by sea in the conventional way and was lost, then carried aloft in the beak of a large bird – an explanation that was suggested to Mrs Connolly, but which she rejected. The light tap that she felt as the notecase hit her does at least suggest that it cannot have fallen a great distance – from an aircraft, for example.

Still, things that fall from the sky are often supposed to have come from planes. The grilled halibut that fell over Barnes might have been an inflight meal, though it is hardly usual for an aircrew to jettison food in mid-air, rather than stowing it until the aircraft lands. The excrement that fell onto Craiglockhart Tennis Club was initially assumed to have come from a malfunctioning aircraft toilet, since there are several authenticated instances of 'blue ice' – urine mixed with water and disinfectant – plummeting to earth. This explanation seemed even more obvious because the Edinburgh-to-Birmingham flight was actually passing overhead at the time. But a careful check on all the shuttle's toilets ruled the aircraft out as the solution.

That is the strangest thing about things that come from the

sky. Chunks of ice certainly do form on high-flying aircraft and then fall to earth, but many well-documented ice falls predate manned flight. Charles Fort's favourite example was a gigantic hailstone, reportedly the size of an elephant, which fell at Seringapatam, India, around the year 1800. (Fort's source for this unlikely sounding tale was impeccable: the case was cited in the *Annual Report of the British Association for the Advancement of Science*.)

Another explanation is often advanced to account for the fall of frogs and fishes: the hapless animals were scooped up from a river or a pond by a passing waterspout, and deposited later some way off. This theory has something to recommend it: for one thing it has long been recognised that a number of falls really are caused by waterspouts. A whirlwind dropped fish at Quirindi, New South Wales, in November 1913, and fish fell from a waterspout in Louisiana in June 1921. Nevertheless, the waterspout hypothesis has weaknesses. There do not seem to be any accounts of rains of tadpoles, nor of smelly mud, broken bottles, old bicycles and the rest of the detritus that normally lurks in ponds alongside the frogs and the fish. And the theory cannot easily explain a number of the most peculiar cases. There are instances of extremely localised falls: at Mountain Ash, in south Wales, a large number of freshwater minnows and sticklebacks fell from the sky, in February 1859, covering a rectangle of ground, some eighty yards by twelve, with fish. (For a long time it was supposed that none had landed outside this extremely limited area, but one recent researcher has shown that a few came down in the surrounding hills.)

An even more peculiar example of the same phenomenon seems to have occurred on the other side of the world in the spring of 1986. Three fishermen from Kiribati, an island chain several thousand miles north-east of Australia, spent four months adrift on the Pacific in an open boat after their outboard motor failed. They survived by catching shark, but soon tired of eating the same food day after day. Then, as one of their eventual rescuers explained, 'One Saturday night, while they were praying for a different kind of fish because they were sick of shark, something fell into the boat. It was a rare blackish fish which you can never catch trawling. It never comes to the surface, and lives about 620 feet down.' Even setting aside the extraordinary fortuitousness of this deliverance, the Kiribati fish fall is remarkable because it is hard to see how such a fish could have been picked up by a waterspout, or even dropped by a passing bird.

The most mysterious of all the odd substances that fall from the sky used to be 'angel hair', thin strands of an apparently gelatinous material, which floats down from the heavens and generally dissolves on contact with the earth. It was sometimes associated with UFOs, and there are a number of cases on record to suggest that it was actually the solid exhaust matter expelled by a flying saucer. On 17 October 1952, for example, a narrow cylinder accompanied by about thirty smaller objects was seen high over Oloron, France. All were trailing angel hair behind them. A large number of strands fell to earth and clumps hung from bushes and telephone wires for several hours afterwards.

Since the 1950s, reports of angel hair have become exceedingly scarce, perhaps, in part, because in the 1970s the Center for UFO Studies arranged for two early samples of the material to be analysed, and they were found to be nothing more than the webs of a balloon spider. But spiders' webs themselves sometimes seem to have mysterious properties. They occasionally appear in unusual quantities – amounts so spectacular that one wonders how many spiders must have been involved in their manufacture. During the night of 28 October 1988, for instance, coastguards patrolling the English Channel off Dorset reported a cobweb cloud with an estimated area of thirty square miles. Webs have also acquired sinister connotations on the modern battlefield. During the Bosnian conflict there were several reports that a 'mysterious web-like substance' had been released over Croatia and drifted down onto the heads of the local populace. A few samples of the material were secured for analysis. Under the microscope they seemed to be synthetic rather than natural spiders' webs, though the Serbians' motive for producing such apparently harmless material remains a matter for conjecture.

Noise from Nowhere

A few places in the world are associated, not with falls of matter, but with repeated reports of strange sounds. Usually they take the form of a persistent low-frequency hum, associated with a specific area and capable of driving those who hear it to distraction. Not everyone can hear the hum, though, and for years the official explanation was that those who did, were probably suffering from a form of tinnitus – a hearing disorder, which causes sufferers to experience a buzzing noise inside their heads. In Britain, it took until 1992 for the government to acknowledge that the phenomenon of the noise from nowhere actually existed, by which time new cases were being reported from the UK at the rate of about 500 a year.

Not that strange hums are unique to Britain. One of the best-documented recent cases comes from Hueytown, Alabama, a small coalmining town. Beginning in December 1991, and continuing for more than a year, residents complained of a loud buzz, similar to the sound of a dentist's drill. The hum invaded the town irregularly, seeming louder at night (when there is less background noise), and loudest of all when it was cloudy or raining. A number of potential culprits were suggested, including electro-magnetic fields generated by power lines, microwave radiation and the throbbing of the twelve foot fans that ventilated Hueytown's mines. In Britain, similar noises have been explained as resonating gas mains; while in Taos, New Mexico, site of perhaps the most persistent humming phenomenon of recent years, blame has been variously attributed to secret military experiments with ultra-low-frequency radio, communications from UFOs and the grinding of the tectonic plates lurking below the town in the Rio Grande Rift – an explanation that links the humming phenomenon with the mystery of earthlights.

Another phenomenon of the upper regions, which fascinated Fort, is the mystery of unexplained aerial detonations: booming retorts that echo across the skies and seem to come from nowhere. Today they are sometimes called skyquakes, and are often associated with the passage of supersonic aircraft overhead. In the 1970s, the area around Bristol was plagued by these mystery detonations for several years, and they were popularly ascribed to Concorde as it accelerated through the sound barrier on its way to New York, a theory that did not entirely accord with the facts as noted in the new plane's schedule. In any case, skyquakes, like ice falls, were recorded many years before the advent of aircraft. Some were attributed to the explosion of meteors as they entered the atmosphere. Others have been put down to UFOs.

One area was once associated with aerial detonations above all others: Barisal, a village at the eastern end of the swamplands of the Ganges delta, seventy miles south of the Bangladeshi capital, Dacca. These skyquakes were called the Barisal Guns, because they resembled the muffled boom of an old cannon. The guns were frequently heard by British travellers in India, all the way from the coast to a point about 300 miles inland, in the foothills of the Himalayas, over a period of at least fifty years. It was never ascertained whether the detonations were occurring on land, at sea or in the air, and they were variously explained as fireworks, the sound of bamboo bursting in jungle fires, ball lightning, submarine eruptions and the rumble of river banks collapsing into the morass.

The sheer variety of the theories advanced to explain mystery noises seems as interesting as the noises themselves. Technicians and scientists – caught off-guard, perhaps – hazard guesses without investigation. Where there is proper research into the phenomenon, the most obvious explanations frequently turn out to have flaws. In many cases, the mystery turns out to be more complex than it first appeared and many of the best-known cases of strange hums probably have multiple causes, one of them being the publicity given to the phenomenon. When hums are in the air, people listen a little more intently, and think they hear a lot more clearly.

Vanishings

During the 1920s, Charles Fort stumbled across a phenomenon so unusual that it had no name. So he coined one to describe it: teleportation, the transportation, usually instantaneously, of solid objects from one location to another.

Fort and his successors developed an elaborate, if not entirely serious, theory, which suggested that teleportation had once been a prime mover in the creation of the earth, shifting continents, then falling into disuse when it was no longer needed and withering away to almost nothing. 'It could be,' Fort suggested, 'that once upon a time this whole earth was built up by streams of rocks, teleported from other parts of an existence. The crash of falling islands – the humps of piling continents – and then the cosmic humour of it all . . . the force that once heaped the peaks of the Rocky Mountains now slings pebbles at a couple of farmers near Trenton, N.J.'

To a Fortean, such a phenomenon could explain many apparently unconnected mysteries. It could account for poltergeists, and also for the mysterious appearance of out-of-place animals thousands of miles from their normal habitat. The fish and frogs that fell from the sky could have been teleported there from rivers and ponds. Perhaps some of the many people who vanished in strange circumstances had been teleported away, and others, who appeared with equal suddenness, had been carried to where they were found by a teleportive force.

There is no shortage of cases of such strange appearances and disappearances. They are central to several religions. A spate of fairly well-known cases occurred in the late nineteenth and early twentieth centuries, and a number of quite spectacular examples are recorded earlier than that. In recent years, however, many of these cases have been reinvestigated and found to be baseless.

One of the earliest instances for which we have some near-contemporary evidence concerns a Spanish soldier of the Manila garrison – his name is given as 'Gil Perez' in one modern account – who, on 25 October 1593, vanished from his post in the Philippines and appeared with equal suddenness in the main square of another Spanish colonial capital, Mexico City. This case was referred to, briefly, in the introductory chapter. The man was immediately arrested and thrown into prison as a possible deserter. Fortunately for him, he possessed one vital piece of information with which to convince his captors of the truth of his unlikely tale: on the same day as he had vanished from Manila, news had reached the city of the death of its governor, Gomez Perez Dasmarinas, who had been struck down and killed off the Philippine coast during a mutiny on board his ship. This awful news took two months to reach Mexico City by conventional means, but when it did the soldier was at last believed, released, and sent back to Manila.

Several modern authors have regarded the case of the teleporting soldier as one of the strongest in the paranormal canon. It had, it appeared, been investigated by the Mexican authorities and by the Holy Tribunal of the Roman Catholic Church (which suspected witchcraft, not surprisingly). Yet a recent reinvestigation by a Canadian researcher, Mr X (his legal name), has shown the whole story to be so full of holes that it should act as a warning to anyone willing to accept such extraordinary claims at face value. X's research showed that there was no contemporary account of the teleportation, though he did find several early suggestions that Dasmarinas's death had been foretold by a few citizens of Mexico City. Indeed the earliest version of the teleportation account dates to a century after the events are supposed to have occurred. Nor does it seem credible that a soldier who vanished from Manila on the day of the fatal mutiny could have been aware of the governor's death; the news could hardly have reached the colony so soon after it happened.

Other staple accounts of apparent teleportations now seem equally open to doubt. In 1809, for example, the British diplomat Benjamin Bathurst, who had broken his journey home to rest in a small Prussian town, is famously said to have gone out to his coach, 'walked around the horses', and vanished. On closer examination, it becomes apparent that there were no witnesses to his disappearance, and that he was probably murdered for his fur coat and money.

Then, during the First World War, an entire battalion of British troops, the First-Fifth Norfolks, about 200 men in all, were said to have marched into a peculiarly shaped cloud, or patch of mist, while advancing on Turkish lines during the Gallipoli campaign, never to emerge. The case of the 'Vanishing Norfolks' became one of the most celebrated mysteries of all and was quickly elaborated. Some fifty years after the event, an eyewitness, a New Zealand soldier, came forward to say that after the Norfolks had marched into the cloud, it slowly lifted off the ground and moved away against the prevailing wind – an account that attracted the attention of ufologists. A decade later, however, an author named Paul Begg was able to show that the bodies of more than half the missing men had been located at Gallipoli after the war. The remainder, he concluded, almost certainly perished in action against the Turks, as did many tens of thousands of other soldiers of the Great War whose bodies were never recovered from the battlefield.

Nevertheless, many perplexing disappearances remain unexplained. The fate of the ten unfortunates who sailed on board the *Mary Celeste* is still a mystery, a century and a quarter after she was found adrift and apparently abandoned off the Azores. Dozens of attempts have been made to explain the mystery, ranging from the suggestion that the ship's crew abandoned her as part of an insurance fraud, via the idea that one crewman went mad, murdered all the others and then jumped overboard, to the more believable theory that the master ordered his men to abandon ship because he feared her cargo – raw alcohol – was about to explode. Yet, although certain key facts are beyond dispute (the ship's boat was missing, indicating that she had been deliberately abandoned, and the popular notion that she was discovered with a meal still warm in the galley is a fantasy), no one explanation can conclusively account for every detail of the case.

It is also possible to disappear utterly on land. One appropriately sinister case occurred in the winter of 1900 on desolate Eilean Mor, a waveswept rock no more than 800 yards by 500, which is, nevertheless, the largest of the seven Flannan Isles in the Outer Hebrides. Until the turn of the century, these islands were uninhabited, and had been for several hundred years. The occasional shepherd might land to graze his sheep, but – at least according to tradition – he would on no circumstances remain overnight, since the lonely isles were supposedly haunted and also believed to be the abode of fairies who did not take kindly to interlopers. Then, a small lighthouse was built on Eilean Mor, and three lighthousemen were sent to the island to operate it.

In December 1900 the crew consisted of James Ducat, Thomas Marshall and Donald McArthur; a fourth man, Joseph Moore, was on shore leave. On Boxing Day, Moore returned to the Flannan Isles on board the supply ship *Hesperus* to take his turn on watch. He was rowed ashore through a heavy swell and laboured up the several hundred steps to the new lighthouse – to find it utterly empty. Everything was in order, the beds were made, the great lamp trimmed, and the log book written up to 15 December. After a careful search, all that seemed to be missing were two of the three sets of oilskins, and a box of tools normally stowed on a platform just below the lighthouse, some 110 feet above the grey, December sea.

The Northern Lighthouse Board, which was responsible for the station, concluded that the lighthousemen must have been washed into the sea during a spell of unusually bad weather. During the 1950s, another keeper at Eilean Mor named Walter Aldebert developed an interest in the mystery and took photographs, which showed that in high winds waves crashing into the islet could send columns of water up to 200 feet up the side of the cliffs – far enough to sweep away unwary lighthousemen who thought they were safe from the fury of the storm. But the real mystery of the disappearances at Eilean

Mor was why all three lighthouse keepers should have gone out together into a storm – one without waterproof clothing. Aldebert's suggestion was that two of the men set off to secure some gear and that one of them was washed over the cliff by an unexpected torrent of water. The survivor went back to the lighthouse to alert his colleague, who ran out into the storm without waiting to don his protective clothing. But when the two keepers returned to the clifftops in the hope of rescuing their friend, a second wave carried them, also, to their deaths.

Aldebert's theory is a convincing one, and has the advantage of being backed up by his photographic evidence. But the Eilean Mor case is an interesting one for another reason: it demonstrates the way in which a body of folklore can attach itself to an unsolved mystery, rendering that puzzle all the more enigmatic in the process. According to the writer Vincent Gaddis, for example, keeper Marshall had made some sinister and perplexing entries in the lighthouse's log before he disappeared. The entry for 12 December noted that Ducat was 'irritable'; that for the 13th observed: 'Ducat quiet. MacArthur crying'; on the 14th, Marshall wrote: 'Me, Ducat and MacArthur prayed'; finally, on the 15th, came the unexplained remark 'God is over all'.

To Gaddis, the implication was unmistakably that the lighthousemen had been menaced by some indeterminate, creeping force, which had subdued them, not in a single moment of elemental fury, but over the course of several days. Yet his reference for the diary entries is not a reliable one – it is an English magazine called *True Strange Stories*, published in 1929. Although the original log is now inaccessible, it seems unlikely that Ducat, who was Marshall's superior, would have allowed him to make insubordinate remarks in an official record. And, even if the entries are truly given, the idea that three men from a sternly Calvinist seagoing community should pray together need not be seen as too remarkable.

That has not, of course, stopped other writers from speculating about the vanishing lighthousemen of Eilean Mor. One author, Carey Miller, states that 'an unseen force on the island would not tolerate intruders and got rid of them', and also that 'when Joseph Moore flung open the door of the lighthouse and called out the names of his friends, three enormous black birds, the like of which had never been seen before, launched themselves from the top of the tower and flew out to sea'. There seems to be no good authority for such remarkable claims. But so long as there are mystery-mongers to invent such details, it is certain that there will still be mysteries to be solved.

Blazing Bodies

They found what was left of Dr John Irving Bentley next to the lavatory in his Pennsylvania home.

It wasn't much. There was no sign of his torso, his arms or his legs. No clothes and no personal effects. All that remained was a skull, resting on some water pipes, and the brown, charred stump of a single foot, sitting next to a hole that had been scorched right through the floorboards to the cellar below.

Across the hole lay the 92-year-old invalid's walking frame, which had fallen at a crazy angle as the doctor struggled, unsuccessfully, to escape the death that was enveloping him. The thing that really perplexed the firemen who arrived to clear up the mess, however, was that though Bentley's body had blazed so fiercely that it had been reduced to a five-inch cone of sooty ashes that had fallen through to the basement, the walking frame's rubber caps had not even begun to melt.

What sort of flame could have turned Bentley's body into a pile of greasy embers – something that takes a crematorium furnace, burning at more than 600 degrees Centigrade, more than ninety minutes to achieve – without setting fire to his home? Why was the remaining foot unburned? The firemen, gathered around the hole in the floor, found themselves forced to consider an unusual possibility: spontaneous human combustion.

The phenomenon of spontaneous combustion has been recognised since the mid eighteenth century, when an elderly

Italian countess, Corenlia Bandi, was found in bed one morning. Her body had been reduced to 'a heap of ashes, two legs untouched, from the foot to the knee, with their stockings on; between them was the lady's head, whose brains, half of the back part of her skull, and the whole chin, were burnt to ashes; among which was found three fingers blackened. All the rest was ashes, which had this peculiar quality, that they left in the hand, when taken up, a greasy and stinking moisture.'

In the eighteenth and nineteenth centuries, spontaneous combustion was generally thought to afflict elderly heavy drinkers, and it was presumed that an excessive intake of alcohol rendered the body in some way more likely to combust. In the twentieth century this explanation has rather fallen by the wayside, and it has been noted that a few much younger people appear to have been killed in the same strange way; but no convincing explanation for precisely what might cause so peculiar a phenomenon has been proposed.

Those who have studied spontaneous combustion are agreed that there are certain specific signs that mark such fiery visitations. In practically every case, the corpse is almost, but not quite, completely consumed. The extremities – usually feet, sometimes hands – are the portions left untouched. Still more unusually, bones, which normally survive ordinary fires, have crumbled into ash. The characteristic sweet odour of roasted human flesh is surprisingly absent, and every drop of blood within the arteries and veins is vaporised. In the rare instances where the remains are still ablaze when found, the fire is seen to burn with a characteristic, electric-blue flame. Finally, the blazing of the body does remarkably little damage to the surroundings.

The latter point is, perhaps, the most anomalous. In one case dating to February 1888, a Dr Mackenzie Booth was called to a hayloft in Constitution Street, Aberdeen, where he found the remains of a 65-year-old, pensioned-off soldier slumped on the floor. The whole body had been consumed – according to Booth, 'both hands and the right foot had been burnt off and had fallen through the floor into the stables below, and the features of the face were represented by a greasy cinder retaining the cast of the features' – but the fire that had killed the old man and burnt through the floorboards had failed to ignite any of the bone-dry straw that was lying next to him.

In all, there are perhaps 300 cases of spontaneous combustion on record. The best-known occurred in the summer of 1951, when a 67-year-old woman named Mary Reeser was killed in her Florida apartment. The room she died in exhibited all the classic signs of SHC. There was greasy soot everywhere, but little fire damage to the fixture and fittings. An easy chair, a table and a lampshade had perished in the blaze, but the police report of the incident mentions that the plastic light switches, cotton sheets and even a pile of papers against one wall were untouched by the flames. When the surviving ashes and fragments reached the pathologists, the twelve stone woman's remains were found to weigh less than ten pounds.

It is important to note that a convincing scientific explanation for deaths that look as if they might be caused by spontaneous combustion does exist. This is the phenomenon known as 'the candle effect' – the idea that a fully dressed human body is little more than a candle in reverse. Clothes act as the wick, and once they catch light, the fire feeds off melting body fat, gradually reducing the corpse to bone. The source of ignition is generally supposed to be a dropped match or a lighted cigarette; in others, the victim suffers a seizure or a heart attack and falls face-first into a hearth. Furnishings such as beds and chairs can add to the intensity of the blaze.

Many of the details often observed in cases of spontaneous combustion favour the candle effect hypothesis. Elderly or drunken people are less likely than the able-bodied to notice and extinguish a blaze in time; moreover, their extra weight would, literally, feed the flames. And the reason that legs and feet seem curiously immune to the effects of spontaneous combustion is simply that heat and flames rise.

Joe Nickell of the Committee for the Scientific Investigation of Claims of the Paranormal has argued that the flaming death of Dr Bentley is a classic instance of the candle effect at work. Bentley, he points out, was infirm and 'had a habit of dropping matches and hot ashes from his pipe, upon his robes, which were spotted with burns from earlier occasions. He also kept wooden matches in both pockets of his day robe – a situation that could transform an ember into a fatal blaze.'

Nickell believes that Bentley woke to find his clothes on fire and staggered to his bathroom where he tried to extinguish the flames – the broken remains of a water pitcher were found in the toilet bowl. 'Once he fell on the floor, his burning clothing could have ignited the flammable linoleum. Beneath that was hardwood flooring and wooden beams – wood for a funeral pyre,' he suggests. 'Cool air drawn from the basement in what is known as the "chimney effect" could have kept the fire burning hotly.' A similar fate probably greeted Mary Reeser: 'When last seen, Mrs Reeser was sitting in a big chair, wearing flammable night-clothes and smoking a cigarette – after taking two sleeping pills and stating her intention of taking two more.'

It is certainly true that some cases of apparent spontaneous combustion involve people whose remains are found lying head down in a fireplace and whose bodies have been largely consumed by flames, leaving only the extremities untouched. And, once it is admitted that the exact symptoms of spontaneous human combustion can be duplicated naturally, the central claim advanced by believers in the phenomenon – that the human body simply cannot be destroyed so completely in an ordinary home – can be dismissed.

Nevertheless, there are still difficulties in accepting the candle effect as a complete solution to the mystery. The principal problem is that it takes several hours – perhaps eight to twelve in total – to reduce a human body to ash in this way. Thus, the candle effect appears an adequate explanation in cases such as those of Mary Reeser and John Bentley, whose remains were found early in the morning, at least eight hours after they were last seen alive. However, Larry Arnold, a Pennsylvania-based researcher who has devoted years to the study of spontaneous human combustion, has recently uncovered a case in which the body of a middle-aged woman was almost completely destroyed in less than twenty minutes, and perhaps in as few as six.

The case began when Arnold got permission to attend a firemen-only course on arson detection. At the end of the seminar, the instructor passed him some astonishing photos of a charred corpse that had been all but consumed by flames. Only the splayed lower legs remained, still adopting an eerily natural pose.

It took Arnold eight months of detective work to track the photos down to their source – the little Pennsylvania town of Drexel Hill and the former home of 51-year-old Helen Conway. It was Conway's legs that he had seen in the arson photographs, and her body, reduced to nothing more than smoking charcoal by the intense heat, that lay slumped above them in a scorched armchair. 'Her lower legs were reasonably intact,' Arnold was told, 'though the epidermis had pulled away and bubbled in some places. The subcutaneous tissue of the upper legs had split asunder – and the rest of her anatomy was a blackened mass of fused tissue, practically unrecognisable as human.'

Investigation soon revealed that Conway's grand-daughter had fetched her a cigarette only three minutes before returning to discover her surrounded by flames. And the fire brigade took about the same amount of time to respond to the call-out and extinguish the fire. Conway had gone from puffing away at her cigarette to smouldering away in her blackened armchair in almost no time at all.

Nickell draws attention to the fact that the victim was smoking shortly before the fire began, and suggests that the abnormally rapid combustion occurred because 'it may have begun at the base of the seated body and burned straight upward, fed by the fat in the torso, and may thus have been a much more intense fire – not unlike grease fires that all who cook are familiar with.' Indeed, Conway's death had come so suddenly that even Arnold believes it may not have been a case of spontaneous human combustion at all. 'As I see it,' he writes, 'it's probable that Helen Conway burned in much less than 360 seconds by an even rarer form of human transition – *spontaneous human explosion.*'

Whoever is right – Arnold or Nickell – more evidence is required before we can pinpoint the solution to this gruesome enigma.

Children of the Wolf

Several hundred miles to the west of Barisal and its guns, in the Bengali district of Midnapore, an Indian clergyman named Singh once rooted two human children and two cubs out of a wolf's lair under a white ant mound. It was the autumn of 1920, and the two youngsters, both girls, one about six and the other three, eventually became the most celebrated of the handful of children who have apparently been reared by animals.

Although the case of the wolf-children of Midnapore is the best-documented, earlier examples might be cited. Romulus and Remus, the mythical founders of Rome, were supposed to have been raised by a she-wolf, and historical cases go back at least to 1341, when hunters from the town of Hesse, in Germany, found a wild boy who appeared to have been brought up in a similar fashion. (Like the Green Children of Woolpit, whose discovery had alarmed the villagers of Suffolk two centuries before, the boy fared badly when forced to adopt the rough Hessian diet; indeed he quickly died.)

Nor are wolves the only animals to have displayed such noble instincts. There are three old Lithuanian records of children being raised by bears, and cases of children supposedly brought up by sheep and pigs. In Australia, at the turn of the century, a Sydney woman was fined £1 for abandoning her child to be reared in a chicken run, with the result, the court heard, that the unfortunate infant could only imitate its feathered friends, even roosting with them at night. More recently, in the 1970s a monkey-boy was found in the jungles of Sri Lanka and a book was written about the 'gazelle boy' of the

Spanish Sahara, who had disproportionately thick ankles, leapt and bounded with the best of his herd, and was never captured.

When he inspected the children he had rescued from the ant-mound, the Reverend Singh discovered several such adaptations to life among the beasts. They were drowsy by day and mostly active by night. Their knees, elbows and hands were covered in thick calluses from going on all fours, their hair was thick and matted and they were unable to stand up. They were also quite wild, scratching and biting ferociously anyone who tried to pick them up, fiercely resisting all attempts to bathe them, and gazing at their rescuers with such blank expressions that it seemed there was little that was human about them.

Singh never found out who the children were or how they came to be living in the forest, among the wolves; but he resolved to care for them and to restore their humanity if that were possible. The girls, whom Singh named Kamala and Amala, were taken back to the orphanage he ran at Midnapore and placed in a makeshift cage until their re-education could be begun. Progress was painfully slow. At first the wolf-children would eat nothing but raw meat, and sometimes, after midnight, they howled. 'This cry was a peculiar one,' Singh noted in his diary:

> It began with a hoarse voice and ended in a thrilling shrill wailing, very loud and continuous, neither human nor animal. I presumed it was a call to their companions, the wolves or the cubs. It could be heard from a good distance, and the more so on a still night when everyone was asleep and no other sound was audible except the screeching of the owl and sounds of animals prowling in search of prey or drink.

Within a year of the rescue, the younger wolf-girl, Amala, died. Kamala lived on for eight more years and was eventually taught to stand upright and wear clothes. She even mastered some thirty words of Bengali, but never enough to say anything about her former life. She succumbed to typhoid fever in the autumn of 1929, having lived almost all her life so protected from publicity and public enquiry that many of those who had heard her story still strenuously doubted that it was truly possible for a human child to be reared by animals.

Children brought up in this way, and feral savages who rear themselves in the wild, raise profound questions concerning human uniqueness, the intelligence and abilities of animals, and the otherwise unbridgeable gap between animals and men. Although it has been suggested that such cases are exaggerated or partially fabricated accounts of autistic children (who do indeed exhibit many of the characteristics of feral children) abandoned by their parents, the evidence that some instances, at least, are genuine seems quite strong. As well as exhibiting internal consistencies, the data throws up some pleasingly anthropomorphic correlations; for example, children raised by carnivores are generally described as sullen and suspicious, whereas those found in the care of herbivores are more open and approachable.

The intense interest that such cases aroused, particularly in the eighteenth and nineteenth centuries, was central to the debate over the divine origins of man. After all, if humankind was specially created by god to be distinct from animals, children raised in the wild should have retained more human characteristics than they apparently had. Another persistent theme in all these stories is the possibility of rehabilitating a child deprived of all guidance and affection as a human being. As such, they have always held a particular fascination for people who are interested in how and when we learn, and for scientists who wish to understand what (if anything) distinguishes humans from animals.

The case of Victor, the wild boy of Aveyron, is especially interesting from this point of view. He came out of the forests of southern France in 1800, aged twelve or thirteen, after living wild for at least three years, and probably more. The boy had apparently survived alone, for, unusually, there was no suggestion that animals had played any part in his upbringing. He appears to have lived chiefly on forest berries and root vegetables, which he stole from the fields of adjoining farms, and to have realised that he was human; during the winters he sometimes visited local people who would give him raw vegetables that he threw onto the fire to cook. Victor could not speak, and was classified as an incurable idiot by a leading educationalist. Then he had the good fortune of coming under the care of Jean Itard, a doctor who spent five years socialising him – among other problems, he suffered from attacks of 'hysterics' that seemed to be prompted by an unchannelled sexuality – and teaching him to speak a few words. Itard's methods, revolutionary at the time, became the foundation of all modern techniques for teaching deaf-mute children.

A rather similar, but very little-known, case occurred on the Kuano, a river in Uttar Pradesh, in the 1970s. In February 1973, the local priest saw a naked boy of about fifteen, swimming and catching fish in the river. When he told the people of Baragdava, the nearest village, about the child, a woman named Somni suggested that the child was her son, Ramchandra, whom she said had been washed away by the river when he was only a year old. A search was mounted, but the amphibian boy was nowhere to be found, and indeed he was not seen again until 1979, when Somni came across him sleeping in a field and positively identified him as her son from a birthmark on his back. Ramchandra awoke and escaped, but the villagers began to keep a strict watch and eventually succeeded in capturing him. Upon examination the child was found to be bullet-headed, mute and nearly hairless, with black-green skin. He ate raw fish and frogs, and also vegetables. Although he soon escaped back to the river, the boy was henceforth less shy of human company and, like Victor, would sometimes approach the settlement to consume bowls of spinach and water left for him by the villagers.

Eventually, the case of the Kuano amphibian boy came to the attention of Hubert Adamson, a British writer with a particular interest in feral children, and in 1985 he travelled to Uttar Pradesh to investigate further. Adamson discovered that Ramchandra had died three years earlier in somewhat mysterious circumstances, following the arrival in the village of police from the town of Morudehahea. The villagers and policemen succeeded in capturing him and made to take him away, but Ramachandra broke free and ran off. A few hours later he turned up in a neighbouring settlement, where he was not known, and approached some women in a tea shop, one of whom was so horrified by his strange appearance that she threw a pan of boiling water over him. In great pain, the amphibian boy ran back to the river, and some time later his blistered body, covered in fish bites, was recovered from the water.

The mystery, for Adamson, was twofold: what had prompted the child to lead a strange, water-borne existence for fifteen years in what was a relatively accessible, agricultural area, and what had finally prompted the villagers of Baragdava to call in the police? Questioning as many people as he could, he eventually concluded that the problem was probably Ramchandra's burgeoning sexuality, which had drawn him to the village women – as Victor of Aveyron had been drawn nearly two centuries earlier. With his strange appearance and inability to communicate, the boy must have made an alarming companion, and it seems to have been the dismay and disgust that his sexual interest aroused that led to the involvement of the town police.

Phone Calls from the Dead

It was dusk when the telephone rang in the Indianapolis home of Viola Tollen. Standing alone in the gathering darkness, Mrs Tollen answered the call, and found herself engaged in a brief but remarkable conversation.

For several years she had enjoyed an acquaintance with her young neighbour, Ruby Stone. A short while before the phone call, the friendship had been cut short when Ruby had died, aged only seven. Now, however, Mrs Tollen heard a small, childlike voice on the other end of the line, a voice she recognised but could not quite place. 'They told me I could not telephone, but I just did, didn't I?' the peculiar caller began, to which a puzzled Viola could only reply: 'I know your voice, but who are you?' 'You know me,' the voice responded. 'I am Ruby.'

What Mrs Tollen had experienced was a rare phenomenon known as a 'phone call from the dead'. There are only a few dozen recorded cases. Indeed the calls are so unusual that almost no one was aware they even existed until the available material was painstakingly pieced together a few years ago by two American psychical researchers, D. Scott Rogo and Raymond Bayless.

Their database included several cases just as unsettling as Mrs Tollen's. For example, a certain Iris Brace, the loyal secretary of Dr Walter Uphoff, an economics professor at the University of Colorado, died unexpectedly after undergoing minor surgery in the summer of 1965. Her boss had asked her to call a colleague as soon as she left hospital to see if he would participate in a series of lectures that Uphoff was organising. On the morning of Mrs Brace's funeral, Dr Uphoff remembered to make the call himself. He had just got through when his colleague exclaimed, 'Just a minute! My other phone is ringing.' Dr Uphoff was asked to hold, and within a few minutes his colleague picked up the phone again to say: 'Your secretary just called to remind me that you wanted me to participate in your programme.'

In a rather different case, which occurred in May 1971, a Mr and Mrs MacConnell of Tuscon, Arizona, were telephoned by an elderly friend whom Rogo and Bayless call Enid Johlson (a pseudonym). Mrs Johlson had recently lost touch with the couple after being moved from one nursing home to another, so they were pleased to hear from her when she telephoned one Sunday.

After answering the phone, Mr MacConnell passed it to his wife Bonnie. 'Do you know who this is?' the voice at the end of the line queried, and Mrs MacConnell immediately recognised it as that of her old friend. They chatted together for about thirty minutes, until Mrs MacConnell offered to visit and bring Enid a bottle of her favourite blackberry brandy. Mrs Johlson was not encouraging. 'I don't need that now,' she said, though she did admit that after being confined to bed she now 'got around fine' and had 'never been happier'. The call then ended on a friendly note, and the MacConnells commented on how much stronger and more lively their friend sounded now than she had on the last time they had spoken.

Five nights later, Bonnie MacConnell found herself thinking about her friend again, and decided to telephone her at the nursing home where she had said she was staying. The receptionist at the home seemed startled by this request. 'Mrs Johlson died last Sunday,' she explained – several hours before the MacConnells had received that lengthy telephone call.

Phone calls from the dead, therefore, share many characteristics that psychical researchers have come to recognise in ghost stories. Some are 'crisis apparitions', others apparently attempts by the dead to contact the living. But, rather like the Old Hag experience, they have the added importance of seeming so uniquely bizarre that the people who receive them are often reluctant to tell anyone about the calls. This means that the database of calls should be relatively uncontaminated by instances in which the witness consciously or unconsciously follows the established pattern in which a case usually unfolds.

Rogo and Bayless draw attention to another point of interest. Because the messages are conveyed mechanically, through the medium of the telephone, it should be possible to say something about their origin and thus perhaps their source. For example, in some cases the calls were placed through an operator, or the witness noticed that all the telephones in the house rang at once. This implies that the call originated at a distance. In others, the recipient of the call specifically noted that the telephone bell rang in a peculiar way to announce a phone call from the dead. This, to Rogo and Bayless, suggested that the call did not literally come down a telephone line. It might have been a 'direct voice' or clairaudient phenomenon – a message created by a spirit using some psychical means.

In such cases, the telephone might have been selected as a method of passing the message in a 'natural' context, thus avoiding the sort of problems that arise when a witness is scared or confused by the sudden manifestation of a psychical phenomenon.

Of course, Rogo and Bayless were working from the assumption that there was something genuinely anomalous about the calls, and that they were not simply cases of fantasy or mistaken identity. A sceptic might point out that Rogo, who died in 1990, has yet to place any phone calls from the spirit world himself. Yet, whether or not phone calls from the dead are a genuinely psychical phenomenon, they are of interest for another reason. They are a fine example of the ways in which strange phenomena evolve to take advantage of new technology.

Comparable cases have been observed before. For example, the invention of the telegraph – which roughly coincided with the heyday of spiritualism – resulted in some interesting cases of apparent telegraphic contact with the dead. The same thing happened when the wireless was developed at the turn of the twentieth century. Mysterious voices have also been heard on television and over CB radios.

Similarly, the telephone has played its part in the creation of other enigmas. The Men in Black have used it to menace UFO witnesses; certain unused lines are occasionally filled with mechanical voices reading endless series of numbers – a mystery that has been linked both to ufology and the possibility of mind-control experiments; and some strange deaths have been caused by lightning, which strikes phone lines and travels down the wires, electrocuting anyone using the telephone at the end of the line.

Charles Fort defined his apparently scattershot approach to chronicling strange phenomena when he observed, 'One measures a circle, beginning anywhere.' Study any strange phenomenon and you will find yourself considering others, drawing parallels, making links. Nothing in the borderlands exists in isolation.

Little Green Men, and Other Bizarre Entities

Wild children are not the only unusual creatures to lurk in forests, nor to venture into towns. Cryptozoologists have all but accepted that ape-creatures and swan-necked lake monsters live out in the wilderness. But alongside such ostensibly flesh-and-blood creatures dwells a sinister menagerie of swamp slobs, mad gassers and little green men so outlandish that it is difficult to believe that they are physically real.

These cases are often so bizarre that they are generally either ignored or dismissed. Yet there seems no reason to distinguish them so sharply from commonplace entity reports of small, aliens and hairy bipeds. The witnesses to these high strangeness cases seem as reliable (or to put it another way, no more imaginative) than those who report more conventional encounters, and some are reluctant to come forward and still profess themselves baffled by what they have seen. If such people are telling the truth, at least as it appears to them, the implications are immense – for while it may be reasonable to believe in a handful of alien visitors and a scattering of undiscovered ape-men, the carnival of charlatans that goes on dancing in the background hints that some answers must lie in the realms of either psychology or parapsychology.

In the southern United States, for example, many swamps and bayous are rumoured to be home to strange, apparently reptilian bipeds. During the summer of 1988, one such creature was at large in the Scape Ore swamp near Bishopville in South Carolina. It was first encountered by a man named George Hoolomon, who was drawing water from an artesian well in the swamp when, he said, a strange creature with big eyes leapt towards him from the woods. Then, on 15 July, Tom and Mary Waye, who lived nearby on Branlett Road, woke to find their car covered with sand, scratches and teeth-marks.

The publicity given to the Wayes' discovery persuaded another witness to come forward and report a much more dramatic encounter. Christopher Davis, a seventeen-year-old from the little settlement of Browntown, had been driving home alone across Scape Ore at about two a.m. on 29 June when he was forced to pull over to change a flat tyre. He had just completed the job and was putting his tools away when he looked up to see a strange creature running towards him across an open field. It seemed man-like, but appeared to be exceptionally tall and its eyes glowed red in the dark. Terrified, Davis leapt back into his car and attempted to drive off, but as he did so the creature reached the vehicle and thrust its hands through the partially wound-down window. Davis pulled back onto the road and pressed hard on the accelerator: 'I could see him from the neck down – the three big fingers, long black nails and green rough skin. He was strong. I looked in my mirror and saw a blur of green running. I could see his toes, and then he jumped onto the roof of my car. I thought I heard a grunt and then I could see his fingers through the front windshield, where they curled round the roof.' According to one version of the story, it was only when the car reached a speed of 35 mph that the creature fell off.

Davis drove straight to his parents' home and parked in the driveway. He refused to leave the vehicle until his father opened the front door. Both his parents and the local sheriff agreed that the boy seemed genuinely terrified – and with good reason. From his disjointed descriptions it appeared that he had been attacked by a foul-smelling entity at least seven feet tall, with skin like a lizard's, long arms, and, according to one newspaper report, 'a disturbing orthodontia problem'.

The writer John Keel collected nearly two-dozen similar accounts of what he called 'abominable swamp slobs' from across the United States. Several involved attacks on drivers and cars – something quite out of character for the more retiring ape-creatures such as Bigfoot. On 1 November 1958, for example, Charles Wetzel was driving near the Santa Ana River in Riverside, California, when the radio station he had tuned to faded into static and a six-foot-tall creature leapt in front of his car. It had glowing eyes, a beaky mouth, and no visible nose or ears, and was completely covered in leaf-like scales. Wetzel braked hard, and the creature came to him, emitting a high-pitched scream and leaving sweeping claw-marks on the windshield. As he accelerated, Wetzel saw his attacker fall backwards into the road and felt the bump as he ran it over. Though a subsequent investigation showed that the car had driven over something that had rubbed grease on its underside, no skin or scales were found, and there were no reports of strange corpses found on the Santa Ana road. It may be significant that of the score or so of 'lizard man' reports on record, all but two occurred after the release of the famous 1954 horror film *The Creature from the Black Lagoon*, which featured a very similar monster.

The Mad Gasser of Mattoon, the Illinois night stalker who made a brief appearance in the introductory chapter, is another example of a being from this mysterious realm. During the few days of his reign of terror in the early autumn of 1944, the people of Mattoon had every reason to believe that the Gasser was physically real. His victims had survived to tell their stories, and they were certain they had smelled his sickly-sweet paralysing gas as it drifted into their bedrooms, felt it burn their lips and throats, and, on a couple of occasions, even watched the black-clad prowler as he made his escape. Yet the gas left no traces, the Gasser could not be caught, and, as the days passed and the police failed to detain any suspects, fear of the intruder caused the case to spiral out of control. A total twenty-five incidents were reported within a fortnight. And then, as suddenly as he had appeared, the phantom anaesthetist stopped his work and vanished.

Was there really a Mad Gasser at work in the Illinois town? The general suspicion, even at the time, was that there was not, and today the Mattoon case is often cited as a fine example of 'mass hysteria'. The local newspaper did not help. It covered the attacks in a sensationalist fashion, and wrote, in its initial report of the case, of 'first victims', as if to imply that there would be more. A psychologist from the University of Illinois, who visited the town to investigate, showed that the witnesses included a disproportionately large number of women from low-income areas and pointed out that the Gasser had not visited Mattoon's two high-income residential areas.

On the other hand, more recent research has shown that Mattoon's gasser was not alone. A strikingly similar series of attacks was carried out in Botetourt County, Virginia, during the winter of 1933–34. Not only did both cases involve the spraying of sickening gasses that caused constrictions of the throat and swelling of the face; there was also the strange detail that at Mattoon an empty tube of lipstick was found outside one victim's home, while at Botetourt the prints of high-heeled shoes were found at several of the crime scenes. The Botetourt case was covered in the local press, but only accorded the briefest of mentions in the national papers; it seems implausible that it could have inspired a panic in Mattoon ten years later. Moreover, the idea of a paralysing gas seems an odd one for a journalist to invent. It is more reminiscent of David Hufford's uncovering of the Old Hag experience in Newfoundland.

Encounters with many less ambiguous but equally perplexing entities can still be found in old case files. In May 1913, three young boys working on a farm in Texas saw a small man, about eighteen inches tall. 'He had on a kind of hat that reminded me of a Mexican hat,' one recalled. 'It was a little round hat that looked like it was built onto him. He didn't have on any clothes. Everything looked like a rubber suit including the hat.' Before the boys could get a better look at the little being, he was torn to pieces by the farm dogs. His innards and blood appeared to be human, but his skin was dark green in colour. At Everittstown, New Jersey, on 6 November 1959, meanwhile, a man named John Trasco went out to feed his dog and encountered a man some three feet tall and dressed in green, who said to him: 'We are peaceful people. We don't want no trouble. We just want your dog.' Trasco's response was to chase the entity away shouting, 'Get the hell out of here!'

Where do such bizarre beings come from? Ufologists might suspect that they were the occupants of a flying saucer, though the reports tend not to mention any such craft, occultists that they are the denizens of a hollow earth. Janet Bord, who is an authority on fairy-lore, has tentatively linked such cases to old folk-tales concerning the little people, whose penchant for green clothing symbolises their association with the countryside. On the other hand, sceptics, pointing to the essential irrationality of these encounters, would argue that many such cases are hoaxes, and the rest merely figments of the imagination.

With luck, we are now in a position to see that every one of these suggestions begs questions of great fundamental importance – problems that are central to the whole question of what actually occurs in the borderlands – issues that the ufologists and the sceptics may not actually have considered at all. Suppose the little green men *are* UFO occupants: that takes us no closer to understanding what UFOs are or where they come from, let alone why they are here. What would they want with someone's dog, anyway, and how is it that a case dating to the late 1950s can contain such incongruous hints of an alien abduction mania that would take two more decades to flourish?

Suppose, on the other hand, that the entities are really fairies. Are they adopting modern guise for reasons of their own? What possible motive could they have for appearing in green rubber Mexican hats? Or is the way in which the little people are perceived in some strange way dependent on the person who sees them?

Presume, then, that the tales are nothing but hoaxes and hallucinations. If hoaxes, does it matter that the Texas farm case received no publicity for decades, had no apparent point, and seems to have earned none of its perpetrators a penny? If hallucinations, can we explain the physical evidence – the dogs' attack, the blood – or the fact that there were several witnesses, or even the reason why the entity was small, and green, and rubbery?

The real quandary, when we venture into the borderlands, is still distinguishing between what is real and what is unreal, but at least the issues that confront us are now better-defined: the reliability of the eye-witness, the interpretation of his testimony, the group dynamics of anomalous experience, and the extent and the validity of the physical evidence. These are problems that will be considered in detail in the second part of this book.

8

Hoax

Shortly after dawn on a February morning in 1948, a resident of the seaside town of Clearwater, Florida, came across a remarkable line of footprints meandering along the sands. They came from the sea and marched along the beach for more than two miles before vanishing back into the waves. That was unusual enough. But as word of the discovery spread, the thing that most alarmed the people of Clearwater was the size of the unknown creature that had apparently called on them during the night.

The sand that dawn was damp, and the prints were clear and sharply defined. Each was three-toed and far bigger than the largest man's – about fourteen inches long and eleven across. Whatever had made them, it appeared, must have been between ten and twenty feet tall.

Men from the Sheriff's Department of Pinellas County went to the beach to investigate. A story spread through the town that a young couple, out on the seafront that night, had seen a huge monster rear out of the waves and come ashore, and that they had reported the incident to the police, who had searched the beach without finding anything. Nevertheless, a few days later, the creature was back, leaving a trail a hundred yards long to the north of the town, tracks on Dan's Island to the south, and two trails in the Indian Rocks area, one of them a mile long. During the autumn, more of the distinctive three-toed footprints appeared forty miles up the Suwannee River.

In New York, a British cryptozoologist and broadcaster named Ivan T. Sanderson heard of the bizarre tracks and travelled south to investigate. He examined plaster casts of some of the footprints, and it did not take him long to locate some witnesses who thought they had seen the elusive beast that had made them. The most important sighting was made by two pilots from Dunedin Flying School, who reported seeing a strange creature swimming off Hog Island on 25 July. They told Sanderson it was about fifteen feet long, 'with a very hairy body, a heavy blunt head, back legs like an alligator' and a long tail. A holidaying couple from Wisconsin, who had been fishing on one of the little islands off Tarpon Springs, said they had watched a large animal with 'short, thick legs, huge feet, no neck, covered with short, grey, thick fur' and with flippers rather than arms waddle out of some bushes and into the ocean. Finally, Sanderson himself saw a strange creature while flying up the Suwannee River. It was twenty feet long, a dirty yellow in colour, and wallowed on the surface of the river as he soared overhead.

Piecing the evidence together, Sanderson came up with a most peculiar theory. He suggested that the mystery animal was a type of giant penguin driven from its natural habitat to the Gulf of Mexico by some natural catastrophe. Though he admitted there were significant discrepancies in the information he had collected – how the notion of a penguin could be squared with the long-tailed animal described by the Hog Island pilots prominent among them – he did not believe the case could be a hoax. The trails were too long, he thought, and the prints too deep to have been made by man. As one of the United States' best-known zoologists, and a man with years of experience tracking large animals through far more difficult terrain than the Florida coast, his views commanded respect, and the strange case of the 'giant penguin' was occasionally noted as an unsolved mystery in books on the unknown.

It was not until fifteen years after Sanderson's death in 1973 that it become clear that Florida's penguin panic had been a hoax all along. The trails of footprints had been concocted by a couple of friends, Al Williams and Tony Signorini, who had been inspired to make them by the recent discovery of dinosaur tracks in New Mexico. Together, they experimented by building giant concrete feet to wear over their shoes; when these proved insufficiently bulky to leave really deep prints in the sand, they went to a local foundry and had a pair of three-toed boots cast in iron. Each boot weighed 30 lbs, and when Tony Signorini eventually confessed his role in the affair to the *St Petersburg Times* in 1988, he still had them, hidden in a box in his workshop. The boots perfectly matched the plaster cast prints taken on Clearwater beach, proving that the affair was a hoax. The tracks had been made as a joke, pure and simple; there was no intention to profit from the furore, nor even any real plan to reveal the truth. Williams had died long before Signorini decided to confess his role in the prank to the local paper; had the surviving friend chosen to remain silent instead, the solution to the mystery would have died with him.

The whole ridiculous business still retains the power to baffle. The principal puzzle is how a naturalist of Sanderson's standing could have allowed himself to be taken in by what was really rather a crude deception. When the tracks were found it was observed that they seemed to have been made by a jointless, flat-bottomed foot, and, while their size may have suggested that they were made by something much taller than a man, the distance between each print was not much more than a single human stride. It was suspicious that all the tracks had appeared overnight, and then there was the problem of the conflicting descriptions given by the witnesses.

Indeed, the existence of so many witnesses – Sanderson included – is extremely revealing. Given that there *was* no giant penguin haunting the Gulf Coast in that remarkable year, what had the courting couple, the Hog Island pilots, the

14. The giant head which washed ashore at Tecolutia, Mexico, early in 1969. It weighed one tonne and was thought to be part of the body of a sea serpent.

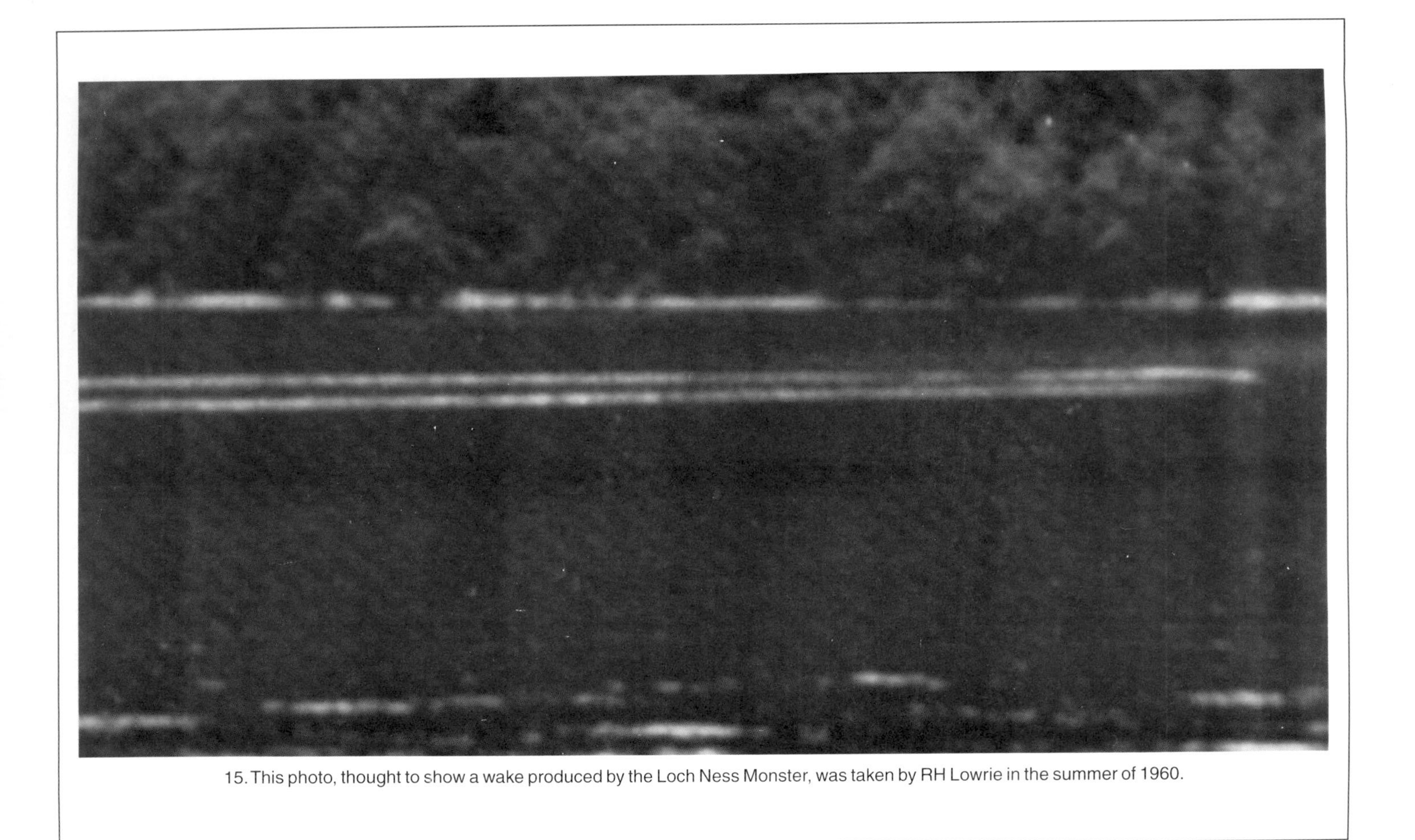

15. This photo, thought to show a wake produced by the Loch Ness Monster, was taken by RH Lowrie in the summer of 1960.

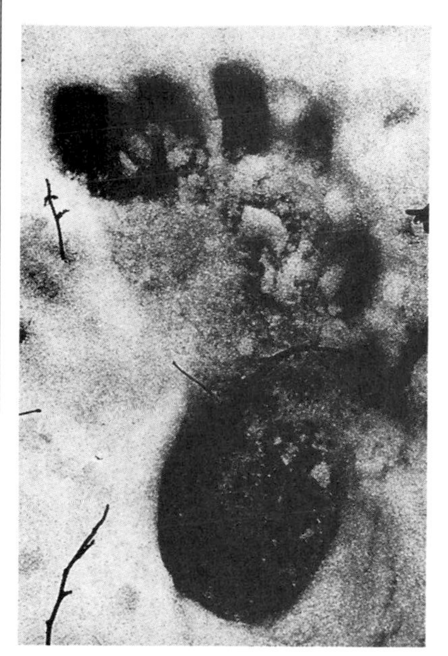

16. One of more than 1,000 footprints left by the 'Bossburg Cripple' – a Bigfoot with a club right foot – in Washington State in October 1969.

17. A giant snake reported from Siracusa, Italy, in August 1954.

18. Satellite photograph supposedly showing the gigantic north polar opening to a hollow earth.

19. Two of the Devil's arrows, a group of megaliths in northern England which form part of the longest generally accepted ley line in Britain.

20. *Above:* A patch of damp in Christ Church, Oxford, which bore a striking resemblance to the late Dean Liddell *(left)* and appeared a quarter century after his death in 1898.

21. *Below:* Some of the fish which fell from the sky over East Ham in 1984 and were recovered by Bob Rickard, editor of *Fortean Times*.

22. *Right:* One of the 'Holy Aubergines' which appeared across the Midlands in 1990, bearing in their seed patterns verses from the Koran.

23. *Below:* The charred remains of Helen Conway, whose body was destroyed in as little as six minutes – by spontaneous combustion?

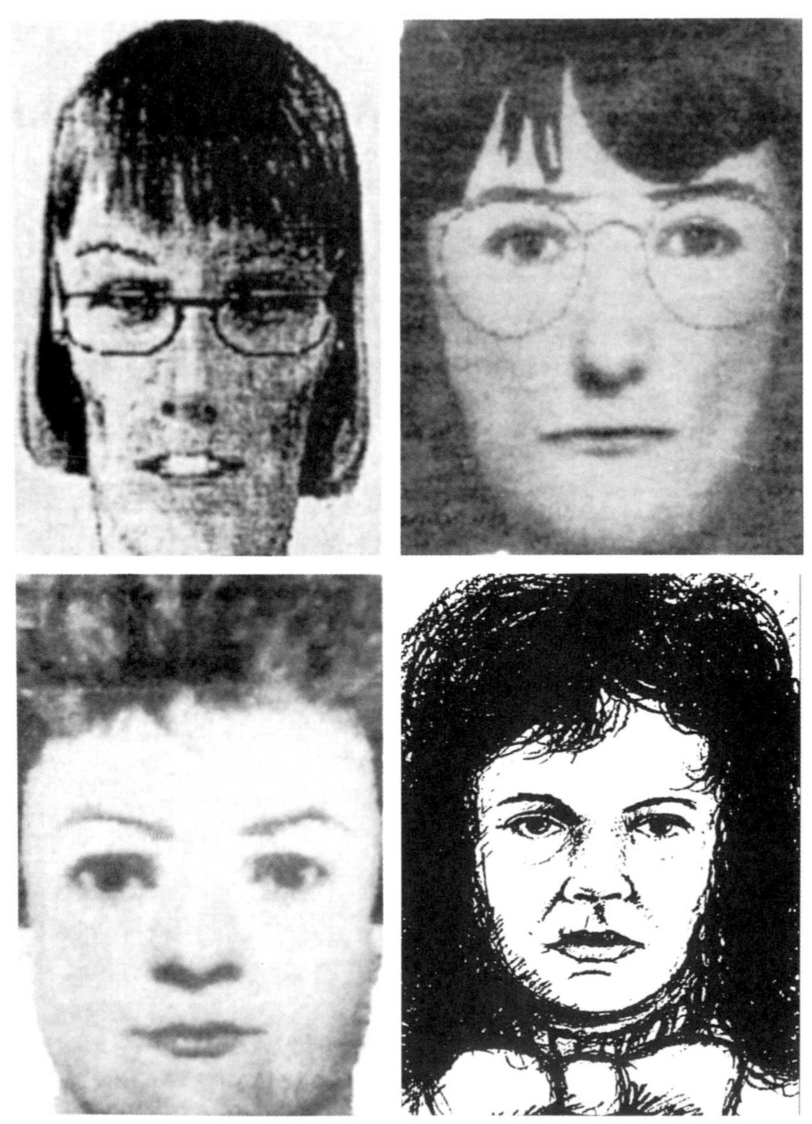

24. Official police photofits showing phantom social workers who appeared at homes in (left to right, top to bottom) Hampton, Bristol, Portishead and Leicester.

25. *Right:* A performance said to show the fabled Indian Rope Trick in the 1920s.

26. An artist's impression of the bizarre Goatsucker, which plagued Puerto Rico in 1995 and 1996.

Wisconsin tourists and the British naturalist actually seen? Another mystery animal, perhaps – but that seems to be stretching coincidence too far. It must be more likely that they had seen nothing at all, and either invented their stories out of mischief or to please their questioner, or, caught up in the excitement of the giant penguin panic, misidentified known animals that they had glimpsed for only an instant.

There is a second great lesson to be learned from the panic, and that is that ordinary people are prepared to go to extraordinary lengths to carry out a hoax. In the Florida case, Tony Signorini was willing to don his thirty-pound overshoes and labour for hours to make a line of prints down Clearwater beach. He described the great effort that was required, to the *St Petersburg Times*: 'I would just swing my leg back and forth and give a big hop,' he explained. 'The weight of the feet would carry me [about six feet]. They were heavy enough to sink down in the sand.' Even if we allow that the trail was probably not quite two miles long, Signorini must have repeated this action well over 1000 times that night. Had he never confessed, and had a sceptic suggested that the Florida tracks were really a hoax, that great line of prints would have seemed the best evidence that the giant penguin was real: after all, why go to all the trouble of making such a track when a line of prints a few hundred yards long would seem to serve the same purpose? The answer must be that the two pranksters took enough pride in their work to want to do it properly.

Florida's penguin panic teaches us that any description of the secret universe that fails to make a generous allowance for man's predilection for hoaxing, playing elaborate practical jokes or exaggerating for effect is certain to be an inaccurate one. This is a vitally important conclusion, not least because there has always been a tendency, among field researchers in particular, to underestimate the number of hoaxes and deceptions that litter the borderlands of belief.

There can, moreover, be no doubt that hoaxing has significantly influenced the development of many familiar mysteries from the moment of their birth. A determined and well-executed hoax can have enormous and unforeseen repercussions – providing the spark for a thousand reports of Bigfoot, perhaps, or the inspiration for the whole extensive apparatus of spiritualism and mediumship.

For this reason, the first step towards assessing the evidence for strange phenomena should be to sweep the case files clear of false reports, practical jokes and outright hoaxes, leaving as a residue only incidents of misperception and a core of genuinely inexplicable events.

This is, of course, much easier said than done. There is no such thing as a generally agreed estimate of the proportion of ostensibly genuine cases which are actually the product of malice and deliberate deception and, though some researchers have been fairly sanguine in assuming that their accumulated experience renders them well able to spot such hoaxes, experience suggests that only the crudest and least well thought out frauds are truly easy to detect. Any hoax carried out with a modicum of care, subtlety and knowledge of the subject – and a fair number that do not – probably has a good chance of eluding detection.

There are several explanations for this failing. A good many investigators seem unable to understand the lengths to which pranksters will go, and are unwilling to concede that the efforts they have put into researching a case have been wasted. They cannot believe that their witnesses may be clever enough and devious enough to fool them, and there may also be a human and understandable reluctance to admit to being deceived, even temporarily, into taking a hoaxed report seriously. Where a hoaxer has also claimed to be a witness, and allowed himself to be named, he is often protected by the additional presumption that no sane person would invite the ridicule and notoriety that tends to attach itself to those who have encountered the unknown. Sometimes it is only when someone seems to be making capital out of an experience that the notion of a scam is readily entertained. Yet, as one recent example shows, it takes only a handful of dedicated pranksters to create chaos in the borderlands.

Round in Circles

Beginning in the summer of 1980, perfect circles of flattened crops began to appear in the rolling countryside of the Thames Valley. The first to attract significant attention appeared in the Vale of Pewsey, within sight of one of the celebrated white horses cut into the local chalk. It was a neat formation of three circles in a field of corn; within each circle, every stalk of grain had been flattened in a clockwise swirl. A day or two after the circles appeared, a reporter from the local paper, the *Wiltshire Times*, visited the site and wrote a story suggesting that the circles were too neat and too precise to have been made by the wind, the rain, or downdraft from one of the army helicopters that exercised on Salisbury Plain. Perhaps they were made by UFOs, the *Wiltshire Times*'s report suggested.

More circles appeared in 1981, including another formation of three – one large, two small – at a place called Cheesefoot Head. After that, each successive summer saw a new crop. Nor was it long before more theories as to what the circles were, and how they came to be sited in the middle of the English countryside, were published. The UFO hypothesis still had its supporters: some knowledgeable ufologists pointed out that very similar reports had been made in tropical Queensland in the late 1960s, where the formations had been christened 'saucer nests'. But the most convincing explanation came from a meteorologist named Terence Meaden, who had a special interest in weather anomalies. He proposed that the crop formations were made by small whirlwinds, or dust devils, which became trapped in the lee of a hill and spun around on the spot, creating perfect spirals. The theory could even, at a stretch, explain a triple formation, such as that at Cheesefoot Head, if it was assumed that three small dust devils formed simultaneously along a miniature weather front.

The next year, though, things got more complicated still. Patterns of five circles – a large one surrounded by four small satellites, like the marks that might have been left by a flying saucer with four landing legs – appeared in five separate locations. The whirlwind theory could not account for the precision of such patterns, but there was now plenty of scope for alternative explanations, which ranged from a new suggestion of Meaden's (electromagnetic energy in the form of 'plasma vortices' – a phenomenon related to ball lightning) to the idea that the circles were the work of rutting hedgehogs. By now research had also uncovered the existence of a few pre-1980 circles. A scattering of more or less reliable reports went back to the 1940s and, eventually, the growing band of researchers uncovered a Restoration pamphlet that seemed to describe a crop circle that had formed in a field in Hertfordshire in 1678. It was said to have been mown by the Devil.

Media interest in the annual phenomenon reached a peak in the late 1980s, and so did the complexity of the crop formations. Simple, single circles of flattened wheat or barley were, by now, practically unheard of. Instead, rings of standing corn began appearing within the circles, and tails outside them. Eventually, in the summer of 1990, the phenomenon reached new levels of complexity with the appearance of a number of beautiful and highly intricate 'pictograms', or hieroglyphs, among the crops. The best was found in a field at Alton Barnes, Wiltshire, on 12 July. It was made up of four large circles and three smaller ones: a formation 130 yards long, connected by narrow swathes cut straight through the crop. There were several 'decorations': three of the circles featured long, toothed projections resembling keys.

Almost no one really believed that such fantastic formations could have been produced by a random meteorological phenomenon, however complex. True, Meaden continued to advance ever more complicated variations on his plasma vortex theory. He thought the Alton Barnes pictogram might have been made by 'an unstable double vortex . . . attracted to tractor-line regions because of local electric field anomalies initiated by the repeated passage of tractors up and down the field', but the bulk of the crop circle fraternity had now split into two broad factions. There were those who thought that the steadily increasing complexity of the patterns was being orchestrated by non-human intelligences of some sort (whether these were ufonauts, nature spirits or demons remained a matter for speculation), and those who believed that the more complex circles, at least, were the work of hoaxers.

Some members of the non-human intelligence faction produced interpretations that backed up their theory. Charles D'Orban of London University's School of Oriental and African Studies speculated that the shapes in the pictogram might be a message in Sumerian, the world's oldest written language. He thought the circles – which had appeared at the height of a severe drought – could be translated as a warning to 'double your wells'. Others thought the 'writing' was a Mongolian dialect, or perhaps Tifinig, an old North African script. A weatherman named Philip Eden suggested that they were meteorological symbols predicting, among other things, a force seven gale from the south-west.

The hoax hypothesis was not too popular in comparison, and seemed unlikely for several reasons. First, the formations were so perfect that it appeared inconceivable that even a team of people could have made them during the brief hours of summer darkness without leaving some trace of their presence. Crop circle experts also pointed to the strange way in which the corn and barley in the formations was swirled down without breaking the stalks, and to the vast numbers of formations that were now being reported – more than 500 in 1990 alone, including several in such out-of-the-way locations as Japan, Bulgaria, and Llanidloes, in Wales.

Yet, just as the phenomenon seemed to have become as inexplicable as it was complex, the world of the crop-watchers imploded with startling suddenness. In September 1991, the *Today* newspaper printed a short series of articles about two Southampton men, Doug Bower and Dave Chorley, who had confessed to hoaxing a large number of crop circles, beginning around 1975. According to the story they told, they had met in the late 1960s and discovered that they shared a number of interests – in art, for one thing, but also in strange phenomena.

Doug, who had a particular interest in UFOs, had spent much of the 1960s in Australia, where he had heard about the Queensland 'saucer nests', and one night he suggested that it would be interesting to create a similar formation in an English field and watch the ufologists argue about it. Together, the men made quite a number of circles in the late 1970s, using an iron bar to flatten the crop at first and then inventing an instrument they called the 'stalk-stomper', a much more efficient tool made from a plank and a length of rope. But no-one seemed to notice their activities (they never even knew of the excitement caused by the 1980 article in the *Wiltshire Times*), and they were on the point of giving up when their 1981 Cheesefoot Head triplet made the news.

Emboldened, the two men continued their activities, their efforts becoming more elaborate by the year. There seemed to be little risk of detection (except by Doug's wife, who had to be convinced that his absences from home at night were not evidence of an affair), and less danger (though during one foray, by bizarre chance, Doug was actually knocked unconscious by a lump of human waste that had fallen from an aircraft toilet), and the two men took great pleasure in creating new effects to baffle Terence Meaden and lead on the believers in non-human intelligences. Gradually, though, they began to realise that they weren't alone. Other circles began to appear – made not by alien beings, but a new generation of hoaxers.

One of these circlemakers was an American journalist, Jim Schnabel, who eventually wrote a history of the phenomenon. His close involvement with the crop circle community helped him to identify several dozen circlemaking groups, which gave themselves names such as 'Merlin & Co.' and 'The Bill Bailey Gang'. Several of their members were closely associated with various groups of believers.

Doug and Dave's revelations created an initial panic among the cropwatchers, especially when the pair displayed their credentials by creating several new and impressive formations to order. But a number of researchers refused to be convinced by their claims, falling back on the argument that real circles were formed with a precision and subtlety that no hoaxer could match. It was only when a number of these experts were fooled by man-made circles, which they unwisely assured the media were genuinely mysterious – 'If this is a hoax, I'll eat my shirt in public,' one said of a prominent fake during the 1992 circle season – that general disillusionment set in. Although small numbers of crop circles continue to appear in the corn each summer, often in spectacular and beautiful formations, the number of enthusiasts researching the subject, which had topped the 1000 mark at its peak, dwindled almost to nothing.

The crop circle saga is perhaps the single best example of a phenomenon riddled so rotten with fraud that it collapses from within. Much can be learned from it, from an understanding of the motivation of theorists who concocted increasingly complex natural explanations to deal with the ever more elaborate formations to a recognition of the pivotal role played by the media, who first encouraged, and then exposed the men behind the phenomenon.

Yet lost among these lessons lies a fragile truth. No one explanation is likely to solve a phenomenon as complex as the crop circle mystery. Not every circle need have been hoaxed; what about the apparently genuine recollections of pre-Doug and Dave formations, for example? There may have been something in the early meteorological explanations for the phenomenon.

Doug and Dave, after all, based their original design on Australian saucer nests whose origin is uncertain. There are also a handful of accounts by eyewitnesses who watched the formation of simple circles, which seemed to be made by dust devils, or even strange electro-magnetic effects. Some people appear to have seen plasma vortices at work in fields. A sequence of photographs, taken in August 1976, shows a whirlwind at work in a recently harvested field of corn. Behind all the many hoaxes, a rare but genuine phenomenon may still be lurking.

Faith and Fraud

The crop circle phenomenon is a modern example of a truly ancient art. There have been hoaxes for as long as there have been strange phenomena, and the motives for carrying them out were probably much the same as they are today – mischief, money, a perverse sense of achievement. In the heavily religious societies of the past, however, there was an additional reason to deceive: the need to inspire or reinforce belief.

It seems a reasonable guess that a disproportionate number of historic hoaxes had a religious inspiration, and that the people who carried them out in the past probably saw them as neither reprehensible nor wrong. Examples of such deceptions can be traced back millennia. At Baiae, in Italy, for example, an underground tunnel complex called the Oracle of the Dead, hacked out under an ancient temple during the days of the Roman republic, did duty as a passageway to the portals of Hades. A 200-yard tunnel led from the surface to a place some 140 feet below the surface, where two boiling volcanic springs fed steaming water into a channel that passed for the River Styx. For many decades, until they were suppressed by Marcus Agrippa around the time of Christ, the priests who tended the Oracle seem to have made a good living by welcoming the curious and those who wished to contact spirits of the dead. These visitors were, perhaps, dosed with hallucinogenic drugs and escorted below ground where, with the help of passageways illuminated by flickering torches and ceremonies conducted by black-cowled figures, they were convinced that they really had paid a visit to hell.

When Christianity became the official religion of the Roman Empire in the fourth century AD, a ready trade in the relics of Christ sprang up. The first customer for such articles of faith was Helena, mother of the emperor Constantine the Great (whose own conversion to the Christian religion was prompted by the appearance of a blazing cross in the sky over his army, shortly before he secured his empire in the Battle at the Milvian Bridge in October 312). In AD 327, at the age of seventy-two, she made a pilgrimage to Jerusalem, where she was escorted to various holy sites, including the supposed burial place of the True Cross. At Helena's demand a search was instigated, and no fewer than three wooden crosses were soon discovered in a cistern beneath an old temple.

The empress is said to have distinguished between the Cross of Christ and those of the two thieves crucified alongside him by laying a dying woman down on each in turn; when she was placed on the one True Cross, the invalid instantly recovered. The Cross was carried back to Constantinople along with Helena's other purchases: the nails with which Christ had been crucified, and a miraculously well-preserved crown of thorns. Nearly 1700 years later, though, few even among the devout believe that these easily located relics – to which the people of Constantinople attributed the survival of their city during a number of sieges over the next thousand years – were not frauds, produced to please a powerful and impatient woman.

More recently, it has been suggested that many of the other miracles associated with Christianity can also be explained as hoaxes and deceptions. A detailed study by an Italian chemist named Luigi Garlaschelli, for example, has made a valuable contribution to the debate that has been raging over the phenomenon of weeping, sweating and bleeding icons. Most come from Christian countries, where there are many miraculous statues of the Virgin Mary, but similar examples have been reported from other parts of the world. The Roman historian Livy reported that a statue of Apollo once wept for three days and nights in succession, while at Chengannur, in the Kerala province of India, an iron sculpture of the Hindu goddess Bhagawati is said to menstruate once or twice a year. The manner of its bleeding is appropriate: the statue stands in a shrine built on a sacred rock that, it is believed, was miraculously formed in the image of the god Shiva's penis. Nor does every example involve a statue; there is a holy tomb in the Lebanon which once trickled blood and is said to have effected at least one miraculous cure.

Garlaschelli began to study the phenomenon in 1995, when

there was a sudden rash of weeping statues throughout Italy. The first of these, a seventeen-inch plaster model purchased at the Marian shrine at Medjugorje in Herzegovina and installed in a garden in the small town of Civitavecchia, began to cry dark red tears in February of that year, and thousands of pilgrims flocked to see it. The statue was said to have wept up to nine times a day, for perhaps five minutes a time, and, as its fame grew, about a dozen similar cases were reported around the country.

In the past it has been alleged that samples taken from bleeding statues have been tested and shown to be human blood, but Garlaschelli's researches suggested a far more mundane explanation, which has the twin virtues of justifying 'blood', 'sweat' or 'tears' being produced from a statue to order, apparently from nowhere, while requiring no suspicious holes and no mechanical, electronic or chemical gimmicks. All that is needed is a glazed, hollow statue made of a porous material such as plaster. If the interior of the statue is filled with liquid – red for blood, clear for sweat and tears – the thin porous shell will absorb it while the glaze prevents it from seeping to the surface. All that a forger then needs to do to produce his effect is make an imperceptible scratch in the glaze, say at the corner of one eye.

Garlaschelli's solution has the virtue of simplicity (the secret could have been discovered in antiquity, and passed on, or rediscovered, many times since then), and the fraud would be difficult to detect: once the liquid was exhausted, there would be few traces of its presence left in the icon. It certainly explains why there are very few cases of statues weeping continuously, or even regularly for very protracted periods – though examples have been reported of icons that wept for up to eight years, on occasion. The best way of accounting for periodic flows (such as in the Civitavecchia case) is to assume that a hoaxer is stopping and unstopping a scratch in the glaze several times a day.

This scientific explanation for weeping and bleeding images turned out to have an unexpected relevance when hundreds of

Hindu statues suddenly began to drink milk in September 1995. The phenomenon began in India and was also reported from London and Hong Kong, New York and Singapore. Religious images, usually statues of Ganesh, the elephant-headed son of Shiva, began supping liquid offerings one morning and continued for anything up to three days, as tens of thousands of Hindus gathered at temples to watch and, if possible, feed their gods. The Gateway supermarket in Southall, London, sold out of 28,000 pints of milk in a morning once news of the miracle spread.

The sceptics' plausible explanation for this all but unprecedented phenomenon was the principle of 'capillary action' – in effect, the weeping and bleeding phenomenon in reverse. Any unglazed statue made of a porous material such as baked clay can absorb liquid with startling rapidity thanks to the interaction between the surface of the liquid and the network of pores that riddle the surface of the stone. Metal statues (many brass idols were also seen to drink) posed more of a problem, but experiments suggested that the milk that was fed to them could disperse across their surfaces in an almost invisible layer, and indeed milk mixed with a red dye was observed to do this when offered to a statue in New Delhi. Nevertheless, the sheer volume of milk some statues were said to have consumed was so great – several litres in some cases – that the phenomenon retains some of its mystery. Curiously enough, neither sceptics nor believers seem to have taken the obvious next step of revisiting the miraculous statues a week or two later to find out whether the temples were reeking of yoghurt.

One final religious hoax deserves consideration here, if only because of its sheer outlandishness. It concerns the supposed discoveries of a seismological team who, at the tail end of the 1980s, bored nine miles into the earth's crust somewhere in Siberia. At that great depth their drill suddenly began to rotate more rapidly, indicating that it had penetrated a cavern of some sort. The joint Soviet-Norwegian team lowered a special microphone into the depths in the hope of recording the sounds of continental plates clashing together. Instead – it was reported in the fundamentalist Christian press – their instruments detected unexpectedly high temperatures of up to 1100° C, and their microphone recorded indescribable moanings, as though millions of souls were writing in torment. Worse was to follow. When the instruments were withdrawn, a certain Dr Dmitri Azzazov testified that 'a cloud of gas escaped and – we could not believe our eyes – a creature appeared. Its teeth and eyes expressed only evil as it howled like a wild beast before vanishing.' Only one conclusion seemed possible: the team had drilled all the way to hell.

News of the remarkable discovery seems first to have appeared in the Scandinavian press in August 1989, but it soon made its way into journals such as *Biblical Archaeology Review* and *These Last Day Ministries*. The source for the story was a Norwegian named Age Rendalin, who claimed to be a 'special counsellor to the Minister of Justice in Norway'. He, in turn, said that he had picked it up from Christian radio stations in California, and had returned to Norway to find the papers there full of similar reports.

Investigation eventually revealed that Rendalin was really an Oslo schoolteacher. He stuck to his story about hearing the bare bones of the tale on American radio, but confessed to having circulated most of the interesting details, including the astonishing revelations of Dr Azzazov, in order to find out how carefully the Christian press checked their stories. The original inspiration for the whole story may have been a news item about the unprecedentedly deep Kola Borehole in Russian Lapland. From there, the tale began to spin out of control with the gradual accretion of layers of speculation and wish-fulfilment. Rendalin's hoax merely whipped the whole whirlwind of rumour to such a pitch of frenzy that it could no longer support its own momentum, and collapsed.

Yaqui Business

A simple fraud such as this is not too hard to detect. Its very outlandishness betrays it, and its principal begetter, who has no particular reason to conceal himself, can be tracked down. But a number of other hoaxers have succeeded in establishing themselves at the centre of quite complex belief systems, and in attracting numerous believers who, in some cases, have been persuaded to surrender all their possessions, leaving the leaders of such groups wealthy and with a motive to spin more elaborate fantasies capable of attracting new devotees.

Any number of modern cults fit this description. We have also seen how the religion of spiritualism grew from the admitted frauds of the bone-clacking Fox sisters. But two more modern, and essentially literary, hoaxes remain much less well known and have continued to fool numerous readers.

In the 1950s, almost the only works available in Britain dealing with unusual phenomena were those of an author who claimed to be a Tibetan Buddhist lama named T. Lobsang Rampa. Rampa published a series of books, beginning with a volume called *The Third Eye* in 1956, which told how he had been educated in a monastery in Lhasa, undergone an operation that opened his 'Third Eye' and accessed his latent psychic powers, and had even flown in combat against the invading Japanese. Later volumes included a number of even more remarkable stories, such as Rampa's account of how he had projected his astral body to Venus, where he had conversed with a number of 'ascended masters', including Christ and Buddha.

After a year or two, Rampa's books had enjoyed enough success to attract the attention of several Tibetan emigres who remarked on the implausibilities of his account of life in Lhasa. Puzzled and suspicious, they hired a British private detective named Clifford Burgess to investigate the author and discover how much he really knew about the mystical side of Buddhism. Burgess's report was not merely devastating but actually farcical. 'Rampa', he reported, was no lama. His real name was Cyril Hoskins, and he was a plumber's son from Plympton in Devon. He shaved his head to cultivate a suitably oriental look, and was certainly an avid student of the occult, but he had never been anywhere near Tibet, had never flown fighter planes, and had certainly never had surgery on his third eye.

Remarkably, perhaps, Hoskins's career survived these devastating disclosures. As he explained in *The Rampa Story*, his most comprehensively autobiographical work, he was indeed Hoskins – but only after a fashion. As Rampa, he had actually died on his journey from Tibet to Britain and his spirit had been forced to find a westerner's body to inhabit. The lama and the plumber's son met on the astral plane where, in exchange for a healthy karmic credit, Hoskins agreed to turn over his physical body to the Tibetan. Disencarnate Tibetan psychic surgeons got to work, and Rampa the homeless, celibate monk inherited Hoskins's English looks, his house and, incidentally, his wife. Burgess's report thus neatly side-stepped, Rampa/Hoskins went on to write nearly a dozen further books, including one, *Living With the Lama*, which purported to be the telepathically dictated memoirs of Rampa's cat. They did not enjoy the success of *The Third Eye*, but did collectively sell more than a million copies during the 1960s.

The Rampa fraud was a crude one. There were many obvious implausibilities about the tales, and it was only the public's general ignorance of Tibet and of the occult that enabled Hoskins to get away with it. The hoax perpetrated by Carlos Castenada, in some respects Rampa's spiritual successor, was sophisticated in comparison. Yet Castenada, who enjoyed considerable success in the 1970s with *The Teachings of Don Juan* and three other books about his encounters with a Mexican Indian sorcerer and his initiation into the mystical 'Yaqui way of knowledge', used essentially the same technique.

Castenada's Don Juan books are the best-selling works in the history of anthropology, attracting an audience of millions with their mix of philosophy, adventure and startling psychic phenomena. Castenada explains that the Yaqui sorcerer and his friend, Don Gennaro, are able to levitate, teleport and generate poltergeists and strange visions at will. They strive to unsettle the author's – and thus also the reader's – sense of reality, replacing it with the vision of an ever-shifting universe underpinned only by the powers of sorcery.

This philosophy proved extremely attractive to readers who grew up in the 1960s and were influenced both by the ideals of that decade and the advocacy of drugs to attain enlightenment (Don Juan and Castenada take a variety of interesting hallucinogens in the name of education). Another factor, which lent the books considerable credibility, was that Castenada had received a PhD from the University of California at Los Angeles for a thesis based on the field notes that he claimed to have compiled during his time with Don Juan in Mexico. His work was hailed as a classic of 'experience-centred' anthropology and a model for colleagues who wished to get inside the heads of their subjects.

Yet, according to Richard de Mille, the author of two critical studies of Castenada's world, there is no evidence that the giggly Don Juan and his friend Don Gennaro (whose love of lavatory humour prompted one writer to label the pair 'the Laurel and Hardy of shamanism') ever existed, nor that the author carried out any field work among the Yaqui Indians. Although Castenada's books boast far more internal consistency than most literary hoaxes, there are one or two significant errors that suggest that they are works of imagination. As for the attractive and intriguing philosophy that underlies the adventure and the strange phenomena, the thesis on which the popular works were based appears to have been written at UCLA. Castenada gambled, successfully, that the professors who would examine him had not read all the books in their own libraries.

De Mille's deconstruction of Castenada extends to the personal history that the author claimed for himself, which was shown to be as fraudulent as Cyril Hoskins's. Yet Castenada's critics and his friends agree that his books have something worthwhile to say. More than one professional anthropologist has insisted that it matters little whether they are works of fact or fiction, since they contain important truths. Few hoaxers can claim that sort of distinction.

Mirabelli, and Other Miracle-Workers

It should go without saying that frauds that involve the creation of additional categories of experience and whole new philosophies are few and far between. Hoaxes that seek to reinforce an existing belief are far more common.

Indeed, a sceptic might argue that almost the whole history of spiritualism and psychical research is the history of such frauds. This is an extreme view, but it is certainly fair to say that the true sources of all the spectacular physical effects produced by mediums – which have helped to define our idea of what a seance should be, from table-rapping to ectoplasm – have been called into question. Many physical mediums, including a number of the most respected, were actually caught in such fraud at least once in their careers.

Among the most puzzling of these cases is that of Eusapia Palladino, a poorly educated Italian woman from the town of Bari, who was the first of this new breed of medium. The orphan daughter of a mother who died in childbirth and a father who was killed by brigands, Palladino travelled north around 1866 to work as a nursemaid in Naples. She was said to have been discovered by the parapsychological community in a strange but very appropriate way when the noted Italian psychic investigator Damiani attended a London seance at which a spirit named 'John King' appeared. King spoke of a powerful medium in Italy who was his reincarnated daughter. The spirit gave the street and the number of the house in Naples where Palladino was working.

Following her discovery by Damiani, Palladino astonished Italy by giving a series of seances at which objects appeared to move or levitate of their own accord, musical instruments played themselves and figures materialised from thin air. Palladino herself also exhibited the rare phenomenon of bodily elongation, appearing to grow up to four inches taller than her normal height at times. Such unprecedented marvels soon attracted the leading psychical researchers of the day, and the medium was invited to hold seances in London, Paris and New

York. Most took place in the dark, as was already traditional, but others were held in reasonable light. On several occasions Palladino, whose hands were held by her investigators and who frequently conducted seances while strapped to her chair in an attempt to exclude the possibility of fraud, produced phenomena that baffled her famous and eminently qualified sitters. One, Ercole Chiaia, noted: 'This woman rises in the air, no matter what bands tie her down. She seems to lie on the empty air, as if on a couch; she plays on . . . organs, bells and tambourines as if they had been touched by her hands or moved by the breath of invisible gnomes. If you place in the corner of the room a vessel containing a layer of soft clay, you find after some moments the imprint in it of a small or a large hand, or a face from which a plaster cast can be taken.'

However convincing they appeared, though, it is evident that Palladino's effects were similar to those achieved by conjurors with the help of threads and accomplices, and she was many times caught in deliberate fraud. At a series of seances held at Cambridge in the summer of 1895, and attended by the well-known stage magician J.N. Maskelyne, the medium was detected raising a table with her foot and using a free hand to produce several levitation effects. She was similarly exposed at a series of seances held later in the United States.

Palladino's frauds have always divided the world of psychical research. Her sceptical critics have argued that, once any supposed medium has been caught in a deception, it is fair to presume that similar effects obtained on other occasions were also the products of fakery. The medium's supporters – including, it has to be said, some of the eminent psychical researchers who had detected her in fraud – argued equally strongly that her seances varied in quality from day to day and place to place, and that on some occasions, which they had observed, the strange things that happened in them were genuinely inexplicable. Palladino, they suggested, turned to fraud because she was unwilling to disappoint her sitters when her 'inner energies' were low or conditions were generally inauspicious.

The case of Eusapia Palladino demonstrates, as we have already seen, that almost any complex phenomenon may contain some evidence that suggests it is genuine and some that proves it a fraud. At this late date it is not possible to say whether the psychical researchers who investigated her and pronounced her at least intermittently genuine (even though some were highly sceptical of her claims), were deceived – and deciding what to believe and what not to seems essentially a matter of taste. The most sensible course may be to suggest that, in cases where fraud has been detected once, the strictest controls should thenceforth be applied, and benefit of the doubt offered sparingly, if at all.

It is fair to say that few other mediums have matched Eusapia Palladino's ability to produce physical effects during seances. One who did, the Brazilian medium Carlos Mirabelli, has also been exposed as at least an occasional fraud. Mirabelli was reputed to produce automatic writing in twenty-eight languages, make trance speeches in twenty-six, materialise and dematerialise solid objects and even the spirits of the dead, and also play billiards without using his hands. He is best remembered today for a photograph taken around 1934, which shows him apparently floating, hands outstretched, in mid air at his home near Sao Paulo.

An examination of the best available print however, produced evidence of retouching in the area just below the medium's shoes and led investigators to conclude that, far from levitating, Mirabelli was actually standing on a step-ladder at the moment the picture was taken. Since his death, the reputation of this king of psychics has declined to the point where most of his feats have been called into question. Physical mediumship is now an almost forgotten art – one of the last British mediums to claim to materialise objects at seances (he specialised in roses) was eventually caught with flowers hidden in the battery compartment of his tape recorder – a good indication that most if not all of its old practitioners were hoaxers.

The Kidnapped Calf

Spiritualism is not the only phenomenon with foundations in a mire of fraud. The American airship wave of 1896–7, which, when rediscovered by ufologists in the 1960s, was hailed as the best evidence that the flying saucer had a history predating 1947, is today generally dismissed as the product of simple misidentifications and outright fakery.

Many late nineteenth-century sightings of 'lights in the sky', it now seems clear, were no more than visions of the planet Venus. Meanwhile an intensive historical reinvestigation involving a search in the archives of some 1500 local newspapers, turned up evidence that many of the most famous and spectacular cases from the wave were outright inventions.

Two of these reports stand out from the rest for their sheer drama and their impact (they have been reprinted as fact in dozens of books). On the evening of 19 April 1897, according to a letter published in a paper called the *Farmer's Advocate*, a strange airship, crewed by six tiny beings, descended over the Kansas farm of a rancher named Alexander Hamilton, lowered a rope, and hoisted one of his prize heifers off into the sky. The next day, a neighbour discovered the hide, legs and head of the unfortunate beast lying on soft ground, with no evidence of footprints leading up to or from it.

This astonishing tale, with its parallels with the twentieth-century obsessions of alien abductions and cattle mutilation, naturally attracted considerable interest, but none of the many authors to reprint it bothered to investigate it further until Jerome Clark contacted some of the older residents of the area in the mid 1970s. Clark was able to establish that Hamilton had invented the story as an entertainment for the local Liars' Club – a group who gathered occasionally to see who could spin the most outlandish tall tale. The farmer had even penned a confession to the hoax, which rested undisturbed in the files of another obscure local newspaper, the *Atchison County Mail*, until its eventual rediscovery in 1982. The find came as a particular blow to the many ufologists who had placed their faith in affidavits that the witnesses had signed and in reassurances, found in other contemporary press reports, that Hamilton was a man of great personal honesty and integrity.

On the same day that the Kansas farmer had his supposed close encounter, another newspaper, the *Dallas Morning News*, published an even more remarkable story – one that again presaged one of the major themes of late twentieth-century ufology. This one concerned the crash of another airship in the little settlement of Aurora, Texas. The ailing craft had apparently flown low over the town before smashing into a windmill owned by one Judge Proctor and exploding into tiny fragments. The body of its pilot – a strange little creature whom the locals assumed was probably a Martian – was reportedly recovered and interred in the local cemetery.

The rediscovery of this story in the 1960s brought several ufologists to Aurora armed with spades and a determination to prise an exhumation order from the local authorities, but it too was eventually discovered to be a hoax. The perpetrator on this occasion appeared to be a local telegraph operator named S.E. Haydon, who span the yarn to while away the hours on a boring shift and in the hope of attracting visitors to a town dying after being by-passed by the railway. As in the case of the Kansas calf-napping, the story of the Aurora airship crash had been bolstered at the time by the addition of bogus endorsements in the local press.

The lesson learned from the discovery of such hoaxes was the unreliability of the American press in the nineteenth century, at a time when journalistic resources were minimal, space had to be filled and modern standards of objectivity and honesty were barely understood. Upon closer examination, late nineteenth-century newspapers have proved to be full of invented tales and hoaxes – and this is true not only of the United States but also the press of other countries. In Britain, for example, the respectable *Illustrated London News* of 9 February 1856 ran a spectacular 'entombed animal' story concerning the discovery, during the construction of a French railway tunnel, of a living pterodactyl the size of a large goose.

This too was a hoax, the fraud being signalled to the paper's more knowledgeable readers in the animal's supposed Latin name *Pterodactylus anas* (*anas* = 'duck' = 'canard'). There is no particular reason to suppose that accounts taken from similar sources of strange sea serpents and the wild men of the backwoods will necessarily be any more accurate.

Ufology has continued to generate a huge number of hoaxes and frauds well in to the twentieth century. Perhaps the most complex was the Ummo affair, a Spanish case that began with a close-up sighting of a flying disc in the Madrid suburb of Aluche on 6 February 1966. The principal witness, one Jordan Pena, described an enormous circular object with three legs and, on its underside, a curious symbol: three vertical lines joined by a horizontal bar. The two exterior lines curved outwards at the edges, which made the pictrogram resemble the alchemical sign for the planet Uranus.

Pena's sighting caused a certain amount of excitement, which grew when the author of a local UFO book received a packet of photos showing the underside of a similar saucer adorned with the same strange symbol. Shortly afterwards, a leading Spanish contactee named Fernando Sesma became involved when he began receiving lengthy, typewritten documents that purported to come from a spacefaring race called the Ummites. The visitors announced that they came from the planet Ummo, 14.6 light years from earth, and their letters addressed a wide range of technological, philosophical and political issues, the last from a noticeably left-wing stance. Over the next twelve months, the Ummites mailed around 150 letters containing a total of 1000 pages of information, data and space gossip. Each page of every letter was stamped with the symbol that Pena had seen on the Aluche saucer.

Although few ufologists outside Spain took the affair seriously – the photographic evidence was highly suspect, and, while the Ummite letters were more sophisticated than most contactee communications, there was nothing in them that could not have originated on Earth – none could doubt that considerable effort had gone into the supposed hoax.

Precisely who, or what, was behind the letters and the photos (it has been suggested that the affair was an extended prank, the work of some foreign intelligence agency, or even an attempt by a socialist group to publish radical material that could not otherwise have appeared under General Franco's dictatorship), the Ummo affair appears to have been a literary equivalent to the Clearwater penguin panic. It proved once again that some hoaxers are prepared to invest an enormous amount of effort in their deceptions for no obvious reward.

A similar case, which occurred in America during the 1950s, has won greater fame. It began when an American ufologist named Morris Jessup received two rambling letters – signed variously 'Carl Allen' and 'Carlos Allende', but evidently written by the same strange person – alleging that the US Navy had conducted a series of bizarre experiments during 1943 which were designed to render an entire warship invisible. According to the mysterious letter-writer, these tests had been all too successful. A destroyer, the USS *Eldridge*, had been surrounded by a force-field so powerful that it not only cloaked the ship from view, but also sent half its crew mad and caused other seamen to spontaneously combust. In another experiment, the *Eldridge* had been teleported from its base to the naval dockyard at Norfolk, Virginia. Because these trials had taken place at the Philadelphia Naval Yard, the case became known as the Philadelphia Experiment.

A few months after Jessup received the incredible letters, a copy of his book, *The Case for the UFO*, was mailed to the Office of Naval Research. It had apparently been annotated by three gypsies – 'Mr A', 'Mr B' and 'Jemi' – who possessed remarkable inside knowledge of the UFO mystery; one of the writers, 'Mr A', seemed to be none other than Carlos Allende. A few ONR officers were sufficiently intrigued by the annotations to arrange for a small private facsimile printing of the book, an action that naturally convinced many ufologists that there may well have been some truth in Allende's bizarre claims.

In fact, as the researcher Robert Goerman discovered, purely by chance, in the summer of 1979, the letter-writer was not a gypsy, nor a Spaniard – and certainly not an extraterrestrial, as one or two later UFO authors had suggested. His name really was Carl Allen, and he came from New Kensington, Pennsylvania. He was an intelligent drop-out who had concocted the whole Philadelphia Experiment story and written the Jessup letters and all three sets of notations in the marked-up copy of *The Case for the UFO* himself. Some of the background for the story came from his own experiences in the Second World War, when he had served on a merchant ship that tied up alongside the USS *Eldridge* at Philadelphia Naval Yard.

Today, the strangest thing about the whole Allen/Allende hoax is not the suggestion that the US Navy possessed, in 1943, technology that should have made the American government's subsequent multi-billion dollar investment in stealth technology an irrelevance, but the absence of basic research by the many people who had written about the Philadelphia Experiment. For example, Allende was always described as an utterly elusive mystery man, who flitted from address to address and could never be traced. As proof of this, it was explained that one of the several return addresses given in his letters was an abandoned New Kensington farmhouse. In fact, as Goerman discovered, the farmhouse was not only occupied, it was owned by Carl Allen's family. Any researcher who had taken the trouble to visit or even write to the address could have discovered the truth about the 'mysterious Carlos Allende' for himself. None did.

In fairness, it should be added that the UFO community is sometimes capable of substantial feats of research. Far more effort has been devoted to attempts to prove or disprove the authenticity of a more recent *cause celebre*, the so-called Majestic 12 affair – and with good reason. 'MJ-12', its proponents say, was, and possibly still is, a top secret US government committee formed to consider the UFO problem. It was supposedly set up by President Truman in September 1947 and its dozen members (who apparently originally included Truman's Secretary of Defense, James Forrestal), were made privy to every scrap of information that the government possessed about flying saucers – including the explosive revelation that a UFO and its four alien pilots had been recovered from the New Mexico desert near Roswell and that news of the retrieval had promptly been covered up with a phoney story that the object had been a weather balloon.

The mere existence of MJ-12 and its amazing fund of secret information remained unknown to anyone in the UFO community until December 1984, when a little-known researcher named Jaime Shandera, who had spent two years working on the Roswell cover-up story with William Moore, received an anonymously posted package containing photographs of two Majestic-12 briefing documents about crashed UFOs. Several years later, the British ufologist Timothy Good also received a copy of the same documents. None of the three researchers has ever revealed where their packages were mailed from, and the original film negatives have not been made available for study. There is therefore no way of proving that either of the remarkable documents is genuine.

On the other hand, several attempts have been made to prove that the MJ-12 papers are fakes. Several sceptics have paid close attention to the non-standard phraseology and rendering of dates in the two documents, but by far the most devastating disclosure was the revelation, by the eternally doubting Philip Klass, that the presidential signature that ends one of the papers appears identical to a known Truman signature at the foot of a mundane official memo, which is freely available to anyone requesting a copy at the National Archives. This one discovery, particularly when considered in the context of the peculiar provenance of the MJ-12 papers, has been enough to cast fatal doubt on the whole affair, even though the identity of the presumed hoaxer has never been revealed. William Moore acknowledges that many ufologists suspect he himself forged the documents that his partner received, but has always denied that this was the case.

The Dark Side

Whatever his role in the MJ-12 affair, Moore has openly admitted to taking an active part in a deception which not only ranks among the most spectacular of frauds, but suggests that the US government is playing an active part in spreading confusion and disinformation among members of the UFO community.

At the end of the 1970s, a New Mexico UFO investigator called Paul Bennewitz began to research a possible abduction case involving a mother and her young son. Under hypnosis, the woman recalled the abduction itself and details of what had happened next. She and her son were taken to an underground base, she told Bennewitz, where they saw a liquid-filled vat in which floated human body parts. They watched as their abductors vivisected a kidnapped calf – this was at the tail end of the cattle mutilation panic – and were themselves subjected to a medical examination during which small metal objects were implanted in their bodies. The objects in the tank, she was to recall, 'horrified me and made me sick and frightened to death'.

Bennewitz was particularly intrigued by the strange implants. He believed the aliens – or EBEs (short for 'Extraterrestrial Biological Entities'), as he called them – were probably monitoring and controlling their abductees, and thought it might be possible to prove this by detecting any electromagnetic signals that they might beam to the implants. He soon became convinced that he was picking up alien low-level transmissions and that he had succeeded in decoding them with the help of a special programme he wrote for his home computer.

The established UFO groups did not take Bennewitz's theories very seriously, particularly when he announced that he had translated enough of the EBE's coded messages to discover that the aliens were behind the phenomenon of cattle mutilations and were also killing, dissecting and even eating humans. According to Bennewitz, they were using the blood and organs they obtained to prolong their own lives and to construct a sinister race of cyborgs from human and bovine body parts. The cyborgs would be used to reduce humankind to the level of slaves or cattle.

Still more dramatically, Bennewitz and his supporters alleged that the US government was well aware of what had been going on and had even struck a secret agreement with the EBEs, under which the aliens were allowed to maintain underground bases, mutilate cattle and even kidnap humans (though they had to promise to give the Americans a list of the people they planned to abduct). In exchange, the US government was promised the secrets of EBE technology and weaponry. Before long, though, the aliens had reneged on the agreement, leaving the Americans powerless to prevent the abduction of their citizens and the mutilation of their livestock.

Much of Bennewitz's material was provided by Sergeant Richard Doty, a member of the Air Force Office of Special Investigations. Doty quickly became a vital source of what appeared to be highly classified US government papers on the UFO mystery, one of them being the document that contained the first known mention of the Majestic 12 group. Favoured ufological contacts, including William Moore, were told that he represented a secretive group called The Aviary, made up of insiders who opposed the American government's cover-up of the UFO mystery. The members of the Aviary gave themselves appropriate code-names (Doty seems to have been known as 'Falcon') and said they could provide spectacular proof that there was a cover-up. A television producer named Linda Moulton Howe was told by Doty that he could arrange for the release of astonishing secret film of crashed flying saucers and meetings between humans and aliens, and even secure an interview with a captured ufonaut known as EBE-3.

Perhaps not surprisingly, Howe's footage never materialised, and her contract to produce a UFO documentary for the cable station HBO expired, though in 1988 Moore did arrange for 'Falcon' and another member of the Aviary, 'Condor', to appear on a networked documentary called *UFO Cover*

Up? . . . Live! Their faces and voices disguised, the two men related a number of extraordinary tales about the EBEs. Apparently, the aliens were in complete control of Area 51, and the US government's captured specimens enjoyed all sorts of earth music – especially Tibetan chanting – and snacked on strawberry ice-cream. Far from buttressing Bennewitz's conspiracy theory, as they had been expected to do, the two members of the Aviary invited nothing but ridicule with such testimony.

It was not until 1989 that William Moore came forward to make some sense of the whole Bennewitz–Doty–Howe affair. He flew to Las Vegas to address the annual Mutual UFO Network convention, declining to release the text of his speech in advance and insisting that he would take no questions from the floor. The latter stipulation may have been unnecessary, since many of the assembled ufologists were left dumbfounded by the address. Moore admitted that he had acted as an unpaid double-agent for the US intelligence services between 1980 and 1984, providing Doty and his superiors with information about Bennewitz and the civilian UFO group APRO. At the same time he had helped to feed a whole stream of disinformation, apparently cooked up by the Air Force Office of Special Investigations, to the hapless Bennewitz, who had not only believed it, but actually been driven to a nervous breakdown by the sinister 'revelations'.

AFOSI's aim appeared to have been to discredit the alien abduction movement, though some ufologists got caught up in the general atmosphere of conspiracy theory and suggested that Moore's disclosures were themselves part of the disinformation campaign. Moore excused his actions by saying that he had gone along with AFOSI in an attempt to learn more about the cover-up.

Photographs of the Known

In the one and a half centuries since the invention of photography, many hundreds of still pictures and films have been offered as evidence of everything from snapshots of flying saucers to photos of the gods. Such images have been extremely influential, not only because they have largely defined our idea of what the Loch Ness Monster, say, or Bigfoot, actually look like, but because the general presumption is that they are better proof than the unsupported testimony of a witness.

Some of the most intriguing of these photographs have been examined by experts and pronounced genuine – or at least not obviously faked. Yet the idea that paranormal photographs are proof of anything remains debatable at best. Cheap computer technology has now made the production of sophisticated forgeries so easy that it is probably fair to say that any still photographic evidence produced after, say, the mid-1980s, is at least theoretically suspect. But even before that date there were many different ways of hoaxing a photograph, and so many of the best images have been exposed as frauds over the years that it has become possible to wonder whether any of the remainder are unquestionably genuine.

Most photographic hoaxes rely either on models of some sort, or on the technique of double exposure. The former can be used to produce pictures of apparently solid objects, such as monsters or UFOs, while the latter is favoured for the manufacture of ghost photographs and other such frauds. It is rare – because there is generally no need – for a hoaxer to retouch an existing print or tamper with a negative, although the most common endorsement given to a picture is that it exhibits no sign of such tampering.

Double exposures were used as early as 1862 to produce 'spirit photographs' that usually purported to show a sitter surrounded by the spirit forms of the departed. A Boston man named William Mumler was the first to practise such deceptions, though they persisted into the 1920s. Mumler's initial effort was to produce an image on a photograph of a client, a Dr Gardner, which the sitter identified as his dead cousin. (He later acknowledged that the figure was actually a living model.) Undeterred, Mumler and his imitators proceeded to produce many similar pictures in which the 'spirits' were generally either exceedingly faint or swathed from head to foot in loose clothing. A minority of the images boasted cloth-draped figures with grotesque faces that were apparently moulded in *papier mache*. To modern eyes most spirit photographs are so crude that it is hard to imagine that anyone was ever taken in by them; but a number of spiritualists did take them seriously, and they offered comfort to many.

The nineteenth-century vogue for spirit photography had its echo in the notorious early twentieth-century case of the 'Cottingley Fairies', which produced a series of pictures that similarly outraged common sense while proving surprisingly difficult to dismiss as hoaxes. The fairy pictures were taken in 1917 and 1920 by two cousins, Elsie Wright and Frances Griffiths, in a small wood near Cottingley in Yorkshire. Cottingley itself is usually described as a village, which lends the pictures a charmingly rural air, though in fact it was by 1917 the largest 'village' in all England (it had its own town hall) and practically a suburb of the industrial town of Bradford. Elsie and Frances, who were sixteen and ten respectively when the first photographs were taken, secured the first two images using a plate camera borrowed from their father. Several years later they shot three more. They took the pictures, they later said, because Elsie's parents declined to believe their stories of encountering fairies in the dell.

The first two photographs were taken in July and September 1917: a portrait of Frances gazing at a troupe of dancing fairies and a picture of Elsie (her fingers weirdly elongated) watching the dance of a grotesque gnome. Arthur Wright developed the first plate in his own makeshift darkroom on the afternoon it was taken, but remained unimpressed by the image. He was certain the two girls had been 'up to summat', a view that was only reinforced when he developed the second photograph a few months later. Elsie's mother, a Theosophist, was more equivocal. She wanted to believe her daughter was telling her the truth.

Eventually, she showed the photographs to some friends at a local Theosophist meeting. From there the matter came to the attention of the president of the Blavatsky Lodge in

London, Edward Gardner. He, in turn, passed the two photos to Arthur Conan Doyle, the creator of Sherlock Holmes and a noted spiritualist, who paid for the girls to be supplied with a superior camera in the summer of 1920. Using this, they secured the three further images. One caught a female fairy in mid-leap, close to Frances's face; another showed a fairy offering Elsie a miniature bouquet. The third, and least clear of all the five photographs, pictured what the girls said was a 'fairy bower' in a bush and Gardner interpreted as a 'fairy sun bath'.

News of the Cottingley photographs broke in December 1920, when Conan Doyle published an article on the subject in the Christmas edition of the *Strand* magazine. A further piece, discussing the second series of photos, appeared a few months later, and general controversy reigned. Doyle's celebrity was enough to convince some of the veracity of the pictures, while others denounced them as obvious hoaxes. What must certainly have been clear, from the perspective of the Wright and Griffiths households in Yorkshire, was that matters had gone too far for Elsie and Frances to back down and admit their deception – if deception it was.

Of course – of *course* – the Cottingley photographs were fakes, and simple fakes at that. The fairies were paper cut-outs, mounted on hat-pins. (On close examination, the tip of one pin can be seen protruding from the gnome's stomach. Conan Doyle had noticed it in 1920 and suggested that it was the creature's belly-button, thus proof that the process of birth was much the same in the fairy realm as it is in our own world.) Some had been drawn by Elsie, a talented artist, and others cut from a wartime volume called *The Princess Mary Gift Book* and embellished with wings. (This explained the suspiciously modern hairstyles sported by the fairies, and their emphatically twentieth-century dress sense.) The 'fairy bower' shot appeared to be an unintentional double exposure.

It was not until 1981 that Elsie (then aged eighty) and Frances confessed, but evidence of fraud had always been there in the pictures for all to see. In the first photograph – showing

Frances surrounded by dancing fairies – a cascade in the background was blurred where the waters tumbled down into Cottingley Beck. Yet the fairies' wings and bodies were not, indicating that they were not in motion when the picture was taken. With hindsight it also became obvious that the photographs were far more carefully posed than the girls' accounts suggested, and that some had been retouched.

The Cottingley fairies saga is among the most instructive of hoaxes. Elsie and Frances's essentially simple deception endured for so long thanks to a curious combination of circumstances, many of which turn out to be present in other cases. To begin with, even doubters had to concede that the girls seemed too young and too inexperienced to produce such photographs. The two 1917 photos were said to be the first exposures Elsie and Frances had ever made. Experts from Kodak, who conceded that the pictures could have been hoaxed, added that they did not think two young girls from a Yorkshire village would have the knowledge and the ability to produce such forgeries.

This comment became one of the principal pieces of ammunition available to those who believed that the fairy pictures were genuine. Another was the telling conclusions of Harold Snelling, the expert consulted by Gardner. He was given the picture of Frances with the dancing fairies, examined it closely, and somehow felt able to announce: 'The plate is a single exposure. These dancing figures are not made of paper nor of any fabric; they are not painted on a photographed background – but what gets me most is that all these figures have *moved* during exposure.'

In retrospect, it seems that it was largely the weight of such apparently expert opinion – combined with the girls' protracted insistence that the pictures were genuine – that prevented the manifest flaws in the photos from being given due weight much earlier than they were.

Precisely similar situations have occurred several times since 1920. In the 1970s and 1980s, for example, one of the most colourful figures in modern monsterdom, an itinerant magician and entertainer called Tony 'Doc' Shiels, produced his own fairy photographs, and a whole series of pictures supposedly depicting sea serpents and the monsters of several different lakes. 'Doc' explained his amazingly high success rate by making the dubious assertion that he 'raised' the beasts from their lairs with psychic powers, but also insisted so adamantly that his photos were genuine that a number did appear in books and magazines about the unknown.

In 1992 Shiels's amiable hoaxes were finally exposed by Mark Chorvinsky, the editor of *Strange Magazine*, who showed that he had probably faked at least some of his snaps by photographing Plasticine models on glass. Chorvinsky also pointed out that the hoaxes were entirely predictable, since 'Doc' had published a number of books advocating hoaxing and setting out the techniques of forgery. Because these had been circulated among magicians rather than anomalists, they had never attracted the attention they deserved. In short, the Shiels affair demonstrated once again that the most apparently sincere of witnesses can be hoaxers.

Nor should it be forgotten that it is possible to fake moving images as well as still photographs of the unknown. Some of the earliest films of the Loch Ness Monster – those shot by a newsreel cameraman called Malcolm Irvine in 1933 and 1936 – appear to have been shot using models towed through the water. (Again, Irvine's phenomenal luck in capturing the monster twice on film should have aroused suspicion sooner than it did.) It has also always been rumoured that perhaps the most influential of all 'monster' films, a twelve-second sequence of 16 mm cine camera film showing what appears to be an adult Bigfoot, shot in 1967 by Roger Patterson and Roger Gimlin, shows a 'man in a monkey suit'.

The hoax – if that is what it is – must have been a relatively sophisticated one, since the Bigfoot in question appears to be a female endowed with pendulous breasts. Several analysts have pointed to a realistic-looking ripple of muscles under the skin, and Patterson and Gimlin backed up the film with a number of plaster-casts of footprints apparently left by the creature. Yet John Napier, an anthropologist with an interest in the Bigfoot story, points out that there is nothing in the creature's gait that could not have been duplicated by a human, and a recent reinvestigation of the ape-suit rumours by Mark Chorvinsky has shown that professional Hollywood make-up artists generally believe the film to be a hoax.

In these circumstances, it does seem that, at the very least, photographs and films of the unknown need to be backed up by other evidence that something strange is going on – and that the case files of many psychical researchers and UFO investigators require urgent reassessment.

Practising Deception

For many years, a spectacular parade of hoaxes and frauds has coloured the way in which strange phenomena are perceived. Millions of people who have never attended a seance imagine the experience as a display of physical mediumship involving rappings on tables and the manifestation of ectoplasm. For tens of thousands more, the Loch Ness Monster is the elegant, long-necked beast portrayed in the Surgeon's Photograph. Though ufologists dismiss the nightmare visions of Bennewitz and Lear as ludicrous, the media have nevertheless presented their theories to an avid public. It would be easy simply to condemn such frauds as dangerous and irresponsible and then to dismiss them. But this is to ignore the important truth that a strange relationship exists between a hoaxer and his public.

Every deception exploits a certain need. In the borderlands of reality this is often a need for proof, for spectacular confirmation of an existing hope or an established faith: Conan Doyle and his spiritualists wanted to believe in paranormal entities, and the Cottingley fairy photographs supplied the proof they sought. It may also be something as simple as a need for excitement – the horror of Paul Bennewitz's suggestion that aliens are farming human flesh with the knowledge and approval of the very people who ought to be protecting us is considerably more stimulating than the contemplation of yet another insoluble 'lights in the sky' UFO case.

Yet a good hoax generally offers more than this. In an essay to mark the supposed fiftieth anniversary of the Philadelphia Experiment, the ufologist Jacques Vallee identified no fewer than thirteen additional factors that helped to make Carl Allen's story so memorable, beginning with a startling but seemingly verifiable central fact: that the USS *Eldridge* had been rendered invisible and then teleported from one location to another. Vallee also stressed the importance of interesting witnesses (and the elusive 'Carlos Allende' was surely one of the most unusual and compelling witnesses of all), to which one might add 'authoritative witnesses' – after all, Eusapia Palladino's reputation rested as much on the public's knowledge that distinguished scientists had tested her and pronounced her genuine as it did on the phenomena that she produced.

A dramatic sequel helps: a second set of Cottingley fairy photos revived interest in the first, just as the arrival of Lear and Doty lent some credibility to the otherwise unsupported allegations of Paul Bennewitz. So, too, does any hint of official secrecy, or the suggestion that a key witness is risking all to expose that cover-up; as Vallee points out, 'as an "underdog" on the run, Carlos Allende had a degree of believability he would not have enjoyed had he been, say, a drugstore owner in Toledo or the manager of a Safeway store in Tuscon.'

Finally, the best and most believable paranormal hoaxes should appear to be beyond mere fabrication by humans. Those who believe that the Ummo letters were genuine communications from the people of another planet point to some lengthy technical passages in the papers, which discuss an extraterrestrial version of physics that seems much more advanced than our own. The drinking statues of Ganesh supped milk in full view of hundreds of the faithful. Doc Shiels's photographs were examined by several experts who could detect no definite evidence for fraud.

Many hoaxes that fit these criteria have been uncovered over the years, but the chances must be that very many more remain undetected. The only conclusion can be *caveat lector*: let the reader beware.

9

Hard Evidence?

There are many ways of classifying the unknown. Here is one that is rarely used, but which makes particular sense to anyone trying to assess and categorise the world of the unexplained as a whole.

There are two sorts of strange phenomena: those that may not be fully understood, but are undeniably real, and those that are not fully understood, and equally, may not be real at all. The first category includes mysteries such as ball lightning, falls of animals and objects from the sky, submarine light wheels, out of place animals and entombed frogs and toads. The second encompasses ghosts, ESP, extraterrestrial spacecraft, religious visions, monsters and miracles.

This classification takes into account the fact that the majority of reports of any strange phenomena are always shown to be hoaxes or mistakes, and focuses on the core of cases that have been investigated and labelled 'unexplained'. For example: the carcasses of out of place jungle cats, swamp cats and even the odd puma found littering the British countryside show that some, at least, of those who have reported sightings of big cats were telling the truth. So, while a study of those cases that were the product of mistakes and misperceptions might well produce some insights into witness psychology, the problem is where do the real cats come from. Are they simply beasts that escaped from human owners, or were deliberately released; are they members of an unknown breeding population of wild animals; or are some even being teleported from their natural habitat in Africa? Similarly, no one who has actually studied the evidence can really deny that fish, frogs, sand and so on, do fall from the sky. The question is, how they do so and, particularly, whether the popular scientific theory – waterspouts – is actually an adequate explanation.

Confronted by the evidence, even a sceptic would accept that some such cases involve real falls, real animals and so on. The same sceptic would, however, argue that there has never been a monster in Loch Ness (though there may be some large fish); that there's no evidence that earth has ever been visited by beings from outer space; that cases of telepathy, clairvoyance, precognition and psychokinesis can all be explained as lucky guesses, chance and fraud, and that most ghosts are simply the product of the imagination.

Considering these two broad categories, we can say that mysteries of the first type should prove to have rational, scientific explanations, though they may perhaps involve the development of existing theories in new directions. Should the mysteries of the second type prove to be in any way real, however, some major scientific theories (accepted because they have been tested and repeated) will have to be rejected or rethought. It is not surprising, therefore, that science has disregarded the evidence that has been offered for the reality of monsters and miracles, and demanded higher standards of proof.

Sheep and Goats

This demand confronts us with the problem of what sort of proof actually exists for the reality of strange phenomena. It must be said at once that the ideal – a testable and repeatable effect that can be obtained under laboratory conditions – does not exist. Psychical researchers, who have been tackling this difficulty since the 1930s, generally account for it by suggesting that psi is a weak and capricious effect, which is far stronger in some people than in others. Even those with strong psi powers, 'psychics', in other words, are thought to be highly sensitive to all manner of influences.

One of the most thoroughly explored is what is known as the 'sheep-goat effect' – the proposition that belief in psi, in itself, helps to determine whether or not a subject is able to demonstrate extrasensory perception. Gertrude Schmeidler, a former president of the American Society for Psychical Research, tested 1200 subjects in an attempt to prove her hypothesis that those who 'asserted with certainty that ESP was completely impossible under the experimental conditions would score lower than other subjects', and found that while believers and neutral subjects ('sheep') scored just above chance, her disbelievers ('goats') scored so far below chance that they seemed to be exhibiting what Schmeidler termed 'psi-avoidance'. Similar tests carried out with pairs of children suggested the corollary that the dominant partner would tend to score better than his more submissive friend.

Even a single subject is thought to be prey to a range of influences, ranging from his general state of mind, his motivation and whether or not he is suitably relaxed to his relationship with the experimenter. The difficulties of making the correct allowances for all these variables proved so great that much of the 1960s and 1970s was spent in a fruitless search for a suitably 'psi-conducive' experiment, and failure was taken to suggest that, even if every condition is favourable from the subjects' point of view, the outcome of the test can be affected by the experimenter himself, whose own state of mind, motivation and so on are also vital, and who may, even unconsciously, use his own psi to distort the results. This phenomenon is known as the 'experimenter effect'. Since it is virtually impossible to allow for such a wide range of variables while designing an experiment, it seems quite probable that, even if psi exists, a repeatable experiment that proves as much will never be developed

The Eye of the Beholder

Of course, the majority of strange phenomena are not testable under laboratory conditions. In fact, as we have often noted, most of them are not only encountered in isolated or out of the way places, but are observed by only a single witness. Almost everything we know about these phenomena depends on the accuracy of eyewitness observation in these given conditions.

The first point to make about such testimony is that it is generally of a poorer quality than most investigators and researchers understand or will admit. Indeed, eyewitness evidence is so fallible that quite extraordinary errors have been reported. A moment's reflection suggests that almost everyone has had personal experience of this problem in the form of what might be called 'the car-crash scenario': when two vehicles collide, not only the drivers, but any witnesses, will tend to give highly contradictory accounts of what has taken place. There is no reason to suppose that the same inaccuracies will not recur in eyewitness accounts of strange phenomena.

Allan Hendry, who was employed full-time as principal field investigator by the Center for UFO Studies, once published a volume called *The UFO Handbook* in which he drew attention to the unexpectedly poor quality of most eyewitness reports that he looked into. In case after case, Hendry – who found himself acquiring a detailed knowledge of the major natural causes of saucer sightings – was able to identify the supposed 'UFO' as a planet, a star, a satellite, an aircraft or a balloon. In one particularly dramatic incident, he was able to show that a witness who had nearly battered down his neighbours' door in an attempt to warn them of a huge UFO hovering overhead had actually been looking at the moon. (Even more remarkably, the witness accepted Hendry's explanation.)

It cannot be stressed too strongly that, had Hendry not

arrived on the scene, this case could have gone on record as a spectacular sighting of an entirely typical and physically real UFO. Most UFO books – indeed most books on strange phenomena – are largely filled with just these sorts of cases.

With this observation in mind, let's reconsider one of the accounts with which we opened this book – Tony Clark's experience of the non-existent *tchae khana*, where he enjoyed the best meal of his life. Clark and his companion, both level-headed engineers, came upon the restaurant during a long drive through an unfamiliar landscape; when he retraced his route a few months later he was unable to relocate the spot.

At first glance this seems a wonderfully eerie mystery, particularly when it is remembered that several similar cases are on record. Between 1952 and 1969, for example, John and Christine Swain made 250 journeys through the New Forest in search of a mist-shrouded lake they were convinced they had once passed whilst on holiday near Beaulieu Abbey. They were sure that they would recognise it because they clearly recalled a small island on which stood a sword embedded in a stone. There is also a tradition, a little further to the west, of a phantom cottage in a wood near Haytor in Devon, which baffled an Ordnance Survey worker who spied it from a hill and noted smoke rising from the chimney and washing on the line. Later, descending to the wood, he could find no trace of the building or its ghostly occupants.

But suppose Clark was mistaken? On the one hand, he was able to identify the village he had visited because of an unusual rock formation just outside it. On the other, he was, by his own account, unfamiliar with the area – a desolate part of northern Iran – and had been hungry and tired when he chanced onto the *tchae khana*, hardly the perfect conditions for accurate observation. Nor does he seem to have established the name of the village where the restaurant was located.

Whether or not Clark's phantom diner was genuinely inexplicable, it is certainly instructive to compare his case to the mystery of a vanishing hotel once thought to stand in the Sussex countryside. A British couple who passed this building one day made a note of its location because they were so enchanted by its appearance that they planned to return to stay; despite making many enquiries and a detailed search, however, they could not find the building again. But when an account of their quest appeared in the *Journal of the Society for Psychical Research* under the headline 'Hallucination of a non-existent building', a sceptic named Denys Parsons decided to retrace the couple's route himself. He successfully identified a wrong turning that had confused the pair and, working back from that, arrived at the very real hotel.

What, then, are the factors that affect the accuracy of an eyewitness report? First, we have to consider the physical conditions at the time: the weather, the visibility, the distance between the witness and the phenomena he was observing and so on. Then there is the problem of the duration of the encounter itself. (In most cases it is very short, perhaps in the order of a few seconds.) Next, there is the length of time between the event and when it was reported, which may be protracted because many witnesses are reluctant to come forward immediately. Finally, there is the eyewitness himself. Is he a good observer? Is his eyesight good? If there was another witness, did they discuss the incident in detail before making a report? (Most will, thus tending to produce an account in which there is an impressive agreement in matters of detail.) And, perhaps most important of all, what was the witness's 'state of mind' at the time that he had his encounter? Was he alert and focused, or disoriented and terrified? Are there any signs that he was in a state of high expectancy, or in a suggestible frame of mind?

It is an unfortunate fact that a resolution to consider only cases in which the conditions were favourable and the experience was prolonged, in which a report was made immediately by witnesses who were alert and proven good observers, and in which there is no hint that the observers had any expectation of making a sighting or were anything other than calm and sceptical for the duration of the encounter, would trim our casebook from several tens of thousands of cases to a few hundred incidents or less. From my own experience, I would estimate that less than five per cent of the material received by *Fortean Times*, the journal of strange phenomena, is considered worthy of publication – and almost all of that does not meet the conditions outlined above.

When Allan Hendry sat down to sift through the cases that remained when he had discarded every report of an unidentified flying object that proved to be identifiable, he found that he was left with 113 'genuine' UFO reports from a total of 1300 received by CUFOS between August 1976 and November 1977 (8.7 per cent). Few of those matched the ideal criteria, either. And when Susan Blackmore first visited the archives of the Society for Psychical Research, expecting to find them packed with documented examples of strange occurrences, she was told: 'Everyone expects our archives to be packed with cases but they're not. Only the very best ones – the ones that have had some sort of investigation – make it into them.'

In recent years, psychologists and physiologists who have taken an interest in the problems of perception and memory have been able to demonstrate just how fallible they are. One recent survey by Richard Wiseman and Peter Lamont of the University of Hertfordshire considered the fabulous Indian rope-trick – 'the world's best-known secular miracle' – a conjuring performance in which a magician makes a rope stand on end, after which a small boy climbs it. The trick has several known variations, ranging from the unimpressive (the boy climbs the rope and climbs down again) to the remarkable (while climbing the rope, the boy vanishes, only to reappear from a basket, which has been in plain view of the audience). In the classic version of the trick, the boy vanishes at the top of the rope and his voice is heard, refusing to come down. The magician climbs after him, and also disappears. Shortly thereafter, the parts of a dismembered body rain down from nowhere. The magician reappears at the top of the rope, descends, covers the bloody hunks of boy with his cloak and, hey presto, the child emerges from its folds alive once more.

Ranking their cases in order of impressiveness, Wiseman

and Lamont discovered that the average lapse of time between the event and the witness's report of the event was a mere four years in the least notable examples, but a remarkable forty-one years in the case of the most complex and striking accounts. This suggested that the witnesses embroidered their stories over the years, perhaps in telling and retelling their experiences. After several decades, what might originally have been a simple trick had become a highly elaborate performance in their minds.

How, though, did these witnesses come to elaborate their tales in such a consistent way? One answer would be that they already knew, or subsequently discovered, how the full-blown Indian rope-trick was supposed to look, and drew on this knowledge when they were embroidering their accounts. If this is true, we would also expect some witnesses who misperceive, say, the planet Venus as a UFO and who are familiar with flying saucer lore, to submit an elaborated account of their experience. Instead of seeing a bright but stationary light in the sky, they will report a fast-moving, brilliantly lit spacecraft. Similarly, some visitors to Loch Ness will see wave formations, but report a series of long, low humps moving swiftly through the water, and some sitters at a seance who see an object moved by the trickery of the medium will report that they witnessed a genuine and inexplicable psychokinetic effect. There is not even any reason why the witnesses in such cases should require years to elaborate their accounts; many will misinterpret the natural as supernatural during the experience itself. And, indeed, the literature of the unexplained is littered with reports of this variety.

A psychologist would say that such experiences are the product of 'expectant attention': people will see and feel what they want or expect to see and feel. Many telling experiments have been conducted to prove that expectancy exists. In one trial, subjects were told to walk along a corridor until a light flashed and, though no light ever did flash, some would duly stop. Similarly, a subject asked to hold two metal rods connected to a battery may well jump when the device is switched on, even if the battery is dead. He expects to feel an electric shock and, moreover, the shock of jumping will probably persuade him that he has felt one.

One product of this sort of expectant attention was noted by Tim Dinsdale, who drove to Loch Ness from his home in Reading in 1960 in the hope of filming the monster. It was an arduous journey, which took the best part of two days to complete. Once at the loch, Dinsdale had only six days in which to find and film the monster before he would have to return. He was a confirmed believer in the creature and had a good idea of what the monster should look like and how it would behave.

Arriving at Loch Ness on the afternoon of his second day at the wheel, Dinsdale drove along the southern shore. Suddenly he noticed a family pointing towards the water and waving their arms about in excitement. Knowing that this could presage a sighting of the monster, Dinsdale sped on and, sure enough,

> two or three hundred yards from shore, I saw two sinuous grey humps breaking the surface . . . I looked again, blinking my eyes – but there it remained as large as life, lolling on the surface!
>
> I swung the car across the road and locked the wheels, pulling up in a shower of gravel; and flinging open the doors, I lifted the camera out with its long ungainly tripod. I struggled to set it up on the uneven ground and with palsied hands set about the task of getting it into action. I knew the seconds must be flying by, but the unfamiliar camera would not be hurried. By now my hands were shaking to such an extent that I could do little useful with them – but when at last, almost in despair, I squinted through the sight ready to film, the humps were still in place, calmly awaiting events – floating on the surface, strangely docile and inanimate.
>
> For a moment I hesitated, my finger on the button, and then on a sudden impulse I reached for my binoculars and focused them upon it. Expanded seven times, the humps looked more impressive, larger than life it seemed, and yet when I examined them carefully it was just possible to see a single hairlike twig

> sprouting out of the one on the right – with a solitary leaf upon it, fluttering gaily in the breeze!

The 'monster' was, of course, a floating log, but one that Dinsdale's need, expectation and inexperience had transformed into a living creature.

At the end of the 1970s, Adrian Shine, the leader of the Loch Ness and Morar Project, designed an experiment to test the perceptions of volunteers who arrived at Loch Morar eager to hunt for Morag, the cousin of the Loch Ness Monster. He found a long, straight pole of wood, attached it to a pulley apparatus and a long rope, and sank it some distance out into the loch. Normally, the pole was completely submerged, but by releasing the rope it could be made to rear out of the water like a surfacing monster.

Newcomers to the project's site were led down to the shore and left alone for a few moments – at which point Shine's wooden monster would put in a very brief appearance. The excited volunteer would report the sighting and be told to sit and sketch what he had seen. Although the wooden pole had no protrusions of any sort, Shine discovered that a significant number of his 'witnesses' sketched in a tiny head at the end of a long neck. They knew what Morag was supposed to look like, and drew what they expected to see, not what had actually appeared.

Flaps, Panics and Contagion

Single reports by isolated witnesses may be potentially inaccurate, but the problems of assessing them are nothing compared to the difficulties of understanding how and why a whole mass of similar reports can be logged within a few short weeks as some new phenomenon sweeps through a community.

Such 'waves' or 'flaps' are among the most remarkable features of the borderlands. Perhaps the best example of all was the sudden flurry of reports of 'flying saucers' that occurred in the months after Kenneth Arnold's sighting of a formation of unidentified flying objects over the Cascade Mountains on 24 June 1947; one early study catalogued a total of 850 sightings in June and July 1947, but it is now estimated that – thanks, no doubt, at least in part to the influence of the media – a total of about 4000 were logged worldwide in about five weeks, creating such an explosion of interest that an entirely new subject was born.

Incidences of 'flaps' go back further than this, however, and it is evident that they can spread swiftly and devastatingly by word of mouth alone. In July and August 1789, revolutionary France was convulsed as the Great Fear – the rumour that unstoppable armies (variously said to be Austrians, Britons, Swedes, Spaniards or even released galley slaves and brigands in the pay of French royalists) were killing, raping and looting their way through the land – shot from one village to another.

The most important point to note about the Great Fear is that, while there was no truth whatsoever in the story, thousands of people heard alarmingly realistic accounts of the devastation as it gripped community after community. On 28 July 1789, for example, nineteen-year-old Lucy de La Tour du Pin was at the village of Forges-les-Eaux in Normandy when she heard a commotion and went into the street to find an agitated crowd surrounding a man riding a grey horse that was still foaming at the mouth and bleeding from the flanks from being harshly ridden. The man had come from Gaillefontaine, five miles away, where, he assured his audience, an Austrian army was already 'pillaging everything and setting fire to barns'. Had Lucy not physically restrained the village priest from ringing the church bells, and then promised to ride to Gaillefontaine with her husband to prove that the village was not in enemy hands, the Fear would certainly have struck Forges-les-Eaux. As it was, when the de La Tour du Pins did reach Gaillefontaine, they found the village intact but its inhabitants convinced that it was Forges-les-Eaux that was in Austrian hands.

A series of similar, but even more supernatural, panics began in the city of Nanking in 1876 when rumours erupted that invisible demons were travelling the country cutting off people's pig-tails. Since the queues were worn as a sign of obedience to the Manchu government, and removing them was an act of rebellion punishable by death, this panic spread with great swiftness to Shanghai, Hangchow and Amoy. It finally reached Peking, and took three years to die down completely. In the meantime, whole provinces were convulsed, and to be a stranger in any community afflicted with the panic was to risk lynching. At least three Chinese converts to Christianity were beheaded on the suspicion that they were responsible for the hair-cutting, and the peddlers of various preventative charms did a roaring trade as tales of flying paper men, armed with scissors and created by sorcerers, spread through the towns.

Similar hair-cutting scares were recorded in China as early as the fifth century AD. Their modern equivalent is probably the penis-severing panics which spread periodically through some West African communities, when it is rumoured that black magicians are on the lookout for fresh genitalia to fuel their magic potions. Since the story goes that the sorcerers can magic away a man's privates simply by touching him anywhere on his body, the most obvious symptom of this panic is a sudden reluctance to shake hands, coupled with an increased tendency for men to walk about with their hands in their pockets, the better to carry out occasional surreptitious checks.

The real point to make about these remarkable panics is that in no case has there ever been evidence that any victim has had his pigtail or his genitals removed by supernatural means. Just as there were no Austrian soldiers in France in 1789, there seem to have been no invisible paper men in China in the 1870s and no penis-severing sorcerers in Africa in the 1990s. The rumours spread solely because they played on the local people's basest fears. They may, on rare occasions, have been helped along by the odd 'genuine' case – there seem to have been a handful of authentic hair-cutting incidents in China, though they appear to have been pranks or acts of malice – but these are hardly necessary. The flaps take on a life of their own.

Surely the best modern example of the social panic is Goatsucker, the mysterious mammal mangler which appeared in Puerto Rico in the spring of 1995. The scare began with the killing of an unusual number of domestic animals – goats, chickens and rabbits on the whole. Several dozen such carcasses were discovered in the provinces of Orocovis and Morovis. What terrified the local farmers was the manner in which they had been despatched: each of the dead animals seemed to have been killed with puncture wounds, and to have been drained of blood by an unknown predator.

It was not until some time after the initial killings that the first descriptions of the animals that appeared to be responsible for it came in. A policeman in Orocovis, investigating reports of a dead sheep, saw a humanoid creature some four feet tall lurking in the shadows. It had orange-yellow eyes and an overpowering stench. On 26 March 1995, Jaime Torres encountered a similar monster in the same field. It had a small round head, elongated eyes, a small mouth, and multi-coloured skin that varied from grey and purple to brown and yellow.

The panic in Puerto Rico was considerable. Search parties of up to 200 people searched the island's backwoods and there was considerable speculation as to the creature's identity. Though a few favoured the idea that Goatsucker was a previously undiscovered animal indigenous to the island, perhaps a bat, the majority preferred to argue that it was either some sort of alien 'pet' that had escaped from a UFO, or a genetic experiment gone horribly wrong.

Soon a composite description of the Goatsucker emerged. It was a strange-looking creature: bipedal, with legs like a kangaroo's, long arms terminating in vicious claws, and a head much like that of a Grey, with huge black eyes and a tiny mouth. Most peculiarly of all, it possessed a long line of quills or spines that ran from its head all the way down its back. At least one witness saw the spines quivering and vibrating, generating enough lift to allow the Goatsucker to fly away.

That was the combined representation, but a closer look at what each witness actually saw suggests that there was little real agreement as to what the Goatsucker looked like. Some described it as a predatory animal, others seem to have thought of it as something from a UFO. Some thought it had wings, and in at least one reconstruction it was provided with a suitably diabolical forked tail. In Guanica, in December 1995, a witness named Osvaldo Rosado was seized by a black-haired, five-foot 'gorilla'.

There was a similar disagreement over the manner in which Goatsucker carried out its murderous depredations. Although the prevailing opinion was that the creature despatched its victims with a single puncture wound, the first dead sheep found right at the beginning of the scare, in March 1995, bore three wounds apiece. Some animals had had their throats slit. In 1996, the majority of the dead animals were despatched with a deep double puncture wound to the neck. Hardly surprisingly, sceptics on the island began to suggest that Goatsucker did not really exist: the deaths were simply the work of everyday predators such as cats and dogs.

The manner in which the Goatsucker panic spread seemed to suggest that the sceptics were right. In 1996, the creature appeared to extend its area of operations; there were reports of similar livestock depredations in Mexico, Venezuela and in the southern United States. In the autumn of 1996, Goatsucker even reached Europe, being blamed for the deaths of six Portuguese sheep killed with a single puncture wound at Idanha-a-Novo. But wherever it went, the killer confined itself to the same Hispanic communities that were aflame with media coverage of *El Chupacabras*. The sceptics' logical explanation looked likely to be correct.

Was there ever a real Goatsucker? Although a handful of eyewitness reports remain perplexing, it seems that the most likely answer to this question is no. The differing descriptions of the creature and the varied manner in which Goatsucker's victims met their ends point to a variety of different phenomena being incorporated into a new and vigorous belief system. Livestock deaths that would normally have been attributed to dogs, and entity sightings that would normally have been linked to UFOs (Puerto Rico is a noted UFO hot-spot), all became, for a time, part of the Goatsucker legend.

The sociologist Ron Westrum noted examples of this effect whilst investigating UFO sightings:

> A considerable folklore has grown up around UFOs . . . For instance, one rural witness told an investigator matter-of-factly that 'they say that when you get within a quarter mile of "one of them" your CB don't work'. Now this is a very precise piece of knowledge, whatever its reliability, and the wide circulation of such 'facts' throughout society is making 'naive' UFO witnesses more scarce. This folklore tends to set up an expectation that certain kinds of things will be seen or will happen during a UFO experience and this affects not only what the witness feels he ought to relate to others but also what the witness remembers as happening. I suspect that many experiences which would previously have been labelled in a different way are now labelled 'UFO' as a result of stereotypes.

Psychologists call this phenomenon 'contagion', and it has been argued that it plays a major role in determining how some strange phenomena are reported. Any case that is not confined to a single incident, the theory goes, is liable to be influenced by the expectations of its witnesses. The more a strange event is discussed and wondered at – the more media coverage a phenomenon receives – the more likely it is that a witness's heightened expectations will lead him astray. A light in the sky that would have attracted little comment before June 1947 becomes a flying saucer in July. A wave that, seen on Loch Lomond, would be identified as a wave, becomes a monster as it rolls across Loch Ness.

A striking example of contagion occurred in Britain in December 1881. A member of parliament named Walter Powell went missing in a balloon called *Saladin*, which floated off from its moorings at Bridport on the English channel with him still on board. He was an influential man, and a good deal of publicity was given to his mysterious disappearance. Before long, reports of strange lights and objects in the sky were received from the English Channel, Dartmouth, Hartlepool (hundreds of miles to the north), and from Alderney, Montrose Ness, as well as Mount de Fuerte and Bilbao, Spain. Perhaps some of them were the *Saladin* – which was never found – but they could hardly all have been. A similarly instructive incident occurred in Holland in 1978, when a small panda escaped from a zoo in Rotterdam. The story was released to the media, and before long the authorities had received about 100 reports that the slow-moving and readily-identifiable animal had been sighted in locations throughout the country. In fact, it transpired, not one of the sightings was genuine. The panda was killed by a train only a few yards away from the zoo, and everyone who thought they had seen the animal elsewhere had been mistaken.

A related phenomenon, usually termed 'mass hysteria', seems to have been responsible for many other peculiar incidents. Mass hysteria differs from contagion in that its effects are frequently more dramatic but remain confined to a much more restricted area. There are often spectacular physical symptoms: in Cairo, in April 1993, up to 1300 schoolgirls attending more than thirty-two schools were affected by a mysterious wave of nausea and fainting fits that seemed to have no physical cause. The incident appeared to have its beginnings in a village in the Nile delta, where a teenager reading aloud to her class suddenly swooned. Some of her friends followed suit and the malady spread from there. Numerous similar examples might be given.

The phrases 'hysterical contagion' and 'mass hysteria' are conventionally applied to these sort of incidents to describe the way in which sufferers can experience physical symptoms that do not really exist. But 'mass hysteria' is not an *explanation* in itself. In fact the precise mechanism by which the hysteria is communicated from one person to another, and the reasons why it affects some people but not others, are not fully understood. It seems clear that the phenomenon is sometimes related to stress and flourishes in conditions of uncertainty; a number of cases have been connected to political unrest, for instance. Expectancy, too, probably plays its part. Psychologists have suggested that six factors play a part in generating cases of hysterical contagion:

> First, regional conditions must be conducive. In order for a rash of Bigfoot sightings to occur, the geography must permit the creature to make sudden appearances and then to evade capture – very few Bigfoot encounters are reported in urban settings. Also, channels of communication must be available for the reports to spread . . . Social and economic stress, as well as a lack of faith in the authorities, predispose people to embrace unconventional interpretations. [In addition,] every culture has marginal traditions that offer alternative explanations for various experiences. A triggering episode often serves as the pebble that commences the avalanche of reports; as stories of strange happenings are transmitted through the community, people begin actively to seek the experience and, not surprisingly, many are successful. Finally, outbreaks of unusual manifestations are aided by breakdowns in official control of public expression. The more tolerant a society is regarding a particular unconventional idea, the more likely it is that this idea will influence anomalous experiences.

Mysterious though their mechanisms may be, it seems clear that the phenomena of contagion and mass hysteria can provide at least a partial solution for some cases in which there is either a suspicious lack of physical evidence, or in which the evidence that does exist is being forced to fit preconceived models (the cases of mass demonic possession, which occasionally occurred in renaissance nunneries, seem much more likely to have been caused by mass hysteria than genuinely supernatural assaults). Nevertheless, it is always a poor idea to explain a mystery with a mystery. Much more work needs to be done on the causes and consequences of hysterical contagion before we can know for certain what it is and why it occurs.

Multiple-Witness Cases

It seems, then, that eyewitness testimony can be unreliable to a degree never suspected by many field investigators. People make gross errors when describing and interpreting the things they have seen. They can also 'see' and experience things that were never there at all. So many factors – the physical conditions, the duration of a sighting, the witness's reliability and state of mind, the passage of time between an encounter and a report, and whether or not the witness makes critical checks to confirm his initial impression that whatever he has seen is anomalous, not to mention suggestion, expectation and contagion – can combine to produce misinterpretations and outright errors, so that in even the best cases there will always be some doubt as to what, precisely, occurred.

The first step towards compiling a more accurate impression of what is happening in the borderlands is to search for multiple-eyewitness accounts. There are an enormous number of them – a check on a catalogue of 24,000 UFO reports indicates that two-thirds involve more than one witness – though one revealing survey has suggested that 'high strangeness' encounter cases are much more likely to involve only a single person. Unfortunately, however, multiple-witness reports are seldom much more illuminating than single-witness encounters. In most cases the witnesses had ample time to discuss what they had seen before they told their story, with the result that the final account tends to reflect a consensus view of the encounter.

Nor is there any guarantee that several witnesses will observe an event more accurately than one, particularly if expectation is in the air. A fine example of this problem concerns the mid-nineteenth-century medium, Daniel Home, perhaps the most controversial figure in the history of psychical research. To his supporters he was 'the greatest physical medium in the history of spiritualism'; to his detractors, a charlatan, a humbug and a fraud. (Browning's poem *Mr Sludge the Medium* is a thinly veiled attack on him.)

Home's most famous feat, which took place on 13 December 1868, was to levitate and float out of one third-storey window and in through another, a dozen feet or more away – an achievement still frequently the subject of debate amongst parapsychologists today. He did this at a seance attended by three sitters. An examination of their accounts, however, shows that they actually saw almost nothing of the incident. Home began by requesting that they all remained in their seats; he then went next door and the sitters heard the sound of a window being opened. After a few moments, Home opened the window of the seance room and stepped in. Of the three witnesses, one, the Master of Lindsay, was sitting with his back to the window; he later stated, however, that he had noted from a shadow on the opposite wall that Home appeared to be levitating in a horizontal position. A second witness, Captain Charles Wynne, is variously stated to have seen Home remain in his own seat throughout the performance, and to have told Home, 'The fact of your having gone out of the window and in at the other I can swear to.' The third, Lord Adare, remembered seeing Home standing outside the window (where there was a small balcony) but added that the room was in near total darkness at the time.

The famous seance, in short, is among the worst-documented of all those given by Home in his twenty-five-year career, so much so that it is possible to explain the medium's feat as a remarkable case of suggestion; as a conjuring trick (Houdini once offered to duplicate the 'illusion' in its original setting, and the sceptical psychical researcher Frank Podmore suggested that, having noisily opened a window next door, Home slipped back into the seance room under cover of darkness, hid behind a curtain, opened the second window and then stepped back into the room); or as a genuine and remarkable instance of levitation.

Not every multiple-witness case is this ambiguous, but there are, nevertheless, other problems to be considered. One, once again, is expectant attention. A fine multiple-witness case that might be explained in this way occurred at Ballinspittle, a small Irish village near Cork, in the summer of 1985. A teenage girl named Clare O'Mahoney was walking past the village's Marian grotto at dusk when her attention was drawn to its life-size concrete statue of the Virgin six or seven yards away and about twenty feet above her. She noticed that it appeared to be swaying backwards and forwards, as though someone was standing behind it and pushing it. This impression was quickly confirmed by her mother and sister. Word of the odd phenomenon quickly got around the village and the next evening forty people assembled to stare at the statue, which obliged by appearing to sway once again. A week after the initial report, the grotto at Ballinspittle was packed with thousands of anxious pilgrims, most of them saying their rosaries and all staring intently at the statue.

The phenomena reported from Ballinspittle ranged from movements of the statue to religious visions – one woman said she saw the face of Christ appear over the Virgin's, others that the virgin's hands had moved. The apparent miracle attracted considerable media coverage. Within a few days, other Virgins in other grottoes were also seen to sway about. At the height of the moving statue flap, more than four-dozen statues scattered through sixteen of Ireland's twenty-six counties were said to be in motion.

Lionel Beer, who investigated the flap at first hand, has pointed out that it had several interesting features. It occurred in July and August, during the traditional 'silly season', when the press had space to give the phenomena plenty of coverage. It happened to be the second wet summer in succession, at a time when there was considerable anxiety in Irish farming communities about the state of the crops. And, oddly, there were no reports of moving statues in the Ghaeltacht (those areas of Ireland where Gaelic remains the principal language) or in Northern Ireland, where perhaps different cultural conditions prevail.

The most interesting proposed solution to the mystery, though, was produced by a team of psychologists from University College Cork, who went to Ballinspittle armed with a video camera. To their considerable surprise, the scientists discovered that they, too, could detect movement in the statue. However, when they played back their videotape they realised that the concrete image had in fact been quite stationary all the time. What they had experienced was an optical illusion called the autokinetic effect: a misperception caused by the fact that, even when stationary, the human head and body themselves sway imperceptibly, while the eye continues to make minute scanning motions even when it is gazing at a fixed object. The effect is that the brain receives the impression that it is the object itself which is in motion.

The importance of this finding is not merely that it satisfactorily explains an apparently mystical phenomenon witnessed by many thousands of sincere people – not to mention suggesting a solution to many 'lights in the sky' UFO sightings, among other strange phenomena – but that it recalls an important study carried out in the 1930s by a psychologist named Sherif. He used the phenomenon to test the group dynamics of perception, and established

> that autokinesis is subject to group suggestion influences; when several subjects observed a light together, their estimates of the degree of movement tended to converge towards a single value. Later, when these subjects viewed the light individually, they continued to perceive the same amount of movement seen by the group. [Sherif's] research powerfully demonstrated that consensus cannot be relied upon to determine the objective reality of a witnessed phenomenon; multiple observers of an ambiguous stimulus are quite capable of erring together.

Some groups of witnesses are also prey to other misperceptions. In a few cases, one dominant witness appears to lead another, a phenomenon known to psychologists as *folie a deux*. (One extreme incident involved a total of twelve members of the same family, who were found to live in one remarkable and delusional world – a unique case of *folie a douze*.) This, too, is a little understood phenomenon. It does appear, though, that *folie a deux* tends to occur among family and close friends;

strangers do not seem to have the necessary knowledge of each other, let alone the requisite reservoir of common experience, to manifest the disorder.

Perhaps, then, we need to look for multiple-witness cases in which the witnesses were unknown to each other, and in which they occupied different vantage points. Again, in the ideal case these witnesses would not meet before their accounts were noted down – indeed it would be best if they were interviewed by different investigators, in order to minimise the risk that their stories might be influenced by leading questions. Unfortunately, such cases are very few and far between.

One that has attracted an enormous amount of attention in the last decade is what appears to be the first independently witnessed alien abduction. This is the case of Linda Napolitano, a New York woman who has recalled, under hypnosis, being repeatedly abducted from her Manhattan apartment by grey aliens who beamed her through her bedroom window into a hovering UFO. She was introduced to the abduction researcher Budd Hopkins, who found her account interesting, 'but thought no more about it [because] it was just so similar to so many other cases'.

Some time later, however, astonishing confirmatory evidence arrived in the form of a letter that Hopkins received from two police officers named Richard and Dan. The men explained that they had been parked below Linda's apartment building on the night of one abduction (30 November 1989) and had seen her exit her apartment suspended in a beam of light and ascend to a waiting UFO. The saucer then plunged into the East River.

Further details were added in several subsequent letters from the same policemen. Better still, Hopkins was later contacted by two other witnesses, one an important political leader whom the two policemen had been guarding that night, and the other an independent witness, an elderly woman who explained that her car had stalled while she was crossing Brooklyn Bridge at the time of the abduction. This woman had seen Linda – accompanied by three aliens – ascending a beam of light to a UFO.

So far, this seems an extremely exciting case. First, Hopkins had a witness who consciously recalled being abducted, and who was able to relive the experience under hypnosis. Second, he had received several detailed letters from three witnesses travelling in the same car, who had seen the same astonishing sight. Third, another witness had watched the encounter from a separate vantage point.

There are, however, enormous difficulties in accepting Hopkins's version of events. To begin with, all four of the witnesses who contacted him have remained anonymous. Everything we know about the things that they saw is contained in their letters – none has come forward to be interviewed face to face by Hopkins or any other investigator. Furthermore, one of the witnesses – the woman on Brooklyn Bridge – is now said by Hopkins to be dead.

There are other problems, particularly inconsistencies in the witness's stories. Despite a thorough search, Hopkins was unable to locate any police detectives named Richard and Dan who could have been in the area at the right time, and a subsequent letter from the men explained that this was because they were not policemen at all, but bodyguards. The woman on the Brooklyn Bridge wrote that, far from plunging into the river, the UFO had flown off over her car. Finally, Hopkins has attracted a fair amount of hostility from fellow ufologists by hinting that the important political leader involved in the Napolitano abduction was none other than Perez de Cuellar, the secretary general of the United Nations. Perez de Cuellar has not commented publicly on this suggestion.

No one doubts Hopkins's *bona fides* as a sincere and dedicated abduction researcher. Indeed his dedication to the Napolitano case is such that it is probably the most intensively investigated abduction incident of all. It is, then, all the more remarkable that this apparently perfect case – replete with independent and apparently reputable witnesses and supported by eyewitness evidence recalled both consciously and under hypnosis – should remain so thoroughly opaque.

All these findings are of great importance for two reasons: first, because, since eyewitness testimony is often all we have, it is vital to understand how unreliable it is, and, second, because this new understanding provides guidance when we come to consider the many strange phenomena that literally defy belief.

A simple example: can Bigfoot be real? It is a large animal and would require a substantial amount of food, not to mention a large area of trackless woods in which it could live without coming across too many humans. It seems reasonable to suppose that it might survive in the forests of Oregon and Washington State, but perhaps not too much further east. How credible, then, are the sightings that are now on record from New Hampshire, New Mexico and New York? The only American state with no Bigfoot reports is Hawaii.

The same problem crops up in a consideration of Irish *peistes*, or lake monsters. During the late 1960s and early 1970s, sightings were reported from more than a dozen small lakes in Connemara, and there was a surge of interest in the region among Loch Ness researchers who saw an opportunity to hunt monsters with a much greater chance of success. A typical example of these reports came from Lough Nahooin, near Clifden, where, on 22 February 1968, a local farmer named Stephen Coyne was down by the shore at dusk when he noticed a black object in the water:

> The object was an animal with a pole-like head and neck about nine inches to a foot in diameter. It was swimming around in various directions. From time to time it put its head underwater; two humps then came into view. Occasionally, a flat tail appeared. Once this came out near the head, which argued length and a high degree of flexibility. The thing was black, slick, hairless, with a texture resembling an eel.

All in all, seven members of the Coyne family saw the beast

and estimated its total length at about twelve feet. The monster swam about the lough for at least half an hour, and at one point came within nine yards of the people assembled on the shore – close enough for them to see that the interior of its mouth was pale and that it appeared to have no teeth. Even allowing for the poor light, the encounter is probably the best close-up lake monster sighting on record.

A team led by Lionel Leslie visited Nahooin that same summer with the aim of netting its monster. They found a lake no more than a hundred yards by eighty, with a maximum depth of twenty-three feet. Gazing at the tiny lough, the monster hunter F.W. Holiday remembered saying: 'If there's one in here, then it's ours.' The team's biologist, Roy Mackal, on the other hand, 'experienced a sinking feeling as I contemplated this small body of water; not even one animal could have more than a transient relationship with this little pond.' Sure enough, despite spreading a net from one side of the lough to the other, and rowing an electronic fish-stunning device around the perimeter, no monster appeared. After a while even Holiday found himself despondent:

> The investigation was fast becoming paradoxical. Although everything suggested that *Peistes* were indigenous to these lakes, there was nothing to indicate what they ate. Nahooin contained a stable population of small brown trout. However, to suppose that a creature the size of a crocodile lurked in the pool and fed on these fish was obviously nonsense. The fish would have been cleared out in a few days.

Pages could be devoted to such cryptozoological imponderables, but one final example of the problems of taking eyewitness testimony literally will probably suffice, since it concerns repeated sightings of that least likely of sea creatures, the mermaid. Gwen Benwell and Sir Arthur Waugh, the leading authorities on the subject, list several dozen examples in their book *Sea Enchantress*, and point out that belief in mermaids was commonplace for many years – and not only among fishermen. In 1723, for example, a Danish Royal Commission was set up to establish whether mermaids really existed. After considering the available evidence, the commissioners reported that they did, and amongst the eyewitness reports that they put forward was their own sighting of a merman off the Faroe Islands.

Since the conventional explanation for such cases is that witnesses are mistaking manatees and dugongs for 'fin folk', it seems worth noting that a number of extremely close encounters with mermaids were reported as recently as the last century. Most of these cases come from Scotland, a particular stronghold of belief in such creatures. In 1830 a group of crofters on Benbecula, an island in the Outer Hebrides, were cutting seaweed when one of them stumbled across an animal 'in the form of a woman in miniature' on the shore. The men in the party tried and failed to capture her, but as she tried to swim to safety a boy hurled a stone that struck her in the back. Two days later, her dead body washed up two miles from where she had been seen, and a careful examination was made of it: 'The upper part of the creature was about the size of a well-fed child of three or four years of age, with an abnormally developed breast. The hair was long, dark and glossy, while the skin was white, soft and tender. The lower part of the body was like a salmon, but without scales.' After the examination, the little body was buried – not in a Christian cemetery, but down by the sea – under a mark-stone which stood as late as 1961. Its existence has prompted some cryptozoologists to speculate that it might yet be possible to recover the skeleton and study it.

The most dramatic of all known sightings of mermaids likewise comes from Scotland: in 1833, the six-man crew of a small fishing vessel from the Shetland island of Yell found a mermaid entangled in their nets one day and hauled her on board. The fishermen kept her on the boat for three hours, and described her as about three feet long, with a monkey's face and small arms which she kept folded over her breasts. She had a crest of bristles on her head and neck, which she could raise and lower at will, no fins or gills, and a fish-like lower body, which ended in a tail like that of a dogfish. Eventually they released her back into the water, alive.

It is unfortunate that this case, like that of the Benbecula mermaid, lacks a first-hand source. Indeed it comes to us third-hand, having been reported to Robert Hamilton, the professor of natural history at Edinburgh University, by a Mr Edmonston, a 'well-known and intelligent observer' who had interviewed the skipper and one of his men. Unacceptable as evidence as it may be, however, it certainly suggests that eyewitnesses are capable of seeing things – under ideal observational conditions – that no cryptozoologist would dare suggest might be physically real. Moreover, such reports are, to all intents and purposes, indistinguishable from the more acceptable sightings of a west coast Bigfoot or the Loch Ness Monster. Had the six Scottish fishermen of Yell netted a baby sea serpent, for example, there can be little doubt that (third-hand or not) their report would have been taken seriously by the monster hunters.

What can we conclude from our survey of eyewitness testimony? Not, certainly, that every piece of unsupported evidence for the unknown must be rejected out of hand; but, perhaps, that before it is accepted, however tentatively, it needs to be carefully considered in the light of everything that has been discovered about the fallibility of such testimony and the specific conditions under which witnesses are most likely to have supplied a distorted account of what they have seen. And, of course, that it is always a bonus if an eyewitness can back his story up with a photograph, a film, or some other form of permanent record – a tape recording, a sonar chart, or physical evidence in the form of a plaster-cast footprint or even a carcass.

Films and Footprints

Many hundreds of photos purporting to show paranormal occurrences, unidentified flying objects and unknown animals exist. For example, a recent work by the ufologist Wendelle Stevens, which sought to collect and publish every known UFO photograph, ran to two volumes and a total of about 900 pages. To this total must be added a lesser number of films and video sequences, which are generally more important in that they convey a better sense of what the phenomena in question looked like and are also more difficult to hoax.

Unfortunately, the great majority of these images fall into two broad categories: either they are outright hoaxes, or they are accompanied by insufficient information to enable investigators to make a proper evaluation. Should we elect to consider only those for which a reasonable case might be made, the total available for study falls to no more than a couple of dozen.

By way of illustrating this contention, let's consider the photographic evidence for one particular phenomenon, the Loch Ness Monster. At the time the last full survey of such images was published, in 1986, this totalled twenty-six still photos (excluding known hoaxes), twenty-six film sequences and one short video clip, all of them obtained in the five decades between 1933 and 1983. There has been a handful of additions in the last decade, but it is safe to say that none of them is of great significance.

Of this total of fifty-three pieces of evidence, twenty-five were obtained at such long range, are so indistinct, or are accompanied by so little supporting information, that they cannot be said for certain to show any animate object. A further fifteen are thought to be misidentifications, generally of birds or logs floating in the water. Of the balance of thirteen photos and films, five are known hoaxes and two are suspected hoaxes, leaving a meagre total of six images that might possibly show something interesting.

Among the photos we have just rejected are many of the best-known pictures of the Loch Ness Monster. The most famous of all, the Surgeon's Photograph – a 1934 plate showing a thin head and neck curving over the water – was recently exposed as a fraud executed by fixing a model neck to a clockwork submarine. The three angular humps photographed by a forester named Lachlan Stuart in the summer of 1951 are now strongly suspected of being a hoax. And all five of the well-publicised underwater photographs said to depict the monster, which were secured by an American team from the Academy of Applied Sciences in Boston during the 1970s, are now thought to show nothing more than portions of the loch bottom.

What of the images that remain? One, the very first photograph ever taken of the monster, is both utterly indistinct and thoroughly bizarre. It resembles nothing so much as a half turtle shell with a single flipper at the rear, and looks unlike any other supposed picture of the monster. The photographer, a local man named Hugh Gray, was so busy with his camera that he left only a fragmentary description of the object he had seen. It has since been suggested that the picture actually shows a Labrador swimming towards the camera with a stick in its mouth.

The second remaining photograph was secured by one member of a team of watchers assembled by the insurance magnate Sir Edward Mountain to keep the whole loch under observation for a five-week period. It shows what appears to be a long, shallow hump in the middle of the lake. It would probably be identified as a wave were it not for suggestions of a splash of spray rising above its centre, and it is certainly not sufficiently distinct to allow anyone to state what it really shows.

The third picture, shot in July 1955 by a bank manager named Peter McNab, is one of the most dramatic photographs of the monster. As well as showing two huge, black humps crossing the mouth of Urquhart Bay, about half-way down the loch, it clearly shows the tower of ruined Urquhart Castle. This provides a useful scale that has enabled investigators to estimate that the visible portions of the monster are 55 feet long – bigger than almost every estimate of the total length of the largest lake monster. The real problem with the McNab photo, however, is that there should be two of them: according to the photographer's account, he secured pictures of the creature with two different cameras. Upon examination, however, one of the two images can be seen to be a rephotographed version of the first. McNab's son, his companion at the time, can shed no light on the photos because he did not see the monster at all: he was 'busy under the bonnet of the car' at the time.

Of the three remaining pictures, the best-known is undoubtedly Tim Dinsdale's minute-long film of the monster, secured only a couple of days after his abortive attempt to film a log in April 1960. It was shot at a distance of about a mile and showed, so Dinsdale claimed, a single hump moving across the loch and then swimming parallel to the far shore.

Critics have sought to explain the sequence as a film of a motorboat crossing the lake. There are certainly a number of problems which suggest that they might be correct: the 'hump' is moving at the same speed as a boat with an outboard engine, and one or two frames from the film even seem to show what might be the head of a man sitting in the stern. The best evidence that it does indeed show a monster is Dinsdale's eyewitness statement, particularly his observation of the hump through binoculars. He was certain he could see a red-brown back, with a large dapple on one side and the 'fullness and girth of an African buffalo'. As it moved off, paddle strokes were visible on either side. The sceptic Ronald Binns has, however, demonstrated that Dinsdale's reconstruction of the view through his binoculars is inaccurate and that he greatly exaggerates how well he would have been able to see the object. Knowing what we do about his state of mind in April 1960, it might be best to discount this portion of the evidence.

What photos are we left with? One short film sequence, showing a long and narrow wake, shot by Dick Raynor of the Loch Ness Investigation Bureau in June 1967, and a set of still pictures taken by R.H. Lowrie of the yacht *Finola* on 7 August 1960. The latter case is probably the stronger of the two, since the incident lasted for ten minutes and the single published photo is not only backed up by the evidence of other family members on the yacht, but was independently witnessed from shore by a monster hunter named Torquil MacLeod. The eyewitnesses described a large animal, travelling at over six knots and displaying three humps and a 'neck-like protrusion'. But what does this 'best of all' monster photographs show? Nothing but a broad 'V' wake proceeding parallel to the shore. It is so inconclusive that we have to rely on the witness's assertion that the wake was too substantial to have been made by an otter or some ducks.

In general, it has to be admitted that the evidence for most forms of strange phenomena is little better than that for the Loch Ness Monster. Very few photographs of ghosts, for example, seem to have been taken deliberately. It is more common for phantoms to appear unexpectedly in the midst of carefully-composed studies, say of the interior of a church, and for the photographer to swear that he saw nothing of the sort when he took his picture. Several such portraits show 'classic' ghosts – literally, figures dressed in sheets or loose robes – that are quite unlike the sort of apparitions normally reported at present. The most famous of the few ghost photographs shot deliberately was obtained in 1936 and shows a faint and amorphous shape descending the main staircase at Raynham Hall in Norfolk. It is said to portray the Hall's 'brown lady', a ghost sometimes seen around the house. Though accepted as genuine for many years, the photograph has more recently been considered a possible hoax. It is certainly remarkably well composed.

What, then, is the value of photographic evidence? Today, thanks to the rapidly increasing sophistication of computer image enhancement techniques, the answer to that question is 'Practically nothing', since it is hard to envisage an image that could not be hoaxed. Even film footage can be convincingly faked by someone with enough time and money. Older images are of slightly higher value as evidence, though, as we have seen, photographic hoaxing has a long and distinguished history. Yet one thing indelibly etched on the brains of anyone who studies mysterious photographs is the maxim that the clearer the photo, the more likely it is to be a hoax. All too often, pin-sharp pictures – particularly of apparently extra-terrestrial spacecraft – are exposed as frauds, and it does make a certain sense to assume that the witness who is able to snatch a photo of what is generally a short-lived phenomenon is quite likely to secure only a blurred and indistinct image. From this point of view, photographic evidence seems very unlikely to produce any definite answers soon.

In fact, by far the most compelling evidence for the reality of some strange phenomena lies in what might be categorised as 'physical traces'. Not only does such evidence have the great virtue of being available for leisurely examination by experienced investigators; it also suggests that here, at least, is a mystery that has a degree of physical reality and which cannot be explained as some sort of hallucination.

For example, the best proof that Bigfoot is a real animal and not the product of the witness's imagination lies not in the debatable Patterson film but the dozens of good quality casts of abnormally large footprints assembled by crypto-zoologists over the years. Although many such prints might be hoaxes, a few are harder to explain this way. Grover Krantz, a professor of anthropology at Washington State University, has drawn attention to the fact that the best prints exhibit a number of interesting characteristics. Though full-size Bigfoots appear to be flat-footed, for example, perhaps because of the weight the feet have to bear, prints left by smaller specimens do seem to exhibit some arching.

In another interesting case, which occurred at Bossburg in Washington in October 1969, a half-mile trail of more than 1080 prints appeared in the snow. A study of the prints suggested that the creature that had made them had a normal left foot but that its right was a club foot in which the third toe was squeezed out of its natural alignment. This subtle abnormality was sufficient to convince John Napier, a British anthropologist, that the prints were genuine, and certainly it might be suggested that if they were a hoax they were a pointlessly cunning and protracted one. On the other hand, those who remember Tony Signorini and his concrete overshoes may prefer to reserve judgement.

There are, in addition, a number of cases in which apparent sasquatch tracks have been left so deeply imprinted in the earth that it would have been difficult for a hoaxer to have duplicated the effect, but Krantz, at least, believes that the best Bigfoot prints are the minority in which the 'dermal ridges' – patterns on the sole of the foot, equivalent to fingerprints – can be clearly seen. The best such case comes from Mill Creek, on the Oregon–Washington border, where, in June 1982, a series of prints fifteen inches in length were found in mud on the forest floor. They exhibited clear dermal ridges, and casts of the prints have impressed a number of scientists. There is, however, some reason to suspect fraud in this case, principally because Paul Freeman, the man who found the tracks, has admitted to hoaxing other Bigfoot trails. In addition, a Forestry Service investigation suggested that there was evidence that detritus such as pine needles had been brushed aside before the prints were made, and that there was no sign of the sort of variation between strides or the slippage that would have been expected as the prints ascended a muddy hill.

Very occasionally, some physical evidence has also emerged from the murky world of ufology. In one of the most bizarre cases on record, a plumber named Joe Simonton, who lived at Eagle River, Wisconsin, looked out of his window on 18 April 1961 and saw a silvery UFO land in his back yard. A hatch opened and three small 'men' wearing black uniforms stepped out. One wordlessly indicated that he wanted Joe to fill a bucket full of water for him. When Simonton complied, the entity went back into the UFO and emerged with four warm and greasy pancakes. When he cautiously tasted the extra-terrestrials' breakfast, Simonton discovered that it tasted like cardboard, but a chemical analysis later showed that the objects were indeed ordinary oatmeal pancakes. Ufologist John Rimmer seems to explore all the possibilities when he observes: 'Now this might prove that Joe Simonton was a fraud. On the other hand it might prove that pancakes are pretty much the same wherever they come from. Or it might prove that humanoid creatures from other worlds can exist quite happily on Earth foods when they have to do so.'

Altogether more intriguing evidence materialised in Brazil in September 1957, when the society columnist for the *O Globo* newspaper received a remarkable letter through the mail. The writer claimed that he had been fishing near Ubatuba, in Sao Paolo state, when a disc-shaped craft appeared overhead. It seemed to be about to crash nearby, but at the last moment shot vertically upwards instead and exploded in a flash of light, showering the whole area with fragments of metal. Although the letter was signed, the signature was illegible – but as proof of the story, three samples of a light, grey metallic substance were enclosed.

The 'Ubatuba residue', as it is known, has caused an extraordinary amount of controversy over the years. Different portions of the fragments have been subjected to a battery of chemical tests, which established that the material was magnesium of remarkable purity. At one point it was claimed that the residue was so unusual that it could not have been manufactured on earth, but it is now generally conceded that very similar samples of magnesium were made in the United States as early as the 1940s. And though one analysis did suggest that the fragments exhibited a 'directional crystal growth', indicating a possible extraterrestrial origin, this finding has to be set against the fact that no witness to the spectacular explosion itself has ever come forward. On balance, the Ubatuba case looks like a hoax.

There are, however, a handful of close encounters of the second kind that are much harder to explain. One of the best occurred in the French village of Trans-En-Provence on 8 January 1981, when a local man called Renato Nicolai heard a whistling sound and looked up to see a 'ship' shaped like two saucers joined together landing in his garden. Nicolai ran to a small cabin a short distance away and watched as the object took off again, emitting the same strange sound. The case has impressed ufologists, not only because Nicolai seemed uninterested in his experience and professed to know nothing about UFOs, but because it was investigated by the local police and an official French government agency, GEPAN, the *Groupe d'Etude des Phenomenes Aerospatiaux Non-Identifies.*

GEPAN's report noted a number of interesting physical traces produced by the landing: a weakening in the chlorophyll pigment of leaf samples, marks on the ground corresponding to the craft's 'landing legs' and traces of heat damage to the soil. Though it might be easier to agree that the Trans-En-Provence case was truly remarkable had the effects been a little more pronounced, ufologists have labelled the detailed GEPAN investigation 'perhaps the most significant investigation ever undertaken of a single UFO report'.

Dramatic effects were certainly not lacking in a second notable close encounter, which occurred in the Manitoban wilderness around Falcon Lake in May 1967. A prospector called Stefan Michalak reported that he had watched two glowing, cigar-shaped objects appear overhead, one of which landed not far from where he was working a quartz vein. He approached, assuming – he later said – that it was an experimental American plane, and stuck his head though an open hatch. 'The inside was a maze of lights. Direct beams running in horizontal and diagonal paths and a series of flashing lights, it seemed to me, were working in a random fashion with no particular order or sequence. I took note of the thickness of the walls of the craft. They were about 20 inches thick at the cross section.'

As soon as Michalak withdrew his head, the hatch closed, and though he thought he had heard voices from within the UFO, he did not see any occupants. His entry barred, he began to examine the craft's hull, noting that it burnt his glove as he touched it. A few moments later, however, and without warning, a small 'exhaust' on the bottom of the object began to belch hot gas, forcing Michalak back, setting his shirt and vest on fire and searing his chest as the object soared upwards. Badly hurt, the prospector staggered back to his motel.

In the aftermath of the Falcon Lake encounter, Michalak

reported sensations of nausea, headaches, appalling odours from his burns, depression and anorexia. He lost about twenty-two pounds in weight in the aftermath of his experience.

Although there is no doubt that Michalak certainly did suffer thermal burns to his chest and chemical burns to his abdomen at the time of his experience, attempts to pin down other possible physical effects met with less success. One analysis detected low but significant levels of radiation on samples taken from the landing site – about the same as might be emitted by a luminous watch. Others found nothing of the sort. Some thought it suspicious that Michalak had tried to get himself a ride home after the experience by offering to tell his story to the Winnipeg *Tribune*, while others found it hard to believe that a hoaxer could or would exhibit all the physical symptoms Michalak complained of, and was treated for. In sum, the case was highly ambiguous. The ufologist Jerome Clark sums it up as 'the sort of exercise in frustration and ambiguity that drives UFO investigators to distraction'.

Examining the Physical Evidence

There are, therefore, only a few rather isolated instances where some physical evidence of apparently good provenance is actually available for examination. Of these, perhaps the most remarkable are a few small lumps of some dark substance kept in a golden reliquary in an Italian cathedral. They are the principal component of what is known as the 'blood miracle of Naples': the liquefaction of what is said to be the dried blood of St Januarius, which takes place with almost complete predictability on eighteen separate feast days in May, September and December each year. Indeed the phenomenon occurs so regularly that any failure of the blood to liquefy is regarded as a very bad omen. In 1527 it remained resolutely solid and there was a severe plague; in 1569 failure was followed by a terrible famine; and in 1990 the Italian football team failed to win the World Cup, despite enjoying home advantage.

Surprisingly little is known of St Januarius himself. He is said to have been an early Christian bishop martyred by the Roman emperor Diocletian, but his relics did not finally come to rest in Naples until 1497 and there is at least a one-hundred-year gap between his inferred death in about 305 and the first records of his supposed effects. The likelihood must therefore be that the dark clots contained in holy phials in the cathedral of Naples are not saint's blood. Nevertheless, many thousands of pilgrims can attest that they certainly appear to possess miraculous properties. In 1970 a Neapolitan doctor named Giorgio Giorgi found himself only about three feet from the spot where the archbishop of Naples was holding one of the glass phials out to his congregation, slowly rotating it as he did so. After about four minutes,' Giorgi wrote later, 'I was disconcerted to see, just in front of my nose, that the clot of blood had suddenly changed from the solid state into that of a liquid. The transformation . . . happened suddenly and unexpectedly. The liquid itself had become much brighter, more shining; so many gaseous bubbles appeared inside the liquid . . . that it appeared to be in a state of ebullition.'

An explanation for the phenomenon remained elusive for many years. Even Father Herbert Thurston, the great Jesuit authority on religious phenomena and by no means a credulous man, professed himself puzzled: a study of the sources suggested that liquefactions had occurred in temperatures varying from 15° F to 85° F, and after the holy phials had been displayed for anything between a few minutes and twenty-four hours. Still more remarkably, the blood changes colour from brown or black to bright red as it liquefies, and it appears to vary in volume, sometimes filling the phials halfway, sometimes completely. In 1906, however, and again in 1991, a more or less plausible solution was proposed, based on the scientific principle of thixotropy.

Thixotropic substances are solids that quickly liquefy when shaken. Certain clays are thixotropic, and can cause terrible landslides if suddenly agitated. The same principle is used to make non-drip paints, and, in 1991, a University of Pavia chemist named Luigi Garlaschelli created several thixotropic mixtures from clays, beeswax in alcohol, and chalk, water and salts. Garlaschelli's compounds look fairly similar to the clotted blood in the holy phials and can be readily and repeatedly liquefied. Although it cannot be said that the thixotropic theory easily explains every anomaly associated with the blood, one point in favour of it is that a key ingredient in Garlaschelli's favourite compound – hydrated ferric salts – is abundant on the slopes of nearby Mount Vesuvius. This might explain why Naples, apparently uniquely, boasts anything up to twenty similar relics, including three bottles of the blood of St John the Baptist, a phial of St Lawrence's fat, and even the remarkable liquefying milk of the Virgin Mary.

The Elusive Final Proof

One last category of evidence must be mentioned. There are a scattered handful of reports which hint that researchers in a number of fields have come tantalisingly close to obtaining the irrefutable evidence they seek. These immensely frustrating cases generally involve cryptozoologists, who – if all the whispers are true – have, on several occasions, nearly succeeded in obtaining the close-up photographs and the carcasses they covet.

In 1965, for example, the monster hunter F.W. Holiday began to hear rumours of two astonishing film sequences said to have been obtained in the mid-1930s by a Highland doctor named McRae. One showed a sea serpent on the shore of a Scottish sea loch, writhing a long, maned neck over a bed of seaweed. The other, taken at Loch Ness at a range of about a hundred yards, was a close-up view of a three-humped monster close inshore, its neck held low over the water. On its bluntly conical head could be seen two hornlike sense organs, and its neck was covered with a stiff, bristly mane. The strangest feature noticed by McRae was that the monster's skin seemed to be in permanent motion, rippling as the muscles played under the skin. Unfortunately, Holiday was told, McRae had consigned the two sequences to a bank vault and created a trust to ensure that they did not fall into the wrong hands after his death. The trustees – who are themselves now dead – were powerless to do anything other than give a verbal description of their content, and the film, if it ever existed, has probably decayed by now to the point where it would be unwatchable.

A similarly unfortunate fate befell what Bernard Heuvelmans reports may have been the first sea serpent carcass to come into human hands. In the spring of 1885 a Mr Gordon, the president of the United States Humane Society, went sailing along Florida's Atlantic coast. One morning, having moored for the night in the remote New River Inlet, he found his anchor had become fouled by the body of a huge sea creature. Hauled up from the mud, it turned out to be a slender body some forty-two feet long, minus its head and part of what appeared to be a lengthy neck, but still possessing a pair of flippers and a long and narrow tail. It was in an advanced state of decomposition (always a warning sign when it comes to considering sea monster carcasses), but Gordon attempted to preserve it by having it hauled above the high water mark. Before any further investigation could be conducted, however, a storm blew in and the sea reclaimed the strange remains.

This loss might not matter so much had it not been for the soft heart of Captain William Hagelund, a retired Canadian whaler who actually claims to have caught a baby sea serpent in a net in August 1968. Hagelund and his family were yachting in the Gulf Islands, off the coast of British Columbia, when they heard a disturbance in the water one evening off De Courcy Island. Lowering a dinghy, the old whaler rowed out to investigate and discovered a small eel-like creature some sixteen inches long and an inch in diameter, swimming about on the surface. After some effort he managed to bring it on board for a closer examination and found that he could not identify it. It had a large head with a hooked jaw, whiskers and a myriad tiny teeth, plates or scales running along its back, a pair of anterior flippers and a large forked tail. It was black-brown on top and covered with a yellow 'fuzz' underneath. Hagelund decided to take the mysterious creature to a nearby biological station the next morning and deposited it in a bucket of sea water, but, during the night, the sound it made as it tried to escape so moved him that he went on deck and – to the enormous frustration of every cryptozoologist in existence – lowered the bucket into the water to give the monster its freedom.

Nor are sea monsters the only unknown animals to find themselves in human hands. In December 1967, two students out hunting in the Tenton Forest in Wyoming claimed to have shot and killed a seven-foot creature that they took to be a bear. Closer examination showed it to be a giant ape covered in dark brown hair. Never, apparently, having heard of Bigfoot, 'and thinking it must belong to someone, they decided to leave the corpse where it was and keep quiet about the affair'. By the time they realised the importance of their kill, it was too late to recover the body. A couple of years later, in the summer of 1969, a party camping near Auburn in Washington State heard noises in some bushes and the next morning discovered a bear trap containing a gigantic severed foot some twenty inches long. The creature that had left it seemed to have retreated from the trap, leaving huge footprints alternating with patches of blood. Astonishingly, the party decided to leave the foot where it was, and it was never heard of again.

Such tales should, of course, be treated with caution. Most will strike experienced cryptozoologists as too good to be true. And, even if the reports are genuine, they are worthless in the absence of a body. Perhaps the New River Inlet carcass, had it been preserved, would have been identified as yet another decomposing shark, as so many washed-up 'sea serpents' turn out to be. Certainly, in the rare cases where elusive remains have finally fallen into scientific hands, analyses have proved inconclusive or downright disappointing. A notable example of this trait was a mummified 'Yeti hand', tracked down in an obscure Nepalese monastery by the Texan oil millionaire Tom Slick and smuggled out of the country by the film actor Jimmy

Stewart, who concealed it in his underpants. Given up to scientific examination, it proved to be ancient, but human.

As human, perhaps, as the source of some of the greatest mysteries of the borderlands?

10

Answers From Inner Space

One of the most remarkable events ever to occur within the borderlands took place in Canada, in the summer of 1973, when the members of the Toronto Society for Psychical Research conducted a series of seances at which they conjured up the ghost called Philip.

Philip told them much about his life and times. He had been an English aristocrat who fought on the king's side in the English Civil War. Though married, he had begun a romantic liaison with a gypsy girl, whom he loved dearly. But she had been arrested during one of the periodic witch-manias that swept through the country, and was brought to trial as a sorceress. Though Philip tried desperately to save her, the girl was eventually burned at the stake. The guilt that he felt for failing to prevent this tragedy was so great that his ghost found itself tied to earth, unable to progress further in the afterlife.

Though Philip's ghost never actually materialised at any of the society's seances, it made its presence felt in other ways. The group's meetings were plagued by knocks and raps; the table at which they sat tilted from side to side; noises were heard in far corners of the room and lights blinked on and off. Philip seemed to be an unusually bold spirit, too: though most ghosts prefer to restrict themselves to the confines of a darkened room, Philip was happy to be summoned into the presence of an audience of fifty for the benefit of a local television station, which broadcast one of the seances live.

This sort of behaviour was unprecedented, even by the standards of the great days of spiritualism, but what made the case truly extraordinary was the fact that 'Philip' did not exist. He had been invented by the Toronto Society for Psychical Research as part of an attempt to discover whether it was possible to create a purely artificial ghost. The eight members of the group had spent months creating his character and elaborating a believable, but suitably dramatic, personal history for their creation, and during that period they themselves had come to think of him as something rather more than simply a fictional character.

It is appropriate to sound a note of caution at this point. The Toronto group has made some dramatic claims for the experiment. The most significant is that, once Philip's personality had been sketched out in sufficient detail, the ghost took on a life of his own. Not only could no one member direct him; he also became independent of their collective control, to the extent that he would occasionally contradict the life story that had been invented for him. This, if true, would be good evidence for the existence of some form of extrasensory perception. It has also been suggested that the raps and the table-tilting that occurred during the seances, supplied proof of the reality of psychokinesis, since they were evidently not the work of spirits from the great beyond. Furthermore, the Toronto seances seemed to show that belief is a vital component of the anomalous experience. When one member of the group told Philip, 'We only made you up, you know,' the phenomena abruptly ceased. The ghost did not reappear until all the members of the group had spent some time reacquiring their belief in him.

The problem here is that, although the story of the Philip seances is certainly exciting, and potentially highly significant, the experiment has not been repeated by other researchers.

Until it is, it would be unwise to accept the Toronto group's claims at face value. Though collective fraud seems an unlikely explanation in this case (which was moderated by the respected parapsychologist A.R.G. Owen and run by his wife), it might have been possible for one member of the group to hoax the others.

For the moment, though, it does not matter whether we accept the Philip seances as evidence for ESP and the existence of some sort of group consciousness, or whether we attribute the ghost's activities to expectation, hallucination, or even hoaxing. The point is that the members of the group convinced themselves that what they were experiencing was real.

What can the Philip case tell us about wondrous events? It suggests that strange phenomena may have an internal rather than an external source. It shows that some strange phenomena may appear to be objectively real even though they are evidently *not* objectively real. And it demonstrates that it is possible for a group of alert, inquisitive and intelligent witnesses to experience such phenomena collectively. In short, it implies that many unexplained mysteries might be solved if we look, not for a parapsychological explanation, but for a psychological one.

The Goblin Universe

Before proceeding to examine the sort of psychological processes that may be responsible for these sort of phenomena, it is only fair to point out that a number of researchers have proposed an alternative theory to resolve the dichotomy we have just identified: that while many strange phenomena do not appear to be physically real, they nevertheless do exhibit signs of intelligence.

This other theory is sometimes called the 'ultraterrestrial hypothesis'. It suggests that a number of the mysteries we have been considering – including UFOs, poltergeists and even Bigfoot – may all be manifestations of one controlling intelligence, or perhaps a group of such intelligences, which exist in some sort of alternate reality. The cryptozoologist and occultist F.W. Holiday called this place the Goblin Universe – 'a hall of distorting mirrors into which we are born with yelling protest'. It is generally conceived of as some sort of higher dimension, whose inhabitants, the 'ultraterrestrials', can pass to earth when they so choose. Alternatively, it has been suggested that these intelligences simply live further up what the UFO researcher John Keel has called 'the Superspectrum' of existence than mere human beings. This means that they are generally invisible, but may be seen by people with special psychic abilities. It also means that we cannot hope to catch, hurt or even understand them.

Though the ultraterrestrials are not usually thought to be actively hostile to human kind, a number of authors have suggested that they often seek to mislead us for mysterious purposes of their own. This is presumed to explain the red herrings produced by complex phenomena such as the UFO enigma, and the sort of baffling 'high weirdness' reports in which one sort of mystery shades into another, and abductees are plagued by poltergeist infestations or a priest is called in to exorcise the ghost of the Loch Ness Monster.

A typical incident of this variety occurred at the home of Thelma Arnold, in Uniontown, Pennsylvania, on 6 February 1974. Hearing a clattering at her front door, Arnold grabbed her 16-gauge shotgun and stepped outside. By the porch light she saw a large ape-like creature standing only a few feet away. It raised its arms above its head in a gesture of apparent surrender, but Arnold was so scared she pointed her shotgun at the monster's belly and opened fire anyway. She didn't kill it. 'It just disappeared in a flash of light,' she told investigators.

A few years later, in the spring of 1979, Sam and Ruth Frew, who lived not far from Uniontown, saw a large object 'tumbling from the sky', and a fortnight later they began to hear strange animal noises in the hills. The sounds continued for three years until, on 12 August 1981, Sam Frew became convinced he had received a telepathic message: 'Come back down to the gas line.' He went out into the woods, and encountered a hairy creature some twelve feet tall. Frew got the impression that the monster was trying to communicate with him. 'They are intelligent. It tries to communicate. It is not from this dimension – that is why you only find a few footprints and then they disappear,' he told the reporter who arrived to interview him.

Although supporters of the ultraterrestrial hypothesis prefer not to make the comparison themselves, their theory is really a restatement of the old spiritualist idea of the 'astral plane', on which enlightened spirits rub shoulders with demons that descend to possess the unwary, and with mischievous elementals who delight in alarming or perplexing ordinary people. And it has the same purpose: to account for the essential illogicality of complex phenomena. It seeks to explain, for example, why apparently real monsters can be shot, but never killed; how they can be hunted, but never caught; and how they can survive in habitats that could not possibly support one animal, much less the sort of numbers needed to sustain a species.

If all things are possible, then it is possible that the ultraterrestrial hypothesis may be true – but it would be very difficult to prove that such an elusive and deceptive realm exists. It is altogether simpler to suppose that strange phenomena are complex because the human brain is complex, and that some of the answers we are seeking can be found not by searching for an alternate reality, but by looking within our own minds.

Fantastic Voyages

Perhaps the best place to begin an exploration of the ways in which witnesses experience unusual events is the relatively new psychological concept of 'fantasy proneness'. This theory, proposed by Sheryl Wilson and Theodore Barber, suggests that a relatively small proportion of the adult population – perhaps four per cent, according to the current estimate – experience fantasies of a vividness and frequency unknown to the rest of us. Wilson and Barber suggest that fantasy proneness stems from a failure to abandon childhood immersion in fantasy and imagination, and that it is likely to be more common among those who enjoyed particularly complex and rewarding fantasy lives during their infancy. If they are correct, we would expect to discover that 'fantasy-prone personalities' are likely to have had childhood 'imaginary friends', enjoyed make-believe games, and believed firmly that their toys had personalities and that Santa Claus was real. It appears that there may also be some connection between fantasy proneness and childhood traumas such as abuse, since abused children can turn to fantasy to provide an illusion of the control that is lacking in real life.

What, though, are the characteristics of the adult fantasy-prone personality? Wilson and Barber compared a small sample of apparently fantasy-prone people to a control group, and concluded that they spent much of their time attending to fantasies in which they could 'see', 'hear', 'smell' and 'touch' the things they were imagining. Not only were they sometimes able to orgasm without physical stimulation; they were more likely to experience vivid dreams and waking hallucinations, including visions of ghosts and monsters. Half believed that they were receiving special messages from some higher intelligence. Others underwent apparently psychic experiences, and almost all of them tended to be susceptible to hypnosis. Indeed, the psychologist Robert Baker has observed that 'the behaviour we commonly call "hypnotic" is exhibited by these fantasy-prone types all the time'. Wilson and Barber stressed that though the fantasy-prone may have low self-esteem and cope poorly with stress, they are not disturbed or mentally ill and are capable of living perfectly happy and apparently normal lives.

This is an important and testable hypothesis, particularly when it is remembered that Wilson and Barber may have underestimated the number of people who turn to fantasy in special circumstances. The author Hilary Evans has noted that many witnesses to the unknown appear to be going through difficult or traumatic periods in their lives. They may be adolescents encountering the problems of puberty (like many poltergeist 'epicentres' and visionaries who receive visits from the Virgin Mary), or adults dealing with the stresses of unemployment, poverty or a failing marriage. Might they, at least temporarily, adopt the strategy of the fantasy-prone personality to help themselves through such difficult times? Evans puts it this way:

> The individual has a need (not necessarily one that he is aware of) which can be either an immediate crisis, usually of a personal nature, or a temporary awkward phase in his development which he finds it difficult to surmount, such as adolescence or menopause, which may well be accompanied by an identity crisis; or a long term uncertainty, such as a religious doubt, or a chronic frustration, such as a boring or humiliating existence. Unable to resolve this by normal means, his subconscious mind devises and projects to his conscious mind as simulated reality a dramatic episode in which he seems to encounter an otherworldly being which, to him, represents authority together with whatever other attributes are required.
>
> To make the incident effective, it must be believable; to be believable, it must be lifelike. So it is presented in such a way that the conscious mind accepts it as reality.

It should be emphasised, at this point, that the concept of fantasy proneness is still at an early stage of development. Few studies have been made of the trait, and only a small sample of apparently fantasy-prone people have been interviewed. Moreover, it was quickly recognised that adults who are fantasy prone soon learn that they will be ridiculed if they indulge in these satisfying alternative realities too publicly, and are thus likely to conceal the extent of their rich imaginative lives, even from close family and friends. This makes it difficult to establish exactly how frequent fantasy proneness is. Without further research, it is not even safe to say that fantasy proneness exists at all.

Nevertheless, it is obvious that Wilson and Barber's theory may help to explain a great number of reports of strange phenomena such as alien abductions, ghostly visitations, sightings of creatures such as Bigfoot, and out of the body experiences. It would account both for the vivid realism of such reports and for their strange unreality and bizarre logic, as well as providing an explanation for the preponderance of single-witness sightings and the difficulty of producing physical evidence to back up eyewitness statements. It even has the advantage that no apparently inviolable scientific laws need to be suspended for the experiences to become a reality.

Another of the attractions of the fantasy-prone personality hypothesis is that it explains why a proportion of those who encounter strange phenomena experience a variety of different enigmas – like Sam Frew, who watched a UFO land, heard noises and then had his telepathic contact with Bigfoot. This sort of agglomeration of the bizarre can be seen in a number of high-strangeness cases – notably the Maine UFO incident, which featured not only a UFO sighting and an abduction but unexplained sounds, mystical visions, poltergeist effects, men in black and telepathic messages. Sometimes this sort of pattern is sketched out over a lengthy period that culminates in one major incident; one French ufologist has christened this phenomenon the 'build-up phase', and it might be explained as a series of increasingly elaborate fantasies dreamed up by a fantasy-prone witness.

It is possible to test the proposal that many of those who report unusual experiences will prove to be fantasy-prone personalities? Apparently, yes. There is considerable anecdotal evidence that many UFO abductees and mediums exhibited signs of fantasy proneness as children. When she was eight years old, the great mental medium Mrs Leonore Piper was playing in the garden when she 'suddenly felt a sharp blow on her right ear, accompanied by a prolonged sibilant sound. This gradually resolved itself into the letter "S", which was then followed by the words "Aunt Sarah not dead, but with you still".' A few weeks later the child cried out at night that she could not sleep 'because of the bright light in the room and all the faces in it'.

Her contemporary, Mrs Gladys Leonard, experienced even more obvious symptoms of fantasy proneness. As a child, she recorded in her autobiography, 'in whatever direction I happened to be looking, the physical view of the wall, door, ceiling or whatever it was, would disappear, and in its place would gradually come valleys, gentle slopes, lovely trees and banks covered with flowers of every shape and hue. The scene seemed to extend for miles, and I was conscious that I could see much farther than was possible with the ordinary physical scenery around me.'

Similarly, Catherine Muller, the Martian medium of the 1890s, spent her childhood in revolt against what the psychologist Theodore Flournoy termed 'the humdrum surroundings in which fate had caused her to be born'. Though physically healthy, she was prone to hallucinations, visions and premonitions, and even seriously questioned whether she was really her parents' child: was it not possible, she asked them, that her nurse had brought the wrong baby home from an afternoon walk? Catherine Laboure, the French nun whose vision of the Virgin Mary in 1830 is among the most formative strange experiences on record, 'had a penchant for seeing apparitions, notably of St Vincent de Paul, the founder of her order, and also claimed to have a personal "angel", a "child of about five who was radiant with light".'

One of Nigel Watson's UFO witnesses, Paul Bennett, saw his first flying disc when he was nine years old. It shot past his window while he was lying in bed, almost close enough to touch but making no noise. Subsequently, he saw several other UFOs and even what appeared to be an extraterrestrial robot, all of which appeared near his home in Bradford while he was in the company of friends. Bennett experienced apparent psychokinetic effects, too: his bedroom light had switched itself on and off and alarm clock fell to the floor. He also dreamed of UFO sightings, and sleepwalked about once a month.

Several attempts have been made to conduct a more rigorous analysis of fantasy proneness among UFO abductees and those who undergo near death experiences. Keith Basterfield, Robert

Batholomew and George Howard surveyed 152 people who claimed to have been abducted and concluded that 132 of them – 87 per cent – exhibited at least one of the characteristics of fantasy proneness. Joe Nickell conducted a similar survey of thirteen abductees whose experiences had been uncovered under hypnosis by the Harvard psychologist John Mack, and published by him in the book *Abduction*. He reported that all thirteen showed definite signs of fantasy proneness; one exhibited four of the seven major indicators, one five and the balance of eleven displayed all seven. One recalled that as a child, he had heard animals speaking to him; another that she could 'feel people's auras'; most had received telepathic messages from extraterrestrials. Nickell also claimed that the published accounts suggested that all but two of the abductees were elaborating fantasies under hypnosis: experiencing astral flight, seeing earth spirits or even, in one case, 'becoming' an alien and speaking in a robotic voice.

It can hardly be said that the fantasy-prone personality hypothesis has been welcomed by researchers who have devoted years to working with witnesses to strange phenomena. Abduction specialists, in particular, have argued that the theory cannot explain the complexities of their cases, and pointed to three rival surveys that do not seem to show the same correlations between fantasy proneness and unusual experiences. One, conducted by a team from Carleton University in Ottawa, produced equivocal results and has been used to bolster the arguments of both sides. The second, carried out by members of the Center for UFO Studies and based on a small sample of only nineteen abductees, concluded that the great majority appeared to be neither especially fantasy prone nor hypnotically suggestible.

The third is the work of a psychologist named Kenneth Ring, who has researched both abductions and near death experiences. Ring considered fantasy proneness as a possible cause of both phenomena, but found no link. His research did, however, suggest that witnesses to both close encounters and NDEs do undergo what he calls 'alternate reality experiences'

– strange experiences that seem real. The distinction between fantasy proneness and alternate reality experiences has eluded other psychologists; one, Leonard George, comments: 'Most researchers would include "alternate reality experiences" under their definition of fantasy proneness.' So it seems that at present the evidence does favour fantasy proneness as an explanation for some types of strange phenomena.

Invisible Realms

One of the most striking things about many of the strange events we have been studying is their apparent realism. If they are hallucinations, as the fantasy-prone personality hypothesis supposes, they are subtle and vivid ones. But what exactly are hallucinations, and how can we identify them for what they are?

A consideration of the evidence suggests that, broadly speaking, we may be dealing with two separate categories of experience. The first, and to some degree the most common, involves the intrusion into the waking world of figures and objects that in some way interact with our ordinary surroundings. These most psychologists would recognise as 'true hallucinations', which are generally defined as disturbances of perception that appear to have substance. An hallucination will therefore appear entirely real, throw shadows and interrelate correctly to objectively real features in the environment. (It is, however, possible for a true hallucination to appear translucent or be of a figure or object that appears much larger or smaller than it should.) As such, hallucinations could account for some encounters with aliens, monsters and ghosts, as well as meetings with giants and fairies.

Psychologists recognise several species of hallucination, including the Doppelganger, in which the percipient sees another figure but recognises himself, even though this other figure may well appear only partial, monochrome and 'jelly-like'. Another is the 'pseudo-hallucination' or vision, which differs from the 'true' hallucination in that the percipient is aware at the time that the thing he is experiencing is not real. Pseudo-hallucinations are often associated with mental disorders such as hysteria. In general, though, most psychologists now agree that hallucinators do find it difficult to distinguish between signals that are generated internally (by their brains) and externally (as a result of inputs from the five senses) – that is, between hallucinations and objective reality. This is really the key finding when it comes to considering whether or not hallucinations are a plausible explanation for some encounters with the unusual.

The second broad category of unusual events is perhaps even stranger, for it involves cases which, far from being accounted for by presuming that a single hallucination has intruded into the waking world, seem to involve a witness entering a different reality altogether. There is no question that those who undergo such experiences are simply 'seeing things'; for the duration of their experience they have in effect crossed into the borderlands and encountered a secret universe. A psychologist would say that they were experiencing an altered state of consciousness (ASC).

Ordinarily, we all live in a world known as 'consensus reality'. One writer defines this as 'the waking state . . . the world view taught to us in our earliest years by the representatives of our culture – in most cases, our parents. In this state, we tend to have roughly similar experiences to other members of our society. In part, this similarity arises from the fact that we live in the same environment, but in part it is due to the influences of our shared world view, which guides us in choosing what to notice, what to value and what to disregard.'

An altered state of consciousness, on the other hand 'is one in which [an individual] clearly feels a *qualitative* shift in his pattern of mental functioning, that is, he feels not just a quantitative shift (more or less alert, more or less visual imagery, sharper or duller, etc.), but also that some quality or qualities of his mental processes are different. Mental functions operate that do not operate at all ordinarily, perceptual qualities appear that have no normal counterparts, and so forth.'

What counts as an altered state of consciousness? Anything from sleep to an hypnotic trance, the state of calm induced by meditation to the state of euphoria induced by drugs. What is the ASC's significance when it comes to understanding the unknown? It calls into question everything that we think we see, hear, feel and know.

One of our most fundamental assumptions is that our eyes see the world as it really is, that they transmit this information accurately to our brains, and that the signals passed down the optic nerve are decoded and processed efficiently in the visual centres of the mind and then properly and permanently stored within our memories. If we were not comfortable with this notion, we would spend our time questioning every sensory input that we receive, rather than working, resting, playing, and generally getting on with our lives.

For most people, most of the time, it is a justifiable assumption to make. But in an altered state of consciousness, our perceptions of reality are hopelessly askew. In such states, reality becomes an illusion, and our illusions, reality.

The vital importance of altered states of consciousness lies in the fact that they are characterised by features that appear time and again in eyewitness accounts of strange phenomena. These include hallucinations; extreme emotions, from fear to ecstasy; feelings of profound insight and revelation; distorted body images; a different sense of time; and greatly enhanced suggestibility. Is it possible, then, that some anomalous experiences are not real, but actually the product of altered states of consciousness?

The answer to this question appears to be 'yes'. Moreover, recent research has pointed increasingly to one specific ASC as a possible source for many of the strange accounts we have been considering.

Sleep researchers have identified two little-known transitory stages between wakefulness and sleep, in which the normal distinctions between what is real and what is a dream become blurred. On falling asleep, the brain passes briefly through the 'hypnagogic state', which is characterised by an upsurge in disconnected but vivid and often extremely bizarre imagery. Peculiar sounds and smells may also be sensed. On awakening, it passes through a very similar 'hypnopompic state', though it is more common for hypnopompic images to have meaning, perhaps because the brain is anticipating the events of the coming day.

Between them, the hypnagogic and hypnopompic states occupy perhaps five per cent of our sleep, but the sights and sounds that occur in them tend to be even more ephemeral than dreams. The most common form of hypnagogia seems to be a parade of unrecognised faces (and the fact that they *are* unfamiliar is very often commented on) that flash into the brain following no particular pattern. Sometimes, though, the hypnagogic and hypnopompic states do seem to be capable of presenting brief stories more reminiscent of ordinary dreams. (For example, one sleeper had a vision of an immensely bright light, through which he could see a room where three British army officers were bent over a map table, apparently arranging troop movements. He was 'panic-stricken' lest they should turn and see him.) This seems to be particularly true of sufferers of narcolepsy – excessive sleepiness.

In general, though, as one writer notes, 'the hypnagogic experience is probably the most elusive kind of image-seeing there is. Not only is it never shared with others, but the images flash across the mental vision of the percipient with such rapidity, and at a time when his intellectual forces are particularly inactive, that the experience is so fugitive as to be virtually unseizable.'

One of the principal attractions of hypnagogia as a possible explanation for a variety of strange experiences, is that it is the very first stage of sleep. For this reason it is possible that some apparently waking experiences, even those that took place in the middle of the day, are actually examples of hypnagogic hallucinations. All we have to do is assume that the witness was, perhaps unwittingly, on the verge of drifting into sleep. Such an assumption may not be justified in many cases, but it is worth considering in others.

Although the few psychologists who have studied hypnagogia state that the majority of such hallucinations seem unthreatening, it is clear that a sub-category of highly realistic and terrifying visions do exist. These alarming experiences vary from a sensation of dread and the feeling that 'something' has entered the bedroom to full-blown visions of monsters, hags, ghosts and aliens. They are often accompanied by something at least as terrifying – a feeling of helplessness that amounts to the conviction that the witness is utterly paralysed. Sleep researchers suggest that this latter phenomenon is actually the result of the brain disconnecting itself from the rest of the nervous system so that the body does not rise to act out its dreams. For this reason sleep paralysis is more commonly reported in the hypnagogic than the hypnopompic state. We can recognise in this description the essential characteristics of David Hufford's 'Old Hag' experience.

Of course, none of this precludes the possibility that in some cases 'something' really has entered the bedroom – whether it be an Old Hag or an alien abductor – and that the witness who recalls what appears to be an instance of hypnagogia is really accurately remembering a physical experience. However, research into hypnagogia has established that it has several defining characteristics, and if we bear these in mind we may be in a better position to distinguish between real and essentially hallucinatory experiences.

Robert Baker defines the five characteristics of hypnagogic and hypnopompic hallucinations as follows: 'First, it always occurs before or after falling asleep. Second, one is paralysed or has difficulty in moving or, contrarily, may float out of one's body. Third, the hallucination is unusually bizarre. Fourth, after the hallucination is over, the hallucinator typically goes back to sleep. And fifth, the hallucinator is unalterably convinced of the "reality" of the entire experience.'

Comparing these characteristics with the abduction researcher David Jacobs' summary of a 'typical abduction', it is immediately obvious that there appears to be a close correlation between the two:

> An unsuspecting woman is in her room preparing to go to bed. She gets into bed, reads a while, turns off the light, and drifts off into a peaceful night's sleep. In the middle of the night she turns over and lies on her back. She is awakened by a light that seems to be glowing in her room. The light moves towards her bed and takes the shape of a small 'man' with a bald head and huge black eyes. She is terrified. She wants to run but she cannot move. She wants to scream but she cannot speak . . .
>
> Often the abductee forms 'screen' memories that mask the beginning of an abduction event. For example, one abductee said she saw a wolf in her bedroom one night. She clearly remembered its fur, fangs, and eyes. Other abductees say they have seen an 'angel' or 'devil'. They sometimes remember that they felt themselves floating out of the bed but then 'fought it' and were able to lower themselves back into bed.

At the very least, it must be admitted that this classic form of alien abduction account has such strong similarities with the hypnagogic hallucination that hypnagogia must be considered as a possible explanation for some abduction cases. Indeed, it might adequately explain a great many of them.

Of course, not all hallucinations occur in sleep states. Some are produced outside the brain – for example, in the eye ('entoptic phenomena') and the ear ('entotic phenomena', including tinnitus). Entoptic phenomena commonly centre around form constants – geometric images produced by neural firing in the visual system behind the eyeball. It is thus possible to see form constants in the dark, or when one's eyes are shut. As we have seen, one typical form constant is a vision of the sort of tunnel sometimes encountered in a near death experience, but witnesses can also experience bright, pulsating lights or even, in some exceptional cases, recognisable figures.

There are also hallucinations of touch, such as the 'cocaine bug' – the vivid sensation that the skin is crawling with insects, commonly encountered during withdrawl from drug addiction.

The familiar feeling of 'coldness' that many witnesses experience before and during a ghost sighting might also be an hallucination of sorts, since temperatures do not seem to drop physically during an encounter. The psychical researcher Celia Green, who published an analysis of apparitions, notes one nineteenth-century case in which three women felt a 'cold wind' as a ghost walked past them, though the candles they were holding did not even flicker, and a twentieth-century encounter on the Greek island of Poros in which the witness said she 'seemed to grow colder and colder' though she knew it was in fact a warm night.

Green's study also threw up another interesting pattern. When she analysed what witnesses had been doing when they saw an apparition, she discovered that 38 per cent had been lying down, 23 per cent were sitting, 19 per cent standing still, 18 per cent walking and 1 per cent driving or riding. This implies that the likelihood of experiencing a strange phenomena is inversely proportional to physical activity. Perhaps the brain needs a certain amount of leisure to concentrate on something other than attention-intensive tasks.

Such a suggestion is certainly reminiscent of the altered state of consciousness known to psychologists as 'absorption', which is commonly thought to be closely related to, or even identical to, fantasy proneness. A simple example of absorption might be becoming so engrossed in a book that one fails to notice someone else entering a room. In extreme cases, concentration becomes totally focused on a single object, with the effect that (perhaps unnoticed), other objects disappear, and time seems to slow or stop.

Absorption, in other words, can lead to the blurring of normal perceptions and create suitable conditions for fantasies. One piece of research concluded that 'objects of absorbed attention acquire an importance and intimacy that are normally reserved for the self, and may, therefore, acquire a temporary self-like quality'. This is a finding that might help to explain some monster sightings and perhaps also many cases of apparent psychokinesis (though another study found no relation between absorption and reports of PK). It could certainly account for the strange sense of detachment from the environment that is common in many borderlands experiences, including close encounters.

The ufologist Jenny Randles coined the term 'Oz factor' to describe this sort of experience, and gave, as an example, the case of a pair of UFO witnesses, Mr and Mrs W, who saw a dark disc hovering in the sky near Manchester on the evening of 21 July 1978. During the sighting, which lasted for about one and a half minutes, the Ws realised that the street they were standing in was strangely quiet; there were no vehicles and no other pedestrians. In other cases, witnesses have described a sudden silence descending around them, so that even birdsong ceased. This sounds very much like absorption.

Faulty Diagnoses

All those who have studied fantasy proneness and the propensity to enter altered states of consciousness agree that such conditions are not illnesses. Nevertheless, any analysis of unusual experiences must also consider the possibility that a variety of medical problems could help to explain some unusual events.

One obvious example is the phenomenon of possession, the apparent displacement of the human soul from the body by some other entity, usually a demon. This alarming experience has been reported from all over the world, and the historical cases go back to antiquity. There is, however, broad agreement as to the symptoms of possession, which include astonishing contortions of the face and body, foaming at the mouth, vomiting, exhibitions of tremendous strength, and the tendency to spew obscenities in a deeper, much gruffer voice.

For example, in 1491, a French nun called Jeanne Potier (who seems to have been an hysterical nymphomaniac), initiated a spate of possessions at a convent in the town of Cambrai. Possessed nuns barked like dogs, showed superhuman strength and claimed to foretell the future. In Wertet, in Holland, in 1550, nuns 'climbed trees like cats' and claimed they were being lifted several feet into the air and pinched or beaten by invisible hands. Though such cases routinely led to witch-hunts, torture, trials and executions, it was generally recognised, even at the time, that many incidents of apparent 'possession' were the products of hysteria and psychological contagion.

Today we can also recognise the characteristics of epilepsy in many surviving descriptions of possession; *grand mal* seizures typically involve unconsciousness followed by frenzied spasming and foaming at the mouth. Another condition that may have contributed to the classic portrait of possession is Tourette's Syndrome, a rare neurological disorder whose symptoms range from facial tics to astonishing verbal outbursts, from barks and screams to uncontrollable swearing. Questioning the 'possessed' man might even produce further evidence that demons really were at work: it is common for a Tourette's sufferer to feel that some invisible entity is dictating these bizarre patterns of behaviour.

One of the most intriguing characteristics of epilepsy is the way in which seizures are often preceded by what is known as the 'epileptic aura'. This can feature a variety of hallucinations and the sensation of 'presences' which may vary from the Virgin Mary to the devil, combined with episodes of *deja vu* or the rarer phenomenon of *jamais vu* (familiar places seeming new and different). Epileptic auras are frequently accompanied by feelings of foreboding, though they can also be ecstatic. Certainly, it seems that the experience of an aura could convince an epileptic that he was experiencing a supernatural event, as easily as his companions were overawed by the seizures themselves. Furthermore, a significant proportion of epileptics never experience seizures at all. Knowing only the epileptic aura, they might well believe that they have been chosen to experience profound religious or occult events.

One particular part of the brain, the temporal lobe, appears to be the seat of such strange visions. Lobes can be found at the base of both the left and the right hemispheres and account for about forty per cent of the wrinkled outer layer of 'grey matter' that deals with the higher functions of the brain, including the interpretation of sensory inputs from the eyes and ears and the storage and retrieval of memories. Damage to the temporal lobes, whether during epilepsy or, perhaps, as the result of a head injury, can produce remarkable changes in the way that the brain perceives the world around it. One of the most common is the creation of what is often termed the 'dreamy state', in which extremely vivid visual and auditory hallucinations are common. Sufferers may well also experience intense feelings of dread.

It is important to realise that this particular variety of seizure does not lead to the characteristic 'fit' of thrashing limbs that most people associate with epilepsy: the temporal lobes do not control the muscular system. Furthermore, the symptoms of the disorder may not occur with any great frequency and it is quite likely that many sufferers never realise they have the condition.

Those who suffer from temporal lobe epilepsy exhibit a number of interesting personality traits, including 'excessive moral zeal and a tendency to find profound meaning in mundane events'. Most intriguingly of all, people with temporal lobe malfunctions (not just epilepsy) have been shown to be more likely to report that they have experienced unusual and inexplicable encounters, not to mention the strange sensation of floating, commonly reported by abductees and those who have out of the body experiences.

It thus seems fairly clear that a clinical study of witnesses to events such as UFO abductions and religious visions might show that at least some apparent mystical and paranormal events were actually episodes of temporal lobe epilepsy. But several recent studies have suggested that the minor temporal lobe abnormalities, which fall far short of epilepsy, may also cause people to see and hear bizarre things.

In one preliminary study, the brain activity of a dozen mediums was monitored using an EEG, and ten of the twelve were found to have temporal lobe abnormalities. Another piece of research suggested that damage to the right temporal lobe correlated with experiences of extrasensory perception and visions of ghosts and spirits. But perhaps the most interesting examination of the possible links between unusual experiences and temporal lobe abnormality is being conducted by Michael Persinger, the Laurentian University neurophysiologist who is also one of the chief proponents of the earthlights theory. Persinger believes that some reports of strange phenomena may be the product of 'microseizures' in the temporal lobes, triggered either by fatigue, anxiety or a personal crisis, or even by variations in the earth's natural magnetic fields. In order to test the theory, he sought volunteers and asked them to don a special helmet equipped with solenoids positioned over the temporal lobes. Using this helmet, he was able to deliver magnetic pulses to his subjects' brains, which stimulated bursts of electrical activity within the lobes.

The parapsychologist Susan Blackmore volunteered to have her lobes stimulated by Persinger's helmet in a 'dungeon' deep within the university and found it an alarming experience:

> I was wide awake throughout. Nothing seemed to happen for the first ten minutes or so. Instructed to describe aloud anything that happened, I felt under pressure to say something, anything. Then suddenly my doubts vanished. 'I'm swaying. It's like being on a hammock.' Then it felt for all the world as though two hands had grabbed my shoulders and were bodily yanking me upright . . .
>
> Something seemed to get hold of my leg and pull it, distort it and drag it up the wall. It felt as though I had been stretched halfway up to the ceiling. Then came the emotions. Totally out of the blue, but intensely and vividly, I suddenly felt angry – not just mildly cross, but that clear-minded anger out of which you act – but there was nothing and no one to act on. After perhaps ten seconds, it was gone. Later, it was replaced by an equally sudden attack of fear. I was terrified – of nothing in particular.

For all Persinger's magnetic terrorism, Blackmore saw no

aliens; nor did she report the sensations of actually being abducted. To that extent the idea that the temporal lobes play a central part in many strange experiences remains unproven. But add an element of suggestion, she theorised, and there might be a tendency for the victims of microseizures to try to rationalise their experiences: 'Of course, I knew it was all caused by the magnetic field changes, but what would people feel if such things happened spontaneously in the middle of the night? Wouldn't they want, above all, to find an explanation, to find out who had been doing it to them? If someone told them an alien was responsible and invited them to join an abductees' research group, wouldn't some of them seize on the idea, if only to reassure themselves they weren't going mad?'

Many abduction researchers would answer this question with a resounding 'No'. David Jacobs criticises Persinger's belief that magnetic fields generated by the grinding of tectonic plates prior to earthquakes could stimulate the temporal lobes, and indeed there is as yet no direct proof for this theory. Nor was Persinger able to test abductees, rather than run-of-the-mill student volunteers, in his laboratory. Unless sceptics manage to produce better evidence for a direct link between brain abnormalities and hallucinations that more precisely resemble the aliens and monsters that seem to wander the earth, the problem will remain a matter of interpretation, though the negative evidence that has been produced to date is enough to make many people wonder whether it is sensible to accept abductees' reports at face value.

Epilepsy and temporal lobe abnormalities are not the only clinical problems that can result in remarkable hallucinations. Oxygen starvation wreaks havoc with perception and leads directly to some extremely bizarre reports. We have already seen that some of the features of near death experiences may be the product of oxygen starvation; here are two other cases that appear to have had a similar cause.

During the Great War (when pilots flew in open cockpits without oxygen), one flier reported that 'at a very great height he had seen a curious dragon-like animal apparently floating in the air and approaching him rapidly'. Fearing he was about to be attacked, the pilot descended, and the dragon presently vanished. A rather similar incident, though apparently one with a slightly different cause, occurred in August 1971. A scuba-diving instructor named Ian Skinner was swimming at a depth of about 130 feet off Malta when

> [I] saw a light ahead of me and was drawn towards it both by curiosity and what seemed like an unknown force. Over the next ridge and very much further down I saw a very beautiful young woman, tall and slim, with a lovely figure, standing at the entrance to a large cave . . . The incandescence of the surrounding area added to the serenity and calm of the sight.
>
> I thought I must be suffering from nitrogen narcosis, described in the early days of diving as 'the rapture of the deep'. A look at my depth gauge revealed that I was 230 feet down. Then she spoke: 'Hello, I have been waiting for you, do not be afraid, with me you are safe.' I backed away but she smiled, walked towards me and held out her hand. It felt warm, sensual and safe, and my fear disappeared.
>
> 'When you return to me I will be waiting for you, then you will stay with me for ever. I have a gift for you.' She handed me a small jar shaped like an amphora. As I ascended, I saw her waving as she slowly faded from view.

Skinner surfaced still carrying the amphora, which was later identified as a Phoenician scent jar.

The Mysteries of Memory

Even if we accept that fantasy proneness, temporal lobe epilepsy, oxygen starvation and indeed other psychological and medical factors may help to explain why some witnesses experience strange phenomena, we are little closer to understanding *why* they see the things they see.

Where do the monsters and aliens that are reported time and time again actually come from? Although they could be real, the best guess seems to be that they are dredged up from a memory that stores information on most of the things we have experienced during our lives.

It is important at this point to recognise that perhaps the most popular conception of memory is not correct. It is not an infallible filing system in which our thoughts and experiences are preserved for ever, and from which they can be retrieved intact – if not directly, then by using special techniques such as hypnosis. Recent evidence suggests that memories are actually little more than brief summaries, which our brains flesh out for us as required. When we relive a moment in the past, we are actually experiencing not a true recollection, but an imaginative reconstruction of events, which is inevitably flawed. The central details that concern us are emphasised, irrelevancies are forgotten, and recollections are reinterpreted with reference to our own beliefs and needs.

Memory, moreover, is a plastic phenomenon. It can be shaped and moulded, and recall can easily be influenced by an incautiously phrased enquiry. In one experiment, members of a group were shown a film of a traffic accident and then asked one of two questions: 'Did you see a broken headlight?' or 'Did you see *the* broken headlight?' Twice as many of those who were asked the second question said they had seen a shattered light. In fact no broken headlight was shown in the film.

Most alarmingly of all, it is possible to introduce entirely false memories into the brain, either deliberately or quite unconsciously. Once implanted, false memories are indistinguishable from true recollections, and will continue to seem real even in the face of convincing evidence that they are fantasies. It is even possible for false memories to pass lie-detector tests.

One example, which shows how a false memory can be implanted, and how the witness can then elaborate on it, concerned a four-year-old boy who was told, once a week for eleven weeks, that he had experienced an entirely imaginary event: 'You went to hospital because your finger got caught in a mousetrap. Did this ever happen to you?' The researchers recorded his replies over the weeks:

> *First interview*: No, I've never been to hospital.
> *Second interview*: Yes. I cried.
> *Fourth interview*: Yes. I remember. It felt like a cut.
> *Eleventh interview*: I was looking and then I didn't see what I was doing and it got in there somehow . . . I went downstairs and said to Dad, 'I want lunch', and then it got stuck in the mousetrap . . . My brother pushed me into the mousetrap. It happened yesterday. I caught my finger in it yesterday. I went to the hospital yesterday.

Over the last decade, false memory syndrome, as it is known, has featured in a number of strange legal cases involving outlandish claims of ritual child abuse, often by well organised gangs of Satanists. Several dozen cases of alleged Satanic Ritual Abuse have occurred in the United States, Britain, Holland, Brazil, Australia and New Zealand, and several have resulted in convictions and long jail sentences for the accused.

These cases have several factors in common: they are based on the often unsupported testimony of one young child, or at best a handful of children; there is no physical evidence that the abuse ever took place; and the courts are asked to believe that the child witnesses' frequently astonishing claims are literally true. Children have recalled numerous incidents of babies being sacrificed and burnt, of apparitions of ghosts and monsters, and (in one instance) of victims being fed alive to sharks kept in a large tank by the leader of a Satanic cult. Despite extensive inquiries by the police, not a single dead baby has ever been found, let alone any tanks of man-eating sharks. There is a strong presumption that they involve the implantation of false memories, probably unintentionally, by therapists and social workers who themselves actively believe in the reality of Satanic Ritual Abuse.

That some incidents are definitely the product of false memories was demonstrated by a remarkable case that occurred in Olympia, Washington, in 1988–89. Paul Ingram, the local police chief and, incidentally, a committed Christian, was accused of sexually abusing his two adult daughters. During several months of therapy, the women gradually recalled an astonishingly protracted and complex story of ritual abuse at the hands, not only of their father, but other police officers, their mother and several other members of a Satanic coven.

When the charges were put to Ingram, he denied them at first, but eventually confessed and even added some more recollections himself. Some of his memories were so bizarre that Richard Ofshe, a psychologist employed by the prosecution, became convinced they were fantasies. He tested this theory by telling Ingram that his daughters had recalled an incident in which he forced them to have sex while he watched. They had made no such allegation, and at first Ingram denied the abuse had ever happened. Within a few days, however, after 'thinking it over', he wrote a detailed account of the non-existent incident, complete with 'remembered' dialogue. Ofshe 'now had serious doubts whether Ingram was guilty of anything, except of being a highly suggestible individual with a tendency to float in and out of trance states and a patent and rather dangerous eagerness to please authority.' He concluded that the policeman was so sure that his children would not lie that he had convinced himself he must be repressing his own memories of the abuse.

Not every memory of Satanic Ritual Abuse is consciously recalled. Many are retrieved under hypnosis, a technique that has also been widely used to investigate past lives and alien abductions, with spectacular results. No matter how well the abductors seem to have masked their activities by erasing conscious memories and planting screen recollections in their place, hypnotic regression by an experienced therapist generally seems to be able to reconstruct events as they really happened.

Over the past several decades, hypnosis has acquired a potent reputation as a devastating tool for uncovering hidden truths. It is widely regarded as a sort of universal truth-serum, one that leaves a witness incapable of telling lies or evading answers. Unfortunately, this is far from the truth. Although it has been shown that hypnosis can improve some people's ability to recall the details of past events, there is also ample evidence that it greatly enhances suggestibility, leaving the subject highly vulnerable. A hypnotised witness may seize on cues offered by an inadvertently leading question and fantasise a suitable response. It has also been demonstrated that hypnosis actually increases the chances of simple error. According to Leonard George, 'there is no evidence that hypnotised people have consistently better memories than non-hypnotised ones; rather, hypnosis tends to increase *confidence* in one's ability to remember, rather than *accuracy*. A hypnotised person may thus be more likely to mistake a fantasy for a true recollection.'

Many valuable experiments have been conducted to assess the reliability of evidence given under hypnosis. In one case, a vivid false memory of a bank robbery was implanted into a volunteer's memory; he was subsequently able to 'pick out' the criminal responsible from a set of photographs. In another, three women who were driven past an elaborately staged hold-up were hypnotised and asked to recall what had happened. They disagreed as to the number and the sex of the robbers and the colour and make of their getaway car. Even if an investigator is scrupulously careful not to ask leading questions, research suggests that witnesses may unconsciously offer up fantasies under hypnosis. This is because hypnotic trances appear to inspire the subject with a strong desire to please the therapist.

We have already noted that forgotten memories of films once seen and novels once read are one source of these past lives. Psychologists know this phenomenon as cryptomnesia, and it is surprisingly common. Mediums who claim to channel new symphonies composed by the likes of Beethoven may well be producing pastiches based on works they heard performed years earlier. (Research has shown that the majority of auditory mediums have had a fair degree of musical training.) Similarly, the psychologist William James discussed one case of apparent demonic possession in which an illiterate German woman, laid low by fever, began to ramble in Latin, Greek and Hebrew. Though the local priest suspected the worst, it was eventually discovered that the woman had boarded with an old professor while she was a child. The scholar was in the habit of reading aloud to himself while wandering the corridors; in her fever, the 'possessed' woman had recalled his words without understanding their meaning or remembering where she had heard them.

Several other recognised memory phenomena also appear to be relevant to the analysis of unusual experiences. One is cryptaesthesia, the subconscious acquisition of information. The term was coined by Theodore Flournoy, the Swiss psychologist who investigated one of the Martian mediums of the 1890s. Flournoy gives the example of a man who walked into a deserted campsite in a forest and heard a 'voice' ordering him to leave the spot at once. He was so surprised to hear words apparently issuing from thin air that he complied; immediately afterwards a large tree fell across the clearing, crashing across the spot where he had been standing. Under Flournoy's questioning, the near-victim recalled that he had noticed termites swarming over the tree as he entered the clearing, and he concluded that his unconscious had recognised this sign that the tree was unsafe and fashioned an auditory hallucination in order to warn the conscious brain of the danger. Many people, it seems safe to say, would have been more inclined to attribute such a spectacular escape to the warning of a helpful spirit or seen it as an example of precognition.

Another phenomenon, pareidolia – the brain's tendency to translate random sensory cues into meaningful images and messages – can help to explain a wide variety of other unusual events. This intriguing but well-understood freak of memory and perception has been experienced by anyone who has looked up at the clouds and seen images of lions, dragons and the like, and it accounts for the great majority of simulacra – from visions of the face of Christ in the flaking paint on a henhouse door to the holy tortilla pulled burning from a New Mexico oven in 1978, which bore the saviour's likeness in the scorch marks on its underside. A related term, *Fata Morgana*, describes the peculiar appearances of what seems to be a celestial city floating in the air. What is actually being seen is a mirage of pinnacles of rock or ice that form themselves into fantastic shapes which the brain interprets as towers, spires and castles. This unusual example of pareidolia, which probably explains sightings of Alaska's beautiful 'Silent City', is most often seen in the colder latitudes.

Nor is pareidolia a purely visual phenomenon; it explains how some fundamentalist Christians can find messages extolling Satan on records, when they are played backwards. (Not only does it seem unlikely that such messages exist; research has shown that they cannot be understood, either consciously or unconsciously, if they are created.)

Perhaps the most striking recent example of pareidolia was the short-lived enthusiasm among psychical researchers for the electronic voice phenomenon (EVP). First discovered by a Swedish film producer named Frederick Jurgenson at the end of the 1950s, EVP was publicised by a Latvian, Konstantin Raudive, in a book that appeared in English at the beginning of the 1970s. Essentially, it purported to consist of messages from the dead, picked up either by a tape recorder left running in an empty room or by listening carefully to the white noise produced by a radio tuned between stations. (Later on, one entrepreneurial company produced a special machine, the Spiricom, which it claimed would amplify and record the voices for a modest outlay of two or three thousand pounds.) One British researcher claimed to have received 10,000 different messages by using the radio method.

There were two obstacles to accepting EVP as a psychical phenomenon. One was the problem of picking up the messages in the first place. Most were so faint that they could hardly be heard, and it was soon discovered that no two people interpreted any given communication the same way. The second was the brevity of practically all the messages and nonsensical character of most. (Something also true of some apparent 'phone calls from the dead'.) One transmission, recorded by Philip Rogers of Sheffield, included an apparent conversation between flying saucer occupants, which Rogers transcribed as follows:

> *First man*: 'Space. Take part in air arm. Yar-var nianna donnova-ionosphere.'
> *Second man*: 'I've gone! Yonskaler yes! You touch. You've jammed it. Go on!'
> *Woman*: 'He's shifting in time-space.'
> *Second man* (adopting broad Yorkshire accent): 'Shut up.'
> *Third man*: 'My stoicranz is stuck.'
> *Second man*: 'Space.'
> *First man*: 'Good old Einstein.'

Frankly, it is easier to invoke pareidolia as an explanation for this exchange than to assume that ufonauts really do speak such gibberish.

Problems with the Psychological Source Hypothesis

Taken together, this collection of strange psychological conditions and eccentric brain phenomena does have the potential to explain many of the greatest mysteries of the borderlands. Perhaps the reason why UFO abductions are so rarely observed is that they never really happen. Perhaps people who describe past lives or remember the horrors of Satanic Ritual Abuse are reliving false memories. Perhaps evidence produced under hypnosis is no more real than a dream of flying.

I suspect that a great many of the most perplexing reports we have on record have their origins in the human brain – a suggestion that might be called the 'psychological source hypothesis'. But I cannot prove it, and nor can the massed ranks of sceptics with their statistical analyses and their correlations. There is a fundamental difficulty in trying to fit broad theories to specific data, and researchers into alien abductions or reincarnation will always be able to point to astonishing details in individual cases, which cannot be explained by theories as broadly based as the fantasy prone personality hypothesis. Once we see things from this point of view, it becomes pretty obvious that believers and sceptics will be able to argue their respective corners for some time to come.

For psychological theories to be worth anything, though, they must be more testable than the unproveable ultraterrestrial hypothesis. Is there any way of measuring the significance of the role played by human imagination and human memory in the reporting of strange phenomena?

Observing witnesses while they actually undergo a strange event is difficult, but not always impossible. It is obvious, for example, that people who are undergoing an out of the body experience do not physically travel to the places they visit; their bodies remain still and their minds seem fixed in a trance state of some sort. There are, moreover, only a handful of anecdotal accounts to suggest that any witness has seen the astral body that is supposed to float around the ceiling at the start of an OBE – and without such evidence it would certainly be difficult to prove that this 'body' was in any sense real. In addition, attempts to film abductees who claim to have been forcibly taken from their beds on a semi-regular basis have always proved unsuccessful. For whatever reason, the aliens simply do not come when the cameras are on.

The situation is nearly as unsatisfactory when it comes to carrying out tests with the witnesses themselves. Much of the research that has been done on concepts such as the fantasy prone personality involved not reinterviewing the witnesses, but a much less satisfactory process of reviewing published case summaries, with all the problems of avoiding implicit biases that this implies. There are several reasons for this: lack of resources, lack of time and the problem of assembling a suitable sample from case histories investigated by rival researchers, to name but three. The upshot, though, is that surprisingly little work has been done with the witnesses themselves.

One early experiment that did show some promise was

carried out by Richard Haines, a physiologist and UFO investigator, in the mid-1970s. Haines wondered whether the eyewitnesses who sketched the flying saucers they had seen on his sighting reports were remembering clearly and reporting their experiences accurately, or simply drawing their sighting 'as it ought to be' and basing their perceptions on material they had read or seen in UFO books or science fiction movies. Haines asked 424 people, the majority of whom had a previous interest in ufology, to 'draw what you think a UFO looks like'. Of these, 137 thought they had seen a UFO. Reviewing the mass of sketches, Haines found that there were significant similarities between the drawings made by the two groups. The principal difference was that UFO witnesses sketched fewer adornments – doors, portholes, landing legs and insignia – than did non-witnesses. The implication seemed to be that both groups were drawing on a common, culturally based image of what UFOs should look like, and that this image was strong enough to affect the ways in which witnesses perceived 'real' UFOs.

Another UFO researcher, Alvin Lawson, conducted a rather similar experiment in the hope of discovering how people who had little or no knowledge of ufology, and who had certainly never claimed to have experienced a close encounter, might fantasise an abduction experience. He advertised for creative people to take part in his experiment and selected eight subjects, who were each hypnotised and asked eight highly leading questions, suggesting that they had been abducted and subjected to a medical examination. Lawson then compared their statements to the experiences of 'real' abductees.

Lawson's research seemed to show not only that his volunteers fantasised surprisingly elaborate encounters, but that their imaginary experiences closely paralleled the cases collected by field investigators specialising in abductions. People who had alleged no knowledge of UFOs described typical features of an abduction experience such as beams of light, telepathic communication and examinations of the sex organs by humanoid occupants.

Ufologists have criticised the Lawson experiments on several grounds. It is certainly true that a sample of only eight people is hardly enough to allow general conclusions to be drawn, and it is regrettable that more effort was not made to establish just how much these 'ignorant' volunteers had really managed to absorb about the UFO experience. A third criticism – that the aliens imagined by the hypnotised subjects were so highly varied that fewer than twenty per cent were humanoid, compared to a seventy per cent incidence of humanoids in 'real' cases – is also worth noting, although the experiment took place some years before small, grey aliens began to appear in abduction reports to the exclusion of other ufonauts.

On balance, Lawson's limited experiment does seem to suggest that reports closely resembling supposedly real encounters can be produced by the human brain alone – particularly when it is in a highly suggestible state. What it does not do is show where our mental imagery of ghosts and aliens, demons and monsters comes from. Is it the product of a lifetime's exposure to ancient folklore and to modern media overflowing with fictionalised accounts of strange phenomena – memories of which are stored deep in our subconscious, just waiting to be accessed – or is some of it 'real' in some other way? And, if it is the latter, just what sort of phenomenon are we dealing with?

11

Strange Fashions

The phantom social workers came for Elizabeth Coupland's children on a winter's day in 1990.

There were two of them – young women, attractive and assured – and when they knocked at the door of Coupland's Sheffield council flat they explained that they represented the National Society for the Prevention of Cruelty to Children. Because her visitors were smartly dressed and authoritative, Coupland let them in and allowed them to examine her children, one aged two and the other five months.

The visitors soon left, and Coupland assumed that she would hear nothing more of the matter. But a day or two later, one of the women returned, this time accompanied by a male colleague, to announce that she had been given the authority to take both the children into care. Shocked and then scared, Coupland resisted. When she threatened to call the police, the social workers beat a diplomatic retreat.

Coupland *did* phone the police, and the police called the NSPCC. But the NSPCC denied that any of their workers had paid a visit to an Elizabeth Coupland. The local authorities in Sheffield knew nothing about the incident, either.

Before long it became evident that bogus officials were

calling at other homes. The publicity given to the Coupland case prompted several dozen other parents to come forward and report that they too had received visits from neatly turned out young men and women who presented themselves as health visitors or social workers and announced that they had come to check up on their children. On several occasions an examination did indeed take place, and sometimes the visitors explained that they were searching for bruises or other signs of sexual abuse.

The obvious suggestion was that a gang of paedophiles was at work. With this in mind, the police launched a major investigation in the spring of 1990. By the time it was wound down a few months later, 'Operation Childcare' had become Britain's biggest ever police hunt and involved twenty-three separate forces. The results, though, were hardly what had been expected. After many thousands of man-hours spent taking statements, searching for witnesses and combing the paedophile community for clues, the police concluded that only two of a total of 250 reports were worthy of further investigation. The remainder, they decided, were false alarms caused by calls from a motley selection of Mormons, door-to-door salesmen, canvassers, market researchers, portrait photographers and even one or two genuine health visitors.

Although the story has long since disappeared from the pages of the national press, the phantom social workers have continued to knock on doors the length and breadth of Britain. They were in Edinburgh in April 1995 and in Leicester a month later. They have called at homes in Bristol, Bath, Blackburn, Battersea and Barnsley. And since that January morning in 1990, not a single person has been convicted or even charged with impersonating a social worker, nor with any related incidents of sexual assault. In only one case were children actually removed from their house. (In that instance, the infants were taken to the local park, bought an ice cream, and then brought safely home.)

Unsurprisingly, the police have never been able to assign rational motives to these uncatchable, phantom social workers.

The theory that the visits were the work of organised paedophile gangs seems to be ruled out by the fact that in the great majority of cases the visitor was a woman – female paedophiles are practically unknown – and that attempts to seize the children concerned were, at best, half-hearted. A more likely explanation is that some of the phantoms are actually vigilantes looking for evidence of child abuse; journalists investigating local cases have identified at least two instances involving self-appointed 'child-savers'.

Operation Childcare did turn up some interesting evidence about the appearance and behaviour of the phantom social workers. Most witnesses said that they were visited by one or two women; less frequently, by a woman accompanied by a man. All the women were young, in their late twenties and early thirties, heavily made-up and smartly dressed. One witness, Katharine Millett of Sheffield, described her visitor as 'like a model. Her hair was tied back in a bun, she had a nice figure, and wore a dark two-piece suit.' Few had local accents, and several called in advance to make appointments, and carried identification. They even displayed an inexplicable preference for driving red, A-registered Vauxhall Cavaliers.

The real question, though, is not so much who the social workers were, as why they appeared in Britain, and why during the winter of 1989–90. In fact, it is not hard to guess at the likely solution to this mystery. The phantom social worker flap erupted in the midst of the greatest panic over child abuse the country had ever experienced. During those winter months, the newspapers were full of reports of what appeared to be the ritual abuse of children by gangs of Satanists operating in Manchester, Rochdale and Nottingham. It was said that infants were being raped and tortured at secret religious ceremonies; that babies were being murdered and eaten; and that foetuses were being deliberately aborted and ritually sacrificed to the devil. None of these allegations was ever proven.

During the months when the phantom social workers were knocking on doors, real social workers were conducting dawn raids on the homes of children who had been identified as potentially at risk from the Satanic covens, and taking the infants forcibly into care. Coming as they did only a couple of years after the notorious 'Cleveland scandal', during which more than 120 cases of supposed child sex abuse were diagnosed by a paediatrician employing an inaccurate new test, these raids seemed to prove that no family was safe from social workers who might decide at any moment that its children were at risk, and who so obviously possessed all the powers they needed to take them into care and keep them there for months at a time.

The parents who received a call from a Mormon missionary, and reported the matter to the police as a visit from a bogus health visitor, would doubtless always have been wary of a stranger calling. Like any parent, they would have felt occasional fear for their child's safety, and concern that they might be hurt or injured one day. Looking at the phantom social worker flap from that point of view, one could argue that it flared into being in response to a fundamental anxiety. But perhaps the most interesting thing about the panic was the way in which the fearful abductors were portrayed. They did not appear as stereotypical paedophiles and obvious perverts, but as something that was much more subtly frightening, because it was so much more difficult to deal with. Although the underlying anxiety of the parents might help to explain *how* the strange visitors appeared, we can only comprehend *why* they came as social workers and *when* they chose to make their entrance if we make the effort to understand the whole cultural background to the case.

The Many Monsters of Lake Saint-François

The idea that our minds arrange matters so that strange phenomena manifest themselves in a manner appropriate to the time and the place in which they occur is known as the 'cultural source' or 'psychosocial' hypothesis. The theory first came to prominence at the end of the 1960s, and although it has been developed considerably since those early days, it still has many of the characteristics that marked it out when it first appeared. It is, for example, much more popular in Europe – and particularly France – than it is in the United States, where it is often regarded as a needlessly complex theory, not to mention an essentially unprovable one. Moreover, its critics point out, it has its Achilles heel in the fact that it cannot easily account for cases that produce physical evidence, nor for those that display precise similarities in the detail of weird experiences. The cultural source hypothesis's very subtlety works against it, it is argued, since witnesses to strange phenomena have such varied backgrounds and such different expectations that each new encounter should be very different to the last.

Nevertheless, it has to be admitted that the theory does neatly account for many of the broader trends in unexplained phenomena – the strange fashions of the borderlands. In the field of ufology, for example, where the idea first surfaced, it provides an explanation for the mystery of why the unidentified flying objects of the 1890s appeared as airships, the UFOs of the mid-1940s were ghost rockets and those of the 1950s looked like flying saucers. To psychosocial theorists, all were reflections, not of up-to-the-minute technology but of contemporary hopes or fears. In this interpretation, the airships of the great flap of 1896–7, crewed by their brilliant American inventors, fulfilled the turn-of-the-century desire to conquer the skies. The ghost rockets of 1946 reflected the doubts and uncertainties of the post-war world – when who knew what the Russians might be up to with their captured German scientists – and the flying saucers of the 1950s anticipated the dawning of the space age or became a metaphor for the fear of communist invasion, depending on your point of view.

The cultural source hypothesis also seeks to explain some of the mysteries of psychical research and many of the mysteries of cryptozoology. At its most obvious, it provides one ready explanation for the problem of why the Blessed Virgin Mary appears so frequently to Catholics, whose religion places a special stress on her veneration, and so rarely to members of the Protestant Churches, who appear simply to lack the cultural conditioning necessary to fuel such visions. Similarly, the great success of spiritualism, and the eagerness with which spiritualists embraced the phenomena of the seance room, might be viewed as a cultural response to the declining influence of the established churches and the vacuum in belief and authority that that created.

These are, of course, broad, indeed crude, arguments that are open to considerable criticism and liable to require extensive amendment when examined in detail. But the cultural source hypothesis also has some interesting things to say when it is applied on a more personal level. It predicts, for example, that if a man, seeking to discover whether he can recover suppressed memories, visits a therapist who believes in reincarnation and alien abductions, and if he half-expects and half-hopes to rediscover a past life or an abduction under hypnosis, he is very likely to recall just such an experience.

This sort of hypothesis can be verified experimentally. One psychologist, Robert Baker, assembled sixty volunteers and split them into three groups. Twenty were told that hypnosis could uncover past lives; twenty were told that hypnotic regression was a fallacy; and the rest were given a non-committal introduction to the subject. Baker then hypnotised all his subjects and attempted to explore their memories of past lives. His results showed that subjects who had been encouraged to believe in the reality of reincarnation experienced more past lives. Similarly, a study of the past lives recalled by the subjects of different hypnotists showed that the therapists' beliefs seemed to influence their subjects' recollections. One who believed that reincarnation occurred immediately after death found his subjects reporting an unbroken stream of incarnations. Another, who thought that the soul waited a while before returning to earth, found gaps of decades between past lives.

Ian Stevenson's research on reincarnation – which, it will be recalled, does not depend on the use of hypnosis – also throws up the possibility that cultural influences are at work. An analysis of his casebook shows that, while Stevenson's Indian and Sri Lankan subjects almost invariably reincarnate a few miles from the place where their previous life ended, his Alaskans are generally reborn within the same families. Similarly, Stevenson's Asian subjects almost never change sex as they progress through successive incarnations, while those studied by British and American-based therapists such as Arnall Bloxham and Joe Keeton often do. It seems more probable that these differences are the product of cultural and religious influences than it does that reincarnation is a fact, but one that works very differently for British souls than it does for Indian and Sri Lankan ones.

A French folklorist, Michel Meurger, has elaborated the most detailed version of the cultural source hypothesis yet proposed. Meurger began his work with a field study of some twenty lakes in the Canadian province of Quebec, which local tradition asserted are haunted by lake monsters. Though cryptozoologists have attempted to investigate some of these traditions, they have concentrated only on the handful of accounts that resemble modern monster sightings, ignoring the context in which they appear. Meurger emphatically rejects this reductionist approach and seeks, instead, to demonstrate that it is fundamentally impossible to separate folklore from reality so neatly. By ignoring the folkloric context of a report, cryptozoologists fail to comprehend its original purpose and meaning, and find themselves tentatively accepting the reality of lake monsters that simply cannot exist.

Meurger's work in Quebec showed him that the lake monster is in fact only one of a number of recurring motifs that appear again and again in local folk traditions. Lakes that teem with monsters are also said to have no bottom and to be riddled with underwater caverns, or connected to each other by submerged channels, filled with terrifying whirlpools and navigated by mysterious submarines. How, asks Meurger, can we be justified in rejecting these inconvenient pieces of folklore as mere legend, while accepting traditions of lake monsters because they, alone, conform to the notions of cryptozoological reality which happen to prevail today?

Even if the study of Quebecois lakes *is* restricted solely to reports of lake monsters, cryptozoology still struggles to make sense of the wide variety of creatures that are being seen. Meurger gives the example of Lake Saint-François, an isolated body of water south-east of Montreal, surrounded by thick pine forests and riddled with lake monster lore. It is twenty-one miles long – about the same as Loch Ness – and some 180 feet deep, hardly one of the world's great bodies of water. Yet according to the accounts of local people (whose sightings were made within the last three decades or so), it is home to up to five different species of monster. Meurger collected reports of giant sturgeon, some thirty feet long; animals with backs like saw-toothed logs; a large, finned fish; a creature like a whale; and a spotted monster with a crocodile's head. Yet zoologically speaking it is highly improbable that so many different creatures could co-exist in one small lake, or indeed that monsters of any sort could dwell in a score of different lakes in this single Canadian province.

How, then, does Meurger prefer to interpret such accounts? He believes that the variation in reports may be accounted for by the merging of European lake monster traditions – all horse-headed beasts, dragons and giant snakes – with local Canadian Indian lore, which has its emphasis on horned serpents, thus creating a broad cultural palette from which lake monster motifs may be drawn.

From this starting point, he goes on to argue that lake monster lore needs to be viewed in the widest possible context – that the monsters themselves are part of what he terms a 'mythological landscape', a place where the human imagination can be given freer rein, where the terms fact and fiction lack meaning (or rather, mean what the witness thinks they mean), and where monsters are more than merely monstrous. Wanderers in the mythological landscape invest them with some of the supernatural powers and the traditional magic of folklore. They become protean beasts, uncatchable, unknowable, ever-changing and eternally elusive – just like the religious visions, the aliens and the monsters we have already met.

This does not mean that the entities we are dealing with emerge solely from hallowed tradition and ancient myth. Modern folklore, modern fiction and urban legends have added their own motifs to the mythological landscape – blue-clad virgins and ectoplasmic rods in the nineteenth-century, mystery submarines and small, grey aliens in the twentieth. (It should be recognised, however, that some of the potency of these new images stems from the way in which they draw on older and better-established legends and motifs.)

Meurger's concept of the mythological landscape, then, may be the missing link we have been seeking – a place where the real and the unreal, the old and the new can meet, merge, and intertwine. Should it exist, it might not only account for the zoological improbabilities of lake monster lore and the medical implausibilities of alien abduction experiences, but solve the central problem that bothered us when we were considering the role that psychological anomalies play in the understanding of strange phenomena. We saw *how* such experiences might have their origins within our own minds, the products of altered states of consciousness or temporal lobe epilepsy, but not *why* they featured ghosts, humped monsters and alien abductors, and not troops of pink elephants.

The answer, surely, is that these nightmare creatures are already roaming the mythological landscape and that, while the topography of this landscape varies subtly from one person to the next, the general cultural influences to which we are all subject are sufficient for it to remain broadly familiar as we move from community to community, if not necessarily from country to country. For this reason most Europeans and Americans who endure an alien abduction will report that it was carried out by grey aliens, even though an Algerian or a Malaysian witness may have a very different experience.

The question, then, is whether there is any proof that Meurger's mythological landscape exists within the borderlands, and, if it does, how we can distinguish the phenomena that exist there from those that have a genuine reality.

In Search of the Mythological Landscape

Throughout this book, we have grappled with one central problem: whether the strange phenomena we are encountering are real.

Far too frequently, the evidence has appeared contradictory and the eye-witness testimony fatally flawed. Some enigmas have appeared to be cultural artefacts and others products of the backwaters of the human mind. In many cases, however, we have acknowledged that a phenomenon may yet have a basis in physical reality.

Now it is finally time to suggest a method of determining which strange events are 'real' – that is, which have an unknown source, whether this is external to the witness or internal – and which are 'unreal', by which I mean the products of hoax, misidentification and misinterpretation, influenced, perhaps, by social or cultural factors. Of course, it will prove difficult even now to draw a firm dividing line between the two alternatives: many apparently real phenomena are undoubtedly distorted by a witness's expectations, prior knowledge and state of mind, while, tellingly, many evidently unreal enigmas are, to all intents, indistinguishable from undoubtedly genuine cases. Nevertheless, if we make allowances for such factors it is at least possible to move towards some more definitive solutions.

It seems to me that the key to the problem may lie in a study of the historical continuity of strange phenomena. If an enigma is reported in essentially similar ways at many different times, in many countries, it seems likely to be real and to have an external source or to be a product of the involuntary functions of the human central nervous system. If the same phenomenon is apparently confined to a particular religion or culture, or it changes and mutates down the years, appearing in very different forms depending on the time and the place in which it manifests itself, it is likely to be unreal or the product of an internal stimulus generated by the higher functions of the brain.

Hunting the Holy Aubergine

The first thing to be said in favour of the cultural source hypothesis is that strange phenomena are as subject to the dictates of fashion as the everyday world. Although people with only a casual interest in the unexplained may not realise it, the borderlands are in a constant state of flux. Old mysteries fade away, and are reported less and less until eventually they disappear. New ones are born. Other enigmas change their name or their public face, and reappear in different guises.

One phenomenon that is still less than a decade old is the holy aubergine, an apparently ordinary looking vegetable which, cut open, is found to contain a devotional message written in the pattern of its seeds. Aubergine morphology being what it is, the seed patterns resemble only Arabic script and the devotional messages discovered to date have all appeared in Moslem communities.

What appears to have been the earliest example of this phenomenon turned up in the Leicester kitchen of Farida Kassam in March 1990. This one announced *Ya-Allah* ('Allah exists'). 'We were really shocked when we first saw the seeds,' Farida's husband Zahid said. 'We couldn't believe our eyes. Our insurance man was the first non-Muslim we showed it to, and even he could match the writing [with a plate bearing the same words].' Towards the end of the month, the Kassams received permission from the local mosque to announce their discovery, and within a week more than 5000 people had called on them and seen the miraculous vegetable. When the aubergine finally started to rot, it was buried in holy ground.

News of the find spread rapidly throughout the Moslem community in the Midlands. The manager of the grocery store where Farida had bought the vegetable was besieged by customers, and within a few days three more holy aubergines had been discovered in Leicester and others were found in Nottingham, Burton-on-Trent and Birmingham. One contained the word 'Allah' and the seeds of another appeared to form a verse from the Koran. Shortly afterwards, a Kenyan family, whose son was studying in Britain, found seeds spelling 'Allah' in a vegetable purchased in Nairobi. The most celebrated aubergine of all was owned by Hussain Bhatti of Nottingham, whose son, studying for A level chemistry, successfully preserved it in a saline solution.

To the people who found them, the holy aubergines were true miracles – a distinct sign sent by God. Reductionists, on the other hand, argue that the seed patterns were nothing more than simulacra that have always been present, and that once publicity was given to the Kassam's claim, other Moslems found messages in their own vegetables because they had started looking for them. There is probably more than a grain of truth in this suggestion, but we should also consider the idea that other, greater, forces were at work.

The holy aubergine was only one of several Moslem phenomena that surfaced around the same time. In Algeria, three days after the Islamic Salvation Front won the general election of June 1990, a cloud seen to the east also appeared to spell out 'Allah', while in Hyderabad, southern India, Haji Mohammed Multani discovered a mango that bore the inscription *La Ilaha Illallah* ('There is no god but Allah'). The timing of this wave of Islamic simulacra is particularly interesting. The images all appeared around the time of the Gulf War, which set Moslem against Moslem, as well as seeing the reappearance of 'Christian' armed forces in the Middle East, and coincided with a remarkable upsurge in Islamic fundamentalism throughout the region. Yet it is also important to note that, once implanted, the seeds of a new phenomena may still bear fruit years later. In 1996, another holy aubergine turned up in Bolton, Lancashire, in the kitchen of Mrs Ruskana Patel. This, too, spelled the now-familiar phrase *Ya-Allah*. One interesting feature of the case was that Mrs Patel said she had dreamed the previous night that one of the three aubergines she had bought that day was blessed.

The Mystery of the Five Wounds

Seven-hundred-and-seventy years ago, another miraculous event occurred in somewhat similar conditions of heightened expectation and religious longing. Of all strange phenomena, stigmata (the appearance of wounds paralleling those received by Christ on the cross) are among the most mysterious, the best-documented and the most controversial. It is also an especially good example of an enigma which, though it has evolved significantly over the years, nevertheless displays great continuities, which makes it possible to compare cases that have occurred centuries apart.

To begin with, the phenomenon of stigmata has a very definite date of birth: 14 September 1224. On that day, Francis of Assisi – the future saint, and already a noted ascetic and holy man – was preparing to enter the second month of a retreat, undertaken with a few close companions in spartan conditions on Monte La Verna, overlooking the River Arno. He had spent the previous few weeks in a prolonged contemplation of the suffering that Christ had undergone on the cross, and it seems likely that he himself was in a weakened condition attributable to protracted fasting. As Francis knelt to pray in the first light of dawn,

> he began to contemplate the Passion of Christ . . . and his fervour grew so strong within him that he became wholly transformed into Jesus through love and compassion . . . While he was thus inflamed, he saw a seraph with six shining, fiery wings descend from heaven. This seraph drew near to St Francis in swift flight, so that he could see him clearly and recognise that he had the form of a man crucified . . . After a long period of secret converse, this mysterious vision faded, leaving . . . in his body a wonderful image and imprint of the Passion of Christ. For in the hands and feet of Saint Francis forthwith began to

appear the marks of the nails in the same manner as he had seen them in the body of Jesus crucified.

In all, Francis received five wounds: two on his palms and two on his feet, where the nails that fixed Christ to the cross were traditionally supposed to have been hammered home, and the fifth on his side, where the Bible says Jesus received a spear thrust from a Roman centurion. Later stigmatics have almost invariably received identical marks, though in a few cases only one or two are present, and in others scratches appear on the stigmatic's forehead in the area where Christ is presumed to have been injured by his crown of thorns.

Why did stigmata materialise so suddenly in thirteenth-century Italy? Part of the answer seems to lie in the theological fashions of the time. The Catholic Church had recently begun to place much greater stress on the humanity of Christ, and was shortly to introduce a new feast day, *Corpus Christi*, into the calendar to encourage contemplation of his physical sufferings. Religious painters had responded to this trend by producing a series of frankly gory depictions of the crucifixion, featuring a Jesus who was plainly in agony, and who displayed wounds that were dripping blood. Such portrayals replaced the much more stylised and peaceful images of an earlier era. Indeed, the contemporary obsession with the marks of crucifixion can perhaps best be demonstrated by an incident that occurred in Oxford two years before St Francis's vision: a young man was brought before the Archbishop of Canterbury, charged with the heresy of declaring that he was the Son of God. In court it was discovered that his body bore the five wounds, and it seems that he had actually allowed himself to be crucified, either because he genuinely thought he was Christ, or, perhaps, to encourage others to believe his claims.

It is unlikely that news of this peculiar case ever reached Francis of Assisi. On the other hand, it is indisputable that the saint's great celebrity ensured that the story of his stigmatisation was soon known throughout Europe, and it was not long before other cases of stigmata began to appear. At least ten more were recorded in the thirteenth century, and a recent estimate sets the total number reported since 1224 at just over 400. These include such noteworthy cases as that of Johann Jetzer, a Swiss farmer who displayed the marks of stigmata in 1507; Therese Neumann, a controversial German stigmatic who was afflicted with a whole range of woes and who displayed the stigmata on Fridays from 1926 until her death in 1962 – though never convincingly in the presence of scientific observers; and Padre Pio, a Capuchin monk who, as well as being probably the best-known of all stigmatics, is also supposed to have experienced a number of other strange phenomena and to have effected numerous miraculous healings (it is a characteristic of stigmatics that they are associated with other miraculous events). There is presently a strong movement within the Catholic Church to have Pio canonised.

Today, there are approximately twenty-five known stigmatics scattered around the world. Their numbers include at least five Italians, two Britons and four Americans; one lives in Korea and another in Japan. Since cases of stigmata were, until the present century, entirely confined to Catholic Europe, this is in itself a fascinating development. Equally noteworthy is the dramatic change that has occurred in the ratio of male to female stigmatics. The vast majority of those who have displayed the wounds of Christ have been women: 353 in total, compared to just 54 men. This is a ratio of almost seven women to every man. According to an analysis conducted by Ted Harrison, the leading contemporary authority on the subject, however, the ratio has changed dramatically in the last half-century. Among the forty-four cases of stigmata reported since 1946, it has swung to 2.4 to 1, and among living stigmatics it is a mere 1.5 to 1.

Harrison has suggested that this dramatic shift may be explained 'by the changes in the balance of authority between men and women both in the church and society', and proposed that in previous centuries women may have manifested stigmata to draw attention to themselves in a society dominated by men and in a church that excludes women from the priesthood. Even more importantly, he draws attention to 'the role stigmata plays in granting to individuals and congregations a direct spiritual authority', citing as examples stigmatics who became either the leaders of messianic sects, or were, at the very least, instrumental in effecting a religious revival in their local churches.

A study of the records of stigmata throws up other interesting patterns. Before 1900 there are no cases of priests receiving the stigmata (Padre Pio was the first); since then there have been several. Cases appear in clusters: only a single event occurred in the whole of the Iberian peninsula between the thirteenth century and the fifteenth, and there have been a mere seven since 1800, but a total of fifty-four were recorded between 1600 and 1799. Perhaps most intriguingly of all, the location of the wounds has begun to change as medical knowledge has advanced. Traditionally, two of the five wounds have appeared on the palms, where countless icons have shown the nails that were supposed to have been hammered into Christ's hands prior to crucifixion. We now know that nails positioned in this way could not have supported the weight of a body, and that the Romans crucified their victims by driving a nail into the arm just above the wrist. Sure enough, in at least two recent cases the stigmatic has bled from wounds in the newly-approved areas.

What all this suggests is, first, that stigmata is a culturally based phenomenon: there are no parallels in any of the major non-Christian religions and, with the exception of the odd twentieth-century Anglican or Baptist stigmatic, there are no sufferers who are not also members of the Roman Catholic Church. Second, it would appear that wounds are not literally marks inflicted by Heaven; if they were, there seems no reason why a gap of twelve centuries should have occurred between the death of Christ and their first appearance. Nor is it easy to argue that the stigmata have been bestowed solely upon the devout and the deserving: one of the most notable recent cases involved a Spaniard named Clemente Dominguez, who, having been rejected as a candidate for the Catholic priesthood, set himself up as the pope of his own heretical church and was subsequently excommunicated for his pains.

In fact, the one characteristic that the great majority of stigmatics do appear to share is extremely low self-esteem, a history of psychiatric illness, or a tendency towards hysteria and self-mutilation. Teresa Musco, a stigmatic from Naples, endured a lifetime of bad health and a total of more than 100 operations in the years leading up to the early death she had predicted for herself. (She was thirty-three when she died in 1976 – significantly, the same age as Christ.) While she lived, Teresa habitually described herself as 'a dungheap' and her diary frequently contained the exhortation 'Lord, use me as your cleaning rag!' Therese Neumann alleged that as a teenager she was twice the victim of attempted rape, suffered blindness and convulsions as a result of head injuries, and claimed that she had lived for more than three decades on nothing more than the bread and wine she received daily at Communion. She was strongly suspected of inflicting her stigmata on herself. Even more curiously, the English stigmatic Jane Hunt began to display the signs of the Passion in 1985 after suffering a series of miscarriages, and ceased to do so following a hysterectomy performed in 1987.

Very tellingly, it has been shown beyond reasonable doubt that in the great majority of cases, stigmatics appear to have begun by inflicting the five wounds on themselves. Father Herbert Thurston, the great Jesuit expert on the physical phenomena of mysticism, considered that there had been no completely believable case of stigmata since that of St Francis. Magdalena de la Cruz, the famous Spanish stigmatic of the sixteenth century, whose frequent self-mortification and spectacular wounds made her a favourite at court, eventually confessed to having inflicted her injuries on herself. Magdalena's Portuguese contemporary, Maria de la Visitacion, would surely also have been exposed as a fraud after a fellow nun glimpsed her through a crack in the door of her cell, painting nail-wounds on her hand, had the priest who was handed a bar of soap and despatched to examine her not accepted her plea that the slightest touch to her wounds was agony. Similarly, the remarkable Johann Jetzer, who claimed to have experienced not only recurrent poltergeist phenomena but a series of religious visions in his cell, and before whom an image of the virgin was seen to weep, confessed in 1507 that his stigmata were fakes. Four friars from his monastery were subsequently burned at the stake, and Jetzer escaped only when his mother smuggled him a set of women's clothes in which he bluffed his way out of his death cell.

What, then, *are* stigmata? Judging from the evidence, they appear to be an essentially psychological condition, but one whose manifestations are determined by the cultural expectations of the stigmatics themselves. Self-loathing, attention-seeking and low self-esteem might well compel the sufferers to mutilate themselves, but without the pervasive iconography of several centuries of Christian tradition to draw on, it seems more than likely that most stigmatics would inflict such injuries in a less systematic and less symbolic way.

The tentative acceptance of this conclusion does not deprive the phenomenon of stigmata of all its mystery. After setting aside such outright frauds, we are left with a large number of stigmatics who appear to have mutilated themselves, either consciously or unconsciously, perhaps while in an altered state of consciousness brought on by semi-starvation or excessive prayer. In these cases, investigators such as Harrison have argued that there is substantial evidence that the original wounds can recur spontaneously and apparently psychosomatically, generally on significant dates such as Good Friday.

In one nineteenth-century case, a French girl named Louise Lateau (who received the stigmata five years after being trampled by a cow, an incident that caused severe abscesses to develop inside her body) had her arm encased in a sealed glass cylinder by two doctors, Warlomont and Crocq. Within twenty-four hours, 'the lower end of the receptacle was occupied by a little pool of liquid blood . . . The back of the hand showed clots of coagulated blood, black, hard and adhering strongly . . . The wound which produced [them] was about a centimetre and a half long and five millimetres wide. Its epidermis had disappeared; the base occupied by the dermis was red and muddy.' More recently, Domenica Lo Bianco, an Italian, was videoed in a laboratory as she relived one incident of stigmata in a trance state. Marks are seen to appear spontaneously on her arm as she is filmed.

This latter piece of evidence is especially interesting because while Lo Bianco habitually exhibits the stigmata on Good Friday, her wounds recurred in the laboratory on an ordinary day that she apparently persuaded herself was the festival itself. This suggests that Harrison may be correct in suggesting that some cases of stigmata may be attributable to psychosomatic causes – in other words, to the power of suggestion.

Ian Wilson, another author who has written on the subject, has drawn attention to parallels between stigmata and apparently psychosomatic illnesses. In 1951 a British doctor, A.A. Mason, used hypnotic suggestion to clear up a congenital skin condition that lent his patient's skin an unsightly reptilian appearance. During ten days of treatment, the condition on various parts of the patient's body improved by between 50 and 95 per cent. Another physician, Robert Moody, wrote in 1946 that a patient whose army colleagues had frequently tied him with ropes to prevent his sleepwalking, occasionally developed weals and indentations on his skin corresponding to the rope marks while under his care. More recently, an American, R.D. Willard, who 'lightly hypnotised' twenty-two female volunteers and asked them to imagine that their breasts were becoming 'pleasingly warm' reported that nine of the women in his sample subsequently needed to buy a larger bra.

It is important to remember that, attractive though the notion of autosuggestion may be, such cases are not fully accepted by science, and the precise mechanism by which the brain might directly influence the body is not at all understood. Nevertheless, there is no doubt that such a mechanism – should it ever be shown to exist – could help to explain a number of strange phenomena.

Beyond the Body

Stigmata may, in essence, be confined to a single culture – Catholicism – but some strange phenomena occur almost everywhere. As we have seen, among the most widely distributed is the near death experience, which, as well as occurring in practically every society throughout the world, apparently irrespective of the witness's own religious beliefs, also has a persuasive physical explanation. Nevertheless, the evidence shows that the NDE, too, is subject to significant historical and cultural influences – not what we would expect if it were a purely medical phenomenon.

One of the most obvious differences between twentieth-century accounts and their precursors of the medieval era is the journey undertaken by the dying soul. Modern near death experiences generally involve a journey down a lengthy tunnel towards a pinprick of bright, white light that, if reached, seems to reveal itself as a sort of ante-room to heaven. This was not the case in the earlier period. Surviving accounts of medieval NDEs frequently include vivid descriptions of two alternative afterlifes – one in heaven, and the other in purgatory or hell.

There are other fundamental differences between medieval and modern experiences: earlier accounts lay great emphasis on judgement and the tests and torments a soul must undergo before entering heaven. This accords to contemporary religious belief. Similarly, modern cases tend to involve an educational and non-judgmental 'life review', which the dead person is encouraged to conduct himself – a view of the afterlife perfectly in keeping with the self-obsession of the late twentieth century. Carol Zaleski, who has made a particular study of the history of the near death experience, suggests that the medieval NDE reflects the period's universal faith in the reality of post-mortem reward and punishment, while its modern equivalent has been shaped both by a sharp decline in belief in the existence of hell (something that has not stopped most people from at least hoping for a heaven) and new imagery of the afterlife that has been developed and popularised by spiritualism. Zaleski concludes with the suggestion that the near death experience is 'a work of the narrative imagination, shaped not only by the universal laws of symbolic experience, but also by the local and transitory statues of a given culture'.

Support for this contention comes from a study of the NDEs of medieval China and Japan, most of which do contain the core features of guides, god-like beings, a structured afterlife and the dramatic reform of the witness's previous lifestyle upon recovery. There are, for example, differences between Taoist near death experiences, which focus on heaven, and Buddhist NDEs, which are much more concerned with hell. Indeed, it would appear that the experiences of a number of monks who returned from the dead with accounts of many-tiered hells ruled over by different gods played a significant role in shaping Buddhist concepts of what happens after death. Moreover, once a strong image of the afterlife was well established in Chinese Buddhist scripture, subsequent NDEs became substantially less concerned with the topography of hell: a number of 'visitors' who wished to witness souls in torment were informed that tours were no longer allowed. In consequence, Chinese NDEs came to resemble more closely modern accounts of the near death experience during the late medieval and early modern periods.

All of this suggests that physiology alone cannot explain every aspect of the near death experience and that NDEs do have a cultural component that can substantially shape the experience itself.

It is also well worth pointing out that events that seem remarkably like near death experiences can occur when the brain is not in fact in the process of dying through progressive oxygen starvation. One western case concerned a typical NDE reported by a man who had plunged from a cliff and imagined that he was certain to die on the rocks below, but survived. Another, from medieval Japan, is told of the monk Honen, who is reputed to have introduced the Pure Land school of Buddhism to the country late in the twelfth century. As a gesture of devotion, Honen took to chanting the name of

Amida, the king of the Pure Land – heaven – up to 70,000 times a day (about 100 times a minute). This enormously repetitive task seems to have helped to induce altered states of consciousness in which the monk experienced many visions, which he carefully recorded between the years 1198 and 1212. Among them are a number of apparent NDEs.

Another interesting variation concerns experiences that occur while the witness is in a coma, rather than undergoing a near death experience. These suggest that the NDE need not be as limited in duration and scope as is implied by recent western cases, which generally involve the rapid resuscitation of the witness at or before the moment in which he encounters the 'being of light'. There may even be a correlation between the degree of detail in the experience and the length of time that the witness was unconscious.

Among a number of ancient Chinese records of apparent near death experiences is the case of Chao T'ai, a native of Hupeh province who spent ten days in a coma. His NDE was particularly complex, and involved being met by two horsemen who took him along a road east to a large city. After passing through the gates, Chao was taken before an entity dressed in scarlet and told to list his sins. The entity then informed Chao that he had been chosen to make an inspection of the heavenly city's water-works, which among other things serviced an underground inferno. Chao's lengthy tour of inspection gave him the opportunity to witness the various punishments inflicted on souls consigned to the different levels of hell, and also the efficacy of the diverse Buddhist rituals performed by the living for the dead. Eventually it was discovered that Chao had been called to the city prematurely owing to a bureaucratic error (a characteristically Chinese detail that it is hard to imagine could have been repeated in, say, an NDE account from Dark Age Europe), and he was instructed to return to the waking world and inform those still living about the afterlife.

There are other noteworthy parallels between the near death experience and other types of strange phenomena. Peter Rogerson, one of the social historians of ufology, has pointed out that 'like UFO abductees, medieval returnees have old scars healed and new ones imprinted – St Fursa bore a permanent burn-mark on his jaw and shoulder from a flaming soul flung at him by a demon! There are also the psychological stigmata common to both classes of experience: loss of memory or the power of speech, or the possession of wild talents. Other familiar motifs occur: Knight Owen, in St Patrick's purgatory, encounters the room much larger on the inside than it is on the outside.'

If Rogerson is correct, these parallels suggest that there is, indeed, an important cultural dimension to the near death experience and to close encounters and alien abductions, and that all these phenomena may stem, at least in part, from a common physiological or psychological source, rather than having different causes that are independent of the witness's mind. What we perceive as the evolution of a phenomenon or the metamorphosis of one enigma into another could, therefore, be explained as a single, unchanging experience, perhaps of a physiological nature, which the brain interprets with reference to prevailing cultural conditions – a phenomenological equivalent of the old nature/nurture argument.

Yet even invoking the witness's culture, knowledge and expectations may not be enough to explain one especially peculiar anomaly associated with the near death experience. This concerns one of the most detailed historical references to an apparent NDE. The great Dark Age writer Bede describes the experience of a man named Drythelm, who was suffering from a severe illness and who appeared to die one evening in AD 696. In the morning he revived and reported meeting a man 'of shining countenance and bright apparel' who led him through a huge valley. One side of the valley was covered in flames while the other was blanketed with snow, and souls were being tossed from one side to another. Drythelm thought this was hell, but his guide explained that these souls were held temporarily in the valley and that they could be released if prayers and masses were said for them. Next, the 'dead' man was shown the true Hell – a bottomless pit infested with demons – and then taken over a huge wall into a flower-strewn meadow filled with happy people. He took this to be heaven, but his guide explained that it was merely a place in which slightly imperfect souls awaited entry to the real heaven, which was far brighter and more fragrant. He thereupon regained consciousness, renounced his worldly goods and retired to a monastery to begin what one scholar calls 'a life of devotion, austerity, fasting and frequent cold baths'.

Now, the odd thing about this experience – and more than half-a-dozen similar cases survive from the Dark Age and early medieval periods – is that at the time that it occurred, the Church had not adopted the doctrine of purgatory, and the suggestion that there were any states in the afterlife other than heaven or hell was neither theologically acceptable nor even actively considered. The question thus arises of why Drythelm and his fellow-travellers encountered an apparent purgatory during their journeys through the afterlife. Is his experience evidence for an unsuspected interest in the exact hierarchy of the afterlife among Dark Age Englishmen, or something more – perhaps even a genuine experience of life after death?

The Camels Are Coming

Religious and psychical phenomena are not the only ones to follow unsuspected but illuminating fashions. The history of cryptozoology also demonstrates peculiarities that have gone quite unremarked-on by cryptozoologists. Among these is the problem of land sightings of the Loch Ness Monster.

Although not very widely known outside the hard core of researchers, there are in fact two score of these exceptional reports on record, and monster hunters have always been excited by them, principally because the witnesses describe parts of the beast that are generally not seen. Among these records, the sighting made by Mr and Mrs George Spicer on 22 July 1933, is the one most often cited. Rupert Gould, who interviewed the couple, summarises it as follows:

> They had passed through Dores and were on their way towards Foyers when, as the car was climbing a slight rise, an extraordinary-looking creature crossed the road ahead of them, from left to right, in a series of jerks . . .[Spicer] saw no definite head, but this was across the road before he had the chance to take the whole thing in properly – it was only in sight for a few seconds. The creature was of a loathsome elephant-greyish colour. It had a very long and thin neck, which undulated up and down, and was contorted into a series of half-hoops. The body was much thicker . . . He saw no indications of any legs, or of a tail – but in front of the body, where this sloped down to the neck, he saw something 'flopping up and down' which, on reflection, he thought might have been the end of a long tail swung round to the far side of the body. The whole looked like a 'huge snail with a long neck'.

What is less often commented on, even in the most specialist studies, is the bizarre distribution of the land sighting reports. With the solitary exception of a monster seen half-ashore at very long range in 1960, all date to the summer of 1934 or before, and seven to the period before April 1933, when stories of the monster first began appearing in the press. In fact there seem to have been only a handful more water sightings than land sightings in this early period.

A second significant problem is the astonishing difference between the creatures described by witnesses who saw the monster on land before 1933 and the popular, current perception of Nessie as a plesiosaur-like animal with a long neck, flippers and a tail. Spicer's monster might conceivably match that description, but on the other hand a chauffeur named Alfred Cruickshank, driving by the loch one night in April 1923, saw what appeared to be quite a different creature:

> My view of the Monster was: Body 10–12 ft long, 5 ft 6in–7 ft in height, tail 10–12 ft. Colour, green-khaki, resembling a frog, with a cream-coloured belly which trailed on the ground. It had four legs, thick like an elephant's and had large webbed feet. In reality it looked like an enormous hippo . . . It gave out a sharp bark, like a dog, as it disappeared over the road.

Cruickshank – who is, incidentally, the only witness who has ever heard the monster utter anything other than a breathing sound – drew a sketch of the creature he had seen dimly illuminated with his flickering headlamps. It shows a low fat animal with a large, dog-like head, almost no neck, four short legs with fingers or claws, and an immense tail.

Still more bizarrely, at least five other early witnesses who saw the monster on land describe something quite unlike either the aquatic Nessie or Cruickshank's weird 'hippo'. Around 1879 a group of children picnicking on the north shore of the loch near an old graveyard heard a noise and turned to see an animal walking down the slope behind them towards the water. It was grey, with a long neck and small head, and 'waddled' into the loch. A year later, a man named E.H. Bright was walking with his cousin near the same spot when a similar animal emerged from the woods. It, too, was grey, had four legs, a long neck, and generally looked something like an elephant. Around 1912, a party of five or six children, including a boy called William MacGruer and his sister Margaret, were at Inchnacardoch Bay, at the south end of the loch, when an animal lurched out of some bushes and headed for the water. Margaret said it was grey, moved like a caterpillar and had two short legs under its massive body. William recalled that it was a pale yellow colour and looked like a camel, with a long neck, angled back and long legs. It was 'humping its shoulders and twisting its head from side to side'.

Finally, Colonel L.McP. Fordyce, driving with his wife along the south shore of the loch in April 1932, was astonished to see 'an enormous animal coming out of the woods on our left and making its way over the road about 150 yards ahead of us towards the loch. It had the gait of an elephant, but looked like a cross between a very large horse and a camel, with a hump on its back and a small head on a long neck. I stopped the car and followed the creature on foot for a short distance. From the rear it looked grey and shaggy.' Never having heard of the Loch Ness Monster, the Fordyces concluded that they had come across some sort of freak, escaped from a menagerie.

But was it? Perhaps these beasts are actually creatures from the mythological landscape suggested by Meurger – proto-traditions, ill-defined but ready to take on a specific shape and adopt a more regimented pattern of behaviour. Looking at the evidence, it seems plausible that there was, before 1930, a tradition that a land animal looking like a hippo, a camel or an elephant lived near and perhaps also in Loch Ness. It may have been quite an ancient legend: in 1771, one Patrick Rose is supposed to have heard about a monster, 'which was a cross between a horse and a camel with its mouth in its throat' and had recently been seen in the loch. The first part of this description sounds like the Loch Ness Monster, all right, but the detail that it had its 'mouth in its throat' is far more reminiscent of one of the monstrous hybrids of folklore and legend.

Does folklore offer a candidate to fill the role? Surely this strange creature is none other than the fearsome water-horse long said to guard the highland lakes. Compare the descriptions of E.H. Bright, the MacGruers and Colonel Fordyce to that of the water horse which haunted a place called the Children's Pool at Loch Oich, just a few miles to the south along the Caledonian Canal:

> Tradition has it that many years ago some children residing at Inchlaggan were playing on the loops of the Garry at this spot when a huge 'beiste' in the shape of a deformed pony appeared on the bank of the river. Curious to learn whether the creature was not a real pony on which they could enjoy a ride, the children went up to it and, the story has it, they found the 'beiste' so docile that one of them ventured on its back. No sooner had the child done so than the 'beiste' plunged into the pool with the rider . . . No trace was ever found of the bodies thus mysteriously drowned.

All that can be said for sure is that once reports of water-borne Nessies began to be logged in the mid-1930s, land sightings rapidly died out. Did the monsters' habits change suddenly, as some circumstance drove them from land into the water? Were two quite different creatures involved in land

and water sightings? Or is there a folkloric connection here, involving the birth of a cryptozoological water monster from old traditions of lake guardians and fairy creatures? If so, what does that suggest about the reality or the unreality of all sightings of the Loch Ness Monster?

Enigma Variations

It is not difficult to cite similar examples that illustrate how traditions can mutate and ancient archetypes evolve into modern mysteries. Histories of science may suggest that the medieval alchemist, crouched over his cauldron and engaged in the perpetual quest for the Philosopher's Stone – a substance capable of transmuting base metal into gold – was merely a precursor of the modern chemist, but a better parallel might be the eccentric inventor who appears brandishing a magic substance capable of turning water into the present-day equivalent: petrol.

A good half-dozen such cases have been recorded in the last quarter-century, of which perhaps the best involved Thomas Munson, a Welshman from Blaenau Ffestiniog. Munson turned up on television in 1974 demonstrating 'Tracanath', a special powder he said he had discovered in Germany at the end of the Second World War and which, added to water, would run engines at a cost of four pence a gallon. (Munson imitated the alchemists of old by vanishing on the eve of a demonstration laid on for him by potential investors. A subsequent analysis of the fuel he produced revealed it to be '95.3% distilled water, benzene, methanol, iodine crystals, ignitable oil, borax and Fairy washing-up liquid'.) In 1996, an Indian named Ponnaiah Ramar Pillai demonstrated a 'wonder herb' that had a similar effect (though this time the cost was nine pence a gallon) to government scientists at the Indian Institute of Technology in New Delhi. Initially incredulous, the scientists later announced that they had been hoaxed and that Pillai had used a spoon hollowed out and filled with real petrol in his demonstration.

Similarly, the intriguing 'Men in Black' who menace UFO

witnesses appear to have both antecedents and successors. The folklorist Peter Rojcewicz (who himself encountered a possible MIB one day in his university library, after entering what appears to have been an altered state of consciousness) has suggested that there are analogies between the MIB, and the tell-tale awkwardness that so often betrays them as inhuman, and classical encounters with the devil. Certainly Satan is often described as black-skinned, and in various legends his cloven foot could always be relied on to give him away. The phantom social workers also seem to have several things in common with the archetypal man in black. The phantoms were typically described as bland, smartly dressed (often wearing black suits) and better-informed about the people they were calling on than any normal visitor would be – just like the men in black. Moreover there are several descriptions of very peculiar-sounding 'social workers' – one caked in unnaturally heavy make-up, another who dressed as a woman but moved so awkwardly that the witness suspected 'she' might be a man. Both these patterns of behaviour are characteristic of the stranger MIB encounters.

There is, in fact, something suitably modern about the men in black. Hilary Evans describes the MIB as 'the entity enigma at its most accessible and yet in some respects its most ambiguous'. Though in one way less strange than most of the alien inhabitants of the borderlands, they are, nevertheless, far more directly menacing, and their detailed knowledge of the witness, combined with the hint of quasi-governmental powers, is enough to make them unusually threatening to members of a modern society that may not believe in ghosts but knows it has every reason to fear the unelected and non-accountable representatives of the state. From this point of view, it is clear that the men in black and the phantom social workers do fulfil something of the role played by a medieval devil, the one offering his victims eternal damnation and the other the loss of liberty or children. Where the devil tempted, though, the MIB threaten – perhaps quite appropriately in a more regimented world, where the state possesses the information and resources it needs to make good the devil's threats.

Is it possible that the men in black, the phantom social workers and the archetypal devil are all culturally-specific manifestations: the externalisation of a basic human fear – loss of liberty – dressed up in clothes appropriate to the day? Certainly there are elements to MIB reports which suggest that they may be a form of hallucination: consider the circumstances in which a trio of men in black appeared to Albert Bender, the founder of the International Flying Saucer Bureau, in September 1953 – just as he was on the verge of publishing his final solution to the UFO mystery. Having been overtaken by a sudden fit of dizziness, Bender was lying down in his bedroom when he became aware that he had been joined by three shadowy figures: 'The figures became clearer. All of them were dressed in black clothes, they looked like clergymen, but wore hats similar to Homburg style. The faces were not discernible, for the hats partly hid and shaded them. Feelings of fear left me . . . The eyes of all three figures suddenly lit up like flashlight bulbs, and all these were focused on me. They seemed to burn into my very soul as the pain above my eyes became unbearable. It was then I sensed that they were conveying a message to me by telepathy.'

Such bizarre manifestations certainly sound like the products of an altered state of consciousness, and one can see how Bender's mental condition – particularly the stress he felt under as he completed his work on the saucers – could have contributed to this. On the other hand, witnesses seem to be able to interact with the MIB in ways they simply cannot with ghosts, monsters and other supposed hallucinations; men in black carry on lengthy conversations, sit where they are asked to, and accept drinks and even bowls of jelly from their hosts. They are satisfyingly surreal. The presence of such characteristics has important implications, which will become apparent later.

The Secret Life of Fairy-Folk

Not every ancient tradition, then, yields to the forces of the modern world. Some seem enormously plastic, and capable of adapting themselves to circumstances as they change.

Take fairies, for example. Contrary to popular opinion, fairies are not solely creatures of legend. At one time little people were fairly commonly encountered in the real world too (albeit not the fey and gossamer-winged creatures of children's stories), and a surprising number of cases involving sprites, nature-spirits, gnomes and even brownies are still reported today.

Two relatively recent examples – one from the nineteenth century and the other from the twentieth – will have to suffice. In the summer of 1884, the driver of a mail-cart on the Isle of Man set out to collect his mail-bags in the evening, as was usual. He was due back at one thirty a.m. but did not reappear until nearly half past five.

Interviewed by William Martin, a collector of local tales, some three years later, the man explained the reason for his delay by recounting a story which is not only a typical fairy-tale but also contains echoes of the traditional behaviour of poltergeists: 'He solemnly related that when about six miles from home he was beset by a troop of fairies, all of whom were particularly well-dressed in red suits and provided with lanterns. They stopped his horse, threw the mail-bags into the road, and danced around them in the well-known manner usual with fairies. The poor postman struggled with them in vain. No sooner did he succeed in replacing a bag than it was again immediately thrown out. This continued until the appearance of daylight.'

A second encounter with what appeared to be dancing fairies occurred on 10 August 1977, and the witness was a Hull policeman, PC David Swift. He was walking his beat an hour or two after midnight when he came across a peculiar patch of mist swirling about some playing fields. As he approached the mist, he could make out three figures dancing within it, whom he at first supposed were drunks. One was a man 'dressed in a sleeveless jerkin, with tight-fitting trousers', and the other two were women 'wearing bonnets, shawls and white dresses'. All three had an arm raised – as if, it was later suggested, they were dancing around an invisible maypole. Before Swift could reach them, all three figures vanished, and, when the policeman reported the incident to his desk sergeant, he found that he was not believed. When the incident was reported in the local press, PC Swift was subjected to such ridicule that he has refused to discuss the case ever since.

The apparent survival of fairies into the twentieth century is surprising enough in itself, but perhaps the most intriguing thing about the modern reports is the way in which they sometimes contain details suggesting that the little people are changing with the times. One witness, Marina Fry of Cornwall, recalled (many years after the fact) that in 1940, when she was three years old, she and her elder sisters had heard a buzzing noise one night and looked out of their bedroom window to see a little man about eighteen inches tall, sporting a white beard and wearing a red pointed hat. He was 'in a tiny red car driving around in circles'. This could be nothing more than a fantasy, a dream or a false memory, but in September 1979 a group of children aged between four and eight who were playing in Wollaton Park, Nottingham, had a very similar experience. The details of their account were recorded by their headmaster, who interviewed the witnesses separately (but after they had had time to discuss the details of the case among themselves). It was dusk when:

> the children saw around 60 little men, about half as tall as themselves. They had long white beards with red tips (though one boy was positive the beards were black), and wrinkled faces. They wore caps on their heads, described as being like old-fashioned nightcaps, Noddy-style with a bobble on the end. They also wore blue tops and yellow tights. For most of the 15 minutes that the children were with them, the little men were in little cars. There were 30 cars, with two men in each. (One child said the cars were green and blue, one said they were red,

one said red and white). The cars didn't have steering wheels, but a round thing with a handle to turn. There was no sound of engines, but they travelled fast, and could jump over obstructions like logs. The little men chased the children but didn't catch them, although they could have done. The children were sure it was only a game.

There is even a case involving what seemed to be a fairy aircraft: in 1929, an eight-year-old boy and his five-year-old sister were playing in their garden in Hertford when a tiny plane (apparently it was a biplane, in common with most contemporary aircraft) with a wingspan of twelve or fifteen inches, swept down over the fence, landed by the dustbin and then took off again and flew away. The pilot was a small man wearing a leather flying helmet who waved to the children as he took off.

Many readers will probably prefer to treat these cases as fantasies, and there are details that suggest that they are products of the imagination; for example, the Wollaton Park 'go-karts' sound very much like dodgems, with which infants aged four to eight might be expected to be familiar. The fact that every report of mechanised fairies comes from children is probably also significant.

Nevertheless, one does not need to believe that such stories are literally true to find them highly illuminating. After all, if fairies that used to get around on foot or on horseback can now drive cars and fly aeroplanes, there seems to be no reason why they could not also pilot UFOs.

A number of prominent ufologists have suggested that close encounters, and alien abductions in particular, may be closely linked to fairy lore. It is certainly true that the fairies of folk-tales were always keen on abducting human beings. The motif of the changeling – an ugly fairy baby left in a crib in place of a gold-haired human infant carried off to fairyland – is one example (compare the general purpose, the strengthening of fairy stock by the admixture of human traits, with David Jacobs' theory of an alien hybrid breeding programme), but there are also many stories involving men and women who enter a fairy ring and find themselves permanently entrapped in a dance there, or who are permitted to visit the fairies' underground kingdom but find it hard to leave. There is even a parallel here with the familiar theme of the missing time experience: in many of the tales in which a man does return from the fairy lands, he is sure that he has been away for only a day or perhaps a week, only to find that several years have passed in the human world. (It is possible that this might be the product of a trance state of some sort.)

Of all the tales of fairies collected by folklorists, the one that sounds most like a close encounter is the strange account given by a man named David Williams, a Welshman who lived at Penrhyndeudraeth in Gwynedd. He was a servant who had been walking home one night some way behind his mistress. When he arrived at her house, he was told that she had returned three hours earlier, though he thought he had been only three minutes behind. By way of explanation, he said that he had watched

> a brilliant meteor passing through the air, which was followed by a ring or hoop of fire, and within this hoop stood a man and woman of small size, handsomely dressed... When the hoop reached the earth these two beings jumped out of it, and immediately proceeded to make a circle on the ground. As soon as this was done, a large number of men and women instantly appeared, and to the sweetest music that was ever heard commenced dancing round and round the circle. The sight was so entrancing that the man stayed, as he thought, a few minutes to witness the scene. The ground all around was lit up by a kind of subdued light, and he observed every movement of these beings. By and by the meteor which had first attracted his attention appeared again, and then the fiery hoop came to view, and when it reached the spot where the dancing was, the lady and the gentleman who had arrived in it jumped into the hoop, and disappeared in the same manner in which they had reached the place. Immediately after their departure the Fairies vanished from sight, and the man found himself alone and in darkness.

There are several possible interpretations of this peculiar tale, of which the most likely is that Williams believed the genteel couple were Oberon and Titania, the king and queen of the fairies, paying a ceremonial visit to some of their subjects. Whatever the truth, probably the most remarkable thing about this unusual account is that it dates to the early nineteenth century and was set down in Elias Owen's *Welsh Folk-Lore* in 1888, seven decades before the first modern close encounter occurred. If it is literally true, it might be evidence for the historicity of alien entities. If, however, it is fiction (as seems more likely) – whether a folk-tale or a wild excuse spun by a tardy servant to explain his absence – it is just as remarkable as an example of how an apparently modern and objectively real phenomenon is actually an accumulation of fictional elements, long known to folklorists.

Other ufological motifs can also be found in old folk-tales. The idea that UFOs possess the power to stop car engines, for example, leaving their occupants helpless to escape, is paralleled in tales of the fairies' 'invisible barrier.' In one such case, which occurred at Lis Ard, a fairy fort in County Mayo, around 1935, a girl who was trying to leave the hill found herself unable to pass through a gap in the outer bank. Each time she approached it, some force turned her around and walked her back towards the centre of the fort. As it got dark, she 'felt' a growing hostility around her, and when she called out to a search party with torches, which came up the hill looking for her, her would-be rescuers were unable to hear her. She was able to escape only when the invisible barrier that had constrained her mysteriously vanished. The girl's alarming experience could certainly be compared to that of an abductee, taken from a stalled car and confined within a UFO until released and allowed to drive away by the entities who had seized him.

A number of researchers have gone so far as to suggest that such fairy-tales are actually folk memories of real encounters with alien abductors, expressed in the only terms familiar to a non-technological society. Others, such as the French ufologist

Jacques Vallee, have proposed that fairies and alien abductors are both products of a single core phenomenon, which manifests itself in culturally specific ways. (Whether this phenomenon is an internal one – in other words, a form of fantasy or hallucination that is a characteristic product of the human brain – or external, and perhaps part of some mysterious ultraterrestrial control system, as Vallee once seemed to propose, has never been adequately debated.) On the other hand it may be that twentieth-century encounters are simply modern folk-tales, representing nothing more unusual than an understandable and universal fear of abduction.

Certainly, the abduction motif may be found in the legends of many different societies. For example, the people of Haiti believe that they are systematically oppressed by powerful voodoo sorcerers (*zobop*), who regularly abduct victims to sacrifice in hideous magical rites. In the early 1940s, it was rumoured in the capital, Port-au-Prince, that a spectral automobile (*motor-zobop*), driven by sorcerers, toured the island at night, ferrying victims to such ceremonies. It could be identified by the unearthly blue light cast by its headlamps.

One man who encountered the *motor-zobop* was Divione Joseph, himself a voodoo magician, who had travelled to a lonely crossroads late one night to cast out spirits. Suddenly he was blinded by a bright blue light and lost consciousness. When he came to, he was inside a *motor-zobop* and surrounded by hideous semi-human figures wearing masks. After trying to bribe him not to speak of what had happened, the masks threw Joseph out of the vehicle. He then found himself back in his own bed.

The ufologist John Rimmer, who first drew attention to Joseph's account, has this to say about his strange encounter:

> The story has many close and obvious parallels with UFO abductions. Firstly, the blinding light and the loss of consciousness are amongst the most frequently reported features of the initial stages of abductions. Subsequent awakening surrounded by strange semi-human figures is common to almost all abduc-

> tion accounts. Here Divione sees masked men – a sight which would obviously be more familiar to a voodoo practitioner than space-suited aliens. Some other aspects of this Haitian story demonstrate a close relationship to the UFO abduction, particularly in the way that the percipient and the abductors behave: there is the basic irrationality of abducting someone, then just offering him money not to tell everyone else about it – the kidnapping appeared to have no other purpose.

To this I would add that we should bear in mind both the pattern of expectation – Joseph was doubtless aware that the appearance of a bright light at night might presage an abduction by a *motor-zobop*, just as many modern abductees assume that bright lights in the night sky may be UFOs, and 'know' that aliens are visiting earth to abduct us – and the final detail that the victim awoke in his own bed. There is a suggestion that the experience was an elaborate fantasy of some sort, perhaps even a vivid dream, which would certainly explain the irrationality that Rimmer comments on.

Abduction rumours are just as common in western societies. In the late nineteenth century, much of Europe was swept by lurid speculation about the existence of a white slave trade dedicated to luring young western girls into, first, prostitution and, latterly and more romantically, the clutches of desert sheikhs. As late as May 1969, the French town of Orleans was convulsed by rumours that girls were being seized in the changing rooms of certain boutiques, drugged and packed off to the Middle East. One of the more sinister aspects of the panic was that all the shops concerned had Jewish proprietors, which added an unpleasant taint of anti-semitism to the cocktail of speculation.

In an attempt to demonstrate that the stories were ridiculous, the head of the local Jewish association invented the detail that the victims were being delivered into slavery through a network of tunnels that led down to the river Loire, where a submarine was waiting to ship them to their destination. A day later he had this story repeated back to him as fact.

From our point of view, the most interesting thing about this case is its demonstration of how an apparently absurd rumour can be spun from nothing – not a single woman or girl was actually reported missing in Orleans for the duration of the panic – and be believed by hundreds, perhaps thousands, of people who themselves unconsciously elaborate and reinforce it by constantly discussing and repeating one or two basic accounts. It is not even necessary for a single dramatic event to spark the panic. The sociologist Edgar Morin, who arrived in Orleans in time to document the rumour as it developed, believed that he had traced its source to a number of vague newspaper stories about unexplained disappearances and a tabloid article about the abduction of a woman in Grenoble. But there seems little doubt that the stories spread as rapidly as they did because they touched on some much more deep-rooted fears – of alien and unscrupulous Jewish businessmen on one hand, and of foreigners' lust for French girls and increasingly overt teenage sexuality on the other. From this point of view it is perhaps unsurprising that the panic centred on boutiques selling 'indecent' teenage fashions.

Nevertheless, it may be dangerous to make too much of the apparent folkloric antecedents of alien encounter and abduction stories. Michel Meurger has recently pointed out that there is no proof of continuity between ancient rural folk-belief and modern urban mass-belief, and suggested that the search for parallels between the two has distorted a complex issue. His conclusion is that 'the quest for purely formal analogies has blinded researchers to the obvious rootedness of the body of UFO narratives in a specific time (the second half of the twentieth century) and space (initially the USA)'.

Meurger believes that all the elements of the alien abduction scenario may be found in late nineteenth- and early twentieth-century science fiction. Certainly such accounts regularly include the medical examinations and surgical procedures characteristic of a typical abduction case, which were never a feature of fairy-lore and seem to have their basis in now-forgotten nineteenth-century fears of body-snatchers and vivisectionists. The Martians in H.G. Wells's influential *War of the Worlds* abduct humans in order to extract their blood. Pulp adventure comics of the 1930s frequently depict aliens and the villains of the future as large-brained but spindly-limbed creatures ruling over an entirely mechanised universe: 'an abnormally developed head is the morphological sign of the superman'. It is not uncommon for such stories to include dispassionate surgeon-scientists who are prepared to vivisect captured humans with as little compunction as a human might dissect a lower animal. Other, similar, works often feature surgical machines equipped with long needles, another characteristic of the abduction experience.

Taken together, the similarities between the abduction motifs and ufology, on the one hand, and folklore and science fiction, on the other, are sufficiently striking to suggest that even apparently sincere accounts of alien abductions are unconscious fantasies produced by the witnesses, which draw on a universal human fear and a common store of source material compiled over many generations, to which practically every westerner – and many individuals from other cultures – will have been exposed. This theory seems to explain the similarities between individual abduction experiences and the pattern such encounters follow as well as the extra-terrestrial hypothesis; it also accounts for the illogicalities and incongruities that appear to be characteristic of such cases, and explains the similarities between the abduction experience and other strange phenomena, the peculiarities of witness psychology and the general absence of physical evidence for abductions better than the ETH.

In support of this contention, it has been observed not only that there is a near-total absence of solid evidence that any given alien abduction actually took place or was witnessed by anyone other than the abductee, but that the abductors themselves are simply too nearly-human to be 'real' aliens, whose technology and society might well be thousands or even millions of years more advanced than ours. We have no reason to suppose that any aliens we do encounter will look anything like us, much less that they will share our urge to explore and explain. Indeed, the sexual and medical obsessions of the average Grey all too accurately mirror our own, and might well have a psychological explanation.

Although the precise mechanism by which the human brain is able to call upon the sort of source material we have been discussing here and use it to elaborate an experience that appears entirely real is still not properly understood, it does appear that in the case of the abduction experience, at least, the strange fashions of folklore and fiction can suggest some very worthwhile lines of enquiry.

Ghost and Poltergeist

In sharp contrast to the phenomenon of alien abductions, which hardly existed before 1960 and still remains practically unknown outside the United States, ghosts have been reported in every era by every society. Moreover, with the exception of a few modern parapsychological theories of hauntings, there has been a remarkable unanimity down the centuries as to what ghosts are: they are uniformly seen as spirits of the dead.

Such unanimity makes it all the more remarkable that there seem to be definite fashions in the way that ghosts appear and are reported. An historical study of apparitions demonstrates convincingly that the phenomenon has evolved dramatically over the years, and that the ghosts seen today by members of undeveloped societies differ from those that appear in the industrialised world.

Throughout recorded history, the ghosts that are seen in primitive societies have always tended to be perceived as malignant and something to be avoided. Human souls may frequently return in the form of animals – for example, some African tribes believe that wrong-doers become jackals after death, while the Tapuya Indians of Brazil have a tradition that virtuous souls are able to enter the bodies of birds. Even when they do adopt a human form, primitive ghosts do not appear to be good communicators. The ghosts of Algonquin Indians chirp like crickets, while those of the Zulus and the Maoris 'speak' in thin, whistling tones that can only be interpreted by witch doctors and shamans. In somewhat more urbanised societies, ghosts are sometimes described as 'gibbering'.

Historically, there was general agreement that when the dead assumed a human form and returned to earth, it was usually for a specific reason – to avenge a murder, perhaps, or point out the location of buried treasure – thus unburdening themselves of some wordly problem and permitting an ascension to heaven. In the second century AD, for instance, the Roman writer Pliny the Younger recorded that:

> There was a house in Athens haunted by an old spectre who came out at night rattling his chains; an old man, skinny and dirty, with scruffy hair and beard, wearing fetters on his legs and chains at his wrists. A philosopher decided to spend a night there to find out what was going on. As he read his book he heard the noises, then saw the figure. It beckoned him; he followed into the garden where the ghost suddenly vanished. The scholar picked some grass and leaves and marked the place of the disappearance. Next day he had the local magistrates dig there, and a skeleton in chains was found; after proper burial rites the haunting ceased.

This story, which must come to us third hand at best, is of no value as evidence of anything other than the prevailing belief in ghosts during the middle Roman Empire. But taken in this context it is quite revealing, providing us with a source for the image of the fettered ghost still popular in gothic works of fiction today, and with confirmation that ghosts were supposed to be abroad only at night, that they were recognisably the spirits of specific dead people, and that they returned with a purpose, which, once fulfilled, ended the haunting.

Fashions in ghosts changed again during the medieval and early modern period. Now apparitions – apparently on day release from hell – appeared wreathed in flames, or dragging blackened bodies along with them. These ghosts seem to have fulfilled a similarly moral but decidedly more religious function, appearing to warn the living not to risk the perils of damnation. One such case concerns two friars who met the ghosts of three men that they knew had died without being absolved of their sins. Two of the spectres spoke, but the third remained silent and his companions explained that he had been a slanderer and was now condemned to hell, where his torment was to hold in his mouth a red-hot stone that perpetually burned his tongue and prevented him from speaking.

A further change in emphasis occurred during the Reformation, when the concept of purgatory was under attack by the new Protestant Churches, and apparitions in the Catholic lands became even more explicit in confirming the reality of an intermediate realm in the afterlife. In the seventeenth and early eighteenth centuries, however, ghosts seemed to take much less interest in religious affairs and become more concerned with either legacies and possessions or revenge. It was only in the succeeding 150 years that a more romantic view of ghosts began to prevail, which continues to influence reports of apparitions today. This was the era of the ghostly monk or the woman in grey, as well as of a handful of ghosts not tied to a specific location, such as the Flying Dutchman.

Perhaps most significantly of all, the nineteenth century was also the era of the 'anonymous ghost'. Throughout the preceding millennia, ghosts had generally been readily identifiable to the people who saw them. Indeed they were typically friends, relatives or victims of the percipients, and it was vital to their purpose – whether that was imparting a warning, avenging a wrong or pointing out the location of a hidden legacy – that they were immediately recognisable to the people they visited. Identifiable ghosts did continue to be seen during the Victorian period – and they still appear today – but an increasing number of reports began to feature ill-defined, shadowy or otherwise unidentifiable spirits, which seemed to have no clear purpose.

It is only fair to point out that the scarcity of historical sources makes it difficult to say to what extent this pattern of evolution genuinely reflects witnesses' experiences of apparitions before the nineteenth century, and it has been argued that many early reports have been deliberately distorted to turn them into religious parables. Certainly, it was only with the founding of the Society for Psychical Research in the 1880s that any concerted effort was made to collect reports of apparitions from the general public, and this may go some way to explaining the perceived shift to reports of the 'anonymous ghost' in the nineteenth century. Nevertheless, there seems be little doubt that the popular modern image of a ghost – a tall, grey and anonymous figure dressed in loose robes, which appears suddenly, communicates nothing and perhaps vanishes through a wall – would have seemed as alien to Pliny or a medieval friar as the apparition of a blazing corpse fresh from purgatory would appear to us today.

None of this makes a great deal of sense if we presume that the apparitions seen throughout history are all examples of a single phenomenon with an external source. There seems to be no reason why appearances of the dead should vary so dramatically from century to century unless reports of ghosts are substantially shaped by the expectations of the witness and thus the culture from which they spring.

This is not to say that all apparitions can be explained as purely mental constructs. The cultural source hypothesis cannot explain those few cases where what appears to be the same apparition is reported independently by several witnesses over the years, nor the equally rare incidents in which a ghostly figure is seen by a number of different people at the same time; and it is necessary to look a little further to explain cases that feature an apparently successful prediction or that are discovered to have occurred at a particularly significant time – so-called 'crisis apparitions'. Nevertheless, it is fascinating to compare the varied history of encounters with ghosts with the numerous surviving accounts of a, supposedly, closely-related phenomenon: the poltergeist.

Records of 'noisy ghosts' date back as far as 856 BC. Since then, well over 500 cases have been reported from a wide variety of locations and many different cultures, providing us with a database comparable to that available to students of apparitions. Hereward Carrington, one of the most prominent psychical researchers of the first half of this century, noted that cases of stone-throwing poltergeists had been reported from China, Iceland, Java, South Africa, Britain, France and Germany, and his database included incidents from more than thirty countries. In stark contrast to the ever-changing ghost, however, the poltergeist has always manifested itself in essentially the same way.

The remarkable similarity between ancient and modern accounts of the phenomenon is best illustrated by comparing an ancient case with some modern ones, and one of the earliest detailed accounts of apparent poltergeist phenomena appears in *The Journey Through Wales*, a well-regarded chronicle written by a monk called Gerald of Wales around the year 1190. Gerald describes a tour that he had made of his homeland two years earlier, and in the course of a description of the area around Manorbier, he breaks off to note:

> In these parts of Pembroke, in our own times, unclean spirits have been in close communication with human beings. They are not visible, but they are present just the same. First in the home of Stephen Wiriet, then, at a later date, in the house of William Not, they have been in the habit of manifesting themselves, throwing refuse all over the place, more keen perhaps to be a nuisance than to do any real harm. In William's house they were a cause of annoyance to both host and guests alike, ripping up their clothes of linen, and their woollen ones, too, and even cutting holes in them. No matter what precautions were taken, there seemed to be no way of protecting these garments, not even if the doors were kept bolted and barred. In Stephen's home, things were even more odd, for the spirit there was in the habit of arguing with humans. When they protested, and this they would often do in sport, he would upbraid them in public for every nasty little act which they had committed from the day of their birth onwards . . .
>
> If you ask me the cause and the explanation of an event of this sort, I do not know what to answer, except that it has often been the presage, as they call it, of a sudden change from poverty to wealth, or more often still from wealth to poverty

> and utter desolation, as, indeed, it was in these cases. It seems most remarkable to me that places cannot be cleansed of visitations of this sort by the sprinkling of holy water, which is in general use and which could be applied liberally, or by the performing of some other religious ceremony. On the contrary, when the priests go in, however devoutly and protected by the crucifix and holy water, they are among the first to suffer the ignominy of having filth thrown over them.

It seems to me that these two paragraphs are extremely revealing in their different ways. The first is immediately identifiable as a description of two classic varieties of poltergeist infestation, directly comparable to modern instances. For example, a case reported from Runcorn, Cheshire, in the autumn of 1952, featured clothes being torn, objects moved about, and bedding disarranged. Another, the famous Enfield Poltergeist of 1977 (which remains among the most heavily investigated and controversial cases of all), was notable not only for incidents in which excrement was smeared about the house, but for protracted attempts to communicate with the poltergeist, which 'spoke' through one of the children in the house – with frequent recourse to obscenities – and also left messages lying around, scrawled on pieces of paper or written on the walls. This voice claimed to be a variety of different people, some of whom had died in the house and said they had come from the local graveyard; on one occasion it demanded 'I want some jazz music. Now go and get me some, else I'll go barmy.'

Indeed, the phenomena reported by Gerald of Wales have recurred many times in the intervening centuries. A statistical analysis of 500 hauntings and cases of poltergeist infestation, carried out by Alan Gauld, shows that the movement of small objects is the most common characteristic of such cases, occurring in 64 per cent of the sample, followed by rapping noises, which occur in 48 per cent. (A sceptic would add at this point that such 'phenomena' are far easier to fake than some other habits attributed to poltergeists.) Nevertheless, talking poltergeists are also relatively common: one case in six features some sort of communication between humans and some sort of entity. Torn clothes are rarer, but still occur in 6 per cent of cases, while the hurling of filth and excrement occurs in almost one case in twenty.

The second of Gerald's two paragraphs is, if anything, even more revealing. First, the monk relates some local folklore concerning the poltergeist: that an infestation is a sign that the inhabitants of the house concerned will soon experience a sharp swing in their fortunes. (And, sure enough, both Wiriet and Not soon find their circumstances sadly diminished.) The motif is not encountered in poltergeist cases nowadays, yet, as we have just seen, the phenomena themselves have remained precisely comparable. This suggests that a firm line may be drawn between folk-belief in the poltergeist phenomenon, which has indeed changed and evolved over the years, and an underlying phenomenon which appears to be in some way real. Second, Gerald himself (a churchman of such standing that he aspired to an archbishopric) is evidently puzzled as to why the poltergeists in question proved immune to the usual religious remedies. This suggests that he is recounting the case history as he heard it. Were he telling the story for effect, or to suggest a moral, it would make more sense for him to have the priests succeed in their attempts to exorcise the troublesome spirits.

There are other cultural aspects to the history of the poltergeist, but though they can help us to understand the ways in which such phenomena were interpreted, they do not seem to have influenced the phenomena themselves. For example, Gauld notes that there are far fewer cases of apparent 'possession' by poltergeists now that few people believe in demons, and adds that 'the hundred years or so following the Reformation saw a marked drop in the percentage of reported cases in which the phenomena were ostensibly linked to a deceased person', a fashion he plausibly attributes to the fact that 'the idea of return from the dead was anathema to early Protestant theological writers'. But an analysis of the score or so of cases that were recorded in the years in question shows that the usual mixture of objects hurled about rooms, voices speaking from thin air and knockings and rappings disturbing the occupants of a house remained unchanged, whatever the explanation the witnesses chose to apply to them.

The general sceptical view of poltergeists – which might be summarised as the 'naughty little boy or girl' theory – is that they are all fakes, and there is no doubt that some are, indeed, hoaxes. For example, a series of mysterious blazes that occurred in one Alabaman home in 1959 and that were originally attributed to a poltergeist proved to be the work of a nine-year-old boy who wanted to drive his family back to the city from which they had recently moved.

Nevertheless, the suggestion that infants or adolescents have hoaxed most or all poltergeist infestations appears difficult to sustain in the absence of direct proof of fraud in most cases and in the face of evidence for the historical continuity of the phenomenon. Were the supposed hoaxers adult, it might be permissible to suggest that they had become aware of a tradition of what poltergeists are and do, and modelled their fraud along these lines – though even then the similarity between cases that occurred hundreds of years apart on different continents would appear remarkable. It is altogether less plausible to suppose that children as young as seven or eight are equally aware of how a poltergeist is supposed to behave, particularly as surprisingly few cases of poltergeist-like phenomena appear in the sort of folk-tales that children might have heard and drawn upon. It does seem, then, that the poltergeist – perhaps unlike the common or garden ghost – is a physically real phenomenon with characteristics that have been reported fairly consistently throughout its recorded history. The question of what the phenomenon is – whether it involves the psychical manifestation of physiological change, for example – remains unanswered.

Problems with the Cultural Source Hypothesis

For all the attractions of the cultural source hypothesis, the suggestion that the society in which a strange event occurs can affect the way in which that event is actually experienced has been criticised by some researchers, including a number of folklorists.

The best-researched and most significant of these rebuttals comes from Thomas Bullard, an American folklorist with a special interest in ufology. In 1987 he published a substantial dossier of information on more than 300 abduction experiences – virtually all those that had been reported up to that date – in which he analysed the components of the reports in a search for patterns and parallels. Like Meurger, Bullard concluded that there appeared to be no direct links between the fairy abductions recorded in folklore and the alien abductions reported by folklorists. He also noted that there did not seem to be any significant disparities between consciously remembered abduction experiences – which made up about a third of his sample – and those recorded under hypnosis, and that the memories retrieved by different regression therapists were strikingly similar in detail. This suggests that such reports are not produced simply by over-eager ufologists and over-confident therapists implanting false memories in the minds of witnesses. If they *are* fantasies, they would appear to have a different source.

Nevertheless, Bullard's exhaustive research did demonstrate that the classic abduction experience follows a set pattern that could be deconstructed to produce a set of motifs – 'capture', 'examination', 'return' and so on – just as folklorists dismantle fairy stories and label their component parts. Though critics of the cultural source hypothesis have pointed out that Bullard also found unexpected patterns that recurred even though no attention had been drawn to them, these experiences did appear to be distinctly fantastic in character – as much like the details of a piece of science fiction as anything. For example, Bullard's analysis revealed a high incidence of what he called 'doorway amnesia', the abductee typically having no memory of passing through any door or portal when entering a UFO. Another oddity was abductees' frequent obsession with the source of concealed lighting on board the 'saucer'.

David Hufford, the folklorist and behavioural scientist who was the first to study the Hag experience, is another critic who has suggested that the cultural source hypothesis is too limiting. Reviewing the evidence for Old Hag apparitions in different cultures, he noted that, while the precise form adopted by the 'bedroom invader' did vary from place to place, apparently relative to the cultural expectations of the witness, the core details of the experience – the sensation of paralysis, the slow approach of impending assault, rising panic and the feeling of being crushed by the attacker's weight as it crouches on the chest – remain the same, and are reported whether or not the witness has ever heard of the Hag experience. Hufford found that approximately six in ten of the Newfoundland students he questioned at the outset of his research, were unaware of the Old Hag; 6.5 per cent of those who had experienced the Hag had not discussed it and had no idea that anyone else had ever had such an encounter, but they nevertheless reported essentially the same experience.

Hufford concluded that 'the distribution of traditions about the experience has frequently been confused with the distribution of the experience itself' and that the physical symptoms seemed to fit sleep paralysis during a hypnagogic hallucination. Nevertheless, at the close of his investigation, he had to concede that 'the contents of the experience cannot be satisfactorily explained on the basis of current knowledge'.

It seems, then, that neither the psychological nor the cultural source hypotheses can stand on their own. A number of complex and widely reported phenomena resist attempts to reduce them to a single explanation.

It is, however, possible to combine the two theories to produce much more satisfactory broad solutions. Thus the Old Hag may be viewed as a physiological phenomenon that is experienced through the lens of cultural influences and expectations. The alien abduction experience, rather than being the product of a physically real assault by extraterrestrials, may have a psychological source, but if it does then it can only be one overlaid with a substantial cultural component – in this case, detailed knowledge of the pattern that a typical abduction is supposed to follow, gleaned either from journalistic coverage of earlier cases or (in the case of the earliest abductees) dim recollections of ancient pulp fiction.

If it could be shown conclusively that the witness had had no exposure to any of this, the cultural component of this solution would of course fail; but such is the pervasiveness of the media today that it would be difficult to find such a person, particularly in the knowledge – gleaned from research into recollections of past lives – that the brain retains vivid impressions of books and magazines read once, decades previously, and is quite capable of weaving a convincingly real fantasy based on such recollections. And, in the absence of such a perfect witness, the problem of alien abductions, like the problems of so many of the strange phenomena considered in this book, must remain, for the moment, unsolved.

12

A Sense of Wonder

Transcription of a tape-recorded phone message:

> Hi. My name is Virginia Staples, and in 1948 I lived in Bremerton, Washington. The apartment where I lived had a gigantically huge basement. There were huge holes in the walls and the apartment house manager used to tell me that it was rumoured there was a passage to the water. The huge apartment houses were so close together and they all had basements and they were all old buildings. There was a washer and a washtub and clotheslines. And on this particular day I had gotten my clothes all hung up but I kept feeling that someone was staring at me or looking at me. And it was such a creepy feeling I finally turned around and looked towards the back of the basement and froze. I was so scared I can still feel it. I couldn't move. In one of the huge holes in the basement there stood this huge thing. [She breaks down here.] Oh, it was horrible! I stand five foot tall and this creature was as tall as I was. It had a bright orange coloured body and little spidery thin legs and antennae on its head that kept moving back and in and out. [Crying now.] That thing started towards me. I backed out of the basement and got up to my apartment and I packed all my things and moved. I was so scared. I moved over to Seattle to my cousin's. I went to an aquarium to see if I could see anything that looked like

> what it was, and the only thing that I could find that looked anything like it was this little tiny shrimp. But it just doesn't make sense. I had horrible nightmares for years. I finally got up enough nerve a couple of years ago to go back and revisit Bremerton. But the apartment house on Denny Street has been torn down. Really nobody would believe this, but, as God is my witness, it really happened.

And, indeed, I have no doubt that it *did* happen, at least as far as Virginia Staples is concerned. The real question is what 'it' was.

There can be little doubt that the incident made a strong impression on the witness's mind – one so profound, in fact, that half-a-century later it was still one of the defining moments of her life. Staples herself is evidently convinced that the creature she saw was in some way real – either a flesh-and-blood monster, possibly one that had made its way up from the sea through the secret passageway she describes, or a paranormal entity of some description – a monster from another dimension, perhaps, or a being from the depths of hell.

She may even be right, though the giant shrimp that she describes is, to my knowledge, unique in all the many records of the borderlands. But by now it should be evident that there are other explanations for her experience, some of which may also be in some way true.

Consider, first, the psychological background to the case, insofar as we can understand it. Was Staples merely being sensible in packing and leaving the building so precipitately, or did she already have some ulterior motive for leaving – one that she may not even have admitted to herself, but which the vision in the basement gave her every reason to indulge? (We cannot know.) Does her enduring fearfulness reflect a genuine terror, or indicate an unusually vivid imagination – perhaps, even, a fantasy-prone personality? (We cannot say.) Might, in fact, the entity that Staples saw have been an hallucination of some sort? Certainly the witness seems to have found that the atmosphere made the basement area a frightening and oppressive place – everything about it is characteristically 'huge' in her account – and she was, perhaps, a little 'spooked' by the landlord's tales of its legendary connection with the sea. One might well argue that a certain degree of expectancy was present that day in 1948 – the strange sensation Staples had that she was being watched, for instance.

Of course, most of us have experienced that uneasy sensation from time to time without turning to find a five-foot-tall king prawn advancing towards us. And if we do take the common-sense approach of presuming that the terrible creature was not literally, physically real, it seems unlikely that we will ever know for certain why Staples's vision took the form it did.

Consider, though, the cultural aspects of the case. It occurred during the heyday of the pulp science fiction magazine, the 'B' movie and the Saturday morning adventure serial. Perhaps a related form of bug-eyed monster featured in one of the pulps a month or two earlier, or in a newspaper comic strip the previous year. (On the other hand, perhaps Staples had simply dined on shrimp the night before.)

What can be said, with some certainty, is that the memory that caused Staples to break down while she was leaving her message on the answer-phone in 1995 simply cannot be an accurate record of the monster she saw in 1948. The whole terrifying incident must have been relived so frequently over a period of almost five decades that, quite unbeknown to the witness herself, it quickly mutated into a false memory of indeterminate reliability.

It is, naturally, quite impossible to say now what, if anything, provided the initial stimulus for Staples's experience. Perhaps an entity looking something like a giant shrimp actually did materialise on the far side of the basement; more probably, though, what the witness really saw in the hole in the wall was something relatively formless: an ill-defined, bright-coloured haze produced by nerves firing unexpectedly in her temporal lobes, perhaps, or even something quite mundane, such as an item of orange clothing glimpsed from the corner of an eye – something that acquired greater form and substance as Staples replayed the experience in her mind time and time again, first consciously, as she fled back to her apartment, packed, and left the area for good, then subconsciously, in the nightmares that she experienced for years afterwards.

The mental process that might have turned a hazy initial stimulus into an extraordinary memory is even harder to define. One point that can be made is that Staples may well have used her innate story-telling abilities to shape an indeterminate and thus, in some sense, an unsatisfying experience into something with more meaning. She would have done this by selecting the 'best' elements of the story and elaborating them, quite possibly adding others at the same time that did not in fact occur.

Indeed, I can vouch from my own experience of writing up the case that such an elaboration is possible. Making notes for this section of the book, I recalled Staples's account and jotted on a scrap of paper the words 'Giant bipedal shrimp in cellar', together with a reference. Yet when I reread the transcript of the witness's phone message, I realised that nowhere does she state that the creature walked on two legs, or even that it stood upright. That is certainly the *impression* one gets from a casual reading of the account, but that is because years of watching second-rate films with inadequate special effects conditions one to expect most monsters to be humanoid. Similarly, and returning now to Staples's own account, the idea that the creature should advance towards her might have been suggested by the conventions of fiction and film. It is not only the sort of thing that monsters *do*; it adds a definite sense of purpose – indeed a suitable aura of menace – to the whole experience.

What this analysis teaches us – and what most of what has gone before suggests – is that everything that occurs within the borderlands is utterly subjective. The key to understanding these events lies in a painstaking, and ultimately entirely speculative, interpretation of witness testimony, since in only a minority of cases is there any hope of finding confirming physical evidence.

This subjectivity makes it very difficult for an open-minded observer to reject any case with complete confidence, let alone be quite certain that he has properly understood even a single phenomenon. Yet, thankfully, it does seem possible to advance a few general conclusions.

The first is that unusual experiences refuse to be neatly compartmentalised. Some mystery animal reports contain parapsychological elements; some UFOs appear to be the products of earth phenomena. It is, therefore, both pointless and dangerous to consider any strange phenomenon in isolation. The same applies to the grand unifying theories that have been advanced to account for them. Neither the psychological source hypothesis nor the cultural source hypothesis can stand alone, because culture influences psychology and psychology, culture. Only a combination of the two theories can hope to explain complex phenomena such as the Old Hag or the Black Dog.

The second conclusion is that there seems to be no such thing as a consistently inexplicable phenomenon. If one case of spontaneous human combustion yields to the explanation that the victim fell head-first into a grate, then the whole idea that spontaneous combustion is somehow uniquely strange and terrible fails. If one persuasive lake monster sighting turns out to be a misperception of a wave or a diving bird, we can never be sure that every other equally persuasive witness is not also in error. This problem has profound, and scarcely explored implications for the whole study of strange phenomena, and places an insupportable burden on the generally scarce and ambiguous physical evidence.

Finally, we must acknowledge that more of the answers we have been seeking lie within ourselves than ever was suspected. At root, the reason for this is that the human mind possesses an inherent sense of wonder – a capacity to enjoy and be stimulated by the unknown – which has been responsible for a good deal of mischief and misunderstanding. But since this same sense of wonder has also driven us out of the caves and into our present state of civilisation, it would be quite wrong to wish it away.

Mysterious and mystical experiences possess a powerful capacity to change lives. Because they are important, they should always be considered with an open mind, with a reluctance to rush to definite conclusions and with an eagerness to savour the rich variety of human experience. With, in short, a sense of wonder.

The things that happen in the borderlands are terrifying, confusing, perplexing, maddening, yes. But we go because we want to go.

And everyone visits the borderlands at least once in their lives.

Notes

Introduction

Tom D'Ercole D'Ercole told of his encounter with the strange cloud in 'True Mystic Experiences: My Own Little Cloud', *Fate*, (February 1979) pp 54–5. The incident took place at Oyster Bay, New York, in the summer of 1975 and the test on the shirt was conducted at Garden City Junior High School. D'Ercole estimated that the growing cloud reached a final size of around six feet by eighteen inches at which point it had become 'an abstract, multicurved, dark, vaporous "something" '.

The mysterious tchae khana Tony Clark, 'Lunchtime at the Phantom Diner', *Fortean Times*, 69 (June/July 1993) pp. 34–5. A sceptic would note that Clark exhibited a tendency to believe in mystical experiences when he wrote to *Fortean Times*, 88, (July 1996) to tell the strange experience of an engineer friend's encounter with an invisible bedroom entity in Nigeria.

Edward Baldock Daily Telegraph 2 and 16 February 1991, cited in *Fortean Times*, 58 (July 1991) p. 6. Wigginton turned out to be a less successful murderer than she was a vampire: she dropped a credit card by her victim's body and was arrested, tried and sentenced to life imprisonment.

Nonquawuse J.B. Peires, *The Dead Will Arise: Nonquawuse and the Great Xhosa Cattle-Killing Movement of 1856–7* (Johannesburg, Raven Press, 1989).

Prince Paul Sieveking, 'Rover's Return', *Fortean Times*, 70 (August–September 1993) pp. 38–41.

Bobbie Ibid.

The Bermuda Triangle Lawrence Kusche, *The Bermuda Triangle Mystery – Solved* (London, New English Library, 1981).

The bedroom invader David Hufford, *The Terror That Comes in the Night*

(Philadelphia, University of Pennsylvania Press, 1982); Hilary Evans, *Visions•Apparitions•Alien Visitors: A Comparative Study of the Entity Enigma* (Wellingborough, Aquarian Press, 1984).

'Randy P.' Strange, 16 (1995) p. 23.

Fatima Kevin McClure, *The Evidence for Visions of the Virgin Mary* (Wellingborough, Aquarian Press, 1983) pp. 71–86. According to this careful and level-headed researcher, 'Nothing about Fatima has turned out to be in the least bit simple or straightforward . . . I have never seen such a collection of contradictory accounts in any of the research I have done in the past 10 years.'

Fatima has been back in the news again recently, thanks to the efforts of officials at the Iranian embassy in Lisbon. They have translated the works of a local scholar into Persian, noting his theory that the miracle site was named after the prophet Muhammad's daughter by African Muslim invaders in the early middle ages. According to this theory, the apparition seen by Lucia Santos was of Fatima herself and not of the Virgin Mary. Planeloads of Iranian religious tourists were daily expected at the site, ready to turn it into a place of Islamic pilgrimage. *Fortean Times*, 86 (May 1996) p. 11.

The location of Troy Iman Wilkens, *Where Troy Once Stood* (London, Rider, 1990); *Guardian*, 25 and 26 June 1990.

The Holy Land in Arabia Kamal Salibi, *The Bible Came from Arabia* (London, Cape, 1984).

Comyns Beaumont John Michell, *Eccentric Lives and Peculiar Notions* (London, Thames & Hudson, 1984). Beaumont's theories parallel those of the once-influential Anglo-Israelite movement, which suggested that the British were none other than the Ten Lost Tribes of Israel, and thus God's chosen people. Donna Kossy, *Kooks: A Guide to the Outer Limits of Human Belief* (Portland, Feral House, 1994).

The Green Children. The discovery of the children can be dated to between 1135 and 1154. It was not recorded for at least sixty years, however, first appearing in the chronicles of Ralph of Coggeshall (*Chronicon Anglicarum*) and William of Newburgh (*Historia Rerum Anglicarum*), both of which were edited in scholarly editions in the last century: Ralph by J. Stevenson (London, Rolls Series, 1875), and William by R. Howlett as one of the *Chronicles of the Reigns of Stephen, Henry II and Richard I* (London, Rolls Series, 1884). The most recent of several re-examinations of this case is Paul Harris, 'The Green Children of Woolpit', *Fortean Times*, 57 (1991) pp. 39 and 41.

Encounters with trolls Michel Meurger, *Lake Monster Traditions: A Cross-Cultural Analysis* (London, Fortean Tomes, 1988) p. 17.

UFOs in non-western cultures Thierry Pinvidic, 'An Algerian Case Study', *Magonia*, 14 (1983) pp. 3–7.

Misidentification of a television crew Mike Dash, 'The Case of the Phantom Social Workers', *Fortean Times*, 57 (1991) pp. 43–5.

Scottish UFO abduction Personal conversation with Malcolm Robinson, Strange Phenomena Investigations, who looked into this case.

The Flying Dutchman Michael Goss and George Behe, *Lost At Sea: Ghost Ships and Other Mysteries* (Amherst, New York, Prometheus Books, 1994) pp. 46–52. Goss and Behe ably examine the report, and suspect a 'spicing up' of the journal entry.

The King of Bhutan's lake monster National Geographic, September 1961, cited in Peter Costello, *In Search of Lake Monsters* (St Albans, Panther Books, 1975) p. 294.

Jimmy Carter's UFO Robert Sheaffer, *The UFO Verdict* (Buffalo, Prometheus Books, 1980); Steuart Campbell, *The UFO Mystery Solved: An Examination of UFO Reports and Their Explanation* (Edinburgh, Explicit Books, 1994) p. 88.

Father Gill Kim Hansen, 'Papua-New Guinea, 26–27 June 1959' in Hilary Evans and John Spencer (eds) *UFOs 1947–1987: the 40-Year Search for an Explanation* (London, Fortean Tomes, 1987) pp. 59–62; Martin Kottmeyer, 'Gill again: a fresh look at an old classic', *Magonia*, 54 (November 1995) pp. 11–14.

Falkville, Alabama encounter Margaret Sachs, *The UFO Encyclopedia* (London, Corgi, 1981) p. 99.

Paul Ingram Lawrence Wright, *Remembering Satan: Recovered Memory and the Shattering of a Family* (London, Serpent's Tail, 1994).

The Halifax Slasher Mick Goss, *The Halifax Slasher: An Urban Terror in the North of England* (London, Fortean Times, 1987).

Alabama fish fall 'The Chilatchee, Alabama Fish Fall', *INFO Journal*, 46, p. 24. All the species of fish involved were indigenous to the area, but the closest body of water was Chilatchee Creek, a little more than a mile to the west. Mr and Mrs Phillips stated that no whirlwinds or tornadoes were reported at the time and they could see nothing in the local weather patterns to suggest how they had been drawn into the strange cloud. Because the fall was so localised, and the cloud so unusual, Mrs Phillips stated that she felt the event was somehow intentional.

Hessdalen Hansen, 'Hessdalen, 1981–1985' in Evans and Spencer, *UFOs 1947–1987*, pp. 88–92.

Gulf Breeze Jerome Clark, 'Gulf Breeze sightings', in *The UFO Encyclopedia: UFOs in the 1980s* (Detroit, Apogee Books, 1990) pp. 121–8.

The Veronicas Ian Wilson, *Holy Faces, Secret Places: the Quest for Christ's True Likeness* (London, Doubleday, 1991). It is now generally accepted that the images are paintings, though some argue that these works of art were divinely inspired.

The Holy Prepuce 'Preposterous prepuce', *Fortean Times*, 44 (Summer 1985) p. 8.

Adamski's flying saucer photograph Curtis Peebles, *Watch the Skies! A Chronicle of the Flying Saucer Myth* (Washington, Smithsonian Institution Press, 1994) p. 303 n. 8. Other possibilities include an eight-inch model closely based on plans for a spaceship published eight months before Adamski's photos were taken, and a tobacco humidor equipped with three ping-pong balls. Jerome Clark, *UFO Encyclopedia: The Emergence of a*

Phenomenon: UFOs from the Beginning Through 1959 (Detroit, Omnigraphics, 1992) pp. 1–12.

Morgawr A. Mawnan-Peller, *Morgawr, the Monster of Falmouth Bay* (Exeter, Centre for Fortean Zoology, 1996); Tony 'Doc' Shiels, *Monstrum: A Wizard's Tale* (London, Fortean Times, 1990); Mark Chorvinsky, 'Tony "Doc" Shiels: magic and monsters', *Strange*, 8 (Fall 1991) pp. 4–20. Doc, incidentally, has never confessed to this forgery, nor to charges that he similarly hoaxed his well-known photos of the Loch Ness Monster and rather obscure snapshots of fairies.

Spirit photographs 'Spirit photography' in Leslie Shephard (ed), *Encyclopaedia of Occultism & Parapsychology* Detroit, Gale Research, 1984 (2nd edn) pp. 1261–62.

Faked moon landings See, for example, David Percy, 'Dark Side of the Moon landings', *Fortean Times* 94 (January 1997) pp. 34–39.

The Turin Shroud David Sox, *The Shroud Unmasked: Uncovering the Greatest Forgery of All Time* (Basingstoke, The Lamp Press, 1988); Mike Dash, 'Shrouded in mystery', *Fortean Times*, 51 (winter 1988/89) pp. 4–7. Since 1988, the shroud has also become involved in a new controversy; authors Lynn Picknett and Clive Prince have suggested that it is actually an early experiment in photography conducted by Leonardo da Vinci.

There have been 3000 sightings of the Loch Ness Monster . . . The figure of 3000 was first given by David James, MP, the founder of the Loch Ness Phenomena Investigation Bureau, in *The Field*, 23 November 1981, pp. 951–53. That of 10000 appeared on the jacket of Roy Mackal's *The Monsters of Loch Ness* (London, Futura, 1976). A careful listing of known sightings from all sources, compiled by the German Fortean Ulrich Magin forms an appendix to Henry Bauer, *The Enigma of Loch Ness: Making Sense of a Mystery* (Urbana and Chicago, University of Illinois Press, 1986). See also ibid., p. 10 n. 32.

133, 306, 688 demons fell with Lucifer . . . These are the figures cited in Richard Cavendish, *The Powers of Evil* (London, Routledge & Kegan Paul, 1975) p.234.

Poodles in microwaves 'Nuking the poodle', *Fortean Times* 80 (Apr–May 1995) p. 180.

1 Strange Planet

Red snow The Mirror of Literature, Amusement & Instruction (London), vol. XXV no. 702, (1 January 1835) p. 44, citing the contemporary 'Voyage in the South Atlantic Ocean by HM Sloop *Chanticleer*'.

Blood-red clouds Notes & Queries, 8th series, vol. 12 p. 228, cited in Charles Fort, *The Book of the Damned*, p. 257, in *The Complete Books of Charles Fort* (New York, Dover Publications, 1974).

Fall of sand on Baghdad Annual Register, 1857, p. 132, cited in Charles Fort; *The Book of the Damned*, pp. 234–5. The original account was by Charles Murray, the British Envoy to Persia.

Fall of rose-coloured frogs on Stroud Bob Rickard, 'When pink frogs fell', *Fortean Times*, 51 (winter 1988–89) pp. 14–15. There were also falls of pinkish-red frogs in Cirencester two weeks earlier, and at Cheltenham somewhat later on. Ian Darling, of the Gloucestershire Trust for Nature Conservancy, said the frogs were not really red, or pink; they were an albino strain whose colouring came from blood showing through their pale skins. The GTNC suspected that the airborne amphibia might have come from the Sahara, carried north by hurricane force winds along with quantities of red Saharan sand, some of which fell on England at around this time. Rickard notes various flaws in the GTNC's theories, and also that, at around the time the frogs came tumbling down, the film *The Love Child* was released, the poster for which showed pink frogs falling, and the story of which featured a band and a song called 'The Pink Frogs'. In a follow up, 'More on pink frogs', *Fortean Times*, 52 (summer 1989) p. 79, four more reports of such animals, one dating back to the late 1920s, were noted, casting further doubt on their supposed Saharan origin.

Ghosts and water A theory formulated by G.W. Lambert, president of the Society for Psychical Research 1956–58, in the *Journal of the SPR*, June 1955, in relation to poltergeist cases, and subsequently elaborated into a major alternative to the generally accepted 'person-centred' theory of poltergeist incidents before also being applied to hauntings. Renee Haynes, *The Society for Psychical Research 1882–1982: A History* (London, Macdonald, 1982) pp. 106–08.

Odd things tend to happen on Wednesdays A theory proposed by the author John Keel, based on his analysis of 700 UFO reports from 1967, which showed that more occurred on Wednesday than on any other day of the week. Subsequently analysis of a wider range of sightings failed to substantiate the theory. 'Wednesday phenomenon' in Jerome Clark, *UFO Encyclopedia*: *High Strangeness: UFOs 1960 through 1979* (Detroit, Apogee Books, 1996) p. 58.

Yellow rain 'Scientists say yellow rain is a lot of crap', *Fortean Times*, 42 (autumn 1984) p. 16.

Green UFO near Astrakhan 'From the KGB Archives', *INFO Journal*, 71 (autumn 1994) p. 31.

The Virgin Mary and the lizard Hilary Evans, *Gods•Spirits•Cosmic Guardians: Encounters with Non-Human Beings* (Wellingborough, The Aquarian Press, 1987) p. 54.

The Big Muddy Monster 'Big Muddy Monster Returns', *Fortean Times*, 51 (winter 1988–89) p. 16. The witnesses were Charles Staub, a security guard, and Bob Reiman, owner of the salvage yard. The incident took place on 3 June 1988, a dozen years after the Monster's last reported appearance.

The silent city Dwight Whalen, 'Silent Cities in the Sky', *Fortean Times*, 66 (Dec 199/Jan 1993) pp. 36–40. For Greenland's mid-western cities, see Howard Abramson, *Hero in Disgrace: the Life of Arctic Explorer Frederick A. Cook* (New York, Paragon House, 1991) p. 92.

Japanese Airlines UFO Jerome Clark, *UFO Encyclopedia*: *UFOs in the 1980s*

(Detroit, Apogee Books, 1990) pp. 146–48 outlines the history of this well-documented case and the various unsuccessful attempts to explain it. Steuart Campbell, *The UFO Mystery Solved* (Edinburgh, Explicit Books, 1994) pp. 168–76 has subsequently noted that only Terauchi reported the giant UFO; other crew members saw only two widely-spaced white lights flying in formation. His book suggests that the report can be explained as a mirage of the airfield lights at Allan Army Air Field at Delta Junction, Alaska. Campbell's theory requires the lights to have been switched on at the time and for a temperature inversion to have existed between the base and Captain Terauchi's plane. Neither factor is now proveable, so the objects remain unidentified.

Burlington skyquakes Res Bureaux Bulletin, 31 (23 March 1978) pp. 3-6.

'*Caddy*' Paul LeBlond and Edward Bousfield, *Cadborosaurus: Survivor from the Deep* (Victoria, British Columbia, Horsdal & Schubart, 1995).

The phantom ship of Northumberland Strait Larry Arnold, 'Ahoy Mate! Which Flaming Phantom Ship Sails Thar?', *Pursuit*, vol. 11, pp. 109, 116, 144–50; George Behe and Michael Goss, *Lost At Sea: Ghost Ships and Other Mysteries* (Amherst, New York, Prometheus Books, 1994) pp. 73–5.

Gravelbourg footprints 'Footprints in the . . .', *Pursuit* (July 1971) pp. 69-70.

Clarendon's disembodied voice Light, (December 1889) cited in John Michell and Robert Rickard, *Phenomena: A Book of Wonders* (London, Thames & Hudson, 1977) p. 83.

The Mad Gasser of Mattoon Most accounts of this peculiar case, which lasted from 31 August 1944 until 12 September the same year, are based on a sociological study by an undergraduate student, Donald Johnson, 'The Phantom Anaesthetist of Mattoon: a field study of mass hysteria', *Journal of Abnormal and Social Psychology*, 40 (1945) pp. 175-86, which inclined, as its title suggests, towards dismissing the mystery as lacking a physical reality. More recently, the case has been re-evaluated by Loren Coleman in *Mysterious America* (London, Faber & Faber, 1983) pp. 191–201 and by Willy Smith in 'Mattoon Revisited', *Magonia*, 48 (January 1994) pp. 3–6. Both authors incline to the view that there was more to events than Johnson realised, or admitted.

The Smurfs Newsweek, 4 April 1983, cited in 'Smurfs on rampage', *Fortean Times*, 42 (autumn 1984) p. 14.

Dwendis Loren Coleman, *Curious Encounters: Phantom Trains, Spooky Spots and Other Mysterious Wonders* (London, Faber & Faber, 1986) p. 55.

Teleported to Mexico City Mr X, 'The Aparecido and the death of Gomez Perez Dasmarinas', *Fortean Times*, 52 (Summer 1989) pp. 55–9.

Goatsucker Scott Corrales, *The Chupacabras Diaries: an Unofficial Chronicle of Puerto Rico's Paranormal Predator* (Derrick City, Pennsylvania, Samizdat Press, 1996); and numerous postings to the Forteana e-mail discussion group and Goatsucker web site.

Giant snakes Tim Dinsdale, *The Leviathans* (London, Futura, 1976) pp. 130–7, cites the Brazilian papers *Diario de Pernambuco*, 24 Jan 1948 and *Provincia do Para*, 28 Apr 1949, and gives pen-and-ink sketches of the photographs. Bernard Heuvelmans, *On the Track of Unknown Animals*

(London, Rupert Hart-Davis, 1962) pp. 292–8, mentions, but does not print, two further photographs published in *A Noite Illustrada*, 1 Jun 1948. As these are the only known photos of the *sucuriju gigante*, the near-coincidence of publication dates is certainly remarkable.

Villas Boas abduction The Villas Boas account was not published until 1964, apparently because ufologists believed it was too unlikely and feared that publicising its remarkable details would discredit their subject. Nevertheless, it has turned out to be a remarkable precursor to the current glut of sexually-explicit abduction accounts emerging from the United States. Gordon Creighton, 'The Amazing Case of Antonio Villa Boas' in Charles Bowen (ed.) *The Humanoids* (London, Futura, 1977) pp. 200–238.

The Patagonian plesiosaur Peter Costello, *In Search of Lake Monsters* (St Albans, Panther Books, 1975) pp. 257–268. Tales of the Patagonian plesiosaur continue to emerge from the region. Most, nowadays, centre on Lake Nahuel Huapi, whose denizen has been nicknamed Nahuelito. One recent report of Nahuelito was made by Jessica Campbell, of Barilouche, who saw a grey-green monster eleven yards long exhibiting several humps at the lake surface, probably at the tail end of 1993 (the source is not specific). She particularly remarked on the beast's audibly heavy breathing. Photographs were reputed to have been taken during this sighting, but none have been published to my knowledge. *Animals & Men*, 3 (Oct 1994) p. 11, citing *New Zealand Northern Advocate*, 5 Jan 1994.

Doubtful islands Henry Stommel, *Lost Islands: the Story of Islands that have Vanished from Nautical Charts* (Vancouver, University of British Columbia Press, 1984). Rupert Gould, 'The Auroras, and other doubtful islands' in *Oddities: A Book of Unexplained Facts* (London, Geoffrey Bles, 1945) pp. 124–162, deals with the same subject; Gould discusses the Kerguelen story in the same volume, in his essay on 'The Devil's Hoof-Marks', pp. 20–1 &n.

Uganda's talking tortoise UPI wire, 24 August 1978, cited in *Fortean Times*, 27 (autumn 1978) p. 39.

Uganda's talking goat AFP wire, 3 June 1992, cited in *Fortean Times*, 66 (December 1992/January 1993) p. 9. Tales of talking animals seem to be a speciality of this country; in 'Country File: Uganda', *Fortean Times*, 87, (Jun 1996) p. 45, the *Monitor* of Kampala is quoted as reporting tales of talking birds on the road between Kidongole and Kolin; telling of them caused the witness to lose his or her voice (*Monitor*, 5 Oct 1994). The same paper (*Monitor*, 11 Jan 1994) also carried the story of a cobra that spoke to its victim in the Ateso language.

Burundi's vampire mermaid Karl Shuker, 'Menagerie of Mystery', *Strange*, 15 (spring 1995) p. 32.

Kenyan stone showers David Barritt, 'Tales from Africa', *Fortean Times*, 44 (summer 1985) pp. 36–7, 40.

Orang bati Karl Shuker; 'Menagerie of Mystery', *Strange*, 16 (autumn 1995) p. 28.

Irkuiem Loren Coleman, 'Cryptozoo News', *Strange*, 2 (1988) p. 24.

Cloud-busting planes Wall Street Journal, 6 August 1985, cited in 'Spanish mystery aircraft', *Fortean Times*, 47 (autumn 1986) p. 8.

Icelandic elves Guardian, 18 October 1995.

Bottineau 'The wizard of Mauritius' in Gould, Oddities, pp. 173–93.

Orffyreus Ibid pp. 89–116.

Dr Bachseitz 'The Talking Toilet', *Fortean Times*, 38 (autumn 1982) pp. 24–5; 'Reflections' *Fortean Times*, 39 (spring 1983) pp. 27–8.

Flying pigs Over Wales – *Cambrian Natural Observer*, 1905, p. 35, cited by Charles Fort, *New Lands* pp. 484–5, in *The Complete Books of Charles Fort* (New York, Dover Publications, 1974). In California – *The Register*, Santa Ana, California, 26 Feb 1982, cited in *Fortean Times*, 45 (winter 1985) p. 36.

Giant chicken Sunday Express, 9 June 1985, cited in *Fortean Times*, 46 (spring 1986) p. 29. Baizi called in the police, who observed that the area around the footprint was covered in a grey powder of unknown origin, but who advanced no explanation.

Goatman Mark Opasnick, 'On the trail of the Goatman', *Strange*, 14 (autumn 1994) pp. 18–21.

Caldwell's sky thread Caldwell, New Jersey *Progress*, 6 August 1970, cited in *INFO Journal*, 7 (fall-winter 1970) pp. 11–12.

Greenfield, Ohio sky thread St Louis Post Dispatch, 24 September 1978, cited in *Fortean Times*, 29 (summer 1979) p. 38.

Black dogs 'Mysterious black dogs' in Janet & Colin Bord, *Alien Animals: A Worldwide Investigation* (St Albans, Granada, 1980) pp. 77–111; Graham McEwan, *Mystery Animals of Britain and Ireland* (London, Robert Hale, 1986) pp. 119–149; Jerome Clark, *Unexplained! 347 Strange Sightings, Incredible Occurrences, and Puzzling Physical Phenomena* (Detroit, Visible Ink Press, 1993) pp. 38–41. For a modern American case (Georgia, 1978) see 'Phantom black dog', *Strange*, 13 (spring 1994) pp. 28 and 50. Pierre van Paassen wrote of his experience in *Days of Our Years* (London, Heinemann, 1939) pp. 237–40.

The tatzelwurm Bernard Heuvelmans, *On the Track of Unknown Animals* (London, Rupert Hart-Davis, 1962) pp. 32–36. Also Roger Hutchings, 'Alpine enigma', *Animals & Men*, 2 (Jul 1994) pp. 20–1. For the *tzuchinoko*, see Bernard Heuvelmans, 'Tzuchinoko, a 'tatzelwurm' from Japan' in *INFO Journal*, 49 (June 1986) pp. 7–8.

The cochion Lewis Spence, *The Fairy Tradition in Britain* (Rider 1948) pp. 78-79, cited in Philip Canning, 'Questionables', *Fortean Times*, 21 (spring 1977) pp. 5–6.

The Siwash 'Nevada's red-haired people eaters', *INFO Journal*, 8 (winter – spring, 1972) pp. 28–29, citing St Paul, Minnesota *Sunday Pioneer Press*, 27 Sept 1970.

Navajo skin-walkers 'The abominable werewolves of the Southwest', *Strange*, 7 (April 1991) pp. 40–1.

Dacianos and Brujeria For the former, see Daniel Mannix, *Freaks: We Who Are Not As Others* (San Francisco, Re/Search Publications, 1990) p. 113; for the latter, Bruce Chatwin, *In Patagonia* (London, Pan Books, 1979) pp.

102–05 and Michel Meurger, 'The Mythical Landscape of Chile' in Meurger, *Lake Monster Traditions: A Cross-Cultural Analysis* (London, Fortean Tomes, 1988) pp. 274–89. ('*Invunche*', incidentally, translates as 'midget' or 'dwarf', *chivato* as 'young goat'.) One further and unexpected parallel: Mannix, on the page opposite his description of the Dacianos, has a photograph of Martin Laurelle, exhibited at the New York World's Fair in 1940 – a man who could turn his head 180 degrees so that his chin rested on his spine, without any assistance from the Brujeria.

The manananggal AP wire, 8 May 1992, citing *Manila People's Journal Tonight*.

The tuyul 'Tuyul hunters disappointed', *Fortean Times*, 47 (autumn 1986) p. 9.

Killer kangaroo 'Kangarooiana', *INFO Journal*, 5 (fall 1969) p. 14.

2 Lands of Gods and Angels

UFO abduction story This is a precis of the abduction story recounted by Linda Napolitano, who was supposedly taken from her Manhattan bedroom one night in 1989. The case became celebrated when its principal investigator, Budd Hopkins, announced that he had traced four independent witnesses who claimed to have observed Napolitano as she ascended towards a hovering UFO, making this case almost unique in the annals of ufology.

New animal species 'Vietnam's lost world', *Fortean Times*, 66 (Dec 1992 – Jan 1993) p. 6; 'New mammals pop up in 'Nam', *Fortean Times*, 78 (Dec 1994 – Jan 1995) p. 19; Karl Shuker, 'The cave time forgot', *Fortean Times*, 88 (Jul 1996) p. 42 and 'Wild kthing, I think I love you', *Fortean Times*, 91 (October 1996) pp. 42–3.

Experience-centred phenomena David Hufford, *The Terror That Comes in the Night* (Philadelphia, University of Pennsylvania Press, 1982); James McClenon, *Wondrous Events: Foundations of Religious Belief* (Philadelphia, University of Pennsylvania Press, 1994).

Phantom scrotum-squeezer Paul Vincent, post on the Forteana e-mail group, 22 Oct 1996.

Devil in the pit Steve Howells, post on the Forteana e-mail group, 21 Oct 1996.

Frankenstein Bill Jacobs, post on the Forteana e-mail group, 21 Oct 1996.

Survey demonstrating the worldwide appearance of OBE, Dean Sheils, 'A cross-cultural study of beliefs in out of the body experiences, waking and sleeping', *Journal of the Society for Psychical Research*, 49 (1978) pp. 697–741.

Encounters with Castor and Pollux Steve Moore, 'Close encounters: a mythic perspective', *Fortean Times*, 37 (spring 1982) pp. 34–39, 64. It must be admitted that the remaining seven records of such meetings are not even as well-evidenced as this, but at the very least there clearly was a Graeco-Roman tradition that such encounters were possible, and for some reason cases involving Castor and Pollux outnumber those involving the many other deities of that pantheon.

The witness as a special person Hilary Evans, *Gods•Spirits•Cosmic Guardians* (Wellingborough, Aquarian Press, 1987) pp. 25–6.

The call to Muhammad Philip Hitti, *The Arabs: a Short History* (London, Macmillan, 1968) p. 24.

Joseph Smith and the foundation of Mormonism Richard Bushman, *Joseph Smith and the Beginnings of Mormonism* (Urbana, University of Illinois Press, 1984); Robert Lindsay, *A Gathering of Saints* (London, Simon & Schuster, 1989) pp. 27–35, 100–03; Robert Gottlieb and Peter Riley, *America's Saints: the Rise of Mormon Power* (San Diego, Harcourt Brace Jovanovich, 1986) pp. 32–6.

Hong Xiuquan Jonathan Spence, *God's Chinese Son: the Taiping Heavenly Kingdom of Hong Xiuquan* (London, HarperCollins, 1996).

Visions of the Virgin Mary For Walsingham, see Kevin McClure, *The Evidence for Visions of the Virgin Mary* (Wellingborough, Aquarian Press, 1983) pp. 14–15. For Juan Diego's vision, see Jody Brant Smith, *The Guadalupe Madonna: Myth or Miracle?* (London, Souvenir Press, 1983). For La Salette see McClure, *Visions* pp. 27-35. For a purely sceptical perspective, see Joe Nickell, *Entities: Angels, Spirits, Demons and Other Alien Beings* (Amherst, Prometheus Books, 1995) pp. 159–72.

'*The children . . . Made no specific claims as to her identity*' This leads us to one of the most perplexing oddities of this peculiar subject. According to one survey of 'Marian' visions, the figure that appears actually identifies itself in less than half of recorded cases, and in those in which it does, it frequently adopts a locally-known but by no means generally-familiar identity – in Alsace, in 1873, as 'Our Lady of the Rhine', for example. Hilary Evans, *Visions•Apparitions•Alien Visitors* (Wellingborough, Aquarian Press, 1986) p. 108.

The vision of Bernadette McClure, *Visions*, pp. 36–48; Evans, *Visions•Apparitions•Alien Visitors*, pp. 106–09. The freshness and accuracy of Bernadette's recollection is debatable: her statement dates only from 28 May 1861, by which time she must have retold her story countless times and had also become a nun.

The healing waters of Lourdes The 'miracles' claimed at Lourdes are studied by a panel of Catholic doctors who make up the Lourdes Medical Bureau. In the first century after its foundation in 1884, the Board accepted only eighty-four of the 6000 cases submitted to it as real miracles. Joe Nickell, *Looking for a Miracle: Weeping Icons, Relics, Stigmata and Healing Cures* (Buffalo, Prometheus Books, 1993) pp. 149–52.

One of only two . . . The other was St Catherine Laboure, whose vision of the Virgin occurred in her convent in Paris in 1830. It has been suggested that this experience was central to the development of the modern Marian vision, in that Catherine's vision of the Virgin was immortalised on more than a million religious medals struck to commemorate it and distributed throughout Catholic France. It is certainly not beyond the bounds of credibility that Bernadette Soubirous – and, perhaps, even the visionaries of La Salette – saw copies of this medal before enjoying their own visions, and thus had a good idea of what Mary was supposed to look like.

Fatima and late visions McClure, *Visions*, pp. 71–132; Nickell, *Entities*, pp. 166–70.

Mary's 'schedule' Mike Dash, 'Apparitions and the Marian Year', *Fortean Times*, 51 (winter 1988/89) pp. 19–23.

'The great selectivity with which the Virgin reveals herself . . .' Not infrequently, the vision is even more selective; at Fatima, for example, it is, even now, not entirely clear whether the two youngest of the three children who saw the Virgin ever heard her speak and evident that the apparent catalyst of the whole series of visions was the eldest and only surviving witness, Lucia de Jesus dos Santos. At Beauraing, too, one child among the five principal witnesses – eleven-year-old Albert Voisin – acted both as an instigator and as the primary spokesman for the little group.

Jean Bernard Hilary Evans, *Gods•Spirits•Cosmic Guardians* (Wellingborough, Aquarian Press, 1988) pp. 54–7.

'The Virgin appears hardly at all in Protestant or Orthodox territories . . .' One rather spectacular exception to this general rule was a series of visions at the Coptic church at Zeitoun, Cairo, between 1968 and 1971. In this case, the vision was not only visible to everyone in the crowd, but was actually photographed as it floated around the roof of the local church. The resultant pictures, which show an entirely conventional 'Virgin' with a perceptible halo, have never been conclusively shown to be hoaxes, but certainly fall into the 'too good to be true' category in the opinion of many researchers.

Visions at Llanthony Abbey McClure, *Visions*, pp. 118–20.

Nonquawuse's experience J.B. Peires, *The Dead Will Arise: Nonquawuse and the Great Xhosa Cattle-Killing Movement of 1856–7* (Johannesburg, Raven Press, 1989) pp. 78–9, 87–94. Interestingly, some of Nonquawuse's later visions were in fact shared by a few other people, in circumstances not dissimilar to those that led to the vision of the miracle of the sun at Fatima.

The wandering Nephites Loren Coleman, *Mysterious America* (Boston, Faber & Faber, 1983) pp. 218–32.

1947 visions of the Virgin Evans, *Visions•Apparitions•Alien Visitors*, p. 120.

Amparo Cuevas Evans, *Gods•Spirits•Cosmic Guardians*, p.11. See *ibid.* pp. 12–13 for a nineteenth-century French case of this variety reported by the psychologist Pierre Janet.

False prediction at Fatima Kevin McClure, *The Fortean Times Book of the Millennium* (London, John Brown, 1996) p. 56.

Luminous globe at Fatima Joao Quaresma, cited in McClure, *Visions*, pp. 76–7. This writer subsequently became Vicar-General of Leiria, the diocese in which Fatima lay.

Photos of the gods Bob Rickard, 'Photos of the gods', *Fortean Times*, 36 (winter 1982) pp. 32–42; 'More photos of the gods', *Fortean Times*, 44 (summer 1985) pp. 24–6; *Sunday People*, 13 Nov 1977; 'Bleeding nun snaps Jesus', *Fortean Times*, 75 (Jun-Jul 1994) p. 15; Dash, 'Apparitions and the Marian Year', p. 23.

Religious relics Joe Nickell, *Looking for a Miracle: Weeping Icons, Relics, Stigmata, Visions & Healing Cures* (Buffalo, Prometheus Books, 1993) pp. 73–100.

St Teilo's skull Paul Sullivan & Quentin Cooper, 'Saint's Day Almanac', *Fortean Times*, 79 (Feb – Mar 1995) p. 50; Andy Roberts & David Clarke, 'Heads and tales: the screaming skull legends of Britain', *Fortean Studies*, 3 (London, John Brown, 1996) p. 155.

Incorruption Joan Carroll Cruz, *The Incorruptibles: a Study of the Incorruption of the Bodies of Various Catholic Saints and Beati* (Rockford, Illinois, Tan Books, 1995), esp. pp. 43–6, 256–9; Herbert Thurston, *The Physical Phenomena of Mysticism* (London, Burns Oates, 1952) pp. 233–270; Nickell, *Looking for a Miracle*, pp. 85–93. In the case of St Cecilia there seems to be some doubt that her supposedly incorrupt corpse was adequately examined on its second disinterrment, and so this less-than-satisfactory case must be regarded as 'unproven'.

Non-Christian cases of incorruption Andrew White, *A History of the Warfare of Science with Theology in Christendom* (New York, George Braziller, 1955) vol. 2 p. 10; Aleister Crowley, *The Confessions of Aleister Crowley: an Autohagiography*, ed. John Symons and Kenneth Grant (London, Arkana, 1989) p. 206. My thanks to Brian Chapman for these references.

3 World of Spirits

Wiertz's hypnotic telepathy experiment Leslie Shepard (ed.) *Encyclopaedia of Occultism and Parapsychology* 2nd edn (Detroit, Gale Research, 1984) 2 p. 648, citing S. Watteau, *Catalogue Raisonne du Musee Wiertz* (Brussels, 1865). There has, from time to time, been considerable controversy over whether death by guillotine is instantaneous. An investigation was made by three doctors following the execution of a man named Prunier. Their report, given in the *British Medical Journal* for December 1879, says, *inter alia*, 'We have ascertained, as far as is humanely possible to do so, that the head of the criminal in question had no semblance whatever of the sense of feeling; that the eyes lost the power of vision; and, in fact, the head was perfectly dead to all intents and purposes.' (See John Laurence, *The History of Capital Punishment* (Secaucus, New Jersey, Citadel Press, 1960), p. 85). A somewhat similar but more gruesome idea ran in the mind of Lieutenant Anastay, a French murderer who was executed at the Roquette Prison, in Paris, in 1892. While in the condemned cell he demanded that doctors should be present at his execution, as he wished to communicate with them after death as to his subsequent experiences. This he had a firm faith that he would be able to do. His plan was that the doctors should ask questions of his decapitated head, to which he would reply by turning his eyes to the right for yes and to the left for no. No such experiment was tried, though Anastay asked on the scaffold if a doctor was present. 'I should be very glad to have the tests made,' were his last words on earth [ibid., p. 148]. Educated opinion now holds that decapitation – or the snapping of the spinal cord by hanging – probably results in immediate unconsciousness, even if death may take a little longer. My thanks to Brian Chapman for the latter references.

Mesmer Shepard, *Encyclopaedia of Occultism and Parapsychology* vol. 2, pp. 642–53, 872–5; EJ Dingwall (ed), *Abnormal Hypnotic Phenomena* (London, J. & A. Churchill, 1967) vol. 1 pp. 2–13, vol. 2 pp. 103–07.

The Fox sisters Shepard, *Encyclopaedia of Occultism and Parapsychology*, vol. 1 pp. 488–52; Alan Gauld, *Mediumship and Survival* (London, Heinemann, 1982) pp. 3–4; Joe Nickell, *Entities: Angels, Spirits, Demons and Other Alien Beings*, (Amherst, Prometheus Books, 1995) pp. 17–24. The ages of the Fox sisters are variously given as eleven and fourteen and eight and six, as well as the generally-preferred ten and seven. 'Splitfoot', incidentally, was an old nick-name for the Devil.

Spiritualism Spiritualism soon became an organised religion, with its own churches. Though closely related to Christianity, it does not admit that souls are either rewarded or punished in the afterlife, arguing that, instead, each soul is left to contemplate its own sins and omissions. Evil souls, particularly, may remain chained to earth for a while, but gradual enlightenment leads to an ascension to successively higher planes. Nevertheless, the spiritualists do not believe in a heaven as such. Shepard, *Encyclopaedia of Occultism and Parapsychology*, vol. 3 pp. 1264–82; Ruth Brandon, *The Spiritualists: the Passion for the Occult in the Nineteenth and Twentieth Centuries* (London, Weidenfeld & Nicholson, 1983); Janet Oppenheim, *The Other World: Spiritualism and Psychical Research in England* (Cambridge, Cambridge University Press, 1985).

'And so the next big step . . .' John Mulholland, *Beware Familiar Spirits*, cited in Nickell, *Entities* p. 19.

Oliver Lodge and the 'Raymond' sittings Oliver Lodge, *Raymond, or Life and Death, with Examples of the Evidence for Survival of Memory and Affection After Death* (London, Methuen, 1916); Renee Haynes, *The Society for Psychical Research 1882–1982: A History* (London, Macdonald, 1982) pp. 183–5.

Antecedents of spiritualism Max Sexton, 'Spiritualism, ancient and modern', *The Skeptic*, vol. 9, n. 5 (1995) p.19.

Spiritism Guy Lyon Playfair, *The Flying Cow: Research into Paranormal Phenomena in the World's Most Psychic Country* (London, Souvenir Press, 1975).

Madame Blavatsky James Webb, *The Flight from Reason*, vol. 1, *The Age of The Irrational* (London, Macdonald, 1971) pp. 44–65.

The age of the irrational Ibid. pp. 9–14.

The Society for Psychical Research Haynes *op. cit.*; Ivor Grattan-Guinness (ed.), *Psychical Research: A Guide to its Principles and Practices in Celebration of 100 Years of the Society for Psychical Research* (Wellingborough, Aquarian Press 1982).

Ectoplasm Some authorities state that ectoplasm was a linear descendent of the Mesmerists' 'magnetic fluids'. See Shepard, *Encyclopaedia of Occultism and Parapsychology*, m. pp. 384–8; Gauld, *Mediumship*, p. 4.

Harry Bastien Shepard, *Encyclopaedia of Occultism and Parapsychology*, vol. 1, p. 136.

Confession of the Fox sisters. Shepard, *Encyclopaedia of Occultism and Parapsychology*, vol. 1, pp. 491–2; Nickell, *Entities*, pp. 21–4. It is only fair to point out that the Fox case is still the subject of considerable controversy in spiritualistic circles. Within a year of the exposure, Maggie had retracted her statement and gone back to being a medium; it has been suggested that the 'confessions' were simply the act of two impoverished, and (by now) alcoholic women desperate to earn money from the expose. It has also been argued that some, at least, of the sisters' performances would be difficult to explain as trickery; and it seems incontrovertible that a human skeleton, together with a tin box of the sort carried by peddlers, was indeed discovered buried in the cellar of the house of Hydesville, just as the girls had predicted.

Ectoplasm Shepard, *Encyclopaedia of Occultism and Parapsychology*, vol. 1, pp. 384–8, vol. 3, p. 419; Hilary Evans, *Visions, Apparitions, Alien Visitors* (Wellingborough, Aquarian Press, 1984) pp. 231–2; Kevin Jones, *Conan Doyle and the Spirits: The Spiritualist Career of Sir Arthur Conan Doyle* (Wellingborough, Aquarian Press, 1989) pp. 139–45. It is worth noting both the bizarre and quasi-sexual content of Crawford's experiments, which involved insisting that twenty-year-old Kathleen change into clean stockings and knickers before a seance and conducting a minute inspection of her thighs and the fabric of her underwear – while she was still wearing it – for stains afterwards (the investigator eventually concluded that the ectoplasmic rods were materialising from her vagina), and that Frau Vollhardt figured in court proceedings after being caught in apparent fraud during a seance in the 1920s. Furthermore, Crawford is alleged to have confessed to Eric Dingwall that his results were faked. See Susan Blackmore, *In Search of the Light: The Adventures of a Parapsychologist* (Amherst, Prometheus Books, 1996) p. 211.

Kluski Shepard, *Encyclopaedia of Occultism and Parapsychology*, vol. 2, p. 726.

Super-ESP Gauld, *Mediumship*, pp. 119–46.

The cross-correspondences H.F. Saltmarsh, *Evidence of Personal Survival from Cross-Correspondences* (London, G. Bell & Sons, 1938).

Book tests Gauld, *Mediumship*, pp. 47–9.

New Age psychics 'who channel the disencarnate spirits of ancient Atlantaens . . .' The psychic in question, a celebrated American channeller named J.Z. Knight, was recently involved in an entertaining law case brought by a German rival, Julie Ravel, who claimed exclusive rights to Ramtha, the 35,000-year-old spirit in question. An Austrian judge ruled that Ravel had infringed Knight's copyright, a landmark ruling where supposedly independent and certainly disencarnate intelligences are concerned. 'Ancient Egyptian in custody battle', *Fortean Times*, 81

(Jun–Jul 1995) p. 7; 'Fortean follow-ups', *Fortean Times*, 102 (Sept 1997), p. 16.

Barbie 'Lawyers gag Barbie', *Fortean Times*, 78 (Dec 1994–Jan 1995) p. 7.

Martian mediums Hilary Evans, 'Talking with Martians', *Fortean Times*, 76 (Aug–Sept 1994) pp. 22–7.

Broad categories of ESP These categories were first defined by the parapsychologist Louisa Rhine in the 1950s. In cases of apparent telepathy and clairvoyance, waking intuition is the most common form of experience; cases of precognition most commonly feature realistic dreams. Leonard George, *Alternative Realities: The Paranormal, the Mystic and the Transcendent in Human Experience* (New York, Facts on File, 1995) pp. 86–91.

Rosalind Heywood Renee Haynes, *The Seeing Eye, the Seeing I* (London, Hutchinson, 1976) p. 208.

The lost watch Myers cited in Grattan-Guinness, *Psychical Research*, p. 102.

Telepathy within families Berthold Schwarz, *Parent–Child Telepathy* (New York, Doubleday 1971).

Precognition of racing winners Kilbracken cited in Danah Zohar, *Through the Time Barrier: A Study of Precognition and Modern Physics* (London, Heinemann, 1982) pp. 41–3.

Premonitions of Aberfan Ibid. pp. 38–41.

Cox's rail statistics Ibid. p. 36.

Barker's psychic bureaux Ibid. pp. 40–1.

The No-War Prophecies Kevin McClure, 'The 1939 no-war prophecies', *Common Ground*, 6 (nd *c.* Sept 1982) pp. 14–18; Sid Birchby, 'The Falklands war – why weren't we told?' *Common Ground*, 7 (nd *c.* Jan 1983) pp. 11–12.

End of the world prophecies Kevin McClure, *The Fortean Times Book of the Millennium* (London, John Brown, 1996).

Stanislawa Tomczyk Shepard, *Encyclopaedia of Occultism*, vol. 3 pp. 1366–7.

Alexei Frenkel Mike Dash, 'From our files: Russia', *Fortean Times*, 53 (winter 1989) p. 22; 'Healer, heal thyself', *Fortean Times*, 56 (winter 1990) p. 18. A similar incident was reported from China three years later: a man named Wei, a practitioner of the mystical art of *qi gong*, was run over by a twenty-eight-car freight train near Shanghai while attempting to prove his psychokinetic powers to his mother. 'Blood on the tracks', *Fortean Times*, 66 (Dec 1992–Jan 1993) p. 15.

Ninel Kulagina Joe Nickell, *Missing Pieces: How to Investigate Ghosts, UFOs, Psychics and Other Mysteries* (Buffalo, Prometheus Books, 1992) pp. 175-6.

McDonnell laboratory case Ibid. pp. 176–7.

J.B. Rhine Grattan-Guinness, *Psychical Research*, pp. 51–3, 162–3; Nickell, *Missing Pieces*, pp. 57–8, 161–2.

Samuel Soal His technique was to change ones into fours. Zohar, *Precognition*, pp. 66-9; Blackmore, *Adventures of a Parapsychologist*, pp. 116–8.

'Such displacement of ESP . . .' Martin Gardner, *Fads and Fallacies in the Name of Science* (New York, Dover Publications, 1957) p. 304.

Rat tests Zohar, *Precognition* pp. 87–8.

The Ganzfeld Susan Blackmore, 'A report of a visit to Carl Sargent's laboratory', *Journal of the Society for Psychical Research*, vol. 54, n. 808 (Jul 1987) pp. 186–98; Trevor Harley and Gerald Matthews, 'Cheating, psi and the appliance of science: a reply to Blackmore', ibid. pp. 199–207; Carl Sargent, 'Sceptical fairytales from Bristol', ibid. pp. 208–18; Adrian Parker & Nils Wiklund, 'The Ganzfeld experiments: towards an assessment', *Journal of the Society for Psychical Research*, vol. 54, n. 809 (October 1987) pp. 261–5; Blackmore, *The Adventures of a Parapsychologist* (Buffalo, Prometheus Books) pp. 99–107, 129–30, 246–59.

Child psi Blackmore, *Adventures* pp. 72-89; Susan Blackmore, 'ESP in young children: a critique of the Spinelli evidence', *Journal of the Society for Psychical Research*, vol. 52, n797 (Jun 1984) pp. 311–15; Zohar, *Precognition*, pp. 99–100. The 'vestigial psi' theory, incidentally, was first propounded by Sigmund Freud.

Out of the body experiences George, *Alternative Realities*, pp. 204–18; Susan Blackmore, *Beyond the Body: an Investigation of the Out-of-the-Body Experience* (London, Heinemann, 1982); Blackmore, *Adventures* pp. 168–71.

Remote viewing Russell Targ and Harold Puthoff, *Mind-Reach: Scientists Look at Psychic Ability* (London, Jonathan Cape, 1977); Various, 'Reports on government-sponsored remote viewing programmes', *Journal of Scientific Exploration*, vol. 10, n. 1 (1996) pp. 1–110; Ray Hyman, 'Evaluation of the Military's Twenty-Year Program on Psychic Spying', *Skeptical Inquirer*, Mar/Apr 1996, pp. 21–4 and 'The evidence for psychic functioning: claims vs. reality', ibid. pp. 24–7; Bob Rickard, 'Psi spy – watching us watching them: SRI, CIA, NSA, DIA and ESP', *Fortean Times*, 87 (Jul 1996) pp. 28–30.

'*An exciting programme of defence-related ESP studies*'. See S. Ostrander and L. Schroeder, *Psychic Discoveries Behind the Iron Curtain* (Eaglewood Cliffs, New Jersey, Prentice Hall, 1970).

Near death experiences Susan Blackmore, *Dying to Live* (Buffalo, Prometheus Books, 1993); Kenneth Ring, *Life at Death: a Scientific Investigation of the Near-Death Experience* (New York, Quill, 1982); William Barrett, *Death-Bed Visions: The Psychical Experiences of the Dying* (Wellingborough, Aquarian Press, 1986); Karl Jansen, 'Using ketamine to induce the near-death experience', *Jahrbuch fur Ethnomedicin*, 1995, pp. 55–79; George, *Alternative Realities*, pp. 105–07, Robert Baker, 'A classic work on the nature of death', *Skeptical Inquirer*, vol. 18, n 5 (fall 1994) pp. 524–8.

Reincarnation Jeffrey Iverson, *More Lives than One? The Evidence of the Remarkable Bloxham Tapes* (London, Souvenir Press, 1976); Ian Stevenson, 20 *Cases Suggestive of Reincarnation* (Charlottesville, University Press of Virginia, 1992); Ian Wilson, *Mind Out of Time? Reincarnation Claims Investigated* (London, Victor Gollancz, 1981); George, *Alternative Realities*, pp. 242–5; Leonard Angel, 'Empirical evidence for reincarnation? Re-examining Stevenson's "most impressive" case', *Skeptical Inquirer*, vol.

18, n 5 (fall 1994) pp. 481–7; Roy Stemman, *Reincarnation International Yearbook 1996* (London, Reincarnation International Ltd); Paul Edwards, *Reincarnation: A Critical Examination* (Amherst, Prometheus Books, 1996).

Ghosts Celia Green and Charles McCreery, *Apparitions* (London, Hamish Hamilton, 1975); Andrew MacKenzie, *Hauntings and Apparitions* (London, Heinemann, 1982); Nickell, *Entities*, pp. 39–77.

Lancaster castle hauntings Neale Mounsey, 'Spirits behind bars', *Fortean Times*, 92 (Nov 1996) pp. 34–6.

Tower of London cylinder Notes & Queries, 1860.

Faces of Belmez 'The faces of Belmez return', *Fortean Times*, 83 (Oct–Nov 1995) p. 13.

'Stone tape' theory C.D. Broad, *Lectures on Psychical Research* (London, Routledge and Kegan Paul 1962) p. 137.

Cheltenham case MacKenzie, op. cit. pp. 40–64.

McConnel case Ibid. pp. 22–4.

Animal ghosts Shepard, *Encyclopaedia of Occultism*, vol. 1, p. 53.

Chinese ghosts Ibid. pp. 226–30.

Japanese ghosts Carmen Blacker, 'The angry ghost in Japan', in H.R.E. Davidson and W.M.S. Russell, (eds), *The Folklore of Ghosts* (Cambridge, D.S. Brewer, 1982) pp. 95–108.

West Indian ghosts Venetia Newell, 'West Indian ghosts' in Ibid. pp. 73–94.

Charlottenburg case Alan Gauld and A.D. Cornell, *Poltergeists* (London, Routledge & Kegan Paul, 1979) pp. 148–57.

Distinctions between ghosts and poltergeists ibid. pp. 176–223.

Poltergeist assaults & the case of Eleonora Zugun Ibid. pp. 116–42.

Bristol poltergeist case Blackmore, *Adventures of a Parapsychologist*, pp. 195–99, 202–07.

4 Alien Universe

Maine UFO incident Brent Raynes, 'The twilight side of a UFO encounter', *Flying Saucer Review* vol. 22 n. 2 (July 1976) pp. 11–4; also Shirley Fickett, 'The Maine UFO encounter: investigation under hypnosis' and Berthold Schwarz, 'Comments on the psychiatric-paranormal aspects of the Maine case' in ibid. The witnesses went under pseudonyms at the time, but their real names are given by Jerome Clark in *The UFO Encyclopaedia: High Strangeness: UFOs from 1960 Through 1979* (Detroit, Omnigraphics, 1996) pp. 357–63. The Maine case has not been subjected to much sceptical scrutiny but there does not seem to be any suggestion that it was a hoax. A sceptic would probably suspect that the experience was the product of two fantasy-prone personalities feeding off each other (see chapter 10); and even the most wide-eyed believer would have difficulty in suggesting that the entire experience was literally true.

Earlier reports Jerome Clark, *The UFO Encyclopaedia: The Emergence of a Phenomenon: UFOs from the Beginning Through 1959* (Detroit,

Omnigraphics, 1992) pp. 61–2. Perhaps the ships were supposed to come from the fairy realms. At any rate, the intention seems to have been to show that they were so much lighter than air that the lower reaches of the sky was their equivalent of the sea – and perhaps as dangerous. In another sky-ship story, set in Ireland in AD 956, a crewman swam down from a ship that appeared over Teltown. When he was seized by the people on the ground, he begged to be released, saying 'I am being drowned.' If not outright inventions, the references to sky-sailors and flying ships nevertheless appear hard to explain. Sky-ships continued to be seen until at least the 1640s. On Magonia, see Jaques Vallee, *Passport to Magonia: From Folklore to Flying Saucers* (London, Tandem, 1975); Jean-Louis Brodu, 'Magonia: a re-evaluation', *Fortean Studies*, 2 (London, John Brown, 1995) pp. 198–215.

The first UFO report is sometimes said to have occurred during the reign of the great pharaoh Thuthmosis III, the 'Napoleon of Egypt', who ruled 1479 to 1447 BC. In 1457 BC, according to a papyrus once supposed to have been in the Vatican Egyptian Museum, 'the scribes in the House of Life found there was a circle of fire coming in the sky . . . It had no head, the breath of its mouth had a foul odour, its body was one rod [16 and-a-half feet] long and one rod wide.' A few days later, 'these things became more numerous in the sky than ever. They shone more in the sky than the brightness of the sun, and extended to the limits of the four supports of the heavens.' *Doubt* 41 (1953) The papyrus is supposed to have been sold after the death of its owner, and is now lost; the report was identified as a possible hoax by the US Air Force-sponsored University of Colorado UFO project. Edward Condon (ed), *Scientific Study of Unidentified Flying Objects* (New York, Bantam Books, 1969) pp. 497–500.

Odd clouds over France J.B. Delair, 'UFOs, clouds & pseudo-planes', *Fortean Times*, 24 (winter 1977) pp. 42–6.

Lady of the Lake, Mr X, 'A UFO from 1872?', *INFO Journal*, 59 (Mar 1990) p. 23.

Oklahoma sky serpent 'The family that has archetypal visions together . . .', *Strange Magazine*, 6 (1990) p. 5. The chief witness, a man named Nahu, linked the sighting to Aztec and Native American tales of flying serpents and, following Jung, suggested it was an 'archetypal experience'.

Japanese 'jellyfish creature' 'Jellyfish mutilations', *Strange Magazine*, 14 (fall 1994) p. 38, citing *Japanese Space Phenomena Society UFO Information*, spring 1992. It sounds as though this incident, which occurred in Kinryuu, Saga Prefecture, may have been caused by ball lighting.

Crawfordsville sky serpent Vincent Gaddis, *Mysterious Fires and Lights* (Garberville, California, Borderland Sciences, 1994) pp. 25–6.

Early airships The first powered flight was made by Frenchman, Henri Giffard, in 1852, using a steam airship equipped with a 3 hp engine. L.T.C. Rolt, *The Aeronauts* (Brunswick, Alan Sutton, 1985) pp. 208–11.

Anomalous airship sightings One of the principal peculiarities of the pre-1947 UFO waves is the way in which the objects that are reported are always a little ahead of the technology of the day. It is not surprising, therefore, to discover that the airship wave of 1896–97 was preceded by a series of reports of mysterious balloons seen over Canada, and that these balloons subsequently reappeared over Poland. There were also a handful of earlier airship reports, the first of which may have appeared in the *Santa Fe Weekly New Mexican* of 29 March 1890. It described an incident that had occurred on 26 March at Galisteo Junction, New Mexico, when three men on an evening stroll heard loud voices and the sounds of music coming from a 'large balloon' shaped like a fish which was drifting over from the west. Though they saw no engines, the men were sure that the balloon was fully under the control of its eight to ten occupants who, as they passed overhead, threw a number of objects out of their passenger car. One proved to be a flower accompanied by a piece of silk-like paper on which Chinese characters had been painted. A few days later, a wealthy young Chinese man who was visiting the district recognised this as a note from his fiancee, who was flying from China to New York on what was hoped to be the maiden voyage of a regular aerial service. The young man left by train for New York and a reunion; to the best of our knowledge, neither he nor the airship ever arrived in the city. This was a few years after the first tentative experiments with dirigibles (which were prominently in the public eye in this period), but the Chinese had no such advanced craft flying at that time.

The 1896–97 airship wave is probably the best-investigated of all historical anomalies. The files of almost 1500 newspapers from across the United States have been combed for reports, an astonishing feat of research. The general conclusion of investigators was that a considerable number of the simpler sightings were misidentifications of planets and stars, and a large number of the more complex the result of hoaxes and practical jokes. A small residuum remains perplexing. Clark, *The Emergence of a Phenomenon*, pp. 17–39; Brookesmith, *UFOs: the Complete Sightings Catalogue* (London, Blandford, 1995), pp. 22–3.

Sacramento sighting Clark and Brookesmith, passim. The incident occured at about seven p.m., and San Francisco is only seventy miles from Sacramento, suggesting that the airship was moving at the rather startling speed of just over four miles per hour. Should the airship wave really be linked to extraterrestrial visitations, it is interesting to speculate on the problems such a limited performance would pose for would-be intergalactic travellers.

Other airship waves Cf. Carl Grove, 'The airship wave of 1909' *Flying Saucer Review*, vol. 16, n. 6 (Nov–Dec 1970) pp. 9–11, vol. 13 n. 1 (Jan–Feb 1971) pp. 17–19; Willy Wegner, 'The Danish airship of 1908', *Metempirical UFO Bulletin*, NS9 (winter, 1977–8) pp. 11–12; Joseph Trainor, 'The New England airship invasion of 1909', *Fortean Studies*, 1 pp. 59–70; Nigel Watson, 'Airships & invaders: background to a social panic', *Magonia*, 3 (spring 1980) pp. 2–7, 'UFOs 1900–1946' in Clark, *The Emergence of a Phenomenon* pp. 361–83, among many other sources. There were also isolated sightings of 'airships' and 'cloud cigars' throughout the period 1897–1914 in the United States and several other countries.

Foo fighters Loren E. Gross, *Charles Fort, the Fortean Society and Unidentified*

Flying Objects (Fremont, the Author, 1976). From a catchphrase in an American comic strip, 'Where there's foo, there's fire'. Not all foo fighters were simply lights. Some of them appeared to be metallic and resembled the 'flying saucers' that would begin to be reported in 1947. However, no evidence has ever emerged to suggest that either the Allies or the Axis had anything to do with the foos. Conventional explanations have included St Elmo's fire and reflections from light crystals. Oddly, particularly given the prevalence of airship sightings immediately before it, there seem to have been virtually no UFO experiences during World War I.

Ghost fliers Ole Jonny Braenne, 'The Norwegian 'ghost fliers' of 1933–37'. *INFO Journal*, 73 (summer 1995) pp. 6–11 is based on 1400 pages of reports from the archives of the Royal Norwegian Air Force and Royal Norwegian Defence Department, and effectively replaces a series of earlier and less critical articles on the subject by John Keel, which appeared in *Flying Saucer Review* in the early 1970s. Braenne believes that most of the cases in the archives are attributable to misidentification of stars and planets, and some to sightings of genuine Norwegian-built aircraft.

Ghost rockets Anders Liljegren and Clas Svahn, 'The ghost rockets' in Hilary Evans and John Spencer, (eds), *UFOs 1947–1987: the Forty Year Search for an Explanation* (London, Fortean Tomes, 1987); 'Ghost rockets' in Clark, *The Emergence of a Phenomenon*, pp. 168–76. There have been a few ghost rocket reports since the 1940s. In 1984, two rockets trailing pink, red, yellow and green glowing smoke appeared over Andros Island in the Bahamas. *Strange*, 11 (spring–summer 1993) p. 39.

Arnold sighting Kenneth Arnold, 'What happened on 24 June 1947?' in Hilary Evans and Dennis Stacy (eds), *UFOs 1947–1997* (London, John Brown, 1997) pp. 25-32, Clark, *The Emergence of a Phenomenon*, pp. 216–19. The sighting has been been explained by sceptics as blasts of snow blown from the tops of ridges; clouds; and suspended water droplets in the air, but each of these explanations has been refuted. Arnold did not claim he had seen space-ships, and after several years of active part-time investigation eventually concluded that UFOs were 'living organisms in the atmosphere'.

One problem that emerges from Arnold's estimates of speed and distance is that the objects appeared to have been more than 100 miles away from him when they came into view, but seemed smaller than a DC-4 airliner. It seems unlikely that objects of such a size would be visible from so great a distance, however bright they were. Either Arnold's estimate of speed or his estimate of distance must have been wrong.

Green fireballs The reports began in December 1947 and persisted into July 1948. Loren Gross, *UFOs: A History*, vols 1 and 2 (Fremont, the Author, 1982)

Why 1947? On various aspects of this question, see the special issue of 'Why 1947? The coming of the UFOs', *Common Ground*, 10 (1983). On invasion cinema see Nigel Watson. 'The day the flying saucers invaded the cinema' in Evans and Spencer *UFOs: The 40-year search*, pp. 333–37.

Origin of the term 'flying saucers' The phrase which became so closely associated with the UFO mystery did not, as is commonly supposed, originate with newspaper coverage of the Arnold sighting, though it came into use shortly afterwards as an attention-gratting headline description for the objects that were being seen. The description 'saucer' had in fact been first applied to an aerial anomaly as early as January 1878. Clark *The Emergence of Phenomenon*, pp. 218 and 357.

Formation of civilian UFO groups Curtis Peebles, *Watch the Skies! a Chronicle of the Flying Saucer Myth* (Washington DC: Smithsonian Institution Press 1994).

'Trained witnesses' such as airline pilots ... It has nevertheless been argued that pilots are no more trained to observe UFOs than anyone else and, while perhaps more reluctant to report UFOs than most, for fear of ridicule, are equally likely to be taken in by unusual mirages and the like.

Mantell Edward Condon, *Scientific Study of Unidentified Flying Objects* (New York, Bantam Books, 1969) pp. 504–05; Steuart Campbell, *The UFO Mystery Solved* (Edinburgh, Expliot Books 1994) pp. 74-5 suggests the object was probably a mirage of Jupiter.

Coyne helicopter case Jennie Zeidman, 'UFO-helicopter close encounter over Ohio', *Flying Saucer Review*, vol. 22, n. 4 (Nov 1976) pp. 15–19; Zeidman, 'More on the Coyne helicopter case', *Flying Saucer Review*, vol. 23, n. 4 (Jan 1978) pp. 16–18; Jerome Clark, *The UFO Encyclopaedia: High Strangeness: UFOs from 1960 Through 1979* (Detroit, Omnigraphics, 1996) pp. 121–6.

Manchester case Harvey Elliott, 'UFO 'buzzed' airliner at Manchester airport', *The Times*, 2 Feb 1996; Independent Joint Airmiss Working Group, commercial air transport airmiss report no. 2/95. Ufologist Jenny Randles has suggested that the object was a meteorite.

McMinville photos Clark *High Strangeness* pp. 238–40.

Trindade Island photos; Willy Smith, 'UFOs in Latin America' in Evans and Spencer, *UFOs: the 40-Year Search*, pp. 109–11. Although some critics, such as Donald Menzel, have suggested that Barauna was himself a UFO photo hoaxer, it seems he had merely intervened in an earlier dispute to show how a photograph *could* have been hoaxed. There also appears to have been a fifth Trindade photograph, taken by a sergeant of the island's garrison some time prior to Barauna's sighting, which has never been published, but which formed part of a dossier the Brazilian navy compiled on the case.

Close encounters Part of the system for classifying UFO reports developed by J. Allen Hynek, an astronomer who moved from being a consultant to the United States Air Force's Project Blue Book to the founder and director of the Center for UFO Studies. In Hynek's system, UFO reports are divided into [1] Nocturnal lights, [2] Daylight discs, [3] Radar/visual cases, in which a UFO seen by witnesses on the ground or in the air is also detected on radar, and [4-6] close encounters of the first, second and third kinds. Some later ufologists have suggested adding two further categories, close encounters of the fourth and fifth kinds (abductions, and encounters mentally initiated by humans or that have other parapsychological elements), but these additions have not been generally accepted. J. Allen

Hynek, *The UFO Experience: A Scientific Enquiry* (London, Corgi Books, 1974) pp. 54–206.

Lakenheath-Bentwaters radar-visual case Clark, *The Emergence of a Phenomenon*, pp. 225–7; Philip Klass, *UFOs Explained* (New York, Random House, 1974) pp. 175–233; Ronald Story, *UFOs and the Limits of Science*, (London, New English Library, 1981) pp. 124–9. Martin Shough, 'Radar and the UFO' in Evans and Spencer, *UFOs: the 40-Year Search*, pp. 217–26. Condon, *Scientific Study*, pp. 163–4.

Vehicle interference reports Mark Rodeghier, *UFO Reports Involving Vehicle Interference: A Catalogue and Data Analysis* (Evanston, Illinois, Center for UFO Studies, 1981); Clark *The Emergence of a Phenomenon*, pp. 228–9;

Delphos physical trace case Story, *UFOs and the Limits of Science*, pp. 77–82; Kim Hansen, 'UFO casebook' in Evans and Spencer, *UFOs: the 40-Year Search*, pp. 79–82; Michael Swords and Erol Frank, 'Research note: Delphos, Kansas, soil analysis', *Journal for UFO Studies*, NS 3 (1991) pp. 115–38; Clark, *High Strangeness*, pp. 148–51.

Another problem with physical trace cases is the number of occasions on which traces have been reported despite there being no apparent connection to an actual UFO sighting. See Bill Chalker, 'Physical traces' in Evans and Spencer, *UFOs: the 40-Year Search*, pp. 182–99.

Cash-Landrum CE2 Jerome Clark, *UFOs in the 1980s* (Detroit, Apogee Books, 1990) pp. 43–6; Peter Brookesmith, *UFO: the Government Files* (London, Blandford, 1996) p. 86.

Dundy County UFO crash Jerome Clark, 'Spaceship and saltshaker', *International UFO Reporter* vol. 11, n. 6 (Nov–Dec 1986) pp. 12 and 21.

New Mexico UFO crash Clark, *Emergence of a Phenomenon*, pp. 300–03. The Aztec, New Mexico crash case still reappears periodically as a true story, most recently as the subject of William Steinman's and Wendelle Stevens's *UFO Crash at Aztec* (Tuscon, UFO Photo Archives, 1987).

Stringfield's crash-retrieval research Leonard Stringfield, 'Retrievals of the Third Kind part 1', *Flying Saucer Review*, vol. 25, n. 4 (Jul – Aug 1979) pp. 13–20; 'part 2, *FSR* vol. 25, n. 5 (Sep–Oct 1979) pp. 6–12; 'The UFO crash/retrieval syndrome: status report II, part I' FSR vol. 28, n. 2 (Nov 1982) pp. 3–8; 'part I continued', *FSR* vol. 28, n. 3 (Jan 1983) pp. 6–15; 'The UFO crash/retrieval syndrome: Status report II: new sources, new data', *FSR* vol. 28, n. 4 (Mar 1983); 'The UFO crash-retrieval syndrome', *FSR* vol. 28, n. 5 (Jun 1983) pp. 9–12; 'UFO Crash/retrievals status report III: amassing the evidence' (Cincinatti, the Author, 1983).

The Roswell Incident Among the plethora of sources on this much-discussed event are Kevin Randle and Don Schmitt, *UFO Crash At Rowell* (New York, Avon Books, 1991) and *The Truth About the UFO Crash at Roswell* (New York, Avon Books 1994); Jenny Randles, *UFO Retrievals* (London, Blandford, 1995) pp. 31–55; *Skeptics UFO Newsletter*, Jan 1995; *Saucer Smear* vol. 43, n. 5 (1 Jun 1996); William Barrett, 'Now where was it that UFO crashed?' in Joe McNally and James Wallis (eds), *Weird Year 1996* (London, John Brown, 1996) pp. 64–70; and Brookesmith, *Government Files*, pp. 146–63.

Estimate of the Situation Brookesmith, *Government Files*, pp. 27–8. Not only did the Air Force decline to accept the conclusion of Project Sign's Estimate of the Situation; it replaced it with Project Grudge, manned on the whole by more sceptical investigators.

CIA panel Brookesmith, *Government Files*, pp. 73–92.

Royal Air Force investigation Timothy Good, *Beyond Top Secret: the Worldwide UFO Cover-Up* (London, Sidgwick & Jackson, 1987) p. 42. Again, officialdom insisted that a cover-up existed only in the ufologists' own minds, 'About 90% of the reports have been found to relate to meteors, balloons, flares and many other objects,' the Under Secretary of State for Air told the House of Commons. 'The fact that the other 10% are unexplained need be attributed to nothing more sinister than lack of data.'

Stoljarov committee Ion Hobana and Julien Weverbergh, *UFOs From Behind the Iron Curtain* (New York, Bantam Books, 1975) pp. 33–5; Gordon Creighton, 'Dr Felix Zigel' and the development of ufology in Russia: part I', *Flying Saucer Review* vol. 27, n. 3 (November 1981) pp. 8–13.

'Mr Wilson' Wallace Chariton, *The Great Texas Airship Mystery* (Plano, Texas, Wordware Publishing, 1991) pp. 182–89.

Hopkins encounter Jerome Clark, *The Emergence of a Phenomenon*, pp. 33 and 35. Although Hopkins's careful choice of the phrase 'my imagination' sounds ominous to any sceptic aware of the prevalence of hoaxing during the airship wave, Clark suggests that the encounter may have been an hallucinatory or visionary experience, and draws a parallel with a 1950 contactee case that involved a meeting with nude Venusians.

Greek CE3 Strange Magazine, 13 (Spring 1994) pp. 28 and 50.

More exotic encounters It must also be noted that by the early 1950s, still more spectacular claims were being made of meetings with UFO occupants. These reports came from a new breed of witness, the contactee. They were the first to involve humans actually boarding flying saucers. Among those who did so – and there were nearly a dozen of them in all – the best-known was George Adamski. At least eight prominent claimants emerged in America during the 1950s: George Adamski, Orfeo Angelucci, Truman Bethurum, Daniel Fry, Howard Menger, George Van Tassel, George King and Buck Nelson. Their accounts tended to be light on evidence but heavy on philosophy and mysticism, and to contain many of the features that remain common in New Age circles. King, indeed, founded his own saucer religion, the Aetherius Society, which continues to attract converts even today. Some of his fellow contactees were less ambitious. Nelson hawked bags of hair that he said came from a 385-pound Venusian St Bernard dog.

UFO historian David Jacobs identified an interesting pattern in the stories of successive contactees – each claiming a closer encounter, or enjoying a more spectacular journey into space, than his predecessor, while also insisting that his first meeting with the space brothers had occurred earlier than anyone else's. Not surprisingly, Jacobs surmised that the contactees were inventing, or at best elaborating, their claims in an attempt to enhance their own importance. Jacobs, *The UFO Controversy in America* (Bloomington, Indiana University Press, 1975) pp. 103–04.

Although the contactees began to claim frequent encounters with benign space people from the early 1950s (one, the South African Elizabeth Klarer, even reporting that she had been seduced by a handsome saucer pilot named Akon, by whom she had a child), UFO occupants did not begin to feature heavily in other sighting reports until the 1960s.

Close encounters of the third kind in the 1950s In fact, probably the best of the more credible early close encounters took place not in the United States, or even Europe, but in Papua New Guinea.

The New Guinea incident occurred during an intense local UFO wave. On 26 June 1959, an Anglican missionary, Father William Gill, went outside to gaze into the early evening sky. Above him he saw the planet Venus, shining brightly, but to his surprise there was a second, still more brilliant light above it, which sparkled and then began to descend towards him. After a few moments, Gill called two of his staff out to join him, and before long the rest of the people at the mission came out to stare into the sky, bringing the total number of witnesses to thirty-eight. As it approached, the light grew in size, so that it appeared to be about twice the size of a man's fist held at arm's length, and the people on the ground made out a circular object with a wide, thick base and a narrower upper 'deck'. Two pairs of struts projected downwards from the base, while a bright shaft of blue light flashed on at intervals, darting upwards into the sky at an angle of forty-five degrees. Most remarkably of all, Gill and his companions could dimly make out several apparently human figures standing in the open on top of the upper deck, illuminated by a soft glow that completely surrounded the craft.

The sighting on that remarkable evening lasted for about three-and-a-half hours. During that time, the figures on the upper deck went back into the craft and re-emerged on several occasions, and the craft itself floated around the sky, sometimes appearing below the clouds and at other times disappearing into them. It did not finally vanish until about 9.30 p.m. when the witnesses saw it change colour and suddenly pick up speed, darting off to the west.

The initial sighting was remarkable enough, but what followed was almost unprecedented. The peculiar object returned the next evening at about the same time, this time accompanied by two other lights. Once again, figures could be seen moving about on top of the craft. More in hope than anything, Gill waved at them . . . and the strangers waved back. One of the mission people followed Gill's lead, waving both his arms over his head; two of the figures on the object did likewise. Eventually all four of the figures on the craft began waving at the little group outside the mission.

Father Gill sent for a torch and flashed a series of long Morse dashes at the object in the sky. After a few moments, the object began to sway from side to side, apparently in answer. It seemed to be coming closer, and some of those on the ground wondered if it was preparing to land. In fact, the contact was almost over. As Gill reported, 'After a further two or three minutes, the figures apparently lost interest in us, for they disappeared below deck.' Eventually (and rather remarkably, perhaps), Gill and his companions grew so blase about their guest that they went back into the mission for dinner, and then to Evensong. When they emerged at about 8 p.m. the sky had clouded over and their visitor had gone.

The importance of the New Guinea case lies not just in its witnesses – though the figure remains a record for any close encounter – and the apparent probity of its principal, but also in its resistance to debunking. Menzel, the first critic to attack it, invoked his mirage hypothesis to suggest that the object was the planet Venus; yet Gill was quite specific that Venus was visible in the night sky below the object when it appeared, and that the craft appeared below the layers of clouds that swept over the mission later on that evening. A brightly-lit squid boat on a false horizon or a mirage of the planet Mercury have also been suggested as an explanation. Such theories do have a certain attractiveness; for example, the distortions that a mirage creates could explain why the object appeared to be much thicker than most UFOs, and the unusual duration of the sightings appears consistent with the misidentification of celestial bodies. Yet the mirage hypothesis cannot explain how so many witnesses were sure they had seen figures on the upper deck, and the idea that the UFO was really a squid boat requires a spectacular misidentification of a relatively familiar and nearby object.

To accept that Gill and his companions saw a genuinely unidentified flying object, though, raises a number of interesting questions. Why did the sighting last for so long – or, to put the question another way, why are most other sightings so brief? Why was the missionary's description of the craft, with its 'landing struts', its apparently human figures waving from an open upper deck, and its flashing blue searchlight, so different from almost every other UFO report? If Gill is telling the truth, are other witnesses lying, or are there simply many different sorts of UFOs, and occupants? Jerome Clark, 'Close encounters: history's best case', *Fate* Feb 1978, pp. 38–46. For analysis, see Kim Hasen, 'UFO casebook', in Evans and Spencer, *UFOs: the 40-Year Search*, pp. 59–62; Steuart Campbell. *The UFO Mystery Solved* (Edinburgh, Explicit Books, 1994) pp. 66–8; Martin Kottmeyer, 'Gill again', *Magonia*, 54 (Nov 1995) pp. 11–14.

Kelly-Hopkinsville CE3 Isabel Davis and Ted Bloecher, *Close Encounter at Kelly and Others of 1955* (Evanston, Illinois, Center for UFO Studies 1955).

Bebedouro abduction Clark, *High Strangeness*, pp. 44–9.

Genoa encounter Luciano Boccono, 'Italian night watchman kidnapped by UFO', *Flying Saucer Review*, vol. 26, n. 1 (spring 1980) pp. 4–9.

Problems with occupant reports Frederick Malmstrom and Richard Coffman, 'Humanoids reported in UFOs, religion and folktales: human bias towards human life forms?' in Richard Haines (ed), *UFO Phenomena and the Behavioural Scientist* (Metuchen, New Jersey, Scarecrow Press, 1979) pp. 60–88; Patrick Huyghe, *A Field Guide to Extraterrestrials* (New York, Avon Books, 1996), esp. pp. 122–32.

Number of UFO sightings Hilary Evans, 'A global phenomenon' in Evans and Spencer, *UFOs: the 40-Year Search*, 7.

Intelligent 'super-bees' Cited in Peebles op.cit. p. 90.

Other alien home planets Clark, *High Strangeness*, pp. 245–6, 307–11.

Donald Menzel Remarkably, the name of this arch-sceptic appears on the list of members of the US government's supposed top secret Majestic 12 committee – the group that many ufologists suspect is organising a deliberate cover-up of the fact that America has at least one crashed flying saucer locked away in a secret research facility (see chapter 11). For Menzel's career and theories, see Clark, *Emergence of a Phenomenon*, pp. 158–62; Condon *Scientific Study*, pp. 15, 33, 556–7. For his sighting, see Donald Menzel and Lyle Boyd, *The World of Flying Saucers* (New York, Doubleday, 1963) pp. 60–2 and Campbell *UFO Mystery Solved*, esp. pp. 61–4. Campbell challenges Menzel's identification of the object as Sirius and suggests that it was probably Saturn.

US Navy transport case Philip Klass, *UFOs Explained* (New York, Random House, 1974) p. 52.

La Rubia encounter Huyghe, *Field Guide*, pp. 108–09.

Jean Hingley Albert Budden, 'The mince-pie Martians: the Rolwey Regis Case', *Fortean Times*, 50 (summer 1988) pp. 40–4.

Watson on high strangeness cases Nigel Watson, *Portraits of Alien Encounters* (London, Valis Books, 1990) pp. 146–7.

The men in black. One of the arguments against taking the MIB seriously was that the first man to receive a visit from them appears to have been a practical joker named Harold Dahl, one of the two men responsible for the 'Maury Island caper' of 1947 – the first modern UFO hoax. Kenneth Arnold helped to investigate this incident, which actually happened the day before his own sighting over Mount Rainier, though it was not reported until afterwards. The crew of a lumber boat captained by Dahl were cruising off Maury Island, near Tacoma, when six doughnut-shaped craft (complete with holes in the middle) appeared overhead. As Dahl and his companions watched wide-eyed, two of the objects collided, and there was a loud thump as one began to spew out sheets of metal and a black, rock-like substance. About twenty tons of debris landed in the water, on the island and in the boat, killing Dahl's dog and injuring his son's arm. The crew took some of the debris back to Tacoma, and when the first flying saucer sightings appeared in the papers a few days later, Dahl's partner Fred Crisman told a reporter what had happened. Before long, Arnold arrived in Tacoma to find out for himself what had been going on. He interviewed the witnesses and examined the physical evidence before, perplexed, calling in the Air Force. Arnold cannot have been an aggressive interrogator. The two officers who flew to Tacoma the same day and spoke to the principal witnesses quickly determined that the whole affair was a hoax, hatched by Crisman, which had got out of hand. Within twenty-four hours, the Air Force men were on their way home, taking with them a box of classified reports that a colleague had asked them to ship to their base. They never made it; during the short flight their plane caught fire and crashed, killing both men. Although the crash appears to have been an accident, it did not take long for the *Tacoma Times* to get wind of the incident, speculate that the 'classified material' on board was debris from Maury Island, and suggest that the plane had been sabotaged or shot down by secret agents to prevent the truth about flying saucers from becoming known. Peebles, op.cit. pp. 12–15; John Keel, 'The Maury Island caper' in Evans and Spencer, *UFOs: the 40-Year Search*, pp. 40–3. Peebles notes that Crisman had written to the pulp science fiction magazine *Amazing Stories*, the year before, to claim that he had taken part in an underground machine-gun battle with an evil race dwelling inside a hollow earth; Keel that he subsequently had a peripheral involvement in investigations of the Kennedy assassination and was nearly killed in an assassination attempt in 1968. Arnold's appearance at Tacoma was a consequence of his own relationship with the editor of *Amazing Stories*, Ray Palmer, who hired him to write a report on the incident: Keel suggests that the incident actually involved the illegal dumping of radioactive waste over the harbour by a plane operated by the US Atomic Energy Commission.

During the investigation, Dahl breakfasted (he claimed) in a Tacoma diner with a stranger wearing a dark suit who startled him by reciting a detailed version of the incident, which at that time had received no publicity. The stranger concluded by threatening Dahl that his family would be harmed if he discussed the case with anyone else.

Sinister black-clad men feature in many much older stories, and are often associated with evil and the Devil. The earliest report of their appearance in what might reasonably be said to be a UFO-related context was in 1905, when men in black were twice associated with the events of the Welsh religious revival orchestrated by Mary Jones, a preacher who was accompanied on her travels through the country by strange lights in the sky. On one occasion during the revival, a young peasant woman was visited, in her bedroom, on three nights in succession by 'a man dressed in black' who 'delivered a message to the girl which she is frightened to relate'. He precisely resembled, Mrs Jones said, a similar figure she herself had seen in a lonely lane, which turned itself into a fierce black dog and attacked her. This, she was sure, was Satan himself. Kevin and Sue McClure, *Stars, and Rumours of Stars: the Welsh Religious Revival, 1904–5* (Market Harborough, the Authors, 1980) pp. 5–6. There was even a modern British MIB incident, exposed as a hoax played by one member of a UFO investigation group on his colleagues: Martin Shipp, 'The alien amongst us', *Probe Report*, vol. 3, n. 3 (Jan 1983) pp. 3–14.

Albert K. Bender incident Although he never seems to have confided the 'secret', Bender told close associates, including his chief investigator, Gray Barker, about his visit from the three strangers. Barker's subsequent book on the subject, *They Knew Too Much About Flying Saucers* (New York, University Books, 1956) was largely responsible for placing the story of the men in black on record. In the 1960s, Bender briefly re-entered the world of ufology, authoring a peculiar book, *Flying Saucers and the Three Men* (Clarksburg, Saucerian Press, 1962) which revealed that his MIB were the agents of a civilisation from the planet Kazik, which maintained a base in Antarctica.

'Major Richard French' John Keel, *UFOs: Operation Trojan Horse* (London, Abacus, 1973) pp. 185–86. French did not drive a black sedan; he arrived in a white Mustang which turned out to be a rental vehicle from Minneapolis.

Alien abductions Clark, *UFOs in the 1980s*, pp. 1–14; Philip Klass, *UFO Abductions: A Dangerous Game* (Buffalo, Prometheus Books, 1988); David Jacobs, *Secret Life: Firsthand Accounts of UFO Abductions* (London, Fourth Estate, 1993); Jim Schnabel, *Dark White: Aliens, Abductions and the UFO Obsession* (London, Penguin Books, 1995); Peter Brookesmith, *UFO: the Complete Sightings Catalogue* (London, Blandford, 1995) pp. 164–5.

Betty and Barney Hill In addition, Betty's sister had had a UFO sighting in 1957. At the start of the encounter, when Barney was inclined to think that the object was an aircraft, it was Betty who suggested that it was a UFO. Once persuaded, the idea that they might be about to experience a close encounter seems to have occurred to the Hills: Barney stopped the car and retrieved a .22 revolver from the boot.

In retrospect, it can be seen that another odd detail cropped up towards the end of the encounter as Betty engaged the alien leader in conversation. When she expressed an interest in learning more about the universe, he 'went over to the wall and pulled down a [star] map', explained to her where his home planet was and then 'snapped the map back in place'. A pull-down map might well have seemed a logical item of equipment for a UFO in 1961 but already, three-and-a-half decades later, it seems hopelessly archaic; a modern abductee might expect a map to be flashed onto a computer console. Who knows what further technological advances will have occurred by the time the human race is building its own interstellar spacecraft?

The most obvious alternative to the idea that UFO abductions are real is that they are dreams. This was the view held by Benjamin Simon, the therapist who regressed the Hills. He believed that Betty Hill's 'nightmares', which ufologists interpreted as the externalisation of her suppressed memories, really were no more than bad dreams, and pointed to the sexual symbolism of her aliens' long noses and large needles. Simon concluded that the abduction experience was essentially a fantasy of Betty's which she had persuaded her more suggestible husband to share, and he noted important internal contradictions in the testimony. For example, Betty recalled both being surprised that the aliens seemed to have no conception of time, and being called back, as she prepared to leave the UFO, with the words 'Wait a minute'. The whole incident seemed to have been triggered by the Hills' sighting of a light at just the point where Jupiter was shining brightly in the night sky. As for the details of the close encounter, some ufologists have suggested that it may have been inspired by an episode of the session science fiction series *The Twilight Zone*, which had been broadcast only two weeks earlier. The Hills, however, denied ever having seen the episode and continued to believe that their experience had been real.

Parker and Knapp Jacobs, *Secret Life*, pp. 120–5.

Leah Haley Bob Rickard, review of Leah Haley, 'Cato's New Friends', *Fortean Times* 82 (Aug–Sept 1995) p. 61.

Melissa Bucknell Jacobs, *Secret Life*, pp. 258–9.

'*One interesting thing happened . . .*' 'Comments and questions on Dick Haines' talk Novel investigative techniques' in Andrea Pritchard, David Pritchard, John Mack, Pam Kassy and Claudia Yapp (eds), *Alien Discussions: Proceedings of the Abduction Study Conference Held at MIT, Cambridge, MA* (Cambridge, Massachusetts North Cambridge Press, 1994) p. 472.

Malaysian encounter Ahmad Jamaludin, 'A wave of small humanoids in Malaysia in 1970', *Flying Saucer Review*, v 28, n. 5 (Jun 1983) pp. 247.

Algerian UFO beliefs Thierry Pinvidic, 'An Algerian case study', *Magonia* 14 (1983) pp. 3–7.

5 Where the Wild Things Are

Vu Quang ox 'Vietnam's lost world', *Fortean Times*, 66 (Dec 1992–Jan 1993) p. 6; 'New mammals pop up in 'Nam', *Fortean Times*, 78 (Dec 1994 Jan 1995) p. 19

Zoology had not been presented with such a cornucopia of novelty for well over 100 years It had not; but perhaps this says more about the failings of zoology than it does about the diversity of life on earth. Cryptozoologist Jonathan Downes, who runs the Centre for Fortean Zoology in Devon, and has made a special study of the fauna of Hong Kong, believes that this ostensibly urban wasteland will prove to be at least as important a source of new species as Vu Quang. Recent discoveries in the territory include a new species of rat (February 1996). *Animals & Men*, 9 (April 1996) pp 6, 32–36.

Still more spectacular discoveries may yet be made It is worth remembering that a number of now-familiar species have been catalogued only comparatively recently, even though, in most cases, the animals were familiar to the local people. In the 185 years since Baron Georges Cuvier, the father of palaeontology, made the rash suggestion that 'there is little hope of discovering new species of large quadrupeds', their numbers have included unknown tapirs, baboons, gibbons and must ox, not to mention the pygmy hippopotamus, the giant panda, the okapi, king cheetah, and the mountain and pygmy gorillas. Admittedly all of these creatures had close relatives that were already known to science, but then cryptozoologists have only to move to the lizard kingdom to point to the man-eating Komodo Dragon, the largest and fiercest of lizards, discovered when an airman made a forced landing on an island in the Malay archipelago in 1912, or beneath the waves to trumpet the giant squid or the rediscovery of the coelacanth, a bony fish thought extinct for 65 million years, which turned up in the Comoros Islands in 1938 and has since become the most celebrated of all living fossils. (Again, the coelacanth's existence was news only to scientists. Among the Comoros Islanders, the fish was so well-known that its scales were used as a sort of sandpaper to help mend bicycle punctures.) Cf. any cryptozoolgical text-book or popular work.

New discoveries Rarer by far than identification of individual species are the discoveries of new phyla; yet these, too, happen occasionally. One new phylum, the Locifera, was identified in 1983; it comprises tiny creatures who live on the sea shore in the gaps between grains of sand. Another, the Cycliophora, turned up in 1995. These asexual beasts, each about one-third of a millimetre long, behave like animated cold sores and are found only on the lips of Norwegian lobsters. The Cycliophora are only the 36th phylum ever derscribed; the other 35 are reckoned sufficient to classify somewhere between 30 and 100 million species. *Nature*, 378 Dec 1995 p. 709.

The coelacanth Michel Raynal and Gary Mangiacopra, 'Out-of-place coelacanths', *Fortean Studies*, 2 (London, John Brown, 1995) pp. 156–65.

Porcupines in Devon 'Feral Himalayan Porcupines in Devon', *Nature in Devon*, No. 10.

Wild boar 'Other exotics', *Animals & Men*, 1 (1994) p. 6.

Wolverines Karl Shuker, 'Who's afraid of the big bad wolverine?', *Fortean Times*, 85 (Feb–Mar 1996) pp. 36–7.

Bernard Heuvelmans After gaining his PhD for a thesis on the hitherto unclassifiable dentition of the aardvark, Heuvelmans was called up for military service at the outbreak of World War II. During the occupation, he eked out a living as a professional jazz singer and, after the war, moved to Paris where he began his life's work, researching all manner of unknown animals and producing hugely influential works on the sea serpent, the giant squid and the giant octopus, living dinosaurs and surviving neanderthals. It is no exaggeration to call him the father of cryptozoology; he is also a fierce opponent of the rival folkloric school, which suggests that many, perhaps most, of the creatures he has devoted his life to have no physical reality.

British big cats Trevor Beer, *The Beast of Exmoor, Fact or Legend?* (Barnstaple, Countryside Productions n.d. *c.* 1984); Janet & Colin Bord, *Alien Animals: A Worldwide Investigation* (St Albans, Granada, 1980); Nigel Brierly, *They Stalk By Night: The Big Cats of Exmoor and the South West* (Newtown, Devon, Yeo Valley Productions, 1989); Di Francis. *The Beast of Exmoor and Other Mystery Predators of Great Britain* (London, Jonathan Cape, 1993); Ministry of Agriculture, Fisheries & Food, *The Evidence for the Presence of Large Exotic Cats in the Bodmin Area and Their Possible Impact on Livestock* (London, MAFF Publications, 1995); Karl Shuker, *Mystery Cats of the World* (London, Robert Hale, 1989); John Michell & Robert Rickard, *Phenomena: A Book of Wonders* (London, Thames & Hudson, 1977) pp. 124–5. Regular annual sighting updates, compiled from local newspaper reports, appear in *Fortean Times*; for the most recent round-ups, see *FT*, 59, 18–20 (covering 1990–1); *FT*, 64, 44–45 (1992); *FT*, 73, 41–44 (1993); *FT*, 80, 37–43 (1994); and *FT*, 88, 28–31 (1995).

Jane Fuller Richard Halstead and Paul Sieveking, 'An ABC of British ABCs', *Fortean Times*, 73 (Feb–Mar 1994) p. 42.

Sally Dyke Paul Sieveking, 'Beasts in our midst', *Fortean Times*, 80 (Apr–May 1995) p. 38.

Other big cats For Australian big cats, see Paul Cropper and Tony Healy, *Out of the Shadows: Mystery Animals of Australia* (Sydney, Pan Macmillan, 1994) pp. 55–97; David O'Reilly, *Savage Shadow: the Search for the Australian Cougar* (Perth, Creative Research, 1981). For American big cats, Loren Coleman, 'On the trail: maned mystery cats', *Fortean Times*, 31 (spring 1980) pp. 24–27; 'On the trail; an answer from the Pleistocene', *Fortean Times*, 32 (summer 1980) pp. 21–22. For German big cats, Ulrich Magin, 'The Odenwald beast', *Fortean Times*, 55 (autumn 1990) pp. 30–1. For big cat corpses, see Karl Shuker, 'British mystery cats – the bodies of evidence'. *Fortean Studies*, 2 (1995) pp. 143–52.

Bilbo 'London pride', *Fortean Times*, 75 (June – July 1994) p. 11.

Escapees Cases of escaped big cats in the British Isles include two jaguars that escaped from Colwyn Bay Zoo in September 1982, and were killed shortly afterwards; a puma that got away from the Jane Miller Circus in Leicestershire, in March 1988, but which died after jumping into a freezing river; and a black panther cub found on the banks of the Medway in January 1975, which appeared to have come from Colchester Zoo. In addition, the body of a dead lioness was hauled from a small lake near St Helens, Lancashire, in May 1980, and an apparent lynx was trapped near Inverness in January 1927. Shuker, 'Mystery cats: The bodies of evidence', *Fortern Studies* (1995) pp. 146–9.

Out of place crocodiles John Michell and Robert Rickard, *Living Wonders* (London, Thames & Hudson, 1982) pp. 56–8; Loren Coleman, 'Eratic crocodilians and other things', *INFO Journal*, 12 (February 1974) pp. 12–18, which gives a complete listing with sources for the accounts given in these paragraphs.

Chipping Norton crocodiles The Gentleman's Magazine (Nov 1866) p. 640, (Jul–Dec 1866) pp. 149–54; Charles Fort, *The Complete Books of Charles Fort* (New York, Dover Publications, 1974) p. 592. The other popular explanation for such finds – albeit one that is very hard to prove – is that the animals escaped from a travelling circus or menagerie.

Charleston crocodile fall Coleman, 'Erratic crocodilians', citing *Charleston Evening Post*, 11 Aug 1971.

Crocodile in a Zeppelin Paul Thompson, 'An errant aerial alligator?', *INFO Journal* 39 (Mar/Jun 1981) p. 11, citing John Toland, *Ships in the Sky* (New York, Henry Holt, 1957) p. 279.

Crocodile at Brooklyn Museum Coleman, 'Erratic crocodillians', citing *New York Times*, 7 Jun 1937.

Crocodile in a German train toilet Ibid., citing *Washington Post*, 7 Feb 1973.

Crocodile on the M55 at Preston Michell & Rickard, op. c. 7.

The Hackney bear 'Out of place', *Fortean Times*, 37 (spring 1982) pp. 44–5.

Living mammoths Bernard Heuvelmans, *On the Track of Unknown Animals* (London, Rupert Hart-Davis 1962) pp. 331–53.

Living moas Karl Shuker, 'The case of the missing moa', *Fortean Times*, 69 (Jun–Jul 1993) pp. 42–3.

Thylacine survival Steven Smith, *The Tasmanian Tiger–1980* Wildlife Division Technical Report, 81/1, Tasmania. (National Parks and Wildlife Service, 1981); Paul Cropper and Tony Healey, *Out of the Shadows: Mystery Animals of Australia* (Chippendale, Ironbark, 1994) pp. 1–54.

Dinosaur survival Roy Mackal, *A Living Dinosaur: In Search of Mokele Mbembe* (Leiden, Holland, E. J. Brill, 1987); Karl Shuker, *In Search of Prehistoric Survivors: Do Giant 'Extinct' Creatures Still Exist?* (London, Blandford, 1996).

South America's mystery animals Heuvelmans, *Unknown Animals*, pp. 252–328.

Surviving giant sloth Jan Williams, 'Giant ground sloth in Amazonia', *Animals & Men*, 1 (1994) pp. 8–9; 'The mother of all sloths', *Fortean Times*, 77 (Oct–Nov 1994) p. 17; Shuker, *Pretistonic Survivors*, pp. 144–5, 173. Commenting on the difference in size between a twelve foot *mylodon* and the six-foot *mapinguary*, Oren suggests that forest dwellers commonly tend to be smaller than related species that live on more open ground.

The question of *mylodon* survival was first raised by the 1895 discovery, in a cave at Last Hope Inlet, far to the south in Chile, of an apparently fresh *mylodon* skin, the quest for which forms the backbone of Bruce Chatwin's evocative *In Patagonia* (London, Picador 1979) cf pp. 5–7, 9–11, 175–80. The skin, when carbon dated, proved to be around 10,000 years old.

Giant snakes of the Amazon Heuvelmans, *Unknown Animals*, pp. 284–98; Tim Dinsdale, *The Leviathans* (London, Futura, 1976) pp. 112–37. South America is not the only possible habitat of giant snakes; in August 1959 a Belgian pilot, Rene Van Lierde, was flying low over scrubland in southern Zaire when he came upon a monstrous serpent which, he said, reared up and attempted to attack his helicopter. Recovering from his initial shock, Van Lierde managed to take a single photograph of the giant. His picture does show a large snake but, in the absence of significant ground features that could provide a scale, the only way of estimating its size is to base a calculation on the altitude of the helicopter. Van Lierde reported this as forty-five to fifty metres, and there were more reports from the region, but at present the South American rainforest seems to be the only region in which giant snakes are seen with any regularity. Bernard Heuvelmans, *Les Derniers Dragons d' Afrique* (Paris, Plon, 1978) pp. 59–61. There are also a few circumstantial reports of huge snakes in Sibera – see Paul Stonehill, 'Giant serpents of the Russian Far East', *Strange Magazine* 13 (1994) p. 29.

Monsters of Australia Heuvelmans, *Unknown Animals* pp. 191–220; Cropper and Healy, *Out of the Shadows* pp. 99–110; Rex Gilroy, *Mysterious Australia* (Mapleton, Queensland, Nexus Publishing, 1995) pp. 115–28.

Worldwide ape-man reports Janet and Colin Bord, *The Evidence for Bigfoot and Other Man-Beasts* (Wellingborough, Aquarian Press, 1984); Myra Shackley, *Wildman: Yeti, Sasquatch and the Neanderthal Enigma* (London, Thames & Hudson, 1983); Healy and Cropper, *Out of the Shadows*, pp. 111–58; Ulrich Magin, 'Meet the European snowman', *INFO Journal*, 54 (Feb 1988) pp. 26–7, 36; Sergio de la Rubia-Munoz, 'Wild men in Spain', *INFO Journal*, 72 (winter 1995) pp. 22–5.

Ivan Sanderson and Bigfoot Ivan Sanderson, *Abominable Snowmen: Legend Come to Life* (New York, Pyramid Books, 1968) p. 60.

Fulton case Janet and Colin Bord, *The Evidence for Bigfoot and Other Man-Beasts* (Wellingborough, Aquarian Press, 1984) pp. 19–20.

Roe case Sanderson, *Abominable Snowman*, pp. 108–11. Roe's statement has been edited from a longer affadavit. Perhaps the most notable consequence of the publication of Roe's story, in the pages of the sasquatch researcher John Green's paper the 'Agassiz-Harrison Advance', was that a retired Swedish-Canadian logger named Albert Ostman came forward to tell possibly the most bizarre tale in the history of cryptozoological research. pp. Ibid. 85–95.

Bigfoot has been seen Bord and Bord, *The Evidence for Bigfoot*, p. 111.

True giants Mark Hall, 'True giants around the world', *Wonders*, vol. 1, n 3 (Sept 1992) pp. 31–47.

Abominable snowman Some controversy surrounds the origin of this evocative phrase. It appears to have been invented c. 1930 by a journalist, Henry Newman ('Kim' of the *Calcutta Statesman*), as the result of a mistranslation of the Tibetan *metoh kang-mi*, which may, it is said, be rendered as 'disgusting man-of-the-snows'. It was certainly a fortuitous slip, as the phrase, however much it is disliked by serious researchers, has an undeniable way of sticking in the mind. Ralph Izzard, *The Abominable Snowman Adventure* (London, Hodder & Stoughton, 1955) pp. 23–4.

The yeti is rarely seen A table of cases prepared by the anthropologist, John Napier for his book *Bigfoot: the Yeti and Sasquatch in Myth and Reality* (London, Abacus, 1976) pp. 174–5, mentions only two sightings by westerners, among a longer list of footprints. It is not quite complete, but gives a good idea of how unusual it is for anyone other than the native Sherpas to see the yeti. It is noteworthy, also, that none of Napier's reports come from a lesser altitude than 12,000 feet.

Abbot's yeti sighting Ibid. p. 44. Napier speculates that this sighting was of a bear.

Pamir mountains snowman Bord and Bord, *The Evidence for Bigfoot*, pp. 47–9; Mike Dash, 'In search of the yeti', *Fortean Times*, 67 (Feb–Mar 1993) pp. 32–4; Dmitri Bayanov, *In the Footsteps of the Russian Snowman* (Moscow, Crypto-Logos, 1996).

Wildman as wild men Michael Shoemaker, 'Searching for the historical Bigfoot', *Strange Magazine*, 5 (1990) pp. 18–23, 57–62; Mark Chorvinsky, 'The monster is a man: hairy people, wild people and the Bigfoot legend', *Strange Magazine* 5 (1990) pp. 24–9.

Ray Wallace and the birth of Bigfoot Mark Chorvinsky, 'New Bigfoot photo investigation', *Strange Magazine*, 13 (spring 1994) pp. 10–11, 51;

Chorvinsky, 'From the Editor', *Strange Magazine*, 16 (fall 1995) p.1; Loren Coleman, 'Was the first 'Bigfoot' a hoax?; Cryptozoology's original sin', *The Anomalist* 2 (1995), pp. 8–27.

Wildman evidence Mike Dash, 'Manimals', *Fortean Times*, 54 (summer 1990) pp. 18–23.

MacDonald sighting Rupert Gould, *The Loch Ness Monster and Others* (London, Geoffrey Bles, 1934) pp. 94–6. Miss MacDonald had earlier (February 1932) seen a strange creature resembling a crocodile in the shallow river Ness, which connects the loch to the sea via the town of Inverness. She is the only witness to have claimed such a sighting. Ibid. pp. 38–9.

MacKay sighting Ibid. pp. 39–40. Sceptics have made capital from the fact that Mrs MacKay was the landlady of the Drumnadrochit Hotel, one of the principal places to stay around the loch, and therefore in a position to benefit directly from an increased tourist trade, However, as Gould points out, she initially declined to be identified as the witness for fear that people would not take her sighting seriously. A more potent criticism of this first modern report is that Mrs MacKay initially believed that the disturbance in the water was caused by two ducks fighting, and that her husband, who was driving her along the shore road at the time, stopped the car in time to see only a disturbance in the water and waves rolling in to the shore.

Sightings in Loch Lochy Peter Costello, *In Search of Lake Monsters* (St Albans, Panther, 1975) pp. 153–4; 'Good month for monster hunters', *Fortean Times*, 95 (February 1997) p. 18.

Kenneth MacKenzie's sighting R. Macdonald Robertson, *Selected Highland Folk Tales* (Edinburgh, Oliver and Boyd, 1961) pp. 143–4.

McDonnell-Simpson sighting Elizabeth Montgomery-Campbell with David Solomon, *The Search for Morag* (London, Tom Stacey, 1972) pp. 138–40.

The water-horse K.M. Briggs, *The Fairies in Tradition and Literature* (London, Routledge & Kegan Paul, 1977) pp. 57–8.

A-Mhorag Montgomery-Campbell and Solomon, *The Search for Morag*, pp. 108–11.

Lord Malmesbury and the water-horse of Loch Arkaig Costello, *Lake Monsters*, pp. 148–9.

Ogopogo Mary Moon, *Ogopogo: the Okanagan Mystery* (Vancouver, J.J. Douglas, 1977); Arelene Gaal, *Ogopogo: the True Story of the Okanagan Lake Million Dollar Monster* (Surrey, British Columbia, Hancock House Publishers, 1986).

Lake Storsjon Costello, *Lake Monsters*, pp. 215–26; Ulla Oscarsson, *The Great Lake Monster* (Ostersund nd).

Giant sturgeon '80-year-old sturgeon found dead', *INFO Journal*, 54 (Feb 1988) p. 24; 'Largest fish clarification', *Fortean Times*, 69 (Jun–Jul 1993) p. 63.

Migo One of the peculiarities of this essentially crocodilian monster is that it fails to exhibit characteristic horizontal flexion. In the last few months it has been suggested that the object in the film might be a dead crocodile towed behind a boat. Jon Downes, 'Crocodile tears II', *Animals & Men* 5 (1995) p. 22; Karl Shuker, 'The Migo movie: a further muddying of murky waters' ibid. pp. 22–5; Darren Naish, 'Analysing video footage purporting to show the Migo, a lake monster from Lake Dakataua, New Britain', *Cryptozoology Review*, 1, n 2 (autumn 1996) pp. 18–21.

Lake Tianchi monster Joe McNally and James Wallis (eds), *Weird Year 1996* (London, John Brown, 1996), p. 92.

The Daedalus sea serpent Rupert Gould, *The Case for the Sea-Serpent* (London, Philip Allan, 1930) pp. 94–126.

Captain Cringle's sea serpent Ibid. pp. 188–94.

Stronsay beast Bernard Heuvelmans, *In the Wake of the Sea Serpents* (London, Rupert Hart-Davis, 1968) pp. 118–30.

Tecolutla carcass Rafael Lara Palmeros, 'A marine monster in Tecolutla, Mexico', *INFO Journal*, 71 (autumn 1994) pp. 24–6.

Naden Harbour carcass E.J. Bousfield and P. H. LeBlond, 'An account of *Cadborosaurus willsi*, new genus, new species, a large aquatic reptile from the Pacific coast of North America', *Amphipacifica: Journal of Systematic Biology*, 1, supplement 1 (1995); Bousfield and LeBlond, *Cadborosaurus: Survivor of the Deep* (Victoria, British Columbia, Horsdal & Schubart, 1995).

Heuvelmans and Magin Heuvelmans, *In The Wake of Sea Serpents*, pp. 537–73; Heuvelmans, 'How I conquered the Great Sea Serpent', *Strange Magazine*, 3 (1988) pp. 10–13, 56–7; Ulrich Magin, 'St George without a dragon: Bernard Heuvelmans and the sea serpent', *Fortean Studies*, 3 (London, John Brown, 1996) pp. 223–36.

6 The Good Earth

Stonehenge Roger Sandell, 'Notes towards a social history of ley-hunting', *Magonia*, 29 (April 1988) pp. 3–7.

Definition of earth mysteries Paul Devereux, 'The earth remembered: the nature of earth mysteries', *The Ley Hunter*, 96 (Summer 1984) pp. 4–7.

The ley-line theory Alfred Watkins, *The Old Straight Track: Its Mounds, Beacons, Moats, Sites and Mark Stones* (London, Abacus, 1974), was originally published in 1925; see also Paul Screeton, *Quicksilver Heritage: The Mystic Leys – Their Legacy of Ancient Wisdom* (London, Abacus, 1977).

What is a ley? Watkins, *The Old Straight Track*, pp. 197–204; Paul Devereux and Ian Thompson, *The Ley Hunter's Companion: Aligned Ancient Sites – A New Study with Field Guide and Maps* (London, Thames & Hudson, 1979) pp. 27, 38–43, 72–3.

Examples of leys Ibid. pp. 47–8, 187–9. See also Screeton, *Quicksilver Heritage*, pp. 38–51; Philip Heselton, *Earth Mysteries* (Shaftesbury, Element Books, 1995) p. 22.

Worldwide ley networks Watkins, *The Old Straight Track*, pp. 180–3; Heselton, *Earth Mysteries*, pp. 20–1. German ley research is not yet dead:

cf. Ulrich Magin, 'A church alignment in Worms, Germany', *INFO Journal* 67 (October 1992) pp. 6–9.

'The spirit of the British countryside' ... Watkins, *The Old Straight Track* p. 218

Ley hunting has 'Transformed the countryside into a place of mystery' ... Sandell, 'social history of ley-hunting', p. 5.

Feng-shui A good general guide is Derek Walters, *The Feng Shui Handbook* (Wellingborough, Aquarian Press, 1991). See also John Michell, *The New View Over Atlantis* (London, Thames & Hudson, 1983) pp. 59–66. There are few western parallels to the resultant, exquisitely realised, Chinese landscape. One might be the supposed 'terrestrial zodiacs' that some earth mysteries researchers believe they have identified etched into the landscape at sacred sites. Glastonbury, one of the most mystical of all religious centres, is supposedly ringed by a mile-diameter circle of twelve giant figures, each one representing a sign of the zodiac, formed from the hills and rivers of the area. Some writers speculate that the existence of such alignments is the reason why places like Glastonbury are chosen as sacred sites (the same is supposedly true of the mysterious French Pyrennean village of Rennes-le-Chateau); others have argued, convincingly, that terrestrial zodiacs are no more than giant simulacra, existing more in the mind's eye than in reality. Katherine Maltwood, *A Guide to Glastonbury's Temple of the Stars* (London, James Clark, 1929); Heselton, *Earth Mysteries*, p. 72.

Icelandic road construction Ulrich Magin, 'The Akureyri fairies revisited', *INFO Journal*, 66 (June 1992) pp. 18–19 gives a sceptical overview of such stories.

Moving churches Michael Goss. 'The devil and Barn Hall: the folklore of siting legends', *Fortean Studies*, vol. 3 (London, John Brown, 1996) pp. 159-175

'Earth mysteries research is ...' Devereux, 'The earth remembered', p. 4.

Simulacra of Dean Liddell John Michell and Robert Rickard, *Phenomena: A Book of Wonders* (London, Thames & Hudson, 1977) pp. 58–9, citing *TP's and Cassell's Weekly* of 11 Sept 1926.

Simulacra of George Bernard Shaw 'Shaw simulacrum', *Fortean Times*, 42 (autumn 1984) p. 9.

Gaia hypothesis J.E. Lovelock, *Gaia: A New Look at Life on Earth* (Oxford, Oxford University Press, 1979).

Rollright stones Janet and Colin Bord, *Secret Country: More Mysterious Britain* (St Albans, Granada, 1978) pp. 107–111; Michell & Rickard, *A Book of Wonders*, pp. 86–7.

The Blaxhall stone Heselton, *Earth Mysteries*, p. 28.

The hollow earth Practically the only reliable resource in this crank-infested realm is Walter Kafton-Minkel, *Subterranean Worlds: 100,000 Years of Dragons, Dwarfs, the Dead, Lost Races & UFOs From Inside the Earth* (Port Townsend, Washington, Loompanics Unlimited, 1989).

'A world within a world ...' Ibid., p. 7.

'Supposed conquest of the North Pole' In fact, as is now generally recognised by geographers, Peary almost certainly never came within a hundred miles

of the pole, and lied to conceal this fact. Rather remarkably, the first unchallenged conquest of the North Pole by land did not take place until the 1960s.

Shaver's hollow earth theory Kafton Minkel *Subterranean Worlds*, pp. 139–67; some of the more lurid details, including the Parisienne's abduction by the Dero, are drawn from Warren Smith, *This Hollow Earth* (London, Sphere Books, 1977) pp. 129–43.

Nazi interest in the Hollow Earth These theories are set out in the influential book, by Louis Pauwels and Jacques Bergier, *The Morning of the Magicians* (St Albans, Granada, 1982) pp. 185–200 and in occultist Trevor Ravenscroft's book *Spear of Destiny* (London, Putnam, 1973). They have been severely challenged. It has nevertheless been demonstrated that the Nazi party's historical roots, including elements of its racial theories, partly rest in several of the occultist groups that flourished in Germany in the aftermath of the Great War, and, in particular, the Thule Society. Nicholas Goodrick-Clarke. *The Occult Roots of Nazism: the Ariosophists of Austria and Germany 1890-1935* (Wellingborough, Aquarian Press, 1985). It also seems that both Goering and Himmler did pay some attention to the theories of a German aviator named Peter Bender, who believed not only that the earth is hollow but that we ourselves live on the inside, and that the moon and planets rotate with the earth around a tiny central sun. Bender paid for his theory with his life during the Second World War when Goering sponsored an expedition to the Baltic island of Rugen, where a disgruntled Nazi physicist was instructed to point a special camera heavenwards in the hope of capturing images of the British fleet manoeuvring – overhead – in the North Sea. The complete failure of the tests led to Bender's incarceration and death in a concentration camp. Kafton-Minkel, *Subterranean Worlds*, pp. 217–22.

UFOs and Bigfoot from the Hollow Earth Ibid. pp. 228–9.

T.E. Lethbridge Tom Lethbridge wrote prolifically after his retirement, covering everything from earth mysteries to a proto-'Chariots of the Gods' ancient astronaut theory. His key works, for dowsers, are *Ghost and Ghoul* (London, Routledge & Kegan Paul, 1961); *Ghost and Divining Rod* (London, Routledge & Kegan Paul, 1963) and *The Power of the Pendulum* (London, Routledge & Kegan Paul, 1976). For a concise, albeit entirely positive, overview of his theories, see Colin Wilson, *Mysteries: an Investigation into the Occult, the Paranormal and the Supernatural* (St Albans, Granada, 1979) pp. 49–115.

Experiences of earth energies Screeton, *Quicksilver Heritage*, pp. 171 and 178; Paul Devereux, *Earth Lights: Towards an Understanding of the UFO Enigma* (Wellingborough, Turnstone Press, 1982) p. 151.

Hitching's experiments Francis Hitching, *Earth Magic* (London, Cassell, 1975); Devereux, *Earth Lights*, pp. 122–68.

Dragon Project Devereux, *Earth Lights*, pp. 142–51; Devereux, *Places of Power* (London, Blandford, 1990); Heselton, *Earth Mysteries* pp. 47–51.

More is attributable to chance . . . Paul Devereux, 'It was 20 years ago today', *The Ley Hunter*, 124 (winter 1995–96) p. 1.

Consciousness research Ibid; Heselton, *Earth Mysteries*, p. 102; Julian Thomas, 'Monuments ancient and modern', *The Ley Hunter*, 125 (autumn 1996) pp. 17–19.

'*What I am suggesting* . . . Paul Devereux, *Shamanism and the Mystery Lines* (Quantum Books, 1992) cited by Heselton, *Earth Mysteries*, p. 81.

Corpse ways, death roads and ghost paths Heselton, op. cit. p. 80; Ulrich Magin, 'My life on the path of ghosts', *Fortean Times*, 89 (July 1996) p. 49.

The theories of Aime Michel Jerome Clark, 'Orthoteny', in *The UFO Encyclopaedia: the Emergence of a Phenomenon: UFOs from the Beginning Through 1959* (Detroit, Omnigraphics, 1992) pp. 264–5.

Orthotentic lines From the Greek *orthoteneis*, 'stretched in a straight line'.

Earthlights hypothesis Paul Devereux, *Earth Lights: Towards an Explanation of the UFO Enigma* (Wellingborough, Turnstone Press, 1982) and *Earth Lights Revelation: UFOs and Mystery Lightform Phenomena: the Earth's Secret Energy Force* (London, Blandford, 1989); Michael Persinger and Gyslaine Lafreniere, *Space-Time Transients and Unusual Events* (Chicago, Nelson-Hall, 1977); Kevin McClure, 'Serious faults', *Common Ground*, 7 (1983) pp. 7–10; 'Letters', *Common Ground*, 9 (1984) pp. 11–15; 'The earthlights debate for the defence', *Magonia*, 12 (1983) pp. 8–12.

Bridgend case Devereux, *Earth Lights*, p. 205, citing Jenny Randles and Peter Warrington, *UFOs – a British Viewpoint* (London, Robert Hale, 1979) pp. 208–09.

Hessdalen Jerome Clark, *The UFO Encyclopaedia: UFOs in the 1980s* (Detroit, Apogee Books, 1990) pp. 131–4.

Dr John Derr Quoted in a documentary about Devereux's work. *Equinox* – 'Identified Flying Objects', broadcast by Channel 4 6 November 1996.

Jim Byerlee Quoted in ibid.

Dyfed UFO wave For the proponents' view see Randall Jones Pugh and F.W. Holiday, *The Dyfed Enigma* (London, Faber & Faber, 1979). Among other things, the authors attempted to resurrect Michel's orthoteny theory by plotting Welsh sightings on a map and hunting for alignments. Most of the resulting 'leys' had no more than two or three points. For the opponents' point of view, see Hilary Evans, 'The truth about the Welsh Triangle', *The Unexplained* (London, Orbis, 1981) pp. 874–8

Will o' the wisp John Michell and Robert Rickard, *Phenomena: A Book of Wonders* (London, Thames & Hudson, 1977) pp. 26–7.

Luminous owls David Clarke, 'The luminous owls of Norfolk', *Fortean Studies*, vol 1 (London, John Brown, 1994) pp. 50–8.

7 Reign of Frogs

Charles Fort Martin Gardner, *Fads and Fallacies in the Name of Science* (New York, Dover, 1957) pp. 42–54; Damon Knight, *Charles Fort, Prophet of the Unexplained* (Garden City, New York, Doubleday, 1970); Robert

Rickard, 'Charles Fort and Fortean Times', *Fortean Times*, 29 (summer 1979) pp. 2–8.

Inspector of Invading Oddities 'Imperial Forteanism', *Fortean Times*, 30 (winter 1979) pp. 67–8.

Robert Ripley Ripley (1983–1949) is discussed in Otto Minyak, 'A carnival of curioddities', *Fortean Times*, 74 (Apr May 1994) pp. 33–5, and in 'Robert Ripley', *The People's Almanac Presents The Twentieth Century* (London, Aurum Press, 1996) pp. 766–7.

Norbert Pealroth Obituary in *New York Times*, 15 Apr 1993.

Falls Charles Fort, *The Book of the Damned* (London, John Brown, 1995) pp. 14–19, 38–119.

Dunmarra fish fall 'Diary of a Mad Planet, February to March 1994', *Fortean Times*, 75 (Jun – Jul 1994) p. 49.

Fall of grilled halibut 'Falls', *Fortean Times*, 37 (spring 1982) p. 50.

Brazilian bean-fall 'Falls', *INFO Journal*, 8 (winter – spring 1972) p. 26.

Fall of excrement 'Well, it doesn't smell like rain', *Fortean Times*, 84 (Dec 1995–Jan 1996) p. 11. See also *INFO Journal*, 50 p. 22 for a fall of sewage.

Norrkoping troll fall 'Fall of mystery animal', *Fortean Times*, 6 (Sept 1974) p. 15. The original source, as *FT* reported several years later ('A reprise for Living Wonders', *Fortean Times*, 40 (summer 1983) pp. 4–15) was Gustaf Otto Bilberg's *Almanackia*, of 1709, where the date of the incident is given as the night of 8–9 August and the creature is described as something that 'somewhat resembled a beaver, but its body was a little smaller . . . its head was a bit larger, and its lower jaw a little longer than its upper jaw. It had rather small eyes, short hind legs and tail, and rough brownish fur.'

Other strange falls Jerome Clark, *Unexplained! 347 Strange Sightings. Incredible Occurrences and Puzzling Physical Phenomena* (Detroit, Visible Ink, 1993) pp. 131–2.

Fall of a silver notecase 'Falls', *Fortean Times*, 15 (April 1976) p. 17; A.J. Bell, 'Precession of the gracious: fallout of the damned', *Fortean Times*, 20 (February 1977) pp. 14–17.

Seringapatam ice fall Fort, *Book of the Damned*, pp. 16–17, citing *Annual Report of the British Association for the Advancement of Science*, 1851 p. 82.

Waterspouts Robert Schadewald, 'Fish falls and whirlwinds', *Fortean Times*, 22 (summer 1977) pp. 31–33. See also W. Scott Home, 'Waterspout up for Mr Fort!', *INFO Journal*, 35 (May–Jun 1979) pp. 2–3.

Mountain Ash fish fall Robert Schadewald, 'The great fish fall of 1859', *Fortean Times*, 30 (winter 1979) pp. 38–42.

Kiribati fish fall 'Fish fall answers castaways' prayer', *Fortean Times*, 48 (spring 1987) p. 16 citing *Daily Telegraph*, 25 Aug 1986.

Angel hair Jerome Clark, 'Angel hair', *The Emergence of a Phenomenon: UFOs From the Beginning Through 1959* (Detroit, Omnigraphics, 1992) pp. 44–47. Reports of angel hair date back to at least 1741: 'Falls!', *INFO Journal*, 14 (Nov 1974) pp. 28–30.

Dorset cobweb cloud 'Cobweb cloud', *Fortean Times*, 54 (summer 1990) p. 30, citing *Daily Mirror*, 29 Oct 1988.

Bosnian mystery webs Paul Sieveking, 'The webs of war', *Fortean Times*, 71 (Oct – Nov 1993) p. 34.

Strange hums 'The Hueytown hum', *Fortean Times*, 65 (Oct–Nov 1992) pp. 12–13; 'The Taos hum', *Fortean Times* 71 (Oct–Nov 1993) p. 12.

Bristol mystery booms 'Heavens Above!', *Fortean Times* 19 (Dec 1976) pp. 21–2.

Barisal guns 'Three strange sounds' in Rupert Gould, *Enigmas* (New York, University Books, 1966) pp. 39–45.

Teleportation Fort's coinage of term is recorded in chapter two of *Lo!* (New York, Claude Kendall, 1931), and his claim to authorship accepted by the *Oxford English Dictionary.* It is true to say that Spiritualists already had a term to describe the phenomenon, or one very like it: they called transported objects that materialised at seances apports; also that the tradition of such a phenomenon is a very ancient one. For example, the prophet Muhammad is said to have been instantaneously transported from Mecca to Jerusalem around the year AD 618, prior to his ascent to the seventh heaven.

'It could be . . .' Charles Fort, *The Complete Books of Charles Fort* (New York, Dover Books, 1974) p. 571.

Spanish soldier Mr X 'The Aparecido and the death of Gomez Perez Dasmarinas', *Fortean Times*, 52 (autumn 1990) pp. 55-9. The story entered the phenomenological literature via M.K.Jessup's *The Case for the UFO* (New York, Citadel Press, 1955) and Jessup himself (this is the same Jessup who popularised the contentious case of the Philadelphia Experiment, see chapter 8) seems to have come across it while he was working in Mexico. The earliest version of the tale appears to date from Father Gaspar de Sant Agustin's *Conquista de las Islas Filipinas*, written in 1698 and translated and reprinted several times since then. The name 'Gil Perez' first appears in Margaret Sachs, *The UFO Encyclopaedia* (London, Corgi, 1981), and must surely be a corruption of the name of the governor of the Philippines, Gomez Perez Dasmarinas. There is a very similar story, dating supposedly from 1655, concerning the teleportation of a Portuguese soldier from the Indian colony of Goa back to Lisbon, 'in the air, in an incredible short time'. The unfortunate man was supposedly denounced as a witch and burnt at the stake. The source for this case is the English diarist John Aubrey's *Miscellanies* (London, 1695); no Portuguese source appears to have been discovered. It is noteworthy that the British source for the Goa case predates the earliest Spanish source for the Mexico City case by three years.

Benjamin Bathurst Mike Dash, 'The disappearance of Benjamin Bathurst', *Fortean Times*, 54 (summer, 1990) pp. 40–44.

The vanishing Norfolks Paul Begg, *Into Thin Air* (Newton Abbot, David & Charles, 1979) pp. 40–51.

The Mary Celeste There are dozens of books on this celebrated case, some good, some intriguing, many plain bad. Probably the most careful account, which includes a careful refutation of the major errors made by earlier authors, is that of Charles Eden Fay, *The Story of the Mary Celeste* (Salem, Peabody Museum, 1942). This tends towards the theory that there was a small explosion in the hold, caused by a spark from a metal band on one of the 1700 barrels of alcohol that made up the cargo. Fearing a larger explosion, the captain, Benjamin Briggs, ordered the ship's boat to be lowered, transferred his crew and himself to it, then fell back astern at the end of a tow rope to wait until it was judged safe to reboard. Instead, the tow-rope parted in inclement weather, leaving the crew sitting helplessly in the wake of the fast-disappearing ship. As the weather deteriorated, the small boat foundered and sank, but the *Mary Celeste* sailed on, to be found a day or two later.

Incidentally, the almost universally-held belief that the ship's name was *Marie Celeste* is incorrect. The faulty spelling was popularised when Arthur Conan Doyle used it in a short story. 'J. Habbakuk Jepherson's Statement', based on the mystery, published in the *Cornhill Magazine* in 1884.

The mystery of Eilean Mor For the mysterious log-book entries, see Vincent Gaddis, *Invisible Horizons* (New York, Ace Books, 1965) pp. 177–83; for the freak wave explanation and an interview with MacArthur's surviving daughter (then ninety), see Joan Simpson, 'Boxing day at Flannan Rock', *The Times*, 26 Dec 1990; for the rooks, see Carey Miller, *Baffling Mysteries* (London, Panics, 1976) pp. 19–25.

'Haunted and also the abode of fairies' Such folktales may not actually have existed, though given the isles' undoubted eeriness it would not be surprising if they had.

Spontaneous human combustion Jenny Randles and Peter Hough, *Spontaneous Human Combustion* (London, Robert Hale, 1992); Larry Arnold, *Ablaze: The Mysterious Fires of Spontaneous Human Combustion* (New York, M.Evans & Co., 1995); Joe Nickell, 'Investigative files: not-so-spontaneous combustion', *Skeptical Inquirer*, (Nov–Dec 1996).

Children raised by animals Charles Maclean's *The Wolf Children* (London, Allen Lane, 1977) is the most complete account of the Midnapore case, and is based on rediscovered primary sources including the papers of the Reverend Singh. See also R.M. Zingg, 'Feral man and extreme cases of isolation' in *American Journal of Sociology*, 53 (1949), 'Wild children' in Francis Hitching, *The World Atlas of Mysteries* (London, William Collins, 1978) pp. 207–09, and 'Children brought up by animals' in Michell and Rickard, *Phenomena: A Book of Wonders* (London, Thames & Hudson, 1977) pp. 108–09.

Victor, the wild boy of Aveyron Harlan Lane, *The Wild Boy of Aveyron* (St Albans, Granada, 1977). Victor lived until 1828, when he was about forty.

The Kuano amphibian boy 'Tales from India', *Fortean Times*, 32 (summer 1980) p. 40; 'The water boy', *Fortean Times*, 47 (autumn 1986) pp. 74–5.

Phone calls from the dead D.Scott Rogo and Raymond Bayless, *Phone Calls from the Dead* (London, New English Library, 1980).

MIB use of telephones See Brad Steiger and Joan Whritenour, *The New UFO Breakthrough* (London, Tandem, 1973) pp. 5–19.

'Mind control experiments . . .' 'Killer phones', *Fortean Times* 45 (winter 1985) pp. 8–9; Martin Cannon, 'The numbers game', *The Anomalist*, 1 (1995) pp. 33–45.

The Scape Ore swamp monster Paul Sieveking, 'Lizard man', *Fortean Times*, 51 (winter 1988–89) pp. 34–7; Mark Opasnick and Mark Chorvinsky, 'Lizard man', *Strange Magazine* 3 (1988) pp. 32–3; Loren Coleman, 'The strange case of the two Charlie Wetzels', *Fortean Times*, 39 (spring 1983) pp. 44–6; Coleman, *Curious Encounters* (Winchester, Massachussets, Faber & Faber, 1985) p. 34.

The Mad Gasser of Mattoon Donald Johnson, 'The 'phantom anaesthetist' of Mattoon: a field study of mass hysteria', *Journal of Abnormal and Social Psychology*, 40 (1945) pp.175–86; Coleman, Curious Encounters, pp.191–211; Willy Smith, 'Mattoon revisited', *Magonia*, 48 (Jan 1994) pp. 3–6; Michael Shoemaker, 'The mad gasser of Botetourt', *Fate*, 38, n 6 (Jun 1985) pp. 62–8. In the course of his research, Smith made the important discovery that Johnson, on whose work most other writers based their summaries of the Mattoon case, was only a first-year university student at the time the article was written, with probably nothing more than an introductory course in psychology to guide him in his fieldwork.

Little green men Janet Bord, 'I spy little green men', *Fortean Times*, 91 (Oct 1996) pp. 30–3.

8 Hoax

Florida's giant penguin Ivan T. Sanderson, *More 'Things'* (New York, Pyramid Books, 1969); Bob Rickard, 'Florida's penguin panic', *Fortean Times*, 66 (Dec 1992 – Jan 1993) pp. 41–3. Before altogether writing off the idea of out-of-place penguins, it is worth noting that, in January 1995, five of the birds were spotted in the sea off Genoa. The Italian authorities were trying to discover how they had got there. *Daily Telegraph*, 7 Jan 1995.

Crop circles Pat Delgado and Colin Andrews, *Circular Evidence* (London, Bloomsbury, 1990); Ralph Noyes (ed), *The Crop Circle Enigma* (Gateway Books, 1990) Jim Schnabel, *Round in Circles: Physicists, Poltergeists, Pranksters and the Secret History of the Cropwatchers* (London, Penguin, 1994); Ian Mrzyglod, 'A last word on whirlwinds', *The Probe Report*, v 2 n 4 (Mar 1982) pp. 6–9; crop circles special issue of *Fortean Times*, 53 (winter 1989–90); 'This year's crop', *Fortean Times*, 55 (autumn 1990) pp. 7–13.

'Writing was Tifinig . . .' This North African language also figures prominently in a quite different mystery, the question of what lies at the bottom of the Oak Island Money Pit in Nova Scotia.

Oracle of the Dead Peter James and Nick Thorpe, *Ancient Inventions* (London, Michael O'Mara Books, 1995) pp. 419–21. One of the great mysteries of this remarkable complex was how its builders knew with such certainty that they would strike the vital volcanic springs when they started digging their tunnel.

Constantine the Great The apparently incredible tale of the emperor's vision was told by him to the historian Eusebius, who describes it in his *De Vita Constani* (in H. Wace and B. Schaff (eds), *A Select Library of Nicene and Post-Nicene Fathers of the Christian Church* (Oxford, Parker & Co., 1890) pp. 27–8).

Helena and the discovery of the True Cross John Julius Norwich, *Byzantium: the Early Centuries* (London, Viking, 1988) p. 68; Gordon Stein, *Encyclopaedia of Hoaxes* (Detroit, Gale Research, 1993) pp. 235–6. This remarkable story, too, is reasonably well-attested – Bishop Cyril of Jerusalem (probably not an eye-witness) discussed it only twenty-five years later, treating it as common knowledge.

Other miracles of Christianity . . . It is only fair to note that, with very few exceptions, the Catholic Church does not endorse such miracles as genuine. Many churchmen do have faith in them, but the question of whether or not to believe in them remains a matter of private choice rather than an article of dogma.

'*Livy reported that a statue of Apollo once wept . . .*' Cited in Robert Rickard and John Michell, *Phenomena: A Book of Wonders* (London, Thames & Hudson, 1977) pp. 20–1.

The menstruating statue of Kerala province 'Miracles', *Fortean Times*, 36 (winter 1982) pp. 19–21, citing *Probe India* (August 1981).

The bleeding tomb of the Lebanon The tomb is that of one Father Cherbal, and it can be found in a mountain-top convent at Annaya north of Beirut. It is credited with curing Jeanette Howard, 30, of paralysis in about 1967. 'Miracles', *Fortean Times*, 16 (June 1976) pp. 7, 13–15.

'*Samples have been tested and shown to be human blood . . .*' Including, allegedly, liquid collected from a bleeding crucifix in Porto das Caixas, Brazil, c.1968. Ibid.

Weeping and bleeding statues Luigi Garlaschelli, 'Weeping statues', *Chemistry in Britain*, n. 31 n 7 (July 1995) p. 534; Luigi Garlaschelli to Mike Dash, 27 Dec 1995, author's files; on the Civitavecchia statue, see 'Virgin blood floods Italy', *Fortean Times*, 81 (Jun–Jul 1995) p.11; the statue that wept for eight years was the one in the Porto des Caixas case, see note above. Garlaschelli notes that a regular flow is best maintained with the help of distilled water, and says that the mineral deposits from ordinary tap water can cause an erratic flow. This may help to explain the unpredictable behaviour of icons in many of the most celebrated cases.

Drinking statues Hindu statues are regularly offered such sustenance, but are generally believed to consume only the incorporeal portions of the food. It has been suggested that the drinking statues flap gained currency as quickly as it did because it occurred during the season of *pitr baksh*, when the devout offer milk for the souls of their ancestors. Joe Nickell, 'Milk-drinking idols', *Skeptical Inquirer* (Mar–Apr 1996) p. 7; 'It's all in the lap of the gods', *Fortean Times*, 84 (Dec 1995–Jan 1996) pp. 16–17.

Hell discovered in Siberia 'Hell found under Siberia', *Strange*, 7 (April 1991)

p. 44; 'Siberian hell', *Fortean Times*, 59 (Sept 1991) p.16; Paul Sieveking, 'Driller chiller', *Fortean Times*, 72 (Dec 1993–Jan 1994) pp. 42–3.

T. Lobsang Rampa 'Lobsang Rampa', *The Rampa Story* (New York, Bantam Books, 1968); Stein, *Encyclopedia of Hoaxes*, pp. 5–6; Bob Rickard, 'T. Lobsang Rampa: the plumber from Plympton who became a lama from Lhasa', *Fortean Times*, 63 (June–Jul 1992) pp. 24–6. The 'T' in Rampa's name, incidentally, supposedly stood for 'Tuesday'.

Carlos Castenada Richard de Mille, *Castenada's Journey: the Power and the Allegory* (Santa Barbara, Capra Press, 1976); Stein, *Encyclopedia of Hoaxes*, pp. 1–30.

Eusapia Palladino 'Palladino, Eusapia', in Leslie Shepard (ed), *Encyclopaedia of Occultism & Parapsychology*, 2nd edn (Detroit, Gale Research, 1985) pp. 997–1002; Hereward Carrington, *Personal Experiences in Spiritualism* (London, T. Werner Laurie, c. 1910); Gordon Stein, 'Mediumship: is it mixed or just mixed up?'. *Skeptical Inquirer*, vol 19, n 3, (May–Jun 1995) pp. 30–2.

Mediumistic frauds Alan Gauld, *Mediumship and Survival: a Century of Investigations* (London, Heinemann, 1982)

Mirabelli Guy Lyon Playfair, *The Flying Cow: Research into Paranormal Phenomena in the World's Most Psychic Country* (London, Souvenir Press, 1975) pp. 78–110; Playfair, 'Hoax! The great Mirabelli', *Fortean Times*, 71 (Oct–Nov 1993) pp. 43–5. Playfair, too, tends to believe that there may have been something in Mirabelli's earliest performances – a genuine phenomenon that he was later forced to duplicate with some fairly basic conjuring tricks.

Hamilton calf-napping hoax Jerome Clark, *The UFO Encyclopaedia: The Emergence of a Phenomenon: From the Beginning Through 1959* (Detroit, Omnigraphics, 1992) pp. 192–200; *Atchison County Mail*, 7 May 1897, cited in ibid.

Aurora crash hoax H. Michael Simmons, 'Once upon a time in the west, or, the mystery of the Aurora graveyard', *Magonia*, 20 (August 1985) pp. 3–6; Wallace Chariton, *The Great Texas Airship Mystery* (Plano, Texas, Wordware Publishing, 1991) pp.197–214. When reinvestigated, the story was discovered to be a fabrication from beginning to end – Judge Proctor, who did live in Aurora, did not even own a windmill.

Living pterodactyl Michael Goss, 'The French pterodactyl: a Fortean folly', *Magonia*, 21 (December 1985) pp. 8–7, 11

Other inaccurate nineteenth-century press reports One example might be the Winstead Wildman hoax of 1895. This case has been termed 'the first great Bigfoot flap'. Beginning in August, many people reported seeing a naked, hairy 'wild man' about six feet tall along the New York State/Connecticut border. At least twenty-one contemporary press reports concerning the flap, all of them seeming to suggest that something genuinely unusual was going on, were uncovered before it was discovered that the story was said to have started life as a hoax by an impish newspaperman named Louis Stone. One respected investigator, however, has suggested that the attribution of the flap to Stone is itself a hoax, and suggested that the original reports that got the scare underway were sightings of a bear. Michael T. Shoemaker, 'Searching for the historical Bigfoot', *Strange Magazine*, 11 (spring–summer 1993) pp. 30–1, 59.

Ummo affair Jerome Clark, *The UFO Encyclopaedia: High Strangeness: 1960–1979* (Detroit, Omnigraphics, 1996) pp. 512–16; Luis Gonzales, 'The planet of the anonymous correspondents', *Magonia*, 47 (October 1993) pp. 9–14.

Carlos Allende and the Philadelphia Experiment Goerman, himself a New Kensington resident, discovered of the hoax by glorious chance, when he realised that his next-door neighbour was none other than Carl Allen's father. On the history of the experiment, see Charles Berlitz and William Moore, *The Philadelphia Experiment: Project Invisibility* (London, Souvenir Press, 1979); Robert Goerman, *The Allende Dossier* (Brackenridge, Goerman Publishing, 1982); Jerome Clark, 'Allende letters', *The Emergence of a Phenomenon*; Jacques Vallee, 'Anatomy of a hoax: the Philadelphia Experiment 50 years later', *Journal of Scientific Exploration*, 8. n. 1 (1994) pp. 47–71. Extracts from the annotated *Case for the UFO* appear in several popular UFO books, such as Brad Steiger and Joan Whritenour, *The New UFO Breakthrough* (London, Tandem, 1973) pp. 61–6. Although now generally accepted as a hoax, the Philadelphia Experiment has been reborn for a new generation of readers under the guise of 'The Montauk Project'. Several books based on the latter case have suggested that Philadelphia-style experiments, aimed at controlling time, continued at a secret air force base at Montauk. There is little evidence for anything of the sort. (See, for example, Preston Nichols, *The Montauk Project: Experiments in Time* (New York, Sky Books, 1992).) The truth may be much simpler. In his paper, Vallee cites an interview with another sailor who was on board one of the sister ships at Philadelphia. He suggested that a secret experiment really had taken place, but that it involved new equipment for demagnetising hulls so as to render German magnetic homing torpedoes useless.

Majestic-12 The matter of the 'forged signature' remains open. It is not absolutely identical to the Truman signature found by Klass, a fact that the sceptics explain by pointing out that the MJ-12 paper has been copied at least once, which would cause distortions in the relative proportions of the lines. Proponents argue that different parts of the signature appear to have been enlarged by varying amounts, which suggests that one cannot be a copy of the other. For the proponents' point of view, see Timothy Good, *Above Top Secret: the Worldwide UFO Cover-Up* (London, Sidgwick & Jackson, 1987) esp. pp. 250–3, 385–6; Stanton Friedman, *Top Secret/MAJIC* (New York, Marlowe & Company, 1996). For the debunkers', Philip Klass, 'The MJ-12 Papers' parts 1 and 2', *Skeptical Inquirer*, vol. 12 n 2 (winter 1987–88) pp. 137–46 and vol. 12 n 3 (spring 1988) pp. 279–89; Klass, 'New evidence of MJ-12 hoax', *Skeptical Inquirer*, vol. 14 n 2 (winter 1990) pp.136–8; Joe Nickell and John Fischer, *Mysterious Realms: Probing Paranormal, Historical and Forensic Enigmas* (Buffalo, Prometheus Books, 1992) pp. 81–105.

The dark side hypothesis See summaries of this extremely complex conspiracy theory in Jerome Clark, *The UFO Encyclopaedia: UFOs in the 1980s* (Detroit, Apogee Books, 1990) pp. 99–109; Curtis Peebles, *Watch the Skies! A Chronicle of the Flying Saucer Myth* (Washington, Smithsonian Institution Press, 1994) pp. 256–82. One point that perhaps should be mentioned is the manner in which Doty's AFOSI career ended. In 1986 he was transferred from New Mexico to Germany and assigned to liaise with a number of Communist sources. Doty's superiors became suspicious that he was fabricating some of his material and, when he failed a lie detector test, he was reassigned to the United States as a 'food services specialist', spending his last year with the Air Force as a canteen manager.

Spirit photography Stein, *Encyclopedia of Hoaxes*, pp.183–5; Shepard, *Encyclopedia of Occultism and Parapsychology*, pp. 1261–2.

Cottingley fairies Arthur Conan Doyle, *The Coming of the Fairies* (London, Hodder & Stoughton, 1922); Geoffrey Crawley, 'That astonishing affair of the Cottingley fairies', *British Journal of Photography*, 24 and 31 Dec 1982, 7, 21 and 28 Jan, 4, 11 and 18 Feb, 1 and 8 Apr 1983; Joe Cooper, *The Case of the Cottingley Fairies* (London, Robert Hale, 1990); K.M.Briggs, *The Fairies in Tradition and Literature* (London, Routledge & Kegan Paul 1978) pp. 238–40.

Other fairy photos For Doc Shiels' fairy photos, see Anthony Shiels, *Monstrum! A Wizard's Tale* (London, Fortean Tomes, 1990) pp. 55–7; Mark Chorvinsky, 'The Shiels-related fairy photos', *Strange Magazine*, 9 (spring–summer 1992) pp. 24–5, 60. In a second edition of *The Coming of the Fairies*, Conan Doyle published a series of alleged fairy photographs taken in East Prussia. These photographs have never been discussed in the phenomenological literature, and modern authorities do not seem to be aware of their existence.

Shiels monster photos Mark Chorvinsky, 'The 'Mary F.' Morgawr photographs investigation', *Strange Magazine*, 8 (fall 1991) pp. 11, 46–8; Chorvinsky, 'The 'G.B. Gordon' Shiels photograph', ibid., 49; Chorvinsky, 'The Shiels tapes', ibid., 50–1; Alastair Boyd, 'Notes on the Shiels tapes', ibid., pp. 15, 51; Chorvinsky, 'The trickster', ibid., pp.16–17, 54–5. 'Doc is a serial hoaxer, driven to perform hoaxes again and again as an artistic form of self-expression,' Chorvinsky concludes.

Irvine films The possibility of fraud was first mentioned by Constance Whyte, *More than a Legend* (London, Hamish Hamilton, 1957) in relation to Irvine's 1936 footage. This footage has recently been rediscovered and certainly does not look genuine.

Patterson Bigfoot film John Napier, *Bigfoot: the Yeti and Sasquatch in Myth and Reality* (London, Abacus, 1976) pp. 73–80; Mark Chorvinsky, 'The makeup man and the monster', *Strange Magazine*, 17 (summer 1996) pp. 6–10. 51–3. It has recently been revealed that there is another reason to suspect the film's authenticity: Patterson and Gimlin were directed to the Bluff Creek area, where the sequence was filmed, by Ray Wallace, the road constructor strongly suspected of hoaxing the first modern Bigfoot sighting (see chapter 5). This opens the possibility that the two men were the innocent dupes of a third hoaxer.

Practising to deceive Vallee, 'Anatomy of a hoax'; Marcello Truzzi, 'The sociology and psychology of hoaxes' in Stein, *Encyclopedia of Hoaxes*, pp. 291–7.

9 Hard Evidence

'*A testable and repeatable effect does not exist . . .*' Psychical researchers, who have been tackling this difficulty since the 1930s, generally account for it by suggesting that psi is a weak and capricious effect, far stronger in some people than in others. Even those with strong psi powers – 'psychics', in other words – are thought to be highly sensitive to all manner of influences. One of the most thoroughly explored is what is known as the 'sheep-goat effect', the proposition that belief in psi in itself helps to determine whether or not a subject is able to demonstrate extrasensory perception. Gertrude Schmeidler, 'Some guidelines from research findings' in Ivor Grattan-Guinness (ed), *Psychical Research: a Guide to its History, Principles and Practices* (Wellingborough, Aquarian, 1982) pp. 268–83.

Hendry's UFO investigations Allan Hendry, *The UFO Handbook: a Guide to Investigating, Evaluating and Reporting UFO Sightings* (Garden City, New Jersey, Doubleday & Company, 1979).

Phantom lakes and cottages John Michell and Robert Rickard, *Phenomena: A Book of Wonders* (London, Thames & Hudson, 1976) pp. 51–2.

The case of the phantom hotel Skeptical Briefs (December 1995) p. 2. There is also a folkloric element to this story-cycle, since there are parallels with the tale of a mother's journey with her daughter to the Paris Exhibition of 1889. Upon their arrival, *en route* from India to London, they repaired to room 342 of their hotel, which was rather distinctively decorated. The mother felt ill, and so the daughter went out alone for medicine; on her return a few hours later, however, she found her mother missing, her room mysteriously and comprehensively redecorated, and a disbelieving hotel manager who insisted that he had never seen either lady before and who demonstrated that the register, which both had signed, bore no trace of the mother's name. Greatly distressed, the young woman sought help, unsuccessfully, from the police and the British ambassador. Only later did it emerge that her mother had died suddenly of plague and that, fearing a panic that would ruin the Exhibition, the hotel management and the city authorities had connived to cover up all trace of her existence. This account made its first appearance as a short story titled 'Too Long at the Fair', but it has since been reported as fact by a number of books on strange phenomena, such as the *Reader's Digest Book of Strange Stories, Amazing Facts* (London, Reader's Digest Association, 1979) p. 361.

Blackmore and the SPR archive Susan Blackmore, *The Adventures of a Parapsychologist* (Amherst, Prometheus Books, 1996) p. 179.

The Indian rope-trick Richard Wiseman and Peter Lamont, 'Unravelling the

Indian rope-trick', *Nature* vol 383 n 6597 (19 Sep 1996) p. 212; Rupert Gould, 'The Indian rope-trick' in *The Stargazer Talks* (London, Geoffrey Bles, 1943) pp. 7–13; Eric Dingwall, 'The end of a legend: a note on the magical flight', in Allan Angoff and Diana Barth, (eds), *Parapsychology and Anthropolgy: Proceedings of an International Conference Held in London, England, August 29–31 1973* (New York, Parapsychology Foundation, 1974) pp. 241–61.

Expectancy Graham Reed, *The Psychology of Anomalous Experience* (Buffalo, Prometheus Books, 1988) pp. 58–60; Tim Dinsdale, *Loch Ness Monster* (London, Routledge & Kegan Paul, 1961) pp. 81–2; personal discussions with Adrian Shine, 1984.

1947 UFO flap Ted Bloecher, *The Report on the UFO Wave of 1947* (Washington DC, the Author, 1967); Jan Aldrich, Project 1947 press release, November 1996.

The Great Fear Simon Schama, *Citizens: a Chronicle of the French Revolution* (London, Viking, 1989) pp. 429–36. Schama notes that a similar phenomenon had occurred in France in 1703, but there are in fact many historical parallels.

Chinese hair-cutting panics Steve Moore, 'Tales from the Yellow Emporium', *Fortean Times*, 39 (spring 1983) pp. 51–3; 'Tales from the Yellow Emporium', *Fortean Times* 40 (summer 1983) pp. 42–3; 'Chinese hair-cutting panics: a tail-piece', *Fortean Times*, 59 (Sep 1991) pp. 48–50.

Vanishing penis panics Bob Rickard, 'Jewel heist panic', *Fortean Times*, 56 (winter 1990) p. 33.

Goatsucker Scott Corrales, *The Chupacabras Diaries: an Unofficial Chronicle of Puerto Rico's Paranormal Predator* (Derrick Hill, Pennsylvania, Samizdat Press, 1996); Corrales, 'How many goats can a goatsucker suck?', *Fortean Times*, 89 (August 1996) pp. 34–8; 'Euro-sucker?', *Fortean Times*, 95 (February 1997) p. 8. Goatsucker's principal chronicler, Scott Corrales, noted two possible precursors to the panic: one a wave of cattle mutilations in 1975, and the other a little-known 1989 flap concerning a plague of 'vampire birds'. He also explored the highly sensationalist coverage of the flap in the Puerto Rican press.

'*A considerable folklore . . .*' Ron Westrum, 'Witnesses of UFOs and other anomalies', in Richard Haines (ed), *UFO Phenomena and the Behavioural Scientist* (Metuchen, New Jersey, Scarecrow Press, 1979) p. 91.

'*Contagion' theory* Joe Nickell, 'The Devil's Footprints: solving a mystery', *Skeptical Inquirer*, vol 20 n 1 (Jan–Feb 1996) pp.18–20; Nickell, *Entities: Angels, Spirits, Demons and Other Alien Beings* (Amherst, Prometheus Books, 1995) p. 43.

Walter Powell and the Saladin Nigel Watson, *Phantom Aerial Flaps and Waves, Magonia Occasional Paper, no.1* (London, Magonia Magazine, 1987) p. 9.

Mass hysteria 'Spring fever', *Fortean Times*, 69 (Jun–Jul 1993) p. 16; Leonard George, *Alternative Realities: the Paranormal, the Mystic and the Transcendent in Human Experience* (New York, Facts on File, 1995) pp. 114–16.

Multiple-witness reports Westrum, 'Witnesses of UFO,' pp.106–07.

High strangeness reports Ibid. A survey of 334 humanoid encounters indicated that sixty-one per cent involved only a single witness.

The mediumship of Daniel Home Eric Dingwall, *Some Human Oddities* (London, Home & Van Thal, 1947) pp. 91–128, 187–193; Leslie Shepard (ed), *Encyclopedia of Occultism and Parapsychology* (Detroit, Gale Research, 1984) vol 2, pp. 621–5, 759–61; Trevor Hall, *The Enigma of Daniel Home: Medium of Fraud?* (Buffalo, Prometheus Books, 1984). It is only fair to state, first, that there is some doubt as to which room on which floor of which house the seance took place, and therefore as to how the two windows were positioned relative to each other, and the distance between them; and second that Home did appear to levitate in front of multiple witnesses on numerous other occasions, to the satisfaction of those witnesses. His case continues to arouse lively debate.

Ballinspittle's moving statue Lionel Beer, *The Moving Statue of Ballinspittle and Related Phenomena* (London, Spacelink Books, 1986); Joe Nickell, *Looking for a Miracle: Weeping Icons, Relics, Stigmata, Visions and Healing Cures* (Buffalo, Prometheus Books, 1993) pp. 64–5.

'That autokinesis is . . .' George, *Alternative Realities*, p. 27.

Folie a deux George, *Alternative Realities*, p. 137; Hilary Evans, *God•Spirits•Cosmic Guardians* (Wellingborough, Aquarian Press, 1987) pp. 239, 256–7.

Linda Napolitano abduction Budd Hopkins, *Witnessed: the True Story of the Brooklyn Bridge UFO Abductions* (New York, Pocket Books, 1996); Philip J. Klass, 'New Hopkins book', *Skeptics' UFO Newsletter*, 42 (Nov 1996) pp. 1–7.

Problems with Bigfoot Janet and Colin Bord, *Bigfoot Casebook* (St Albans, Granada, 1982); John Green, *Sasquatch: the Apes Among Us* (Seattle, Hancock House Publishers, 1978).

The monster of Lough Nahooin F.W. Holiday, *The Dragon and the Disc: an Investigation into the Totally Fantastic* (London, Futura, 1974) pp. 48–62; Roy Mackal, *The Monsters of Loch Ness* (London, Futura, 1976) pp. 40–1.

Mermaids Gwen Benwell and Arthur Waugh, *Sea Enchantress: the Tale of the Mermaid and her Kin* (New York, Citadel Press, 1965); Michel Meurger and Claude Gagnon, *Lake Monster Traditions: a Cross-Cultural Analysis* (London, Fortean Tomes, 1988) pp. 18–22.

Photographic evidence for the Loch Ness Monster See the surveys in Roy Mackal, *The Monsters of Loch Ness* (London, Futura, 1976) pp. 93–122, 273–6; Ronald Binns, *The Loch Ness Mystery Solved* (Shepton Mallet, Open Books, 1983) pp. 107–125; and Steuart Campbell, *The Loch Ness Monster: the Evidence* (Wellingborough, Aquarian Press, 1986) pp. 35–74.

Lowrie photos Tim Dinsdale, *Loch Ness Monster* (London, Routledge & Kegan Paul, 1976) pp. 104–06; Dinsdale, *The Leviathans* (London, Futura, 1976) pp. 19–21.

Raynham Hall ghost Robert Rickard and Richard Kelly, *Photos of Unknown* (London, New English Library, 1980) p. 1.

Bigfoot prints John Napier, *Bigfoot: the Yeti and the Sasquatch in Myth and Reality* (London, Abacus, 1976) pp. 96–119; Janet and Colin Bord,

Bigfoot: the Evidence (Wellingborough, Aquarian Press, 1984) pp. 90–6; Michael R. Dennett, 'Evidence for Bigfoot? An investigation of the Mill Creek 'sasquatch prints', *Skeptical Inquirer*, vol 13 n 3 (spring 1989) pp. 264–72.

Joe Simonton's extraterrestrial pancakes John Rimmer, *The Evidence for Alien Abductions* (Wellingborough, Aquarian Press, 1984) p. 79; Jerome Clark, *The UFO Encyclopaedia: High Strangeness: UFOs from 1960 Through 1979* (Detroit, Omnigraphics, 1996) pp. 168–75. There seems to be some doubt as to Simonton's occupation. He is sometimes said to have been a chicken farmer.

Ubatuba residue Jerome Clark, *The UFO Encyclopaedia: The Emergence of a Phenomenon: UFOs from the Beginning Through 1959* (Detroit, Omnigraphics, 1994) pp. 331–3; Jenny Randles, *UFO retrievals: the Recovery of Alien Spacecraft* (London, Blandford 1995).

Trans-En-Provence CE2 Jerome Clark, *UFOs in the 1980s* (Detroit, Apogee Books, 1990) pp. 205–07; Eric Maillot and Jacques Scornaux, 'Trans-En-Provence: when science and belief go hand-in-hand', in Hilary Evans and Dennis Stacy (eds), *UFO 1947–1997: 50 Years of Flying Saucers* (London, John Brown, 1997) pp. 151–9.

Falcon Lake CE2 Clark, *High Strangeness*, pp. 191–200.

The blood of St Januarius The best recent summary of this well-known phenomenon is Bob Rickard, 'Seeking red: the blood miracle of Naples', *Fortean Times*, 65 (Oct/Nov 1992) pp. 36–41. For Garlaschelli's views on thixotropy, see Luigi Garlaschelli and Sergio Della Sala, 'Working bloody miracles', *Nature*, vol 353 p. 507 (10 Oct 1991). It seems well worth noting that Januarius's blood originally liquefied only once each year, on his feast day.

Failure of the blood to liquefy There appears to be a sharp distinction made here between the seventeen expositions of May and September, when a failure of the blood to liquefy is taken very seriously, and the single December exposition, at which failure is quite common. According to the tabulation of Alfana and Amitrano, *Il Miracolo di San Gennaro* (Naples, 1924) (cited in ibid.), there had been seventy-eight failures in the last 200 December expositions, but only a handful – perhaps fewer than fifty – among the 3400 May and September expositions during the same period. The great discrepancy between these ratios of failure (1:2.6 in December, 1:60 in May and September) does not appear explicable by relying solely upon the thixotropic theory.

The elusive hard evidence Another example is the so-called Silpho Moor Saucer, a miniature UFO some eighteen inches across which turned up at the top of an earth bank near Fylingdales early warning station in Yorkshire towards the end of the 1950s. The saucer seemed to contain nothing but a hollow copper rod, with a metal coil wrapped tightly around it on which were etched a series of hieroglyphic symbols. Closer investigation showed that the tube was packed with seventeen wafer-thin copper scrolls covered with similar hieroglyphics which, when translated, turned out to be a 2000-word message to mankind purportedly written by an alien called Ullo. After passing through several hands, the Silpho Moor Saucer was last seen on display in a fish and chip shop somewhere in east Yorkshire, and attempts to relocate it have not been successful. Presumably it was a hoax, albeit it an elaborate and largely pointless one. Jenny Randles, *UFO Retrievals*, pp. 77–82.

Dr McRae's monster films It is worth noting that Holiday's principal informant, the Scottish landscape painter, Alaister Dallas, later contradicted this version of events in an interview with Alan Wilkins. F.W. Holiday, *The Great Orm of Loch Ness* (London, Faber & Faber, 1971) pp. 113–17; Mackal, *The Monsters of Loch Ness*, pp. 116–17; Campbell, *The Loch Ness Monster* p. 53.

New River Inlet carcass Bernard Heuvelmans, *In the Wake of the Sea Serpents* (London, Rupert Hart-Davis, 1968) p. 131.

Hagelund's baby monster Paul LeBlond and Edward Bousfield, *Cadborosaurus: Survivor From the Deep* (Victoria, British Columbia, Horsdal & Schubart 1995) pp. 57–9, 121.

Bigfoot remains Bord and Bord, *Bigfoot Casebook*, pp. 128–9.

Mummified yeti hand Loren Coleman, *Tom Slick and the Search for the Yeti* (Boston, Faber and Faber, 1989) pp. 90-91

10 Answers From Inner Space

Philip the Imaginary Ghost Iris M. Owen and Margaret Sparrow, *Conjuring Up Philip* (New York, Harper & Row, 1976). Had Philip materialised, he would have become what occultists call a 'thought form'. Hilary Evans, in *Visions•Apparitions•Alien Visitors* (Wellingborough, Aquarian Press, 1986) pp. 216–21, gives two examples of apparently successful attempts to create thought forms. One, a psychical experiment conducted in St Petersburg, in 1913, led to the temporary creation of the fairytale character 'Puss in Boots'.

The Goblin Universe F.W. Holiday, *The Goblin Universe* (St Paul, Minnesota, Llewellyn Publications, 1986), p. 214.

Ultraterrestrials Jerome Clark, *The UFO Encyclopaedia: High Strangeness: UFOs from 1960 Through 1979* (Detroit, Omnigraphics, 1996) pp. 551–2.

Thelma Arnold's Bigfoot B. Ann Slate and Alan Berry, *Bigfoot* (New York, Bantam Books, 1976) pp. 118–19. 'Arnold' is in fact a pseudonym.

Telepathic Bigfoot Janet and Colin Bord, *The Evidence for Bigfoot and Other Man – Beasts* (Wellingborough, Aquarian Press, 1984) pp. 115–16.

Fantasy-prone personalities Jerome Clark, *The UFO Encyclopaedia: UFOs in the 1980s* (Detroit, Apogee Books, 1990) pp. 111–12; Robert Baker, 'The aliens among us: hypnotic regression revisited', *Skeptical Inquirer*, vol 12 n 2 (winter 1987–88) pp. 147–62; Mark Rodeghier, Jeff Goodpaster and Sandra Blatterbauer, 'Psychosocial characteristics of abductees: results from the CUFOS Abduction Project', *Journal of UFO Studies*, NS, 3 (1991) pp. 59–90; Leonard George, *Alternative Realities: The Paranormal, the Mystic and the Transcendent in Human Experience* (New York, Facts on File, 1995) pp. 4–5, 51–2, 96–7; Joe Nickell, 'A study of fantasy proneness in the thirteen cases of alleged encounters in John Mack's 'Abduction', *Skeptical Inquirer* v 20 n 3 (May–Jun 1996) pp. 18–20, 54.

'The individual has a need . . .' Hilary Evans, *Gods•Spirits•Cosmic Guardians* (Wellingborough, Aquarian Press, 1986) p. 268.

'Build-up phase' theory John Rimmer, *The Evidence for Alien Abductions* (Wellingborough, Aquarian Press, 1984) pp. 49–50

Mrs Piper Leslie Shepard, *The Encyclopaedia of Occultism and Parapsychology* (Detroit, Gale Research, 1985) vol. 3 p. 1037.

Mrs Leonard Ibid., vol. 2, p. 755.

Catherine Muller Hilary Evans, 'Talking with Martians', *Fortean Times*, 76 (Aug–Sep 1994) pp. 22–3.

St Catherine Laboure Joe Nickell, *Looking for a Miracle: Weeping Icons, Relics, Stigmata, Visions & Healing Cures* (Buffalo, Prometheus Books, 1993) p. 170.

Paul Bennett Nigel Watson, *Portraits of Alien Encounters* (London, Valis Books, 1990) pp. 16–70.

'Most researchers . . .' George, *Alternative Realities*, p. 97.

Altered states of consciousness Ibid., pp. 11–13, 126–7; Graham Reed, *The Psychology of Anomalous Experience* (Buffalo, Prometheus Books, 1988) pp. 168–9.

'The waking state . . .' George, *Alternative Realities*, 11–12.

'. . . is one in which [an individual] clearly feels . . .' Ibid., citing C.T. Tart (ed.), *Altered States of Consciousness: a Book of Readings* (New York, Wiley, 1969); Hilary Evans, *Alternate States of Consciousness* (Wellingborough, Aquarian, 1989).

Sleep phenomena Peretz Lavie, *The Enchanted World of Sleep* (New Haven, Yale University Press, 1996) pp. 79–80.

Hallucinations Reed, *The Psychology of Anomalous Experience*, pp. 46–68.

Hypnagogia and hypnopompia Although I use the term 'hallucination' to describe these visions, there is still some debate about whether they are true hallucinations or simply images – in other words, things that the percipient knows are not real. I prefer the term hallucination here because it seems clear that some experiences, which may fairly be presumed to be hypnagogic or hypnopompic, do appear entirely real to the percipient, to the extent that he may well find it difficult later to rationalise the experience. Ibid. p. 65. In general, see David Hufford, *The Terror That Comes in the Night: an Experience-Centred Study of Supernatural Assault Traditions* (Philadelphia, Alternative Realities, University of Pennsylvania Press, 1982); Evans, *Visions•Apparitions•Alien Visitors*, pp. 45–58; Baker, 'The Aliens Among us'; George, op. cit. pp. 126–8

'An unsuspecting woman . . .' David Jacobs, *Secret Life: Firsthand Accounts of Alien Abductions* (London, Fourth Estate, 1993) pp. 49–50.

Hallucinations and absorption George, *Alternative Realities*, pp. 4–5, 83–4, 105–7, 117–19.

Sensation of cold Celia Green and Charles McCreery, *Apparitions* (London, Hamish Hamilton, 1975) p. 117.

Oz factor Jenny Randles, *UFO Reality: a Critical Look at the Physical*

Evidence (London, Robert Hale, 1983); Jerome Clark, *UFOs in the 1980s* (Detroit, Apogee Books, 1990) pp. 169–70.

Possession T.K. Osterrich, *Possession, Demoniacal and Other, Among Primitive Races in Antiquity, the Middle Ages and Modern Times* (Secaucus, New Jersy; Citadel Press, 1974); Rossell Hope Robbins, *The Encyclopaedia of Witchcraft and Demonology* (London, Bookplan, 1964) pp. 392–8; Marc Cramer, *The Devil Within* (London, W.H. Allen, 1979); Barry Beyerstein, 'Neuropathology and the legacy of spirit possession', *Skeptical Inquirer*, 12 n 3 (spring 1988) pp. 248–62.

Temporal lobe abnormalities Robert Durrant, 'Temporal lobe epilepsy', Mutual UFO Network Investigator's Edge series, no. 11, 1991; Beyerstein, 'Neuropathology' pp. 251–5; George *Alternative Realities*, pp. 276–7; Susan Blackmore, 'Alien abduction: the inside story', *New Scientist*, 19 Nov 1994, pp. 29–31; Richard Restak, 'Complex partial seizures present diagnostic challenge', *MHI* September 1995.

Jacobs's refutation of Persinger Jacobs, *Secret Life*, pp. 296–7.

Cases of oxygen starvation Nigel Watson, 'Historical aerospatial anomalies', *Fortean Times*, 36 (winter 1982) pp. 44–46; Ian Skinner, 'Mystery of the deep', *Fortean Times*, 92 (November 1995) p. 51.

Memory and false memory Reed, *The Psychology of Anomolous Experience* pp. 69–90; George, *Alternative Realities*, pp. 93–5; Lawrence Wright, *Remembering Satan: Recovered Memory and the Shattering of a Family* (London, Serpent's Tail, 1994); Ted Goertzel, 'Measuring the prevalence of false memories', *Skeptical Inquirer*, v 18 n 3 (spring 1994) pp. 266–72; Martin Gardner, 'The tragedies of false memory', *Skeptical Inquirer*, v 18 n 5 (fall 1994) pp. 464–470.

'Ofshe now had serious doubts . . .' Wright, *Remembering Satan*, p. 146.

Hypnosis Baker, 'The Aliens Among us'; Evans, *Visions•Apparitions•Alien Visitors*, pp. 186–8; Ian Wilson, *Mind Out of Time?: Reincarnation Claims Investigated* (London, Victor Gollancz, 1981) pp. 95–114; Peter Reeven, 'Fantasising under hypnosis: some experimental evidence', *Skeptical Inquirer*, v 12 n 2 (winter 1987–88) pp. 181–83; Jonathan Venn, 'Hypnosis and reincarnation: a critique and case study', *Skeptical Inquirer*, v 12 n 4 (summer 1988) pp. 386–91.

Cryptamnesia George, *Alternative Realities*, pp. 59–60; Melvyn Willin, 'Music from beyond the veil – or within ourselves?', *The Skeptic*, v 10 n 5/6 (Dec 1996) pp. 37–40.

Cryptaesthesia George, *Alternative Realities*, pp. 57–8.

Pareidolia Ibid. pp. 97–8, 212–14. For Christ on the henhouse door, see 'Henhouse "Images" ', *Fortean Times* 18 (Oct 1976), for the holy tortilla, see Robert Rickard and Richard Kelly, *Photos of the Unknown* (London, New English Press, 1980) p. 95.

Electronic Voice Phenomenon Konstantin Raudive, *Breakthrough: an Amazing Experiment in Electronic Communication* (Gerrards Cross, Colin Smythe, 1971); William Welch, *Talks With the Dead* (New York, Pinnacle Books, 1975); Alan Cleaver, 'But are the voices lying? The Electronic Voice Phenomenon: tape recordings or . . .?', *Common Ground*, 1 (1982) pp.

23–6; Alexander Macrae, 'Breakthrough! Again?' *Common Ground*, 6 (1983) pp. 32–4.

UFO drawings Richard Haines, 'What do UFO drawings by alleged eyewitnesses and non-eyewitnesses have in common?', in Haines, (ed), *UFO Phenomena and the Behavioural Scientist* (Metuchen, New Jersey, Scarecrow Press, 1979) pp. 358–95.

Lawson's abduction experiments Clark, *UFOs in the 1980s*, pp. 2–3; Evans, *Visions•Apparitions•Alien Visitors*, pp. 174–85; Jacobs, *Secret Life*, pp. 292–3.

11 Strange Fashions

Phantom social workers Mike Dash, 'The case of the phantom social workers', *Fortean Times*, 57 (spring 1991) pp. 43–5; Bob Rickard, 'Social panics', *Fortean Times*, 61 (Feb 1992) p. 36; Bob Rickard, 'The spectral inspectorate', *Fortean Times*, 66 (Dec 1992–Jan 1993) pp. 48–9; Bob Rickard, 'Fear on the doorstep', *Fortean Times*, 77 (Oct–Nov 1994) pp. 36–8; Joe McNally, 'It's all right missus, we're from the social', *Fortean Times*, 87 (Jun 1996) p. 18.

The cultural source hypothesis Jerome Clark, *The UFO Encyclopaedia: UFOs in the 1980s* (Detroit, Apogee Books, 1990) pp. 172–85.

Baker's reincarnation experiments Robert Baker, 'The effect of suggestion on past lives regression', *American Journal of Clinical Hypnosis*, 25 (1982) pp. 71–6.

Tendency of past life regressees to reflect beliefs of hypnotists Ian Wilson, *Mind Out of Time?: Reincarnation Claims Investigated* (London, Victor Gollancz, 1981) pp. 95–114.

Wilson's analysis of Stevenson's reincarnation data Ibid. pp. 53–60.

Michel Meurger and the cultural source hypothesis Michel Meurger, *Lake Monster Traditions: a Cross-Cultural Analysis* (London, Fortean Tomes, 1988).

Lake Saint-François Ibid. pp. 59–77, 117.

Strange fashions Strange phenomena are not only born: they die. Many of the unexplained mysteries that perplexed previous generations are all but forgotten now, and some flourished and then withered away in a single lifetime.

A fine example of just such a short-lived phenomenon is the lost art of *nauscopie*, which flourished for a few years in the late eighteenth-century on the Indian Ocean island of Mauritius. *Nauscopie*, according to its inventor, an obscure French naval officer named Bottineau, was a method of detecting the approach of vessels while they were still up to 600 miles away by making a close study of the skyline. With practice, he claimed, it was possible to isolate certain atmospheric effects that betrayed the presence of ships below the horizon:

'When a vessel approaches land, or another vessel, a *meteor* appears in the atmosphere, of a particular nature, visible to every eye, without any difficult effort: it is . . . the necessary result of the approach of one vessel towards another, or towards land. The existence of this *meteor*, and the knowledge of its different modifications, constitute the certainty and precision of my announcements.'

Whatever the mysterious *meteor* was, it seems unlikely that it was quite as easy to spot as Bottineau contended, and he seems, at first, to have put his remarkable discovery to use, principally, to make money. He made bets with the officers of the French garrison as to the when the next ship to reach the island would make its landfall, and between 1778 and 1782 seems to have successfully predicted the arrival of 575 vessels at Mauritius, some of them four days before they reached port. From surviving papers, it appears that the governor of the island, Viscount de Souillac, and several of his senior officers were quite satisfied that Bottineau had made a remarkable discovery, and that the 'wizard beacon keeper', as he became known, had managed to explain away his occasional lapses to the satisfaction of his superiors.

We will probably never know whether *nauscopie* was a fraud, a genuine meteorological phenomenon akin to mirages, or perhaps a form of remote viewing. Even now, though, years after the perfection of radar, proof of its existence would be of great interest to scientists and some practical use to sailors – and in the 1780s, the idea that a fleet could be detected at a great distance was revolutionary and of such import that, had the French been able to master the art, they could conceivably have seized command of the sea from Great Britain and emerged triumphant from the Napoleonic Wars. Yet Bottineau was never able to convince his government to back him, and he died in great poverty in 1802. Though two elderly pupils were still practising *nauscopie* as late as 1826 – an Indian journal of that time records that one of them 'was invited to Paris by the Institute, but he could not observe the same appearance there, and came back' – therefore, the secret appears to have been lost in the first half of the nineteenth century. Nothing quite like Bottineau's discovery seems to have been made before or since. Rupert Gould *Oddities* (London, Geoffrey Bles, 1944) pp. 173–93; *The Mirror of Literature, Amusement & Instruction*, vol. 7 n 200 (17 Jun 1826) p. 379.

Holy aubergines 'Muslim signs and wonders', *Fortean Times*, 55 (autumn 1990) pp. 4–5; 'Islamic simulacra', *Fortean Times*, 53 (winter 1989/90) p. 8; 'Holy fruit and vegetables', *Fortean Times*, 88 (July 1996) p. 8.

Stigmata Herbert Thurston, *The Physical Phenomena of Mysticism* (London, Burns, Oates, 1952) pp. 32–129; Ian Wilson, *The Bleeding Mind: An Investigation into the Mysterious Phenomenon of Stigmata* (London, Weidenfeld & Nicholson, 1988); Joe Nickell, *Looking for a Miracle* (Buffalo, Prometheus Books, 1993) pp. 219–225; Ted Harrison, *Stigmata: A Medieval Mystery in a Modern Age* (New York, Penguin, 1994); Harrison, 'What a way to spend Easter', *Fortean Times*, 95 (February 1997) pp. 34–38.

'*He began to contemplate . . .*' This passage is drawn from the *Fioretti* ('Little Flowers'), a compilation of St Francis's sayings and doings, which was not, in fact, set down until about a century after the saint's death. However, written evidence that he received the stigmata dates to no more than two years after the incident occurred.

'A young man was brought before the Archbishop . . .' The court found against the man and sentenced him to life imprisonment.

Out of the body experiences Carol Zaleski, *Otherworld Journeys: Accounts of Near-Death Experience in Medieval and Modern Times* (Oxford, Oxford University Press, 1987); James McClenon, *Wondrous Events: Foundations of Religious Belief* (Philadelphia, University of Pennsylvania Press, 1994) pp. 151–84.

'A man who had plunged from a cliff . . .' Ian Stevenson, 'Survival after death: evidence and issues', in Ivor Grattan-Guinness (ed.), *Psychical Research: A Guide to its History, Principles & Practices in Celebration of 100 Years of the Society for Psychical Research* (Wellingborough, Aquarian Press, 1982) pp. 109–10.

'Like UFO abductees . . .' Peter Rogerson, review of Zaleski, *Magonia*, 29 (April 1988) p. 16.

Purgatory The Catholic doctrine of purgatory was first defined in a Papal letter of 1253, set out at the council of Lyon (1274) and elaborated at the council of Ferrara-Florence (1438–45). Prior to that there had been a belief in a less defined realm of limbo, which was a transitional place for souls on their way to heaven and provided a home for unbaptised babies. The notion of purgatory was, however, more ancient than this. It may have been borrowed from the much older Persian faith of Zoroastrianism, which incudes a belief in the soul's journey through a purifying fire. Among the attractions of the doctrine was its ability to explain the appearance of ghosts, which were viewed as souls still awaiting entry to heaven. Protestants suggest that since believers are freed from sin through faith in Christ, the dead soul will go straight to heaven. The Orthodox Church also rejects the notion of purgatory, while continuing to encourage prayers for the souls stranded in some undefined, intermediate state following death. James Lewis, *Encyclopaedia of Afterlife Beliefs and Phenomena* (Detroit, Visible Ink, 1995) pp. 224–5, 295–6.

Land sightings of the Loch Ness Monster Roy Mackal, *The Monsters of Loch Ness* (London, Futura, 1976) pp. 262–4; Rupert Gould, *The Loch Ness Monster and Others* (London, Geoffrey Bles, 1934) pp. 43–6; Tim Dinsdale, *Loch Ness Monster* (London, Routledge & Kegan Paul, 1976) pp. 111–12; Peter Costello, *In Search of Lake Monsters* (St Albans, Panther Books, 1975) pp. 36–7; Ronald Binns, *The Loch Ness Mystery Solved* (Shepton Mallet, Open Books, 1983) pp. 49–51; Mike Dash, 'The camels are coming', *Fortean Times*, 58 (Jul 1991) pp. 52–3. Cruickshank's description of the monster as a sort of giant frog is reminiscent of the account of a diver, Duncan MacDonald, who supposedly went into the loch near Fort Augustus, around 1880, to examine a wreck. At a depth of thirty feet he saw a large animal 'like a huge frog' lying on a ledge above him and apparently watching him intently. In fact this dramatic encounter must be a hoax or a tall tale, as the visibility in the loch at that depth is nowhere near good enough for MacDonald to have seen any such thing. Nicholas Witchell, *The Loch Ness Story* (London, Corgi, 1982) pp. 26–7.

The beiste of the Children's Pool Peter Costello, *In search of Lake Monsters* (St Albans, Panther, 1975) pp. 154–5.

Alchemists 'April fuels', *Fortean Times*, 11 (Aug 1975) pp. 3 and 19, Alchemy & elixirs', *Fortean Times*, 35 (summer 1981) pp. 39–40; 'Water power baffles scientists', *Fortean Times*, 85 (Feb–Mar 1996) p. 16; 'This man cooks up kerosene', *Fortean Times*, 94 (Dec 1996) p. 17. Though it falls outside the remit of this book, it seems worth nothing that a handful of cases involving apparently successful transmutations of lead into gold are on record – see Gaston de Mengel, 'The evidence for authentic transmutation', *Journal of the Alchemical Society*, 1 n 4 (April 1913) and Rupert Gould, 'The last of the alchemists', *Enigmas: Another Book of Unexplained Facts* (New York, University Books, 1965) pp. 137–87.

Men in Black Peter M. Rojcewicz, 'The 'Men in Black experience and tradition: analogies with the traditional devil hypothesis', *Journal of American Folklore*, 100 (Apr–Jun 1987) pp. 148–60; Hilary Evans, *Visions•Apparitions•Alien Visitors* (Wellingborough; Aquarian Press, 1984) pp. 136–145.

'The figures became clearer . . .' Bender cited in Evans, op. cit. p. 140.

Fairies Katharine Briggs, *The Vanishing People: Fairy Lore and Legends* (New York, Pantheon Books, 1978); Janet Bord, *Fairies: Real Encounters with Little People* (London, Michael O'Mara Books, 1997). One explanation for the prevalence of fairy lore, incidentally, is that it comprises a folk-memory of a period when *homo sapiens* co-existed on earth with Neanderthal man, who was slowly driven into the far reaches of Europe by his more aggressive rival. This might explain the survival of such stories in Celtic countries. Another is that fairies reflect an ancient belief that the human soul was incarnated in the form of a miniature human figure.

Fairies and alien abductions Bord, *Fairies: Real Encounters*, 5; Jacques Vallee, *Passport to Magonia: from Folklore to Flying Saucers* (London, Tandem, 1975); Katharine Briggs, *The Fairies in Tradition and Literature* (London, Routledge & Kegan Paul, 1977) pp. 115–22; John Rimmer, *The Evidence for Alien Abductions* (Wellingborough, Aquarian Press, 1984) pp. 41–8; Michel Meurger, 'Surgeons from outside', *Fortean Studies*, 3 (London, John Brown, 1996) pp. 308–21.

Abductions in Orleans Edgar Marin, *Rumour in Orleans* (London, Blond, 1971).

Ghosts Leslie Shepard (ed.), *Encyclopaedia of Occultism and Parapsychology*, 2nd edn. (Detroit, Gale Research, 1984) vol. 1 pp. 52–64; R.C. Finucane, *Appearances of the Dead: a Cultural History of Ghosts* (London, Junction Books, 1982); Alan Gauld, review of Finucane, *Journal of the Society for Psychical Research* 52 n 797 (Jun 1984) pp. 330–3.

Pliny the Younger Cited in Finucane, *Appearances of the Dead*, p. 2.

The friars' ghosts Ibid. p. 60.

Poltergeists Gerald of Wales (trans. Lewis Thorpe), *The Journey Through Wales* (London, Penguin 1978) pp. 151–2; Hereward Carrington and

Nandor Fodor, *The Story of the Poltergeist Down the Centuries* (London, Rider & Company, 1953); Alan Gauld and A.D. Cornell, *Poltergeists* (London, Routledge & Kegan Paul, 1979); Guy Lyon Playfair, *This House is Haunted: the Investigation of the Enfield Poltergeist* (London, Sphere Books, 1981); Shepard, *Encyclopaedia of Occultism*, vol. 3 pp. 1049–55; Joe Nickell, *Entities: Angels, Spirits, Demons and Other Beings* (Armherst, Prometheus Books, 1995) pp. 79–107; McClenon, *Wondrous Events*, pp. 57–77. It is only fair to point out that in the Enfield case, an investigator from the Society for Psychical Research submitted a critical report that suggested that the disturbances could have been the work of the two young girls in the house.

Bullard's work on abductions Jerome Clark, *UFOs in the 1980s* (Detroit, Apogee Books, 1990) pp. 1–14; Hilary Evans, 'Abducted by an archetype', *Fortean Times*, 33 (autumn 1980) pp. 6–10.

David Hufford's work on the Old Hag David Hufford, *The Terror That Comes in the Night: an Experience-Centred Study of Supernatural Assault Traditions* (Philadelphia, University of Pennsylvania Press, 1982) pp. 171–245.

'The distribution of traditions . . .' Ibid. pp. 245–6.

12 A Sense of Wonder

Giant shrimp 'A giant shrimp?', *Strange Magazine*, 6 (1990) p. 5. For an intriguingly similar case, involving the apparition of a werewolf associated with two stone Celtic heads, see 'A Celtic werewolf', *Fortean Times*, 15 (Apr 1976) pp. 4–5). This particular case is especially interesting in that the supposedly ancient ritual objects at the centre of events were subsequently shown to be clay figures made as playthings as recently as the 1960s – a conclusion that certainly suggests that the werewolf (which was seen on three separate occasions by three different witnesses) somehow had a psychological rather than a parapsychological origin.

Photo credits

Fortean Picture Library	1, 2, 3, 4, 8, 9, 10, 12, 16, 18, 19, 20, 21
Mary Evans Picture Library	5, 6, 7, 13, 17, 25
Larry E. Arnold/*Ablaze!*	23
Harry Trumbore	11a–h
Photographer unknown	14
RH Lowrie	15
Ross Kinnaid	22
John Sibbick	26

Index

(The notes are not indexed)

abductions 43–4, 303, 335–7, 424–5, 426–7, 435–6
  by aliens 163–71
  by fairies 422–4
  false 384
  hypnagogia, as explanation for 370
  and temporal lobes 375–6
Aberfan disaster, foretold 89
Abominable Snowman (yeti) 196, 198, 202, 353–4
absorption, state of 371–2
Adamski, George 16, 155
Adamson, Hubert 265–6
aerial detonations, *see* 'skyquakes'
Aerial Phenomena Research Organisation (APRO) 136, 305
Agnagna, Marcellin 191
Agobard, bishop, Book Against False Opinions 128–9
Air Force Office of Special Investigations (AFOSI) 305
airships 131–2, 297–8
Alaska, UFO lights over 23–4
alchemists 415
Aldebert, Walter 255–6
Algeria, difference in reporting UFOs in 172
aliens, bodies of 148
  see also extraterrestrial biological entities
alignments, *see* ley-lines
Allen(de), Carl(os) 300–1, 312
Almirante Saldhana 138, 139
Altered States of Consciousness (ASC) 366–77
Alton Barnes (Wiltshire) 282
Alvarez, Jose 141–2
Amazing 229
Amazon region, animals of 193–6
America, *see* United States
America, wild men in 198–201
anacondas 194–5
Andros Island (Bahamas), yay-ho in 197
Angel, Leonard 113
angel hair 249
animal ghosts 121
animals:
  curious 44
  as nurturers of children 262–6
  parapsychological tests on 94–5
Anna Ali, Sister 68
Anthony of Padua, Saint 71
ape-men 177
apes 196–205
Apollo, weeping statue of 287
apparitions of living persons 115
  see mainly under ghosts
apports (materialisations of objects) 79
APRO (UFO group) 136, 305
Arbor Low (Derbyshire), stone circle at 220
Arc, Joan of 4, 52

Index

Arnold, Kenneth 133, 135, 147, 323–4
Arnold, Larry 260–1, 262
Arnold, Thelma 358
astral experiences 96–105
astral plane 359
Ataska, Mary 68
Atlanta 229
aubergine, holy 398–400
aural hallucinations 370
Aurora (Texas), airship crash 298
Australia:
  animals of 186–7, 196
  big cats in 180–1
autistic children 264
autokinetic effect 334
autosuggestion 405–6
Aviary, The 304–5
Azzazov, Dr Dmitri 290

Bachseitz, Dr, plagued by talking toilet 23, 30–2
Baiae (Italy), Oracle of the Dead at 286
Baker, Robert 104, 360, 369, 393
Balanovski, Eduardo 233
Ballinspittle (Co. Cork) 332–4
Bandi, Countess Cornelia 258
Banner, Frederick 130
Barauna, Almira 138, 139
Barber, Theodore 359–62
Barisal (India), aerial detonations at 251
Barker, J.C. 89, 89–90
Barrett, Sir William 104
Bartholomew, Robert 363–4
Basterfield, Keith 363–4
Bastien, Harry 80
Bathurst, Benjamin, vanishing of 253–4
Bayless, Raymond 267, 268–9
bears 184–5
  as Bigfoot 203–4
Beaumont, Comyns 10
Beauraing (Belgium), Virgin Mary appears at 60
Bede 410
bedroom invaders 7, 45–7
Beer, Lionel 333
Begg, Paul 254
'Believe it or not' strip (by Ripley) 245
Belmez (Spain), faces on hearth at 117–18
Benbecula (Hebrides), mermaid stranded at 338
Bender, Albert K. 161
  and Men in Black 417
Bennett, Paul 363
Bennewitz, Paul 303–4, 305, 312
Bentley, Dr John Irving 257, 260
Benwell, Gwen 338
Bermuda Triangle 6–7
Bernadette, St 56–60, 64, 71
Bernard, Jean 61–2
Bernard, Dr Raymond 231
Bernstein, Morey 106
Bhagawati, goddess 287
Bhutan, king of 13, 14
Bigfoot 196, 198–201, 231, 330, 337, 358–9
  filmed 310–11
  footprints 345–6
  perhaps bears 203–4
  wild men as explanation of 204
  possible body of 353
  see also Abominable Snowman; America, wild men in; ape-men; bears; wild men; *wodewoses*; Yay-ho; *yeren*, yeti
Binns, Ronald 343
birds, giant 177
Bishopville (South Carolina) 270–1
Black Dog 34–5
Blackmore, Susan 95, 97–8, 99, 320
  lobes stimulated 375–6
Blavatsky, Madame Helene Petrovna 78, 228
Blaxhall Stone (Suffolk) 226
Bloxham, Arnall 106, 394
blue objects 22
boa constrictors 195–6
Boas, Antonio Villas 27
Bodmin Moor (Cornwall), cat 179, 183

Bonacase, Serge 195
book tests, in seances 83–4
Booth, Dr Mackenzie 258–9
Bord, Janet and Colin 201, 274
Bossburg (Washington) 345
Botetourt County (Virginia) 273
Bower, Doug 283–5
von Boxberger, Leo 188–9
Brace, Iris 267
Brady, Ben 238
brain, and visions 373–4
Brazel, Mac 147–8, 149
Brazil, UFOs in 27, 138–9
Bridgend (Glamorgan) UFOs 237–8
Bright, E.H. 413
Broad, C.D. 118
Brookesmith, Peter 145
Brujeria, secret society, in Chile 37–9
Bucknell, Melissa 170
Buddha, photo of 68
Buddhism, and reincarnation 105
Buddhists, near-death experiences of 408
Bullard, Thomas 435–6
Burgess, Clifford 291
Burundi 29
  mambu mutu in 39
Byerlee, Jim 239–40

Cairo, mass hysteria in 329
Caleuche (ghost ship) 37–8
Cameron, Kevin 187
Campbell, Steuart 241
Canada 24–5, 45–7, 200, 208, 225–6, 348–9, 352–3, 355–7, 364, 375–6, 394–5
candle effect, as explanation for spontaneous human combustion 259–60
Carey, James 172–3
Carleton University (Ottawa) 364
Carrington, Hereward 431
cars, etc, interference with, by UFOs 140–2
Carter, President Jimmy, UFO sighting by 13, 14
Cash, Betty 144–5
Castenada, Carlos 292–4
Castor and Pollux 49
Catherine of Genoa, St 71
cats, big 177–8, 178–83, 314–15
cattle:
  kidnapping of 297–8
  mutilation of 303–4
caves, inside the earth 227
Cazcarra, Manuel 197
Cecilia, St 70
Centre for UFO Studies, survey by 364
Chamberlein, Frances 95
Chao T'ai 409
Cheesefoot Head, crop circles of 281, 284
Cheltenham hauntings 119–20
Chiaia, Ercole 295
childbirth, woman in, and near-death experience 104
children, and poltergeists 123
Chile, Brujeria brotherhood in 37–9
China:
  Christianity in 51–2
  feng shui 224
  ghosts 121
  hair-clipping panics in 324–5
  Inspector of Invading Oddities 245
  lake monsters of 212
  near-death experiences in 408–9
Chipping Norton (Óxfordshire), crocodile 183
chivato (monster) 38
Chorley, Dave 283–5
Chorvinsky, Mark 205, 310–11
Christ 48
  foreskin of (Holy Prepuce) 15–16
  alleged photographs of 67–8
  relics 286–7
  see also stigmata
CIA and UFOs 150
Cicero 49
circles:
  crop 281–5
  stone 242
Civitavecchia (Italy), weeping statue of 288

clairvoyance (visions at a distance) 86, 87
Clark, Jerome 297–8, 349
Clark, Tony 2–4, 318
Clearbury Ring 220
Clearwater (Florida), footprints 276–9
Cleveland, Mrs Willis 85
Clonmacnois (Ireland), sky-ship over 129
Close Encounters of the Second Kind (CE2) 140
Close Encounters of the Third Kind (CE3) 150
cochion ('Red Ones') 36–7
coelacanths 178
concentric spheres, inside earth 227
Congo, 'dinosaurs' of 188–93
Connolly, Lynn 247
consciousness research 234
'contactees' of UFOs 155
'contagion' 328–30
Conway, Helen, spontaneous combustion of 261–2
Cornell, A.D. 124
corpseways 235
Cottingley fairies 307–10, 311–12
Coupland, Elizabeth 388–9
Cox, William 89
Coyne, Lawrence 137
Coyne, Stephen 337–8
Craiglockhart (Edinburgh), shower of excrement 246–7
Crawford, O.G.S. 221
Crawford, W.J. 81
Crawfordsville (Indiana), sky serpent 130
Crew, Jerry 198, 204–5
Cringle, Captain R.J. 213
crocodiles, in Britain etc 183–4
crop circles 281–5
cross, Christ's 287
cross-correspondences between mediums' messages 83, 84
Crowley, Aleister 72
Cruickshank, Alfred 412–13
cryptaesthesia 382
cryptomnesia (hidden memory) 110, 112, 381–2
cryptozoology 36, 176–216, 351, 353, 394–5
  reputation 215–16
Cuevas, Amparo 65–6
'cultural source' hypothesis 391–8, 408
  problems with 435–7
Cyborgs 304

Da Silva, Jose Antonio 152
Dacianos (gypsies) 38–9
Daedalus, HMS 212–13, 215
Damiani, Signor 294
Davis, Christopher 270–1
de la Cruz, Magdalena 404
de Mille, Richard 293
death, *see* soul
death roads, 235
Defense Intelligence Agency, US 101, 102
deja vu 373
Delphos (Kansas), UFO 142–4
demons, numbers of 18
Dennis, Glenn 148
D'Ercole, Tom 1–2
Deros (race) 229, 230
Derr, Dr John 239
Despard, Captain and Mrs 119–20
Devereux, Paul 225, 233, 234–5, 236–7, 240–1, 242–3
Devil's Arrows (Yorkshire) 219–20
Diego, Juan 53–4
dinosaurs, surviving 188–93
Dinsdale, Tim 322–3, 343
direct voice 79
disappearing pupil, East Anglia 8–9
Divine, encounters with the 48–66
dodos 186
Dominguez, Clemente 403–4
Don Juan, *see* Yaqui way of knowledge
Doomsday, forecasts 90
Doppelgangers 365
D'Orban, Charles 283
Doty, Sergeant Richard 304, 305

dowsing 218, 232
Doyle, Sir Arthur Conan 67
and Cottingley fairy photos 308, 311
Dragon Project 233
dreams, realistic and unrealistic 86
Drexel Hill (Pennsylvania) spontaneous combustion in 261
Drythelm, near-death experience of 410–11
Ducat, James, vanished 255–6
Dundy County (Nebraska) 146
Dunmarry (Australia) 246
duppies (West Indian ghosts) 121–2
Dwendis (little people) 26
Dyfed (Wales), earth lights 240
Dyke, Sally and Nick 179

earth:
as Gaia 226
hollow 227–31
earth lights 236–43
earth mysteries/magic 217–43
see also ghost paths, ley-lines
earthquakes, and lights in the sky 238–9
EBEs, *see* extraterrestrial biological entities
EBE-3, ufonaut 304–5
ectoplasm 78, 79, 81–2
Eden, Philip 283
eels, as monsters 210
Egryn peninsula (Wales) 240–1
Eilean Mor (Hebrides) 255–7
El Repilade (Andalusia), Virgin Mary visits 60
Elawar, Imad 113, 114
Eldridge, USS 300–1, 312
Electronic Voice Phenomenon (EVP) 383–4
elves 224
endorphins, and near-death experiences 103, 104
England 8–9, 10, 11, 14–15, 53, 86–7, 88–9, 93, 106–9, 115–17, 119–21, 129, 137, 140, 159–60, 163, 179, 180–1, 183–5, 218–19, 220–2, 225–6, 231, 232–3, 240, 247, 255–6, 262, 281–2, 283–5, 289, 291–2, 307–12, 318–19, 328–9, 331–2, 344, 388–9, 398–400, 410–11, 418–19, 420, 432
Enfield (Middlesex), poltergeist 432
entoptic and entotic phenomena 370
epilepsy 242, 373–4
Euler, Leonhard 228
Evans, Hilary 240, 360–1, 416
'Evans, Jane' 106–9
Everittstown (New Jersey) 273
excrement, shower of 246–7
expectant attention 321
extrasensory perception (ESP) 82–3, 86–95, 316, 356
extraterrestrial beings 166
see also UFOs, abductions
extraterrestrial biological entities 303
extraterrestrial hypothesis (ETH) 153–4
eye witnesses, multiple 331–40
evidence of 317–23

fact and fiction, defining 41–2
fairies 224
abduction by 422–4
Cottingley fairy photographs 307–10, 311–12
fairy-folk 418–27
Falcon Lake (Manitoba), UFO encounter at 348–9
Falkland Islands, war not predicted 90
falls from the sky 15, 44, 246, 248–9
false memories 378–9, 384
'fantasy proneness' 359–65
fashion, effect on visions 398
Fata Morgana 383
Fatima (Portugal), Virgin Mary appears at 9–10, 60, 61, 63, 66
faults, geological 240–3
Fawcett, Percy 194–5
feng shui 224
feral children 262–6
Fickett, Shirley 163, 165, 175

film:
 of Loch Ness etc 310–11, 341–4
 UFOs 341
fish, falls from sky 15, 246, 248–9
flaps, panics, contagion 323–30
Flournoy, Theodore 85, 363, 382
Flying Dutchman 13, 14
flying pigs 32–3
flying saucer clubs 136
flying saucers, *see* UFOs
folie a deux 64, 334–5
folklore 388–437
Foo fighters 132
footprints 345–6
 mystery 276–8
Fordyce, Colonel L.McP. 413
foreknowledge, *see* precognition
Forrest, Robert 219, 221
Fort, Charles 244–6, 248, 269
 The Book of the Damned 246
 on falls from the sky 244, 246
 on teleportation 252
Fortean Society 245
Fortean Times 320
Fox, John, and family 76–7
Fox, Kate and Maggie 80
France 4, 35, 52, 54–6, 56–60, 61–2, 64, 71–2, 75–6, 249, 324, 348, 363, 372, 424–5
Francis of Assisi, St 400–2
Frankenbury Camp 220
fraud:
 in ESP 91–2
 in mediums 80, 81–2, 86
 in poltergeists 124–5
 see also hoaxes
Freeman, Paul 346
French, Major Richard 161
Frenkel, Alexei 91
Frew, Sam and Ruth 358–9, 362
Fry, Marina 419
Fuller, Jane 179
Fulton, Charles 199
Fund for UFO Research 145

Gaddis, Vincent 130, 256
Gaia 226
Ganesh, drinking statues of 312–13
Ganzfeld research 94
Garabandal (Spain), Virgin Mary in 60
Gardner, Edward 308
Gardner, Martin 93
Garlaschelli, Luigi, investigates weeping, sweating, bleeding icons 287, 351
gas, used by creatures 272–3
 see also Mad Gasser of Mattoon
Gauld, Alan 124, 432–4
Geller, Uri 4
gender, of stigmatics 402–3
Genoa (Italy), UFO 152–3
geomancy 218
George, Leonard 365, 381
Gerald of Wales 431–2, 433
Germany 23, 30–2, 69, 75, 122, 132, 181, 230, 254, 262
Gervase of Tilbury, chronicle mentions UFOs 129
ghost paths 235
ghost rockets 132, 133
ghosts 115–25, 427–34
 of animals 121
 duppies 121–2
 as hallucinations 118, 119, 121
 noisy 430–1
 photographs of 344
giant birds 177
Gill, Fr William 13, 14
Gimlin, Roger 310–11
Giorgi, Giorgio 350
Giraud, Maximin 54–6
glutamate, in brain 105
Goatman, Maryland 33
Goatsucker, Puerto Rico 26, 326–8
'goblin universe' 357–9
gods, photographs of 66–9
Goerman, Robert 300–1
Goligher, Kathleen 81
Good, Timothy 302
Gordon, (Mr) 352
Gould, Rupert 411–12
Grant, Joan 105
Gravesend (Kent), UFOs 129

Gray, Glen 126–8, 157–8, 161, 162, 163, 164, 165, 172–5
Gray, Hugh 342
Great Fear ('mass hysteria') 324
Great Sea Serpent 212–15
Greeks, and gods 49
Green, Celia 99, 371
Green Children, of Woolpit 11
green objects 22
Greenhaw, Jeff 13, 14
'Greys' 46, 166–71, 335
Griffiths, Frances 307–9
Grinyova, Nina 203
Ground Saucer Watch group 138
ground sloth 193–4
Groupe d'Etude des Phenomenes Aerospatiaux Non-identifies (GEPAN) 348
guillotining, and life after death 73–5

Hackney (London), bears 184–5
Hagelund, Captain William 352–3
hailstones, *see* ice
Haines, Richard 386
hair-cutting panics in China 324
Haiti, abduction in 423–4
Haley, Leah 170
Halifax (Yorkshire), razor-slashing in 14–15
Hall, Mark 201
hallucinations 86, 365–6, 369–71, 374
  ghosts as 118, 119, 121
  UFOs as 155, 169, 173
Hamilton, Alexander 297–8
Hamilton, Professor Robert 340
Harrison, Ted 402–3, 405, 406
haunted houses 119
hauntings, *see* ghosts
Haydon, S.E. 298
Haytor, phantom cottage 318
Heard, Gerald, suggests UFOs are crewed by bees 154
heaven, according to Bede 411
Heim, Albert 103–4
Helena, Empress 286–7
hell:
  in Bede 410–11
  drilling to, in Siberia 290
  Roman 286
Hendry, Allan 317–18, 320
Hertford, fairies in 420
Heselton, Philip 220–1
Hessdalen (Norway), earth lights over 15, 238
Hesse (Germany), wild boy of 262
Heuvelmans, Bernard 36, 178, 214, 352
Heywood, Rosalind 86–7
Hiba-gon (monster) 197
'high strangeness' in UFO cases 157–63, 331
Hill, Betty and Barney 165
Himalayas, yeti in 202
Hindu drinking statues 289
Hinduism, and reincarnation 105
Hingley, Jean 159–60, 163
Hitching, Francis 232–3
Hitler, Adolf 230
hoaxes 14–15, 16, 41, 276–313
  of Bigfoots 204–5
  of poltergeists 434
  of UFOs 155, 169
Holiday, F.W. 338, 351–2, 358
Hollow Earth theory 227–31
holy relics 69–72
Home, Daniel, medium 331–2
Honen, monk 408–9
Hong Xiuquan 51–2
Hoolomon, George 270
Hopkins, Budd 167–8, 335–7
Hopkins, Dr Herbert 161, 163–4, 175
Hopkins, W.H. 151–2
horse racing bets, forecasting 88–9
Hoskins, Cyril, *see* Rampa, T. Lobsang
Houston (Texas):
  UFO near 144–5
  vicious smurfs in 25–6
Howard, George 364
Howe, Linda Moulton 304, 305
Howells, Steve 47
Hueytown (Alabama), noise 250

Hufford, David 45–7, 273, 369, 436
Hull (Yorkshire) 247
  fairies in 418–19
hums 250–2
Hunt, Jane 404
Hunt, Lord John 202
Hurst, Harry 109
Huxtable, Graham 106
Huyghe, Patrick, *The Field Guide to Extraterrestrials* 153
hybrids, alien programme to breed 168–9
Hynek, J. Allen 140
hypnagogic state, as explanation for some phenomena 367–9
hypnopompic state 368
hypnosis:
  and cultural source hypothesis 393
  used at guillotining 73–5
  and Mesmer 75–6
  and regression 106–11
  and satanic abuse 380–1
  of UFO victims 163–4, 165, 175
Hyslop, James 85
hysterical contagion 328–30

ice falls on earth 248
Iceland, elves of 30, 224–5
icons, weeping, sweating, bleeding 287
Idaho, UFOs over in 1947 133
Illustrated London News, hoax in 298–9
imagination, place of 42
incorruptibility of sacred bodies 70–2
Independent Joint Airmiss Working Group 138
Indian rope-trick 320–1
Indonesia, *orang bati* of 30
Ingram, Paul 14, 379–80
Inkberrow, big cat of 179
inner space 231
intelligence, controlling goblin universe 357–9
International Flying Saucer Bureau 161
intuitive impressions (hunches) 86
invunche (monster) 38
Iran, missing *tchae khana* of 2–4
irkuiem, mystery Russian mammal 30
Irvine, Malcolm 310
Islam, *see* Moslems
Isle of Man, fairies of 418
Italy 15–16, 67–8, 70, 71, 152–3, 286–8, 294–5, 312, 349–51, 400–3
Itard, Dr Jean 265

Jacobs, Bill 47
Jacobs, David 167–9, 170, 369–70, 376, 420
jamais vu 373
James, William 381–2
Jansen, Karl 104–5
Januarius, St, blood of 287, 349–50
Japan 36, 121, 196–7, 408–9
Java, *tuyul* of 39–40
Jessup, Morris 300–1
Jesus Christ, *see* Christ
Jesus dos Santos, Lucia de 60, 63–4, 66
Jetzer, Johann 402, 405
Joan of Arc 4, 52
Joao Pessoa (Brazil), food from the sky in 246
'Johlson, Enid' 267
John Baptist, three relic heads of 15
Johnson, Ronald 142–4
Joseph, Divione 423–4
Judenmann, Claudia 31–2
Jung, Carl, and mediums 85
Jurgenson, Frederick 383

Kafton-Minkel, Walter 227
kangaroos, killer 40
Kardec, Allan 78
Kassam, Farida 398
Kavoi, Peter 29
Keel, John 271, 358
Keeton, Joe 394
Kelly (Kentucky), close encounter at 152
Kentucky, creature in 199
Kenya, stone showers 29–30

ketamine anaesthetic, an explanation for near-death experiences 104–5
Khe Tre 176–7
Kilbracken, Lord, premonition of 88–9
Kiribati, fish fall near 248–9
Klass, Philip 137–8, 156, 302
Kluski, Franek 82
Knapp, Tracey 167–8
Krantz, Grover 345–6
Kuano, river (India) 265–6
Kulagina, Ninel 91
Kusche, Lawrence 6
Kwanyin (Buddhist goddess), picture of 68

La Rubia, Antonio 158–9, 162
La Salette, vision of Mary at 54–6
de La Tour du Pin, Lucy 324
Laboure, St Catherine 71–2, 363
Lady of the Lake, barque, and UFOs 130
Lake Dakataua (New Britain) 212
lake monsters, *see* Loch Arkaig; Loch Canisp; Loch Lochy; Loch Morar; Loch Ness; Loch Oich; Lough Nahooin; Lake Dakataua; Lake St François; Lake Storsjon; Lake Tianchi; Okanagan Lake; *peistes*; Quebec, lake monsters of; water horse; zeuglodon
Lake Saint-François 395
Lake Storsjon (Sweden), monster 209–10
Lake Tianchi, monster 212
Lakenheath/Bentwater air bases (Suffolk), UFOs over 140
Lamont, Peter 320–1
Lancaster prison, ghosts of 115–17
Landrum, Vickie and Colby 144–5
Larkin, Lt J.J. 120–1
Lateau, Louise 405
Lawson, Alvin 386–7
Leicestershire, earth lights 240
Leonard, Mrs Gladys, medium 84, 363
Leslie, Lionel 338
Lethbridge, T.E. 232
Levelland (Texas), UFO landings at 141–2
levitation 332
  of mediums 78
  of objects 90–1
Lewis, Bill 232–3
ley-lines 217–23
  as lines of energy 231–4
  doubts on 221
  see also earth mysteries, ghost paths
ley-hunting 231–4
  and UFOs 236
Liddell, Dean 225
life after death 73–5, 115–25
  see also ghosts, hauntings, reincarnation
lightning 269
  as UFO 142
lights in the sky, during World War II 132, 297
Likouala-aux-Herbes river 190–1, 193
Lisaird (County Mayo), fairies in 422
Little Green Men 270–5
lizard man 272
Llanthony Abbey (Wales), Virgin Mary at 62
Lo Bianco, Domenica 406
Loch Arkaig, monster of 208
Loch Canisp, monster of 207
Loch Lochy, monster of 207
Loch Morar, monster of 207–8, 323
Loch Ness, monster of 17–18, 44, 203–6, 208, 211–12, 215, 323, 411–15
  false sightings 322–3, 328
  films 310, 341–4
  photographs 311, 341–4
Loch Oich, water horse of 414
Lodge, Sir Oliver 78, 84
Long, James 142
Lough Nahooin 337–8
Lourdes (France) 56–60
Lovelock, Jim 226
Lowrie, R.H. 343–4

McArthur, Donald, vanished 255–6
McClenon, James 47–8
McClure, Kevin 63, 240
McConnel, David 120–1
McConnell, Mr & Mrs 267
McCoy, Colonel Howard 149
MacDonald, Kathleen 205–6
McDonnell, Duncan 207
MacGruer, William and Margaret 413
Mack, John 166–7, 364
Mackal, Roy 189–91, 338
MacKenzie, Kenneth 207
MacLeod, Torquil 344
McMinville (Oregon), UFO photographed at 138, 139
McNab, Peter 342–3
M'Quhae, Captain Peter 212–13
McRae, Dr, films of lake monster 351–2
Mad Gasser, of Mattoon 25, 272–3
Madrid (Spain), UFOs and 299–300
Magin, Ulrich 215, 235
Magonia, as source of UFOs 128, 129
Majestic 12 (MJ-12) 301–3, 304
Malmesbury, Lord 208
mambu mutu (vampire) 29, 39
mammoths 185
manananggal (vampire) 39
Manchester, UFO sighted over 137
Mansfield (Ohio), UFO 136–7
Mantell, Thomas 136
mapinguary 193–4
Marfa (Texas), earth lights 238
Markwick, Betty 93
Mars 154
Marshall, Thomas, vanished 255–6
Martians, contacted by mediums 85
Martin, Ronald 142
Martin, William 418
Marto, Francisco and Jacinta 64
Mary, Virgin 52–66, 392–3
  at Fatima 9–10
  statue of at Ballinspittle 332–4
  weeping 287
Mary Celeste 254–5
Maryland, Goatman of 33
Maskelyne, J.N. 295
Mason, Dr A.A. 406
mass hysteria 272–3, 329–30
  see also Great Fear
Mathieu, Melanie 54–6
Matto Grosso 193–5
Mattoon (Illinois), 'Mad Gasser' of 25, 272–3
Mauritius, *nauscopie* and 30
Meaden, Terence 281–2, 284
medical conditions, and fantasy 372–7
mediums 77, 79–86, 362–3
Medjugorje (Croatia), Virgin Mary appears at 60
Meier, Billy 155
memory 377–84
  false 378–9, 384
Men in Black (MIB) 160–2, 269, 416–17
Menzel, Donald 155–6
mermaids 338–40
  vampire 29
Merry Maidens (Cornwall) 232
Mesmer, Franz 75–6
meteors, as UFOs 137–8
Meurger, Michel 394–7, 414, 425–6, 435
Mexico:
  Dwendis of 26
  Vision of Mary in 53–4
Michalak, Stefan 348–9
Michel, Aime 236–7
Midnapore (Bengal), wolf-children of 262, 263–4
Migo, lake monster 212
Milingo, Archbishop Emanuel 68
Mill Creek (Oregon) 346
Miller, Carcy 256–7
mind over matter, *see* psychokinesis
Mirabelli, Carlos 296
mirages 42
  of stars 156
  as UFOs 138–9
moas 185
Mohammed Multani, Haji 399
mokele mbembe 188–93
Mondongo, Nicolas 190

monsters, in the sky 130
Moody, Dr Robert 406
Moore, Joseph 255
Moore, William 302–3, 304–5
Morin, Edgar 425
Mormonism 51, 65
Moroni, angel 51
Morris, Robert 94–5
Moses 48, 50
Moslems:
  find messages in aubergines 398–9
  other messages 399–400
motor-zobop 423–4
Mounsey, Neale 115–17, 122
Mount Hiba (Japan) 196–7
Mountain, Sir Edward 342
Mountain Ash (Glamorgan), fish fall at 248
Muhammad 48, 50
Mulholland, John 77
Muller, Catherine 85, 96, 363
multiple personality disorder (MPD) 110–11
Mumler, William 306–7
Munson, Thomas 415
Musco, Teresa 404
Mutual UFO Network 145
Myers, F.W.H. 87
mylodon (sloth) 194
mythology 394–8
  and Loch Ness monster 414–15

Naarding, Hans 186–7
Nanking, demons infest 324–5
Napier, John 311, 345
Naples (Italy):
  blood relic liquifies at 349–50
  other substances 351
Napolitano, Linda, abduction of 335–7
narcolepsy 368
National Investigations Committee on Aerial Phenomena (NICAP) 136
National Security Agency, USA, 101
nauscopie (remote viewing) 30
Navajo Indians, and skin-walkers 37
Nazis, and hollow earth 230–1
near-death experiences (NDEs) 96, 102–5, 364–5, 407–11
  explanations for 103
Nephite tribe, and Mormons 65
Neumann, Therese 402, 404
New Apollonia (Thessalonica), UFO lands near 152
New Hampshire, UFO 165
Newfoundland 45, 46, 47
Nickell, Joe 63, 71, 125, 259–60, 364
Nicolai, Renato 347–8
night terrors 104
  see also bedroom invaders, hypnagogia, Old Hag, near-death experiences
Noble, Ted 182
noises, mysterious 250–2
Nombanda 65
Nonquawuse 4–5, 64–5
Norfolk, First-Fifth, disappearing battalion 254
Norrkoping, troll at 247
Norway (Maine), *see* Stephens, David
Nottingham, lion at 180
Nugent, Rory 192
n'yamala 189

OBEs, *see* out-of-the-body experiences
occupants, of UFOs 150–7
Ofshe, Richard 380
Ogopogo, lake monster 208
Okanagan lake (Canada) 208
Old Hag (bedroom invader) 46–7, 273, 369, 436–7
Old Straight Track 218, 222
Olssen, Karin and Marta 209
Olsson, Peter 209–10
Olympia (Washington), false memory 379–80
O'Mahoney, Clare 333
Onelli, Dr Clementi 27–8
Operation Childcare 389–90
Operation Stargate 101–2
onyro (angry spirits), Japan 121
Oracle of the Dead 286

orang bati (flying men) 30
Oren, Dr David 193–4
Orleans (France), abductions and 'mass hysteria' in 424–5
orthotentic lines 236–7
ostention 18
Ostman, Albert 200
out-of-the-body experiences (OBEs) 48, 96–102, 385
explanations 98
Owen, A.R.G. 357
Owen, Elias, on Welsh folklore 422
owls, luminous 241–2
oxygen starvation, as explanation for hallucinations 376–7
Oz factor 372

van Paassen, Pierre 35
paedophiles, alleged 389–91
Palladino, Eusapia 294–6, 312
Palmer, Ray 229, 231
Pamirs, yeti in 203
pareidolia 382–3, 384
Parker, Will 167
Parsons, Denys 319
Patagonia, plesiosaur survival in 27–8
Patel, Mrs Ruskana 399–400
Patterson, Roger 310–11, 345
Pearlroth, Norbert 245
peistes (Irish lake monsters) 337–8
Pembroke, poltergeists in 431–2
Pena, Jordan 299
penguin, giant 277–9
penis-severance 325
Penrhyndeudraeth (Gwynedd), fairies in 421–2
Pereira, Maria Gomez 117–18
'Perez, Gil', teleportation 252–3
Perez de Cuellar 336
Persinger, Michael 241, 242, 375–6
petrol, alchemical creation of 415
pets, homing of 5–6
Pewsey, Vale of (Wiltshire), crop circles 281
phantoms, *see* ghosts
'Philadelphia experiment' case 300
'Philip', imaginary ghost 355–7
Philippines, vampire 39
Phillips, Para Lee 15
Phillips, Ted 143
philosopher's stone 415
phone calls from the dead 266–9
photographs 306–11
of ghosts 344
of the gods 66–9
of the Loch Ness monster 311, 341–4
spirit 306–7
of UFOs 138–40, 340–1
physical evidence 349–51
Pillai, Ponnaiah Ramar 415
Pinvidic, Thierry 172
Pio, Padre 402, 403
Piper, Leonore, medium 84, 362
Pitnov, Derek 114
Piute Indians, Nevada 37
plasma vortices 282, 285
plesiosaurs:
as lake monsters 210
in Patagonia 27–8
Pliny the younger 428
Podmore, Frank 332
poltergeists 122–5, 252, 431–4
epicentre 122, 123
infestations, 123, 124
plague Dr Backseitz 30–2
Pontmain (France), vision of Virgin Mary 55
Popobawa, in Zanzibar 29
possession 372–3
post-mortem consciousness, experiment on 73–5
Potier, Jeanne 372
Powell, James 189–91
Powell, Walter 328–9
precognition (foretelling the future) 86, 88–90
Project Sign, *see* United States Air Force
Proyart, Abbe 188
pseudo-hallucinations 365–6
Psi 86, 92, 94, 95, 316
psychic warfare 100–1
psychics, testing 316

psychokinesis (movement of objects by mental means) 86, 90–2, 94, 356, 371–2
psychosocial hypothesis, *see* cultural source hypothesis
pterodactyls, alive 299
Puerto Rico, Goatsucker of 26, 326–8
pumas 182
  see also cats
purgatory 411
Puthoff, Harold 100
Puysegur, Marquis de 75–6

Quebec, lake monsters of 394–5

radar/visual reports, on UFOs 139–40
radiation, suffered from UFOs 144–5
Ragsdale, Jim 148–9
Ramchandra, wild boy 265–6
Rampa, T. Lobsang (i.e. Cyril Hoskins) 291–2
Randles, Jenny 372
random number generators 94, 95
'Randy P' 7–8, 10, 45
rappings 80, 122
rationalism, rejection of 78–9
Raudive, Konstantin 383
Raynes, Brent 172
Raynham Hall (Norfolk), ghost 344
Raynor, Dick 343
realism, apparent 365
reality 366
  nature of 42
recurrent spontaneous psychokinesis (RSPK) 123–4
red objects 21–2
Reeser, Mary, spontaneous combustion of 258, 260
Regulski family 122
Regusters, Herman 191
reincarnation 105–14, 393–4
relics of Jesus Christ and saints 69–72
religion, influence on out-of-the-body experiences 48
remote viewing 100–1, 102
  see also nauscopie
Rendalin, Age 290
repetition of phenomena 33–4
Rhine, J.B. 92–3, 94
Richet, Professor Charles 81
Rimmer, John 423–4
Ring, Kenneth 364–5
Rio de Janeiro, UFO over 158–9
Ripley, Robert 245
Roe, William 199–200
Rogers, Philip 384
Rogerson, Peter 409–10
Rogo, D. Scott 267, 268–9
Rojcewicz, Peter 416
Rollright Stones (Oxfordshire) 226, 233
Romans and gods 49
Rosado, Osvaldo 327
Rose, Patrick 414
Roswell (New Mexico), UFO 147–9
Rowley Regis (Birmingham) 159–60
Royal Air Force, and UFOs 150
Runcorn (Cheshire), poltergeist 432
Russia 91, 150, 203, 289–90

Sacramento (California), UFO 131
St Elmo's Fire, as UFO 142
Saints' relics 69–72
Saladin balloon 328–9
Salibi, Kamal 10
Sanderson, Ivan T. 198, 277–8
Santa Clara liner 213
sao la (ox) 176–7
Sasquatches, *see* Bigfoot
Satan 416
satanic ritual abuse 379–80, 384, 390
satanism 14
Saucedo, Pedro 141–2
'saucer nests', and crop circles 281
Saunders, Anna-Mae 199
Schmeidler, Gertrude 316
Schnabel, Jim 284
Schrenck-Notzing, Baron 81
Schwarz, Berthold 34, 87–8
science fiction (sci-fi) 135, 425–6
Scotland 17–18, 44, 203–6, 207, 208, 211–12, 215, 246–7, 255–6, 310–11, 323, 332–3, 328, 338–40, 341–4, 351–2, 411–15

see also under the word Loch
Screeton, Paul 232
Scully, Frank *Behind the Flying Saucers* 146–7
sea-serpents 11, 16, 177, 352–3
  classification 215
  giant 212–15
seances 77–8, 80
  with 'Philip' 355–7
Secret Masters 228
secret weapons, UFOs as 42
Seringapatam (India), ice fall 248
serpents, South American 27, 194–6
Shackley, Myra 197
Shakleton, Basil 93
Shamanism 234
Shambhala 228
Shandera, Jaime 302
Shankar, Ravi 114
sharks, as sea-serpents 214
Shaver, Richard 228–9
Shaw, George Bernard, simulacrum of 226
Sheffield, Martin 27–8
Sherif, psychologist 334
Shiels, Tony 'Doc' 16, 310, 313
Shine, Adrian 323
Shoemaker, Michael 204
Siberia, drilling to Hell in 289–90
Sidgwick, Eleanor, 84
Signorini, Tony 278–9
Silent City 23
silver objects 22–3
silver threads 33–4
Simon, Dr Benjamin 165
Simonton, Joe 346–7
Simpson, William 207
simulacra 225, 399
Singh, Reverend 262, 263
Singh, Gurnam 68
Singh, Veer 113
Sirius 156
Siwash cannibals 37
'sixth sense' 88
skin-walkers 37
Skinner, Ian 377
'skyquakes' 24–5, 238, 251
sleep 367–70
Slick, Tom 353–4
Smith, Mr & Mrs A.P. 33–4
Smith, Joseph 51
Smith, Steven 186
Smurfs, in Houston 25–6
snakes, South American giant 27, 194–6
Snelling, Harold 309
Soal, Samuel 93
social workers, phantom 388–91
Society of Psychical Research (SPR) 79, 84, 115, 320, 430
somnambulism 75–6
Soubirous, Bernadette 56–60, 64, 71
soul:
  after death 105
  journey to death 407
  and near-death experiences 102
  and out-of-the-body experiences 98
sounds, anomalous 250–2
South America, mystery animals of 193–6
  giant snakes 27, 194–6
Soviet Union:
  supposed originator of UFOs 132, 133, 134
  and UFOs 150
spacecraft, alien, UFOs as 42
Spain, anomalous drought in 30
Spicer, Mr & Mrs George, *see* Loch Ness monster on land 411–12
spider's webs 249–50
Spinelli, Ernesto 95
spirit guides 84–5
spirit photographs 306–7
spiritism 78
spirits, world of 73–125
spirits of the dead, *see* ghosts
spiritualism 76–86, 393
spontaneous combustion, of humans 257–62
spoon-bending 90
Sprinkle, Leo 167
'Stanislawa, P.', medium 81
Staples, Virginia 438–41
stars, as UFOs 156

statues:
  drinking milk 289
  weeping etc 287–8
Stephens, David (UFO witness) 126–8, 157–8, 161, 162, 172–5, 362
  hypnosis 163–4
Stevens, Wendelle 341
Stevenson, Ian 109, 111–14, 393–4
Stewart, James 353–4
stigmata, 15, 400–6
Stoljarov, General Porfiri 150
Stone, Ruby 266–7
stone circles 242
'Stone tape' theory of ghosts 119
Stonehenge, and ley-lines 220
stones:
  movement of 226
  shower of, Kenya 29–30
Story, Ronald 143
Strieber, Whitley 166
Stringfield, Leonard 147
Stuart, Lachlan 342
sturgeons, as explanation for sightings of lake monsters 210–11
Sudden Unexplained Nocturnal Death Syndrome (SUNDS) 40
Sujith 112–13
sun:
  second star at centre of earth 228
  dancing and whirling, at Fatima 9–10
Super-ESP 82–3
supersonic aircraft, as explanation for anomalous sounds 251
Surrey puma 180
Swain, John and Christine 318
swamp slobs 270–1
Swann, Ingo 101
Swanson, Mildred 67
Swift, PC David 418–19
Swifte, Edmund 117
Symmes, John Cleves 227, 231

Taiping Rebellion 52
talking toilet 23, 30–2
tama, Japanese ghost 121
Taos (New Mexico), hum 250
Targ, Russell 100
Tart, Charles 99
tatzelwurm (Alpine lizard) 36
tchae khana 2–4
Tectonic Strain theory 241
teenagers and poltergeists 123–4
Tele, Lake 189, 191–2
telegraph 269
telepathy (mind-reading) 86, 87–8
telephone 269
teleportation 252–3
temporal lobe, of brain, as source of strange phenomena 373–5
Tenton Forest (Wyoming) 353
Terauchi, Captain Kenju 23–4
Teros (race) 229, 230
testing:
  of imagination and memory 385–6
  of phenomena 315–16
Thailand, early deaths in 40
theosophy 78, 308
  and astral bodies 96
  and interior of the earth 228
Theresa, St, of the Sacred Heart 70
theurgy 78
Third Eye 291
thixotropic substances 350–1
Thurston, Fr Herbert 72, 350, 404
thylacine 186–7
Tighe, Virginia 106
tinnitus 250, 370
Tollen, Viola 266–7
Tomczyk, Stanislawa 90–1
Toronto Society for Psychical Research 355–7
Torres, Jaime 326
touch hallucinations 370–1
Tourette's syndrome 373
trances, *see* hypnotism
Trans-en-Provence, UFO landing at 347–8
Trasco, John 273
Trent, Paul 138, 139
Trier cathedral, holy tunic of 69
Trindade Island, UFO photographed over 138, 139

Tripp Pond (Maine) 157–8
trolls 11, 247
Troy, Wandlebury Ring as 10
true giants 201
Truman, President Harry S. 301
tunnel effect, of near-death experiences 103
Turin shroud 16–17
tuyul 39–40
twins:
 and psi 95
 and telepathy 87
tzuchinoko, Japanese snake 36

Ubatuba, residue from UFOs 347
UFOs (unidentified flying objects):
 and car interference 140–2
 and crop circles 281
 drawings of 386
 early reports of 128–30
 and earth lights hypothesis 237
 explanations usually found for 317
 fake photographs of 16
 at Falcon Lake 348–9
 food from 346–7
 'genuine' reports 320
 'high strangeness' cases 157–63
 later reports 131–50
 and Little Green Men 274
 Maine case 126–8, 157–8, 161–2, 163–5, 173–5
 MJ-12 affair 301–3
 multiple witness cases 331, 335–7
 nature 42, 155–6
 nests 281
 numbers 154
 occupants 150–7
 and orthotentic lines 236
 and other worlds 171–5
 photographs and films of 16, 138–9, 340–1
 physical traces of 142–5
 remnants of 146–50
 residue from 347
 Trans-en-Provence case 347–8
 types 392
 variety of ways of seeing 12–13
 see also abductions, aliens, close encounters, lights in the sky, Men in Black, Ummo affair, United States Air Force
The UFO Handbook 317
Uganda, talking animals of 28–9
Ultrasound emissions 233
'Ultraterrestrial' hypothesis 357–8
Umfuli, SS 213
Ummo affair 299–300, 312
Underworld 227
Ungava Bay (Quebec) 225–6
Uniontown (Pennsylvania) 358–9
United States 1–2, 7–8, 13, 14, 15, 16, 23–6, 33–5, 37, 40, 76–7, 80, 87, 92–3, 101–2, 106, 114, 122, 126–8, 130, 131–2, 133, 135–6, 137–9, 141–5, 146, 147–9, 152, 155, 157–8, 161, 162, 163–4, 165, 167–8, 170, 172–5, 181, 198–201, 204–5, 227, 229, 238, 250, 257, 260–1, 262, 266–7, 270–2, 273, 276–9, 292–4, 297–8, 300–2, 303–4, 305, 310–11, 312, 316, 323–4, 335–7, 345–6, 353, 358–9, 379–80, 417, 438–41
United States Air Force 142, 147, 149
 and Project Sign 135–6, 149
United States Army and Marine Corps 145
United States Government, *see* Majestic 12
United States Intelligence Services 305
Uphoff, Dr Walter 267
urban myths 18
 see also folklore
USSR, *see* Soviet Union

Vallee, Jacques 312, 423
vampires 4, 29, 39
vanishings 252–7
Vatienus, P. 49
Venus (planet) 155, 297
Veronica cloths, miraculous image of Christ on 15
Victor, wild boy of Aveyron 264–5
Villas Boas, Antonio 27, 165

Vincent, Paul 46
Virgin Mary, *see* Mary
de la Visitacion, Maria 404–5
visual hallucinations 370
Vollhardt, Maria 81
Vu Quang ox 176–7

Wales 36–7, 62, 89, 106, 237–8, 240–1, 248, 415, 421–2, 431–3
Wallace, Ray 204–5
Walsingham (Norfolk) 53
Wandering Jew 65
water horse 414
  in Scottish lochs 207–8
waterspouts 248, 315
Watkins, Alfred 218–19, 221, 222, 231–2
Watson, Nigel 162–3, 363
Waugh, Sir Arthur 338
Waye, Tom and Mary 270
Webb, James 78
weeping, sweating or bleeding inanimate objects 287–8
Wetzel, Charles 271–2
Wells, H.G. 426
West Indies, ghosts of 121
Westrum, Ron 328
whales, as sea-serpents 214
Wheatley, Dennis 47
Wheeler, Jim 141
whirlwinds:
  and crop circles 281, 285
  and falls from the sky 248
white slave trade 424
Wiertz, Antoine Joseph 73–5
Wigginton, Tracey 4
wild men:
  Chinese, hair from 205
  Pamirs 203
  real 204
  of the woods 197–8
  see also Bigfoot
Wilkens, Iman 10
will-o'-the-wisp 241
Willard, R.D. 406
Williams, Al 278
Williams, David, and fairies 421–2
Williams, Frank 142
Williamson, Alf 146
Wills, Captain Roger 137
Wilson, Ian 109–11, 112, 406
Wilson, Sheryl 359–62
Winchmore Hill (London), lioness of 181–2
Wiseman, Richard 320–1
witches, and out-of-the-body experiences 96
wodewoses 197–8
wolf-children 262–6
Wollaton Park (Nottingham), fairies 419, 420
Wonthaggi monster 187
Woodcock, Percy 25
Woolpit (Suffolk), Green Children of 11, 262
World Wars, not forecast 90
Wright, Elsie 307–9
Wright, Newell 142

X, Mr 253
Xhosa nation 4–5

Yanacsek, Robert 137
Yaqui way of knowledge 292–4
Yay-ho 197
  see also Bigfoot
yellow objects 22
yeren 205
  see also Bigfoot
yeti 196, 198, 202
  hand of 353–4
  see also Bigfoot
York, Andrew 240

Zaleski, Carol 407–8
Zanfretta, Fortunato 152–3
Zanzibar, demon buggerer of 29
Zdorick, B.M. 203
Zeidman, Jennie 137
Zener cards 92, 95
zeugoldon (whales), as explanation for lake monster sightings 210
zobop 423
Zugun, Eleonore 123, 124